NECKER
AND THE
REVOLUTION
OF 1789

Robert D. Harris
University of Idaho

UNIVERSITY
PRESS OF
AMERICA

LANHAM • NEW YORK • LONDON

Library of Congress Cataloging in Publication Data

Harris, Robert D.
  Necker and the revolution of 1789.

  Bibliography: p.
  Includes index.
  1. Necker, Jacques, 1732-1804.   2. France—Politics
and government—1774-1793.   3. France—History—
Revolution, 1789-1799.   4. Statesmen—France—Biography.
I. Title.
DC146.N36H37   1986   944.04'092'4   [B]   86-15881
ISBN 0-8191-5602-7 (alk. paper)

CONTENTS

Preface. v

I   A Catechism for Sovereigns and
    Administrators 1

II Necker's Successors at the Contrôle
    général 31

III The State's Secret 73

IV Calonne and the Notables. 103

V   The Battle of Figures 145

VI The Reform Program of the Notables. . . . 193

VII The Fifteen Months of the Archbishop. . . 219

VIII The Rejection of the Brienne-Lamoignon
     Ministry and the Return of Necker. . . . 261

IX The Representatives of the Nation 297

X   The Convocation of the Electoral
    Assemblies 339

XI The National Mandate. 377

XII The Opening of the States-General 403

XIII The Failure of Mediation. 445

XIV The Sway of Circumstances 497

XV The Minister of the Nation. 531

XVI The Struggle for Liberty and Order. . . . 589

XVII The Struggle for Executive Power. 623

XVIII The October Catastrophe 667

XIX Necker and the Constituent Assembly . . . 707

XX   End of a Career 741

   Conclusion. 769

   Bibliography 773

   Index. 793

PREFACE

This is a continuation of my study of Necker's political career, initiated by my book published in 1979, Necker, Reform Statesman of the Ancien Régime, which was devoted exclusively to his reform ministry from 1776 to 1781. In the volume now offered I have thought it useful to examine in detail the ministries of Necker's successors at the Contrôle-général in order to show why Necker remained a prominent figure in the public eye even during the years he was out of office. His book published early in 1785, On the Administration of Finances in France, was a great success with the public and particularly influential among the "notables." Those who attended the Assembly of Notables in 1787 were largely "Neckerist" in their views on the kind of reforms they wanted. It was necessary for me to study the ministry of Loménie de Brienne in detail because Necker's policies when he returned to the government in August 1788 were to a great extent determined by the experiences of the preceding ministry.

The chief purpose of this study is to explain Necker's thoughts and acts as he tried to steer the nation through the initial stages of its revolution, and to see those ideas and acts in the context of the often intractible circumstances that he faced. The prevalent view today seems to be that Necker was an able administrator but an inept political leader. It is not my purpose to overturn this judgment, but rather to understand his policies and try to view the situations as he saw them. As in the case of his first ministry I find that his policies and intentions have at best not been correctly understood, at worst the prevalent view has been too often influenced by the violent libel literature propagated by his enemies.

That Necker has been a comparatively neglected figure in the history of the French Revolution no doubt calls for some justification for this undertaking. When Necker returned to power in August 1788 he saw his role as entirely different from that of his first ministry. He recognized that the revolution was inevitable and he welcomed it, seeking to guide it in the channel he thought the most enlightened part of the nation desired. His objective was to found a constitutional monarchy in which a bicameral parliament would exercise full legislative powers, but leave to the royal government full executive power. There would be a bill of rights guaranteeing basic liberties to all citizens, especially security of persons and property. There would be an end to arbitrary government such as many believed had existed in the ministries of Calonne and Loménie de Brienne. Responsible financial administration was particularly desired by those who were government creditors and feared default, and those who wanted to establish institutional checks on government expenditures. In addition, under such a polity it would finally be possible to carry out all those social and economic reforms for which Necker had been the protagonist, and were desired by most of the nation. This was the revolution that Necker envisaged, and also many of the most educated and responsible persons involved in the events of 1789. Yet it has been all but forgotten in the general histories of the French Revolution. "Necker and the forgotten revolution" might have been the title of this volume.

Perhaps not so much forgotten as misnamed. The "aristocratic revolution" is often written about, but it is seen as a "whiggish" or "archaic" attempt to return to an age of feudal aristocracy and therefore was unrealistic and doomed to failure. This, in my opinion, is a mistaken interpretation of the "pre-revolution" of 1787-1788. That event was aristocratic only in that it was not democratic. It was not archaic in

the sense of looking backward to the regime that preceded absolutism. On the contrary, Necker's revolution was forward-looking based upon the experiences of
the Anglo-Saxons. It may be argued that far from being emphemeral it was the revolution that finally en-
dured after all the vicissitudes of the twenty-five
year period, and that it was the radical revolution
that was ephemeral. To be sure, the Year Two of the
Republic was also "prophetic" as Ernest Labrousse has
written. The republic, democracy, and social democracy eventually came and prevail today. But does the
historian study the past only from the standpoint of
what it contributed to his own time? It has long been
recognized that the "Whig interpretation of history"
was unsatisfactory for that reason. Is it not possible that historians of our democratic and socialist
age have succumbed to a similar fallacy?

In the later years of his life, after 1790,
Necker's reputation suffered a precipitate decline because he was condemned by those who detested the Revolution, and equally by those who placed him in the
camp of the counter-revolution. There seems to be a
tendency in revolutionaries to project their enemies
as "counter-revolutionary" when to the outside observer
the revolutionary credentials of those enemies are as
valid as their own. To the end of his life Necker remained a constant defender of the moderate revolution,
never abandoning it as so many did who became disillu-
sioned by the violence and atrocities that accompanied
it. In his own memoirs Necker compared his fate to
that of Michel de L'Hôpital who, in the sixteenth century, sought to moderate the rival factions that were
tearing the kingdom apart in the Wars of Religion. It
seems to me that there is much truth in that comparison.

This study is based predominately on primary
sources. Necker's own writings, edited and published
by his grandson in 1821, have been the most important.

I have also made considerable use of the dispatches of foreign ambassadors at the court of Versailles. I think nearly all the published memoirs, correspondence, and diaries have been consulted, while recognizing that the authenticity of some has been questioned. Government documents in the form of decrees, remonstrances of sovereign courts, proces-verbaux of deliberative assemblies have been important sources. I have not attempted to include in the bibliography all secondary works on the prerevolution and the revolution of 1789 that have appeared in recent years. My intention has been to study Necker's career from primary sources without regard to interpretive controversies that are raging today around the subject of the French Revolution.

There are some secondary works that I have used and should mention. The different articles and books of Jean Egret on the "prerevolution" have been important in my discussion of the ministry of Loménie de Brienne and the events in Dauphiné, although I disagree with Egret in some of his judgments on Necker. I have derived information about the troop movements during the July Days from Jacques Godechot's La Prise de la Bastille. On the assignats I have derived some information from the monograph of my namesake (but no kin), Seymour Harris. Finally I have continued to make use of Henri Grange's book on Necker's thought, Les Idées de Necker. Professor Grange read Chapter 12 of this manuscript, "The Opening of the States-General," and made some important suggestions that were used. I wish to acknowledge his friendly interest and help but of course I remain responsible for the final version of that chapter.

There are other acknowledgements to be made of both institutions and persons who have given me support in this endeavor. The Research Council of the University of Idaho granted me a summer research stipend in 1980. Two years later the Sabbatical Leave

Committee of the University of Idaho granted me a sabbatical for the fall semester, 1982. Still two years later, in 1984, the History Department of the University relieved me of teaching duties during the fall semester in which this manuscript was largely completed. In the preparation of the manuscript I have had the loyal assistance of my graduate student, Elizabeth Barker Mattson, who typed the entire manuscript before it was submitted to the final typing. Again I wish to express my appreciation to Mrs. Florence Anderson for such a professional final typing job, and for saving me from some lapses in style. Those that remain of course are my responsibility. Finally, and again, I must thank my wife, Ethel, for being so supportive in what must seem an obsession in my preoccupation with Necker.

After the above was written my manuscript was accepted for publication by the University Press of America, and I have further debts of gratitude for necessary assistance. The College of Letters and Science of the University of Idaho has prepared the manuscript for the photo-production process. I wish to thank Linda Main, Linda Boyd and the word-processing unit for the many hours they have devoted to this project. For the proof-reading I have been able to call upon friends and colleages. Bernie Wegmann Proctor, Janet Groff Greever and William S. Greever have purged the manuscript of countless errors, most of which were mine and not the word-processors. Any that remain are my responsibility, for I was the last to read the manuscript and make the final decisions. The translations from the French have been my own, except in some rare cases where I have used a translated book.

CHAPTER 1

A CATECHISM FOR SOVEREIGNS AND ADMINISTRATORS

The day on which Jacques Necker submitted his resignation to Louis XVI as director of the royal finances, May 19, 1781, has not become one of those fateful days in French history which have given rise to a series of monographs by French historians. Two other finance ministers of the French government in the eighteenth century have become subjects in the series "Thirty Days Which Made France," namely John Law and Jacques Turgot.[1] But history has little remembered the Genevan banker whose first ministry spanned the years 1776-1781, who was recalled to the government by Louis XVI in the severe crisis of 1788, and whose popularity reached a peak during June and July, 1789, perhaps unparalleled for ministers in the history of the French monarchy.

There is a striking contrast in the neglect of Necker by historians and the opinion held of him by the French public during the years of his first ministry and immediately following. At the time of his resignation "Mr. Necker took with him the regrets of the nation," wrote Jean-Joseph Mounier in his memoirs.[2] "His resignation was generally thought to be a calamity," wrote the comte de Lally-Tolendal in his brief biography of Necker. He added that if Necker had not resigned he would have succeeded to the position of the comte de Maurepas who died the following November. "Then there would have been neither deficit nor notables nor revolution."[3] In November 1783, after the successful conclusion of the American War the Austrian ambassador at Paris, Mercy-Argenteau, wrote to Emperor Joseph II that if France could find an able and powerful minister she would be prosperous and flourishing, for the country was favorably endowed

1

with great resources. "The general cry of the Nation, even in the remotest provinces," he wrote, "calls for the return of Mr. Necker."[4]

But what was "the Nation" in the year 1781? The term appeared often in the publications of that day such as the remonstrances of the Parlement of Paris. The general meaning of the term seemed to be that part of France which was separate from the royal government. In the time of Louis XIV there was no such distinction between the king and the nation. After the passing of the grand century there grew up an independent force alongside the monarchy, a force often described in the eighteenth century as "public opinion," which spoke for the nation. During his first ministry Necker had paid court to this new power, recognizing its legitimacy, so to speak, not only in his writings but in his deeds as the most important administrator of the domestic affairs of the kingdom. And public opinion for the most part gave its support to the ideas and the policies of the Genevan banker.

Where were the spokesmen for public opinion to be found? In a broad spectrum of social and cultural forces in the eighteenth century. The intellectuals and writers of the time, those called "philosophes" were for the most part favorable to Necker and his policies during his first ministry. Many of the most prominent prelates of the French Catholic Church were avowed "Neckerists." Some of the most esteemed ministers in the government during the 1780s admired the talents of Necker, among them being the secretary of state for the navy and colonies, the Marquis de Castries, who remained a loyal supporter of the Genevan.[5] The highly-regarded Marshal de Beauvau was also a constant friend and supporter as was his beautiful and influential wife, the Maréchale. In general, that class of the most educated of the prelates, the higher ranks of the nobility who saw the need for reform, as well as the wealthy members of his own class, the

2

third estate, was the basis of Necker's support. These were people designated at the time as "notables," a term historians have adopted since then to denote the class.

Certainly Necker did not enjoy the undivided support of this class in the decade of the 1780s. He had powerful enemies as well, and it was because of them that he submitted his resignation to the king in May 1781. For the most part his enemies at that time were those opposed to his reforms, who thought any change in the traditional customs and institutions of the absolute monarchy was unnecessary and dangerous. They did not recognize that new power to which Necker paid court, public opinion; they maintained it was his own creation or a figment of his imagination. The France of the ancien régime, of the absolute monarchy of Louis XIV, such was their France. They deplored what they called "the thirst for novelty."

Many of his enemies had good reason for hating the reform statesman. It was against their interests that his reforms were carried out. Courtiers who sought lavish pensions and other pecuniary favors from the king, financiers whose profits at the expense of the royal government were curtailed, and especially those whose offices were abolished. Yet it would not be true to say that only those whose interests were curtailed became Necker's enemies. The greater number were sincere conservatives, those who believed that the France of the ancien régime was just what it ought to be and could see no reason for change.

Even his enemies did not deny that Necker continued to enjoy great prestige in the public after his resignation in 1781. One of the prominent journalists of the day who was a confirmed anti-Neckerist was Louis Petit de Bachaumont, whose "Secret Memoirs" kept readers informed of Necker's activities during the decade of the 1780s. When memoirs of the former min-

3

ister of war, Claude-Louis, comte de Saint-Germain, were published in April 1784, Bachaumont took note of them. He had to admit that Saint-Germain held Necker in very high esteem, even describing him as "the greatest administrator he ever knew." "It is entirely possible that he believed that," remarked Bachaumont with acerbity, "and that he was duped by Necker, as so many other enlightened persons were who knew little about the state of finances and were unable to discern the hypocritical measures of the charlatan."[6]

But usually when the "Secret Memoirs" mentioned Necker it was only to report to readers without indulging in comments of that kind. In the fall of 1784 when Necker and his wife left Montpellier to return to Paris they passed through the city of Moulins. Bachaumont told his readers that the citizens of Moulins turned out to give a hearty reception to the Neckers. The reason for this enthusiasm for the former director-general of finances is that Moulins and the province of Bourbonnais were to be the beneficiaries of a provincial assembly and provincial administration to replace the dictatorial authority of the intendant. The intendant of Moulins had refused to obey Necker, knowing that the Parlement of Paris was becoming increasingly hostile to Necker's provincial assemblies. It was this issue that compelled Necker to insist on the support of the king, failing which he submitted his resignation. The same person was still intendant when Necker passed through Moulins in November 1784, and Bachaumont told his readers that he was so unpopular that he was compelled to leave the city during the honors paid to the Neckers.[7]

In February 1786 one of the important social events of the season was Mademoiselle Necker's presentation at court. This was the debut of the precocious 20-year-old daughter of the Neckers, who later in the year was to be married to the Swedish ambassador, Baron Eric Magnus de Staël-Holstein. Bachaumont reported that 300 carriages stopped at the Necker estate at Saint-Ouen so their owners could pay their respects to the Neckers, adding that this event caused a new rash of rumors that Necker was about to return to his old post in the government of Louis XVI.[8] In August of the same year the sister of Marie-Antoinette, the Archduchess of Saxe-Teschen and her husband, who were governors of the Austrian Netherlands, paid a visit to Necker at Saint-Ouen, which, according to Bachaumont, "again gave rise to rumors that they would attempt to persuade the king and queen to bring Necker into the government."[9]

Such was the prestige and fame of the former director of the royal finances. Like the great minister of Louis XV, Choiseul, Necker seemed as important a figure in retirement as he was in office. Yet, unlike Choiseul, Necker's prestige did not derive from a flamboyant, "charismatic" personality. Rather, it was based on his "ideas" and on his policies regarding the administration of the internal affairs of the country. He was not diffident in proclaiming those policies, and his Compte rendu au Roi published in February 1781 described in detail for the king and his subjects the reforms that Necker had achieved in the past four years and what he hoped to accomplish as soon as the war was over and he could devote undivided attention to reform.

For a work on the government finances the Compte rendu was an amazing publishing success in 1781. Equally surprising was the success of a three-volume work that came from Necker's pen early in 1785, De l'Administration des Finances de la France. The bookseller Hardy noted in his manuscript journal "Mes Loisirs" on January 22 "nearly 12,000 copies had been sold at the Librairie Panckoucke," even though publication had begun only a few days before. He reported that the sale had been delayed by the Calonne administration so that when it appeared a critique of

5

the "Introduction" might also appear at the same time. The critic, reported Hardy, was none other than the "sieur Bourboulon, an employee in high finances, known as an antagonist of the sieur Necker." It is probable that the appearance of this refutation simply added to the interest of Necker's new book, for Bourboulon had been a notorious and unpopular critic of the Compte rendu in 1781. It is also probable that the evident hostility toward the book of the Controller-General, Charles-Alexandre de Calonne, added to the public's interest. Hardy wrote that Calonne hoped the king would forbid its publication, but when he entered the king's room and found him reading it, Louis remarked: "I don't see why it should concern you; I see nothing unfavorable in it about you."[10]

According to baron de Staël's letters to King Gustavus III of Sweden, not only Calonne but Vergennes, the foreign minister and chairman of the Council of Finance, and Hue de Miromesnil, Keeper of the Seals, were also hostile to the book and sought to persuade the king to exile Necker from France. The secretary of state for the navy and colonies, the marquis de Castries, remained loyal to Necker and countered the "intrigue" of the other ministers. Castries asked the king about rumors that he had forbidden Necker to come to Paris. The king told Castries that he was well disposed toward Necker, but "in view of the great sensation that his book has caused, it would not be a bad idea for him to remain away from Paris for a time." Hardy reported that Castries wrote accordingly to Necker, who was in southern France. Baron de Staël, who was on good terms with the queen at that time, wrote that she told him the same thing "while adding expressions very flattering to Mr. Necker."[11]

By March 10 Hardy had finished reading Necker's work and described his impression in the diary. Although not well versed in the subject, Hardy found it

"highly interesting for a citizen." He paid tribute
to the writer's "sublime ideas, delicate feelings, and
superior talents, who expresses himself with as much
eloquence as energy." Despite himself, Hardy was
drawn to read it a second time. He admitted that
Necker had one fault, a little too much boasting, but
he thought the author could be pardoned that because
of his "zeal, the purity of his intentions, and his
high moral principles." He praised Necker's defense
of the poorer classes, and his unveiling for the
reader the mysteries of financial administration
"which affect all orders of the state." Necker gave
advice freely to his successors in the Contrôle-
général, and even to other ministers as well. In
fact, wrote Hardy, the book might well have been entitled "a catechism for sovereigns and ministers."[12]

In view of Necker's past disputes with the parlements arising out of his reform of the vingtième tax
and his provincial administrations it is noteworthy
that they were in general favorable to his book published in 1785. The Provincial Estates of Brittany
took offense at Necker's proposal to reform the salt
monopoly (gabelle) by extending it to that province
which had been free of it even though Necker proposed
a modest price for salt and a reduction of other taxes
in compensation. The Estates asked the Parlement of
Rennes to suppress the book in the area of its jurisdiction. The Parlement adjourned consideration of the
book for five years, which in effect meant refusing to
denounce it. The Parlement of Bordeaux decreed that a
copy be placed in its archives to be shown to the
royal government the next time it asked for an increase in taxes. Finally, according to Hardy, the
most important and powerful of the parlements, that of
Paris, "refused to give heed to the violent objections
to the book by some courtiers."[13]

That there was vehement opposition to Necker's
book in some quarters is attested by Metra. "No one

7

can be neutral," he wrote on January 18, "one either violently detests it or admires it." At Paris a brochure denouncing the book was solemnly burned at a club. On the first of February a new large volume appeared denouncing the introduction of Necker's work. "These bitter remarks are directed against the person of the author, against his style, his vanity, his turn of phrase, etc. but not at all against the principles [expressed in it] or against the system of justice and economy which is the foundation of this honorable work." Referring to Necker the publicist wrote: "Out of office, without a motive to seek praise, this former administrator is winning new partisans every day, even among people whose interests are harmed, such is the grandeur and power of integrity which shines forth from this writing where the cause of the [common] people is defined with truly heroic courage."[14]

That Necker's treatise "On the Administration of Finances in France" had a strong appeal to the reading public is incontestable. What needs to be explained is why it had such wide readership and influence. A book on government finances is not usually a best seller in any age. The attention of both friends and critics was attracted first of all by the "Introduction" to the three-volume work. Here the former minister of finance explained what he thought were essential qualities for a person called to administer such a vast and powerful department of the government as the finances. After which he took the reader into his confidence and described his own feelings about his five-year ministry and his regret at not being able to carry out the reforms he had so ardently hoped for during the years of the American War. The style of this passage was not unlike that of his late compatriot, Jean-Jacques Rousseau:

> I do not conceal my regret at being interrupted in my career without finishing what I had planned for the good of the state and

the glory of the king. I am not hypocritical and vain enough to affect a serenity
which would tend too much toward indifference to be praise-worthy. I will never forget the moment when, a few days after my
resignation I was putting my papers in order, I came across those in which I had
sketched my various ideas for the future;
especially those projects I had formed for
the amelioration of the gabelles, for the
suppression of all interior custome duties,
and for the extension of the provincial administrations; suddenly I was unable to continue, and throwing aside all papers, I covered my forehead with my hands and tears
flowed from my eyes. And yet even then I
did not forsee everything. For when, after
having made such efforts in public affairs,
when, after having seen such painful victo-
ries over one's own sensibilities, either
for having established greater order in the
finances, or for having laid down rules of
administration which I thought were sound, I
was yet required to witness the abandonment
of part of those policies. . . .Ah, let the
reader glimpse into my heart and pity me for
an instant![15]

One might expect such an outpouring of the heart
from a writer like Rousseau who made a _coeur_ _sensible_
his special trademark, but it was no doubt unusual for
a minister of the government. It would be difficult
to imagine such a passage in the memoirs of a Richelieu or a Mazarin. Yet it may be just that quality
that explains Necker's great popularity. This was the
age of the "tearful comedy" in the theatre and the
sentimental novel on tables in all the boudoirs. Of
course Necker laid himself open to the sardonic jeers

9

of his enemies by such exposure. But we may imagine that many of his readers wept with the author when they came to that passage. The interest of posterity and the historian of course is neither to jeer nor to weep, but to try to understand the reason for the great vogue for Necker in the decade preceding the French Revolution.

There was a constant theme throughout this oftentimes intricately detailed work, namely the necessity for morality in government. The most important quality for a minister responsible for the affairs of the state, Necker said, was personal integrity and a dedication to using the powers of his position to pursue moral ends. The insistence on this quality in a minister, which another age may not have found so important, seemed to make a profound impression on the French reading public in 1785.

The enthusiasm with which the French embraced the cult of morality in government was possibly due to the special character of French absolutism in the eighteenth century. The royal government could not levy unlimited amounts of tax revenue, as was demonstrated by the resistance of the sovereign courts led by the Parlement of Paris. But there were no checks on the way in which the king's money was spent that did come into his coffers. The parlements would remonstrate if they felt abuses of the king's confidence were perpetrated, but they could go no further than repeat their remonstrances until the royal government silenced them. This gave the finance minister enormous discretion about how royal revenue was handled. It is true that there were chambers of account that existed for the purpose of auditing the king's funds, but they were years behind in their accounts, and furthermore a certain part of royal expenditures, discharged through acquits de comptant, were withheld from the scrutiny of the chambers of account.

It was this matter of power over the king's revenue that made the finance minister such a crucial figure in the government. While the great spectacular malversations of government revenue by ministers of the seventeenth century were no longer the rule in the eighteenth century, there was extreme pressure on the finance minister to grant special favors to highly-placed and influential courtiers, or to friends and relatives. It required strong character to resist these importunate demands of the powerful and ingratiating. Necker had demonstrated that he had such character during the years of his first ministry, and he was not modest in letting the public know about it. It was not only the pressure of high-ranking beggars but special interests of various kinds: the military services, the various sections of the royal households, including those of the queen and the king's brothers, the swarm of office-holders, financiers who handled the king's money for exorbitant commissions, tax-farmers, private firms that supplied the government's many purchases, the list of the kinds of people trying to expand the government's expenditure was endless. There was no institutional means of surveillance over these expenditures except for the finance minister. He was the only servant of the king interested in preventing useless expenditures, in protecting the king against "surprises to his religion" as the saying was, or in protecting the tax-payers from an endless increase of their burdens.

To protect the interests of the many from the grasping elites was often an unrewarding task. It was so much easier to be openhanded, never turn down a request, bask in the sunshine of popularity among the recipients of royal favors! But Necker did not feel entirely alone. He had three allies that he relied upon. One was the king himself. Louis XVI was a moralist also, who thoroughly approved of the precepts of Necker: the need to prevent useless expenditure, to lighten the tax burden, to control the debt of the royal government. But he never overcame the habit of depending upon others which had been instilled in him by his "mentor" of the early years of his reign, the comte de Maurepas. After the latter's death in November 1781, his place came to be occupied by the minister of foreign affairs, the comte de Vergennes, who had acquired an intense dislike of Necker by 1781 and it was his influence which usually prevented Necker's recall to the government. Vergennes was a minister of the ancien régime. Concerned with foreign affairs during his career he had no sympathy for the reform program of Necker. Since his own power depended completely on the king's grace he was opposed to any innovation that he feared would weaken royal power. After Vergennes' death in 1787 it was the queen who came to have the most influence over the king's decisions on ministerial appointments.[16]

The second ally of the "virtuous minister" was public opinion, that force to which he often appealed, and for which he admitted in later years he had almost a religious veneration. It was to take the public into his confidence that Necker propounded the doctrine of publicity in all the government's actions. Secrecy should be held to a minimum. It was particularly necessary to publicize the situation of the government's finances to let the public know that the king's money was being handled responsibly. It was also necessary for the king to take his creditors into his confidence, let them know exactly where he stood financially, just as an individual would take his banker into a similar confidence.

The third ally, in case of default of the other two, and the one that Necker relied upon most in his later years, particularly after the bruising defeats of the third ministry by 1790, was his own conscience, his own sense of what was right, and the solace that he had not betrayed his principles. Ultimately it was his firm religious belief that preserved him from de-

12

spair in the gigantic upheavals of the French Revolution and his own dramatic participation in them. For Necker the social and political order was based upon the divine order. In the years of his retirement after 1781 he became increasingly preoccupied with religious questions, disturbed by the evident weakening of Christianity in Europe and what this might mean for the future. It was not surprising that his second book to be published during this period between ministries was "On the Importance of Religious Opinions," published in 1788 just before the entry on his second ministry.[17]

One of the deplorable consequences of a minister submitting to the pressure of courtiers and others for special favors was that the interests of the lower classes, those who had no means of making their influence felt at court, were overlooked. In his book published in 1785 Necker once again, as in previous works, insisted on the responsibility of the royal government for the welfare of the lower classes. "The primary duty of the minister entrusted with internal affairs," he wrote, "is the care of the people and the protection of the poor." By the "people" he meant those without property, who were dependent on the work of their hands for subsistence. The finance minister especially has the responsibility for protecting those classes from the fluctuations of the economic cycles. The state can be indifferent to the impact of the fluctuations on the well off, but not on the less fortunate. If there should be a crop failure and a threat of shortage in the grain supply the government must take measures to enter the market and purchase supplies for storage, to regulate export, and in general do whatever is necessary to assure sufficient grain supplies at a price level the lowest class can afford. Necker did not trust the theoretical principles of the free-trade advocates to bring about that result. But again, as in his previous works, Necker made it clear that he was no believer in the leveling

13

of fortunes. Great inequalities of wealth would necessarily exist, and any attempt of the government to
equalize them would "endanger the order of society,
and also interfere with the growth of industry and labor."[18]

But there were certain powers within the hands of
the finance minister for protecting the lower classes.
Most important were the methods and sources for raising the king's revenue. The tax burden should be distributed in accordance with ability to pay. The existing tax system was brutally repressive, falling on
the classes least able to pay. Most flagrant was the
corvée, a labor tax of about one week per year levied
on peasant villages for the upkeep of the state's
roads and bridges. This, Necker wrote, should be converted to a monetary tax and partitioned according to
ability to pay. The government's salt monopoly was
also harsh on the poorer classes, and particularly
disastrous because of the great temptation for smuggling salt from the provinces where it was free of the
monopoly into the provinces of the grande gabelles
where the government price of salt was many times the
market price. Necker proposed to lower the price of
salt and make it uniform throughout the kingdom,
granting certain indemnities to the "salt free"
provinces so that they would not be paying a greater
tax burden because of the reform.

As for the three major direct taxes, it was the
taille which seems most repressive and unjust to the
present-day observer because the nobles and the clergy
were exempt and many others too. It was levied on the
produce of the land, and that meant, the burden fell
on the rural peasant class. But Necker shared what
seems to have been a common assumption of that time:
the apparent inequity of the taille was greatly mitigated by the fact that those exempt from it who leased
out their land to farmers actually paid the taille because it was deducted from their rent. Only the no-

14

bles who exploited directly their lands were exempt
from the taille, and even this privilege was limited
to a certain number of acres. In practice it was the
poorer nobility who enjoyed this exemption, the large
wealthy land-owners did not.

For the other two direct taxes, the capitation or
poll tax and the twentieths (vingtièmes) only the
clergy was exempt because it paid a subsidy to the
government called a don gratuit. It was the common
opinion that this was far below what the clergy would
pay if subject to the direct taxes. But it was also
acknowledged that the French Catholic Church provided
social welfare services and education as well as maintaining the churches and serving the cult. As for the
nobility, it was not exempt in theory from the capitation nor the vingtièmes, but in practice they were
able to evade them, especially the latter, because
they insisted on the right to declare the value of
their lands and the income from the land. Necker
sought to counter this abuse by establishing a system
of assessment whereby those subject to the vingtièmes
would meet in a common assembly of the parish and
agree on the equitable share of each proprietor. This
innovation was strenuously resisted by the parlements,
and Necker's successor, Jean-François Joly de Fleury,
discontinued it in July 1782 when he added a third
vingtième to the other two. Once again the directors
of the vingtième had to accept the valuations of the
proprietors, and they insisted that the land values
and income should not be assessed any higher than the
first year that the vingtième was imposed, namely
1749. The third vingtième was imposed to meet the
great costs of the American War and was to end three
years after the end of that war, as it turned out, by
the end of 1786. It was a general assumption in 1787,
by the Controller-General, Calonne, his successor,
Loménie de Brienne, and the Assembly of Notables that
if the vingtième were assessed according to the actual
value of the landed income the increase in yield would

15

be equal to the third vingtième. Hence it was the expiration of that wartime tax that focused attention on the evasion of taxes by the wealthy proprietors. In his 1785 book on French finances Necker gave his endorsement of that policy in advance: the actual or current value of the landed income must be the basis of assessment. He was extremely apprehensive about the consequences of an increase of the tax burden on the lower classes. If circumstances should require an increase of taxes to meet some extraordinary expenditure then the burden should fall primarily on the rich.

Throughout this book Necker emphasized the excessive amount of tax money that was being taken from the substance of the people. So much space was devoted to this matter that it is apparent he was opposing a powerful force that was arguing the opposite thesis, namely that taxes were not too heavy in France, they were in fact heavier in England and other European countries. France was wealthy, her economy was expanding, fully one-half of the currency in Europe was in the French kingdom, so that there should be no concern about the tax burden. Necker believed that such arguments were sponsored by those who had a definite interest in the royal revenue:

> Whenever the public debt increases, whenever [royal] gifts, pensions, or the profits of financiers expands and multiplies, there is created in the state a very considerable party whose interests are often opposed to those of the people. For all those persons whose fortune consists in obligations on the king, or on favors of the court, easily agree to an increase of the tax burden, so much does it harmonize with their interests to have the revenue of their debtor increased, or that the royal treasure have more money to lavish.[19]

More government loans which eventually would have to be liquidated by more taxes, this was an unending spiral looked upon complacently by the swarm of courtiers, the holders of rentes and other obligations of the king, the wealthy financiers who had purchased lucrative offices that managed the royal finances for high fees and commissions. Only the virtuous king supported by the strong character of his finance minister could defend the people from this rapacious horde. No wonder the courtiers, the office holders, those who battened on the public treasure hated the Genevan banker with a ferocious passion which they vented in numerous libels published during the last year of his ministry![20]

As for the argument that the English per capita tax burden was greater than in France, Necker admitted that fact, but denied it was a valid reason for raising French taxes. He believed, mistakenly perhaps in view of recent research, that the British were able to make the wealthy pay their fair share of the taxes rather than shift the burden to the poor.[21] Anyway, Necker asserted that high taxes were not good for any people, and the English were too heavily taxed for the good of their economy. Furthermore, it was not simply a matter of the quantitative burden of a tax system that mattered, it was the manner, the techniques by which it was administered that could make the difference between an oppressive system and one that would not create resentment. In England the needs of the government were discussed openly in Parliament, tax laws were clear and the assessments public and above board; whereas in France everything was done secretly, no one outside the government could know what the basis for tax burden was nor could the individual taxpayer know what his burden was compared to his neighbor's. It was secrecy which created distrust and gave full rein to the imagination, which exaggerated the already existing inequities.

The greatest evil in the French tax system was the number of exemptions from the tax burden which made it all the more onerous for those who were not exempt. These privileges were not only attached to persons but to corporations and regions. For the administration of the salt monopoly (the gabelle) the kingdom was divided into six different regions ranging from the most heavily taxed provinces (the area of the grandes gabelles) to provinces that were completely free of the tax, such as Brittany. The internal transit duties (customs, tariffs, tolls) were similarly levied differently in the provinces, ranging from the large central area of relatively free trade (the "Five Great Farms") to those eastern provinces that were treated like foreign countries in the administration of tariffs. Certain provinces retained their traditional assemblies of estates and administration dependent upon them. These pays d'états raised the royal taxes independently of the central administration which administered the direct taxes in the pays d'élection and the more recently acquired provinces since 1648 (the pays conquis). The corporations that enjoyed special exemptions and privileges were the financial companies such as the General Farm which contracted with the royal government to administer the collecting of the indirect taxes.

Necker's method of reform did not include the use of the meatax. Privileges and immunities that had been granted by the king in past centuries by formal charter or patent could not be summarily abolished. It was necessary to "compose with them," to use Necker's own expression. That meant it was necessary to negotiate with the privileged. If their offices were suppressed the capital value of the offices would be returned to them. If a province were to be asked to give up an immunity, as in the case of the gabelle being extended to Brittany, compensation of some sort would be offered. For those who like to see bold, slashing reforms, or who believe that only violent revolution can bring any real change, Necker's method would seem paltry and uninspiring, or at least ineffective. His own argument to that viewpoint was that, on the contrary, it was the brutal reform that was really ineffective. Changes that are truly ameliorative come about by negotiation, not by force. It does not improve the over-all situation to leave people humiliated and resentful. No doubt some privileges were manifestly unjust and indefensible. But in those cases the government must use persuasion, not force, in bringing about a reform.

In his 1785 book on "the administration of finances in France," Necker set forth in elaborate detail just how he would propose to reform the entire fiscal structure of the government. For the indirect taxes, the rule was to establish uniformity throughout the kingdom for the salt and tobacco monopolies and the excise and sales taxes. The internal customs duties and tolls would be eliminated and the entire realm would become a free-trade area; for Necker agreed with the physiocratic doctrine that the fiscal system should promote economic growth rather than hinder it.

For the reform of the direct taxes there were two leading ideas in the book: the necessity for publicity in the entire fiscal operation from the time the amount to be levied was decided through the apportionment, assessment, and collection of the tax. The second idea was the need to decentralize the administration of the direct taxes. The provincial assemblies and their administration that he had set up in the Berri and in Haute Guienne during his ministry were to be established throughout the pays d'élection. These regional governments were to take over most of the functions of the intendant as far as administering the direct taxes were concerned. They were to have other important responsibilities for local government as well. These assemblies were to be composed, as in

Berri and Haute Guienne, of notables of all three orders, the clergy, nobility and third estate; but the
third estate would have the same number of seats as
the other two orders combined, the doublement that was
to become so famous with the convening of the States-
General. Deliberation and voting was to take place in
a common assembly, not separate bodies of the three
orders. The leading prelate of the region would serve
as president of the assembly. The king would choose
one-half the members initially who would select the
remainder by co-option.

Removing the injustices of the taxes was an important matter in Necker's reform plans. But what
must have made the strongest impression on his readers
was the assertion that the taxes need not be as high
as they were at the time, and that government debt not
only should not be increased by loans, but could be
decreased. About 207 million livres per year went to
service the debt. The remedy he proposed was to cur-
tail expenditures. During his first ministry Necker
had made a substantial reduction in expenditures. In
his 1785 treatise he showed in some detail how more
could be done. The government spent 58 million livres
in order to collect 585 million, the latter being the
total amount collected from the taxpayers. The method
of collection was obviously inefficient. Necker
showed how at least 16 million could be pared off that
cost of collecting the taxes, both direct and indirect. In every branch of the administration he stipulated how savings could be made: in the services of
supply for the army, in the King's household and also
that of the Queen and the princes, the king's brothers.

An important feature of Necker's reform program
was to reduce the great number of venal offices.
There was a strong inclination for finance ministers
to multiply useless offices because of the capital
that would be realized at the time of their sale.

About 700 million livres was owed by the government to office-holders in 1781. This was an unsatisfactory situation for Necker because it made the government dependent upon the financiers for the management of its finances. He did not believe in a blanket sweep of these offices and their replacement by a bureaucracy that could be administered directly by the minister. He thought such a radical institution was not feasible in France because of the general habits and outlook of those who served in the government. It was necessary to give them some incentive to perform efficiently, and venality of office provided a scheme that tied the officer's duty to his self-interest. So the system of venal offices was not to be eradicated, but it could be reformed. There were too many useless, unnecessary offices. And each one was endowed with commissions, salaries, emoluments, fees, immunities and special privileges, all at the expense of the public and the royal government. Necker had brought about a great reduction of such offices during his first ministry: the farmers-general reduced from 60 to 48, the receivers-general from 48 to 12, treasurers in the armed forces and the King's Household greatly reduced in number. But in 1785 Necker thought that these offices could be even further reduced.[22]

Two observations are usually made about Necker's economies. One is that the capital of the abolished offices had to be returned to the former officer, and therefore savings were illusory. The second is that it is a mistake to think the government's financial embarrassment was due to the lavish grants and favors of the king, or Marie Antoinette's expensive taste for jewelry, or the comte d'Artois's spectacular gambling debts. The true cause of the government's gigantic debt and financial straits during the century, it is said, was the wars that France engaged in from the time of Louis XIV to the Revolution. Necker would have agreed with the facts stated but not the critic's conclusions. It is true that the capital of the of-

21

fice was either returned to the individuals who had purchased the office or the interest was paid regularly on the unreturned portion. This was a new expenditure. The advantage for the abolition of offices could only be realized over a period of time. Once the office had been paid off the government would be free of an encumbrance which was not just financial but also administrative and social as well. A plethora of useless offices made it difficult for the administration to function efficiently. The great number of unnecessary offices contributed to that social class which Necker saw as having interests fundamentally opposed to the interests of the general public.

As for the second criticism, Necker recognized that the wars of Louis XIV and the eighteenth century were the main reason for the government debt and he deeply deplored it. "Sad fate of human nature! The course of the public fortune resembles that of life; the good days of one and the other are precursors of a long night!"[23] Certainly there was no more pacifist-minded statesman of the eighteenth century than Necker. But once the king had incurred those debts his promise to repay them was sacred. There could be no thought of repudiation, or even a reduction as in the time of abbé Terray. But how could one handle a huge government debt whose carrying charges threaten to keep its ordinary budget perpetually unbalanced? Here was one of the most important lessons that a banker could teach both sovereigns and administrators. Where the finance minister has a sharp eye for savings throughout the vast administrative apparatus of the royal government, the cumulative effect could be enough to balance the ordinary expenditures by ordinary revenues. When that point is achieved, and peace-time succeeds wartime so that no more loans are necessary, then the government can see its way clear to amortize a great part of its debt, and consequently to reduce the tax burden on the king's subjects.

This fact was the main message, and certainly the one that must have made the greatest impact on his readers, in the entire book. When it is realized that almost all who attended the Assembly of Notables in 1787 had a copy of Necker's book and were intimately familiar with its description of the royal finances, one can understand what an impact Calonne's disclosures had on that assembly.

After a detailed accounting of the government's revenue and expenditures for 1784, Necker summed up his discussion by showing that the government's income was about 600 million livres, and its expenditures amounted to 610 million livres, about a 10-million deficit. His own Compte rendu nearly four years before had shown a 10.2 million surplus of ordinary revenue over ordinary expenditures. Now, in 1784, it was incumbent upon him to show how the financial posture of the government that year tied in with his earlier official report to the king on the state of his finances.[24] The surplus announced in the Compte rendu of January 1781 was almost used up in the two life rente loans of February and March of that year. So by the time of his resignation in May the ordinary income was about even with expenditures. The 10 million livres estimated deficit in 1784 was explained by listing all the new sources of royal revenue since that time and the new expenditures. The former included the new tax measures of Joly de Fleury and Ormesson, Necker's successors at the Contrôle général, and other sources such as the extinction of obligations on debts, and the increase of income from indirect taxes. The fixed expenditures incurred since May 1781 were due mostly to new loans of Joly de Fleury, Ormesson, and Calonne's first major loan of December 1783. The total of new revenue came to 63 million livres, the total of expenditures came to 73 million livres. The third vingtième would expire at the end of 1786. That would mean a loss of 21.5 million livres per year. But Necker did not think the financial outlook was particularly worrisome. The indirect taxes would continue to increase in yield, and the government was steadily amortizing its debt which would continually reduce ordinary expenditures.[25] Furthermore this was not even considering the enormous possibilities for savings which he had just enumerated. With wise management there seemed to be no reason for apprehension about the royal finances.

There was one lingering debt from the American War that ended in 1783. About 220 million livres of naval notes were yet to be redeemed by the government. This debt was not included in the accounts of expenditures because interest was not paid on it currently but only at the time the notes were liquidated. Once this debt had been paid Necker could see no reason for more government loans. It so happened that soon after Necker wrote that comment in his book Calonne issued his second major loan, in December 1784, with a capital value of 125 million livres. He explained in the loan edict that this was to be used to liquidate the remainder of the war debt. But he had also said that in his first loan of December 1783.

So the readers of "On the Administration of Finances in France" had little reason to suspect that the royal government was on the brink of a major financial disaster that would convulse the nation and bring on the Revolution. But readers were also forcefully impressed with the thought that this favorable situation required continuation of the policies Necker had initiated during his ministry: great integrity on the part of the finance minister, his stern resistance to importunate and unjustified requests of courtiers, and particularly the high ranking aristocrats and princes near the king; a minister willing to cut costs wherever possible, to carry on his management of the royal finances above board, publicizing his acts and achievements. Did France have that kind of finance

minister in 1785?   By that date it was apparent to
many observers that it did not.

[1]Edgar Faure, La Disgrâce de Turgot, 12 mai 1776 (Paris, 1961); La Banqueroute de Law, 17 juillet 1720 (Paris, 1977).

[2]Jean-Joseph Mounier, Recherches sur les causes qui ont empèché les Français de devenir libre (Genève, 1792), II, 27.

[3]Trophime-Gérard de Lally-Tolendal, "Necker", in La Biographie universelle (Paris, 1811-1849), XXX, 268.

[4]Florimond-Claude, comte de Mercy-Argenteau, Correspondance secrète du comte de Mercy-Argenteau avec l'empereur Joseph II et le prince de Kaunitz (Paris, 1889-1891), I, 225-226.

[5]Duc de Castries, Le Maréchal de Castries (Paris, 1955), 134.

[6]Louis Petit de Bachaumont, Mémoires secrèts pour servir à l'histoire de la République des Lettres en France depuis 1762 jusqu'à nos jours (Paris, 1777-1789), XXV, 219-220.

[7]Ibid., XXX, 59-60.

[8]Ibid., XXXI, 87.

[9]Ibid., XXXII, 265-266.

[10]"Journal du libraire Hardy," Bibliothèque nationale (BN), MSS Fonds Français, 6685, fol. 53. The journal of Metra reported earlier in January that Panckoucke was ready to sell 6000 copies on January 6 but that the sale was being held up by Calonne until his loan was closed out. Presumably he referred to the loan of December 1784. Metra, Correspondance secrète (1967 reprint), III 237.

[11]Correspondance diplomatique du baron de Staël-Holstein, Ambassadeur de Suède en France (Paris, 1881), 15.

[12]Hardy, op. cit., fol. 74.

[13]Loc. cit.

[14]Metra, Correspondance secrète (1967), III, 349.

[15]Jacques Necker, De l'Administration des finances en France, in Oeuvres complètes, IV, 97-98.

[16]In the enormous memoir literature of the French Revolution the following seem to present a just description of the character of Louis XVI: J. de Norvins, Mémorial (Paris, 1896), 204-206; Marmontal, Mémoires de Marmontal (Paris, 1891), publiés par Maurice Tourneux, III, 120; J. N. Moreau, Mes Souvenirs (Paris, 1898-1901), Seconde partie, 327.

[17]Jacques Necker, De l'importance des opinions religeuses (London et Paris, 1788).

[18]Necker, De l'Administration des finances en France, in Oeuvres complètes, IV, 70-71.

[19]Ibid., p. 75.

[20]Baron Besenval was an intimate in the circle of the duchess de Polignac and knew from the inside the character of Necker's enemies. He made the following comment about the entrance of Necker to the ministry in August, 1788: "Mr. Necker has against him only the people who seek to enrich themselves at the expense of others, to profit from the public distress in order to make a fortune, as well as the courtiers who fear [Necker's] austerity in opposition to the sums they hope to receive by favor." Pierre-Victor de Besenval, Mémoires (Paris, 1851), 345. Questions have been raised, however, about the authenticity of these memoirs.

[21]Peter Mathias and Patrick O'Brien, "Taxation in Britain and France 1715-1810. A Comparison of the Social and Economic Incidence of Taxes Collected for the Central Governments," Journal of European Economic History , 5 (Winter, 1976), 601-50; 7 (Spring, 1978), 209-213.

[22]See my Necker, Reform Statesman of the Ancien Régime (Berkeley, 1979), 139-159. In a review of this book, which was generally favorable, J. F. Bosher asked, however, why I had failed to point out that "Necker's goal . . . was to establish a stronger treasury and a single or consolidated revenue fund, a technical objective which does not appear in his writings but only emerges from a close study of the system he was trying to reform and the legislation by which he began to reform it." The Journal of Modern History (March, 1981), 53(1), 81. I had made a close study of all Necker's legislation and it does not seem to me that he ever intended to go that far, certainly not during his first ministry. The consolidation of all

28

the different <u>caisses</u> into a single one had been urged
by Isaac Panchaud when he was an advisor to Joly de
Fleury in 1782. See BN MSS Joly de Fleury, 1434, fol.
10.

[23]Necker, <u>De</u> <u>l'administration</u> <u>des</u> <u>finances</u>, in
<u>Oeuvres</u> <u>complètes</u>, v, 125-126.

[24]Marcel Marion maintained that Necker's motive
in writing this three-volume opus was to cover up the
fraudulent sleight-of-hand in his <u>Compte</u> <u>rendu</u> of
1781! <u>Histoire</u> <u>financière</u> <u>de</u> <u>la</u> <u>France</u> (Paris, 1914),
I, 370.

[25]Necker, <u>De</u> <u>l'administration</u> <u>des</u> <u>finances,</u> in
<u>Oeuvres</u> <u>complètes</u>, V, 238-240.

CHAPTER 2

NECKER'S SUCCESSORS AT THE CONTROLE GENERAL

Necker's resignation on May 19, 1781 came nearly
two years before the conclusion of the American War.
Those later years were the most costly for France
during the long conflict. Extraordinary war expenditures amounted to about two hundred million livres
in each of those years. Hostilities ended on January
20, 1783, but the final Peace of Versailles was not
signed until September of that year. Just before
leaving office in May 1781, Necker gave to the king a
statement of the financial situation for the remainder
of the year 1781 which indicated that there would be a
surplus in the Treasury at the beginning of 1782 of
about 64 million livres.[1]

The new minister of finance took the same title
as Necker's, "Director General." He was Jean-François
Joly de Fleury, a member of an old and distinguished
family of the robe. It appears that Necker had considerable respect for this magistrate, even though the
new finance minister was a defender of the ancien
régime who had little taste for most of Necker's reform ideas. The magistrate class in general disliked
Necker's view of the institution of venality of office, and especially his scheme to expand his provincial assemblies and administrations throughout the
kingdom as a substitute for the overweening authority
of the intendants. The magistrates feared those new
assemblies as a threat to their power as well, and
their resistance to Necker's attempt to expand those
assemblies was the incident that led to his resignation.[2] It is probable that Joly de Fleury was chosen
in order to mollify the courts of magistrates. In any
case it proved to be advantageous to have a person who
was influential with the Parlement of Paris in the

31

post of finance minister during the last two years of the war. There was no serious protest by the Parlement throughout the ministry of Joly de Fleury of new taxes and more loans.

At first there was fear that the resignation of Necker might jeopardize the government's credit which the Genevan had managed to maintain at an impressive level. Necker's last loan, the life rente loan of March 1781, did slacken in the market place and Joly de Fleury withdrew about thirteen million livres worth of the bordereaux which had been let out to brokers, so that only about 25 million livres worth of the loan was actually subscribed.[3] Eventually the remaining bordereaux were sold, probably in the ministry of Henry Lefevre d'Ormesson who succeeded Joly de Fleury on March 31, 1783.[4] Uneasy about the government's credit in the first months of his ministry, Joly de Fleury decided that it was necessary to increase tax revenue. In July 1781 a 10% surtax was placed on all indirect taxes. This yielded an increase in revenue variously estimated at from 20 to 25 million livres annually. With that increase in revenue Fleury believed it was feasible to attempt another large loan of life rentes. This loan edict was published in January 1782. To the relief of the minister the loan was eagerly bought up by investors so that it was soon raised to a capital of 120 million livres and 12 million rentes.[5]

The victory at Yorktown in October 1781 gave hope that the war would soon be concluded and with it the end of the enormous strain on the royal finances. But in the following summer Admiral de Grasse suffered a severe naval defeat at the hands of the British fleet. It appeared to Joly de Fleury and his staff at the Contrôle Général that plans must be made to finance another full year of war. In July 1782 he imposed a third vingtième on the other two vingtièmes, which amounted to a direct tax on agricultural income of

32

thirteen percent.[6] By December of that year it was decided that another major loan would be necessary. It was feared that the market for life rente loans had been exhausted. So a new loan of perpetual rentes at 5% was offered investors. The investors could purchase the rentes by paying one-half the price in money and the other half in notes of government loans that had been issued many years ago and were no longer at par value on the market place. But the government would accept these notes at par value in payment for the rentes now being offered investors. The capital of this loan was to be 200 million livres. A month after the loan was promulgated hostilities came to an end. The finance minister could breathe a sigh of relief.

In March 1783 Joly de Fleury submitted a financial statement to the king entitled "The Situation of the Finances for 1783" in which it was shown that the Treasury would be well supplied for the needs of 1783 and could begin the following year with a surplus of 34,735,750 livres.[7] Certainly the American War had been different than the Seven Years' War when the royal government encountered stubborn resistance to new taxes by the Parlement of Paris, and where the credit of the government had deteriorated to such an extent that loans could not be marketed, no matter how advantageous the terms offered to investors.

One might have thought that the difference was due to the exceptional financial capabilities of Jacques Necker. Many did draw that conclusion but not Joly de Fleury. As already mentioned, this honorable and capable magistrate was a firm upholder of the ancien régime who disliked most of Necker's reform policies. He especially defended the institution of venality of office. The government, he maintained, needed to draw upon the fortunes of the wealthy. If those who made money in private enterprise invested it in government offices the benefit was mutual. The officer enjoyed various privileges, and the government could use the money. Joly de Fleury could see no harm in a strong, flourishing class of venal office-holders. On the contrary, they were the guarantee not only of cheap government loans at 5% but were loyal, responsible government servants. Most officers had inherited their offices and like Joly de Fleury himself came from families that had served in courts of magistrates and financial companies for generations. For Joly de Fleury a large class of venal officers was the guarantee of honesty, efficiency, and competence in carrying out the tasks of the government.[8]

The result of this thinking was that much of Necker's reform concerning the liquidation of superfluous offices was undone. The 48 receivers-general who collected the direct taxes for the royal treasury were restored. Necker had reduced the number to 12. Even offices abolished by Necker's predecessors, Turgot and Terray, were restored by Joly de Fleury. The alternate receivers of revenue in the élections numbering 204, which had been abolished by Turgot, were restored by Joly de Fleury. The offices attached to the Bureau of Finance and the Chamber of the Domain which had been abolished by abbé Terray were all restored by an edict in 1781. These offices included the 36 Treasurers of France.[9] Alternate treasurers of the different departments which had been abolished by Necker were restored by Joly de Fleury. The high profits that treasurers made by administering government money were resumed. He wished to restore the six intendants of finance in the Contrôle Général, but the king resisted that change.[10]

Other reforms of Necker were not abolished outright but were "counter-reformed" to remove those features that were most objectionable to the conservatives hostile to his reforms. For example the intendant's authority over the provincial assemblies and administrations in Berri and Haute Guienne was restored. The privileges of the numerous offices in the King's Household were restored.[11] In the interests of the landed proprietors subject to the direct land tax of the vingtièmes the edict of Joly de Fleury imposing the third vingtième in 1782 revoked Necker's reform of 1777 which laid down a new method of assessment that would bring the value of the land and harvests up to current market prices. The law of July 1782 stipulated that the tax rolls of the vingtième could not be revised in the future. In effect, it meant the restoration of the method whereby the wealthy and influential landowners had evaded their fair share of the tax burden.

In a similar matter, Necker had attempted to strengthen the king's hand against unreasonable demands for pensions and other favors by having all such grants from the treasury published each year. This policy was also discontinued by his successors. "All the old abuses are returning in a flood," wrote Mercy-Argenteau to Emperor Joseph in October 1781. In the same letter he referred to the scandalous debts of the comte d'Artois and the affair of Radix de Sainte-Foy, former treasurer of d'Artois who was now suspected of malversation of funds while holding that office.[12] In February 1782 the finance minister reported that a special grant of 1,607,270 livres was made to the comte d'Artois to meet his most pressing engagements, "but this arrangement only suspends momentarily the evil."[13] The financial statement of Joly de Fleury submitted to the king in March 1783 indicated that an extraordinary grant of two million livres was given to Artois that year.[14]

The impetuous rush for royal favors and pensions did not proceed without resistance. The king became concerned about the matter as did the other ministers. The attachment of Joly de Fleury to the institutions and practices of the ancien régime did not imply spendthrift irresponsibility. He was scrupulous about

35

keeping strict account of the finances. In January
1782 one of the most complete accountings of all the
debts of the king since the beginning of 1777 was
drawn up.[15] Joly de Fleury wanted to continue the accounting procedures initiated by Necker whereby all
expenditures of each department of the government
would be submitted monthly and annually to the minister of finance. No less concerned about the increase
of money going to favorites was the minister of foreign affairs, the comte de Vergennes. After the conclusion of the hostilities of the American War in January 1783 Vergennes was promoted to the position of
the Head of the Royal Council of Finances, the post
held by the comte de Maurepas which had not been
filled since the latter's death in November 1781.
This in effect made Vergennes the principal minister
of the government.

In February 1783 Vergennes created a special committee on finances to supervise all expenditures of
the royal government. The Regulation of February 26,
1783 setting up the committee stipulated that it would
be composed of the Head of the Royal Council of Finances, the Director General of Finances, the Keeper
of the Seals (Hue de Miromesnil) and also two officers
of the Chamber of Accounts and two of the Court of
Aides. The Council was charged by the Regulation to
meet at least once a week or oftener. "All ordonnateurs [those entrusted with spending government funds]
without exception will remit to His Majesty without
delay the debt-in-arrears of their respective departments as of last January 1st. Also they will send an
account of their ordinary and extraordinary expenditures that they estimate to be indispensable in time
of peace." All requests for extraordinary expenses
and payments of old claims would be brought before
this Committee. It was especially charged to scrutinize pensions and favors.[16]

The setting up of the Committee on Finances was certainly the kind of "order" that Necker had constantly preached. The "Situation of the Finances for 1783" that Joly de Fleury was able to submit to the king in March must have been the first fruit of this institution. Yet soon after that document was sent to the king Joly de Fleury stepped down as finance minister. The reasons for his departure are not very clear. In his biography of the Marshal de Castries, Secretary of State for the Navy, the duc de Castries asserts that the setting up of the committee was a maneuver by Joly de Fleury supported by Vergennes to force the resignation of Castries. There had been tension between Castries and the finance minister since the beginning of the latter's ministry over the insistence of Joly de Fleury that the Navy Department comply with the restraints Necker had placed upon all the military departments. That is, to send monthly and annual accounts to the Contrôle Général and not to issue letters of credit without authorization of the finance minister. These matters had been the source of tension between Necker and the predecessors of Castries in the Navy Department, Sartine, and the Marquis de Ségur in the War Department. After the replacement of Sartines and Montbary in later 1780 by Castries and Ségur, Necker seemed to enjoy good relations with both secretaries of state. But the Naval Department continued to resist complying with the reforms of Necker in the succeeding ministry of Joly de Fleury, despite repeated edicts which stated expressly that "these rules apply to the Naval Department too." In the last months of hostilities Castries had issued naval letters of credit to pay for expenditures in the East Indies without authorization. The same kind of showdown was looming that had occurred between Necker and Sartine in October 1780. Now the establishment of the Committee on Finance to oversee and control all expenditures was felt by Castries to be an intolerable affront. As his descendent described his feelings: "In order to bridle the minister of integrity and make it appear that he had dilapidated public funds, the king was persuaded of the necessity of setting up a Committee on Finance where would be discussed all the anticipated expenditures of the ministry; such a treatment inflicted upon the budget of the Navy in time of war would be catastrophic."[17] But the war was over, an armistice having been reached about two months before the establishment of the controversial committee. Despite his optimism about the general credit situation of the government Joly de Fleury was none the less concerned about reducing expenditures as soon as possible and begin the process of liquidating the war debt. Castries had ambitions not only for rebuilding the naval vessels destroyed in war but also new ships and undertaking major construction of naval ports, notably at Dunkirk and Cherbourg. Believing that the new Committee on Finance was a personal attack on himself, Castries submitted his resignation to the king, or rather he read his resignation message first to the queen, who persuaded him to delay giving it to the king for a week, so that he would not make the Committee of Finance the issue of his resignation. In the meantime, both Castries and Ségur were mollified with the promotion to rank of marshal.[18] The Committee on Finance was not abolished, although with what effectiveness it functioned is unknown. If this was the reason for the resignation of Joly de Fleury the incident did not augur well for the future administration of the royal finances. It reflected clearly the principal problem faced by the government of Louis XVI in attempting to put the finances in order and to bring spending under control. If the distinguished and highly respected secretaries of state for the armed forces would not tolerate budgetary control by such an institution as the Committee on Finance there was little hope of restraining the two princely brothers of the king or the other grands who looked upon the royal treasury as inexhaustible. If the time

38

should come when the minister of finance himself had no interest in curtailing expenditures and balancing the budget, the future of the country would be in peril.

This did not occur however in the ministry of Joly de Fleury's successor, Henry Lefèvre d'Ormesson. The reasons for the appointment of this 32-year-old magistrate to such a crucial position are as obscure as the reasons for the resignation of Joly de Fleury. The king seemed to have been impressed by his management of the Ecole de Saint-Cyr. The new minister resumed the title of Controller General which had been discontinued at the time of Necker's appointment as Director of Finances. Henry d'Ormesson exhibited some of the parsimonious habits of Necker, without however being a follower of the Genevan banker. Like Joly de Fleury, he was a member of an illustrious family of magistrates and was loyal to the institutions of the ancien régime. He retained the Committee on Finance and it appears that through this institution he was able to offer considerable resistance to pressure for pensions and other gratifications.[19]

Although a conservative of the ancien régime who, like Joly de Fleury, had sought to persuade the king to restore the six intendants of finance, there was a return in some measure to Necker's policy of eliminating offices that were clearly useless. One edict of July 1783 abolishing the offices of treasurers and controllers in a military department stated that "we have by different edicts, eliminated several offices of which we have recognized the lack of necessity or that the privileges attached to them are onerous to our people and our finances."[20]

Even though hostilities ended with the armistice of the 20th of January 1783, the extraordinary expenditures for the military departments were still heavy. Joly de Fleury had planned a new lottery loan of 24 million livres to keep the treasury in that "state of abundance" he always thought necessary to maintain the government's credit. This loan was carried out by his successor in April. Later in the year in October, another lottery loan of 24 million livres was issued. Neither of Ormesson's two major loans seemed to have aroused any opposition from the Parlement of Paris.

Two events in September and October, 1783, led to the undermining of Ormesson's position with the chief minister, Vergennes, and the king, and made possible for those hostile to his policy of economy to have him removed from office. One concerned the Discount Bank, which was a private company and not really the responsibility of the Controller General. But the public tended to see the Discount Bank as having the same relationship to the government as did the Bank of England to the British government. The public perception of that relationship was untrue. The Discount Bank was created to provide a banking facility for private businesses, and its area of operation was limited to Paris. Unlike the Bank of England the Discount Bank was not intended to make loans to the government, nor did its notes that circulated have government backing. The Discount Bank's notes were backed by its own resources consisting of the money invested in it by stockholders and by the commercial paper that it had discounted that was in its vaults. Occasionally the Directors of the bank might over-extend its operation and find themselves compelled to suspend conversion of its notes into cash or other assets, when these notes were presented by the public. But these were only momentary episodes in the history of the Bank which had been founded by Turgot in 1776. The Discount Bank, up to the summer of 1783 had always been prudently managed. Some financial experts wanted it to become like the Bank of England, a source of short term loans for the government and whose notes would become as acceptable in circulation as hard currency by the general public. Necker was wary of this, and he explained why

40

in his 1784 book "On the Administration of Finances."
If the Discount Bank were prudently managed as the
Bank of England such a venture could be successful.
But he understood the nature of the strong credit
power of the British government and the Bank of England as few French magistrates did. He knew the temptation for ministers of the government to borrow from
it without restraint when there were no safeguards
against unlimited government expenditures. In England
the control exercised by Parliament over the British
fiscal system prevented such abuses. The French public and the French journalists of the day were inveterately suspicious of bank notes that circulated as
money. The memory of the "System" of John Law was
still strong in the popular mind. As the Swiss financial expert, Rilliet de Saussure, complained, the
French mistook the "System" for a bank when it was
nothing of the kind. It was a system of unlimited
printing of paper money by the government and which
was given forced circulation.[21]

The events of the Discount Bank that led to trouble began in the early summer of 1783 when it found
itself short of funds to redeem its notes presented to
it by the public. The directors asked the Controller
General to lend the bank 20 million livres to meet
what was only a short-term or temporary over-exten-
sion. Later in the summer, after that crisis had been
weathered, the Controller General sought to get a loan
of 24 million livres from the Discount Bank, something
that had never been done before. Necker, writing
about the incident in 1784, thought the Directors of
the Discount Bank were lacking in character not to
have refused the request.[22] The consequences were
disastrous. The loan caused a panic among holders of
the banknotes who began a run on it. By an order in
council of September 27, 1783, the government intervened and suspended conversion of the notes into money
until the first of January, 1785.[23] This of course
made the panic worse. Both Bachaumont and Hardy re-

41

ported that the "black notes" (of the Discount Bank) were going to be given forced circulation. Manufacturers of ladies fashionable bonnets were now selling "bonnets of the Discount Bank," which were "without fonds [bottoms]." Despite such sarcasm, the crisis was only a temporary one. In October the Bank began partial redemption of its large notes. In November, after a reorganization of the Bank by Calonne, full convertibility was restored. The Bank was basically sound, as was the credit of the government. In October Ormesson managed to float his second lottery loan of 24 million with success. The incident demonstrated not a precarious credit posture of the government but the extreme excitability of the French public about the circulation of bank notes as a medium of exchange.[24]

The second event that seems to have led to the dismissal of Ormesson was the complaint of the Farmers-General over his rewriting of the contract of 1780. An order in council of the 20th of October converted the Farmers-General into a régie. This was not such a drastic change as it might seem, for Necker very largely altered the character of the General Farm in the contract of 1780 making it similar to a régie.[25] Ormesson simply put the final touch to this process apparently without consulting the Farmers-General about the matter. A great outcry arose from the financial company, and this was joined with other sources of dissatisfaction with the youthful Controller General. In the fall of 1783 at the time of the formal signing of the peace treaty with Great Britain there seemed to be a special surge of requests for favors made upon both the king and the queen. The king's two brothers were, as usual, importunate in their demands for more financial assistance to meet their debts. The prince de Conti, the duc de Penthièvre, the prince de Guémenée were all pressing the king to purchase property at terms favorable to themselves in order to save their households from im-

42

minent bankruptcy. "It is said," wrote Bachaumont, "that the four corners of the queen: the Polignacs, the Vaudreuil, the Guiches, and the Périgord, are all united in urging the queen to insist on the dismissal of Ormesson."26 Bachaumont also reported that the Secretary of State for the Navy and Colonies, Castries, and the Secretary of State for War, Ségur, were hostile to Ormesson who was pressing them to comply with the edicts requiring them to submit their accounts to the Contrôle Général. There was also dissatisfaction with the Committee on Finance established in February, although according to the Austrian ambassador it was so weak under Ormesson's ministry as to "provoke derision."27 Ironically, Mercy-Argenteau had urged the queen to oppose the establishment of the Committee on Finance in February because he feared that it would increase the authority of Vergennes who was considered anti-Austrian in his foreign policy. Yet the ambassador was one of those who realized the seriousness of the lack of control over expenditures.28

Finally, Vergennes himself lost interest in defending the Committee as well as the Controller-General, and on November 2 the foreign minister handed to Ormesson the king's request for his resignation.

The next day, November 23, 1783, it was learned that the new Controller-General was the intendant of Valenciennes, Charles-Alexandre de Calonne. The reasons why the king made that choice are not very clear, and the sources on the subject none too reliable. In his letter to the emperor, Mercy-Argenteau said the queen had no part in the decision. But the editors of the published correspondence, Arneth and Flammermont, say that is not true. Relying upon the memoirs of Augeard, a Farmer-General and an officer of the guards in the Queen's Household, they say it was the duchesse de Polignac, baron de Besenval, and Augeard himself who urged the queen to press the king for the appointment of Calonne. The queen was admittedly reluctant at first, but finally acquiesed.[29] Also urging the appointment of Calonne was one of the guardians of the Royal Treasury, d'Harveley (whose wife was said to be Calonne's mistress) and baron de Breteuil, Secretary of State for the King's Household and recently the French ambassador to Vienna. It was, wrote Augeard, a fatal decision. From it came the destruction of the monarchy and the execution of the king and the queen.[30]

Charles-Alexandre de Calonne had spent most of his years of service up until his appointment to the Contrôle Général as intendant in the provinces. He was a servant of the "administrative monarchy" and for that reason he did not have the opportunity of Joly de Fleury to influence the Parlement of Paris. On the contrary, Calonne had been a noted foe of the parliamentary cause in the affair which, before 1789, was always referred to as "the revolution." This was the destruction of the parlementary opposition by Chancellor Maupeou in 1771. Calonne, as a young magistrate, had represented the government's cause in the famous La Chalatois case in Brittany which preceded the showdown in 1771. For that reason alone his appointment was not received enthusiastically by the magistrates of the Parlement of Paris.

Like Necker, Calonne was the victim of scurillous, outrageous libels during his ministerial career, and the historian must treat them with the same critical spirit as the libels against Necker. But with that caveat it does appear that Calonne came to the post of finance minister with a very bad personal reputation. Mercy-Argenteau wrote the emperor that "Calonne has intelligence but the public detests him because of his character and reputation for dishonesty."[31] All other witnesses agree as to his intelligence. He had a quick lawyer's mind that could readily seize complicated subjects and reduce them to es-

44

sentials. He had a particular facility for explaining complex subjects to others of less intelligence. Bachaumont reported on a meeting of the Council presided over by the king in which the Secretary of State for the Navy and Colonies, Marshal de Castries, was reading a lengthy report. The king was obviously bored and began to yawn. Calonne took over the report from Castries and explained the matter in such a lively style as to keep the king interested and awake throughout the meeting.[32]

Calonne's great gift was his ability to ingratiate himself with those who mattered. He was the consumate courtier of the _ancien régime_, representing to a high degree that great change in the character of the French nobility that Necker was to remark upon in his memoirs on the French Revolution. From a spirit of independence vis-a-vis the court which had been typical of the old nobility a great transformation had been brought about by Richelieu, that of the feudal nobility to a court nobility. The most important talent of the latter was not to exercise independent thought and command, but to please the king and those who were powerful at court.[33] In such an environment Calonne had every advantage.

For a finance minister such a character would lead to exactly the opposite policy than Necker's frugality and emphasis upon economy. Weber wrote that "Calonne had a great desire to please, which made refusal difficult, and he had a boundless imagination which led him to depend upon hopes rather than reality."[34] In the milieu to which his tastes and outlook led him, the circle of the friends of the comte d'Artois and the queen, which included such persons as the baron de Besenval, the comte d'Angiviller, the comte de Vaudreuil and Radix de Sainte-Foy, the fundamental conviction was that the grandeur, prestige and the "splendor" (_éclat_) of the throne was the only consideration. A wealthy country could afford great

45

expenditures by the king. The miserly policy of Necker may have been suitable for a city-state like Geneva but not for the greatest kingdom in the world. Besenval wrote in his memoirs that the remedy for financial problems was for the king to repudiate his debts, which after all, were held by creditors who were mostly Jews, Swiss or Dutch protestants, and similarly disreputable bourgeois people. He believed that the bankruptcy following the "system" of John Law was a good example of how to handle the royal debt.[35] If Calonne was not quite as irresponsible and preposterous on this subject as his good friend Besenval, he did believe that Necker's economy was totally unfit and unnecessary for France. As intendant of Valencienne during Necker's first ministry, Calonne was among those intendants who bitterly opposed Necker's plans to establish provincial assemblies which was at the expense of the powers of the intendants in the generalities. He had joined the anti-Necker pamphlet campaign, and according to his friend Augerard, was the author of the pamphlet entitled Les Comments. This was an assault on Necker's Compte rendu of 1781 as well as his policy of economy.

About the "prodigalities" of Calonne there is wide disagreement among historians as to the actual amount that was spent needlessly, and the ultimate consequences of Calonne's policy in bringing about the financial crisis that precipitated the Revolution. Through the nineteenth century the general belief was that Calonne practiced what he preached, and that his free-handed largess did cause the financial crisis. Madame de Staël wrote that if there was any one cause for the French Revolution it was the character of Calonne. "He wished to please at court by lavish distribution of money. He encouraged the king, the queen, and the princes not to deny themselves in any of their tastes, assuring them that [expenditures] for luxuries was the fountain of the prosperity of the states."[36] In his books on the financial origins of

46

the French Revolution, Charles Gomel, writing near the
end of the nineteenth century, was extremely severe
toward Necker, giving him the dubious honor that
Madame de Staël bestowed upon Calonne as the person
who "caused" the Revolution. But Gomel had no brief
for Calonne either, and listed in detail his
"prodigalities."[37] Marcel Marion, in the first volume
of his monumental financial history of France, followed somewhat the judgment of Gomel, but was inclined
to be more indulgent to Calonne, at least to exculpate
him for having brought about the financial crisis of
1787. Marion condemned Calonne's free-handed shower-
ing of "gifts, pensions, forgiveness of taxes, transforming life pensions into pensions of perpetuity,
etc., given with a deplorable facility."[38] The
"amiable minister did not know how to refuse. He tolerated around him . . . waste, profusion, dissipation." But Marion thought Calonne's profusions had
been greatly exaggerated; and above all, Marion could
not agree that Calonne should be saddled with the responsibility for the financial crisis rather than his
too-famous predecessor, Necker. "It is impossible,"
he wrote, "to be precise as to what the prodigalities
of Calonne cost the state, but it is certain that to
see in his open-handedness toward courtiers the principal cause for the ruin of the finances is to exceed
all bounds."[39]

Looking at the famous "Red Book" that was published in 1790 Marion found it records the amount of
extraordinary financial aid given to the king's two
brothers, the comte d'Artois and the comte de Provence
during the years 1783-1787. This sum was 13,814,000
livres for Monsieur, and 14 million livres to the
younger brother, comte d'Artois. "The other gifts and
gratuities were a little under three million livres
(for those same years) out of a total of 6,174,793
livres for the entire reign. The indemnities, advances, and loans were 4,120,000 out of a total of
15,294,101; the acquisitions and exchanges (of prop-

erty) came to 20,868,821 livres."[40] Marion also cites a document in the Archives nationales containing a list of favors granted to individuals each year by the king. "These favors in 1784 were around 270,000 livres; in 1785, 210,000 livres. The sums given only one time came to 660,000 and 495,000 livres respectively. In 1778 and 1779 [years of Necker's first ministry] war years it must be remembered--these figures were respectively 65,000 and 148,000, 300,000 and 122,000 livres. The difference is not so great as to justify the traditional reputation of rigid inflexibility on Necker's part and systematic prodigality on Calonne's."[41]

To a banker's mind the differences in the latter figures may not seem quite so insignificant. Considering all the figures given in the above paragraph as a summary of the "prodigalities" of Calonne, Marion established his comparison of the Necker and Calonne ministries on a narrow basis. As readers of Necker's book on the administration of finances were able to see, the Genevan's policy of austerity was not simply a matter of withholding special favors to courtiers. The central issue in the administration of finances was the ability of the finance minister to control all expenditures throughout the far-flung administration of the ancien régime, not just pensions and gratuities. Establishing control consisted in such policies as publicizing the expenditures of each department of the administration, so that the ministers of the royal council could have a precise knowledge of where the government stood financially. Policies such as the liquidation of useless venal offices were for the purpose of establishing that control. Requiring ministers and department heads to submit to the Contrôle général regular accounts of their operations was essential if "order" was to be established in the financial administration. Furthermore, even in the granting of royal favors the finance minister had it within his power to grant them throughout the adminis-

48

tration of finances. For example, in the compte rendu in 1787 that Calonne drew up the amount allotted for "unforeseen expenditures" was twelve million livres. It had been three million livres in Necker's compte rendu of 1781. Finally the issue between Necker and Calonne was not simply profusion and waste of the royal government's money. A considerable part of Calonne's expenditures for internal improvements--harbors, roads, buildings--would not have been objectionable if the royal finances were in a condition to afford them. But it made no sense to Necker, nor any other prudent person in that day, for the government to spend prodigious amounts of money for such purposes, however laudable they might otherwise be, when Calonne was required to summon an assembly of notables and inform them that the government was facing imminent bankruptcy, and ask them to approve sweeping reform measures in a matter of weeks.[42]

The "prodigalities" of Calonne consisted of various kinds: real estate exchanges by influential courtiers for portions of the royal domain made at disadvantageous terms for the king; creation of offices as in the ministry of Joly de Fleury, with accompanying privileges and excessive profits to the purchasers; and granting of favors to individual subjects. The Committee of Finance set up in February by Joly de Fleury to oversee and control all expenditures, especially those for pensions and gifts, was abolished by Calonne at the beginning of his ministry and there was no substitute. The Farmers-General were restored to their former position before Ormesson's reform of October 24. Pension lists were no longer published, and once again became secret.[43]

Among the exchanges of real estate that provoked the most comment was the king's acquisition of the Château of Rambouillet purchased from the duc de Penthièvre for 18 million livres to be paid over a period of three years. It was a good bargain for the

49

duke, according to Bachaumont, because its annual revenue was only 300,000 livres per year.[44] That would have been an annual revenue equal to 1.66% of the purchase price! Another purchase that provoked much comment in the press was the queen's acquisition of the château and grounds of Saint-Cloud. This was purchased from the duc d'Orleans for 6 million livres. In 1784 the Clermontois lands were purchased from the prince de Condé in exchange for 12 million livres, granted in the form of perpetual rentes of 600,000 per year. The sale of the Porte de l'Orient by the prince de Guémenée to the king was negotiated at a price of 11 million livres, which Bachaumont asserted was hardly worth 4 or 5 million livres; it was paid for in a period of 22 years at 500,000 livres per year. Most discussed of all these exchanges was the contract of March 30, 1785 with the comte d'Espagnac who sold the county of Sancerre for domain lands. This was one of the most notorious of such deals because Calonne purchased some of those lands for his own private estate. Later in his apologia written to Louis XVI after his fall from power Calonne maintained that he had secured the consent of the king and that there was nothing illegal or improper about the transaction.[45] In 1791 the National Assembly set aside the contract for Sancerre after an investigation revealed that it was worth 2,008,616 livres and was exchanged for domain land worth 5,783,282 livres.[46] In his apologia to the king in 1787 Calonne maintained that the negotiations for all the above transactions were initiated by his predecessors and he was not responsible for them. The first part of the claim might be true, but they were all officially authorized by royal acts in his administration. Calonne's plea would have been more convincing if he had shown some evidence of resisting or protesting against those transactions. On the contrary he continually extolled his policy of liberality to courtiers in contrast to the "mean-spirited" parsimony of his predecessor.[47]

Among the offices created for special favorites, one of the most notorious was the order in council of October 30, 1785, which separated the _ferme_ of the postal service from that of the _messagéries_ (stage-coach lines) simply in order to create a special office for the duc de Polignac at a salary of 50,000 livres per year. This added a total increase of expenditure for the new _ferme_ of 600,000 livres according to Mercy-Argenteau in a letter to the Emperor. "I wish," he complained, "that those who enjoy the protection of the queen would show less greed." He added that this was only one of a number of such transactions, "the details of which would be too painful to list."[48]

These extravagant expenditures did not go unnoticed by other ambassadors. Dorset wrote to the British foreign secretary in August, 1785: "Your Lordship will not be surprised at the difficulties in which a Minister of Finance finds himself in this country, when you consider the very profuse manner in which the public money is disposed of; and indeed such is the nature of the Government, the Court and its dependents, that a Comptroller General with the best disposition for economy, and the sincerest intentions of administering well, must necessarily meet with such obstacles as to render it impossible to pursue any steady and digested plan." He referred to one incident he believed typical: the two aunts of the king wished to go to the baths at Vichy for six weeks or two months at a cost of three million livres. "M. de Calonne cannot be supposed to have favoured the undertaking this journey at so unreasonable a cost, but it cannot be supposed, either, that he could venture to oppose it."[49] Calonne's apologists maintain that it was not in his power to resist such extravagance. But the essential matter was that he made no attempt to resist it because that was not his policy.

There were many offices restored or created by Calonne. In December 1783 the office of treasurer-general of the King's Household in charge of buildings which had been abolished by Necker was restored, no doubt to the pleasure of that Necker-hater, the comte d'Angiviller, who was head of the establishment. In January three new offices were created for the division of the marc d'or, with a finance of 300,000 livres; in March 1784 two offices of receivers-general in finance for the city of Paris were created having a finance of 700,000 livres; in April the "droits de contrôle" were restored to the office of the Controller General; these had been abolished by Necker in 1777. They consisted of a variety of commissions, emoluments, profits that accrued to the Controller General and made that post one of the wealthiest in the government. Necker had abolished them all when he came to the helm of finances. But Calonne had no compunction about extending the prerogatives of his office as far as they could reach. In May 1784 came the restoration of the office of treasurer of offerings and alms, which had been abolished by Necker. In September 1784 Calonne created 20 new offices of payers of rentes at the Hôtel de Ville; the purpose was entirely laudable, as will be seen below, but each new payer required an officer called treasurer and another called controller. The total capital of the newly created offices by this edict of September was 7,800,000 livres. In 1786 in order to facilitate the conversion of the gold louis the commissioned money-changers of the Hôtel des Monnaies were transformed into venal offices and 283 new offices of agents of exchange were created for the city of Paris, with the total capital value of the offices amounting to 6 million livres.[50] This is by no means an exhaustive list of the offices restored or created during Calonne's ministry. But it is enough to illustrate the contrast between his policy and Necker's.

During the first two years of his ministry there were a number of positive accomplishments that were entirely beneficial for the government's credit posture, and which Necker would have approved. The crisis of the Discount Bank in September 1783 was overcome soon after Calonne's appointment to the Contrôle général. In November of that year all notes of the Discount Bank were again redeemed in specie. In 1784, probably following the advice of his friend and financial advisor, Isaac Panchaud, Calonne made an effort to shorten the period that rentiers had to wait for the annual payment of their rentes by the Hôtel de Ville. The period had been six months. Payments in Calonne's administration were made as soon as they were due. This required a capital of eight million livres in extraordinary expenditures. A better knowledge of the health of the royal finances might have suggested it was preferable to keep the rentiers waiting six months, so long as they were paid punctually, even if late, until the treasury was in better condition to make that extraordinary expenditure.

In 1784 the Caisse d'Amortissement was founded, also probably due to the influence of Panchaud. This was an imitation of the Sinking Fund, long a custom in the English fiscal system. Each year three million livres would be poured into the Fund, and a definite schedule of amortization of all royal debts was set forth in the edict creating the Fund. In 1785 the Company of the Indies was restored as a government-protected monopoly of the East Indies trade, much to the dismay of the Economists, but Necker would have applauded that act. Calonne was most undoctrinaire in his economic ideas and policies. He was willing to take advice from the Economists also and in the same year as the Company of the Indies was restored he brought Dupont de Nemours into the government to take charge of the Bureau of Commerce. The Bureau of Commerce was also staffed by baron de Corméré who was drawing up plans for the single-duty project, the elimination of internal tariff barriers and transit duties.[51] In 1786, largely through the work of Dupont de Nemours the Eden Treaty was signed between France and England, greatly lowering tariffs and stimulating trade between the two countries.

The first two years of Calonne's ministry seemed to have been the most constructive, and the most serene. He himself firmly believed that it was incumbent on the finance minister constantly to exude optimism, let people think that the country is in capable hands and that there is nothing to be concerned about. The Swedish ambassador was much struck by this feature of Calonne's character. He wrote to Gustavus III in August 1784 that when Calonne talked to him "he always gives a very high opinion of the resources of the King his master; he assures me that they have never been as great as at this moment."[52]

The same note was always struck whenever Calonne had to offer a loan to the public. His preambles to the loan edicts resounded with the health and prosperity of the country and the royal government. It was in December 1783, about a month after he came to the Contrôle Général, that Calonne published his first loan. On December 1st he closed the last loan of Joly de Fleury, issued in December 1782 which had only been half subscribed (5 million livres rentes at 5% rather than 10 million livres, with a capital of 100 million livres rather than 200 million). Apparently Calonne thought this loan had exhausted itself and that little more could be raised by its continuation. The new loan to replace it was a life rente loan with a capital of 100 million livres, offered at 9% on one life and 8% on two lives. The rentes were exempt from the tax known as the dixième d'amortissement, which was a tax of one percent on interest income. But the loan also offered a bonus of 1,500,000 livres of additional life rentes to the subscribers who won the lucky numbers on the lottery wheel at the Hôtel de Ville. This added another 1-1/2% interest cost on the loan, making it the most expensive life _rente_ loan for the royal treasury since the beginning of the reign.

Calonne attempted to disarm the anticipated opposition to the loan edict by stating in the preamble that revenues of the king are steadily increasing due to the "care and regularity that is given to their collection," and also because of the increase in commerce, and the economizing of expenditures "which we do not cease to strive for." The preamble admitted that life _rente_ loans are the most onerous for the treasury but pledged that the king would not have recourse to any more life _rente_ loans in peacetime. Two other promises were made in the preamble of the loan of December 1783. One was that a Sinking Fund would be established in order "to liberate the state of its debts." The other promise was to "take appropriate measures to assure the balance of our expenditures with revenue so that we may eventually lighten the burden of taxation."[53]

It was to be expected that the Parlement of Paris would not register the loan edict without a murmur. Calonne, in his haughty manner, let the first president of the Parlement, d'Aligre, understand that the king anticipated no protest over the loan.[54] In fact the Parlement had made no protest about any government loan throughout the period of the American War. But now it was peacetime and the Parlement did not intend to keep silent. In a remonstrance sent to the king on December 17 the magistrates asserted "it is impossible to deny that the ordinary revenue of Your Majesty, the totality of the taxes, carried beyond what has been seen hitherto, and all the extraordinary measures, unfortunately too frequent in recent times, have been more than sufficient to pay for all the expenses of the war." The Parlement recognized that there was still a naval war debt to be liquidated, but it asked if a life _rente_ loan was the best way to handle it.

Life _rente_ loans, the Parlement stated, should not be used in peacetime. There is a better way to balance the ordinary budget, and that is by economy. "There is no item of expenditure which, by a very simple proceeding, could not be the subject of savings without detracting from the splendor of the throne or the well-being of the service." Specifically, the remonstrance called attention to the _acquits_ _de_ _comptant_ (expenditures not subject to the chambers of accounts), and gratifications; it called for a severe scrutiny of secret depredations, "always more frequent than is thought," and the overpayment of purchases to contractors due to the delay and uncertainty as to when they will be paid.[55]

The remonstrances of the sovereign courts in some ways always seemed alike in the eighteenth century. But this remonstrance bore too close a resemblance to Necker's reform policies to escape unnoticed. At the outset of his ministry Calonne had flaunted before him the record of his illustrious predecessor, the Genevan banker, whose fall from the ministry Calonne himself had played a not inconsiderable role in bringing about. The king's reply to the remonstrance was brief, written no doubt by Calonne. It stated that the entire proceeds of the loan were to be used to liquidate the naval debt arising from the recent war. No further comment was made by the Parlement over the loan of December 1783.

Despite the opposition of the magistrates to the loan, it was successfully marketed. In January Calonne was made minister of state, and his star continued to rise. Seventeen eighty-four was his good year. The Sinking Fund was founded in September and this move had a positive effect on government credit. The government bonds rose on the stock exchange (_bourse_). The spring and early summer brought unanticipated expenditures due to an unusually cold winter followed by a rapid thaw causing devastating floods.

56

Calonne met this emergency by imposing a 5% withholding tax on all pensions over 10,000 livres.[56]

By December Calonne saw that another major loan would be necessary. The new loan would raise a capital of 125 million livres to be sold in denominations of certificates (billets) of 1,000 livres at 5%, and to be amortized over 25 years. It was a lottery loan, each of the 125,000 "billets" was to be numbered, and the lucky numbers would be rewarded by bonuses from 15% to 100% above the capital invested. On the 29th of December the Parlement of Paris made representations about the loan, repeating substantially what it had said a year before. "The yield of (the king's) ordinary revenue and taxes in addition to all the extraordinary resources (loans) which were called upon during the war years should be sufficient to pay all the debts and the return of peace should see the beginning of the end of their acquitment." Again the Parlement condemned the "obscurity and confusion in the expenditures." The king's reply, written of course by Calonne, was that all the proceeds of the previous loan had been used to pay the war debt. "The present loan also will be used for the most part for the same purpose. I know precisely the amount of the debt and the final payments will be made in 1786."[57]

The year 1785 saw the beginning of the decline of Calonne's star. The 125 million loan was not well received by the investors or the public, and began to decline on the bourse. The appearance of Necker's book was a source of anxiety to him because he feared the impact it would have on the bourse, and on government "paper." It had been one of Necker's proudest boasts that throughout the war years the credit of government loans steadily increased on the bourse whereas the British loans had declined on the British exchange. Perhaps it was this source of pride in his arch-enemy that turned Calonne's attention to the bourse and the reception of his loan. Speculation on other non-government paper was active in the first days of 1785, particularly that of the Discount Bank and also a similar institution in Madrid called the Bank of Saint Charles. According to some reports Calonne was dismayed to see the stocks of these two institutions rise so rapidly on the exchange at the same time that the loan of 125 million livres was falling. It was for that reason that he began to use the powers of his office to move against both speculators and the two discount banks.

The first government action was taken on January 16, 1785 which limited the dividends of the Discount Bank to 150 livres per share. Another act of January 24 specifically prohibited speculation in the shares of the Discount Bank and also the government loan of 125 million livres. In the summer, on August 7, another law was issued against speculation in general. It set aside as illegal contracts that purchased shares or stocks on margin, that is, purchasing stocks sometime in the future and paying for them at that time. This type of contract was seen as unhealthful for the economy and immoral as well. If one wished to buy shares of stock at the bourse he must buy it with money that he has at the moment and not simply an expectation of money to come in the future. It was often that expectation which was the great gamble, whether it be for the rise of stocks or their decline.[58]

It would appear by the end of the year, these government measures were ineffective in achieving their aim, for a speculative fever descended on the bourse in 1785. This outcome was not only of no use for the marketing of his loan but proved to be acutely embarrassing to Calonne because of the shady contacts he made in an attempt to influence the stock exchange by publicity. In May 1785 appeared the first of Mirabeau's polemical essays denouncing "agiotage" (speculation). This was a brochure of 300 pages entitled "On the Discount Bank" which denounced the bank as a den of iniquitous bankers and speculators. According to Brissot's _Mémoirs_, it was the Genevan financier, Etienne Clavière, and the advisor of Calonne on fiscal matters, Isaac Panchaud, who set Mirabeau to writing the essay, providing him with the technical information. According to Brissot, Calonne subsidized and secretly promoted the publication. The purpose was to lower the value of the shares of the two banks on the _bourse_, for both Clavière and Panchaud were speculating on the "_baisse_" (the lowering of the price of shares). Two months later appeared Mirabeau's second essay which was on the Bank of Saint Charles, and also, according to Brissot, written under the patronage of Calonne. The technical information for this essay was furnished by Clavière.[59] This work was so extreme in its denunciation of the Spanish bank, and so patently mendacious that Calonne found it necessary to ban further publication if relations with Spain were not to deteriorate drastically. The Spanish government was understandably furious and not only prohibited its distribution in Spanish territory but pointed out the grotesque libels of the author, mentioning among other things, that Mirabeau based his attack on Spanish documents but without being able to read Spanish![60] The liaison of Mirabeau with Calonne was well-publicized in the press and did nothing to remove the already-existing clouds over the "reputation" of the Controller General.

What was most serious about his situation was that another large loan was necessary by the end of the year 1785. He knew that he could expect trouble with the Parlement of Paris this time and he was not mistaken. In December his third major loan was sent to the Parlement for registration. It was to be an issue of four million _rentes_ with a capital of 80 million livres to be reimbursed in ten years, one million each year. The incentive for investors was a lottery in which the winners would be able to exchange the rentes "héréditaires" into life rentes paying 9% on one life and 8% on two lives without being subject to the dixième. This despite the fact that Calonne had formally pledged in his first loan edict that there would be no more life rente loans in peacetime. The original edict of the loan also stated that it would be backed by the income from the three vingtièmes. Whether he had forgotten that the third vingtième was due to expire at the end of 1786, or whether he had slyly hoped that the Parlement would not notice, and therefore be unable to protest after it had sanctioned the loan, can not be known. Either would have been quite in character.

As usual, the preamble glowed with optimism about the future, and the Controller General gave a good account of his stewardship:

All our obligations have been paid punctually, even some reimbursements have been made before the date due; the arrears of rentes have been paid more promptly than they have ever been in the past. Never has so much money been used to retire debts; never has so much been spent for useful public works: for ports, canals, roads, for drainage; never has commerce received so much encouragement; never has aid to the provinces been more generously distributed. Such are the first fruits, such should be the first goals of the plan which we have adopted, the resources which it has enabled us to find in order to satisfy so many needs in the midst of so many obstacles. We are more and more convinced that expenditures for amelioration are the mainsprings of wealth, and that credit is fortified by expenditures. We are on the threshold of liquidating all the debts of the last war, and even those that are in arrears in the different departments. Their entire liquidation should be completed during the course of 1786; and if it is not without regret that in order to do so we are obliged to open again a loan, at the same time we have the satisfaction of being assured that with this help we can carry out the total liquidation (of debts) without which the order that we are seeking to bring to our finances would be impossible.[61]

Certainly no one would have argued that money spent to retire debts would add to the credit and the income of the government. But whether expenditures for public works like canals and roads would increase wealth might depend on the finances of the royal government: whether deficit spending would be for the best might be arguable. But what most disturbed the Parlement was whether the Controller General was quite candid in describing all the expenditures of the government.

The first remonstrance was taken to the palace at Versailles on December 18th. The king was reminded by the Parlement that the magistrates had registered the last two loans upon the assurance that "Your Majesty had given to restore order in all parts of his administration and the most strict economy in his finances." The remonstrance referred to "a series of expenditures of which the profusion and the lack of need formed the greatest contrast to this economy so solemnly promised." The proposed loan, asserted the Parlement, would be at 6-1/2% without considering the great cost of the life _rentes_ that would be exchanged for the perpetual _rentes_. "This is really a life _rente_ loan" which the king had formally pledged not to use again in peacetime. Once again the magistrates called attention to where the king could economize: suppress needless expenditures, cut back on immoderate gifts to individuals, award gratifications only for services that are truly important; reject importunate claims for gifts presented as a right. Finally the Parlement referred to the Committee on Finance set up in February 1783 and abolished by Calonne at the beginning of his ministry, although without naming it directly: "the profusion of useless expenditures is not of long standing. Not very long ago every ordonnateur was obliged to give an account of needs of his department for the year. This had been discontinued and now there was no supervision or control of the expenditures of the different spending departments of the government."[62]

The king replied that he "was more concerned than my Parlement about establishing order and economy in my finances. The Parlement must depend on my judgment about expenditures. Necessary loans are for the good of the state where they free it of debt." The magistrates returned on the 19th of December with a repeated remonstrance: how does a loan liberate the state when the interest cost of the loan exceeds the interest cost of the debts being liquidated by it? The king's answer to the second remonstrance was curt: the Parlement was ordered to register the loan forthwith. It did so, but added in its decree the same objections it had stated in the remonstrance. The king, and no doubt his Controller General, were furious at such impudence. The decrees of the Parlement were published in formal documents and this decree would have announced to the world the opposition of the magistrates to the loan. Certainly this would not have helped the marketing of it. Now the entire Parlement was summoned to Versailles to attend a lit de justice on December 23, 1785.

At this session, which must have been one of the most important lit de justices in the reign of Louis XVI, the king ordered the clerk of the Parlement to bring him the decree and he personally erased the offending passages. In a stern rebuke to the assembled magistrates he concluded: "And furthermore I wish it to be known that I am pleased with my Controller General." According to Bachaumont's account of this lit de justice, as the king left the chamber he told the first president (Etienne-François d'Aligre) that he "wished to have M. d'Amécourt relieved of his post." Lefebvre d'Amécourt, rapporteur of the court, had been given a document by Calonne to clarify for the Parlement the use of all money derived from his loans since the beginning of his administration. Amécourt had not done so, and when Calonne asked him why, "M. d'Amécourt replied that he had done the Controller General a service in not presenting the document because it was so full of errors." And then, concluded Bachaumont, "there was a heated exchange of words between the two."[63]

It was certainly Calonne who was the object of the parliamentary opposition. It was evident by the end of that day that he could not again present a major loan to the Parlement for registration without creating a serious crisis in the state. Whether the king would stand by him in such a crisis was problematic in view of his past relations with finance ministers. Bachaumont's judgment was that "although M. de Calonne appears to have triumphed in the session at Versailles, this event is seen as bound to overthrow him sooner or later. It is certain that there is an open schism between himself and the Parlement."[64]

NOTES, CHAPTER 2

[1]See my <u>Necker</u>, <u>Reform Statesman</u>, 222-223.

[2]<u>Ibid.</u>, 238.

[3]BN MSS Joly de Fleury, 1437, fol. 266.

[4]The statement of the financial situation that
Joly de Fleury presented to the king on March 3, 1783,
indicated that ten million of those <u>bordereaux</u> were
still retained in the Treasury. BN MSS Joly de
Fleury, 1442, fol. 57.

[5]BN MSS Joly de Fleury, 1438, fol. 9bis.

[6]In addition to the two <u>vingtièmes</u> was a four
sous per livre surcharge on the first <u>vingtième</u> which
was equal to one percent increase.

[7]BN MSS Joly de Fleury, 1441, fols. 46-47.

[8]BN MSS Joly de Fleury, 1437, fol. 507.

[9]<u>Collection</u> <u>des</u> <u>édits</u>, <u>déclarations</u> <u>et</u> <u>arrêts</u> <u>du</u>
<u>conseil</u> <u>d'état</u>. BN F. 23630 (319).

[10]In her study of the offices of the six intendants of finance abolished by Necker in June 1777,
Françoise Mosser defends a conservative viewpoint similar to that of Joly de Fleury. The six intendants
who held their office by hereditary purchase gave consistency and stability to the far-flung administration

of the finances. "The suppression of the intendants
of finance by Necker," she writes, "was more destructive (néfaste) than beneficial to the financial administration of the 18th century." Françoise Mosser, Les
Intendants des Finances au XVIII siècle (Geneva-Paris,
1978), 249. She writes that Necker admitted himself
that the minister of finance was overburdened with responsibilities and details which he could not attend
to. Necker did make that statement in his 1778 memorial to the king urging the establishing of provincial assemblies and administrations. His remedy
for the admitted over-centralization of the administration of the finances was to shift much of the
responsibility to the provincial administrations.
There is no doubt that the six intendants of finance
whose offices Necker abolished in 1777 were honorable
and capable magistrates. Henry d'Ormesson was one of
them. But the duties of all six intendants of finances did not devolve upon the minister of finance.
The functions of each were assigned to public servants
who did not hold their position by purchased office.
It was possible for Necker to put in those positions
lieutenants who would be responsible to his own direction, and who shared his ideas on reform. Miss Mosser
writes that "It was not order but disorder and uncertainty that was introduced into the administration." This is a serious allegation. But what contemporary evidence does she produce to substantiate
it? The remark of the anonymous writer of "The Secret
Correspondence" edited by Lescure, and which was made
on July 3, 1777, only eleven days after the publication of the edict of June 22. This was certainly a
"rush to judgment." The only other contemporary witness relied upon for the judgment was Soulavie's memoirs. He was a vehement critic of all Necker's reforms, a stalwart defender of the abuses of the ancien
régime. In contrast to those authors one might look
at the testimony of those "lowly commis " whom Necker
brought into the administration following the edict of

June 22. Several were to distinguish themselves in the ministry of finance: Bertrand Defresne, Michel Dailly, Joseph Coster. Cf. Jean Egret, Necker, Ministre de Louis XVI (Paris, 1975), 52-53; J. F. Bosher, "The Premier Commis des finances in the reign of Louis XVI," French Historical Studies (1964), III(4), 475-495. The testimony of Albert-Joseph Hennet, Théorie du crédit public (Paris, 1816), is quite a contrast to those conservative authors relied upon by Miss Mosser. Unlike them, he was a young clerk in the Contrôle Général during Necker's first ministry and had an intimate knowledge of how the administration was carried on. "Never under the twenty-three ministers who succeeded [Necker] have I seen the bureaux so few in number, put out so much work, and with more care. No aspect [of financial administration], no detail was neglected; never at any epoch have I seen merit, talent, and seniority more assured of obtaining promotion that was its right; and one can judge what emulation this certitude fostered among the salaried officials. Never was a government better served and at less expense" (267-268).

[11]Isambert, et al., eds., Recueil général des anciennes lois, XXVII, 237.

[12]Mercy-Argenteau, Correspondance secrète, I, 65-67.

[13]BN MSS Joly de Fleury, 1436, fol. 14.

[14]MSS Joly de Fleury, 1422, fol. 57.

[15]"Etat de tous les emprunts fait par le Gouvernement depuis 1777, 1781 compris," BN MSS Joly de Fleury,, 1437, fol. 11-51.

[16]Isambert, Recueil des anciennes lois, XXVII, 256-257; Orville T. Murphy, Charles Gravier, Comte de Vergennes. French Diplomacy in the Age of Revolution: 1719-1787 (Albany, State University of New York Press, 1982), 401. Murphy has confused the committee set up in 1783 with the Comité contentieux des finances created by Necker in 1777. The two were quite different in functions. The latter committee, which is the subject of the monograph by Aline Logette that he cites, continued to perform its functions up to 1791, whereas the committee set up by Vergennes was abolished by Calonne in the following November.

[17]Duc de Castries, Le Maréchal de Castries (Paris, 1956), 105.

[18]Ibid., 106-108.

[19]AN, Archives d'Ormesson, 114 AP 136.

[20]Collection des édits . BN F. 23630 (432).

[21]Rilliet de Saussure, Lettre sur l'Emprunt et l'Impôt (Genève, 1779), 168-169.

[22]De l'Administration des Finances de la France, in Oeuvres complètes, V, 526.

[23]G. Susane, La Tactique financière de Calonne (Paris, 1901), 202-203.

[24]Bachaumont, Mémoires secrets, XXIII, 184-190; Hardy, "Mes Loisirs," BN MSS Fonds français, 6684, fol. 369.

[25] See my Necker, Reform Statesman, 147.

[26] Bachaumont, Mémoires secrets, XXIII, 239.

[27] Mercy-Argenteau, Correspondance secrète, I, 181-182.

[28] Ibid., 167.

[29] Ibid., 227, n.1.

[30] Jacques-Mathieu Augeard, Mémoires secrets (Paris, 1866), 121. These memoirs have always seemed suspect to me because of the rather implausible statements Augeard makes.

[31] Correspondance secrète, , 227.

[32] Bachaumont, Mémoires secrets, XXXIII, 148.

[33] Necker, De la Révolution française, in Oeuvres complètes, IX, 118-125.

[34] Joseph Weber, Mémoires (Paris, 1822), I, 151.

[35] Pierre-Victor Besenval, Mémoires (Paris, 1851), II, 200.

[36] Anne Louise Germaine, baronne de Staël-Holstein, Considérations sur la Révolution française, ed. Jacques Godechot (Paris, 1983), 108.

[37]Charles Gomel, Les Causes financières de la Révolution française (Paris, 1892-1893), I, xxviii.

[38]Marcel Marion, Histoire financière de la France depuis 1715 (Paris, 1914), I, 358.

[39]Ibid., 359.

[40]Ibid., 359.

[41]Ibid., 359-360.

[42]Cf. Wilma J. Pugh, "Calonne's 'New Deal'", The Journal of Modern History (Sept. 1939), XI, 289-312. The author reviews this aspect of Calonne's economic policy and finds it irreproachable. But the allusion to the "New Deal" appears only in the title. There is no systematic comparison in the article to the situation in the United States in the 1930s. Granted that French economic historians have found a serious economic crisis in the 1780s, it became general only in 1788 and 1789. In any case there is no evidence that Calonne was conscious of a depression during his ministry that called for a policy of government spending to "prime the pump." If he was a Keynesian before his time he was unaware of it. His preoccupation was entirely fiscal: how to get enough money into the treasury to pay for his "prodigalities."

[43]Bachaumont, Mémoires secrets, XXIV, 94.

[44]Mémoires secrets, XXIV, entry of Nov. 29, 1783, 51-52.

[45]Charles-Alexandre de Calonne, _Requête au Roi adressé à Sa Majesté par M. de Calonne_ (Londres, 1787), 14.

[46]Marion, _Histoire financière de la France_, I, 358.

[47]All the above transactions were recorded in the financial statements turned over to the assembly of Notables by Calonne's successor in 1787. They continued to appear in the _Compte rendu_ of Loménie de Brienne in 1788 and Necker's _Compte général_ of 1789. See _Compte général des Revenues et de Dépenses fixes au ler de mai 1789_, Paris, Imprimérie royale, 1789. BN 4° Lf 76.124.

[48]_Correspondance secrète du comte de Mercy-Argenteau_, II, 4.

[49]Oscar Browning, ed., _Dispatches from Paris, 1784-1790. Selected and edited from Foreign Office correspondence_ (London, 1909-1910), 3rd series, I, 66.

[50]_Collection des édits_, BN F. 23630 (721, 732, 734, 741, and 746).

[51]Gustav Schelle, _De Pont de Nemours_ (Paris, 1888), 259; Bachaumont, _Mémoires secrets_, XXV, 95-96.

[52]Eric Magnus, baron de Staël-Holstein, _Correspondance diplomatique_ (Paris, 1881), 4.

[53]_Collection des édits_, BN F. 23630 (476). The loan was entirely subscribed to by investors within a week of the publication of the edict. Later when

speaking to the Assembly of Notables in 1787 Calonne
asserted that the credit of the government was
"totally destroyed" when he took office on November 3,
1783. Only a month later he issued this loan. The
alacrity with which investors snapped it up shows that
Calonne must have been a miracle-worker or that the
credit posture of the government was not as desperate
as he claimed when addressing the Assembly of Notables.

[54]Bachaumont, XXV, 77.

[55]Jules Flammermont, ed., Remontrances du Parlement de Paris au XVIII siècle (Paris, 1888-1898),
III, 515-517.

[56]Hardy, "Mes Loisirs," BN MSS Fonds français,
6684, fol. 430.

[57]Flammermont, Remontrances du Parlement de
Paris, III, 602.

[58]Isambert, Recueil général des anciennes lois
françaises, XXVIII, 71.

[59]George V. Taylor, "The Paris Bourse on the Eve
of the Revolution," American Historical Review 67
(1962), 952.

[60]Bachaumont, Mémoires secrets, XXIX, 173-180,
XXXI, 212.

[61]Collections des édits, BN F. 23630 (710)

[62]Flammermont, *Remontrances*, III, 640-643.

[63]Bachaumont, *Mémoires secrets*, XXX, 137, *passim*.

[64]*Ibid.*, XXXI, entry of Jan. 14, 1786.

CHAPTER 3

THE STATE'S SECRET

To posterity the most famous "affair" during the years 1785 and 1786 was the affair of the diamond necklace. It was, according to Napoleon, the beginning of the French Revolution. The trial of Cardinal Rohan and his virtual exculpation of any wrong-doing toward the queen by the Parlement of Paris, was a blow to the prestige of the monarchy.

In late 1785 and during the first months of 1786 another scandal much talked about was the "affaire Lemaître." This was a case adjudicated first by the criminal court of the Châtelet and reviewed by the Parlement of Paris. Both courts let the defendant off lightly for the crime he was accused of, and this was a blow to the prestige of the ministers, notably the Controller-General, Calonne, and the Keeper of the Seals, Hue de Miromesnil. The defendant in question, one Lemaître, had been a protegé of Miromesnil when the latter was First President of the Parlement of Rouen. When Miromesnil went from Rouen to Versailles to become Keeper of the Seals he brought Lemaître with him, installed him in an office, and made use of his polemical talents in the writing of brochures against his enemies. Feeling that he was not properly compensated for his services, Lemaître turned against Miromesnil and began writing derogatory brochures against him and also the Controller-General. In the fall of 1785 his clandestine printing press was discovered in the Belleville area of Paris, and Lemaître was arrested for printing libels against the two ministers.[1]

It was Miromesnil who had Lemaître arrested and brought criminal charges against him. The defendant freely talked about his activities. In fact he told

more than the prosecutors wanted him to, for he revealed that while he was an ally of Miromesnil he had
printed libelous brochures at the behest of the Keeper
of the Seals and particularly the mentor of the king,
the comte de Maurepas.   It was in the Belleville
press, according to Lemaître that the libels against
Necker were printed during the latter's first ministry.   Lemaître named some of his fellow-workers in
that sinister enterprise, notably the farmer-general
Augeard, and the minister of police in Paris, Lenoir,
both of whom left Paris when this testimony became
known to the public.   Now the "affaire Lemaître" became a scandal of the first water.   Like all such
"affairs" no one knew just how far it would reach, and
what persons in high places would be implicated.
Augeard was not only a farmer-general but also the
commandant of the Queen's Guard.   The queen let him
know, according to Bachaumont, that she would protect
him as long as no crime against the state was involved.[2]   Augeard was a long-standing friend of the
Controller-General of finances, but apparently it was
not known at this time that Calonne had taken part in
the libel campaign against Necker.   At the trial in
the Court of the Châtelet, according to Hardy's account, Lemaître named Calonne as one of the libelists
against Necker whose brochures he had printed.   The
lieutenant criminelle of the court refused to permit
that testimony to be included in the official record
of the interrogation.   Thereupon Lemaître refused to
sign the interrogation if such testimony was not included.

It was evident that the public who attended the
trial was keenly sympathetic to Lemaître, and came to
look upon him as a victim of "ministerial despotism."
The eminent lawyer, Guy-Jean-Baptiste Target, took
charge of the defense.   The Parlement of Paris took
charge of the case.   On January 15, 1786 by a parliamentary decree of 16 votes against four the case was
dismissed.   According to Bachaumont "the decree was

roundly applauded. All friends of the fatherland who were present embraced each other with great feeling. They looked upon this session as a happy day, where the power of a minister was not able to prevail against the cry of liberty, in an affair of this kind, brought for the first time before a court of law."[3] Hardy reported that the government was highly indignant upon learning of the decree and there was some thought of evoking the case to the King's Council. But this was not done although Lemaître prudently fled to London. The entire affair was seen as an indication of the unpopularity of Calonne. Bachaumont wrote about a month after the trial that Calonne attended a ball at Mme. de Vergennes', and having to leave early, his carriage was caught in a traffic jam, he was recognized by the crowd and harshly treated.[4]

If the king was pleased with his Controller-General it was becoming increasingly evident that his subjects were not. Contributing to this winter of discontent was the decision taken the previous October to call in all the gold coins, called louis, for recoinage at a less weight in gold. The reason for this gigantic operation according to the royal Declaration of October 30, 1785, was the heavier gold content of the French louis in comparison to equivalent foreign coins. This encouraged foreigners to invest in French louis, which were leaving the country at an alarming rate. Within the country the louis were being melted down for use in goldsmith manufactures, although it was illegal. Also the official rate of silver to gold, 14 1/2 to 1, varied from the market price (15 1/2 to 1) so as to contribute to the disappearance of the gold louis.[5] The letters patent putting into effect the recoinage appeared on January 18, 1786. It was registered by the Chamber of Monies on January 27 only after repeated and vigorous remonstrances.

In February the Parlement of Paris took the matter under review, and on March 19 the first president

75

carried a remonstrance to the king. The Parlement objected first of all to the complicated procedure for carrying out the operation which brought hardship to the possessors of the louis. The Declaration had promised that the operation would be completed in six weeks. Now the government stated in the letters patent that the operation would take an entire year. This would give the government possession of the gold louis for a year, and was in fact a forced loan. Contrary to what was promised to the holders of the old louis that they would receive a share of the profits to be realized in the recoinage, the Parlement pointed out that the government would gain 18 livres per marc d'or. "It is actually a concealed tax," asserted the Parlement, "for Your Majesty will gain from all the gold in the kingdom a tax of 18 million livres for every million marc d' or that is coined." Furthermore, the Parlement questioned the reasons given that made the operation necessary. France was the country the most abundantly supplied with coins in Europe, and fully one-third of the coins in France were gold coins. The ratio of 14 1/2 to 1 was the same in Holland, and there obviously had been no loss of gold in that country. Furthermore, even if the ratio were unfavorable for gold, would that require the complete remelting of all the gold coins? A decree of the government could alter the ratio to bring the official proportion in line with the market price.[6]

The king's reply to the remonstrance was the harshest he had ever given to the sovereign courts. The magistrates of the Parlement of Paris were told simply that they did not know what they were talking about, that the matter was beyond their competence. He asserted that the operation would yield a profit to his subjects of 15 million livres out of 600 million gold louis recoined. His own profit from the operation would not be more than 6 million livres since he was relinquishing his old feudal right of seigneurage.[7]

76

It is difficult to judge this matter today. Marcel Marion wrote that Calonne's reform of the coinage
was "irreproachable, necessary, advantageous at once
to the public and for the king."[8] But his opinion is
about as preemptory as the reply of the king to the
remonstrance. The magistrates gave reasonable objections to the operation which deserved a calm and rational rebuttal, which they did not get.[9] In any
case, public hostility to the operation was genuine
and contributed to the unpopularity of the Controller-
General.

To some observers the recoinage operation was
only a symptom of the government's financial distress
and the need to find money wherever possible. This
was the opinion of Mercy-Argenteau, whose letters to
Vienna describing the internal situation in France
took on an alarming aspect. On March 10, 1786 he
wrote to Kaunitz describing the behavior of the government:

> The instability of its operations make it
> difficult to foresee what the consequences
> will be for the future. At a time when
> waste and unheard-of profusion absorbs the
> treasury there arises a cry of distress and
> alarm. Then the Controller-General has re-
> course to brutal measures such as the recent
> recoinage of gold money according to proce-
> dures that are deceptive (sous des propor-
> tions vicieuses.) . . . What can be said for
> certain is that the present government sur-
> passes in weakness, disorder, and extortion
> the previous reign, and it is morally impos-
> sible for this to continue without a catas-
> trophe. . .[10]

During August the Austrian ambassador got wind of
certain reform projects the Controller-General was
preparing but their purport was not yet known, and in

any case Mercy-Argenteau had no confidence whatever in Calonne. On August 20th he wrote to the emperor: "The Controller-General is now seeking the support of the queen for his so-called reform projects, which most likely will not result in anything more than new onerous resources to feed the waste which under the present minister has become irremediable. The best observers in the public believe that France has never had a more dangerous Controller-General because they are convinced he will exhaust the last means (of the government) and will abandon his post only after having made it unmanageable for his successor."[11]

In the autumn of 1786 the court repaired to Fontainebleau as was its custom. These excursions were ordinarily expensive, but in 1786 Mercy-Argenteau wrote the emperor that "the dissipation was truly desolating." Joseph II replied that he "could see no remedy for the evil. For my sister does not have those inner resources for amusement and is obliged to escape boredom in any way possible; in the measure that those who surround her can contribute to that end they gain her favor, and engage her to satisfy their cupidity."[12]

Other ambassadors were expressing alarm over the manner in which royal finances were being managed. In February 1786 baron de Staël wrote to Gustavus III that Calonne was wasting money because of the "great frivolity with which he administers the finances. At the moment royal paper is sinking [on the bourse] and the considerable loans which have been made the last 14 months are in part the cause. Those who speculate claim that the government must necessarily be in great embarrassment about meeting its obligations."[13] In September the British Minister Plenipotentiary at Paris, Hailes, wrote to the foreign office that the loan made by the City of Paris of thirty million livres was intended to be used for public works but that it had all gone into the king's coffers, and would be doled out to the city by the Royal Treasury as the work advanced. Hailes commented that "it is another loan of the Minister [Calonne], and it is well worthy of remark that in this year of profound tranquility the sums that have been borrowed both publicly and privately amount to near two hundred millions. I have taken the liberty of touching frequently upon these extraordinary operations of finance, as they appear to me to be very hasty strides towards a national bankruptcy."[14] A month later Hailes wrote an extended report to the Foreign Office on the condition of French finances and the baffling policy of the government. He mentioned that "according to M. Necker's calculation, the public debts of England and France, by great singularity of accident, at the end of the war, amounted to nearly the same sum." He observed that France had not gained those commercial advantages from her intervention in the American War that she had hoped for. The war was as much a disaster for France as for her enemy:

> Disappointed in those hopes (if she really had entertained them) of securing the trade of the United States to herself, it might have been expected that she would have turned her eyes inward upon her domestic condition, and after having seen the mischief she brought upon herself in common with her enemy, that she would have taken some effectual steps towards the contracting of her expenditure, and have applied to her wounds the only medicament from which she could expect relief, that of economy. Great Britain, by setting that example, made such a conduct doubly necessary; each country being accustomed, and with reason, to measure its own wants and distress by the advantages and resources of its rival. But France, at the present moment, seems to have lost entirely sight of that policy; and your Lord-

ship will have observed that I have particularly dwelt, in the course of my correspondence, upon those operations of finance which I have thought most likely to throw light upon a conduct so opposite of what might have been expected.[15]

Hailes then went on to give details of those "surprising expenditures." The queen's lavish "propensity to every kind of pleasure and expense," the unsavory circle of friends that make use of her weakness for their own ends; the fact that it was this circle that had originally brought about the appointment of Calonne to the Contrôle-Général; the establishments of the king's brothers "which are equal perhaps, to those of some of the most independent Princes in Europe;" the enormous costs of the works at Cherbourg; the additions to the grounds and château at Saint-Cloud which he said "are estimated at eleven million;" similar works were undertaken at several other royal residences. Even the commercial treaty being negotiated with England, Hailes thought, was motivated by the "increase in revenue" that would come as a result of the great influx of British manufactured goods. "If this opinion should prove to be well grounded, and from the attention I have paid to the late conduct of the Comptroller General I am much inclined to think it is. it will be a strong mark of the corruption of that minister, who sacrifices to an immediate and temporary resource the dearest interests of his country."[16]

That the royal government was facing a serious financial crisis was evident by the means used to raise money. Calonne himself had recognized at the beginning of his ministry, according to the apologia he wrote the king after his fall from power in 1787 (La Requête au Roi) that it was an abuse of the finance minister's authority to extend loans that had already been issued and the terms fulfilled. It had

80

become the practice that in an emergency the finance minister could simply reopen an old loan and extend the capital well beyond what was stipulated in the original loan edict, and this could be done without bothering to have it registered by the Parlement of Paris. Calonne pledged to the king that all his loans would be written so as to prevent such extensions.[17] Now, during 1786, he had to resort to extending two life rente loans of his predecessors, that of March 1781 by 52,260,000 livres, with an annual charge of 5,250,000 and the life rente loan of Joly de Fleury, issued in January 1782, was extended by 36 million livres, adding a burden of 3,630,000 livres annually. The pays d' états had become exhausted as a source for loans, for he had already borrowed 25 million from them. Only the city of Paris managed to grant a loan of 24 million livres. The sale of offices, among them the new agents of exchange, yielded another 10 million livres. What reflected unmistakenly the distress of the government was the enormous increase in anticipations (short-term credit by financiers such as the farmers-general and the receivers-general). At the end of 1783 the anticipations amounted to 176 million livres. In 1787 at the end of Calonne's ministry they had increased by 79 million livres to a total of 255 million livres. This was the most onerous of all types of government loans, the one that Necker tried most to keep limited. After the beginning of the year 1787 Calonne made more extensions of old loans by an additional 14 million livres. Also at the beginning of that year he made an unprecedented loan of 70 million livres from the Discount Bank. It had never been the purpose of that bank to serve as a vehicle for government loans. According to Calonne's own figures he also borrowed from office-holders by raising surety bonds by 14.6 million livres, although it is not clear just when that was done. All these "extraordinary sources" of money were used in order to escape having to face the Parlement of Paris with another loan edict. But they could hardly be kept secret, and tended to broadcast to investors, as de Staël said, the serious financial distress of the royal government.[18]

If the foreign ambassadors were alarmed by the internal situation in France, what was the attitude of Calonne's ministerial colleagues? While keeping up his tactic of exuding optimism, on the real financial situation he kept matters to himself. He was not inclined to share his concerns with others. But if ambassadors could observe that all was not well, it would seem that other ministers of state should also. The preeminent minister in the government, the foreign minister and head of the Council on Finance, the comte de Vergennes, was absorbed in the foreign policy crisis regarding events in the Netherlands. He was subject to increasing periods of illness, and was to die in February 1787. The Secretary of State for the King's Household, Baron de Breteuil, did have some inkling of what was going on in the Contrôle-général. He sent agents to the Hôtel de Ville to spy on the sales of rentes from Calonne's secret extensions of the loans of March 1781 and January 1782. He passed this information on to Lefebvre d'Amécourt, reporter of the Parlement of Paris. The Keeper of the Seals, Hue de Miromesnil, also had contacts with the magistrates and was aware of what the Controller-General was doing, and also what his colleague Breteuil was up to. Thus Calonne was becoming increasingly isolated in the Council of State. His only base of support was the king, and behind him, the queen and her friends.

The year 1786 had not progressed far when Calonne realized that the source of loans which he had been able to tap was bound to dry up, and perhaps suddenly. The government's loans were doing poorly on the bourse, even though he sought to bolster them by using all the instruments of publicity at his command. He even used treasury funds to enter into the market and buy up government securities in an attempt to keep them from sinking further.

For Charles-Alexandre de Calonne everything depended upon appearances. If the government seemed well-off financially, if people perceived that it was, then it would be. "The credit of the government is everything," he wrote the king in August, "without credit we are lost." Compared to Necker his understanding of what lay behind government credit was extremely superficial. Several who knew him well remarked about his volatile imagination and frivolity. A close friend of Calonne who left memoirs, the marquis de Clermont-Gallerande, mentioned a conversation he had with Calonne in September 1786 and how appalled he was at the Controler-General's light-hearted attitude toward the royal finances.[19]

It was not surprising that a person of that character should be attracted to the works of the "Economists," those who came to be called the physiocrats. The book of Guillaume Le Trosne, On Provincial Administration and Tax Reform, first published in 1779, came to Calonne's attention. What probably captured his imagination was the extreme facility of reform as propounded by Le Trosne. If the ideas of the Economists were adopted by the government, the country would "pass in an instant from shallows of misery to the heights of prosperity." A somewhat more sober physiocratic influence came from Samuel Dupont de Nemours, who was brought into the Bureau of Commerce by Calonne and entrusted with the office of Commissioner-General of Commerce. Dupont was instrumental in the negotiations of the Eden Treaty of 1786 which reduced tariff barriers between England and France. After that treaty was concluded in 1786 Dupont was given the title of Counselor of State. It was probably through him that Calonne derived his reform ideas which he was to present to the king in August 1786 and later to the Assembly of Notables. Calonne was never

completely captivated by the doctrine of the physiocrats. He took from their program what suited him,
and adopted other measures that were a violation of
the most sacred tenets of the creed. The Eden Treaty
of 1786 was preceded the year before by the edict
restoring the Company of the Indies, a move that was
anathema to the physiocrats.

According to memorials written by Calonne during
1786 for the instruction of the king, it was in February of that year that he began to conceive "the great
project" that would overcome the impending financial
crisis. More loans were out of the question, either
public loans that required the registration of the
Parlement of Paris, or secret extensions of loans, or
private loans from officials. "We cannot," he wrote
the king, "any longer get loans approved on the basis
of war debts." By the end of the year new financial
means must be found or the government would face an
unprecedented catastrophe in 1787. Neither could new
taxes be levied for they would arouse as serious resistance on the part of Parlement as the new loans.[20]

This left only one other alternative: reform.
Reform of the fiscal system which had been propounded
by different ministers since the time of Marshal
Vauban in the last years of the reign of Louis XIV,
reforms that would increase the revenue of the king
but at the same time would not levy new burdens on the
already over-taxed common people. It was to end the
abuses in the fiscal system that would be the chief
aim of Calonne's "great project." The tax system
would be revamped so as to eliminate the unjust and
unconscionable exemptions of various privileged
classes. The most productive source of tax revenue
was the land tax, the tax on income from agriculture.
The vingtième was such a tax, but in the years since
its inception in 1749 all sorts of exemptions had been
granted to landowners. First was the Church, the
largest landowner which was completely exempt. The

great nobles and princes of the blood were able to settle for the tax "by abonnement," that is, they paid a specific sum according to special arrangement with the government. By using their influence at court or by various ways of intimidating collectors of the vingtième they were able to reduce their assessments. The large proprietors, both noble and plebeian, were able to resist the vingtième by claiming that tax collectors must accept their own declarations of the value of their lands and crops, and it was notorious that these valuations were far below the actual market value. Furthermore, the parlements always claimed that the government could not arbitrarily increase the tax levy beyond what was originally authorized in the edict. Thus even though profits from agriculture and land values steadily increased during the century the tax rate must remain stationary, according to the magistrates. The only way the revenue from this source could be increased was by imposing another vingtième which was begun in 1782. This third vingtième was to expire at the end of the third year following the conclusion of the American War. Thus 1786 was its final year, and this loss of revenue was what directed Calonne's attention to the land tax.

In his memorial to the king Calonne explained that if the land tax could be levied uniformly on all lands, without exception, the burden need not be increased for those who already paid the tax in full measure, in exact proportion to the value of their crops. If all proprietors could be brought to pay even one vingtième (and that only for the best lands) then the income from the land tax would be doubled and no greater burden would be imposed on those who already paid their fair share. The increased revenue would come from those who hitherto had enjoyed exemptions or special favors or privileges. Such a reform could hardly be opposed by those privileged classes without revealing their utter egotism and lack of patriotism or concern for the well-being of king and country.

The general land tax was not the only measure of the great project that would increase revenue. Calonne again departed from physiocratic doctrines by acknowledging the necessity of increasing indirect taxes as well. But the proposed tax, like the land tax, would be the least burdensome to the poorer classes. It would be an addition to the tax already existing on legal documents called the droits de contrôl. Calonne's stamp tax would broaden it to yield about twenty million livres of additional revenue. Only the well-off would be affected by it, those who made contracts or carried on litigation in the courts.

Other parts of Calonne's project that would provide immediate relief for the financial embarrassment of the government included the transforming of the Discount Bank into a royal bank similar to the Bank of England or the Bank of Amsterdam. It would become a source of loans for the government, replacing the semi-private caisses that handled the government's money and were the source of short-term loans (anticipations). Such a project had long been urged by Isaac Panchaud, and he was probably the source for Calonne's scheme. But it had been the attempt of Henry d'Ormesson to make use of the Discount Bank as a source of government loans that provoked a panic in the summer of 1783. Now, in 1786, the rumor that Calonne was planning to change the Discount Bank into a Royal Bank, leaked out to the public and greatly perturbed the directors of the Discount Bank. According to Bachaumont this caused a precipitate fall in the stock of the bank. The directors immediately sought a conference with Calonne at Fontainebleau (where the court was having such an expensive good time, according to Mercy-Argenteau) and asked the Controller-General for assurance that no such plan was contemplated. Calonne welcomed the directors and told them the king intended to keep the Discount Bank in its present form, but (still according to Bachaumont) declined to give them a written letter to that effect.[21]

Another purely fiscal part of the great project was to extend the period of amortization of several wartime loans that were "inconsiderately" given heavy reimbursement schedules that were now causing a great hardship. The period of amortization would be extended from ten to twenty years.

Calonne's plan for alleviating the financial crisis consisted of two parts. The first were the measures already described above that were to meet the financial needs for 1787. The second part were the reforms, the fundamental changes that would create a better economic and political environment so as to avoid future crises of this kind. The two were dependent on each other. One could not reveal the "state's secret," that is, the seriousness of the financial crisis and the immediate needs of the treasury, without also promising the public some of the reforms which had been already much discussed and were popular with it. Here Calonne freely acknowledged his indebtedness to previous reform ministers, beginning with Vauban early in the century, and the reform scheme of Turgot. He even deigned to admit that some of his reform ideas were to "be found scattered in the book of Mr. Necker, who perceived the whole problem vaguely, without producing any real change because he could only see isolated parts and not the whole and without paying attention to the source of the obstacles."[22]

The most important of these reforms was Calonne's proposal to establish provincial assemblies throughout the pays d' élection. His model for this enterprise was contained in the book of Le Trosne and the essay of Dupont de Nemours written in 1775 but not published

until 1788 (when Mirabeau pirated a copy and published
it under his own name!). But Calonne must have gotten
his main ideas from his association with Dupont in
1786. The plan followed closely Dupont's scheme of
1775 but contained some departures that, again,
grieved the physiocrats. The system comprised three
layers of assemblies, the first being the parish assembly, the second the "district" (or arrondissement)
assembly, the third and final stage was the provincial
assembly. The parish assembly would represent an area
containing from 200 to 250 homes (hearths or _feux_).
The seats in the local assembly would be based on
landownership; those having an income of 600 livres
per year would have one vote. Large proprietors with
several times that income would have a number of votes
derived from dividing their income by 600. Very small
landowners could pool their income to gain a composite
vote. Each parish assembly would send one delegate to
the secondary or district assembly, which in turn
would send one delegate to the assembly of the
province. Calonne departed from Dupont's original
scheme in granting more representation to cities:
each district, which would have an average of three
cities, would permit each city to send two delegates
to the district assembly. All assemblies from parish
to province would be small and manageable, having no
more than 36 deputies, which would enable the assemblies to accomplish their mission with a minimum of
discussion.

The primary function of all assemblies was to apportion the direct tax quota that would be received
from the higher authority. The assessment of the tax
burden would be carried out in the open, each
landowner knowing what his neighbor was paying. But
Calonne made it clear that the assemblies were consul-
tative only. "They should not be called administrative assemblies," he said in a memorial written in
November 1786, "for assemblies administer badly."[23]
They would have some direction of the common lands at

the parish level, or poor relief, and public works, but Calonne's project was vague about this. He was careful to distinguish his assemblies from Necker's two provincial administrations established in Berri in 1778 and Haute Guienne in 1779. These, he said, were given altogether too much administrative and executive authority. The intendant was required to heed their desires, and in fact the absolute authority of the intendant in Necker's assemblies was greatly mitigated, at least until restored by his successors. Calonne, like Turgot and Dupont, believed that Necker's assemblies were given so much power as to constitute a serious menace to royal authority. In fact, that is why they were so popular. The physiocrats (and Calonne) believed in consulting public opinion, but it was to be a public opinion carefully selected and controlled so as not to get out of hand. This was true even though the president of the assembly was to be elected by majority vote in Calonne's assemblies. Another departure of Calonne from the physiocrats was to prescribe at the provincial level that even though the assembly was to represent landowners, a quarter of the deputies must be of the nobility and a quarter of the clergy. Thus the social composition of Calonne's assemblies was no different than that of Berri and Haute Guienne.

A second reform of Calonne's great project which the physiocrats had very much at heart, and which Necker also had favored, was the elimination of internal barriers to commerce in the kingdom. Tariffs should be pushed to the boundaries of the kingdom, within which free trade would be the rule. Calonne would reform the gabelle by making the regulated price of salt uniform throughout the kingdom and restricting the amount of salt that each family was required to purchase (le sel de devoir). As in Necker's proposal for reform of the gabelles, Calonne expected to make a substantial saving by ending the administrative costs of combating salt smuggling. This would be achieved

89

by ending that barrier between the free salt zone and the region of the "grandes gabelles." The Church would no longer be expected to make its "free gift" to the government if its lands were to be subjected to the general land tax. But the Church lands were encumbered by a debt, most of which had been incurred to pay the king his "free gift." Calonne proposed that the Church could liquidate its debt by selling its feudal or seigneurial rights to non-Church persons. These included quitrents (rentes foncier), hunting rights, and so forth. A better administration was proposed for the king's domain lands and the forests. Finally, the corvée for the maintenance of roads and bridges would be definitively ended and replaced by a surtax added to the taille by each provincial assembly.

Such was the great project which Calonne presented to Louis XVI on August 10, 1786. It was necessary to persuade the king to accept the project first of all and then to keep him firmly standing behind it. Calonne argued that the success of the plan depended upon putting it all into effect at one time. Any piecemeal reform would inevitably fail. That had been the fate of previous reform ministers. What was unique about his plan, wrote Calonne, was that it embraced all parts of the monarchy and each individual reform would be ineffective unless all parts of the plan were implemented. Calonne assured the king that if he would only support the plan with firmness, "I have no fear of guaranteeing its success. And success, Sire, will be the salvation of your empire, the glory of your reign, the happiness of your life. It will assure you more and more the love of your people. It will assure you the supreme satisfaction of rendering them happy. It will ease your mind permanently on the state of your finances. It will elevate your power to the highest peak, and your name above all the great names of this monarchy of which you will be called the Legislator."[24] The enthusiasm of the Controller-General was reminiscent of the authors of the physiocratic persuasion as was also the apocalyptic temperament. If the king did not give his unshakeable support to the Plan the consequences of its failure would be equally dramatic. After making the glowing account of the consequences of success Calonne wrote: "What obliges me to throw myself to the knees of Your Majesty and implore his acceptance is that outside of that I see only misfortune and the abyss."[25]

We have little information as to what Louis XVI thought of this project presented to him with such urgency. Later in the month, on August 20, Calonne wrote another memorial about the project in which it appears that the king was reluctant to go as fast as Calonne was urging. He seemed to think that more time was needed, that each of the elements of the project should be weighed carefully and other ministers of the government brought into the deliberation.[26] Calonne vigorously argued against both proposals. Speed was of the essence for the success of the Plan. It was necessary to get the Plan into operation at the beginning of 1787 in order to provide the revenue to keep the government from catastrophe. The new Royal Bank must be the source of loans. As for bringing others into deliberation about the project, Calonne urged the necessity of keeping it secret: "The moment is urgent. Maintaining secrecy is necessary. A prolonged delay could mean failure (of the Plan) and compromise secrecy. Furthermore the number of persons who are competent enough and can be entrusted with the state's secret is very small." Furthermore, Calonne assured the king, it was unnecessary. "I know Your Majesty detests flattery, but it is true that there is no one better fitted to judge if (the project) is or is not in conformity with sound principles of administration."[27]

After the king had had time to study the complete project (for only a sketch had been given him),

Calonne wished him to submit certain parts of it that might seem most controversial to the foreign minister, Vergennes, and the Keeper of the Seals, Miromesnil. After they had given their consent the king would summon a meeting of the Council and let them know his intentions, which were to accept the Plan of the Controller-General and to present it to an Assembly of Notables. Calonne hoped by that tactic to get the support of public opinion for his project. He knew the sovereign courts would resist the project or at least the fiscal parts of it. If he could take away the basis of popular support for the parliamentary side their opposition would not be dangerous enough to prevent the implementation of the plan. Once the Assembly of Notables had approved the plan the king would send it to the 12 Parlements to be registered. If there were remonstrances he could ignore them. This had been the outcome of Necker's quarrel with the Parlement of Paris in 1777 and 1778 over the reform of the vingtième, when public opinion strongly supported the Genevan, although it is not evident that Calonne had that precedent in mind.

Why an Assembly of Notables? And why did Calonne think that body would support his great project when the magistrates of the Parlements and other sovereign courts would not? He answered that the Notables would constitute the most eminent personages of the realm: lords spiritual and temporal, princes of the blood royal, those distinguished in the service of the king and the nation. Surely they would see the justice and reasonableness of the project: its concern for the well-being of the poorer classes, the moderation of its proposals, which the privileged classes could not object to without blushing. The patriotism and sense of honor and responsibility of the Notables, the pride they should feel in being called upon by the king to lend their advice, counsel and moral support to him in this great crisis, who could foresee that the Assembly of Notables would seriously oppose the project?

Furthermore Calonne was convinced, with some good reason, that public opinion was in favor of the reforms. The evident popularity of Necker with the public might possibly have made an impression on Calonne. But if the great project was to rely on the support of public opinion, why not convene the States-General rather than an Assembly of Notables? Here Calonne pointed out to the king in a memorial written at the end of August the important distinctions between those two bodies. The deputies of the States-General are chosen by constituents of the three orders in the bailiwick assemblies; the king chooses all the delegates to the Assembly of Notables. The Notables do not bring cahiers of grievances to present to the government, they come to listen to the proposals of the king's ministers. "It is the king himself who determines the objects upon which they are to deliberate, and they cannot discuss other matters." They are only an advisory assembly. And yet Calonne was convinced that such an assembly with that restricted role, could represent the nation, that it could be a valid interlocutor for public opinion. Furthermore he was convinced that it would not need a long period of time to fulfill its function. A month would certainly be sufficient. He hoped that the Assembly could be convened in the first days of December, and the royal edicts implementing the great project would be registered by the sovereign courts and be put into effect in January.

The haste with which the Controller-General sought to get his reforms enacted betray his anxiety about the financial predicament of the royal government. This was the Achilles heel of the great project. Since the beginning of Calonne's ministry in November 1783 the sovereign courts had exhorted him to scrutinize the royal government for opportunities to economize on expenditures. The Parlement of Paris in particular seemed to be convinced that economy in government would meet all the financial needs of the royal government without further loans. Calonne had paid no attention to this advice, indeed seemed to want to distinguish his administration from that of Necker on just that basis. The parsimonious policies of the Genevan banker were not suited to the grandeur of the world's most imposing monarchy. The kingdom was rich and flourishing and could afford great expenditures. Now in the summer of 1786 when all sources of new loans were becoming exhausted, when the government's securities were sinking on the bourse, and credit was imperiled, how did the Controller-General view the situation? In the August 10th memorial to the king Calonne explained to him the exact situation of the royal finances. Among the documents presented was a statement of the finances for the coming year in which the deficit was fixed at about 115 million livres. Calonne took pains to demonstrate to the king that this was not his doing. A deficit had existed in the ordinary revenue for meeting ordinary expenditures since the beginning of the reign of Louis XVI, indeed since the beginning of the century, in fact for several centuries. The ordinary expenditures of the monarchy had never been balanced by ordinary revenue. Now the accumulation of deficits had caught up with the government and that was the only reason for the financial crisis it faced. It was not anyone's fault in particular. Calonne admitted that even he had not realized the terrible "secret" until he had started back in February to investigate all the financial accounts of the royal government. The deficit had just become institutionalized for so long that nobody realized it was there. Calonne said he was appalled at the disorderly state in which he found the financial documents. Revenue and expenditures of several fiscal years were inextricably mixed up so it was difficult to determine exactly which belonged to each year. Extraordinary income and expenditures were hopelessly mixed with ordinary ones so that it was difficult to determine what were the ordinary or fixed expenditures of each fiscal year. Finally, after much labor, Calonne told the king, he was able to establish an exact account of the ordinary deficit for each year of His Majesty's reign. Beginning with Abbé Terray's financial statement for 1774 which had indicated only a deficit of 27.8 million livres Calonne said that he found the deficit was actually 40 million livres based upon what he called "the effective accounts." These were accounts not of what was budgeted for the year ahead, which could only be approximate guesses, but on the actual accounts at the end of the year of what was really spent for the bureau or department of the government. In 1776 on the eve of the American War there was a deficit of 37 million. With the American War came the necessity of rebuilding a navy and sending armies overseas which necessarily added to the fixed expenditures because of the service charges on the war loans. In 1781, contrary to the famous <u>Compte</u> <u>Rendu</u> of Mr. Necker, which had claimed a surplus of 10.5 million of ordinary revenue, there was in reality, according to the "effective accounts," a deficit of around 75 million livres in the ordinary budget. In 1783, the year that Calonne assumed responsibility for the royal finances there was a deficit of 80 million livres. Now, as the year 1787 approached there was clearly going to be a deficit of 115 million livres.

Was he to blame for this appalling situation? Certainly not. In a memorial sent to the queen in late December to get her support for the great project and the forthcoming Assembly of Notables, Calonne gave an <u>apologia</u> for his three years of stewardship of the royal finances. It was very much what he was to tell the Assembly of Notables two months later. When he came to the helm of the royal finances in November 1783 he found that the king had neither money nor credit. "The debts were immense, the revenue of the year already spent in advance, and confidence was annihilated. One would think, and indeed I did think, that we were reduced to the cruelest extremities. I did not lose courage, I concealed the horror of the situation, I met all obligations, and credit was restored." Then he called attention to the great contrast between the autumn of 1783 and the autumn of 1786, only three years later. "Today all is acquitted. All the war debts are paid. All the debts-in-arrears of the departments are paid off; the payment of _rentes_ which was in arrears is now current. Several emergency expenditures have been provided; several indirect taxes burdensome to commerce have been abolished; no new taxes have been imposed either directly or indirectly, and the people have received each year substantial relief."

Calonne then went on to tell the queen that he had paid over a billion livres for retiring government debt and for extraordinary expenditures. He had only raised about 300 million in public loans, so he had to rely on other means of raising money which were "much more considerable and infinitely more difficult." In face of such necessary expenditures it obviously was not possible to reduce the annual deficit. And yet the increase in the deficit in those three years was not nearly in proportion to what had to be borrowed "so there must have been economy in administration, and the proof of this economy is contained in the single assertion that I did not make any serious blunder in financial policy."[28]

In his _apologia_ written a year later after his fall from power Calonne admitted to having raised 650 million livres in loans of all kinds. That would have added from 50 to 55 million livres to the annual fixed charges. He claimed that the deficit left by his predecessors in 1783 was 80 million livres, which added to 50 million yielded the figure of 130 million. The deficit for 1787 was 115 million livres, 15 million less. Could he have reduced the ordinary deficit by 15 million livres? He left no account of how he had done so unlike Necker who explained in detail how he

96

had managed to achieve a reduction of 84 million livres in ordinary expenditures during his four and one-half years in office. And what about the 350 million that he spent above what he had raised by loans? Assuming an ordinary deficit in 1783, which Joly de Fleury denied existed, and that it rose to 100 million in the three years of his ministry, the total amount of deficit spending would not equal 350 million livres. "You will be astonished," he wrote to the queen, "that I could have spent that much by credit." Indeed not only the queen but the foreign ambassadors, the journalists, his ministerial colleagues, in fact the public would have been astonished to learn that such a feat could be accomplished when the king's credit "was totally destroyed" at the time Calonne came to the Contrôle général in November 1783.

The basic difficulty Calonne faced when he presented his reform program before the Notables was that nobody believed him. His explanation for the cause of the deficit was not credible. The Notables were not hostile to his reform projects. In fact they accepted most of them, although with some important modifications. But they could not accept without further proof Calonne's assertions about the origins of the deficit of 1787. To do so not only required them to disbelieve Necker, whom most of the Notables held in high regard, but all the other finance ministers of the reign. Calonne's assertions about the origins of the deficit would indicate that not only Necker but abbé Terray, Turgot, Joly de Fleury, and Ormesson were either grossly incompetent, or criminally negligent. But it was well known that all four were public servants of great intelligence and competence. If the private life of the abbé is overlooked, all four were men of integrity and high moral standards at least in public life. They were devoted to the king and the nation and would not consciously have concealed the true state of the finances from the king. All four were diligent in their duties and hard workers. Compare those qualities to the reputation of Calonne. He was not fond of work. The portrait left by Jean-Pierre Papon agrees with other eye-witnesses:

> He was a presumptuous person, frivolous, thoughtless, fond of pleasure which he preferred to work (affaires), of spending, which he rarely did to good effect, of flattery, of which he was the dupe. He possessed also the art of pleasing, the desire to be obliging, boldness in his concepts, broad views, and an uncommon knowledge of administration. He had especially that quickness of mind which enables one to grasp things promptly, and to explain them with ease and even elegance, but which often is an obstacle for combining them and studying them in depth, because such a mind ordinarily springs from vivacity or imagination rather than from solidity of judgment.[29]

That employee at the Contrôle général who had served in his youth during Necker's and subsequent ministries, and who left his impressions in his book, Théorie du crédit public, published in 1816, the chevalier Albert-Joseph Hennet, described the great change in the Contrôle général with the beginning of Calonne's ministry:

> When M. de Calonne came everything changed. No more regular working hours, the intendants of finance, the first secretaries, came without seeing the Controller General; portfolios accumulated from week to week; a change in events caused a change in reports, the business was concluded when one could get to it; the intendant of the province whose query was answered was no longer in office; a retirement pension was granted to a man who had been dead for a week.[30]

Calonne's lackadaisical work habits continued through 1786. His grand project had all the earmarks of being hastily assembled and not carefully thought out. Talleyrand records in his memoirs that the proposals to be submitted to the Notables were not yet ready at the time the Notables were originally scheduled to meet in January 1787. A week before the later opening date of February 22, 1787, Calonne called to his office several close advisors, Talleyrand among them, to prepare the documents that were to be submitted to the Notables. "We accomplished in a week's time a job that the presumption and flightiness of M. de Calonne had neglected for five months."[31]

Talleyrand thought the week's work was "not badly done." But it surely was rash to present such hastily drawn projects for such a distinguished body as the Notables and expect them to be approved with a minimum of discussion. In the coming dispute between Calonne and the Notables it was not so much the program as the person that was the issue. And in that confrontation Necker was to play an unexpected role.

[1]Augeard, *Mémoires secrets*, 142-151.

[2]Bachaumont, *Mémoires secrets*, XXX, entry of Dec. 20, 1785, 119.

[3]*Ibid.*, XXXI, 39.

[4]*Ibid.*, 141-142.

[5]Isambert, *Recueil général des anciennes lois françaises*, XXVIII, 89-97.

[6]Flammermont, *Remontrances*, III, 649-661.

[7]*Ibid.*, 660.

[8]*Histoire financière*, I, 376.

[9]This was the opinion of the British ambassador who wrote to the Foreign Secretary on March 30, 1786: "I enclose to your Lordship the remonstrance of the Parliament against the new coinage, and likewise the King's answer. I cannot too strongly recommend to your Lordship the perusal of the former, as it contains the most incontrovertible reasons against that ill-executed operation." Browning, ed., *Despatches from Paris*, I, 106.

[10]*Correspondance secrète*, II, 11.

[11]Ibid., 40.

[12]Ibid., 57.

[13]Correspondance diplomatique du baron de Staël-Holstein, p. 27.

[14]Despatches from Paris, I, 139.

[15]Ibid., 144.

[16]Ibid., 160.

[17]Requête au Roi, 100.

[18]Ibid., 112-130. Calonne listed here all his loans, amounting to 650 million livres.

[19]Charles-Georges, marquis de Clermont-Gallerande, Mémoires particuliers pour servir à l'histoire de la Révolution qui s'est operé en France en 1789 (Paris, 1826), I, 16, n. 1.

[20]Most of the memorials written by Calonne for the king in 1786 are printed in the appendix of Hans Glagau, Reformversüche und Stürz des Absolutisimus in Frankreich, 1774-1788 (Munich, 1908).

[21]Mémoires secrets, XXXIII, 130 ff.

[22]Glagau, Reformversüche, 357.

[23]Ibid., 150.

[24]"Précis d'un plan d'amélioration des finances remise au Roi le 10 août 1786," in Réponse de M. de Calonne à l'écrit de M. Necker publié en avril 1787 (Londres, 1788), 47.

[25]Ibid., 48.

[26]Glagau, Reformversüche, 345.

[27]Loc. cit.

[28]Glagau, Reformversüche, 345.

[29]Jean-Pierre Papon, Histoire du Gouvernement française depuis l'assemblée des Notables . . . jusqu'à la fin de décembre, 1788 (London, 1788), 6-7.

[30]Quoted in Robert Lacour-Gayet, Calonne (Paris, 1963), 89.

[31]Talleyrand, Mémoires, ed., Paul-Louis Couchoud and Jean-Paul Couchoud (Paris, 1957), I, 86.

CHAPTER 4

CALONNE AND THE NOTABLES

During the last months of 1786 Calonne's position
at court and with the king and queen seemed unshakeable. Neither did he betray in his demeanor any anxiety about the state of the finances. At Fontainebleau
in late October Bachaumont described a party given in
honor of the Controller General by the prince de
Condé. Surrounded by courtiers, "Calonne appeared ra-
diant, ceaselessly untying the strings of the purse
from which favors poured forth." He had just purchased nine horses from Siberia as a gift for Monsieur
the Dauphin, and this greatly pleased both the queen
and the king.[1] The Duke of Dorset was also at Fontainebleau and reported to the British government the
incredible expenditures of moving the royal family
back to Versailles in mid-November:

> Their Majesties, the Dauphin, and the rest
> of the Royal Family are removed from
> Fontainebleau to Versailles. The Dauphin
> set out on Monday, the Queen on Tuesday, and
> the King on Wednesday. The expense attend-
> ing these journeys of the Court is incredi-
> ble. Your Lordship may have a faint idea of
> it from the number of Post Horses that have
> been employed in these last three days. The
> Duke of Polignac told me that he had given
> orders for two thousand one hundred and fif-
> teen horses for this service on roads lead-
> ing from Fontainebleau to Paris, which, con-
> sidering the distance to either of those
> places is not equal to forty English miles,
> is prodigious. Besides this, an adequate
> proportion of horses are ordered for the re-
> moval of the heavy baggage belonging to the

Royal Family. How M. de Calonne contrives
to furnish means to answer such vast demands
cannot be conceived, but he still enjoys
great credit at Court.[2]

Meanwhile Calonne had not succeeded in persuading
the king to convene the Notables in December. It was
later that month that Louis submitted the great plan
to Vergennes and Miromesnil for their opinion. Neither was enthusiastic about it. Vergennes feared that
the king's prestige would be seriously compromised if
the Assembly of Notables turned out badly, and his
fears were borne out by events. Miromesnil, an old
parliamentarian who had distinguished himself in
resisting Maupeou at the time of the "Revolution"
obviously had no enthusiasm for Calonne's attempt to
evade the Parlements. But with the king's help
Calonne persuaded both to yield against their better
judgment. On December 29 the Council was convened and
for the first time the other ministers were informed
of the project. The day after Marshal de Castries
wrote a reproachful letter to the king asking why he
had not been consulted on such an important matter:
"Sire, you have decided to take the most important
step in your reign without deigning to seek my advice
and my fidelity, and it was through public information
that I first learned of it."[3]

The king replied that since the matter concerned
only the finances he had not thought it necessary to
consult the naval secretary. He had placed himself
entirely under the domination of Calonne, and the latter's penchant for secrecy meant the king would be seriously isolated if he should ever have to dismiss the
Controller General. It was an unprecedented situation
for the king. The death of Vergennes on February 13,
removed the only strong support Calonne had in the
ministry. The successor to Vergennes at the Foreign
Office was Armand-Marc, comte de Montmorin, who had

been ambassador to Madrid for several years and whose views on domestic matters were unknown.

On the same day of the council meeting, December 29, a royal proclamation informed the public of the convening of an assembly of Notables. "His Majesty declares his intention," so read the proclamation, "to convene an assembly composed of persons drawn from diverse conditions, who are the most qualified in their rank, in order to communicate to them his views concerning the welfare of his people, the order of his finances, and the reform of several abuses."[4] Letters under secret seal were sent out on the same day to 144 persons requiring them to meet at Versailles on January 29, 1787.

The recipients of the letters included seven princes of the blood, 14 bishops and archbishops, 36 nobles of the sword, among them distinguished marshals and generals, 38 magistrates of the sovereign courts, 12 counselors of state, 12 deputies from the pays d'états, and 25 heads of city governments. The choice of persons invited was largely Calonne's although made with the concurrence of the king. To the former's credit it must be said that he did pick the most notable of the different categories and did not attempt to favor those who were his known supporters. Among the princes of the blood only the comte d'Artois was a firm partisan of the Controller General, "seeing in him," according to Bachaumont, "only the amiable person, always generous, always disposed to be openhanded toward His Royal Highness."[5] According to the same writer Calonne invited the Archbishop of Toulouse, Loménie de Brienne, to suggest the prelates that should be invited, not being aware that the archbishop was "Neckerist" and that most of the prelates who came to Versailles were of the same persuasion.

Among the generals were some known friends and partisans of Necker: Marshal de Beauvau, the duc de

Broglie, and Marshal de Mouchy. But two prominent military figures proved to be firm adherents of Calonne in the coming months, the marquis de Bouillé, and Vice-Admiral d'Estaing. When the marquis de Lafayette first heard of the forthcoming assembly he was eager to be a part of it, and let his desire be known to the Controller General. Calonne expressed surprise that General Lafayette would consider himself qualified, his only distinction being his marriage to a daughter of the Noailles. "However," Calonne wrote to the hero of the American War, he "had no objection to recommending him to the king if he promised to perform his duties with zeal and submission."[6]

On January 29, 1787 the Notables arrived at Versailles on schedule. But they found the Controller General not yet ready to open the assembly. This was not a propitious beginning in his relations with that body. The Notables held responsible positions in the kingdom and it was not a small matter for them to give up nearly a month waiting for the opening of the assembly. The delay was caused partly by Calonne's illness, but also by his laziness. He was chronically behind schedule in his work, as those who knew him best and were his friends have testified.[7] Although he told the Notables in his opening address on February 22 that "the king has seen and approved all my proposals," in fact he had not yet written them all.

Finally on February 22 the august assembly was convened, the king personally presiding. After his brief welcoming address, the Keeper of the Seals, Miromesnil, gave a short, unremarkable speech. The Notables were most curious to hear what the Controller General would say for his was the initiative that had brought them to Versailles.

Calonne spoke to the Assembly for about an hour and a quarter. Knowing that his listeners were most keenly interested in finding out about the financial situation he wasted no time in coming to the point. After the conclusion of the American War, he said, the principal task of the government was to put the finances on a sound basis, "for that is the primary source of public well-being." To carry out that task it was necessary to liquidate the past. That meant to pay off all the debts of the American War and to put the expenditures of the government on a level with its income. During the past three years that had been his constant preoccupation. When he came to the helm of the finances in November 1783, he told the Notables, he found a desperate situation. "All the treasuries were empty, all the government securities were falling on the exchange, the circulation of money was interrupted, there was alarm everywhere, and confidence was destroyed." In the face of empty treasuries, what awesome obligations he was required to meet! "There was 220 million livres of war debts to pay, 80 millions of other debts in arrears that were now falling due, 176 millions of revenue had already been used in the form of anticipations on the revenues of future years, there was a deficit of 80 millions in the ordinary revenue and expenditures, the payment of _rentes_ were excessively delayed. Altogether 600 million livres were owed by the government, and there was neither money nor credit." In case anyone thought the Controller General might be exaggerating or not quite telling the truth, Calonne then said that "the time is too recent to need proof. However, I have placed in the hands of His Majesty all the justificatory documents. His Majesty has examined them all, and they remain in his hands."[8]

After this gloomy description of the royal finances at the beginning of his financial administration, Calonne next invited the Notables to look at the present time, and see the results of three years of his stewardship. "Today money is abundant, credit has been restored, government securities have rebounded and are active on the exchange, and, except for difficulties caused by speculation, they leave nothing to be desired." The Discount Bank had been in trouble at the time Calonne entered the ministry. Now it was back in favor with the public, and "its usefulness can only continue to grow." The war debts have all been paid, and all accounts are now current. There is not the least delay in the payment of rentes; 48 million livres have been spent in extraordinary expenditures to bring about that result. Also 36 million livres have been spent extraordinarily to liquidate the remaining rescriptions of the receivers general that had been suspended in the "partial bankruptcy" of 1771. This was done even before the date due. The other debts of the king are all being reimbursed regularly by the special Sinking Fund (Caisse d'Amortissement) set up by Calonne in 1784.

Continuing in this bright, optimistic vein, Calonne went on to describe other accomplishments to his credit. He had been able to meet great unforeseen expenditures during the three years, due to such matters as the foreign policy crisis over the United Netherlands, the climatic disasters in 1784 and 1785 which required government relief for the victims of floods. But much of the accomplishments of his administration was deliberate and productive. New port facilities were built at Cherbourg, Le Havre, La Rochelle, Dunkirk, and Dieppe. New canals, roads and bridges were constructed. Several indirect taxes harmful to commerce were suppressed. The government had granted subsidies to encourage new industries, making France less dependent on their products from abroad. The "first and most important industry, agriculture," had also been encouraged; agricultural societies for improvement had found an encouraging and friendly government. "Indeed, gentlemen, in the midst of these enterprises, each department has received what it has judged necessary for its service, every intendant has obtained the help he has asked for in his generality; each creditor of the state has received his due; none have complained, no petitioner has been repulsed by the dismal allegation of 'the miserable state of the finances' which had so long been the response of the administration."[9]

Knowing that there were in the audience several magistrates of the sovereign courts who had remonstrated against his loans, and being aware also of the Neckerists in the audience who might wonder if such open-handedness was prudent when the government was facing bankruptcy, Calonne had a word for them all. If anyone thought he had spent money recklessly or in order to curry personal favor, Calonne assured the Notables that he had given to the king "exact and enumerated accounts of all that has been given, acquired, exchanged, borrowed and anticipated since His Majesty deigned to entrust me with his finances. To this information I have appended official authorizations and the use that has been made of them. His Majesty has seen them all, he has retained them, and is continually able to verify for himself every item. And I have no fear that the most venomous malevolence could find a single thing there that would compromise me."

As for the Neckerists who continually harped on economizing at every turn, Calonne read them a lesson on economic policy:

In general the economic policy of a minister of finance can exist under two forms that are so different that one would think there were two kinds of economy. The one which strikes everyone by its severe mien, which attracts attention by denying petitions loudly and harshly, which makes a point of being rigorous over the slightest objects in order to discourage the swarm of petitioners, this makes an imposing impression and captivates opinion, even if it has little impact on the reality of the situation. The other, which springs from a sense of duty rather than from character can do more by paying less attention to small matters and keeping itself in reserve for those of some importance. It does not affect austerity for things that are not austere. It allows publicity about what is granted but keeps silent about what is saved. Because it is seen accessible to requests it is not believed that it rejects the greatest part of them. Because it attempts to sweeten the bitterness of refusal, it is thought to be incapable of refusal. Because it does not have the advantageous and easy reputation of inflexibility, it is not given credit for prudent reserve. And often while by an assiduous application to all the details of an immense administration it protects the finances from the most fatal abuses and the most ruinous blunders, it seems to condemn itself by an appearance of liberality which the desire to denigrate soon turns into profusion. Can anyone fail to realize that in a kingdom such as France the most certain and most important of economies consists in not committing a false operation, that a single miscalculation in administration, a mistaken speculation, a loan badly calculated, a backward step, costs the public treasury infinitely more, although it is not realized, than ostensible expenditures which are most talked about? And that the title of economical administrator should go to him for whom one cannot cite a single abortive operation rather than to him who can only boast of savings that are often illusory and more advantageous to the reputation of the minister who makes them a merit rather than to the State whose useful splendour is incompatible with a sterile parsimony. [10]

It was fairly obvious in the above remarks that Calonne was describing his own ministry and that of Necker. Some in the audience may have been puzzled by the allusions in the last paragraph translated above. But those familiar with the brochures put out by the circle of vehement anti-Neckerists would have recognized the matters referred to. It was only a month or so after the opening of the Assembly of Notables that Mirabeau published his essays on Necker's administration in which he denounced the Genevan's wartime loans as "the most badly organized, the most ruinous, which France has ever been obliged to pay."[11] Mirabeau placed the blame for the financial predicament of the royal government squarely on Necker, not only because of his loans but because he had refused to increase tax revenue at the beginning of the American War. It was Necker's loans according to Mirabeau, which had made France a prey to speculators, whom he had denounced in an earlier essay published in January 1787. It was also an article of faith in the anti-Neckerist circle that the too-famous Compte rendu of 1781 was flagrantly in error, that instead of a surplus of 10.2 million livres of income as claimed by Necker there was in reality a deficit which Calonne was to fix at 75 million livres. If Calonne had acquired a reputation of liberality in spending, he asserted that he certainly was not guilty of such great errors as those attributed to Necker by the circle of Mirabeau, Clavière, Panchaud, and Brissot.

Up to this point in his February 22 speech before the Notables Calonne had described in most optimistic colors the general economy and the finances of the royal government. The Notables must have begun to wonder why they had been summoned to Versailles. But if their attentiveness to the Controller General's

111

speech was beginning to waver, it was arrested by what followed. The Controller General explained that he really did not have a choice about the financial policy he had pursued and which he had just described. The catastrophic situation at the beginning of his ministry required that he adopt a policy of appearing to be continually optimistic before the public. To restore the credit of the royal government it was necessary to reassure the people by statements and attitudes of the Controller General. If he had appeared penurious, it would have made even worse the credit situation of the government. It was necessary to spend money in order to get money circulating once more. The great challenge of the moment was to restore confidence and credit. Without credit the government could get nowhere. Hence the "economics of gaiety" as Necker was to describe his rival's administration. To Necker, of course, it would have seemed like whistling in the dark rather than a sound credit policy. It was the need to influence opinion, Calonne said, that made it imperative for him to make such large payments on the government's debt. But in paying off the naval debt incurred during the war, which did not require any annual interest payment, Calonne borrowed money by loans that were at their costliest. The same was true of the 48 million livres paid extraordinarily to bring the payment of the rentiers up to date, and the 36 million to liquidate the rescriptions suspended in 1771. A banker would not have thought that a propitious policy for restoring the government's credit!

It was necessary to exude optimism, Calonne said, in order "to conceal the wound." Now the Notables probably thought he was getting down to the business at hand. So there was a "wound" to conceal! During the past year, Calonne continued, he had made a profound study of the royal finances, and after ceaseless labor he had acquired "a knowledge more certain than has ever been done before of the situation of the finances." The accounts in the Contrôle Général he found to be utterly chaotic. The income and expenditures of fiscal years were hopelessly mingled, as were the ordinary accounts and what was extraordinary or temporary. After some months of hard work he had succeeded in placing before the king "a general account of his finances which I could guarantee to him and justify the exactness. I carefully distinguished the ordinary revenues for each fiscal year and placed the total amount of each in its column from which was subtracted the amount to be sent to the royal treasury. I followed the same method for expenditures." That is, he separated the ordinary from the extraordinary and assigned each to the fiscal year to which it belonged. "These accounts were drawn up from two points of view: one for the year 1787, the other for the ordinary year, presenting a very correct balance between the annual revenues and expenditures. I gave these to the king, supported by 63 individual accounts which presented a very detailed itemized account of each, and His Majesty has made a thorough study of them and at the present time is better instructed than anyone else could possibly be of the true state of finances of his kingdom."[12]

Well, what was the result of these months of intensive study of the financial documents? "The results of this knowledge," Calonne told the Notables, "are neither in doubt nor satisfying." "I must confess," he continued, "and I am not disguising anything, that the annual deficit is very considerable. I have made known to the king its origin, its progress and its causes." This deficit, he found, had existed for centuries, and had continued in every year of the present reign. It was 74 million livres when Abbé Terray came to the helm of the finances in 1770; it was 40 million when he left in 1774, even though Terray's own Compte rendu to the king gave a deficit of only 27.8 million. "But it is recognized and proven by the comptes effectives of that same year

that it was 40.2 million livres." In 1776, only a
short time before Necker took over the royal finances
he recorded a deficit of 37 million for that year.
Because of the wartime needs, the deficit continued to
mount, for ameliorations and economy could not begin
to pay for the costs of the loans. When he became
Controller General in November 1783 he found that the
deficit of ordinary income compared to ordinary expenditures was 80 million livres. Since he was faced
with an indebtedness of 604 million livres, to which
had to be added the 80 millions of the deficit, it was
obvious that he could not pay all that in 1784, or
even in the following years. The public loans of
1783, 1784, and 1785 which were registered by the Parlement of Paris totalled 305 million livres, so that
was obviously not sufficient to meet all those payments. Therefore it was necessary to raise money by
more indirect methods which was done with the full
knowledge and approval of the king. But with all the
loans he had been able to make [which the following
year he fixed at the sum of 650 million livres], still
they were insufficient to meet the expenditures he was
obliged to make during the past three years. "The
rest was made by establishing greater order, economy,
and other arrangements of which an extensive administration is capable, and everything is paid." That is
to say, the government was meeting its obligations and
was not defaulting on any of them.

> But as a consequence of this, the annual
> deficit has necessarily taken on new dimen-
> sions. The causes are too well known to the
> public for the effects to be mysterious.
> The causes are explained by a single obser-
> vation. The deficit was 37 million livres
> in 1776, and since that time until the end
> of 1786 the government has borrowed 1,250
> million livres. These loans were necessary
> to pay for a war--a "nationalist war."[13]

But Calonne said there should be added to this disturbing situation the more positive aspects of the picture, namely the ameliorations in revenue that have occurred during the past three years and those that can be counted upon in future years. Revenue from the indirect taxes has continued to increase, as shown by the contracts he signed in 1786 with the Farmers General, the Administration of the Domaine, and the Régie générale. Very important also was the fact that amortization of loans each year reduced the deficit by the amount of interest they cost. "In the next ten years 400 million livres of debt will be extinguished. That will increase revenue by 60 million livres annually." But until that time it was necessary to increase revenue by other means to meet the large annual deficit.

In his February 22 speech to the Notables Calonne did not reveal the actual amount of the deficit for 1787, nor did he indicate the precise sums that each of his reforms to be presented to the Notables would yield. All such details were in the hands of the king, and Calonne seemed to think the Notables should be satisfied with these general statements about the royal finances. His purpose in convening them was simply to get their approval for the means he had decided upon to meet the financial crisis. Neither did Calonne let the Notables know just how serious the financial situation was. He had negotiated a loan of 70 million livres from the Discount Bank in January. But that would only furnish the government with sufficient funds until the 15th of April. No wonder the Controller General was in a hurry, and did not want the Notables to ask unnecessary questions!

The final part of his February 22 speech was to outline to the assembly his plan for putting the royal finances on a sound basis. Partial and piecemeal remedies, he said, would not be sufficient. It was necessary to attack the evil at its source, to strike at the principle which governs all the details. And

115

that principle was the existence of a kingdom founded upon privileges and special exemptions from the public burdens that should be shared by all who benefit from the government's protection. When he spoke in that vein, Calonne may well have alarmed the Notables, all of whom enjoyed privileges of various sorts, and it seems to historians that he was the precursor of the Constituent Assembly if not the National Convention. But as the reforms were given to the Assembly they appeared much less alarming, indeed even very piecemeal. The vingtièmes were to be replaced by a general tax on all income from land which would be administered by provincial assemblies to be established in all the pays d'élections, but not in the pays d'états which were to preserve their identity. There were to be no exemptions whatever from the general land tax; the great nobles and the Church, and even the king's lands were to be subject to it. But that would make possible a lighter land tax for the poorer class than the two vingtièmes. The nobles would be freed from the capitation tax. The Church, in return for being subjected to the general land tax, would no longer pay the "free gift." The government would permit the Church to alienate its feudal dues and rights which were not supposed to be enjoyed by Church people anyway. There would be uniformity in the administration of the gabelle, all provinces being subject to a common price of salt and the sel de devoir, which however would be a lower price than hitherto. The savings to be realized from this reform was due to abolishing the elaborate bureaucracy needed to enforce the laws against smuggling. Uniformity would also be established in the customs and tariffs which would be moved to the frontier. Additional revenue would come from an extension of the indirect tax on legal documents, a "stamp tax," and also certain parts of the King's Domain lands would be sold under special legislation called "infeudation." The taille would be reformed so as to be less of a burden on the common people, and the corvée labor service for roads and bridges would be abolished and replaced by a monetary tax on all subject to the taille. As for the Discount Bank some mention was made about "increasing its utility" but evidently Calonne had given up the idea for the moment of transforming it into a national or royal bank.

After Calonne had finished his address to the Notables the king invited anyone who desired to address the Assembly. The First President of the Parlement of Paris, d'Aligre, rose and after making the suitable compliments to the king and the Assembly, said, "Sire, may the spirit of order and economy which animates Your Majesty penetrate into all branches of his administration."[14] It was a reminder of the theses the Parlement had maintained constantly the past three years, that "order and economy" alone would balance the expenditures with ordinary revenues.

The following day, February 23, the Notables met again in a common assembly, this time under the presidency of the king's brother, Monsieur, comte de Provence. They were told of the order in which the deliberations would be made. The members would be divided into seven committees or Bureaux, each presided over by a Prince of the Blood. Each bureau would receive the proposals of the Controller General in the form of memorials, divided into four "divisions." The Notables were to convene the following day in their separate committees and receive the first divisions of memorials from the Controller General. After the bureaux had deliberated on these proposals the presidents and two members from each bureaux would meet under the presidency of Monsieur to collate the results of their deliberations. Then the proposals would be submitted to a general assembly of all the Notables for approval. After that the next division of memorials would be taken up. During the Assembly of Notables of 1787 there were six general assemblies. In addition to the initial meetings on February 22 and 23

117

the general assembly met on March 12, March 29, April 23, and May 25.

The second general assembly of February 23 was delayed until noon because some of Calonne's papers containing his speech to the Notables for that day were accidently burned during the night, or at least such was the explanation. The first meetings of the seven bureaux on February 26 were also delayed because Calonne did not have a sufficient number of copies of his memorials of the first division to hand out.[15] Finally, when the Notables could begin work they took up the proposals of the first division relating to the establishment of the provincial assemblies, the general land tax, and the liquidation of the debt of the Church.

All the bureau welcomed the establishment of provincial assemblies. With the exception of the sixth bureau of the prince de Conti, all accepted the establishment of the assemblies at the parish and district levels as well, and the principle of election of delegates to these assemblies. But they were equally opposed to the proposal that deputies be chosen exclusively on the basis of income from land, and that the wealthier proprietors would be given multiple votes in the parish assemblies equal to their annual income divided by 600 livres. There was a limit, of course, no one deputy could have more than a third of the votes! This was one of the absurd ideas that Calonne took over from Dupont de Nemours' essay of 1775. The Notables thought wealth was a good criteria for eligibility, but why should it be exclusively income from land? Should not the artisans of the towns or the merchants also have a right to take part in the selection of deputies at the primary level? The Notables wanted to give more representation to the cities than was allowed by the dogmas of physiocracy.

118

Furthermore the Notables thought wealth should be the determining criteria for only a part of the delegates. At least one third (according to the first and second bureaux) and one-half (according to the third, fifth and seventh bureaux) of the deputies should be nobles or prelates selected by the two orders. The assemblies of Calonne would completely ignore the social ranks of the deputies not only in the matter of selection but in the proceedings of the assemblies. In the ancien régime there was a great preoccupation with what was called préséance, or protocol. Seating in the assembly was arranged according to social rank, and in the old assemblies of estates much time was taken up over disputes as to who should precede whom. The Notables agreed to the principles of meeting in a common assembly and vote by head, as was the procedure in the two assemblies of Berri and Haute Guienne. But otherwise they thought the ranks should be respected. The president of the provincial assembly should be a nobleman or a prelate appointed by the king. The deputies would sit separately (but in the same chamber) according to their order, and within their order according to rank.

In actuality this insistence on the preservation of social ranks in the assemblies was more a matter of principle than substance. The doubling of the Third Estate meant that the two "privileged orders" could not dominate the decisions of the assembly. The first and second bureaux, containing the most influential of Notables stipulated that only one-third of the delegates must be nobles or prelates. Since deliberation was to be done in a common assembly, and voting counted by head, this certainly did not give the aristocrats a preponderance. Even if Dupont's scheme had been used it is probable that as many prelates and nobles would have been sent to the provincial assemblies as in that of the Notables. Calonne had stipulated in his memorial the previous year to the king the principle of the doubling of the Third Estate, although it was not retained in his memorial to the Notables.

Besides preserving the traditional orders and their _préséance_ in the assemblies the Notables also asked the king to clarify the powers to be granted to the assemblies and particularly the role of the intendant at the provincial assemblies. It appeared from the wording of Calonne's memorial that the assemblies were to be strictly controlled by the intendants. The Notables requested that the assemblies be given sufficient executive and administrative authority to accomplish their tasks. These were to assess and collect the taxes, administer the roads of the generality, take care of poor relief, and other functions of local self-government. The Notables, who held up Necker's assemblies in the Berri and Haute Guienne as models, wanted to broaden the powers and scope of the activities of the assemblies. The defenders of the administrative monarchy wanted to preserve intact the authority of the intendant. They were fearful of too much power accruing in the hands of the local assemblies. As a former intendant himself, Calonne was obviously attracted to the physiocratic idea of provincial assemblies. They would be given no administrative power, and would not be even called "administrative assemblies."

Of course it is possible to see in these differences a class conflict: the aristocrats versus the administrative, or absolute monarchy; the former grasping for power at the local level in order to guarantee their privileges and preeminence in society; the intendants and the king being the real defenders of the lower classes against oppression from the aristocrats. There is some indication in the discussion of the First Bureau that provincial assemblies that ignored the distinction of the orders, as did Dupont's and Calonne's, might leave the two 'privileged orders' helpless against those who would undermine the traditional social order and bring about democracy. But did the aristocrats, the "privileged" in the assemblies set up by Necker in the Berri and Haute Guienne exhibit those characteristics of selfish egotism, of reaction to an older regime of an aristocratic society dominated by the estates rather than the monarchy? The record of those two assemblies, as Necker had pointed out in his book on French finances published in 1785, certainly demonstrated that high ranking aristocrats could be public-spirited, patriotic, eager to serve the public, and as solicitous of the condition of the poorer class as ever any intendant was. Furthermore they were forward-looking rather than reactionary. They knew that the old order was changing, and the new order would not be democracy, as some feared, but a regime of notables, of experienced, responsible, competent, and even public-spirited servants of the nation. In fact the above description of the conduct of the aristocrats in the Berri and Haute Guienne was to fit the Assembly of Notables very closely, although this has not been the general opinion of historians.

What was most crucial in the relations between Calonne and the Notables was the matter of taxation and the new land tax proposed by the Controller General. He pointed out the reasons why the vingtième tax had been so unsatisfactory. In 1772 the government ordered a verification of the landed income from all lands. But this required a complicated and lengthy process of surveying and appraisal of land values. In 1782 this process was discontinued when the third vingtième was imposed, and only about 5000 parishes had completed that survey in the ten-year period, this out of 22,308 parishes in the pays d'élections.[16] But the yield from those 5000 parishes was about double the rate of that from the non-appraised lands of the parishes. Therefore, Calonne concluded that if the vingtièmes were levied fairly and equitably throughout the kingdom the government

121

could expect about twice the amount currently collected, an increase of 55 million livres.

It was not only the expense and delay of survey and appraisal of the lands that prevented the government from realizing the full benefit of the vingtièmes. "The injustice has been greatly aggravated because of the influence, the favor, and the protection which have freed the rich proprietors from a portion of their share, while the less well-off have had to pay the tax rigorously." Furthermore there was a great distinction not only among individual proprietors but between cities, some of which were "free cities" or which had settled by special agreement (abonnement), and the same distinction prevailed among the provinces, where the pays d'états levied their share of the vingtièmes according to abonnement.

The advantage of Calonne's idea of collecting the tax in kind rather than in money was that all the means whereby the wealthy and powerful had hitherto escaped paying their fair share would no longer be possible. There could be no question about the harvest from the land, it would be obvious that the king's share of the crop was one out of 20 or two out of 20 sheaves of grain, or whatever the produce of the land might be. There need be no argument about the value of the crops or the rental value of the land! No need to carry out the expensive and hitherto unsatisfactory surveying and appraisal of the lands. The name "vingtièmes" would be discontinued and instead the new tax would be called the "land subsidy" (subvention territoriale). It would be assessed by the new provincial assemblies in the pays d'élections. The levy would extend to all the lands throughout the kingdom. No exemptions whatever would be permitted. Even the king's lands and the princes' would be subject to it. The Church would no longer be exempt, nor would the great nobles be permitted to settle for the tax par abonnement.

In his memorial to the Notables Calonne did not stipulate exactly what sum would be raised by the general land subsidy. It was to be a proportional tax, a particular rate would be levied on the produce of the land. He evidently expected that the land subsidy would replace exactly the two vingtièmes and the 20% surtax on the first vingtième, about 9% general levy on the yearly harvest from the land. The parish assemblies would divide the land into four categories according to productivity of the soil. The most fertile land would be assessed the full 9%, the next category a lesser rate, and so on. Calonne was convinced that if the tax were levied in that manner without abonnements or exceptions it would yield about twice the amount of the previous vingtièmes.

So confident was he of this increase in revenue that he planned to use about 15 million livres from it to grant tax relief in other categories of taxation, although this was not mentioned to the Notables. Included among the memorials of the first division of reforms was one for the taille. A thorough-going reform of that tax would be left to the provincial assemblies that were to be established. Until that time Calonne proposed granting relief to the poorer classes. A top limit of one-twentieth was fixed for assessment on any taillable. Manual workers and artisans could not be assessed more than the price of one day's labor per year. To assure that these concessions to the poor did not add greater burdens on others, Calonne proposed that the amount of revenue from the taille be reduced by 10% throughout the kingdom. In the countryside, in each parish, the assembly would be permitted to withhold 5% of the taille to use for poor relief, or to assist peasants who had suffered some calamity.

Not only the poor were to benefit from tax relief. The nobility, unlike the clergy, had always been subjected to the capitation established near the

123

end of the seventeenth century. Calonne proposed, in his memorial on the land subsidy, that the nobles would no longer be required to pay the capitation. He believed that the nobility and the clergy should not be subjected to personal taxation. It was their exploitation of land that should be taxable, a réelle tax rather than a personelle tax. Evidently he did not consider this one of the "abuses" against which he had inveighed in his February 22 speech. The taille was to be reformed by the provincial assemblies so as to force the wealthier proprietors of the Third Estate to pay their fair share.

In Calonne's reform program, as well as that of his predecessors (including Necker) there was no thought of forcing the nobles and prelates to pay the taille. No doubt the neglect of the reformers for what seems to the modern observer the most glaring evil of the ancien régime, that society should be divided into taillables and nontaillables, was due to the conviction that the nobles and the Church who rented land to cultivators, as most did, actually paid the incidence of the taille. It was subtracted from their profits from the leased land. Only where the noble or cleric exploited directly the land was he exempt, and then only for a limited acreage. The amount of the exemption from the taille was so small that it was not worth affronting the nobles by an issue that was more of principle than of substance.

The other reforms in Calonne's first division of memoirs to the Notables provided means for the Church to liquidate its debts, for the freeing of the grain trade from any restriction, and for the abolition of the corvée. These were the matters referred to the bureaux in the general assembly of February 23. There were to be three other divisions of reform submitted as soon as the Notables had deliberated on the first division. Those proposed in these later memoirs included establishing the single duty tariff, with the

customs barriers removed to the frontiers of the kingdom, the reform of the gabelle, the stamp tax, which
was to be the only other additional tax proposal, the
new administration of the king's domain and forests,
and the extension of the time limit for amortizing
exigible debts.[17]

The proposals for the provincial assemblies, the
new land subsidy, and the amortization of the Church's
debt were placed in the first division because Calonne
knew they would require the most discussion and he was
anxious to speed up the decision-making process. He
hoped to get the new land subsidy approved and enacted
into law immediately and made retroactive to the first
of January. The intendants would administer it until
the provincial assemblies could be set up. Even if it
did take time for the revenue to come into the king's
coffers, the subsidy would be a good basis for getting
a new loan, absolutely mandatory by the end of April
if not sooner. Thus, haste was the essence of
Calonne's great reforms, and that is probably what led
to his inconsiderate treatment of the Notables. Abbé
Morellet wrote that the ideas of the physiocrats were
"an exotic flower in his hat, which had no relationship to his other ideas."[18] The same could be said of
his attempt to rule with the cooperation of a deliberative assembly. He had little sense of how such a
body should be treated, in that respect his attitude
differed markedly from Necker's deferential attitude
toward the States-General of 1789.

The memorial on the land subsidy was the proposal
that elicited the most discussion from the Notables.[19]
All seven bureaux accepted the principle that "all orders of citizens must pay their fair proportion of
public taxes," as stated by the third Bureau of the
duc d'Orleans. There was some question as to whether
the name of the tax should be changed from vingtième
to subvention territoriale, since the former had become so entrenched in legal and commercial documents.

125

But a majority of the Second Bureau of the comte d'Artois asserted that "a new name could assure all the better the universality of assessment and the equality which His Majesty proposes." There was no question that the principle of equality in the administration of the land tax, with no exemptions, was endorsed by the Assembly of Notables. But there were three qualifications in this endorsement. First, that "this be without prejudice to representations which the orders, corporations, and provinces might make on the changes that they could experience by the resolution which His Majesty has announced, in their rights, constitutions, and former customs." That statement was from the Third Bureau, and it was repeated in identical language in most of the others. Did that mean that after solemnly endorsing the king's plan to assess the land subsidy on all lands without distinction throughout the kingdom, that the Notables really meant that they would insist on their privileges and exemptions, the abolition of which was the essence of the plan? Many have thought so, including most historians who write on the subject in the present century. Observers of that time were more charitable, such as abbé Morellet who wrote that the Church was willing to have the provincial assemblies assess the land tax on its lands but wished to collect the tax by using its own personnel, and according to its own customs. The reason for this, the abbé explained to Lord Shelburne, was not to defeat the king's purpose in establishing the land tax but just the opposite: the lesser benefices would be assessed lightly, and the benefices without pastoral duties would be assessed much more heavily.[20] In any case the statement was ambiguous and it is not possible to know exactly how the Notables interpreted it.

The second qualification was much more threatening to Calonne. The sovereign courts had never admitted the right of the king to tax his subjects without representation. The *vingtièmes* were considered to be emergency tax measures due to the mid-century wars. They were limited in time, and even though the name might indicate a proportional tax (one or two twentieths of a proprietor's income from land), in actuality the vingtième was administered much as the taille. It was a fixed sum for a limited period and divided up or apportioned out to the generalities. The "twentieths" merely fixed the upper limit that a proprietor could be assessed.

The Notables were well aware that Calonne had painted himself into a financial corner, and they were not disposed to help him find an easy escape. They knew his motive in summoning the Assembly was to make it possible for him to ignore the remonstrances of the sovereign courts to new loans or taxes. Therefore in deliberating upon the land tax proposal the Notables asserted that they could not give their assent to a proportional tax that would levy permanently a percentage of the taxpayers' income. The sum authorized by a tax law, whether a new one or an increase of revenue from an existing tax, must be a certain sum and the authorization limited in time. Therefore it would be necessary for the Notables to see those financial statements that Calonne had sent to the king in order to verify the deficit, and to see what specific sum was needed by the general tax subsidy. Further, other financial measures in the remaining divisions, including the stamp tax and the proposals to help cover the deficit by certain economies in some departments must also be submitted to the Notables, who would have to wait and examine these in order to see what precisely the deficit was, and how much revenue was needed from the land tax to cover it. The First Bureau expressed the general thought of the Notables on the subject: "Since the purpose of the tax (the land subsidy) is to fill a deficit, it will be necessary to know exactly what the deficit is, and how it came about . . . It has been observed that such knowledge can only come from a comparison of the situation of the finances in

1781 with that which they are today, beginning with the _Compte_ _rendu_ published at that time, and the one that will be furnished to us." The latter referred to the account Calonne had mentioned in his February 22 speech, which he said had been sent to the king, an account of revenue and expenditures "for the ordinary year."

The third qualification of the Notables in accepting Calonne's land subsidy was that if it were to be approved and enacted into law the collection of the revenue should be in money rather than in kind, that is, a proportion of the harvest as in Calonne's proposal. This was surely the most badly thought-out provision of all Calonne's hastily contrived reforms. In the later years of Louis XIV, the little book of Marshal Vauban, _The_ _Royal_ _Tithe_, became famous. It proposed that the government levy a tenth part of the harvest of the land, in kind, as did the Church. In 1725 the government attempted to implement this scheme, but quickly abandoned it the following year, for it proved to be unworkable. The expense of collecting and storing such huge quantities of produce, the great number of employees needed to care for it, had made the costs of collection from three to four times the cost of levying a tax in money. The Church continued to levy the tax in kind, but the parish priest handled much of the collection and storage which greatly reduced the costs. Even so, the prelates among the Assembly of Notables admitted that the collection of the tithe was very inefficient and did not provide a model for the government. The argument most often made by the Notables in opposition to the collection in kind was the physiocratic one: a collection of a portion of the harvest took no account of the capital investment that went into the land. Loménie de Brienne wrote that "every parcel of land that yields ten sheaves of wheat does not bring the same profit to the owner. One of the parcels can require more expense in cultivation and capital investment . . . If two pieces of land are tithed equally the burden could be different for each owner."[21] According to physiocratic ideas it was the net product, after expenses, that should bear the incidence of taxation, not the gross product.

Needless to say, Calonne was distressed to find his land subsidy, the linchpin of his reforms, meeting such serious objections and delays. The Notables were not rejecting his land tax; they were simply telling him that they could not approve it without knowing what specific sum is needed, and what other measures are being taken to remove the deficit. They did not even know what the deficit was. The Controller General attempted to speed matters by sending a "supplementary instruction" to the bureaux informing them that the king did not intend for them to discuss the "fundamentals" of the tax proposal but only the "modalities," that is, how it should be implemented. It was proper for them to discuss the matter of collection in kind or in money, but not the other matters that were taking up time. The Notables reiterated that they could not proceed with the land subsidy until they had more information. It was an impasse.

Finally on March 2 Calonne agreed to attend a select group of Notables at the residence of Monsieur consisting of all seven prince-presidents and six members from each bureaux. For five and one-half hours Calonne debated with considerable skill the objections of the Notables to his proposals.[22] In the course of the discussion he did reveal certain specific information he had withheld from the first meeting of the Assembly on February 22. The compte rendu given to the king showed a revenue "for the ordinary year" of 474,620,000 livres and expenditures for the ordinary year were 575,486,000 livres. But Calonne added that with unforeseen expenditures the actual deficit would be 110 to 112 million livres. He expected that the new land tax would double the income from the vingtièmes that were to be replaced by it, an increase of revenue of about 50 million livres. The new tax on legal documents, the Stamp Tax, would yield a revenue of about 20 million livres. The new schedule for reimbursement of loans that were falling due in the next ten years would extend the time period for 20 years. This would reduce payments by 25 million livres per year. Finally, savings of another 20 million livres would be realized by economizing in the War Department and in the King's Household.

The Notables, remembering the elaborate documentation Calonne had mentioned giving to the king on the state of the finances asked if they could see those documents in order to learn how the deficit came about. Calonne explained that the Notables would not be able to understand the financial accounts because it required a long practice to see what belongs to each fiscal year and what is ordinary and what is extraordinary in the revenue and expenditures. He evidently forgot that he had claimed to the Assembly on February 22 that after several months of "hard work" he had done just that and had presented the results to the king. The Notables thought, not unreasonably, that if the king could understand this documentation it should not be beyond the capacities of Their Excellencies.[23]

It was at that point that Marshal de Beauvau asked Calonne to explain the contradiction between his statements on February 22 that there had been a large deficit every year during the war years and Necker's Compte rendu of 1781 which claimed a surplus of ordinary revenue of over 10 million livres. Calonne replied that as a result of his study of the origins of the deficit he found the Compte rendu of Monsieur Necker was grievously in error by as much as 56 million livres in the very items listed in that account,

130

and which could be estimated as high as 75 million. He had with him a chart which he circulated among the Notables showing discrepancies on nearly every item of the Compte rendu with what he called the comptes effectives which were the accounts at the end of the year 1781 showing precisely what income was received in the different branches of revenue and what exactly was spent by each of the disbursing departments. Calonne did not have the comptes effectives with him, only the results which appeared on the chart opposite the figures given by Necker's Compte rendu.

The Notables were dumbfounded by this disclosure. For six years most of them had believed firmly in the accuracy of the Compte rendu and the integrity of the Genevan banker. The essay that accompanied the account of 1781 together with Necker's book on French finances published in 1785 was the basic handbook of the Notables on the subject of the royal finances. Archbishop Dillon of Narbonne said that even an error of five million livres in the Compte rendu of 1781 would be a severe blow to the prestige of Necker. Not surprisingly the Notables were skeptical about Calonne's figures. Marshal de Beauvau asked Calonne if those documents could be left with the Notables for further study by a special committee. He was strongly supported by the prelates. Calonne refused to do so, arguing that the matter was not pertinent to the questions at hand. He did agree to present the other accounts for 1787 to the Notables if the king would give his consent. He also withdrew his "supplementary instructions" prohibiting the Notables from discussing the "fundamentals" of his memorials. On the matter of the collection of the land subsidy in kind or in money, Calonne conceded that he could change his view.

Despite the brilliance with which he had defended his projects in that meeting the Notables did not retreat from their positions. In the days following the March 2 conference the Bureaux drew up their "observations" on all the memorials the Controller General had presented in his first division, and these were sent to the king. All the Bureaux wished to see the provincial assemblies implemented but with the traditional social ranks, and with greater freedom from the intendants. All expressed adherence to the king's desire to alleviate the tax burden on the lower classes, and that all subjects should contribute to the needs of the government in accordance with ability to pay. But the decision of the Notables on the proposed land subsidy would have to await further information on the specific needs of the royal government. On the matter of the Church's debts, the Notables expressed a desire to see these debts liquidated, but said that the matter of selling some of its property to do so should be left to the next convocation of the clergy in 1788. The Notables did not think liquidation of the debt was essential for the Church to be able to pay its part of the land subsidy, if that measure were eventually adopted. The provisions of Calonne's memorial on the taille were all accepted by the Notables, although some bureaux pointed out that artisans of the towns were not all such poor people as to be included in the class to be given relief. The Bishop of Nevers submitted a lengthy memorial arguing that the alleviation of the burden on the poorer classes should not result in a heavier burden on those who paid the taille d'exploitation and the taille de propriété. The Notables recommended that the capitation tax continue to be levied on the nobility and the clergy of the frontiers, and the first bureau recommended that the revenue be used to alleviate the burden on the lower classes. All the Bureaux accepted with enthusiasm the proposal to restore freedom of export for the grain trade, and to abolish the corvée labor service.

Having deliberated on the first division of Calonne's memorials the Notables met in the third general assembly on March 12 to receive the second division of reforms from the Controller General. In his address to the assembly Calonne complimented the Notables on their reception of the first division. He was pleased to see that the views of the Notables were "substantially in accord with the king's views." "The objections which you have presented, which are principally on matters of form, do not contradict the essential points which His Majesty has proposed to ameliorate his finances and to give relief to his people by the reform of abuses." The Notables heard these words in astonishment. True, they had approved most measures of the first division, but not all. And the amendments they had made to the proposal for provincial assemblies were something more than an unimportant matter of form. They had suspended their deliberation on the land subsidy until further information was provided them. The memorial on the Church's debt and the proposal to liquidate it had not been approved by the assembly.

Upon return to their separate bureaux the Notables exploded in indignation. The Archbishop of Narbonne, in the First Bureau, said that the king could reasonably conclude from the Controller General's speech that the Notables had accepted all propositions without qualification. Monsieur agreed that "it was neither honest nor decent for the Controller General to have reported the Bureaux as saying what they manifestly had not said." All seven Bureaux drew up a vigorous protest and sent it to the king, pointing out where they had not agreed on the proposals of the first division.

For the Notables this was the crowning insult, following so many instances of arrogant treatment by the Controller General. The long delay in opening the assembly, the insistence on curbing the range of discussion, and now the speech of March 12 seemed to confirm their belief that Calonne looked upon the Notables as a docile rubber stamp to be used to overawe the sovereign courts. Since coming to Versailles the Notables were increasingly conscious of public opinion, which was greatly stirred by the king's announcement of their convocation on December 29. "A slight fever has gripped the country," abbé Morellet wrote to Shelburne. "As soon as the public has seen the Notables seriously occupied with its interests, opinion has given them a power which they would not have had by the manner in which they were convened. The Nation has, so to speak, recognized them as its true representatives, although they were assembled with quite a different intention, and by reason of the confidence acquired they have become like the deputies of our old States General."[24] In the bright glare of publicity the Notables knew they were being watched to see if they were indeed the pliant puppets of the government, as suggested by the hawker in the streets selling dolls and crying "Notables à vendre!" ("Notables for sale!")

The frustration of Calonne in facing that kind of a group can well be imagined. The protests of the seven bureaux, so uniform and united as they made the Notables appear, caused the king to wonder about the character of his Controller General. Despite Calonne's effort to repair the damage of his March 12 speech by insisting that he had been misunderstood, the breach between himself and the Notables was out in the open. It was a serious blow to his prestige. In these circumstances it was understandable that the last act of his ministerial career bore the mark of desperation.

Calonne had always cultivated public opinion, being well aware of its power in the later eighteenth century. He cultivated journalists and often wrote anonymous newstories that were published in journals. Late in March articles in journals and printed brochures began to appear denouncing the nobles and prelates of the Assembly of Notables for blocking the

134

reforms of the Controller General.[25] Then on March 31 and April 1 the royal printing plant published and distributed in enormous quantities and nominal cost the memorials Calonne had presented to the Notables of the first and second divisions. They were prefaced by an article written by the famous lawyer, Gerbier, under the title, "Notice" (Avertissement). The article began by explaining the reason for the memorials being published and distributed to the people. Lies were being spread about the purpose of the king in convening the Notables. It was being said that the purpose was to get their approval for an increase in taxes. This was not true, there was not going to be any increased tax burden placed on the people. On the contrary, the king proposes to lighten the tax burden by as much as 30 million livres per year rot counting the cessation of the third vingtième. The revenue of the king will be increased, but this will come from the abolition of unjustifiable abuses and privileges. It is those whose privileges are threatened by the reforms that are spreading these lies. But the article pointed out that the majority of the Notables have expressed their support of the king's intentions to abolish unjust privileges. It was implied that only a minority of the Notables was blocking the intentions of the king. It was to be expected that those whose interests would suffer by the reforms would act in that manner, but true patriots would not.

Ostensibly the "Notice" was not an attack on the Assembly of Notables, and Calonne could claim to be completely surprised by the reaction it provoked. If the Notables were indignant about the Controller General's March 12 speech, they were incensed by the "Notice." In the context of their relations with Calonne over the past three months, it could only be seen as an attempt of the Controller General to win public opinion to his side in his dispute with the Assembly. It implied that the desire of the entire nation and of all true patriots wanted the reforms just

135

as they were printed and now distributed to the public. There were no nuances, no amendments, no qualifications; the "Notice" stated quite clearly that either you were a good patriot and accepted the Controller General's great plan in toto, or you were an egotistical, selfish defender of unjustifiable privileges. In that context it was apparent that the Notables were being placed in the latter category. They were incensed because they thought it was not proper for the Controller General to make such an appeal to public opinion when the deliberations of the assembly were still in progress and supposedly secret. What caused more indignation was the feeling of being treated unjustly. The Notables had expressed complete agreement with the king's intentions. It was not his goals, but the methods that Calonne was proposing to carry out the reforms that the Notables objected to, and they believed their reasons for objecting were perfectly sound.

The Bureaux all sent a protest to the king about the "Notice" and asked his permission to publish their "opinions" on the reforms of the first division. The king was now in a cruel dilemma. The opposition to Calonne had reached a flood-tide. The "Nation," "public opinion," was overwhelmingly in support of the Notables and Calonne was vehemently denounced. The only options open to the king now were to dismiss either the Notables or Calonne. Either course was perilous. If he dismissed the Notables would the monarchy be strong enough to cope with the outcry? The "Revolution" of 1771 was still strong in the public memory. It was said that Calonne was another abbé Terray, except he was "Terray drunk." Yet to dismiss the Controller General was equally serious for the future of the monarchy. Some thought of Lord Strafford, the unpopular minister of Charles I of England whose dismissal in the face of public hostility was the beginning of the end of Stuart absolutism. Emperor Joseph wrote that if the king dismissed Calonne now it would be the coming of an English type monarchy for France, in which ministers were chosen in accord with the wishes of the nation represented in Parliament. Even those who shared the dislike of Calonne did not want to see the king dismiss him for that reason. "In setting their trap for M. de Calonne, (the Notables) did not see that they were catching royal authority in the same net."[26]

But there is little doubt that such was just the intent of an increasing number of the Notables. Right after the March 2nd conference, the comte de Brienne, brother of the Archbishop, who was in the First Bureau, spoke at length on the need to establish a "suitable kind of control" over the expenditures of the government, and for a compte rendu to be made up every year and submitted to a committee made of members from the "intermediate bureaux" of the provincial assemblies, and also some deputies of the assemblies of the pays d'états.[27] Others expressed similar ideas. It was necessary to establish some regular institution that would guarantee that the fate of 23 million Frenchmen would not be placed in the hands of a single individual, i.e., a minister like Calonne. And in the Bureaux there began to be some expression in favor of the States-General as a more suitable body to carry out that reform than the Assembly of Notables. In any case, the present situation of an irresponsible finance minister dilapidating the royal finances must be prevented in the future. This became the minimum demand of the Assembly of Notables, and was the chief reason why the Archbishop Loménie de Brienne who had just entered the government on May 3, was compelled to dismiss the Notables late in the month.

About the ministerial crisis that came at the end of the first week in April the sources are not entirely complete or in agreement. According to the Journal of Loménie de Brienne, it was the financial

crisis that forced the king's hand. In a meeting between the king and the Controller General it was revealed to the king that there were funds in the treasury for only 15 days more operation of the government. Calonne asked the king for what in effect would
have been dictatorial power: that he dismiss both
Miromesnil, Keeper of the Seals, and Breteuil, Secretary of State for the King's Household. Both had become alarmed about the Controller General's handling
of the Assembly of Notables. Calonne told the king
that Miromesnil was secretly supporting the Assembly
of Notables in their opposition to his reforms, and
apparently produced enough evidence to convince the
king. According to information from the Archbishop of
Aix, Calonne had asked Breteuil to issue lettres de
cachet to the Notables, but Loménie de Brienne could
not verify that report. In any case, it is probable
that Calonne was thinking of dismissing the Notables
for it had become out of the question for him to work
usefully with them. He did tell the king that the Notables were opposing all his reform plans, a flagrant
contradiction of his speech at the March 12 assembly.[28]

It was in order to hasten the king's decision to
yield to his demands that Calonne revealed the desperate financial plight of the government. This was in
fact his chief anxiety at the moment. He was reduced
to living from day to day on anticipations, that is,
short-term promissory notes issued by the Farmers-General and Receivers-General based upon the tax revenue
of future fiscal years. Even those most costly of
royal loans were giving out. The financiers who negotiated them were dependent upon the capital of the
market place, and government notes were doing poorly
on the exchange. Calonne strove to bolster the government's credit by spending, according to several reports, ten million livres to prop up government notes
in the last days of his ministry. It was the final
paroxysm of the famous "tactic": spending the govern-

138

ment into bankruptcy in a vain effort to maintain its credit!

Once the veracity of the Controller General was called into question it was to be expected that the king would wonder about his version of the origin of the deficit. He knew that Necker's adherents in the Assembly of Notables did not believe Calonne's charges about the falsity of the Compte rendu in 1781. And of course the former Director General of Finances was highly indignant when he heard of Calonne's allegations about his Compte rendu at the meeting of March 2nd. Necker wrote to Louis XVI beseeching him to be permitted to appear at a council meeting and to confront Calonne with his pièces justificatives of the Compte rendu. Calonne had already refused a request of the Genevan for a personal conference between the two. Louis XVI did not want a personal confrontation, but he sent word to Necker that he could send his pièces justificatives to the care of his friend in the Council, the marquis de Castries, and they would be examined in a council meeting. But Necker wanted to defend his own record personally, and doubted the ability of Castries, certainly a very competent general and military administrator, to handle a financial debate with the quick-witted Calonne.

It occurred to Louis XVI that the successor of Necker at the Contrôle-Général should be in a position to know of the veracity of the Compte rendu and he told Calonne to write to Joly de Fleury about it. Calonne did so willingly for he had heard that Joly de Fleury believed that the account of 1781 was in error by a substantial amount. But the reply of the former finance minister was disappointing. Joly de Fleury wrote that he had no reason to doubt the correctness of the Compte rendu, and he strongly asserted that there was not a deficit during the time he was entrusted with the royal finances. Calonne did not bother to show this reply to the king. But Joly de

139

Fleury had the foresight to send a copy of his letter to the Keeper of the Seals, Miromesnil. At a meeting of Calonne, Miromesnil, and the king the latter asked Calonne if he had received any communication from Joly de Fleury. Calonne said he had not. Thereupon Miromesnil produced his copy of the letter. Calonne lost his temper, upbraided the Keeper of the Seals for secretly joining with his enemies to defeat the purpose of the Assembly of Notables. Calonne then let the king know that he would need to dismiss from his post either his Controller General or his Keeper of the Seals. The king answered by firing Miromesnil first, whom he suspected had intrigued with Calonne's enemies to undermine him. A day later the king had his foreign affairs minister, Montmorin, carry his message to Calonne that the king no longer required his services.

[1] _Mémoires secrets_, XXXIII, 160.

[2] _Despatches_, I, 156.

[3] Duc de Castries, _Le Maréchal de Castries_, 144.

[4] _Procès-verbal de l'Assemblée des Notables tenue à Versailles, en l'année 1787_ (Paris, 1788), 1-2.

[5] _Mémoires secrets_, XXXIV, 175.

[6] _Ibid._, 185.

[7] Besenval, _Mémoires_, II, 207.

[8] "Discours de Monsieur le Contrôleur général," _Procès-verbal de l'Assemblée des Notables_, 56-58.

[9] _Ibid._, 60-63.

[10] _Ibid._, 64-65.

[11] _Lettres du Comte de Mirabeau sur l'Administration de M. Necker_ (n.p., 1787).

[12] _Procès-verbal de l'Assemblée des Notables_, 57.

[13] _Ibid._, 70.

[14]Ibid., 82.

[15]Etienne Charles de Loménie de Brienne and the comte de Brienne, _Journal de l'Assemblée des Notables de 1787_, ed., Pierre Chevallier (Paris, 1960), 24.

[16]Calonne passed over in silence Necker's reform of the assessment of the _vingtième_ in 1777.

[17]The memorials of all four divisions of Calonne's reform projects were published in the _Procès-verbal de l'Assemblée des Notables_.

[18]André Morellet, _Lettres de l'abbé Morellet à Lord Shelburne, 1772-1803_ (Paris, 1898), 227.

[19]BN MSS Joly de Fleury, 1040, contains the printed "Observations au Roi par les Bureaux de l'Assemblée ouverte par le Roi à Versailles, le 23 Février 1787." The quotations from the minutes of the different bureaux are taken from this source.

[20]_Lettres de l'abbé Morellet à Lord Shelburne_, 228.

[21]Loménie de Brienne, _Journal de l'Assemblée des Notables_, 4.

[22]Besenval is often cited as the witness who greatly admired Calonne's handling of debate between himself and the notables in the conference of March 2. _Mémoires de baron de Besenval_, II, 212. But Besenval was not one of the Notables, nor does any _procés-verbal_ indicate he represented the government in any ca-

pacity at the Assembly of Notables. His famous
"testimony" was certainly secondhand rather than as a
direct eye-witness.

[23]According to Bachaumont Calonne brought the 63
documents and the compte rendu for 1787 to the meeting
and allowed them to circulate among those present but
refused to leave them for further study by the Notables. Mémoires secrets, XXXIV, 243.

[24]Morellet, Lettres à Lord Shelburne, 219.

[25]Bachaumont, Mémoires secrets, XXXIV, 345.

[26]Jean-Pierre Papon, Histoire du Gouvernement
français, 30.

[27]Loménie de Brienne, Journal de l'Assemblée des
Notables, 27.

[28]Ibid., 60.

CHAPTER 5

THE BATTLE OF FIGURES

Voltaire wrote in the early 1760s that the French public seemed to have forgotten every other subject except that of grain. All thoughts, conversations in the salons, writings of journalists and philosophers turned to the subject of the nation's grain supply and whether freedom of export should be restricted or completely free. In the year 1787 it seemed that a subject equally improbable absorbed the public, the deficit of the royal government. Calonne had initiated this topic by his February 22 speech before the Assembly of Notables. He had described the origins of the deficit and indicated that it was "very considerable" at that moment. He did not give any figures on the matter, assuming that his listeners would be content to leave them to the Controller General and the king. But he had described the accounts that he had drawn and sent to the king with great precision: there was an account of the state of the finances for 1786, one for 1787, and then an account for "the ordinary year." The latter was supported by 63 different états or pièces justificatives. Like a magician he waved these accounts before the Notables but expected to conceal the figures. There was, however, a great thirst for figures not only among the Notables but the reading public.

At the conference of March 2 a committee of Notables meeting with the Controller General at the home of Monsieur had pried out of Calonne the amount of the deficit, 112 million livres for 1787 in the ordinary accounts "for the common year." He had, further, become more specific about the deficit in 1781. Contrary to the Compte rendu of that year there was a disparity of 56 million livres in the items listed in the Compte rendu itself and he estimated the deficit as high as 75 million livres instead of the surplus of 10.2 million livres claimed by the author of that account.

Not only the French public but all Europe was fascinated by these disclosures. It was no longer an obscure libellist, secretly supported by a powerful minister. Now it was the Controller General making those charges against Necker before an august Assembly of Notables. Could it be that the Genevan banker, this "genius" of financial administration, so known for his virtue, his candidness, and his belief that the minister of finance must be completely honest and aboveboard, that he must earn the trust of the public; could it be that he had made a mistake in the royal accounts by 75 million livres?

As for Necker, after the shock of his disgrace of May 1781 he had recovered his serenity. Despite the talk about his reentering the government he seems to have had no real expectation of a return to power. Life had become one of tranquil reflection, except for concern about his family. The health of his wife was a constant preoccupation as the Neckers moved from spa to spa in search of a remedy. In 1784 he purchased the château at Coppet near Geneva and became absorbed in the restoration of the buildings and grounds. The future of his daughter was becoming a major concern. Negotiations for her engagement to baron de Staël were complicated and tortuous. But finally the marriage took place in 1786, and "Minette" became Germaine, the married daughter. After the publication of his book on French finances in early 1785 Necker's thoughts had turned more and more to social problems, or perhaps once again to the subjects that had absorbed him at the beginning of his venture into the world of letters, the world of the philosophes. Once again the social problem, the question of the gigantic and appalling inequality of conditions of mankind worried him, and also the direction that eighteenth-century philosophy was taking in the matter of religion. The increasing vogue for irreligion and even atheism was troubling. What would be the consequence of this trend if the common people should absorb these ideas? Would they be willing to accept the great inequality of material life? But Necker was never a believer in the "noble lie," the notion that if God did not exist we should have to invent him in order to keep people submissive and respectful toward their social betters. He was sincerely devout and loyal to his Protestant upbringing.

From these preoccupations and meditations Necker was rudely shaken by the declarations of Calonne before the Assembly of Notables. He was first alerted to the danger by his good friend, the marquis de Castries, Secretary of State for the Navy. After the first of January Castries had acquired knowledge of the speech Calonne was writing for the opening session of the Assembly of Notables. Necker asked Castries to inquire further about it, and let the Controller General know that if he had any doubts about the accuracy of the Compte rendu Necker would like to meet with him privately and go over the account. The answer Castries brought back from Calonne seemed equivocal, so on January 29 Necker wrote a letter directly to the Controller General. He said that he had heard that Calonne planned to declare that all accounts submitted to the king on the state of his finances were in error during the reign, and this necessarily included his own account of 1781.

> Having given the most scrupulous attention to the drawing up of the account which I rendered to the king in 1781, I maintain that it is perfectly accurate, and since during that time I gathered together all the justificatory documents for each item that is susceptible of proof, I am fortunately in a position to verify without question the

entire account. Therefore I believe myself justified, Sir, in requesting that you do not alter in any manner the confidence which the exactness of this account merits; or that if you do have doubts you communicate them to me, so that I can clarify them. I will do this all the more willingly in that my interests in the matter are not separate from general considerations which must concern the minister of finance. For there is no doubt that the sanction which the king gave to the account I presented to him in 1781 is all the more worthy of respect in that it has been for a long time the foundation of public confidence.[1]

Calonne replied the following day. He expressed astonishment at receiving Necker's letter, for he thought his reply to Castries' inquiry should have eased Necker's mind. The Controller General protested that it was not in his character "to accuse, to incriminate, to alter." He could not understand the usage of those terms by the Genevan.

I assured the Marshal de Castries that I had no desire to attack the account which you presented the king in 1781, and that I will avoid mentioning it. You say if I have any doubts you would be willing to clarify them; but I have none at all. The study I was obliged to make has furnished me with incontrovertible facts. The king wished me to acquire a thorough understanding of his finances; to accomplish that task I have accounted for the annual deficit, its causes, its origins, and its progress since the time he came to the throne until the present. I have made up a table based upon the compte effectives of each year, the only way to learn the truth. And if I could not avoid telling the king that they do not agree with the accounts which have been given him at various times by his finance ministers, far from accusing any of them of lacking in diligence in their preparation, I have explained to His Majesty how difficult it is to make a correct and distinct separation of the revenue and expenditures that belong to each year, and to make up an account [at the beginning of the year] which will match exactly the comptes effectives which are made up later, and to present an exact balance for the ordinary year. His Majesty has seen, examined, and compared everything. He has had given to him all the documentary proofs (pièces justificatives) and by a very considerable labor which he has been willing to undertake, he is certain of having acquired a true knowledge of the deficit which has always existed and which exists today. That, Sir, is the path I have followed: it is simple, dictated by duty, and not alloyed to any other feeling.[2]

Needless to say, this was small comfort to Necker. On February 7th he wrote a second letter to Calonne saying that he could hardly remain indifferent to the statement that all accounts presented to His Majesty have actually shown a deficit, for that necessarily included his own account of 1781. "To arrive at the truth, Sir, you have no other means that I have had, and which I did not make use of. And since I attach an infinite value to having justly obtained the confidence of both the king and the entire public, allow me to reconfirm the proposition that I have already made . . ."[3]

Calonne did not reply to this letter. On February 28 Necker received a copy of Calonne's speech of the 22nd to the Assembly of Notables with a note from

149

the Controller General: "Since Monsieur Necker had the kindness to send me a copy of his _compte_ _rendu_ in 1781, I would like to return the compliment by sending him my speech before the Assembly of Notables." He added that Necker would be pleased to see that the Controller General had not mentioned the _Compte_ _rendu_ in his speech. But when Necker read the speech he saw that the Controller General had asserted that there was a deficit of 37 million livres in 1776, by Necker's own admission, that it had grown enormously during the following years because of the need for war loans, that ameliorations could not begin to make up the costs of these loans, which came to about 44 million livres by 1781.

Calonne had a weird sense of humor, like his good friend the late comte de Maurepas. One could almost hear the burst of laughter from the grave. What Calonne was really saying to his rival was: really, you shouldn't feel too badly, old boy, for you haven't been any more incompetent than my other predecessors at the _Contrôle_ _général_. They could not tell ordinary from extraordinary accounts either, and were powerless to untangle one fiscal year from another. Anyway, it's no disgrace if the accounts at the end of the year hardly tally with a prediction at the beginning of the year, even if you did miss the mark by a mere 75 million livres!

Necker was wounded as never before. For a few days he hardly knew what to do, for there was no way of knowing upon what Calonne had based his calculations. Then came the special meeting at the home of _Monsieur_ on March 2. The deliberations of the Notables were supposed to be kept secret, an injunction no one bothered about, least of all the Controller General. Necker learned that Calonne had presented _comptes_ _effectives_ for 1781 showing a deficit of 46 million livres in the very items listed in the _Compte_ rendu, and which by other calculations Calonne had expanded to 75 million livres.

On March 6 Necker wrote a letter to the king expressing in strongest terms the injustice of Calonne's allegations. "I would be the most contemptible man in the world if there were the slightest foundation (for Calonne's allegations)." He would not have been perturbed if Calonne had found a disparity of three or four millions in the account which Necker submitted to the king, "but the minister of finance who should make such a mistake, not of 50 to 60 million, as M. de Calonne dares to allege, but of a sum infinitely less must necessarily be a dishonest man." It was unthinkable to allow such an accusation to go unanswered. "I humbly beg Your Majesty to permit me to appear before my accuser either before the Assembly of Notables or a large committee of this assembly, in the presence of Your Majesty."[4]

Necker asked permission to bring with him his pièces justificatives to confront the Controller General with the latter's comptes effectives. The pièce justificative had a precise meaning in that day. It was a formal document signed by a person in authority who would have unquestioned knowledge of its contents, a kind of notarized statement that would be recognized as such in a court of law. Necker possessed such signed documents for all items in his Compte rendu. A compte effective as described by Calonne was the result of the fiscal year's operations as recorded in the daily, weekly and monthly journals of the bureau or department. This was, said Calonne, the only basis of knowing what really happened during the fiscal year. The account at the beginning of the fiscal year, he said, was only hypothetical, a statement of desires or expectations rather than what would actually happen, a budget of prévision. And he found, so he claimed, that the two hardly ever coincided, and that the figures in the compte effective often exceeded the compte rendu.

It has been mentioned in the previous chapter that the king was willing to have Necker send his documents to the Council, but did not want him to confront Calonne personally. Necker insistently begged to be permitted to defend his Compte rendu himself. Becoming impatient at the king's delay in answering, and expecting a refusal anyway, Necker began to write a defense. Although formally forbidden by the king to say or publish anything on the subject of his Compte rendu, because of the excited state of public opinion, Necker determined to go ahead with publication anyway. On April 8th appeared in print his "Memorial published by Mr. Necker in the month of April 1787 in reply to the speech of M. de Calonne before the Assembly of Notables."[5] To Necker's chagrin, he learned of Calonne's dismissal about the same time as his essay appeared in print. The public reception of his essay was so enthusiastic that Calonne could hardly ignore it as Controller General. But out of office and soon to be in exile from his own country, Calonne was no longer visible to the public. Nevertheless it was some consolation for Necker to see the success of his memorial. Abbé Morellet included a copy in his letter of April 9 to Lord Shelburne saying, "I believe you will find it victorious as well as moving and noble in several passages, despite the dryness of such a subject."[6] Archbishop Loménie de Brienne wrote in his Journal that "the writing of Mr. Necker is making the greatest sensation." He noted that the king had said nothing yet about Necker's disobedience and it is hoped that he would let it pass.[7]

Unfortunately the king was not so disposed. It was the queen who took him a copy of the essay, and he exploded in anger. He insisted on prohibiting its publication but the queen disuaded him, for she was now joining others in an attempt to have Necker reappointed to the administration of finances. "If he (the king) would only read Necker's essay," wrote Loménie de Brienne, "he will see that he has been deceived." By April 13 Louis still wanted to expel Necker from the kingdom, but was advised against it by Breteuil because of the excited state of public opinion. So instead Necker was ordered to leave Paris and remain at a distance of at least 20 leagues. He was deluged with hospitable offers of asylum by friends.

There was no question but what the "writing of Mr. Necker" was a resounding success with the public. The Genevan banker was almost everyone's choice to become the new finance minister. Everyone's but the king's. For Louis proved stubbornly determined not to permit the return of Necker to the council. According to the memoirs of Marmontel who was an intimate of the foreign minister, Montmorin, it was the latter who tried to persuade the king to reappoint Necker. Although he was not personally acquainted with the Genevan banker Montmorin believed that the condition of the finances and of public opinion made Necker's return to the ministry a matter of greatest urgency. The decisive influence on the king at the time, according to Marmontel, was the Secretary of State for the King's Household, baron de Breteuil. He was a conservative of the Old Regime, hostile to anything that would weaken the monarchy, and he persuaded the king that it would be a drastic eclipse of his authority to appoint a person as first minister whom he had exiled from Paris a short time before.[8] Furthermore, due to the liaison to be established between Loménie de Brienne and the king, the archbishop was soon to become the leading minister in the government. Even Brienne wanted Necker to join him in the ministry and take charge of finances. The king again refused. "With you," he told the archbishop, "I can do without Necker." On May 3rd Loménie de Brienne became President of the Council of Finance.

Whether Necker was willing to trade his life of tranquil meditation for another round of traumatic ministerial life is not clear. The excitement in the country was a matter of concern to him, and he was not certain that he knew how to cope with it. Yet he could not be indifferent to the fate of the monarchy. When he heard of Brienne's appointment he said to his daughter: "God grant that the new minister can serve the state better than myself. The present circumstances already make it a great task; soon they will surpass the powers of any (single) person whoever it may be."[9]

Yet he must have savored his victory over Calonne. As his own star rose in the political firmament, Calonne's precipitately declined. Never since the "revolution" of 1771 was a minister of the government so unpopular. He found it impossible to remain in France and sought refuge in London, becoming, it is said, the first émigré. In August of 1787 the Parlement of Paris brought a criminal indictment against him for abuse of power, fraud in his handling of the king's domain lands, using government money to speculate secretly on the bourse, and various other ill-defined allegations. It is probable that he had good reason to feel aggrieved. In the Parlement the ebullient youthful Chamber of Inquests was making its influence felt, and Calonne was an easy target. But he was not a crook, only an easygoing, gregarious nobleman, who by his frivolity had brought the royal government into a serious financial crisis. He fought back valiantly against the public's reprobation of him, convinced that it was due to his attempt to impose taxes on the privileged that had brought about his disgrace and unpopularity.

From London in the late summer of 1787 Calonne wrote his own apologia to the king, under the title Requête au Roi. Like Necker's April essay it was a justification of the three years of his own ministry, a vehement and often convincing retort to the allegations of the Parlement of Paris. The two apologias make an interesting comparison. Necker was concerned to show that he had not deceived the king who had trusted him, or the public who held him in such high esteem. His essay captivated attention by its adherence to a central theme: why there was not a deficit in 1781, even if there was one in 1787 amounting to 112 million livres. Calonne's essay was directed against the bill of particulars brought against him by the Parlement of Paris. It was diffuse and highly emotional. What both essays had in common was the willingness of their authors to talk figures: the amount of loans issued by the royal government since the beginning of the reign, the extraordinary expenditures, the accounts of the fiscal year, and what an accounting of the king's revenues and expenditures should be. Calonne did not specifically refer to Necker in his Requête au Roi. It was his later book, a lengthy treatise published in London in January 1788 under the title Réponse à l'Ecrit de M. Necker, that he devoted his attention exclusively to Necker's Compte rendu of 1781 and why it was in error.

Fascinated as the public was by the royal finances and the causes of the deficit, it was not well educated on the subject. Necker's financial statement of 1781 was the only one to be published until April 1788 when the compte rendu of Loménie de Brienne appeared in print. As will be seen, financial affairs were not the strong point of the archbishop's administration. His understanding of a compte rendu was seriously defective. The same was true of the editor of the collection of comptes rendus published at Lausanne in 1788.[10] Both were influenced by Calonne's notion on the subject.

It is essential to understand what a compte rendu such as Necker submitted to the king in 1781 was intended to be. It was not a speculative account of the king's needs and the projected income to meet them for the year ahead, not a budget in the modern sense. This was Calonne's primary misconception. He said that the Compte rendu was unreal, imaginative, an expression of what was hoped for but not borne out at the end of the year. "Mr. Necker's account," he said, "did not apply to the year 1781 or to any other year." It was based upon the "ordinary revenue and expenditure," and might have been true at the beginning of the fiscal year but the relationship of ordinary revenue with ordinary expenditure altered during the course of the year. Calonne's assertions about the finances of the year 1781 were based upon what he called "the concrete accounts" (comptes effectifs). These were records taken from weekly and monthly journals of what actually happened by the end of the year, not what was only hoped for in the compte rendu drawn up at the beginning of the year. This idea was easily grasped and difficult to dislodge.

In his April essay as in his "Further Clarifications on the Compte rendu" published in August 1788 Necker carefully explained what a compte rendu of ordinary revenue and expenditure was, and why it was the cornerstone of financial administration. "Maintaining constant order in the finances as well as reassuring the government's creditors depends essentially on a just harmony between ordinary revenue and expenditures."[11] Establishing that relationship was like an astral navigator's "fix" to determine the actual position of his sea or air-craft. The compte rendu established the relationship between the ordinary revenue and expenditure at the time it was drawn up, signed, and sent to the king. It did not try to predict what that relationship would be at the end of the year. In fact, it was expected that the relationship would soon be altered by new loans. Just as the navigator wants to know exactly where he is at the moment he is taking his "fix" in order to make the necessary adjustments in his compass course, so the finance minister needed to know exactly where the government's finances stood at the beginning of the fiscal year in order to lay plans for that year; whether to impose new taxes to make up for an existing deficit or to achieve the same result by cutting expenditures. All his operations were determined by what was found to be the exact relationship between the ordinary revenue and expenditure at the time of the drawing up of the compte rendu.

There was another type of financial statement drawn up at or soon after the beginning of the year which was more like a modern budget. The purpose of this statement was not to ascertain the relationship between the ordinary revenue and expenditure but simply to assure the finance minister that there would be sufficient funds to meet the projected needs. It began by listing the amount of money (either in species or in notes) in the treasury, the extraordinary expenditures that were foreseen, and the means by which they would be met, usually through loans. This kind of statement would show a surplus of revenue in the treasury to begin the operations of the following fiscal year. The "Situation of the Royal Finances" that Joly de Fleury sent to the king just prior to his resignation in March 1783 was this type of financial statement, as was the account that Necker sent to the king at the time of his resignation in May 1781. It included both ordinary and extraordinary income and expenditure foreseen in the months ahead.

The limitation of this second type of statement was that while it assured the king of sufficient funds to meet projected needs, it did not tell him actually where he stood financially. Having money in the cash register does not necessarily mean that a business is in sound financial health, particularly when much of it is derived from loans. The compte rendu of ordinary revenue and expenditure does provide that information: is the government's financial posture sound,

157

or is it in an unhealthy state? It is necessary, therefore, to know what is meant by "ordinary income and expenditures." Here was another of Calonne's misunderstandings. He assumed that "ordinary" was synonymous with "average" or "common." His compte rendu of 1787 which his successor submitted to the Assembly of Notables was entitled, "The Account for the Common Year." That is, by taking the accounts of several years and averaging them out he achieved a "mean, average, year." This is why he assumed that all items in such an account were necessarily hypothetical, or "unreal" and that the "reality" could only be seen in the "concrete accounts." Just the opposite was true: the reality of the government's finances could only be seen in the ordinary accounts, and the "concrete accounts" were unreal as far as telling the finance minister anything useful that could guide his operations. Necker tried to avoid this confusion of terminology in the account he submitted to the States General in 1789 by changing the expression "ordinary" to "fixed." It was the fixed income and the fixed expenditures that were the crux of the situation about the royal finances.

It is sometimes thought by modern historians that the distinction between "ordinary" and "extraordinary" was a loose one, and that the finance minister could arbitrarily designate items of his account as one or the other depending upon his needs. In Necker's case it is thought that he did so freely in order to make the royal finances under his administration look better than they actually were. It is true that there was some variation among finance ministers, most notably in what reimbursements on the royal debt should be considered ordinary expenditure and what should be designated as "extraordinary." Where the terms of the loan specified reimbursements at fixed periods there was no doubt that such was an ordinary expenditure. But there was a form of royal debt that had no such fixed schedule of amortization, and there could be disagreement on that sort of debt. With that exception the ministers and officials involved in the financial administration had clear and distinct notions of how ordinary accounts differed from those termed "extraordinary." "There is nothing uncertain, nothing problematic," wrote Necker, "in an account of ordinary revenue and expenditure if that expression is understood in its true sense."[12]

A useful description of the difference between ordinary and extraordinary accounts was given in a printed brochure written by a treasurer of the naval department at La Rochelle, one Bonvallet Desbrosses. One can see in the passages below not only that the distinction was not arbitrary, but also why the compte rendu giving ordinary, fixed income and expenditures was a more useful instrument for the finance minister in making his decisions than any document that was made after the year had passed.

> Almost all branches of the (royal) finances for which there are accounts to make are in arrears. Before judging motives for this delay, it is necessary to consider all the objects that are accountable. I will trace them here and classify them under two categories: revenue and expenditure that are ordinary and revenue and expenditure that are extraordinary.
>
> In the ordinary revenues are included all items coming from the tailles, the capitation of industry, the vingtièmes, in a word, all direct and indirect taxes of a fixed amount, and which are collected each day for the account of the king or for those of the fermes and régies.
>
> In the extraordinary revenues are included all items that are irregular . . .

items for which one cannot attach any kind of stability or depend upon anything positive . . . such as <u>lods</u> <u>et</u> <u>ventes</u>, or free gifts, or enemy prize ships, etc. One can also include in this category funds that are authorized without any specific object but which came under the title of <u>fonds</u> <u>à</u> <u>imputer</u>, such as in the form of loans, which are withheld from a current fiscal year to pay for items belonging to a previous fiscal year . . . .

As for expenditures . . . those which are made under the denomination of ordinary expenditures include the daily service of land and naval forces, the upkeep of arsenals, the maintenance of fortifications, the construction and equipment of naval ships, munitions, provisions, wages and salaries, pensions, payments due on rentes, . . . reimbursements and amortization of debts which are stipulated by law.

Under extraordinary expenditures are included all the payments made by anticipations; . . . payments made for items belonging to previous fiscal years, <u>corvées</u>, canals, upkeep of dikes and roadways, the construction of new ports, in a word, all items that are irregular or improvised.[13]

To recapitulate, a statement of the ordinary or fixed income and expenditure at the beginning of a fiscal year told the finance minister what he needed to know in order to plan future operations. The primary concern was to maintain a balance of ordinary revenue and expenditure. The government's credit depended upon that balance because the interest and other fixed charges on its debt were included in the ordinary expenditures. As long as prospective creditors were assured that the obligations of the royal government could be met out of fixed income they would have confidence in its fiscal soundness. If there should be some doubt about this, if it appeared that the government might have to default on its obligations, then its credit would be seriously threatened. This is why the accuracy of the compte rendu was such a crucial matter. Any attempt to deceive the public and creditors about the fixed income and obligations would be a serious violation of trust. Necker insisted on the "positive" character of compte rendu. It was just the opposite of a "hypothetical," or "unreal account." It assured the public exactly where the government's finances stood as of the date of the compte rendu: what income could be relied upon with certainty, and what expenditures the government would meet without any question[14]

Before he was placed in charge of the royal finances Necker had written to the comte de Maurepas in July 1776 that the government should not only take steps immediately to eliminate the deficit indicated in the compte rendu of Bernard de Clugny, his immediate predecessor, but achieve a surplus of at least ten million livres income above fixed expenditure. It appeared at that time that war was imminent and the government's credit required that it have a surplus on hand to pay for new loans. This is why Necker was so proud to announce in January 1781 that he had achieved that surplus which would be used for new loans. In fact the life rente loan in February and the March loan did absorb that surplus, as Necker had expected, indeed planned. Contrary to Calonne's allegation, it was no deception not to have included the costs of those loans in the Compte rendu. That document gave the fixed accounts as of January 1781, not what might come later.

What Calonne meant by those "concrete accounts" (comptes effectifs) which he said were based upon the

161

journals and registers of each department of the government is not clear because he never produced them. Necker begged to be allowed to see them, certain that the Controller General was under some serious misapprehension that could easily be corrected. The Notables also, at the time of the conference of March 2, asked to see those documents that supposedly discredited Necker's Compte rendu. Calonne resolutely refused to yield them. Nor were his successors at the Contrôle général able to find them and send them to the Assembly of Notables, as was done with the current accounts for 1787.[15] One would think that Calonne would have included them in his January 1788 "Reply to Necker," which was devoted exclusively to refuting the Compte rendu of 1781. If he were seriously interested in persuading those who were knowledgeable about the administration of finances of the correctness of his allegations he would have included those "concrete accounts" as pièces justificatives. But nothing of the kind appears in his 1788 "Reply to Necker." In the appendix of the treatise were eighteen documents which served as pièces justificatives. But none of them qualified for that title: they were not signed and certified by officials independent of his control. And only one or two at most had been written after the passing of the fiscal year, which supposedly the comptes effectifs were. Of the eighteen documents included in the appendix six were compte rendus: his own for 1787, Terray's for 1774, Turgot's for 1776, Clugny's for 1776, Necker's for 1781, and Joly de Fleury's for 1783. On all his predecessors' accounts Calonne wrote on the margin his "corrections" of their figures based upon his own "concrete accounts." He altered each of them to reflect the deficit he had announced to the Notables: Terray's account showed a deficit of 40 million livres, the deficit in 1776 was 37 million livres "according to the minister soon to be entrusted with the finances," by whom he meant Necker. Calonne's corrections to Necker's Compte rendu of 1781 showed a deficit of 75 million livres, which he had revealed at the conference of March 2nd. The account of Joly de Fleury included both extraordinary as well as ordinary accounts. Calonne separated them so as to come out with a deficit of 80 million livres in 1783 in the ordinary accounts.

The remainder of the documents in the appendix was a diverse collection: letters written by officials or first secretaries before or during the fiscal year in question, "projects for funding" from branches of the military service; one of the documents was a criticism of Necker's 1785 book on French finances! Not one was an authentic pièce justificative signed and certified as correct by an external authority independent of the Controller General. In contrast Necker had a copy of such a document prepared by different agencies of the financial administration for nearly all his items in the Compte rendu. When writing his "Further Clarifications" in the summer of 1788 he received answers to all his requests for confirmation of his position by officials in the government. This was before he returned to the post of finance minister and had no power over the officials who replied to his requests. One of these officials was Calonne's loyal premier commis, Achilles-Joseph Gojard. Necker confirmed each item in dispute between himself and Calonne by pièce justificative.

Calonne maintained that his figures were based upon the weekly and monthly journals and registers kept by each branch of the financial administration, and that what these reported at the end of the year was "the reality." In some cases it is clear that he meant the calendar year, and it takes no expert knowledge of accounting to see the fallacy of that basis for attacking the Compte rendu. As Necker described the contrast between the "concrete accounts" and the ordinary accounts of a fiscal year, the two would

163

hardly ever coincide. "The receipts and expenditures of any year would not correspond perfectly to ordinary revenue and expenditure because a multitude of possible and plausible events would prevent that concordance. Sometimes the collection of certain revenues would be in arrears; sometimes payments would be made in advance; sometimes a new levy would not all be received during its first year, sometimes an extraordinary expenditure assigned to the proceeds of a _ferme_ or _régie_ would reduce its yield for one time only."[16] This point hardly needs to be labored. Any small businessman knows that if he paid the insurance bill at one time to cover several years, he would not add that lump sum to his annual costs for that year alone. Or that if all accounts receivable are not yet in by the end of the calendar year his annual income is not thereby reduced by that amount.

If all the errors Calonne claimed to find in the _Compte_ _rendu_ were based upon the lack of concordance between the accounts of the fiscal year and the accounts of the calendar year there should have been no problem in his presenting those accounts to the Notables in 1787 or publishing them in his book in 1788. While many of his claims of error in the account of 1781 were based upon that discordance, obviously not all were. Calonne was too clever a person to attempt such a simple-minded procedure. He did attempt to find out the final results of the fiscal year. But he explained to the Notables that this was extremely difficult. "It takes a long period of study," he said, "to be able to see what belongs to each fiscal year, and to separate what is ordinary from the extraordinary." He was obviously referring to that financial document known in the accounting system of the _ancien_ _régime_ as the "_état_ _au_ _vrai_." Since the time of Colbert the ministers of finance had attempted to get all accountable officers to send the report of their operations of the fiscal year to the Council of Finance before sending them to the Chambers of Account for

164

their final "purification." The function of the Chambers of Account was to see if the accountable officer had performed his duties honestly. They did not attempt to establish a total balance sheet of the year's operations; that was not their function. But the Council of Finance did attempt to finalize such a report. Due to the arrears in the collecting of the government's tax income, and the accompanying delay in paying its obligations, added to the normal lackadaisical habits of financial officers of the *ancien régime*, it was years before the final *état au vrai* could be drawn up in the Council of Finance and signed and sent to the king. And when it was finished it included total expenditures and income, both ordinary and extraordinary mingled together. And the figures often reflected income or payments extending over several fiscal years. This complex procedure was due to the retardation of both payments and receipts of income by the royal government, and by the use of anticipations to provide the lubrication to make such a cumbersome system work. The government had to spend its tax income before it was collected. It did so by the use of anticipations, short term loans negotiated with the receivers-general and the farmers-general. Each year these anticipations were assigned not only to the current fiscal year, but to past and future fiscal years. It was no wonder that Calonne was bewildered when he undertook to investigate the causes of the deficit in February 1786!

Whether Calonne's "concrete accounts" were based upon the results at the end of the calendar year or the *états au vrai*, neither was any substitute for the *compte rendu* of ordinary revenue and expenditure. As Necker explained in his April 1787 essay:

> The exactness of the *Compte rendu* appears to me the most evidently demonstrated truth of its kind, and it is today that for the first time, in order to spread doubt, one talks

165

about the entanglement of fiscal years, of comptes effectives, of the impossibility of forming any account with certainty, all of which are devoid of any sense for anyone only moderately acquainted with these matters. The entanglement of fiscal years does not prevent each year from having its own revenue and its own expenditure. And the comptes effectives of the royal treasury given to the Chamber of Accounts being composed of the ordinary and the extraordinary accounts, of payments in money and payments in notes and of fictitious articles of pure comptability, in order to know the annual revenues and expenditures one must make the same kind of an investigation as do the bureaux of finances when they wish to clarify themselves of the situation of affairs. It can happen that in a year of extraordinary expenditures there can be some difference in the amount of ordinary expenditure designated under the category of unexpected expenditures. But (generally) the extent of fixed revenues and expenditures is well known at the beginning of the fiscal year as at the end. And if it were necessary to wait for ten years after the expiration of a fiscal year to get the same kind of information the kings would always be operating in the dark for the most important of their deliberations.[17]

What were the possibilities that the Compte rendu of 1781 could have been in error? It is certainly true that the items of ordinary income and expenditure, no matter how "positive," would not exactly match the amount received and spent during the year. There would be some variation, but it could not be very great unless the finance minister were deliberately trying to deceive the public. Furthermore, whatever error there might be on one side would most likely be compensated by errors on the other side. While writing his "Further Clarifications" in the summer of 1788 Necker had access to the final results of the fiscal year, 1781. He admitted some discrepancies. The cost of anticipations exceeded what he had entered on the expenditures side of the Compte rendu, and he explained the reason for his miscalculation. But that item was more than offset by the reduction in the amount of pensions actually paid in fiscal 1781. After he had corrected the entire account in this way, Necker found the actual surplus of ordinary revenue over ordinary expenditure in 1781 was 15 million rather than 10 million livres.[18]

Another possible source of error was that in such a vast and far-flung financial administration as that of France under the ancien régime there were bound to be accounting problems that did not have a clear precedent, and finance ministers might not have handled the problems in the same manner. There were such items in the Compte rendu of 1781 and Necker took pains to explain in the text of that document what the problems were and how he had handled them. As long as his method was aboveboard and clear to creditors and others who would read the account, there could hardly be any reproach against the finance minister if another might have resolved the matter differently. But if there were enemies who were determined to bring about the resignation of the Genevan banker or prevent his reappointment when he was out of office, these were targets of opportunity to discredit him and his Compte rendu. And Necker did have enemies, both during his first ministry and afterward. Some occupied important positions in the Contrôle-général after May 1781 and were consequently able to funnel information to the writers of polemical libels.

Since the publication of the Compte rendu in February 1781 it had been sniped at by Necker's ene-

mies in brochures printed and distributed furtively.
Necker could not let such attacks go unchallenged
since he believed the credit posture of the government
was based upon the exactness of the Compte rendu.
While he was in office he was able to contradict them,
as he did when the treasurer of the Household of the
comte d'Artois, Antoine Bourboulon, secretly distributed a memorial claiming a deficit of 25 million
livres in the Compte rendu.[19] After Necker's resignation the underground movement to discredit his Compte
rendu was able to act more boldly. The new finance
minister who succeeded him, Joly de Fleury, was not
sympathetic to his reforms, but he was an honest magistrate. Some who came to surround him at the Contrôle-général were equally conservative but not as
honest. The person who became director of the royal
treasury during the ministry of Joly de Fleury was
Marquet de Bourgade, an uncle of Calonne's first wife.
Bourgade resisted all ideas of reform in the financial
administration. He was often at odds with Isaac Panchaud who had been brought into the Contrôle-général
in 1782 as an advisor of Joly de Fleury. Panchaud was
ambitious to bring about the same powerful fiscal institutions in France that he had observed at first
hand in England. Bourgade and Panchaud often competed
with each other to get the ear of the minister of finance. Both had one thing in common: hatred of
Necker. Panchaud was a fellow Swiss, although originally from Berne rather than Geneva. Why he was such
a persistent foe of Necker is not clear. Possibly it
was due to jealousy or some personal reason. A trait
of several of Necker's most notorious enemies among
the class of financiers was their chronic ill-success
in business. Panchaud went bankrupt a number of
times, the last one occurring in the year of his death
in 1789. On March 5, 1787 Bachaumont reported the
"spectacular" bankruptcy of Antoine Bourboulon, treasurer of the Household of the comte d'Artois. Bachaumont added, perhaps with some exaggeration, that Bour-

boulon fled to England leaving a debt of four to five million livres. "He is a haughty person whom nobody pities," added Bachaumont.[20] In May 1789 a nephew of Marquet de Bourgade and brother-in-law of Calonne, a Receiver-General at Bordeaux, named Marquet Desgrèves, also went bankrupt and fled the country.[21]

It has been seen that Calonne's economic policies were not based upon any consistent economic doctrine. He borrowed from the physiocrats what suited his purpose, but he was just as apt to follow the policies of their enemies. Consistency was not his hallmark. The same eclecticism characterized the evidence he produced to substantiate his assertions before the Assembly of Notables. He insisted that the deficit in 1776 was 37 million livres rather than the 24 million indicated in the compte rendu of Bernard de Clugny. His evidence was a letter he found in the Contrôle-général written by Necker to Maurepas in which the Genevan had given his opinion that the deficit in Clugny's compte rendu was nearer 27 million livres. In order for the government to be in a good credit situation Necker wrote that the aim of the finance minister should be to create a surplus of 10 million livres of ordinary revenue. Calonne misread the document to say that Necker had given the deficit as 37 million livres, and he so stated before the Assembly of Notables. Necker pointed out in his April 1787 essay how Calonne had misread his letter.[22] Yet the ex-Controller General still insisted in the January 1788 "Reply to Necker" that the Genevan had given the deficit as 37 million livres!

Some of Calonne's "corrections" to the comptes rendus of his predecessors were based upon the results of the calendar year; some were based upon haphazard letters or memoranda he found in the records of the Contrôle-général like the above letter written by Necker to Maurepas. A very prominent source for Calonne's figures came from documents drawn up in the

169

Contrôle-général in the summer of 1781. Joly de
Fleury had been in office about two months when a
study was completed of the needs of the government if
the war should continue into 1783. It was decided
that new taxes were necessary, a painful decision for
Joly de Fleury, since his predecessor had acquired so
much glory by successfully issuing war loans without
raising taxes. It was necessary to convince the Parlement of Paris of the need to depart from Necker's
policy. A ten percent surcharge on all indirect taxes
was to be the first of these levies. Joly de Fleury
and his advisors spelled out in rounded figures just
what the needs would be for the next two years, and
why an increase of tax revenue was unavoidable.

Among these documents written in July 1781 was
one entitled "Observations on the Compte rendu by Mr.
Necker in the month of January 1781." It was unsigned
like so many of the documents in the Fleury
manuscripts. It is not certain if it was ever sent
out of the office of the Contrôle-général, but served
as a memorandum of what could be said to the Parlement
if persuasion were needed. Ostensibly it was addressed to the king and written by the minister of finance, Joly de Fleury. Several documents in close
proximity were signed by Marquet de Bourgade. In view
of Joly de Fleury's public professions then and later
that he believed the "account of Mr. Necker to be exact," it seems probable that the actual author of the
"Observations on the Compte rendu" was Bourgade.[23]

The "Observations" began by asserting that "the
finances were not in as good a state as the Compte
rendu of Mr. Necker represented them to be." The
writer recognized the danger of destroying the beneficial effects produced by that account, namely the government's credit. "Concerned by such a strong motive,
we feel constrained to limit our observations to certain articles of this account which are patently inexact or disguised by assumptions which speculation

170

might make plausible but which the execution reveals as illusory." The writer specifically singled out three items of revenue and four items of expenditure in Necker's account which he thought fit that description. On the revenue side, the inclusion of the revenue of the _ferme_ known as the Domain of the Occident which levied duties on products coming from overseas colonies did not yield the peacetime figure that Necker had given, 4.1 million livres. Because of the war and British superiority on the seas, that item of revenue for 1781 came to no more than half a million livres. The income from the tax on offices (the _centième denier_) had been given up by the government for a period of eight years, 1780-1788, in lieu of a loan of 6.97 million livres granted by the owners of those offices. In his _Compte rendu_ Necker had continued the normal income from this source, but had balanced it on the expenditure side by adding the interest cost on that loan. This was a fictitious entry, as Necker admitted. The income was fictitious as was the item of expenditure. The writer of the "Observations" pointed out that the fictitious expenditure did not equal the income reported in the _Compte rendu_ by 811,500 livres. Finally the item of 3.4 million livres received from the Church's "free gift" had already been spent and would not be a real income in 1781. The total corrections of the revenue side of the _Compte rendu_ was 7,811,500 livres.

On the four items of expenditure that were "inexact" in Necker's account the "Observations" listed the interest on anticipations, which exceeded the sum given by 4,500,000 livres. The cost of the two lottery loans, that of 1777 and 1780, were computed at the interest rate of 5%, or 3 million livres. This left out of the account the amortization cost of 1,623,000 livres. Necker gave the cost of "unanticipated expenditures" as only 3 million livres, whereas his predecessors had always given that item as 10 million livres. But to be as moderate as possible the writer of the "Observations" calculated that error at only 3 million livres. Finally the Compte rendu failed to give the interest charges on Necker's last two life rente loans, that of February and March 1781, which would be nine million livres. The total sum of expenditure which the writer claimed should have been included in the Compte rendu was 18,123,000 livres. These calculations showed that there was an actual deficit of ordinary income in 1781 of 15,734,000 livres, and that the actual error in the account of Necker was 25,934,500 livres.

All these items were included in Calonne's attack on the Compte rendu in 1788, and Necker replied to each of them in his "Further Clarifications." A momentary diminution of the revenue from the Domain of the Occident should not eliminate that item from the fixed peacetime income of the royal government. The interruption was not as great as Calonne claimed (he had at first denied any income from that source). Necker produced a pièce justificative from the General Farm showing that imports from overseas picked up dramatically in 1780 due in part to the League of Armed Neutrality. The average income for the three years in 1781 through 1783 was about 350,000 livres over the figure he had given in the Compte rendu.[24] In his own "Reply to Necker" Calonne admitted that it was proper to include that item, but insisted it was only 3.5 million livres rather than the figure given by Necker.[25] This was the reason why Calonne reduced the alleged deficit in Necker's account from 75 million livres to 70 million livres.

On the matter of the income from the Church, Necker pointed out that it met in convocation every five years and bestowed its "free gift" on the government. Necker divided that sum into five equal parts to arrive at the sum of 3.4 million livres as ordinary income for 1781. He mentioned that Calonne had also included this revenue in his compte rendu of 1787, but left it out of the account he printed in his January 1788 treatise and substituted the income from the United States for wartime loans.[26] As for the income reported by Necker for the tax on offices, he had admitted in his April 1787 essay that he was somewhat uncertain how to handle that item. A permanent revenue should not be dropped completely from the ordinary account of the king's income. Those familiar with financial documents would think it had been left out inadvertently. The suspension was for eight years, and then would be resumed. It seemed appropriate to leave that income in the account and balance it by the interest the government would pay to the officers. He explained this matter in the Compte rendu in 1781, and could hardly be accused of deception. Yet he never answered the objection that the amount of interest did not match the income reported, so on this item Necker's explanation was incomplete.

Turning to the expenditure side of the account, Necker admitted that he had underestimated the cost of anticipations, as already noted. As for the charges given for the two lottery loans, Necker had explained this unusual situation in the Compte rendu. There was no annual interest charge on the two loans, or rather the interest was included in the reimbursement payments and they were determined by lottery. Since the exact sum owing in 1781 was not yet known, and to attempt to estimate it would detract from that "positive" quality so essential in the Compte rendu, Necker decided to give the costs of the two loans as the interest of the capital that would be required to reimburse them, which was 3 million livres. His figure for "unexpected expenditures" was admittedly lower than that of his predecessors, but he explained how this was the result of his reforms. Calonne maintained later that the actual amount spent on this item came to nearly 10 million livres. Necker explained and produced a pièce justificative showing that this was due to an extraordinary war expenditure in July of

173

that year.[27] Finally, on the matter of the cost of
the two life rente loans of February and March, 1781
(9 million livre), it has already been shown that
loans made subsequent to the Compte rendu were not im-
properly excluded.

The intention of this memorandum of July 1781 was
not to discredit Necker personally but to explain to
the king and the Parlement of Paris, if necessary, why
more tax revenue was needed. The author of the memorandum went on to estimate the ordinary income and expenditures for the years 1782 and 1783 on the assumption that the war might last into the latter year. It
used the figure of 15,734,000 as the ordinary deficit
for 1781, and built upon it for estimating the deficit
for the following year. It concluded that the deficit
would double and reach the figure of 30,956,000 in
1782 if no more tax revenue were raised. This would
be due to new loans to meet the costs of the war.
Necker had estimated the extraordinary expenditures
for the war at 150 million per year. That would require 9.6 million in ordinary costs to pay the interest on those loans. Also the reimbursement on the two
lottery loans of 1777 and 1780 would increase by
5,622,000 in 1782. Looking to the increase of ordinary expenditures for the following year, the memorandum estimated the ordinary, peacetime expenditure for
the navy would be increased to 36 million livres, thus
adding 6 million to the existing peacetime allotment.
There would be a further increase in the cost of the
two lottery loans. Necker's Compte rendu had not mentioned the reimbursement for the offices that he had
suppressed; he listed only the interest charge on
those offices, an item of 2,367,000 livres for a capital of 47,340,000, the amount of the capital of the
offices that Necker had abolished that had not yet
been returned to the former officers. The memorandum
estimated that a reimbursement of 3,633,000 annually
over a period of ten years would be necessary to dis-
charge that debt. Finally, Necker's Compte rendu had

said nothing of the enormous debt-in-arrears that would remain to be liquidated after the end of the war. This would amount to at least 150 million livres; to liquidate it over a period of ten years would cost 15 million livres annually. The memorandum concluded that, based upon Necker's Compte rendu of 1781, an increase of 57,843,500 livres in ordinary expenditures would be necessary by 1783. That figure joined with the reduction of ordinary income from the figure indicated in Necker's Compte rendu, namely 4,211,500 would mean a disparity of 62,055,000 in the compte rendu of 1783 compared to that of 1781. Since Necker's Compte rendu had indicated a surplus of 10.2 million livres, the deficit projected by the memorandum for 1783 was 51,855,000 livres.

The tenor of the "Observations," as of the other documents drawn up at this time to justify the tax increase, was optimistic. The government's financial posture was far from alarming, particularly when compared to the enemy's financial situation, about which some thorough studies were made at this time. The government succeeded in getting the registration by the Parlement of the ten percent surcharge on indirect taxes which added 25 million livres to the annual ordinary income.[28] The same optimism seemed to prevail at the Contrôle-Général a year later despite the disappointing naval defeat in the Carribean in June 1782. The continuation of the war made another tax levy necessary in order to avoid a deficit. The third vingtième was registered by the Parlement without protest. It yielded another 20 million livres annually, although it was to expire three years after the end of the war. In addition to the major new taxes there was a natural increase of indirect taxes because of the expanding economy, an addition of six million livres; another addition of one million livres in ordinary income came from the ferme of the stagecoach service. Another three million addition to fixed income was derived from the decrease in the government's obligations due to the extinction of life rentes. In 1787 Joly de Fleury asserted that the fixed income of the government had increased by 55 million livres during his ministry. Throughout his ministry the credit of the royal government remained high, its loans easily found subscribers and continued to hold up well on the bourse, or stock exchange. At the end of the war Joly de Fleury was jubilant about the success of the government in maintaining its credit and avoiding the fiscal troubles that had plagued the government of Louis XV during the Seven Years War.

It would appear that the "Observations" were to play a role in later events quite unintended by its authors. It was through his wife's uncle, Marquet de Bourgade, that Calonne became aware of this memorandum about the "inexact" Compte rendu of Necker. He seems to have misread the document, or misunderstood it if it was related to him orally. He was led to conclude that the Compte rendu of 1781 was in error, not of 25,934,500 livres (with a deficit of 15,734,000 livres), as clearly stated in the memorandum, but of 62 millions (later reduced to 56 million), and a deficit of 51,855,000 livres. For the items that he singled out, in addition to those mentioned in the memorandum for the deficit of 1781, were taken from the estimation of the later deficits of 1782 and 1783, and he blithely ignored the fact that those deficits did not materialize because Joly de Fleury had increased the government's ordinary income by 56 million livres.

The clearest example of Calonnne's taking his data from this memorandum of July 1781 is the figure he gave for the ordinary peacetime expenditure for the navy, namely 36 million livres. It is clear the Necker's Compte rendu gave the officially authorized amount of 29.2 million livres. The extraordinary expenditure for the navy in 1781 was 144 million livres. The figure of 36 million livres as the ordinary peacetime cost does not appear in any other official document except the July 1781 memorandum. In 1784 the figure was raised to 34 million livres and was so entered in Calonne's compte rendu of 1787. A year later it was raised to 45 million livres. But it was never officially 36 million livres. To accuse Necker of falsifying the Compte rendu by not including that figure, a speculative one applying to some future year after 1781 and which never materialized, is only an illustration of Calonne's method of discrediting his adversary.[29]

The "Observations" pointed out the debt-in-arrears that had accumulated in the war years and which the finance minister would need to liquidate after the war. In later years this became known as "the war debt." It consisted mostly of notes issued by the naval administration to pay for goods in the overseas area. The memorandum estimated that this debt amounted to 150 million livres in 1781. This was not an "exigible debt" which required annual interest and amortization payments. The notes to be redeemed were somewhat like modernday war bonds, to be paid off with interest at some future time, presumably after the war. The memorandum believed that an arrangement would be made after the war to pay this debt in a period of ten years at an annual rate of 15 million livres per year. Since there were no annual fixed costs, this debt could have no place in a compte rendu of ordinary, fixed expenditures. Yet Necker did not "pass it over in silence," as the memorandum claimed. He did not conceal that extraordinary costs for the war were running at the rate of 150 million livres per year at the time of the Compte rendu. In fact they were to reach 200 million livres per year in the last two years of the war. The "war debt" for the navy was 200 million livres at the beginning of 1783 and 25 million livres for the war department.[30]

Calonne certainly knew that he could not impugn the Compte rendu of 1781 for not listing the war debt for which fixed payments had not yet been determined. He found instead a substitute, a non-war debt-in-arrears which amounted, coincidently, to 150 million livres in 1781 for which he maintained 7.5 million livres in interest was owing. What proof did he have for this debt? Simply a document found in the records of the Contrôle-Général drawn up in the ministry of Bernard de Clugny in 1776. This document listed a debt-in-arrears of 203 million livres.[31] Necker had seen this document, pronounced it "full of errors" and of which only 57 million livres required amortization. The remainder were arrears in the payments of rentes, of salaries, and of pensions. One of Necker's reforms in his first ministry was to liquidate the debts-in-arrears in the King's Household which had accumulated because of excessive prices demanded by the companies who furnished the goods and services. At the time of his resignation there remained only 20 million that had not yet been reimbursed in the sections of the royal household known as "buildings" and "garde-meuble." But the interest on this debt was included in the expenditures for the King's Household. The other types of arrears did not require amortization. Of course if pensions, rentes, etc. could be brought up to date that would be good for the government's credit. But Necker could not see the sense of issuing a loan that would add to the ordinary expenditure as long as those claims were met regularly even if some months behind schedule.[32] If there was such a debt of 150 million remaining of that 203 million "debt-in-arrears" Necker wondered what had become of it in subsequent financial statements. It does not appear in the comptes rendus of 1787 or 1788. There is no mention of this either in the very complete table of royal debts made up by Joly de Fleury in January 1782, which evidently Necker had not seen.[33] It was upon such fragile evidence, a document found in the archives

178

written twelve years before his "Reply to Necker," that Calonne's case against the Compte rendu rested.

He continued to insist upon a large debt-in-arrears unrelated to the war existing at the time he came to the Contrôle-Général in November 1783. He told the Assembly of Notables in his February 22 speech that "when the king entrusted me with the administration of the finances at the end of 1783 they were in an extremely critical state . . . all the treasuries were empty, all government paper (on the bourse) was falling, all circulation was interrupted, alarm was everywhere, and confidence was destroyed. In reality there was 220 million to pay for war debts, more than 80 millions for other exigible debts, whether because of arrears in the payment of current expenditures or for the payment of several items which had been committed by my predecessors; 176 million in anticipations drawn on the year ahead, 80 million of deficit in the ordinary accounts, the payment of rentes excessively in arrears; altogether there was a void of over 600 millions, and there was neither money nor credit."[34]

Nothing in that declaration rings true. As has been seen, nothing required him to liquidate those massive debts in the short space of three years. As for the 176 millions of anticipations that he found were spent, he did not pay off that debt, but simply renewed it and added to it 76 millions by the end of his administration according to his own admission. Was there a deficit of 80 million livres in the ordinary income for the year 1783? Here he had not only Necker to contend with, but Necker's successor at the Contrôle-Général.

Jean-François Joly de Fleury was living in retirement in 1787, unlike his brother, Guillaume-François-Louis Joly de Fleury, who was selected as one of the Notables and who participated in the first Bu-

179

reau. The former finance minister was also highly indignant at the February 22 speech of Calonne before
the Notables and began to collect documents in his
files on the period of his ministry. Unlike Necker he
remained out of the public view, but his role in
bringing down Calonne was decisive. It was on April 3
that Calonne wrote to the former minister of finance
saying that his uncle, Marquet de Bourgade, had told
him that Joly de Fleury did not think in 1781 that the
account of Necker was accurate. Since he had been
hearing people say the opposite he assumed they were
wrong and his uncle was right. Unless he hears the
contrary from Joly de Fleury, wrote Calonne, he would
continue to assume so. Joly de Fleury replied, giving
some vent to his indignation at the Controller General
for his statements about the lack of order in the finances during his ministry; then he stated that he did
not believe there was a deficit in 1781. "Your uncle
may have believed so but he was unable to persuade either myself or M. de Maurepas that there was a
deficit." Calonne wrote a second time calling attention to the specific document drawn up in the Contrôle-Général in July 1781 singling out specific articles in which the Compte rendu was in error. Joly de
Fleury was in process of answering the second letter
and also a further communication to Miromesnil about
the financial situation during his ministry. But he
learned of the dismissal of both ministers before this
memorial could be sent. Therefore, it remained in his
collection of manuscripts. But a copy of the first
letter had been sent to Miromesnil, and as we have
seen, it was this letter and Calonne's lack of
forthrightness about it which led to the king's decision to call for his resignation.

The title of the unsent manuscript was "Project
for a reply to M. de Calonne of April 6, 1787." Here
Joly de Fleury wrote that "it's up to M. Necker to
prove that in 1781 the ordinary expenditures did not
exceed the ordinary revenues, as he claimed in his

Compte rendu. His successor has never denied this assertion and he recognized as true in the month of May, 1781, that the ordinary expenditures, not counting the extraordinary war expenditures, did not exceed the ordinary revenues."[35] For the remainder of the year 1781, Joly de Fleury wrote that he found sufficient revenue already provided by the loans of Necker to meet all the needs of 1781. The loan of March 1781, Necker's last life rente loan, was not doing so well on the stock exchange and Joly de Fleury withdrew 13 million livres of bordereau which he held in the treasury. The loan recovered par value on the exchange. From that time on Joly de Fleury said the credit situation of the royal government never became as dismal as Calonne had described it. "How could M. de Calonne persuade himself that the government's credit was worse six months after the war than it was at the end of the war?" The last major loan of Joly de Fleury was made in December 1782, and it was being successfully filled until Calonne closed it in December 1783 to make room for his own life rente loan. The two lottery loans of Ormesson were also successfully subscribed. It simply was not true, wrote Joly de Fleury, that the government's credit was "destroyed" in November 1783.[36] Nor were the government's bonds and notes declining on the stock exchange, as Calonne claimed. "Looking at the journals of that time would suffice to disprove such an assertion."

As for Calonne's allegation of a deficit of 80 million livres in 1783, Joly de Fleury called attention to his two tax increases that raised ordinary revenue by at least 50 million livres per year. The loans during his ministry of all types could not have exceeded 250 million livres; those of Ormesson were 131 million livres. The new annual costs added to the ordinary expenditures would only equal about one-half the increase in ordinary revenue. If there was not a deficit in 1781 there certainly was not in 1783.

In Calonne's "Reply to the Writing of M. Necker" published in January 1788 he included among his pièces justificatives the "Situation of the Finances" given by Joly de Fleury to the king in March 1783, shortly before his resignation. That account, it will be remembered, was not a compte rendu of ordinary income and expenditures, but a statement of the finances that included both ordinary and extraordinary accounts. It concluded by showing there would be funds in the treasury of over 30 million livres to begin the year 1784. Calonne simply transformed that account into a compte rendu by eliminating, without pièces justificatives, what he thought were extraordinary expenditures and revenues. The result was to show a deficit in 1783 of exactly 80 million. But it was a fraudulent chopping up of Joly de Fleury's account, as Necker pointed out in his "Further Clarifications."[37] To show a deficit of ordinary income Calonne expanded the ordinary expenditures and contracted the extraordinary. He included as ordinary expenditures a special grant to the navy which was clearly extraordinary, a special subsidy granted to the comte d'Artois of two million livres; and most curious of all was his inclusion as a fixed annual charge on the government's income the sum of two and one-half million livres "owing to Mr. Necker." The Genevan banker had loaned 2.4 million livres to the government when he entered the service of Louis XVI upon which he received annually 5% interest. But to receive annually 2.5 million on that initial investment would have been quite a coup even for the financial genius he was reputed to be! The other comptes rendus in the appendix of Calonne's "Reply to Necker" were treated in the same way. In the compte rendu of Bernard de Clugny for 1776 Calonne found an omission of 13 million livres in ordinary expenditure, which raised the deficit of that account to 37 million livres, coincidently the same figure he still maintained Necker had told Maurepas about in 1776. To the compte rendu of abbé Terray for 1774 Calonne found a

182

deficit of 40 million rather than the 29 million Terray had calculated for that year. These corrections, as the others, were supposedly taken from the "concrete accounts" at the end of the year 1774. Curiously, Calonne's corrections happened to match exactly certain items of Turgot's compte rendu for 1775, although that account found a deficit of only 22.5 million livres.[38] One could continue endlessly to recite examples of what Necker called "Calonne's strange method." Enough has been shown to indicate that the Assembly of Notables in 1787 was not entirely unjustified in suspecting the assertions of Calonne about the origins of the deficit he had revealed to them.

Returning to Necker's April 1787 essay, it will be remembered that he did not know exactly the basis for Calonne's attack on his Compte rendu. Much of that essay was taken up in showing how his reforms had increased the ordinary revenue so that it could pay for the costs of the war loans. Then he linked up the compte rendu of 1787 which showed a deficit of 112 million livres with his own account. He calculated the increase in ordinary income from 1781 to 1787 and the increase in the fixed expenditures to show how there could be a deficit of that magnitude in 1787 and yet a surplus in 1781. The reader will be spared these details which have been already discussed in my previous publications concerning the Compte rendu and Necker's loans.[39]

At this point the weary reader might well ask if it makes a great deal of difference whether Calonne or Necker was mistaken, or if both might have been somewhat dishonest. The prevailing opinion has been that Necker was the charlatan. If that view is mistaken, perhaps the Assembly of Notables itself might deserve reconsideration by historians. They were Neckerist with few exceptions. Could it be that they were not the egotistical aristocrats they are usually thought to be, that they were on the contrary, very serious

183

and intelligent men, genuinely seeking to find a solution to the financial crisis that faced the royal government?

[1]Jacques Necker, Oeuvres complètes, II, 161-162.

[2]Ibid., 162-164.

[3]Ibid., 165.

[4]Ibid., 169.

[5]Ibid., 159-235.

[6]Lettres de l'abbé Morellet à Lord Shelburne, 235.

[7]Journal de l'Assemblée des Notables, 62.

[8]Mémoires de Marmontel, III, 126-127.

[9]Madame de Staël, Considérations sur la Révolution française, 112.

[10]Charles Mathon de la Cour, Collection de Comptes rendus (Lausanne, 1788).

[11]"Nouveaux éclaircissements sur le Compte rendu," in Oeuvres complètes, II, 494.

[12]Ibid., 271.

[13]The printed brochure of Bonvallet Desbrosses is found in Archives nationales, AD IX 389, no. 19.

[14]Jean Egret was surely mistaken when he wrote in his otherwise sympathetic biography of Necker that "the compte rendu had only a limited significance, as Necker was obliged to admit." Cf. Necker, Ministre de Louis XVI (Paris, 1975), 205. Necker would never have made such an admission. As he wrote in his letter to

Calonne back in January 1787, the Compte rendu of 1781 had been the foundation of the government's credit.

[15]Pierre Renouvin, L'Assemblée des Notables. La conférence du 2 mars (Paris, 1920), 66. Renouvin was sympathetic to Calonne and hostile to the Notables, but he did admit that it was a "blunder" on Calonne's part to withhold those documents.

[16]"Nouveaux éclaircissements," in Oeuvres complètes, II, 275-276.

[17]Necker, "Mémoire au mois d'avril," in Oeuvres complètes, II, 208-209.

[18]"Nouveaux éclaircissements," in Oeuvres complètes, II, 418-430.

[19]Réponse du sieur Bourboulon au Compte rendu au Roi par M. Necker (London, 1781). A manuscript copy is in Archives nationales, K892.

[20]Mémoires secrets, XXXIV, 253.

[21]J. F. Bosher, French Finances, 1770-1795. From Business to Bureaucracy (Cambridge, 1970), 333.

[22]"Mémoire au mois d'avril," in Oeuvres complètes, II, 177-179.

[23]BN MSS Joly de Fleury, 1438, fols. 217-218.

[24]"Nouveaux éclaircissements," in Oeuvres complètes, II, 319-320.

[25]Ibid., 407.

[26]The version of Calonne's account submitted to the Notables was printed in Pierre Chevallier, Journal de l'Assemblée des Notables de 1787, 134.

[27]"Nouveaux éclaircissements," in Oeuvres complètes, II 375.

[28]BN MSS Joly de Fleury, 1432, "Administration des Finances par M. Joly de Fleury, et leur situation à sa retraite," fols. 163-166.

[29]Necker mentioned in his Compte rendu that the king intended to raise the peacetime fixed expenditure for the Navy after the end of the war. But until that was done the peacetime figure was 29.2 million livres.

[30]BN MSS Joly de Fleury, 1440, fol. 182.

[31]It can be seen today in AN K 892, no. 178.

[32]"Nouveaux éclaircissements, in Oeuvres complètes, II, 578-579.

[33]"Etat de tous les Emprunts fait par le Gouvernement depuis le 1er Janvier 1777, Epoque de la guerre, jusqu'à et comprise 1781." BN MSS Joly de Fleury, 1437, fols. 23 ff.

[34]Procès-verbal de l'Assemblée des Notables, 58.

[35]BN MSS Joly de Fleury, 1042, fols. 94-97.

[36]BN MSS Joly de Fleury, 1432, fol. 153.

[37]"Nouveaux éclaircissements," in Oeuvres complètes, II, 578-579.

[38]Necker did not notice or did not comment on this anomaly. It is true that Turgot added in a footnote that his account did not include what the government owed from an "old and exigible debt," which no doubt referred to that "debt-in-arrears" mentioned above which was calculated by Clugny. But evidently Turgot did not consider the charge of that debt to be an ordinary expenditure. Mathon de la Cour, Collection de Comptes rendus, 166-167.

[39]"Necker's Compte rendu of 1781: A Reconsideration," Journal of Modern History (June, 1970), 42(2), 161-183; "French Finances and the American War, 1777-1783," Journal of Modern History (June, 1976), 48(2), 233-258; Necker, Reform Statesman of the Ancien Régime (Berkeley: University of California Press, 1979). The above chapter repeats some of the material already published. My intention is to bring out more clearly certain matters which are still misunderstood about the Compte rendu, as appears in some critical reviews of my book published in 1979.

For example, in a review by George V. Taylor in The Journal of Economic History (1980, Vol. 40, pp. 877-879) my defense of Necker and his Compte rendu was totally rejected. The latter document, Taylor asserts, "is incomplete, mysterious, and infinitely controversial" (p. 878). It is incomplete, he says, because Necker did not indicate how that portion of the ordinary income collected by the receivers-general, the farmers-general, and other receiving agencies, was spent. Taylor avers that Necker was able to conceal from the public that he had paid for ordinary expenditures with extraordinary income. Such an assumption is entirely gratuitous. Among Necker's pièces justificatives for the Compte rendu in the archives at the Château de Coppet one of the folios, "B", has a collection of sixteen different accounts indicating in specific detail how 160,187,761 livres of that money was spent by the receiving agencies.

Taylor claims that Necker accounted for only 147.2 million "of the 166 million" paid by the receiving agencies. (In reality 163,106,671 livres was spent by those agencies.) That is true in the Compte rendu published by baron de Staël in the Oeuvres Complètes of Necker, Vol. 2, pp. 140-144. But Taylor did not notice that items numbered 11-19 gave only the net

amount turned over to the royal treasury by the pays
d'états. The gross amount was left out by de Staël,
but it is indicated in the copy published by Mathon de
la Cour (p. 180), and in the original publication.
The gross amount received by all the pays d'états was
24,659,571 livres of which 16,106,571 was retained by
the states and 8,553,000 turned over to the royal
treasury. That makes a total of 264,154,000 received
by the royal treasury, and 163,376,571 was received
and spent by the receiving agencies.

Taylor finds that the "debt service" for all
loans made during 1781 amounted to 16.3 million
livres, and that "was enough to wipe out the 10.2 million surplus reported by Necker." (p. 878). But that
was not all that happened during 1781. Necker's successor imposed a ten percent surcharge on indirect
taxes which increased the ordinary income by 25 million, more than enough to pay for the added "debt service."

In my book published in 1979 I discussed in chapter 14 the criticism of Necker's Compte rendu by Antoine Bailly whose work was published in 1830. Professor Taylor confuses the état au vrai used by Bailly
with Calonne's comptes effectifs. The two are entirely different documents. The former gives both ordinary and extraordinary accounts, the latter was limited to ordinary accounts.

On the subject of the états au vrai Professor J.
F. Bosher seems to question my understanding of the
French financial system in his otherwise friendly review of my book in The American Historical Review
(June, 1980, 638-639). He thinks that the état au
vrai is limited to the documents that finance officials submitted to the Council of Finance. But an
over-all état au vrai for the entire fiscal year was
drawn up by the Council based upon the documents of

all the financial officials. Such an *état* *au* *vrai* is
discussed not only in Bailly's book but also in Léon
Bouchard's *Système financier de l'ancienne monarchie*
(Paris, 1891) p. 426, and René Stourm's *Les Finances*
de l'ancien régime et de la révolution, II, 192.

Another author appears to question the soundness
of my defense of the *Compte* *rendu*. Charles P. Kindleberger in his *A Financial History of Western Europe*
(London: George Allen & Unwin, 1984), writes that
"The major point, not noted by Harris, is that
Necker's implicit fiscal model is what economists call
partial equilibrium, rather than general equilibrium.
Partial equilibrium analysis assumes other things
equal, as if there were no repercussions or feedbacks.
In general equilibrium one has to take into account
repercussions throughout the system." (p. 172).

Kindleberger seems to think it unnecessary to
show exactly where those "repercussions" were in the
year 1781. Those awesome expressions alone suffice to
discredit Necker! He mistakenly writes that I admit
that later records showed a deficit, presumably he
means for 1781. Certainly the French government spent
more in extraordinary expenditures than was recorded
in the *Compte* *rendu*. There was a war debt, or a debt-
in-arrears that did not have a fixed expenditure for
1781 and was to be paid off later. But whatever the
government spent could not escape being recorded eventually in later *comptes* *rendus* of ordinary expenditures and income. Kindleberger writes that unlike
families governments can "levy taxes at will and create money." This was not true of the French government of the *ancien* *régime*. It may be true of a modern
state, whether democratic or totalitarian. But the
government of the *ancien* *régime* was not strong enough
to force capitalists to yield their money. It had to
be coaxed from them by appealing to their self-interest. That was the basic wisdom Necker brought to the

French government. Only a policy of "order and good faith" could persuade investors to open their purses.

CHAPTER 6

THE REFORM PROGRAM OF THE NOTABLES

Historians of the twentieth century have dealt harshly with the Assembly of Notables of 1787. Correspondingly they have held Calonne in great esteem, seeing in him the victim of the "aristocratic revolution." The Notables were criticized also at the time of their assembly and later because of their opposition to Calonne. But the contemporary critics of the Notables and defenders of Calonne held those views for quite different reasons than twentieth-century historians. They looked upon Calonne as the defender of absolutism, as the preserver of the authority and prestige of the monarchy against those who were seeking to undermine it. Modern-day critics of the Notables see Calonne as a hero of democracy, the person who attempted to abolish unjust privileges of the nobles and prelates, and who for his pains was brought low by their combined opposition.

Certainly Calonne's contemporary defenders had the clearer view of him. There was nothing of the democrat or liberal in his make-up. He wanted to increase the ordinary revenue of the king without having to make any concessions to the national demand to establish some form of control over the management of the king's finances. The Notables insisted that the fate of twenty-four million people should not be subjected to the whims of one man, namely the Controller-General. This is what Calonne wanted, although he continually invoked the king's authority rather than his own. The provincial assemblies that Calonne proposed were to be strictly under the thumb of the royal government, just as he had expected the Assembly of Notables to be. Any notion that Calonne was a sympathizer of democracy should be dispelled by seeing his career after the eruption of the Revolution in 1789. The "first émigré" remained one, and moved from England to the Rhine to assume civilian leadership of the émigré movement whose object was to overthrow the revolutionary regime with the help of the monarchies of Europe. This at a time when Calonne's great antagonist, the Genevan banker, was struggling with the Revolution from within in order to keep it on the course he thought was the desire of the greatest part of the Nation.

Of course the personality, character, and administrative acts of Calonne were such as to play into the hands of his enemies. "He combined in himself all the abuses of which he sought to be the reformer," wrote Pierre-Victor Malouet.[1] But after April 8, 1787, that objectionable personality was no longer around. Now it would be seen if the opposition of the Notables was due entirely to their personal dislike of the individual who had occupied the post of Controller-General, or if their aims had some more basic substance. It was not long before the latter became known as the case.

The situation that faced the king immediately after his dismissal of both Calonne and Miromesnil was how to replace the two ministers upon whom he had depended for so long. The replacement of Miromesnil was the easier of the two. Chrétien-François de Lamoignon, a president of the Parlement of Paris, noted for his work in attempts to reform criminal and civil law, enjoyed great respect in the legal community. Chosen as one of the Notables from the magistrate class, he had sat in the First Bureau presided over by Monsieur. His appointment as the new Keeper of the Seals seems to have been favorably received by the public. As for Calonne's replacement, the immediate choice was a person experienced in the financial administration and who had been Calonne's assistant and therefore could continue presenting the reform projects. The Assembly of Notables was ready to receive the third division of reform proposals at the time of Calonne's disgrace. The person named as the new Controller-General was Michel Bouvard de Fourqueux. Abbé Morellet described Calonne's successor as "educated, with excellent principles of administration, utterly honest . . . but he is sixty-eight years old and has the gout."[2]

It was evident that Calonne's replacement would have to be someone of greater stature. "The public strongly calls for the return of Mr. Necker," Morellet added in his letter to Shelburne, "but the king does not hear with that ear." Even so the condition of the finances was so critical that for a moment it appeared that the king's determination not to appoint Necker would weaken. The most prominent person in the government now was the foreign minister, Montmorin. He had not been personally acquainted with the Genevan banker but he now tried to persuade the king that Necker was the only person who could calm public opinion, work with the Notables, and rescue the government from imminent bankruptcy. "At the end of April," Mercy-Argenteau wrote the emperor, "the financial situation became such that bankruptcy appeared inevitable. The king came each day to the queen's apartment and was so crushed by the condition in which he found his kingdom that he burst into tears." The Austrian ambassador added that the queen took advantage of this state of the king's mind to try to persuade him to recall Necker to the administration of the finances, but the king absolutely refused.[3] According to the testimony of Marmontel, who was a close friend of Montmorin, the foreign secretary enlisted the aid of Lamoignon to break down the resistance of the king to Necker's reappointment. Along with Necker's partisans who were still in the ministry, the naval secretary, Marshal de Castries, and the comte de Ségur, the secretary of war, it appeared that the pressure on the king to reappoint Necker was

formidable. At the last minute, according to Marmontel, the secretary of the King's Household, baron de
Breteuil, succeeded in changing the king's mind again,
pointing out that to appoint as his new finance minister a person whom he had exiled from Paris a short
time before would be an astonishing admission of weakness and therefore detrimental to his authority.[4]

That the king's authority was seriously undermined by the fall of Calonne and Miromesnil was undeniable. The Emperor Joseph had predicted that if
Calonne was dismissed the king would have to choose
his successor from the ranks of the opposition in the
Assembly of Notables, a situation similar to the English government. In fact this is what happened. It
was on April 12 that Loménie de Brienne submitted his
first memorial to the king suggesting a way out of the
impasse between the king and the Notables. He wrote
that the ideas of Calonne's reforms were all acceptable to the Notables, it was only the means he had
chosen to implement them that aroused objections.
"The ideas of the reforms are the king's, the means
were the minister's," he said, meaning Calonne.[5] He
meant also of course that the ideas were not just the
king's but his own. He denied that they were original
with Calonne. These reform ideas and projects had
been in the air for some time. "In order to propose
them to Your Majesty, the minister needed only to
gather them from some conclusions of books and practically all conversation." Discreetly, Brienne held
himself out as the person who could, as the king's
minister, get the Assembly to accept the aims of the
reforms but with other means.

The king was impressed by the memorial and returned it to the archbishop with marginal comments.
Meanwhile the Assembly was considering the third division of Calonne's memorials when it resumed deliberations after the Easter recess on April 15. A week
later it was ready to receive the fourth and final di-

vision of reform proposals, although, according to Bachaumont, the new Controller-General found that Calonne had not completed them at the time of his dismissal. "That minister was never a day ahead of his work," he wrote. The fourth division concerned the financial proposals for eliminating the deficit: an additional revenue to come from the expansion of the stamp tax and the extension of time for amortizing the debts were the most important items. It was the most delicate of all the divisions to take up with the Notables, and according to Bachaumont, the new Keeper of the Seals, Lamoignon, and the new Controller-General, Bouvard de Fourqueux, were in favor of dismissing the Assembly of Notables and taking their chances with the Parlement of Paris, even if it required a lit de justice. But Montmorin and Breteuil opposed that idea, arguing that it would be "indecent" to dismiss the Notables so abruptly after having convened them for the purpose of seeking their advice.[6]

On April 23 the king addressed in person a general assembly of the Notables and presented the fourth division of memorials. He made several significant concessions to the views of the Bureaux. He would accept the changes in the provincial assemblies desired by the Notables; that is, preserving the distinction of the orders with the presidents of the assemblies appointed by the king from the ranks of the nobility or the prelacy. He expressed thanks to the clergy for giving up its fiscal privileges and said he would listen to whatever proposals the forthcoming convocation of the clergy might make regarding the liquidation of its debt. The gabelle would not be reformed as proposed by Calonne but abolished outright, the provincial assemblies deciding how to make up the revenue that would be lost. The king would take whatever measures were necessary to eliminate the deficit. He promised to cut ordinary expenditures by fifteen million livres. He would order that the financial statements revealing the deficit would be turned over to the presidents of all the Bureaux. Finally, the king laid before the assembly the proposal for the stamp duty and the measure to extend the time for the amortization of debts. The Bureaux expressed appreciation to His Majesty for all those concessions but let it be known that the figure of fifteen million livres in economy was altogether too modest, and they expected much more could be cut from the ordinary expenditures.

It was with no little curiosity that the Bureaux received the financial statements of the royal government. Now they could see for themselves the reasons for the deficit. Yet the documents proved to be disappointing. There were three statements submitted: one for the year 1786, one for 1787, and a statement "for the common year." The latter was a compte rendu for the year 1787 of ordinary revenue and expenditures which gave the deficit at 115,306,165 livres, 6 sous, and 6 deniers! The first two accounts were useless for determining the ordinary deficit. They were statements "of the situation" for the year (1786 and 1787) which included both ordinary and extraordinary accounts, and the fiscal years were "entangled," that is, were not limited to one year. For example, the account for 1786 gave as the expenditure for the naval department a sum of 91,800,000 livres. But a separate item followed which lists two extraordinary payments: the redemption of paper money in the Isle of France in the Indian Ocean, of two million livres and the work in the roadstead at Cherbourg at 7.2 million livres. Thus a total for the department of the navy was 101 million livres. The sum for the "ordinary year" was 34 million livres. The "entanglement" of fiscal years was clearly stated: that total of 101 million included 6 million livres left over from the "ordinary service" of 1785; only 28 million livres for the ordinary service of 1786 was paid in that year; there was a sum of 63 million livres to pay the naval debt-in-arrears.

The statement for the year 1786 gave only the net amount turned over to the royal treasury by the sub-treasuries, amounting to 387,584,000 livres. In addition the account showed extraordinary income of 21,940,000 livres making a total income for the royal treasury of 409,524,000 livres. But unlike the account of Joly de Fleury for 1783, this one did not include the extraordinary income to be raised by loans. This was given separately at the conclusion of the statement. The expenditures included the total amount spent not only by the royal treasury but by all the other sub-treasuries, but without distinguishing them. Thus 150 million is listed as paid for rentes at the Hôtel de Ville, but the proportion paid by the receivers-general, the farmers-general, etc. was not indicated. The total expenditure was given as 592,912,400, which left a deficit of 183,388,400 livres. The conclusion of the statement indicated how that deficit would be met in the course of the year: 80 million would come from the loan of December 1785, 6 million from the sale of offices to the exchange agents, 22 million from the loan of Paris, an increase in anticipations of 53 million, and further extension of the life rente loans of March 1781 and January 1782 by 22 million livres. This balanced out at 183 million livres, the sum of the deficit.

The statement for 1787 was much more summary than that for the previous year. It listed the ordinary revenue taken from the compte rendu for the "common year," 474,389,000 livres, to which was added two items of extraordinary income, 7,680,000 livres which would come into the royal treasury from the third vingtième. (This tax expired at the end of 1786 but the income was not raised and sent to the royal treasury until 1787. This is an example of the "entanglement of fiscal years." A compte rendu of ordinary income would list that sum for 1786 rather than 1787.) Also the profits from the recoinage of the gold louis was listed as 3 million livres. This gave a total of revenue for 1787 of 485,069,000 livres. Expenditures were reported differently than in 1786. A list of expenditures by the sub-treasuries was given, amounting to 236,065,896 livres. The expenditures paid directly by the royal treasury were given in detail, totaling 387,182,667 livres. This combined with the expenditure of the sub-treasuries made a total of 623,248,563 livres, and a deficit of 138,179,563. The end of the statement said the loan from the Discount Bank of 70 million livres would help meet this deficit but a new loan of about 74 million would be necessary in 1787.

Even though those two accounts were of no use in establishing the ordinary deficit, the Notables must have read them with great attention. A number of items seemed to corroborate the public image of Calonne's ministry. During the dispute with the sovereign courts over the recoinage of the gold louis the government had asserted that the king would gain no more than 6 million livres from the operation. The account of 1786 showed that 10 million livres had been received, and the account of the following year another 3 million livres. The impression so widespread among foreign ambassadors as well as domestic critics of Calonne's "prodigalities" could find substantiation in those statements. All the "exchanges," the acquisitions, the construction projects were laid out in those accounts. But a curious entry must have puzzled them. In both accounts, for 1786 and 1787 are recorded an extraordinary expenditure of 2,400,000 livres "to Mr. Necker." That was the capital he had loaned to the government during his first ministry. Only in 1790 did he withdraw 400,000 livres. It was only after 1815, during the reign of Louis XVIII that the government returned the remainder to Necker's heirs. Why that item was included for those two years is a mystery. Could it have been another example of Calonne's wierd sense of humor?

The compte rendu for 1787 of ordinary expenditures and revenue was a great disappointment to the Bureaux. It was not at all what Calonne had described it to be in his speech of February 22. At that time he said: "I carefully distinguished the ordinary revenues for each fiscal year and placed the total amount of each in its column from which was subtracted the amount to be sent to the royal treasury. I followed the same method for the expenditures." This would have been the method Necker used in his Compte rendu of 1781, and is what the Notables expected to find in Calonne's for 1787. Instead they found only the gross sums that were received by the sub-treasuries, with no break-down of what they retained and spent for the king and the net amount turned over to the royal treasury. On the opposite side were the total expenditures of the royal government spent for each item: war department, navy, foreign affairs, etc., but only on the margins was the source of each payment given, whether it was paid by the receivers-general, or farmers-general, or the royal treasury. It was not the kind of a compte rendu that could be controlled and verified by pièces justificatives as was Necker's Compte rendu of 1781. But Calonne had stated specifically that his account was accompanied by 63 such documents. They were not turned over to the Notables, nor were the comptes effectifs, or any other statements that would prove the authenticity of the accounts.

The Bureaux believed that there was not enough information for them to perform their task, namely to ascertain precisely what the needs of the government were. They sent word to the king asking if someone at the Contrôle-général could meet with them to explain certain matters and answer questions. The documents had all the earmarks of having been drawn up hastily, for there were obvious inaccuracies and misspellings, such as the word "extinction" in place of the word "extension" of the loans of March 1781 and January

1782 by Calonne. Some dates were evidently wrong, such as that for the loan of December 1785.[7] It was difficult for someone to be found at the Contrôle-général that could help the Notables. Finally the first secretary of finances, Achilles-Joseph Gojard, was located, that not very assiduous public servant whom we shall meet later in the Ministry of Loménie de Brienne. The special committee that met with Gojard expressed satisfaction with the meeting, and so the Notables were able to get on with determining the real amount of the deficit. How useful their meeting with Gojard was can be surmised by the fact that all seven Bureaux came up with seven different figures for the deficit, ranging from 130 million to over 150 million livres. In any case there was enough in those accounts to discredit the financial administration of Calonne, which perhaps was their primary interest.

The special committee that had examined the documents wrote a report about their findings and submitted it to the Bureaux. According to the minutes of the First Bureau the report of the committee was endorsed and was the basis of a lengthy memorial sent by the Bureau to the king. It stated that accounts which had been given to the Notables "prove that the king has been deceived in the financial statements which had been given to him on the condition of his finances, and that he has been led to approve expenditures which his heart would have refused if he could have foreseen the consequences that would follow."

All the ordonnateurs have spent money in excess of their needs. Desiring to expand and perfect the administration entrusted to them, isolated from the financial administration, and from that standpoint, from the public interest, they have obtained increased appropriations which perhaps ought to have been left to easier times. Positions (of employment) have multiplied,

salaries have increased, and a weak surveillance has not been able to contain personal
interest which always seek to escape from
it.[8]

Unlike the Parlement of Paris later in the year,
the First Bureau did not officially accuse Calonne of
criminal conduct, only of bad judgment in spending
such large sums for objects which may have been worthy
in themselves but were unwise in the financial circumstances.

The Bureau then proceeded to show how the expenditures could be cut as much as 40 million livres from
the "ordinary expenditures." Over 15 million livres
could be cut from the war department purely by administration amelioration. The Bureau did not presume to
interpose its judgment as to the number of troops, or
such matters beyond its competence. It did call for
increased pay for soldiers, one of the recommendations
to be found in Necker's book on French finances. The
Bureau was more reserved about cuts in the naval department, but thought 3.4 million could be trimmed
from the current appropriation of 45 million livres a
year for ordinary expenditures. Over half a million
could be cut from the department of foreign affairs.
The Bureau's eye fell on that 28 million livres given
for pensions. Certainly some pensions were justified
but "it was to be feared that favor and dissimulation
have enormously increased the mass." The Bureau
thought the amount for pensions could be cut to 18
million, but prudently recommended a cut of 4.5 million for the moment. Finally, in its memorial the
First Bureau called attention to the expansion of
treasuries' offices in the different spending departments, and the increase in commissions they were permitted to take from royal funds passing through their
hands. At least half a million livres could be saved
by abolition of those superfluous offices. The
salaries and emoluments of the farmers-general and the

régisseurs had also been greatly increased and could be trimmed by 800,000 livres.[9]

On the proposed reforms of the fourth division having to do with the deficit and means of eliminating it, the First Bureau was obviously more interested in ameliorations of the above type than in levying additional taxes. The Notables remembered Necker's ministry and what he had accomplished by strict supervision of expenditures. The Second Bureau also called for a great reduction of treasurers and the innumerable _caisses_ that handled the king's money by private contract. Often they simply poured money into each other for no reason than to reap the rich commissions they were authorized. And each _caisse_ or semi-public treasury gave rise to other venal officials besides the treasurer. The Second Bureau memorialized the king:

> In this regard the Bureau can best put His Majesty in a position to judge how his finances have suffered by the multiplicity of offices by begging him to compare those of all kinds that existed in 1781 in every part of his service, with those which exist today in the same part; and His Majesty will easily recognize that it is not for the genuine benefit of his service that these positions have thus multiplied, but for the benefit of those who have been gratified by the restoration or the creation of all those new offices.[10]

It was not simply a matter of scrutinizing the _compte_ _rendu_ before them and suggesting economies. The Notables wanted to assure themselves and the nation that the king's finances would not again come under an administration like that of Calonne's. The First Bureau now formally proposed to the king the establishment of a Finance Committee "as the most appropriate measure to maintain order, equilibrium, and proportion in all parts of the administration." This committee would be something more than the finance committee set up by Joly de Fleury early in 1783 and abolished by Calonne later in that year. It would be composed of seven members: the chairman of the Finance Council, the Controller General, and five other commissioners serving without salary and independent of the government. The functions of the committee would be to inspect the records of all branches of the administration and all the treasuries every six months at least. It would verify the general accounts of all expenditures and revenue of the government which would be sent to the royal council each year, and then published. "Publicity alone is the strongest check against depredation." The committee would also control government loans. No loan would be permitted without registration (of the Parlement), and all extensions of loans would be forbidden. Furthermore each loan edict must stipulate the source of funding for its reimbursement. The First Bureau also proposed that the government publish the list of pensions granted each year, as it was according to Necker's reform of 1778.[11]

It is sometimes said that this proposal for a fiscal committee of surveillance was intended to "put the royal government in tutelage." The Notables certainly did not see the proposal in that light. They asserted that taxpayers have a right to know that their contributions are not being wasted or used irresponsibly. If their view of Calonne's ministry was correct, then their proposal was not unreasonable. Yet it proved to be the rock upon which Loménie de Brienne's gallant attempt to have the royal government work fruitfully with the Notables foundered.

It was on May 1, 1787, that the Archbishop of Toulouse was appointed by the king as "head of the Council on Finances," the position held by Vergennes and not refilled since his death in February. Brienne was disappointed that the king refused his request to have Necker join the government as Director General of Finances, and well he might be, for finances was not his strong field. Bouvard de Fourqueux stepped down as Controller General and was replaced by the former intendant of Rouen, Laurent de Villedeuil, a Maître de Requête of the Council of State, who was otherwise not particularly distinguished.

The most urgent matter of the new administration was to find money for the coffers were nearly empty. On May 7 the Parlement of Paris registered a royal loan edict providing for the sale of six million life rentes with a capital of 60 million livres. The preamble was quite a contrast to those of Calonne's loans. It stated that the Assembly of Notables had examined the financial accounts of the royal government and had made suggestions for reducing the deficit. It promised a retrenchment of expenditures of at least 40 million per year, but that increased taxes would still be necessary. The government pledged that these taxes would be fixed in time and amount, and that safeguards would be established to prevent future disorders and deficits. The preamble bore the mark of Loménie de Brienne. It was almost an apology to the nation by the king for the mismanagement of the finances during the past three years. The Parlement registered the edict without a murmur.[12]

On the same day, May 7, the king replied to the memorial of the First Bureau with new concessions. He agreed that 40 million livres could be cut from expenditures. He promised to speed up the system of control so that the accounts of the royal finances would become current rather than remain years behind as in the past. He had ordered that a compte rendu of ordinary revenue and expenditures be published every three years. He would restore the edict on pension reform implemented in Necker's ministry but allowed to lapse

by his successors. The list of pensions would be published each year, and he thought the total amount
could eventually be reduced to 18 million livres per
year. He promised to make no future loans without
stipulating the specific funds that would pay the annual interest and amortization of the loan. He was
determined to bring expenditures into line with revenue. With regard to the proposal of a special finance committee to become the permanent supervisor of
the royal finances, the king said he would "consider"
the suggestion, as to its composition and function.[13]

The First Bureau replied to the royal communication by thanking the king for his concessions, but after deliberating upon it, the Bureau wanted to make
known its desires: (a) the accounts of the royal government should be published every year, not every
three years; (b) the Committee on Finance should be
composed of persons independent of the administration,
and it should be appointed before the separation of
the Assembly of Notables; (c) the Committee on Finance
should fix each year the expenditures for all departments, which would be prohibited from exceeding the
designated sum without the express authorization of
the king. The First Bureau was taking an insistent
tone, and this ruffled the king and some of the ministers who thought the concessions already made were
considerable.

Loménie de Brienne now stepped in to play his me-
diating role. On May 9 he met with a special conference representing each of the seven bureaux at the
residence of Monsieur. His intention was to lay before them the specific proposals for erasing the
deficit. He wanted to retain Calonne's land tax
(subvention territoriale) but said the king agreed
that it have a fixed sum, and that it be collected in
money rather than kind. The total amount to be collected would be 80 million livres, 25 million above
what the two vingtièmes currently yielded. That would

be one-half the amount needed from additional tax revenue. The remaining tax revenue would come from the
stamp duty tax which he expected to yield 16 million
livres, and from a tax on residences, a hearth tax,
which would make up the other 10 million livres. He
estimated the annual deficit at 140 million livres.
The king had promised savings of 40 million. That
would leave 50 million livres of the deficit which he
proposed to meet with loans. He gave a detailed explanation of how the new land tax would be administered. The 80 million livres would be divided among
the provinces and partitioned in each province by the
provincial assembly, and then on down throughout the
district and the parish assemblies. The method of assessment at the primary level would be to make ten
percent of the landed income the basic rule. If the
amount collected exceeded the partitioned sum, then
the assessment could be lowered the following year.
Or it could be raised if the assessed ten percent fell
short of the sum. But Brienne was certain that the
levying of ten percent, equal to the two vingtièmes,
when levied on all lands without exception, would
yield at least 25 million livres more than the amount
reaped in the past by the two vingtièmes. The new
land tax then would be paid entirely by those who had
escaped from the full nine percent levy in the past.
Those who were already paying that full amount of
their landed income would not suffer any additional
burden.[14]

These measures to meet the financial crisis must
have seemed to the archbishop the very essence of moderation and fairness. Yet the meeting of May 9 was a
stormy one. The king's message about the proposed Finance Committee and the annual publication of a compte
rendu being vague and unsatisfactory some of the Notables let the archbishop know their irritation. According to Bachaumont the bishop of Nevers read a
stern lecture to Loménie de Brienne. He was accused
of preaching the same doctrine as his predecessors.

"Pay taxes and be quiet!" The brief era of good feeling following Calonne's disgrace was ebbing. As the public became aware of the difficulties between the Notables and the ministry it became more and more excited about it. The "little fever" that Morellet noted in March was obviously rising, and as the Notables felt themselves supported by public opinion they became more audacious. It was a repetition of Calonne's relationship with the Notables, and a premonition of the States General in 1789. The king felt he had made as many concessions as he could, and was resolved to go no further. He found ready support for this stand among his more conservative counsellors, the baron de Breteuil and Lamoignon. The decision was made to dismiss the Notables.

As might be expected in an assembly so subject to influence by an excited public opinion, some of the Notables were more forward and audacious than others. The young general Lafayette, who had been admonished by Calonne when he agreed to invite him to the assembly to "show zeal and submission," was proving to be exuberant in the one but not the other. Before the end of Calonne's ministry he became especially interested in the matter of the "depredations" of the royal domain by "scandalous" exchanges and purchases of property that were adverse to the interest of the king. He submitted a memorial on this subject to the Second Bureau of which he was a member. He admittedly did not have access to the necessary documents, but simply called attention to the dubious nature of these contracts and demanded an investigation.[15]

As far as policies regarding the finances were concerned, Lafayette was the most orthodox of Notables. He submitted a lengthy memorial to the Second Bureau detailing his ideas on the subject. He thought it regrettable that the seven bureaux could not agree on a precise figure for the deficit. He made an eloquent plea for resolving the deficit by ameliorations

rather than by additional taxes. His memorial included most of what the First Bureau had already proposed, except that he went a step further: ameliorations could take care of all the deficit. The Assembly of Notables did not have the authority to agree to
new taxes. "The imprescriptible right to sanction
public taxes belongs only to the representatives of
the nation." At this point the President of the Second Bureau, the comte d'Artois, spoke up in disbelief
of what he had heard: "What, are you calling for the
States-General?" "Yes, my lord," replied Lafayette,
"and even more." This at least was how the incident
was described in Lafayette's memoirs.[16]

While there had been some mention of the States-
General in previous discussions of specific issues in
the Bureaux, Lafayette was the first to make such a
statement, and he was very much alone. The Notables
were not anxious to go that route. The more audacious
wanted an expansion of the functions of the proposed
Committee on Finances but that was all.

May 25 was the date set for the final general assembly of the Notables. All seven Bureaux drew up
their recommendations on all the proposals submitted
to them. These were signed by the presidents of the
Bureaux and sent to the king. They were printed and
are available today for the benefit of those who believe the Assembly of Notables stood for nothing but
aristocratic reaction.[17] Bachaumont wrote that it
"required an iron arm to write down all the recommendations written by the Notables at this critical end
of the session."[18] There were some variations in the
recommendations of the different Bureaux. On the
whole they were very similar. The most prolific and
perhaps the most influential of the Bureaux were the
first three, those presided over by Monsieur, the
comte d'Artois, and the duc d'Orleans respectively.

The matter that had been given to the Notables for their opinion was how to fill the deficit of ordinary income for ordinary expenditures. The First Bureau noted that there were three ways of doing this. First, the way of amelioration, of reducing expenditures, of improvement of administration such as the abolition of superfluous offices. The king had promised a reduction of 40 million livres in the ordinary expenditures. The Bureau encouraged him to make even more.

The second way of eliminating the deficit was by rewriting the loans. The Bureau agreed to the plan to extend the period of amortization of loans for a period of 15 years. Finally, the third way was to raise new tax revenue. The Bureau warmly endorsed the proposal to establish provincial assemblies as a means of improving the administration of the taxes, for abolishing exemptions and unwarranted privileges where the tax burden was concerned. On the gabelle, the First Bureau had proposed early in the Assembly of Notables that it should not be reformed, as Calonne proposed, but abolished. The provincial assemblies would decide how to make up the revenue that would be lost by the disappearance of the gabelle. In this matter the Bureau declined to follow the proposal made by Necker in his book on the finances, and which was somewhat similar to Calonne's. The Bureau felt that the salt tax, a burden on the poor people primarily, could not be justified and should end immediately. The same was true of the corvée labor service, which should be commuted to a monetary tax for the building and maintenance of roads and bridges. On the taille, the Bureau accepted the recommendations made by Calonne, but in addition called for the abolition of exemptions to the taille. There should be no reason why venal officers, servants of the King's Household, postal employees, the bourgeois of Paris, and the free cities should be exempt. Neither should the title of nobility acquired by purchase be a legitimate reason for

211

exemption from the taille at least until the fourth generation. "If finally the number of those privileged were reduced as much as possible, there would be a much greater relief for the taillables than the measure proposed in the memorials."

Somewhat reluctantly, the Bureau agreed to the Stamp tax as proposed by Brienne. It was the "least painful to bear because it was spread among the people in accordance with their ability to pay." Some modifications were suggested, such as the removal of drastic penalties for those whose documents do not have the required stamp. The Bureau did reject the proposal of Brienne to levy a tax on residences, deeming it an arbitrary tax, difficult to levy fairly. Finally, the most important of the new taxes was the land tax which would raise the revenue of the king by 25 million livres. The Bureau said that this tax "should be borne without any exemptions, in accordance with landholdings, and a method of assessment should be adopted that will be common throughout the kingdom." The Bureau intended for the new tax to be borne by those exempt from the two vingtièmes; those who can prove they have been paying the full two vingtièmes and the four sols per livre on the first vingtième will be excused from paying anything on the new tax. Therefore the Bureau did not envisage a completely new land tax replacing the vingtièmes. The new tax was to be superimposed on the other vingtièmes, but equitably and without any lands or proprietors being exempt from it. But these measures were to be considered temporary, not permanent. The second vingtième was due to expire in 1790, and the Bureau hoped that further ameliorations would make the tax unnecessary after that date.

There was no question but that the First Bureau considered exemptions, privileges, "concession," as the great fault of the tax system. The same was true of trading privileges and monopolies. All the recommendations of Calonne's original memorials for the single duty tariff, for the abolition of restrictions on trade, were accepted by the Bureau almost without discussion.

In the final general assembly of May 25 there seemed to be a desire of both the ministry and the Notables to emphasize harmony or at least to present the appearance of cooperation between the king's government and the assembly. Public opinion was becoming increasingly agitated and there was no doubt some alarm felt on both sides, the government and the Notables, about the situation. Furthermore there was a wide area of agreement between them. In their final speeches to the assembly both the spokesmen of the Bureaux and of the government sought to project the image of perfect concord and unity of aims as well as methods.

In his speech to the assembly Loménie de Brienne sounded a cheerful note as he spelled out all the policies that the king was determined to implement and which were in accord with the desires of the Notables. The most important innovation which the king and Notables had agreed upon was the establishment of provincial assemblies. This meant the end of the harsh administrative monarchy which had been a product of the anarchy in the time of the religious wars. "The king has not believed that a regime dictated by circumstances should persist when those circumstances have ceased to exist. He has felt that authority has the greater power as it has the greater confidence (of the people), and that it is not to weaken royal power but to enlighten it and even to make it more effective by relinquishing a part of administration to the provincial assemblies."

"The Notables," he continued, "had repudiated all distinctions when it comes to payment of taxes to support public needs, or for civil liberty, extended to

213

all estates, and which does not permit special taxation, a vestige of the unhappy days of servitude."
And yet at the same time granting equality of taxation
and civil liberty does not mean that other privileges
and forms that belong to the first two orders of society will not be respected. For "distinctions are necessary in a monarchy." And equality in taxation for
making public contributions does not mean a confusion
of ranks. The social hierarchy must be maintained and
democracy repudiated.

As for the provincial assemblies, the préseance
of the first two orders will be observed. There will
be double the number of deputies for the third estate
as for each of the other two, and deliberation and
voting will be done in a common assembly of the three
orders and votes counted by head. The deputies of the
provincial assemblies will be elected from district
assemblies rather than appointed by the king or by
cooption. Loménie de Brienne stipulated that the experiences of the assemblies in Berri and Haute-Guienne
would provide guidelines.

With regard to the finances, the archbishop told
the assembly that the king has expressed to the Bureaux his intention to take steps to prevent such a
huge deficit in the future as was revealed to the Notables at the beginning of their convocation in February. The Bureaux had established different figures
for the deficit when the financial accounts were submitted to them, but Loménie de Brienne believed the
mean figure was about 140 million livres. The king
had promised to retrench expenditures by 40 million
livres; loans would be made to cover 50 million livres
of the deficit; the remaining 50 million livres would
be covered by new taxation. To justify these new
taxes "His Majesty proposed to publish near the end of
the year an exact account of his revenue and expenditures; and if there is a clear necessity for an increase in revenue, from the moment that the taxes are

214

increased His Majesty will not raise them to the level deemed necessary until this account, made with the greatest precision, leaves no doubt about the sum produced by the existing taxes and upon the results of the ameliorations promised; finally it would be made clear what deficit remains after these ameliorations have been carried to at least a savings of 40 million livres." Here obviously was an attempt to meet the demands most firmly insisted upon during the past months, namely that increased taxes should be the last resort of augmenting the king's revenue, after all possibilities of economy and amelioration have been exhausted; and also that a more adequate method of accounting for the royal finances be adopted, and that these accounts be rendered public by way of publication. It was a fateful promise that the archbishop was making to the Notables, and through them, to the nation. Would he be able to keep it?

He could not leave out of his address on May 25 some reference to the Notables insistent demand for the establishment of a Committee of Finance that would be independent enough of the administration to carry out an effective surveillance of all parts of financial administration. His Majesty, he said, would reorganize the existing Council of Finance which will supervise all loans, taxes, and coordinate all important operations. "It is to the Council of Finance that His Majesty intends that all annual distributions of money to the different departments will be made and verified each year. It is by means of this Council and the publicity given to its acts that the king will be guaranteed against future surprises and errors."

This appeared to be the kind of Council set up by Joly de Fleury in 1783, and there was no guarantee from the speech of the archbishop that it would have that independence from the government that the Notables were insisting upon.

215

Other promises were made in the matter of publicizing the acts of the financial administration. The government debt would be published each year so that creditors and the public could see exactly what was owed by the government. The list of pensions and gratifications and gifts by the king to individuals would likewise be published each year. For each loan edict the source for its payment would be indicated in the preamble. There would be a shortening of the time required to complete the accounts of the fiscal year after it had passed. The payments by secret funds (_acquits_ _de_ _comptant_) would be restricted to what was absolutely necessary.[19]

In his closing remarks the Archbishop of Toulouse made an eloquent plea for harmony, holding out great hopes for the future if concord prevailed. In its pathos it was very like the oration of Necker at the opening of the States-General two years later. Such great hopes, expressed with such eloquence, but soon to be dashed!

[1]*Mémoires*, I, 287.

[2]*Lettres à Lord Shelburne*, 237.

[3]*Correspondance secrète*, II, 95, n. 1.

[4]Marmontel, *Mémoires*, III, 126-127.

[5]*Journal de l'Assemblée des Notables*, 64.

[6]Bachaumont, *Mémoires secrets*, XXXV, 29.

[7]The accounts discussed here are all located in *Observations présentées au Roi par les Bureaux de l'Assemblée des Notables sur les Mémoires rémis à l'Assemblée ouverte par le Roi à Versailles le 23 février 1787*. Bn 8° Le21.10.

[8]*Ibid.*, 353.

[9]*Ibid.*, 362.

[10]*Ibid.*, 419.

[11]*Ibid.*, 363-365.

[12]The preamble is printed in *Collection des édits*. BN F. 23631, (25).

[13]*Ibid.*, 377.

[14] Ibid., 373-377.

[15] Bachaumont, Mémoires secrets XXXV, 59-62.

[16] Gilbert de Motier, marquis de Lafayette, Mémoires, correspondance et manuscrits du general Lafayette, publié par sa famille (Paris, 1837-38), II, 177.

[17] Observations présentées au Roi, 383-394.

[18] Mémoires secrets, XXXV, 131-132.

[19] The final speech of Loménie de Brienne is in AN C¹, fols. 470-491.

CHAPTER 7

THE FIFTEEN MONTHS OF THE ARCHBISHOP

To some of the memoir writers of the time it was
a matter of eternal disappointment that Necker was not
appointed to the helm of the finances in May 1787
rather than Loménie de Brienne. In later years the
foreign minister, the comte de Montmorin, expressed to
Marmontel his keen regret that he had not insisted
more firmly to the king that Necker be appointed.
"How many misfortunes France would have avoided, how
much grief I would have spared the king!" he said to
Marmontel, who added in his memoirs: "What would
(Montmorin) have thought then if he had known that he
was to perish on the guillotine, and that the king
would follow him only three months later!"[1] It is
certain that Necker himself shared the belief that
events would have turned out differently had he been
appointed in May 1787. "If I could only have had the
fifteen months of the archbishop," he said wistfully
to his daughter on the day of his reappointment in August 1788, "now it is very late."[2]

And yet Loménie de Brienne was a known Neckerist
at the time of the Assembly of Notables, as were most
of those invited to that body. He was brought into
the ministry because he was considered the leader of
the opposition to Calonne. But hardly a year of his
ministry had passed when the archbishop found himself
the object of hatred almost as intense as that which
had fallen upon Calonne. What were the reasons for
this striking turnabout? It is too easy to say that
the archbishop simply changed hats, that he was no
sooner appointed to the ministry than he gave up the
ideas he had held as opposition leader and quickly
adapted himself to the outlook of the man in power.
Some of his former colleagues among the prelates ac-

cused him of just such a change of heart. But a glance at all the royal acts passed under his administration shows clearly that they were in many cases exactly those called for by the Assembly of Notables. The ministry of Loménie de Brienne was clearly guided by the previous Necker ministry. The archbishop had studied thoroughly the catechism of administrators.

Yet Necker was himself highly critical of Brienne and his handling of the crisis that he faced. It was not the goals and intentions of the archbishop that were at fault but his political ineptness, his blunders, and lack of coolness when facing opposition. This criticism had some similarity to that of Loménie de Brienne's concerning Calonne's reforms that were submitted to the Assembly of Notables. "The goals of the reforms are the king's, the methods were the minister's," he wrote to Louis XVI in April. Necker might have said the same of the Brienne ministry. The legislative acts were Neckerist, the way in which they were carried out were the archbishop's. It is necessary to ask what these goals and methods were, and how Necker might have succeeded where Loménie de Brienne failed.

Some critics of Brienne's ministry say his first and gravest mistake was dismissing the Assembly of Notables. The fact that necessary financial measures were registered by the Parlement of Paris without protest, such as the loan edict of May 7, would seem to indicate that as long as the Assembly was in session, and the ministry in harmony with it, the future difficulties with the sovereign courts might have been avoided. This was indicated also by the letters patent of May 19 which extended for another three years the king's share of the <u>octrois</u>, or taxes levied by city governments on goods entering the city walls.[3] Necker was of the opinion that Brienne ought to have kept the assembly in session until all the reform measures, certainly the financial measures, had safely passed the reef of registration by the sovereign courts. Parliamentary opposition which came after the Assembly of Notables was both more reactionary and radical than had been the generally responsible and cautious assembly. The convocation of the clergy which met in June 1788 was also far more reactionary, far less progressive than were the prelates in the Assembly of Notables.

But the decision to dismiss the Assembly of Notables was not entirely the archbishop's. His initial appointment was to be head of the Council of Finance. This made him the most prominent person in the government, the one upon whom the king most relied. He was not appointed principal minister until late August 1787. In the meantime his ministerial colleagues had some part in the decisions of the government. Some were more conservative than Brienne, more firmly convinced that the king's authority should not be compromised or shared with any group that claimed to represent "the nation." The secretary of the King's Household, baron de Breteuil, was certainly of that persuasion. As for the Keeper of the Seals, Lamoignon, there are contradictory estimates of his role in the ministry. Some believed he was more responsible, more prudent, less capricious than Brienne, and that if his counsels had prevailed on some crucial issues the failure of the ministry might not have happened.[4] On the other hand there is evidence that Lamoignon was an authoritarian at heart. His manner of dealing with the Assembly of Notables was brusque. His handling of the opposition of the Parlement of Paris was on some occasions as inconsiderate as that of his colleague the archbishop. This was particularly true of the treatment of the peers in the royal session of November 1787.

It has been seen that the final assembly of the Notables was held on May 25. Within two months following their dismissal Brienne got the consent of the

221

king and the registration by the Parlement of Paris of several acts that implemented what he had promised in his final speech to that assembly. Predictably among these were those that had caused very little discussion and which were strongly favored by the Notables. Several of Calonne's proposals were to eliminate internal and external barriers to trade. In June an edict of the king suppressed the tax levied on shipping in various ports of France. The edict referred to the desires of the Notables to form a customs union for the entire kingdom, removing all such tariffs to the frontiers. It stated that this project would take time to implement but "we are hoping to carry it to perfection as soon as possible." But freedom of navigation and commerce need not wait, and could be liberated from those encumbrances immediately.[5]

On June 17 a declaration of the king granted complete freedom to export grain. This superseded legislation of 1774 which, while guaranteeing complete freedom of the grain trade within the kingdom, had placed some restrictions on export. If the price of grain should exceed a certain level (12-1/2 livres per quintal, or 30 livres per setier) the government would be authorized to prohibit for a time export of grain outside the country. Now this prohibition was removed, although provincial assemblies could ask for permission to limit export from their province abroad for a limited period, not to exceed one year, if they could show that there was a serious shortage.[6] The declaration of June 17 reflected the influence of the physiocratic doctrine on Loménie de Brienne. No more than Calonne was he a doctrinaire physiocrat, but his friends were. He listened to the exhortations of abbé Morellet but seldom followed them.[7] It would appear that the declaration of June 17 on the grain trade was intended to appease the doctrinaire physiocrats more than for any other practical reason. Very rarely since 1774 had the price of wheat or any other grain exceeded 30 livres per setier. As fate would have it,

222

the summer after the passage of the declaration of June 17 brought a disaster for the grain crop due to severe climatic conditions. Drought and hailstorms cut the harvest in half, and the price of grain shot up beyond the ceiling set by the legislation of 1774. Yet the archbishop seemed unaware of the impending crisis, and the grain dealers were allowed complete freedom of export, resulting in a depletion of the domestic supply. The declaration of 1787 was only repealed after Necker returned to the Contrôle-général. As we shall see, a great amount of his attention and energy was taken up coping with the subsistence crisis throughout his second ministry and even in some of his third ministry.

Two other acts were promulgated in June 1787 that had the overwhelming approval of the Notables. A declaration of June 27 abolished the corvée labor service for royal roads and bridges. This expenditure would now be met by tax revenue. The provincial assemblies were to assume the responsibility of raising the necessary money. Until they could be organized the money would be raised in each province by a supplement to the taille, although a top limit of one-sixth of the taille was stipulated.[8]

Also in June 1787 came the most important of Brienne's legislation, the edict establishing provincial assemblies and administrations throughout the pays d'élections and the pays conquis. The edict stated that "the benefits which have come from the establishment of provincial administrations on a trial basis in Berri and Haute-Guienne having fulfilled our hopes, we have decided to extend the same benefits to other provinces of our kingdom; we have been confirmed in this resolve by the unanimous opinion of the Notables."[9] The intention of the government was to establish these assemblies and administrations in accord with the ideas of the Notables. There would be three levels of assemblies, the parish, the district, and

223

the provincial levels. The parish assembly would be elected by the citizens paying at least 10 livres per year of direct taxes. They would meet in an electoral assembly (to which the seigneur and the parish priest would not come) and elect three representatives per 100 hearths. The seigneur and parish priest would attend the regular parish assembly by privilege rather than election. The parish assemblies of the district would elect 24 delegates to the district assembly; the district assemblies of the province would elect 48 delegates to the provincial assembly. The principle of the doubling of the Third Estate would apply throughout, including both the assemblies and the intermediate bureaux set up to administer the acts decided upon by the assembly. Deliberation would be in a common assembly and votes counted by head.

The edicts of June indicated that the provincial administrations established by Necker in Berri and Haute-Guienne would serve as guidelines until more elaborate instructions could be worked out. Very crucial in this matter was the power of the intendants and their agents over the local assemblies and administrations. The sovereign courts had been apprehensive that the government might use these administrations, as Calonne had attempted to use the Assembly of Notables, as a way of by-passing the sovereign courts and thereby carry out its fiscal policy unhampered by remonstrances. Necker's provincial administrations had severely curtailed the powers of the intendant over local government. But these had been largely restored by Necker's successors. The Parlement of Paris and all other sovereign courts except Besançon and Bordeaux registered the edicts but not without expressing reservations. On August 5 another edict of the government spelled out the position of the intendants in the new provincial administrations. They were given as much authority as they enjoyed under Calonne, and in some respects, according to a modern authority, even more.[10] The edict came at the climax

224

of the struggle between the Brienne ministry and the Parlement of Paris over taxation. The two matters, provincial administrations and tax reform, were intimately linked, because the new local governments were to administer the new taxes. Increasing suspicion of the Brienne ministry by the magistrates strengthened the resistance of the Parlements of Grenoble, Besançon and Bordeaux to the provincial assemblies. Added to the difficulties of the government were the complex jurisdictional rivalries and questions of boundaries. By the fall of 1787 when Loménie de Brienne had hoped to have all local assemblies established, 17 out of a planned 25 provincial assemblies were able to meet.

The matter that the Notables had most emphasized in the last days of their assembly was the establishment of an independent committee on finance to supervise the financial administration and guarantee the nation against future mismanagement such as had happened under Calonne's ministry. Here Brienne tried very hard to conciliate the desires of the assembly but at the same time not to alarm the king and the defenders of his absolute monarchy. It proved to be an attempt to square the circle. On June 5, less than two weeks after the end of the Assembly of Notables, the government handed down a "regulation of the king for the formation of his Royal Council of Finance and Commerce." The preamble stated that "His Majesty, by giving to this committee a permanent and active status, wished to assure himself against errors, irregularities, and surprises that an extensive administration is exposed to." The Council would be composed of the head of the Royal Council of Finance and Commerce, the Controller General of Finance, the Keeper of the Seals, the six ministers of state, and two counsellors of state. A committee under the chairmanship of the head of the Royal Council of Finance would meet every fifteen days to propose the agenda for the Council. "In general," stated the edict, "all the important operations of finance will be brought to the Council."

It would decide upon the budget requests of each of the ordonnateurs, who would be called before the Council to give information upon their respective departments. The funds for each year would be decided upon in December preceding that year, and allocated to the different departments, and these decisions would be made public by printing. If there were unforeseen expenditures in the department the ordonnateur must get the approval of the Council to exceed the allotment. The members of the Council of Finance and Commerce would receive no pay as members of that body. But of course they were all members of the government and received emoluments from their other positions.[11]

The Regulation of June 5 was obviously an attempt to meet the demands of the Assembly of Notables, but it clearly failed to provide the one thing the Notables most insisted upon: independence of the surveillance committee from the government. It was a resurrection of Joly de Fleury's committee of February 1783 rather than what the Notables felt was necessary to guarantee the nation from "surprises" and abuses. This proved to be a fateful omission. Because of it the Parlement of Paris was to arrogate to itself the function which the Notables had intended to give to the finance committee they recommended to the king.

As Brienne entered into his long and stormy relations with the sovereign courts he never ceased carrying out economies in the different departments of government and ameliorations in the collecting of revenue. These policies had been called for by the Assembly of Notables and were Neckerist in inspiration. One of the most important reasons for the repudiation of Calonne by "public opinion" was his openly expressed contempt for the policy of economy. Whatever may be the disagreements among historians regarding Calonne's "prodigalities," there can be none about his repudiation of the "sterile parsimony" practiced by the Genevan banker. But at the time he revealed the huge deficit to the Notables and presented his array of reforms to deal with it, those proposals did call for a reduction of expenditures of 20 million livres in the war department and in the King's Household. Characteristically he had not consulted with the war minister, Ségur, nor the head of the King's Household, Breteuil, about just where and how those savings would be realized.

During the summer and fall months of 1787, and well into the spring of the following year Brienne resolutely carried out economies and ameliorations on a scale that the country had not seen since Necker's ministry. Deep cuts were made in the expenditures of the war department and the royal households; offices were abolished or consolidated, pensions were cut, the war department and the army were reorganized so as to be more efficient in administration. The postal service was reorganized to eliminate one of Calonne's "prodigalities." And finally, in late April 1788 the principal minister published his compte rendu to the nation that he had presented to the king in March. All these acts were in accord with the desires of the Notables and should have won for Loménie de Brienne the plaudits of the nation as they had for Necker during his first ministry.

A regulation of August 1787 brought about an extensive elimination of superfluous offices in the King's Household, which had always been their most notorious refuge. The holders of these offices enjoyed vast privileges and immunities. Most served only a part of the year in order to create more offices to perform the same function. The reform of August 9 cut the number of offices in the Royal Chamber by one half requiring the remaining officers to serve a semester rather than a quarter of the year! Twenty-eight offices of the Wardrobe were abolished. The Stable was shorn of both horses and officers, the equerries who remained having to serve a semester rather than a

227

quarter of a year. The king's "little stable" and "great stable," two separate departments that provided horses and transportation for the King's Household, were consolidated into a single department, depriving the duc de Coigny once again of his "little stable." (It had been abolished by Necker in 1780 and restored by his successor.) The military section of the King's Household which consisted of several units of troops that were more ornamental than useful was also reduced. There were important cuts in the section having custody of buildings and residences of the king. Five châteaux were either sold or demolished. The Queen's Household also was trimmed by nearly one million livres.[12] The king, queen, and even the two spendthrift brothers of the king, the comte de Provence and the comte d'Artois, all welcomed the economy cuts when they realized the seriousness of the financial situation. Certainly Calonne's modern-day apologists have a difficult time justifying his "tactic" of encouraging extravagant spending by the king, the queen, and the princes at the same time he concealed from them the imminent bankruptcy of the government until catastrophe was almost upon them.

In the war department the first measure of the Brienne ministry was taken in June. It abolished the alternate Treasurer-General which had first been eliminated by Necker and then restored by his successor, Joly de Fleury. It yielded a saving of at least a million livres per year.[13] But the most dramatic cuts in the war department were to come in the fall when a new regime was established for the army.

At the time Loménie de Brienne was appointed principal minister, in late August, the war minister, Ségur, and the naval minister, Castries, both resigned from the government, not wishing to subordinate themselves to the archbishop. Their disagreement with him was over foreign policy rather than his domestic policies. The summer of 1787 brought a serious threat of

228

war due to Prussia's armed intervention in the United Netherlands to support the stadtholder of the House of Orange, whose rule was challenged by the burgers of Holland. By a treaty in 1785 the French government had committed itself to defending the republican cause in that country as it had in North America. Prussian intervention was firmly supported by Great Britain, and for France to resist it meant war once again with the traditional enemy. Loménie de Brienne was utterly certain that France was in no condition to go to war at that time. And so the Dutch were informed that France could not enter into the quarrel between themselves, the prince of Orange, the king of Prussia, and the British. It was a bitter pill for the ardent militarists in France, among them, Lafayette, and was one more contributing factor to the extreme unpopularity which descended on the archbishop from the military sector.

The successor of Ségur at the war ministry was the brother of Loménie de Brienne, the comte de Brienne. As a member of the First Bureau of the Assembly of Notables he had been the most outspoken advocate of the need to set up a committee independent of the government to control the administration of the finances. As war minister he was able to second very effectively the stringent economizing called for by his brother the archbishop. Having little experience of military matters, the comte de Brienne was willing to heed the advice of a brilliant young colonel, the comte de Guibert, who was not only an outstanding tactician but an administrator as well.

In October the Council of War was created which was to exercise the kind of surveillance over the war department as the Council of Finance and Commerce was to do over the entire government. The preamble of the king's regulation explained the functions of the new War Council:

His Majesty, thinking that the publication of the reasons for expenditures in all branches of the administration is invariably a check upon abuses and a satisfaction for his people, intends to include the department of war, the most expensive of all, into the general system he has adopted.[14]

The regulation stipulated that at the end of each year, or at the latest, six months after the passing of a fiscal year, the War Council would publish a table of all expenditures of the department of war, extraordinary as well as ordinary. This was certainly leaning over backwards to implement the Neckerist principle of giving publicity to financial administration. It is understandable that the military would have serious objections to publishing the extraordinary expenditures of the war department, certainly in wartime. One reason Necker did not include the extraordinary expenditures in his Compte rendu of 1781 is that it would have been imprudent to have published so much information to the enemy.

The injunction given to the new War Council was not only to publicize the expenditures of the war department but to economize on expenditures. From the time of its inception in October 1787 until the following March the War Council carried out a number of reforms in the army. The military school in Paris was eliminated, being superfluous because of the military schools established in the provinces by Saint-Germain, a reforming minister of war in the early years of Necker's first ministry, and of whom the comte de Guibert was a disciple. The French army had become top-heavy with high-ranking marshals and generals. In a report written in October Guibert gave the figures: 1,261 lieutenant generals, marshals de camp or brigadiers were on active duty, more than in all the other armies of Europe combined.[15] In an order passed by the department of war in March 1788 there was a drastic reduction of those ranks: 359 brigadiers were eliminated and the number of lieutenant generals was to be fixed at 160 by replacing only half of those who retired. The reorganization of Guibert included the abolition of the supply system which had depended upon private companies to furnish troops with food and clothing. The army established its own supply organization. While the reforms of Guibert were harsh on the upper ranks, he did carry out one recommendation of the Notables, to raise the salaries of the troops and pay more attention to their well-being. The result of all these economies was to yield a saving to the government of eight or nine million livres a year.[16]

The determination of the archbishop to carry out his pledge to the Notables to reduce superfluous expenditures was also proved by his reform of the administration of pensions. Necker had pointed out in his Compte rendu of 1781 that the king of France probably paid more for pensions than all the other courts of Europe combined, and he indicated clearly that here was an opportunity for reduction of expenditures. The annual expenditure for pensions did not decline but rose during the administration of his successors, reaching a figure of 27 million in the compte rendu of Calonne in 1787.[17] The Assembly of Notables insisted that the figure certainly represented unmerited pensions and called for its reduction. In a decree of October 13, 1787, Loménie de Brienne announced his goal of reducing the pensions to 18 million livres per year. A withholding tax was clamped on all pensions, which was progressive, according to the size of the pension. Necker's pension reform of 1778 which had not been enforced by his successors was revived in this decree of October 13. New pensions would be awarded on the same date each year. The list of recipients of pensions would be published every year. When pensions became extinct only one-half the amount would be granted out to new recipients until the total amount of this item in the annual expenditure was reduced to 18 million livres.[18]

Reducing expenditures was only one side of the coin in achieving the goal of eliminating the deficit. The other side was the "amelioration" of administration to make it less costly. The Assembly of Notables had called attention to the great number of semi-private sub-treasuries (caisses) administered by venal officers who handled the king's money. These officers, called "treasurers," received excessive fees for their service, and made enormous fortunes, which did not prevent them however from going bankrupt due to over-expansion of their activities. Several spectacular bankruptcies had occurred during the 1780s, such as that of the treasurer-general of the Navy, Claude Baudard de Saint-James. It was customary for these officers to make use of the king's money entrusted to them in these speculative ventures, and so the government's interests suffered in these bankruptcies. The Assembly of Notables called for a return to Necker's policy of consolidation of these sub-treasuries and elimination of superfluous officers, whether treasurers or receivers. Loménie de Brienne carried out this policy much more thoroughly than Necker was able to do. By an edict of March 1788 all these semi-private treasuries were abolished and a single treasury, administered by five officials, handled all the expenditures of the royal government. One of the disadvantages of the system of a multiplicity of semi-independent and private caisses was the inability of the finance minister to keep track of all the government's funds. Now it was possible to keep account each day of all the expenditures.[19]

In fact, it was lack of accountability which was the chief defect in the administration of finances in the ancien régime. The French government, wrote Isaac Panchaud in 1781, was like an aristocratic landowner, careless about his accounts, unmindful of debts because he did not have to be concerned about them in feudal days. British finances, on the other hand, were administered with the care and exactness of a business enterprise.[20] It was that "bourgeois" spirit which Necker had brought to the administration of French finances in the years 1776-1781. The Assembly of Notables, despite their reputation in history of being "aristocratic reactionaries" were very insistent that the government could no longer be as nonchalant about its financial situation as it was in the days when the institution of absolutism was unchallenged. Loménie de Brienne heeded this demand in his final speech of May 25 to the Notables. He promised that an exact accounting of the government's finances would be submitted to the king and then published, hopefully before the end of the year. Perhaps because of the "ameliorations" that have just been described, that document was delayed until March 1788 when it was finally submitted to the king and published "by the king's orders" in late April.

It was the first statement of the government's finances to be published since Necker's Compte rendu of 1781. But it differed in several important respects from its predecessor. It was, as Frédéric Braesch has hailed it, "the first true budget in French history."[21] Completed shortly after the beginning of the year 1788 it was an attempted forecast of the financial operations of the year. That meant it included both ordinary and extraordinary accounts but tried to separate clearly the two types of accounts. For the benefit of its readers, the author of the compte rendu of March 1788 tried to explain in the preface exactly what sort of account it was and to differentiate it from other types of comptes rendus. But for those whose ideas on such matters had been formed by Necker the result must have been more confusing than enlightening. One type of account, it said, was "the estimation for a common year," and this left out reimbursements on debts and other extraordinary expenditures. The deficit in this type of account, it said, was the deficit or ordinary revenue to cover ordinary expenditures plus the interest cost on loans. But this account presented in 1788 was an account of all revenue and expenditures for that year. If such an account is rendered at the beginning of the year it is an "estimate" (aperçue) of the financial operations of that year. If it is rendered at the end of that year it is the "compte effective" of that year. The "preface" went on to say that the account of the "common year" was unreliable, subject to errors and miscalculations. But the second type, which was now being published, was much more reliable.

If the author had in mind Necker's Compte rendu of 1781, or even Calonne's of 1787 as examples of "the account for the common year" his attempted explanation was seriously in error. Neither Necker's account, nor Calonne's despite the confusing terminology in its title (the common year) were accounts of some mythical, average, unspecified year. The first was an account of

234

ordinary revenue and expenditures for the year 1781, as the latter was for 1787. And ordinary expenditures included amortization costs as well as interest costs on the debt. It is true that if the amortization cost was not known at the time of making up the compte rendu it may not be included in some obligations, but these would be very minor. But where the government had formally committed itself to return a part of the capital to the lender as well as the annual interest payment, that was part of the ordinary expenditure of the year. If the government were unable to meet such payments it would be an unmistakable signal that it was in financial distress. And the purpose of the compte rendu, as Necker tirelessly explained to the public, was to show the financial health or ill-health of the government.[22] The confusion about this matter and what the deficit actually was for 1788 was to have dramatic consequences for the ministry of Loménie de Brienne. The financial crisis that came in August of that year, only four months after the publication of his compte rendu took him completely unaware. His first secretary of finances, Achilles-Joseph Gojard, had failed to tell him that the treasury was about out of money! According to the compte rendu of 1788 the deficit of ordinary revenue to meet ordinary expenditures of that year would be only 54,839,540, quite an improvement it would seem of the deficit of 112 million livres in Calonne's compte rendu for the previous year. But Loménie's ordinary deficit did not include amortization costs that were due that year, amounting to 76,502,367 livres. That sum plus the other extraordinary expenditures came to a total of 105,897,952 livres. Thus, so-called extraordinary expenditures added to the ordinary deficit made a total deficit for the year of 160,737,492 livres. The "budget" of Brienne did not include (as most "statements of the financial situation" before his time that also included both ordinary and extraordinary accounts) the loans and other measures planned to enable the government to meet those expenditures. Thus, the compte rendu failed to achieve its primary purpose, to let the government, the ministers, and the king, know exactly where the finances stood, and how the finance minister proposed to meet the undeniable expenditures falling due in the course of the year.

The handling of his compte rendu certainly illustrates the ineptitude of the archbishop in administering the royal finances, whatever his other talents might have been. This may not have been so serious if he had been able to call on someone to take charge of the finances who was experienced and responsible. But he was unfortunate in that respect. Mercy-Argenteau complained that the assistants Loménie de Brienne was forced to rely upon in financial administration were "beneath mediocrity."[23] The successor to Laurent de Villedeuil as Controller General in the ministerial shake-up in August 1787 was a counsellor of state, Claude Guillaume Lambert, a hard-working and honest public servant but, according to Egret, "as lacking as his predecessor in that experience and that ease in the management of the finances that everyone--even his enemies--had recognized in the administration of a Necker."[24] Probably the most serious mistake the archbishop made was failing to dismiss from his post that first secretary (commis), Gojard, who had been at that post since 1781, and was such a contrast to Necker's first secretary, Bertrand Dufresne. The latter was as gifted and hard-working an assistant as the former was nonchalant, a perfect steward for a landed aristocrat of the old type!

Nevertheless it was some merit for the archbishop to have published the compte rendu for
1788, as were all the other sincere attempts he
had made to fulfill his pledges to the Assembly
of Notables. It was to be expected that all
those whose interests had suffered from his measures would react violently against the reform
minister. Necker had certainly experienced the
wrath of the courtiers, the ordonnateurs, and the
officials whose "charges" were abolished.
Loménie de Brienne had expected to encounter the
same opposition. But what surprised him was his
failure to evoke the same enthusiastic support
from the public that Necker had enjoyed. Instead
of inheriting the mantel of Necker it seemed that
the archbishop was cast in the robes of abbé Terray; and his colleague in the government, Lamoignon, was seen as the successor of Chancellor
Maupeou!

By the autumn of 1787 some of those who had
hoped the principal minister would be another
Necker were expressing their disappointment. In
November the Austrian ambassador wrote to the emperor that "nothing up to this moment justifies
the ideas that had been conceived of the talents
of the Archbishop of Toulouse."[25] A month earlier he had criticized Brienne for "spending too
much time over petty details without seeming to
grasp the large contours of affairs. He shows
little knowledge of finances; he tries to achieve
everything by a policy of conciliation. The major reason for his difficulty is the Parlements,
who have usurped an exaggerated influence."[26]
But at the same time Mercy-Argenteau remarked
that there was nothing serious about the financial situation. The country was prosperous,
there was plenty of money circulating in the
country seeking investment. The credit situation
of the government was good, and loans would be

237

successfully subscribed to. It was evident to the Austrian ambassador that the crisis was a political one, not economic or financial.

After the dismissal of the Notables in late May 1787 it was certainly understood by Loménie de Brienne that the crucial matter of his ministry would be his relationship with the Parlement of Paris. This ancient court, whose seat was the palace of justice of the island of the Cité in the heart of Paris, consisted of 144 members in 1787, divided into three sections: the Great Chamber, the Inquests, and the Requests. The first chamber was where the older and more experienced members sat. Those who were just beginning their career as magistrates sat in the Requests. It was the middle chamber, the Inquests, where were to be found those who were still youthful, but experienced enough to have great confidence in themselves. It was here that those inspired by revolutionary zeal were to be found: Duval d'Eprésmesnil and Adrien Duport, to name the most fiery orators among them. Whenever they wished, the peers of France had the right to sit in the general assemblies of the Parlement of Paris and take part in the deliberations and voting of the assembly. It then became the Court of Peers. There were seven princes of the blood who had this right in 1787, and were the same as those who served as presidents of the seven bureaux of the Assembly of Notables. In addition were seven prelates and twenty-seven lay peers who had a right to sit in the assemblies.[27]

Earlier in the century a great prelate-statesman, the Cardinal de Bernis, had remarked that the Parlements were strong only when they were supported by public opinion. When the public withheld its support from the Parlements in their disputes with ministerial and royal author-

ity, then they were not dangerous to that authority. In the "Revolution" of 1771 public opinion
strongly supported the Parlements and eventually
because of it the magistrates triumphed over the
ministry of Chancellor Maupeou and abbé Terray.
The same juncture of forces occurred in 1787 and
1788. The Parlement of Paris and the other
sovereign courts who resisted the ministry of
Loménie de Brienne and Lamoignon could rely upon
public opinion to support their resistance, the
result being the failure of the last reform ministry before the revolution of 1789.

Of course such an entity as "public opinion"
is difficult to locate with precision. Inevitably it was a heterogeneous thing, a coalition of different factions with differing and
even contradictory interests. The most direct
public support of the Parlement of Paris came
from those engaged in the administration of justice: lawyers, notaries, law clerks, and law
students, the "whole crowd that lives by chicanery," as baron de Besenval contemptuously described them. This was the source of popular
movements that could spring up on the Cité and in
the environs of the palace of justice, the Place
Dauphine being the usual location of their assembly. Another element of opposition was to be
found among the courtiers and officers whose interests had suffered by the reforms of the ministry. Even Besenval was among the courtiers who
were hostile to Brienne although not Lamoignon.
A member of the queen's intimate circle which included several who had benefited from the
largesse of Calonne, Besenval commiserated with
the duc de Coigny who had been deprived of his
"little stable" in the reform of the King's
Household. When the queen complained to Besenval
about Coigny's rude behavior to the king in
protesting the cut, Besenval replied, according

to his own testimony, "It is frightful to live in a country where one cannot be sure of possessing tomorrow what he owns today. That is seen only in Turkey."[28] The reforms of Loménie de Brienne cut into other social layers than had those of Necker. Much of the military class was alienated by the reforms of Guibert and the comte de Brienne, however just and reasonable they appear to the outside observer. Generals placed on early retirement and half-pay, or who did not receive an expected promotion because of the reduction of general officers, became hostile to the ministry. Even the common soldiers whose material condition was improved by the reforms were deeply offended by some Prussian forms of discipline introduced that were alien to French ways, such as punishment by running the gauntlet and being struck by the flat of the sword of the entire unit.

But it would be an incomplete description of the situation, to say the least, to attribute the opposition and hostility to the ministry of Loménie de Brienne and Lamoignon merely to selfish motives. On the contrary, the ardor of the youthful magistrates became potent among other classes of the population because it was seen as genuine patriotism, a cause transcending any particular interests, a loyalty to the welfare of the nation itself. The orations of the magistrates show the sources of inspiration of the movement in the summer of 1787 and in May of the following year. An important part of it came from across the Atlantic, where the new nation was holding its constitutional convention. The announced purpose of that convention as finally printed in the Constitution of the United States, "to grant to ourselves and our posterity a more perfect union," described the aspirations of the leaders of the national movement that got under way in the summer of 1787 in France. A new institutional framework that would give to the nation regular representation in the government and protect the people from "ministerial despotism," and which would include a Bill of Rights, such were the fundamental objectives of the movement.

The archbishop was not hostile to those aims, and he had done a great deal to give new representative institutions to France, namely the provincial assemblies; and his later acts show that he was not opposed to those local assemblies being capped by an assembly at the national level. But he knew it was necessary to bring those desirable institutions into being in a way that would not compromise the authority of the the king. A system of representative institutions should make the king stronger, not weaker. And that could only be done if those institutions were granted in a position of strength, rather than having to surrender them to the national movement out of weakness.

It was particularly the financial recovery and the elimination of the deficit that Loménie de Brienne saw as his primary task in bringing about that position of strength. His plan, it will be recalled, provided for some new tax revenue and some loans in addition to the "ameliorations" he intended to carry out. Early in July 1787 he was ready to submit to the Parlement of Paris for registration a Declaration on the stamp tax, which would raise the king's permanent revenue by 20 million livres. The preamble of the Declaration took note of all the acts of the government since the end of the Assembly of the Notables which had implemented the desires expressed by that assembly. About 20 million livres in ameliorations had already been achieved, and it appeared certain that the king would be able to make good on his promise to reduce regular expenditures by 40 million livres. The Notables themselves had recognized that additional tax revenue would be necessary to erase the deficit revealed during their Assembly, and that this should be done by a stamp tax and also by a new land tax. The Declaration stipulated that 20 million was the amount to be raised by the stamp tax, and if more should be collected that excess would be used to lighten other tax burdens. How long would this new tax last? If the comptes rendus of the king's finances that will be published henceforth every year show that it is possible to do without the stamp tax it will be repealed, and in any case not later than January 1, 1798.

In view of the past history of taxation in the monarchy, the magistrates to whom this proposal was submitted for registration, had good reason to be skeptical of the promises contained at the end of the declaration. But the archbishop hardly expected what issued from the Parlement of Paris: the magistrates asked that the financial statements and pièces justificatives for the ameliorations be submitted to them, so that they could verify the need of the government for additional tax revenue. The king, irritated by this unprecedented demand of the Parlement, refused, saying those accounts had already been submitted to the Assembly of Notables. The peers were now attending the assemblies of the Parlement, at least those interested in the dramatic events of July and August. On July 16 the Court of Peers voted upon and passed the fateful decree asserting that only the States-General could sanction a tax that had no specified quantity or duration, and it formally called upon the king to convene the States-General to resolve his financial problems. The decree was published and from that date the public seized upon the States-Gen-

242

eral as the goal of the national movement. The youthful magistrates of the Inquests managed to carry all before them. The more conservative peers and magistrates hesitated to oppose the popular demand out of timidity or perhaps thinking that opposition would be futile.

The call for the States-General was a great leap in the dark, as many recognized at the time. Some were inclined to think that the peers and magistrates who had favored the decree of July 16 did so only as a tactical measure, to force the government to withdraw its plans for increasing tax revenue, and force it to cope with the deficit by more thorough ameliorations of existing revenue and cutting even more severely the expenditures. It must have been some such suspision on the part of Loménie de Brienne that led him to his next move. Ignoring the decree calling for the States-General the archbishop presented to the Court of Peers his second tax measure, the edict on the land tax. This had been also approved at least in principle by the Assembly of Notables and the stipulation that it would be levied on all landowners without exemptions would make it much more popular than the stamp tax, and therefore he presumed the peers and magistrates would be more hesitant to withhold their approval. But the tactic did not work. When the land tax was presented to the general assembly of Parlement and Peers on July 30 the final vote of the assembly was to reject it and to call for the convening of the States-General for the approval of all new taxes of any kind.[29]

The dispute had now reached an impasse, and the next events followed a familiar pattern that had been seen in other serious disputes between the ministry and the sovereign courts in the preceding reign. The king convoked a *lit de justice* at Versailles on August 6, formally set aside the decree of the Court of Peers and Parlement of July 16, forced the registration of the two tax measures in his presence. Or rather it was the Keeper of the Seals, Lamoignon, who engineered this proceeding. It was the hottest day of the summer, the hall was packed full, the king dozed, and according to one eye-witness, snored.[30]

When they returned to Paris the Parlement and Court of Peers declared in a formal decree that the fiscal laws passed by forced registration in a _lit_ _de_ _justice_ were illegal. The decree was published and distributed throughout the jurisdiction of the Parlement of Paris. This was clearly an act of rebellion and the government's next move was predictable. On the night of August 15 sealed letters (_lettres_ _de_ _cachet_) were delivered to all the magistrates requiring them to leave Paris and take up quarters in the city of Troyes, in the old palace of the counts of Champagne.

It now remained to be seen what the response of the public would be to this act of force. Riots against the government erupted in Paris, and were not confined to the _Cité_. Troops and police were called in to restore order. The critical matter was to see if the other sovereign courts would be as resolute as the Parlement of Paris. The comte de Provence took the two tax measures to the Paris Chamber of Accounts for registration, and the comte d'Artois was charged with the same mission to the Court of _Aides_. The latter was badly treated by a crowd outside the Court, and the Court itself rejected the tax edicts. _Monsieur_ was treated more respectfully at the Chamber of Accounts, since he was known to have some sympathy for the national movement, but that court rejected the tax measures no less firmly

244

than the Court of <u>Aides</u>. At Troyes, the Parlement of Paris sent out directives to all subordinate courts in its jurisdiction to refuse to enforce the tax edicts. Most did so, and sent deputations to Troyes expressing their adherence to the resistance to the ministry.

It was evident to Loménie de Brienne that in the competition for public support the peers and magistrates had clearly won. What made the situation extremely critical for the government was the precipitate decline of government notes on the <u>bourse</u>. This threatened the credit posture of the government and the flow of anticipations from the <u>faiseurs</u> <u>de</u> <u>service</u>, exactly the financial crisis that came a year later. The archbishop was ready to negotiate a truce if possible. It was apparent that the magistrates at Troyes would not be averse to an accommodation with the ministry. Removed from Paris they were less subject to the pressure of the popular elements, and the more prudent and conservative magistrates recovered some influence. The archbishop had never been strongly attached to the two fiscal measures, either the land tax or the stamp tax. After all, both had been original measures of Calonne, even though somewhat modified by the Assembly of Notables. Like all the Notables, Brienne did not like increased taxation and would have preferred to erase the deficit by ameliorations and economy alone. After having successfully achieved the 20 million amelioration he mentioned in his stamp tax declaration, Brienne began to think that perhaps in the long run, say in a period of five years, the deficit could be largely erased by amelioration; and if the <u>vingtièmes</u> were continued but levied on all lands without any exemptions permitted, the total yield would easily reach the 84 million livres that had been the goal of the land tax.

It was on this basis that a treaty was reached between Brienne and the magistrates at Troyes. He would withdraw both tax measures. The vingtième taxes would be continued, but levied on all lands without exemptions or abonnements. In the space of five years, from 1787 to 1792, ameliorations in revenue and cuts in expenditures would, together with the increase in revenue from the vingtièmes, erase the deficit. It was necessary for the magistrates to agree on the extension of the second vingtième for another two years, since it was due to expire in 1790. After this second plan for erasing the deficit had succeeded in its purpose in 1792 it would be possible for the king to convene the States-General without any danger to his authority.

Such was the plan submitted to the magistrates on September 19, and which ended the dispute. The Parlement returned to Paris. But another important aspect of the second plan for dealing with the deficit was that loans would be necessary to tide the government over the period necessary before ameliorations could be realized in the annual compte rendu. Loménie de Brienne cautiously intended to ask for a loan only for the year 1788, thinking that 120 million livres in loans would be necessary, and make the decision for the other years until 1792 at the time the compte rendu was drawn up for each year. It was none other than Duval d'Eprésmesnil who persuaded Loménie de Brienne to ask the Parlement to approve a loan all in one sum that would provide for the needs of the entire five years, 1787-1792. This was estimated to be 420 million livres.

It was the Keeper of the Seals who arranged the plans for a meeting of the ministry and the Court of Peers when the Parlement returned from

its fall vacation on November 19, 1787. He would
lay before the assembly of the three chambers and
the peers the government's new plan for erasing
the deficit. Hoping to avoid the strained and
bitter atmosphere of a lit de justice. Lamoignon
called this meeting a "royal session." The king
would be present at the meeting but would not occupy that forbidding chair (the lit). All those
who participated in the assembly would be allowed
to speak freely about the government's proposal,
so certain were the ministers that these proposals were reasonable and moderate and that there
could be no serious opposition to them. The orators assumed the liberty of even addressing the
king during the session, whether that was quite
intended by the ministers or not. Unfortunately
some logical minds could not be satisfied with
that shadowy area between a lit de justice and a
freely deliberating assembly. Jean-Louis
Séguier, one of the most adamant defenders of the
prerogatives of the sovereign courts, asked Lamoignon, after the Keeper of the Seals had presented the government proposals, if this was a
freely deliberating assembly of the Parlement, in
which the members would vote on the proposals, or
if it were a lit de justice in which the proposals would be registered by the sole authority of
the king. Lamoignon replied, as he was bound to,
that while the king was a member of the Court of
Peers and the Parlement, he was not just another
judge. Of course there could not be a vote taken
on the proposals in his presence. It was most
unfortunate that the issue had to be raised in
the way it was, for, according to most memoir
writers who recorded the royal session of November 19, a majority of the assembly would probably
have approved the government's proposals in a
vote. it was one of those times when logic was
the enemy of fruitful compromise.

During the memorable session of November 19 the king had no trouble keeping awake. He listened attentively to lengthy orations, some of which were directed to him in an attempt to cajole him into promising the convening of the States-General before 1792. On two occasions it appeared that he was almost moved to speak up, but refrained, since he had given his promise to the ministers the evening before not to make any concessions not agreed upon at that council meeting. As could have been expected, some members pressed their liberty too far and failed to show the customary respect for the king's presence. Two of these offenders belonged to the circle of the duc d'Orleans. The duke had been the only prince of the blood that refused to stand by the government in the parliamentary crisis. The motives were personal rather than political, being due to a keen resentment at the way he had been treated by the king and especially the queen. It was the circle of ambitious intriguers around the duke at the Palais Royal who were the real leaders of the "Orleanist faction." The duke himself was without much personal force. As president of the Third Bureau of the Assembly of Notables, he could not get around to perform his function before five o'clock in the afternoon, according to Bachaumont. As so many of the Bourbon princes, Orleans was an ineffective speaker. At the end of the royal session of November 19 the king personally ordered the registration of the government's proposals. The duke, guided by his chancellor, the marquis du Crest, got up and addressed the assembly, stammering that the king's action was illegal. Surprised by this intervention the king muttered, "Well, I don't care." Then, remembering who he was, he added: "Of course it's legal since I ordered it!" Thus ended the royal session.

On the day following the session two dramatic events took place. First the two irreverent counsellors of the Parlement received _lettres de cachet_ and were escorted to prison. The duc d'Orleans also received such a letter ordering him to leave Paris and to reside until further notice at his château in eastern France. The second event was the remonstrance passed by the Parlement of Paris against the acts of the royal session of November 19. But the remonstrance was not taken immediately to the king. The magistrates evidently were somewhat intimidated by the action taken against the duke and the two counsellors, and were not anxious to return to Troyes. Instead the remonstrance was pigeonholed for the moment awaiting an appropriate time. In the meantime the magistrates focused on the issue of the king's use of _lettres de cachet_, which they asserted in repeated remonstrances were illegal

The government proceeded to carry out the fiscal measures that were registered in the royal session. An edict providing for a loan of 120 million livres in life rentes was promulgated in late November. It was easily subscribed to, proving the Austrian ambassador correct in his analysis of the credit situation of the government. The opposition to the magistrates and peers had not, seemingly, had an adverse effect on the ability of the royal government to borrow.

If the new financial plan of the archbishop were to succeed it was necessary to enforce the agreement made with the Parlement on September 19, namely that the two _vingtièmes_ would be levied in strict proportion on the income of all lands without exception. But in order to enforce that agreement the government was faced with the old difficulties of determining what the landed income was. In the absence of a _cadastre_ or general land survey the government had to rely upon the private declarations of the landowners. And that was only one means of escaping the full burden of the vingtième, which was a proportional tax rather than one that was partitioned. The reason Brienne had wanted to substitute the land tax for the vingtièmes was because the former would have been a partitioned tax. That meant it would have been assessed "contradictorily"; since each parish would receive its quota of the tax, each land owner would have a direct interest in seeing that his neighbor did not escape from paying his fair share. But in a proportional tax, such as the vingtième, there was no incentive to see what one's neighbors paid, or to make certain that the burden was shared equally. Proprietors sought to escape the 9 percent proportion of the vingtièmes (which included the 20 percent surtax on the first vingtième) and get by with a lesser percentage.

In the fall of 1787 as the new provincial administrations were being established Loménie de Brienne found a way to transform the vingtième tax from a proportional to a repartitional tax. This was to make an agreement, an abonnement, with each of the provincial assemblies. The sum agreed upon would be higher than the province had paid in the past, in order to make up for the abolition of all exemptions and immunities, and all the other ways in which the large landed proprietors had escaped the full rate of 9 percent of their landed income. This strategy supposed that the provincial assemblies would abide by the treaty made between Loménie de Brienne and the Parlement of Paris in September 1787, namely that the two unpopular fiscal edicts would be withdrawn and the vingtièmes restored but with the understanding that they would be levied on all lands without exception. Five of the provincial assemblies did come to an agreement with the government on a sum to be levied on their province which was substantially higher than they had been paying. But four of the new assemblies failed to come to an agreement.[31]   In the case of the new assembly at Riom (for the province of the Auvergne) it was evident that the resistance was due to the influence of Lafayette.   Now the government ministry felt itself justified in subjecting the landowners in the provinces to the assessment of the controllers of the vingtième.   This was the system inaugurated by abbé Terray in the period 1771-1774.   Agents of the government simply investigated the landholdings of the wealthy proprietors and arbitrarily assessed the vingtième tax.   In 1774 when the Parlements were restored to their former position before the "revolution" they immediately took up the cause of the "persecuted" landowners.   The Parlement of Paris and the government were clearly headed for a confrontation on the issue, when Necker's reform of the method of assessment resolved the issue to the satisfaction of the landed proprietors, if not to the Parlement of Paris.   The resistance in the Parlement in 1778 to Necker's reform of the vingtième was led by a youthful member of the Inquests, Duval d'Eprésmesnil, who at that time was unable to prevail against the more conservative magistrates of the Grand Chamber.   Now, in April 1788, ten years later, the same magistrate took up the cause where he had left it and this time succeeded in taking the Parlement with him.[32]   On the 19th of April 1788, the Parlement ruled that the Court of Peers had not agreed the previous September that the government could increase the amount of revenue to be raised by the restoration of the two vingtièmes. Therefore, the attempts to raise the assessments were illegal.[33]

By the time this decree was promulgated by the Parlement of Paris, its magistrates were well aware of the impending blow that the government was preparing against them, even if they did not know the precise details.   But it was clear that Lamoignon and Loménie de Brienne were preparing another "revolution" like that of Maupeou and Terray in 1771.   Believing that

251

the magistrates had public opinion on their side in 1788 as they had also in the 1770s, Duval d'Eprésmesnil persuaded the members of the Parlement to take a formal oath that none of them would partici- pate in any new type of judicial institution that the government might attempt to set up. This was done af- ter passing a decree on May 3 in which the magistrates set forth their idea of the true constitution of the monarchy. Subsidies to the royal government can only be granted by the States-General periodically con- vened; the sovereign courts have a right to verify all edicts of the royal council in order to make certain they do not violate existing rights before they regis- ter them. The Parlement insisted upon the rights of provinces annexed to the kingdom whose privileges and immunities were granted by the treaty of annexation. Finally, the Parlement insisted upon the rights of all citizens to be judged by their "natural judges" rather than by the tribunals of the administrative monarchy. The most eloquent oration was delivered by Duval d'Eprésmesnil, who seemed to echo the American Decla- ration of Independence and the Bill of Rights attached to the U.S. Constitution.[34]

The ministry could only look upon the decrees of April 29 and May 3 as subversive and intolerable, and decided to arrest the two authors of the decrees, Du- val d'Eprésmesnil and Goislard de Montsabert. Aware that some such measure had been decided, the Parlement of Paris met in an evening session on May 5 and, sum- moning as many peers as it could persuade to attend the proceedings, sent a deputation to see the king at Versailles. The king refused to see them (they had not observed the correct procedure of gaining an audi- ence) and instead ordered the commandant of the French Guards at Paris to surround the Palace of Justice with his troops and arrest the two magistrates. It was a dramatic moment in the history of the "pre-revolu- tion." Most magistrates and peers were well-read in English history and certainly must have been aware of the similar incident in the confrontation between Charles I and Parliament. As the commandant entered the Grand Chamber where the magistrates, together with about fourteen peers, had assembled, he demanded that d'Eprésmesnil and Montsabert be pointed out to him, since he did not know them. The magistrates firmly refused to do so, asserting that they "were all Eprésmesnils and Montsaberts." The stand-off continued throughout the next day until finally, the two magistrates, to avoid further embarrassment, voluntarily surrendered themselves and were taken to prisons far away from Paris.[35]

On May 8 the king summoned the entire Court of Peers to meet at Versailles in a lit de justice. The Keeper of the Seals addressed the assembly and laid before them five edicts to register that came to be known as "the edicts of May." It was the anticipated "revolution," in some ways more drastic than that of 1771, but in other respects much more lenient to the magistrates. Rather than being abolished the Parlement of Paris simply was shorn of all traditional political functions. The power of registering edicts would be entrusted to a new court to be called the Plenary Court. All acts of the royal government that applied throughout the kingdom would be registered by the Plenary Court, so that all the other parlements and sovereign courts were similarly divested of their function of registration of such acts, and along with it, the function of judicial review of these acts. The Parlements would still retain the function of registration of royal acts that pertained only to their jurisdictions. But these would certainly be of minor importance compared to those registered by the Plenary Court. It was a momentous revolution, because henceforth the sovereign courts would have no legal powers to impede acts of the royal government either by reiterative remonstrances or by judicial strikes. The Edicts of May took away all claims of the parlements to act as the defenders of the Nation.

253

The Plenary Court was intended to inherit whatever validity there might be in those pretensions of
the magistrates.   All members were appointed by the
king.   All magistrates of the Paris Grand Chamber were
to be appointed, and all presidents and one counsellor
from each regional parlement, two members each from
the Paris Court of _Aides_ and Chamber of Accounts.
Pointedly excluded were the youthful members of the
Paris Chamber of Inquests.   In addition to the magistrates the Plenary Court would be composed of all
princes of the blood, peers of the kingdom, three
archbishops, two bishops, two marshals of the army,
two military governors, and two lieutenant generals.[36]
It was in fact very similar to the Assembly of Notables, although there were no members of the Third Estate, and the Plenary Court had far more magistrates.
The Plenary Court was to have the right of remonstrance which was taken away from the former sovereign
courts.

In addition to the edict creating the Plenary
Court were other edicts carrying out a thorough reform
of the judicial system in the kingdom.   The parlements
were shorn of jurisdiction in civil cases below 20,000
livres.   For criminal cases they were restricted to
those involving privileged persons of the first and
second estates.   Most of the legal business would now
be done by two new tiers of courts, those of the first
instance and those of the last resort; the former
called "presidial courts" and the latter were the
"Grand Bailiwick courts."   The presidial courts were
to assume much of the jurisdiction hitherto exercised
by the private seigneurial courts of the nobles possessing fiefs.   The latter were left with only police
functions.   With such shorn jurisdictions there was of
course a great reduction of magistrates in the former
"sovereign courts," and an important elimination of
special courts attached to different parts of the administration, such as finances, forests, and royal domain.

The judicial reforms of Lamoignon contained in the May edicts also revamped the procedures to be used in criminal law, continuing and expanding some of the reforms carried out in Necker's first ministry. Torture and mistreatment of suspects was completely abolished. Those who had suffered by miscarriage of justice were to be compensated by the government. Costly procedures and delays in the judicial process were abolished. The ordinary litigant now had easier access to the courts for redress than under the old system. On the whole the judicial reforms were in the spirit of the other reforms of the Brienne-Lamoignon ministry, as laudable and desirable from the modern-day viewpoint as were the reforms in the military establishment by Brienne and Guibert.

Even though the wrath of the magistrates was to be expected it might seem to the historian that an enlightened public ought to have supported the reforms of the ministry. Yet in the four months following the May edicts public opinion roundly rejected the ministry. "If the revolution means a concerted defiance of government," writes R. R. Palmer, "the French Revolution began in the summer of 1788."[37] Was this an "aristocratic revolution," supported only by those whose interests were harmed or threatened by reforms of the ministry? This has become a strongly entrenched view in the twentieth century. But it seems undeniable that the opposition to the ministry extended much further. What the forces were that brought about the fall of the Brienne-Lamoignon ministry is an important subject for the history of the French Revolution. It is important also for the evaluation of Necker's role in the Revolution. For it was his judgment of the question raised that was to determine the policy that led to the "great leap in the dark" of the convening of the States-General.

NOTES, CHAPTER SEVEN

[1]Marmontel, Mémoires, III, 126-127.

[2]Mme de Staël, Considérations sur la Révolution française, 128. She quoted her father as saying: "Now it is too late" (trop tard). But this does not seem to have been Necker's feeling at the time, which was not so discouraged. The vicomte d'Haussonville wrote "very late" (bien tard) which would seem to be a more exact description of Necker's view of the situation. Othenin d'Haussonville, "Le Salon de Madame Necker," Revue des Deux Mondes (1881), Vol. 42, 846.

[3]Collection des édits, BN F. 23631 (31bis).

[4]Marmontel was of this belief. See his Mémoires, III, 154.

[5]Collection des édits, BN F. 23631 (35)

[6]Isambert, Recueil général des anciennes lois françaises, XXVIII, 361-364.

[7]Mémoires de l'abbé Morellet, I, 316.

[8]Isambert, Recueil général, XXVIII, 374.

[9]Ibid., 364.

[10]Pierre Renouvin, Les Assemblées Provinciales de 1787 (Paris, 1921), 135-137.

[11]Isambert, Recueil général, XXVIII, 354-357.

[12]Ibid., 416-419.

[13]Jean Egret, La Pré-révolution française, 105, n. 4.

[14]Isambert, _Recueil général_, XXVIII, 455. A similar regulation establishing a Council for the Navy was promulgated on March 19, 1788, containing identical language as quoted above. _Ibid._, 520.

[15]Egret, _La Pré-révolution française_, 84.

[16]_Ibid._, 91.

[17]Necker had given the figure as 28 million livres in his _Compte rendu_ of 1781, but afterwards it was found that only 24.8 million had been spent for 1781. "Nouveaux éclaircissements," in _Oeuvres complètes_, II, 425.

[18]Isambert, _Recueil général_, XXIX, 442-448.

[19]J. F. Bosher, "The Founding of the Modern Treasury," in _French Finances_ (Ch. 11), 197-214.

[20]Benjamin (Isaac) Panchaud, _Réflections sur l'Etat actuel du Crédit public de l'Angleterre et de la France_ (London, 1781), 39.

[21]Frédéric Braesch, _Finance et Monnaies révolutionnaires_ (Nancy, 1934), II, 58-59.

[22]There is evidence that the writer of the "Introduction" to the _compte rendu_ of 1788 was influenced by the ideas of Calonne and his "Reply to the Writing of M. Necker" which was published in January 1788. Calonne maintained steadfastly that Necker had not included amortization of debt in his account, despite the obvious evidence that 17 milllion livres was

paid out for that purpose and a detailed account was given in the published Compte rendu. This is only one indication of this source of influence on the writer of the "Introduction." There are several others. It is possible that the author was Gojard.

23Corréspondance secrete, II, 138.

24La Pré-révolution, 66.

25Corréspondance secrète, II, 138.

26Ibid., 131.

27Egret, La Pré-révolution française, 149.

28Pierre-Victor Besenval, Mémoires, II, 256. The author of a recent work on Breteuil remarks that "the outrageousness of the statement of Besenval is all the more evident when one knows that baron de Breteuil wrote to the First Equerry that in compensation for this loss he would be created a peer of France with an annual pension of 50,000 livres, without counting 20,000 livres the king gave him annually for an old brevet d'assurance that had not been fully reimbursed and that did not include diverse other favors." René-Marie Rampelberg, Le Ministre de la Maison du Roi, 1783-1788, Baron de Breteuil (Paris, 1975), 75.

29Egret, La Pré-révolution française, 67.

30Ibid., 170.

31Egret, La Pré-révolution française, 198-199.

[32]See my Necker, *Reform Statesman of the Ancien Régime*, 180.

[33]Egret, *La Pré-révolution française*. 199.

[34]*Archives parlementaires de 1787 à 1860*, 1er series (Paris, 1787-1799), I, 284-288.

[35]Egret, *La Pré-révolution française*, 251-254.

[36]*Ibid*., 248.

[37]R. R. Palmer, *The Age of the Democratic Revolution* (Princeton, 1959), I, 458.

CHAPTER 8

THE REJECTION OF THE BRIENNE-LAMOIGNON MINISTRY

AND THE RETURN OF NECKER

The most erudite authority in our time of the
"aristocratic revolution" was the late Jean Egret who
published many special studies on the period, the most
comprehensive being The French Pre-Revolution published first in 1962.[1] From the time of the May
edicts in 1788 until the fall of the Brienne-Lamoignon
ministry some four months later, Egret tends to view
the uprising against the edicts as much less dangerous
and widespread than has usually been supposed. There
were two principal sources of opposition, but they
were at opposite poles of the political spectrum. It
was a case of the extremes joining to defeat the center, in this case the Brienne-Lamoignon ministry which
was trying to bring about moderate reform without convulsions. On one side were the magistrates who were
extremely hostile to the May edicts as might be expected, and also the class of people dependent upon
the sovereign courts, the basoche, consisting of lawyers, notaries, recorders, and bailiffs who did the
more menial tasks of the courts. This class rejected
the May edicts bitterly, in some cases stirring up
popular violence in the provinces. But such incidents
were by no means general. They were limited primarily
to Pau, Brittany, and Dauphiné, and in the latter province chiefly at Grenoble. There was very little activity in Paris, not even on the cité around the
palace of justice. In the provinces unrest was notable only in the cities where the parlements were located.[2]

The protests of the magistrates were based upon
strictly reactionary grounds. They defended all the
old privileges: local rights, provincial rights, the

261

diversity of customary law, in fact the exact opposite of what their temporary allies, the nationalists, were calling for. The magistrates were joined by the Church which met in convocation in June 1788. This assembly came under the influence of conservatives rather that the type of liberal prelates who had played such an inportant role in the Assembly of Notables in 1787. The Church convocation of 1788 denied that the government could impose a general tax on church lands, insisted on the complete autonomy of the church and its right to determine the "free gift" that it would grant to the government. The convocation went further than simply insisting upon its own ancient privileges and immunities; it denounced the May edicts, gave its support to the embattled magistrates and called upon the government to convene the States-General. The Church punctuated its stand by allowing to the government a "free gift" of 1.8 million livres instead of the 8 million asked for by Loménie de Brienne.[3]

On the opposite side of the political spectrum we find the ardent nationalists also opposing the May edicts. Here there is some question whether these radicals, those who became the "patriots" of 1789, actually supported the rebellious magistrates in their opposition to the Brienne-Lamoignon ministry, or whether they simply stood aside from the "aristocratic revolution," having no interest in it. Certainly some of the influential writers and politicians of this group, Mirabeau and Condorcet, for example, saw clearly that they had no real community of interest with the parliamentarians.[4] Others who joined in the campaign of denunciation of the ministry sought a genuine alliance with the magistrates for the purpose of overthrowing the Brienne-Lamoignon ministry and with it the entire policy of reform. Their goal was to bring about the States-General in order to carry out the national revolution. As sometimes happens in political turmoil, the radicals saw their most dangerous opponents to be the moderate reformers rather than the conservatives and the reactionaries of the political right wing.[5] Prominent among the future "patriots" who sought an alliance with the magistrates were Antoine-Pierre Barnave, Guy-Jean Target, Nicholas Bergasse, and Lafayette. But the right wing promoters of the "aristocratic revolution" also proclaimed their goal to be the convening of the States-General. In this perspective the deadlock that immobilized the States-General in May-June 1789 was almost preordained. It was a perfectly logical and understandable outcome of the political situation that had brought the States-General into existence.

The Brienne-Lamoignon ministry had committed itself to the convening of the States-General at some unspecified time, but until August 8, 1788 it had avoided stipulating a certain date. As we have seen, Loménie de Brienne wished to postpone the meeting of the estates until 1792 when his five-year plan for financial rehabilitation of the government should have strengthened the hand of the monarchy. In fact the archbishop dreaded the States-General, realizing how uncertain the consequences of such a meeting might be. He would have preferred to establish the provincial assemblies first throughout the kingdom, and have a national assembly of deputies elected by the provincial assemblies. The Plenary Court created by the May Edicts, he thought, could serve as an upper house of a bicameral legislature.[6]

Furthermore, the archbishop was genuinely puzzled as to what the States-General would be nearly two centuries after the last meeting of that body in 1614. That institution belonged to an entirely different age. He was a well-read prelate in French history, and could not be satisfied with the convictions of conservative magistrates who saw no reason why the medieval assembly of estates could not be reborn in the late eighteenth century exactly as it had been in the late middle ages. It was genuine perplexity about this matter, possibly combined, as Egret suggests, with a sly intention of postponing the dreaded convocation and gaining time to implement the provincial assemblies, that led to the royal decree of July 5, 1788.[7] In this act the king referred to the widespread demand for the convening of the States-General but pointed out the difficulty of fitting that institution into a kingdom that had changed so greatly in the space of 175 years. Therefore the king invited the provincial assemblies and other corporations and even individual citizens to submit to him their ideas on how the States-General should be organized.

If this was a delaying tactic, the archbishop's scheme was rudely upset by a financial crisis that caught him unaware at the beginning of August. Being inexperienced as he was in financial administration, he had set up an advisory committee to keep him informed on the state of the royal finances at the time the compte rendu of March was presented to the king. The principal person relied upon on that committee was the First Secretary of the Contrôle-général, Achille-Joseph Gojard. About the beginning of August Gojard told the archbishop, according to the latter's own account in his brief memoirs, that the treasury was empty. Why he had waited so long to inform him of the desperate situation was inexplicable, and Loménie de Brienne suspected a treasonous relationship of the advisory committee with his enemies seeking to force him out of office.[8]

The reason for the financial crisis, according to the memoirs of Loménie de Brienne, was the loss in confidence of investors and bankers in the financial soundness of the government. The drop in value of government securities on the bourse meant that financiers who normally granted short-term credit in the form of anticipations of future tax revenue, were unable to come forth with more money from such short-term loans. The receivers-general and the farmers-general who were the main source of anticipations were dependent upon the government's credit in order to raise that capital in the money markets. In an attempt to raise the government's credit on the bourse and restore the flow of anticipations, Loménie de Brienne promulgated a royal decree on August 8 fixing the date for the States-General at May 1, 1789.

It was a rear-guard action. The government's credit did not improve and it became increasingly apparent that it would not as long as the detested ministers, Loménie de Brienne and Lamoignon, remained at their posts. By the middle of August the government was in desperate straits, the archbishop even appropriating funds the king had ordinarily earmarked for relief of the indigent and those ruined by the hailstorms in July.[9] A loan was out of the question. On August 16 the government passed a decree-in-council suspending amortization payments on certain exigible debts, amounting to 144 million livres per year. In addition, and what created the greatest sensation, was the announcement that the government would temporarily make some of its payments in the form of notes bearing five percent interest. It is usually estimated that about three-fifths of the regular payments of the royal treasury were to be made by these notes, which in fact were paper money. The preamble of the decree attempted to mitigate the impact on public opinion by stating that the financial emergency was only temporary, until the end of the year, and that the forthcoming national assembly of estates, promised for May 1, 1789, would be a guarantee of the financial solvency of the government.[10]

Inevitably all thoughts turned to the one person who could be relied upon to rescue the government in financial distress. Even those who had been resolutely hostile to the Genevan banker now saw him as the only possibility of preventing the royal government from going bankrupt. The comte d'Artois and his circle of friends who had no attachment to the archbishop because of his financial austerity, now joined forces with others to urge the king to dismiss Brienne and appoint Necker in his place.

The decisive person who brought this about was the queen. Unlike Artois, she was a firm supporter of the archbishop. It had been largely her influence that brought him to the ministry in May 1787. She had been able to put some distance between herself and the former circle of friends (who were the same people as Artois' friends) due to the exhortations of the Austrian ambassador and her brother, the Emperor Joseph. The court at Vienna had been alarmed for some time at the extreme disfavor into which the queen had fallen in the esteem of the nation, and the court seemed to think it was due to the grasping and greedy people who had made up her circle. She had strongly supported the economy slashes of the archbishop, which did not spare her own household.

Both the king and the queen remained firmly attached to the archbishop personally as well as because of their approval of his policy. They could not understand the reasons for the extreme unpopularity into which he had fallen and could only resent what they considered the public's rank injustice. The only criticism the queen had about the archbishop was his apparent inability to handle the royal finances. Therefore she proposed to the archbishop some time after August 16 that he admit Necker into the government to replace the Controller General, Lambert. She found Loménie de Brienne receptive to the suggestion. Then the queen asked the Austrian ambassador, Mercy-Argenteau, to approach Necker on the matter.

On August 20 Mercy-Argenteau had a three-hour conversation with Necker in an attempt to persuade him to accept the finance post under the principal minis-

ter. Necker said that he could not serve in the same
ministry of which the archbishop was a part. By joining a government which had unfortunately fallen so low
in public esteem he would compromise his own standing
with the public without achieving any benefit to the
king. This placed the Austrian ambassador in an awkward position because the queen did not want Necker to
enter the government unless he would be subordinate to
a principal minister. "He needs a brake," the queen
told Mercy-Argenteau, "and the king is incapable of
performing that role unassisted." She thought of
someone else becoming the prime minister, suggesting
the duc de Châtelet. But it was very difficult for
the royal couple to dismiss abruptly the archbishop,
who after all, was a man of honor and integrity. The
Austrian ambassador strenuously sought to persuade
Necker to change his mind, but the Genevan was
adamant. Finally Mercy-Argenteau told the queen that
Loménie de Brienne should be persuaded to resign on
his own initiative. The bitter pill could be sweet-
ened by granting him exceptional favors to show the
royal couple's esteem for him, and their regret at his
departure. In a letter to the emperor the ambassador
said it was the only solution. "The incompetence or
the misfortune of the principal minister was on the
point of ruining the monarchy for a long time, in-as-
much as bankruptcy would have been inevitable had he
remained in the government." Furthermore he pointed
out the longer Loménie de Brienne remained in powere
the queen's reputation would continue to decline, for
she was known to be his strongest support.[11]

Finally on August 24 the queen yielded to the
persuasion of Mercy-Argenteau and admitted that
Loménie de Brienne would have to go. She asked the
ambassador to perform the unpleasant task of intimating to the principal minister that his resignation
would be accepted. It was a bitter moment for Loménie
de Brienne for he thought he had deserved better from
the nation. His acceptance of a large bonus from the

king may have eased the blow somewhat, but certainly did nothing to improve his standing with the public, given the fact that the royal treasury was about out of money. He was also promised the post of co-adjutator of his archbishopric for his nephew, the admission of a niece to the court of the queen, and for himself the cardinal's hat which was bestowed upon him by the Pope at the end of the year.

The queen always looked upon Necker as the minister who was forced upon her by public opinion. This was to cloud the relationship between the two throughout this second ministry, in contrast to the strong support she had given him in his first ministry. When Mme. de Staël was admitted to the queen's circle a few days after her father's appointment she experienced the queen's aloofness toward herself and the pronounced favor shown to the niece of the archbishop.[12]

On Sunday August 24 during the negotiations between Necker and Mercy-Argenteau the king sent a message to the ambassador authorizing him to assure Necker that he would have complete control of the finances and could appoint his own subordinates, and that he would have entrance to the council, the coveted ministerial rank that had been denied him during his first ministry. Also the king gave his firm assurance that the States-General would be convened on the date promised, and that he would work with the estates to find the means for filling the deficit.

On the day of the archbishop's resignation, August 25, the queen wrote to Mercy-Argenteau: "Forgive me such weakness, but I tremble that it is myself who has brought him (Necker) back. My fate is to bear misfortune, and if diabolical machinations cause my decision to again miscarry, or if he (Necker) erodes the authority of the king I will be detested all the more."[13] It was on the following day, Tuesday morning August 26 that Necker had his first audience with the queen. During the interview the king came to her apartment. "Sire, here is your best friend," she said, presenting Necker.[14] Necker recorded that the king was somewhat embarrassed because of the events of the preceding year, but that "I spoke to him only of my devotion and respect, and that from this moment I would resume my duties for the king as I had performed them at another time."[15] Necker was given his former title, Director General of Finances, for he told the royal couple that he did not wish the title or the position of principal minister. As during his first ministry he served without any monetary compensation.

It was with a heavy heart that Necker took up the burdens of his second ministry. Everyone had such high expectations of him, yet he was not certain that he would have the means to cope with the crisis facing the monarchy. He could only envy his daughter, who was transported with joy at the news of his appointment. According to Madame de Staël he told her: "It is the daughter of a minister who has the pleasure, for she basks in the reflection of the power of her father. But for himself power, especially at the present moment, is a terrible responsibility."[16]

During the months preceding his appointment Necker had been deeply engrossed in writing his answer to the new assault on the integrity of his first ministry and his Compte rendu . The "Reply of M. de Calonne to the Writing of M. Necker published in the month of April 1787" was a lengthy and detailed defense of Calonne's allegations before the Assembly of Notables regarding the Compte rendu of 1781.[17] The reply of Necker, "Further Clarifications on the Compte rendu," was in the press at the time of his conversations with Mercy-Argenteau just prior to his appointment.[18] In fact he gave to the ambassador a copy of the first eleven sheets to come off the press.

It was with a gloomy cast of mind that Necker had taken up this task of defending once again his administration and his Compte rendu . For Calonne's book was written in that facile and persuasive style of which he was past master. Necker knew that his own style was often described as "heavy" and "ponderous." According to Necker's grandson, August de Staël, while in London Calonne maintained contact with a "Calonne committee" in Paris of which Mirabeau was the heart and soul, and to which Panchaud also belonged. The latter had intimate knowledge of the records and financial sources of the Contrôle-général, and according to August de Staël, Loménie de Brienne gave the "Calonne committee" unlimited access to the records.[19] Therefore Calonne's "Reply to Necker" bristled with figures that gave the appearance of authenticity. Loménie de Brienne himself read the "Reply" and is said to have remarked that it would be difficult for Necker to refute it.[20] It was from Calonne's book also that the archbishop probably got some of his ideas that were inscribed in his own compte rendu of March 1788, for he was anxious to avoid what he supposed were "errors" in that of Necker's.

Necker of course had his own piéces justificatives and was not at a loss to answer and explain all the matters brought up in Calonne's book. But he wondered if readers would be willing to follow him in the tortuous labyrinths of the royal finances. And what would posterity think of the debate between himself and Calonne? Would they not say in effect, "a plague on both your houses!" Nevertheless Necker went ahead with the laborious task, and fortunately had finished it just as he was recalled to the ministry of finance. It was evident in August 1788 that his reputation had suffered very little from Calonne's onslaught. Apparently the nation caught up in the excitement of the coming States-General gave little thought to the accuracy of the Compte rendu of 1781.

According to the author of the "Secret Correspondence" it was on September 3 that Necker moved into the offices of the Contrôle-général in Paris. He was astounded to see the changes made in the remodeling and the sumptuous furnishings of the hotel carried out by Calonne. According to the correspondent, "He hardly recognized the place, for luxury and magnificence reigned supreme. Mr. Necker exclaimed: 'I'll have to admit that M. de Calonne knows how to furnish a Contrôle-général!'"[21] In these offices Necker carried out his first acts of the second ministry. It was only in November that he moved to Versailles at the time of the convening of the second Assembly of Notables.[22]

The first serious attention of the new minister was of course to see to the royal finances which were in a seemingly desperate situation. According to Mallet due Pan: "The financial distress was at a peak. Four hundred thousand livres remained in the royal treasury. The other caisses were empty. Negotiations for money were made at the rate of 20 or 25 percent. Authority everywhere was spurned, the government without money was at odds with the entire kingdom."[23]

There seems to be no disagreement, even from Necker's most confirmed enemies, that the Genevan banker turned the situation around almost overnight. His appointment in itself was greeted with great enthusiasm, the government paper on the bourse leaping about 30 percent on the day after. The writer of the "Secret Correspondence" reported that "the revocation of the edict (of August 16) which made a part of the debts of the state payable in paper money has reanimated national confidence. All the securities on the Bourse have recovered their vigor. When one sees the French people pass from appalling distress to a state of joy and hope, one cannot refuse to M. Necker the epithet of 'saviour.'"[24] The Swedish ambassador, who was of course the son-in-law of Necker, but whose dis-

271

patches to the king of Sweden were not lacking in objectivity for all that, wrote Gustavus III on the 31st of August that "the nation, transported with the choice of Necker, expects miracles from him. The recall of the Parlements is the general wish. There can be no doubt that France will be regenerated in a few years if Necker is not thwarted in his policies. The confidence of the public in him is boundless. His genius, his moderation, his character, and his morals, have won him a love which it is impossible to exaggerate."[25]

The sudden turnabout in the financial situation of the royal treasury was due to the resumption of the flow of anticipations made possible because of the confidence Necker was able to inspire in the financiers. Of course such a dramatic change might also have given some credence to the allegations of Necker's enemies that a "Necker cabal" had deliberately withheld credit from the Brienne ministry, a charge that was made a year earlier by baron de Besenval when the government notes on the bourse also took a plunge at the time the Parlement of Paris was exiled to Troyes.[26]

But the new finance minister was able to dispense with the paper notes used by Brienne and to meet all government payments in specie. He raised money by a variety of expedients. The writer of the "Secret Correspondence" recorded on October 8 that the director general "certainly knew how to make people open their purses."[27] He made a considerable profit by a "fortunate speculation in (Spanish) piastres." He succeeded in getting a loan of several millions from Paris notaries, and another loan from agents of the bourse. He was able to meet all expenses for the remainder of 1788 by such measures. In September the date for the opening of the States-General was advanced to January 1, 1789 and it was hoped that once the ship of state could be brought into that supposedly safe harbor the financial problems would be resolved. Later, in October, when Necker decided to reconvene the Assembly of Notables to make the decisions on how the States-General would be elected and organized it was necessary to restore the former date of May 1 for the opening of the States-General. Therefore at the beginning of the new year, 1789, the director general was forced to continue piecemeal, palliative financial measures. He was able to borrow 25 million livres from the Discount Bank in January, and this seemed to assure the government of sufficient finances until the States-General would finally meet in early May.[28]

Keeping the treasury supplied with essential money was only one of the emergency measures Necker faced in the first weeks of September. On July 13 in that summer of 1788 a devastating hailstorm struck French grain fields, particularly in the most fertile areas such as the Beauce. Necker restored the funds that the king had designated for relief of the stricken populations (which Brienne had been forced to expropriate). But this proved to be only the beginning of the drain on the royal treasury because of this disaster of nature. It is estimated by some that the storms followed by drought cut the French grain harvest in half.[29] When Necker entered the ministry he found that no one had given any thought to the threat of a severe shortage of flour and a consequent famine. He immediately repealed the edict of June 1787 which had permitted unlimited export of grain, and took steps to see that the country was sufficiently provisioned for the coming winter. It so happened that the winter was one of the severest in European history. The freezing of rivers and streams immobilized flour mills which added to the threat of famine. Even the winds died down during that winter of calamities so that the mills driven by wind could not produce flour either.

Prohibiting export of grain was only the beginning of Necker's measures to assure subsistence for the population. He subsidized imports from abroad, and when that tactic proved insufficient, he sent royal agents to other countries to purchase grain on the king's account. The price of grain was kept within the reach of the working class by government subsidies to merchants to make up for losses they would otherwise suffer. From September until the following July Necker estimated that the king spent over 25 million livres to purchase grain abroad on his own account. The problem was not only one of purchasing sufficient grain supplies abroad, which was difficult enough since France was not the only country in Europe to suffer grain shortages that winter. The panic to which the population was prone in times of scarcity led local authorities in cities and provinces to attempt to impede the free circulation of grain within the kingdom. Troops and police were necessary to assure the free transport of imported grain. When civil order broke down in the summer of 1789 the threat of famine in some regions, particularly the city of Paris, became even more dangerous because of the interruption of transport.[30]

Grave as were the financial and subsistence crises that Necker faced, they were child's play for him to resolve in comparison to the momentous political crisis that faced him at the beginning of his second ministry. The former banker who had built his fortune largely through grain speculation, and whose wizardry in raising money for the royal government was already legendary, certainly lived up to the public's expectation of him when they called for his return to power in late August 1788. But he was obviously not as experienced in handling political matters, and it is here that some of his contemporaries, even friends loyal to him, as well as historians have weighed the Genevan banker and found him wanting. As stated in the preface, it is not the purpose of this book to re-

274

habilitate Necker's political career in his second and third ministry, but to see how he viewed the crisis, what his policies were, and how they turned out. In other words, the purpose is to view the momentous events of the French Revolution through the eyes of the Genevan banker who played such a prominent role in those events during the years 1789 and 1790.

The most important political decision of his career was made by Necker soon after the entrance into his second ministry. It has been seen that the reforms of the Brienne-Lamoignon ministry were very much in the spirit of Necker's first ministry from 1776 to 1781. From that perspective it would seem paradoxical that Necker should have declined the archbishop's invitation to put his talents to the service of a ministry whose aims had been his own. No more than Loménie de Brienne did Necker think the States-General was the best means of carrying out the kind of transformation that he thought most enlightened people of the time wanted: a system of representation for the nation that would at the same time preserve a strong, effective monarchy. Ideally, he would have agreed with the archbishop that a bicameral legislature in which the upper house would be a chamber of peers and the lower house represent the rest of the nation, and whose members would be elected by the provincial assemblies, was the most desirable solution. But as he viewed the political situation at the beginning of September, 1788, he believed that the opportunity for that solution had passed by, and there was no hope of avoiding the States-General which public opinion called for with such insistence and which the king had formally promised before Necker entered the government. Whether to convene or not to convene the States-General was no longer the king's choice, and certainly not Necker's. After his ministerial career was over in 1791 Necker described how the political landscape appeared to him at the beginning of his second ministry:

The unfortunate events which had succeeded
one another for a year, and had spread alarm
in the kingdom and provoked all the people;
the frequent use of the lit de justice, the
undermining of the Parlements, putting them
on vacation without stipulating a date for
their return, the removal of the Parlement
of Paris to Troyes, followed by the exile
and imprisonment of several of its members,
the seizure of the twelve gentlemen from
Brittany; finally the establishment of a
Plenary Court which, under the immediate
control of the government, was henceforth to
be the only defense of the interests of the
people. All these reckless acts of authority, coming in the midst of a ferment (of
public opinion) which had existed for some
time, had sowed the seeds of discord in the
provinces and appeared to be the unmistakable harbinger of a general insurrection.[31]

At the time Necker entered the ministry violence
had already erupted at Grenoble. Other provinces appeared to be a tinderbox ready for explosion: Burgundy, Brittany, and Guienne. Necker believed that
the country was on the verge of civil war. The dismissal of Loménie de Brienne had brought about a temporary relief in the fever that had seized the nation.
Therefore it would have been the blindest folly to
continue the archbishop's policy of overcoming the
movement by a firm use of military force, by delaying
the States-General if not preventing it entirely. To
do all that on the uncertain assumption that the national movement was not very serious, that it was only
the selfish aristocrats whose interests were harmed by
the reforms that were causing the commotion, and that
the enlightened part of the nation would recognize the
justice and benevolence of the reforms, such a policy
would certainly have been as much a leap in the dark
as the one Necker decided upon.

From Necker's viewpiont, if he had adopted such a course he would have lost his popularity--and his influence--in an afternoon. He would have been exactly in the spot that the archbiship had just vacated. The ship of state was now irretrievably headed for the rapids of the States-General. The only thing for the helmsman to do was to try to guide it as best he could. The nation had spoken for the States-General and it expected a new political order--a constitution--to issue from it. This did mean that Necker's primary concern now was to prepare for the forthcoming national assembly rather than to propose and attempt to implement a program of reform on the king's authority. Anything that he would attempt to accomplish in changing the institutions of the kingdom would only be temporary, or at least subject to review by the States-General. This meant his new ministry was not a reform ministry. He was no longer just director-general of finances; he was now the director of a revolution. Looking back from the year 1791 he described the difference between his first and second ministries:

It will be remembered that during the course of my first administration I was ceaselessly active; an important reform, a small saving to realize, a new organization for the financial companies, a consolidation of caisses, an abolition of treasuries, a new order of comptability, changes of all kinds, and preparations for other reforms that could not be implemented immediately; in short, each day I acted in such a manner.

I saw, upon entering the government in the month af August 1788, that in the interests of the state an absolutely different course was required. This meant that the administration of finances was not to be the most visible part of my activity. I realized that if I once again set out to destroy the old abuses, which had reappeared in great number after my resignation from my first ministry, I would only succeed in arousing protests over matters that were ephemeral; and this would diminish my effectiveness where I would need all my forces and attention to bring about the fruition of the single great enterprise that would lead to a fundamental regeneration. I mean the formation of the States-General. I thought that in such a short time before the assembly of the deputies of the nation it would be futile to begin all by myself a new war on abuses, since they would all be very soon destroyed forever by a more vigorous hand; therefore my sole and essential task was to prepare for the convocation of the States-General, and to its reasonable composition and its peaceful reunion.[32]

Jean Egret was sympathetic to the last reform ministry before the Revolution, and he asserted that the opposition to it was not so widespread as Necker believed. "Necker was badly informed and overestimated the gravity of the crisis provoked by the Edicts of May; he believed civil war was imminent. To conjure it, he thought it necessary to hasten the convening of the States-General and restore the parlements."[33] The recall of the parlements made necessary the resignation of Lamoignon, an event that Necker himself regretted, for he held the Keeper of the Seals in high esteem, as did many of the memoir writers of the time. There is no doubt that the revocation of the edicts of May, implemented by a declaration of September 23, did mean a surrender of the royal government to the movement that the edicts of May had aroused. The question is whether this act of September 23 is what left the monarchy in a weakened condition, or whether it was what Necker called the "inconsiderate acts of violence" of the previous ministry that weakened the monarchy. Of course it is always difficult to judge when a nation is on the brink of a revolution or "general insurrection." Sometimes a concerted minority can generate a great noise and attempt to identify its own interests with the interests of the nation. Was the movement generated by the acts of the Brienne-Lamoignon ministry only an "aristocratic revolution," or was it something more fundamental?

There is reason to believe that the "aristocratic revolution" was only the foam on the crest of a gigantic tidal wave of public opinion. It first appeared at the time of the Assembly of Notables, when abbé Morellet referred to the "little fever" that had gripped the population. The "ferment," as Necker called the phenomenon, continued to grow during the summer of 1787. The Austrian ambassador was a close observer of the scene in France, because Vienna was now engaged in a war with the Ottoman Empire, in partnership with Russia, and the internal situation of its French ally could have an inportant bearing on events in the Balkans. In July 1787 Mercy-Argenteau wrote to Kaunitz about the difficulty Loménie de Brienne was having with the Parlement of Paris. "The evil is greatly magnified," he wrote, "because of the increasingly excited state of public opinion. Little by little it can be seen that the agitation is reaching all classes of society. And it is this ferment which is giving the Parlement the power to persevere in its opposition." What most appalled him was the violence of expressions used by the public against the king and queen. "It is not possible to control by repression this license of language. The fever has become so general that even if people were put in prison by the thousands the evil could not be overcome; that would exasperate their anger to the highest pitch and riots would erupt. This is what the police are saying."[34]

Later in November, after the royal session, Mercy-Argenteau wrote that "Despite the wealth of France, nothing is in its place. The revolution which is so evident in the national spirit threatens some momentous change in the constitutional principles of the monarchy. And if the States-General meet, which have already in some fashion been promised, it is more than probable that royal authority will experience a blow from which it could with difficulty recover."[35] The Emperor Joseph replied that it appeared to him, "from the way in which heads have become so heated that a change in the constituion is inevitable."[36] In July 1788 after the passing of the May edicts Mercy-Argenteau wrote the emperor that "the French nation at this moment is seized with such a spirit of vertige that it is difficult to say on which side there is more delirium and inconsequence, whether on the part of those who should command, or on the part of those who ought to obey."[37]

A high degree of excitement in a population might not necessarily mean it is on the verge of insurrection. But other observers besides Necker were convinced that without a change of ministers that event was very probable. The author of the "Secret Correspondence" wrote on June 17, 1788:

> The time for songs and epigrams has passed;
> it has given place to that of anguish and
> consternation. The people are aroused in
> several provinces. It has already had some
> success against regular troops. Brother has
> shed the blood of brother, and one knows
> that such wounds are difficult to heal. It
> is seriously feared that Burgundy, Franche-
> Comté, and Languedoc will join Dauphiné,
> Guienne, and Brittany, and that rebellion
> will be communicated to the entire kingdom.
> A change of ministry is the only way of
> avoiding the evil.[38]

About the same time the bookseller Hardy was recording in his diary serious disturbances. In Burgundy the military commandant was forced to bring in troops. Before he did so the royal official, the provost, had called out the local constabulary (the maréchaussée) and ordered them to fire on the demonstrating crowds. The result was to find himself imprisoned in his château by the irate citizens. Serious discontent was rife in Lyons. In Provence the military governor was the prestigious Marshal de Beauvau, one of the two marshals who had been selected to sit on the Plenary Court and had declined (the other was Marshal de Broglie, who had also declined to serve on the Court). Beauvau refused to carry out the orders of the ministry to deal firmly with the demonstrations. According to Hardy the Marshal wrote an impertinent letter to Loménie de Brienne pointing out that the principal minister might not always remain the principal minister, but he, the prince de Beauvau, would always be the prince of Beauvau![39] The apparent unreliability of such persons in the forces of order did not augur well for the government's success in enforcing the May edicts. Yet, by the beginning of July nothing indicated that the ministry was ready to relent. On June 30, Hardy wrote in his diary:

> On this day it is being heard from all sides that the Principal Minister and the Keeper of the Seals, despite all the rumors that have been spread about them, are more in the king's favor than ever. He has told them to extricate him from the embarrassing situation by pursuing steadily the execution of their plan, provided that they spare the people (from violence) which he has stongly recommended to both of them. The result will be to see established in all parts (of the kingdom) commissioners, a profusion of lettres de cachet, imprisonment, and all other penalties in order to subjugate the

dissidents to the will of the ministry. It is being heard that at this moment an edict or decree in council is in the press, quashing all the decrees of the parlements of the kingdom, which up to now have only been subjected to legal precedents. (It is being heard) that this act will be promulgated on July 9, and before that happens we will possibly see fire ignite in the four corners of the kingdom, and an internal war will tear apart the country; a situation which would be of great advantage to the enemies of France who will certainly put it to profit. To hear a great number of persons, the only recourse is to implore the great protector of the Gauls (Louis XVI) to renew in their favor the former marks of his powerful protection.[40]

The last comment indicates that while the queen was unfortunately the victim of popular dislike, this feeling did not extend to the king. It would seem that the ministers were the target of this great tide of popular wrath, and not the king. Certainly one diarist cannot be presumed to speak for all twenty-four million Frenchmen. But the cahiers that were drawn up in the first months of 1789 indicate that the king was not the object of popular hatred.

The decree Hardy referred to appeared a week earlier than he had expected, on July 2. Signed by the Secretary of the King's Household, baron de Breteuil, it suppressed all meetings and deliberations convened for the purpose of protesting the May edicts. Officers and officials of the government who took part in such protests were considered seditious and would forfeit their posts. On July 24 Hardy reported the resignation of Breteuil and his replacement by Laurent de Villedeuil. His departure was a serious blow to the ministry. Breteuil was a strong personality, as au-

282

thoritarian as anyone in the government and he had evidently decided that the government had embarked upon on impossible course in enforcing the May edicts.

When the Edict of July 5 appeared whereby the government invited citizens and corporations to submit ideas on the organization of the States-General Hardy recorded that "many people doubt the sincerity of the archbishop in really planning for the convening of the estates." A month later, on August 6 Hardy reported that it was being rumored that the government was placing regiments of the army around Paris, supposedly to maintain order and contain the "little people." But Hardy had also heard about the financial straits of the royal government and assumed that it was making preparations to control the riots that would erupt when the government declared bankruptcy and refused to honor its obligations to creditors.[41] The "rumors" reported by Hardy were often dubious, and this one certainly was in that category. But the testimony of Hardy does show that the financial crisis was intimately linked to the general political crisis caused by the May edicts. Egret seemed to look upon the financial crisis in August as a kind of *deus ex machina* that propelled Necker into power. Without that crisis he seems to have assumed that Necker would not have replaced Loménie de Brienne and the latter would have continued with his "laudatory reforms."

It is against this background of the state of public opinion that the acts of the Brienne-Lamoignon ministry must be judged. Granted that the reform measures were entirely praiseworthy in themselves, the way in which they were carried out was also important. As the comte de Ferrand said about the May edicts, "it is not enough to want to do the good, one must want to do it *a propos* and not compromise it by choosing an unfavorable moment."[42]

In political decisions made in the face of an aroused public, timing was the crucial matter. In Necker's opinion this was the basic fault of the government throughout the period from the dismissal of the Assembly of Notables in May 1787 until the violent popular upheaval in the July Days of 1789. He believed that if the leaders had made the necessary concessions in time, further concessions that weakened the monarchy beyond repair could have been avoided. In his later book on the French Revolution published in 1796 Necker strongly denied that the violent and destructive revolution was inevitable or unavoidable. If this seems an excessively humanistic view of a major historical event it nonetheless was the opinion of one who was a close observer throughout the period and an active participant during two vital years. In all his writings after his departure from France in September 1790 Necker was obsessed by this subject: those crucial decisions which, had they been other than they were, would have directed the mighty stream into a different channel.

After the dismissal of Calonne by the king in April 1787 Necker believed that there was still a chance "to form a new pact with public opinion." The greatest and most serious mistake of the new minister, Loménie de Brienne, was dismissing the Notables. "One should at least have left the Notables sufficient time to determine in a regular manner the situation of the finances."[43] Their demand to have the king appoint a committee of surveillance over the administration of the finances was one which had wide support with the public. To dismiss the Assembly without making that necessary concession was to antagonize public opinion. The same was true with the refusal of the government to allow the Parlement of Paris to examine the accounts of the royal finances when the stamp tax edict was submitted by Loménie de Brienne for registration. Necker wrote that "the Parlement's demand to see the accounts of revenue and expenditures before freely giving its consent to new taxes was approved by the public."[44] Granted that the pretensions of the Parlement to approve new taxes was not in accord with its traditional role of exercising only a judicial review of royal acts. But as long as there was no other institution capable of speaking for the interests of the nation, the public supported the pretensions of the Parlement of Paris. Furthermore the Parlement itself recognized that it was not its proper role to approve new taxes and admitted that the traditional constitutional authority for that function was vested in the States-General.

The character of Loménie de Brienne was of some importance in analyzing the failure of his ministry. Necker believed that the archbishop was authoritarian at heart, despite his well-known reputation for liberalism, a reputation based upon his learning in the science and philosophy of the Enlightenment. Ministers of the absolute monarchy were not inclined to work wholeheartedly with assemblies of any kind. Richelieu and Mazarin in the seventeenth century were the ideal types. If they enjoyed the unquestioned support of the king (or the queen mother) they could be arrogant to everyone else. Turgot, Calonne, and Loménie de Brienne all treated the Parlements with hauteur.[45] One important exception which proves the rule was Jean François Joly de Fleury, who was himself a member of a distinguished family of magistrates who served in the Parlement of Paris. During the two years that he was at the helm of royal finances, the peak years of the American War, Joly de Fleury always had his staff prepare elaborate dossiers of information about the royal finances and held conferences with the parlement leaders whenever important fiscal measures were passed in his administration. He was the last finance minister of the ancien régime to get the Parlement of Paris to register additional tax edicts without protest. Necker had little admiration or liking for the Parlements and their pretensions to

285

speak for the nation, but he knew that it was necessary to handle them in such a way as not to allow them to form a coalition with national opinion against the government. This he was able to do adroitly during his first ministry in his only serious confrontation with the Parlement of Paris in 1778 over his reform of the vingtième.

The archbishop had other and graver faults of character. He became frustrated and irritated at opposition which seemed unjustified in view of the moderation of his policies. Near the end of his ministry this became increasingly evident. The Swedish ambassador wrote to Gustavus III on August 3 that "it appears that the archbishop "is moved by a spirit of bitterness against the Parlement. . . His conduct is uncertain and vacillating; he has frequent outbursts of anger, but it's the anger of a child, armed however with all the power of the king of France."[46]

Most of the memoir writers of the time believed that the greatest fault in policy of Loménie de Brienne was rashly and imprudently resorting to force, and then just as precipitately backing down in the face of opposition.[47] This made the success of the reform edicts, particularly such radical reforms as the May edicts, very problematic from the outset. In attempting to implement the new bailiwick courts Lamoignon found that it was difficult to find judges willing to serve because they would be hopelessly compromised if the May edicts were to be repealed.[48] The nominees to the Plenary Court all refused, with greater or lesser determination, to take part in the new institution which was to assume the political role of the parlements. They were reluctant to compromise their reputations with the public. The attempt to carry out such a violent break with tradition was certainly a rash act, as Mercy-Argenteau wrote to the emperor.[49] Necker, as has been seen, believed that the attempt to use force simply discredited the ministry.

286

In his memorial to the king written during his first ministry in 1778 calling for the establishment of provincial administrations Necker warned about the dangers of a precipitate resort to force against corporations such as the parlements that had strong support in public opinion. "To avoid compromising authority too often one must not be so anxious to use it ceaselessly; one becomes exhausted in its futile deployment, and one lacks power just at the time that it is necessary to maintain it."[50] The failure of the Brienne-Lamoignon ministry was ever-present in Necker's mind in the months after his return to power. This explains his seeming passivity in face of certain matters where others believed the government should take decisive action. The actual authority and the power of the royal government was very weak. What remained had to be carefully nurtured as he sought to bring about a reconciliation between the nation and the monarchy.

If the state of public opinion in August 1788 required the dismissal of Loménie de Brienne, did it also require Necker to abandon the reform policies of his predecessor and embark on the dangerous course of convening the States-General? No less a person than Malesherbes strongly urged the king to give up the plans for the States-General, to convene an assembly and himself grant a constitution. Those who claimed in later years that Necker was largely to blame for the disaster of the Revolution base their claims on his decision not to follow Malesherbes' advice. From the vantage point that Necker viewed the political situation he really had no choice. The most compelling reason for going ahead with plans to convene the States-General was that the king had given his solemn promise to do so. No one expressed Necker's feelings on this subject better than Mme. de Staël in her posthumous history of the French Revolution: "Was it possible that a man like Mr. Necker should propose to a virtuous monarch, to Louis XVI, to go back on his word? And of what use would a minister be whose ascendancy consisted of his popularity, if his first act would have been to advise the king to renege on the promise he had made to his people?"[51]

The argument of Necker's critics was that since the crisis was due to the financial embarrassment of the government, and Necker was able to cope with that crisis, he should have found some way to avoid steering the ship of state into the catastrophe. Honesty may not always be the best policy for the man in power, and some of Necker's critics such as Besenval invoked the principles of the Florentine secretary, Machiavelli. This is a viewpoint that has found some favor with later historians who have written on the French Revolution. It is probably true that Necker was constitutionally incapable of Machiavellian statesmanship. Writing on this subject in 1795 Necker remarked bitterly: "They wanted me to be myself in order to have the esteem of the nation and then to be Mazarin to laugh at it and abuse it."[52]

Fortunately it can be said to those who have little tolerance for honesty in statemen, that Necker did have a much more fundamental reason for going ahead with the convocation of the States-General. Despite his apprehension that it was not the most suitable assembly to carry out the "great enterprise," yet once the decision had been made and was irrevocable, Necker looked forward with enthusiasm to the adventure of guiding the ship of state through the turbulent waters. He was caught up in the great national excitement of late 1788 when all thoughts turned hopefully to the States-General. Recalling this climate of opinion in later years, when writing his book on the French Revolution in 1795 Necker exclaimed: "Alas! can one think now of the universal hopes of all good Frenchmen, of all friends of humanity, without bursting into tears?"[53] It was a time of great hope and also genuine idealism. The nation was one and indi-

visible. The general interest would prevail over particular interests. There would be a new burst of
freedom, a better day for all. This feeling was
shared by all classes, aristocrats as well as ple-
beians. Even the king seems to have gotten over his
moroseness of the summer and in the fall months joined
in the enthusiasm for the great enterprise, little
suspecting, as Necker remarked later, that his was to
be the fate of Iphigenia. The spirit of 1788 has been
all but forgotten in the histories of the French Revolution, only the bitter enmities and divisions within
the national movement being remembered.

Certainly it was the aristocrats who began the
Revolution, as Mme. de Staël was to write later. She
said no revolution can begin otherwise. But beneath
the surface events of 1788 "a sincere and generous enthusiasm animated all the French at that time. There
was public spiritedness in the upper classes; and in
all classes the best were those who earnestly desired
that the will of the nation should have some voice in
the management of its own interests."[54]

Because of the experiences of his first ministry,
and his observations of the French scene since then,
Necker was fully convinced that a fundamental change
in the French constitution was necessary. The system
of absolutism of the previous century could no longer
claim the allegiance of the nation. Where the executive and legislative authority was vested in a king
and his ministers without any institutional check the
people could only consider it a despotism. Even
"enlightened despotism" where the king's public spir-
ited ministers and intendants tried to reform the
abuses of the ancien régime could not satisfy the
need, because whatever gains they made could be easily
revoked by succeeding ministers, as Necker's own ministry had demonstrated. Public opinion had grown too
strong by the 1780s to accept absolutism. There had
to be some mediator between it and the executive

power. It was true that the parlements had acted as a check on the absolute monarchy. But Necker thought the magistrates of the thirteen sovereign courts were not suited by training or character to act as mediators between the monarch and the nation. Their training was in jurisprudence but not in finance or other functions of the legislative power. The magistrates who had purchased or inherited their offices certainly were not suitable representatives for the nation. The resistance of the sovereign courts to the royal government was usually motivated by defending regional or local or individual privileges, rather than having a genuine concern for the national interest.

The long quarrel between the absolute monarchy and the sovereign courts had greatly undermined the prestige of both in the eyes of the nation. As long as there was no other mediator the public usually lent its support to the magistrates. But the latter, animated more by a spirit of legal pettiforgery, was obstructive rather than truly serving the national desires. Only a full-fledged national parliament which the nation recognized as its own spokesman could really carry out the reforms that Necker thought were necessary. Only such a body would have the moral authority and the power to do so.

That the France of the _ancien régime_ needed reforms Necker was absolutely convinced. The system of direct taxes on land which fell upon the poorer classes which most needed the protection of the government, and which the wealthier classes were able to escape in great measure; the multitude of indirect taxes that fell with such unequal weight upon the different regions and classes of the _ancien régime_; the great burden of the taxes, which he estimated as over half a billion livres a year; finally the fears of the creditors of the government, which included such a large class of landowners and wealthy bourgeois, all the above factors called for a strong government that would be able to make the necessary changes that the absolute monarchy and the thirteen sovereign courts were unable to do. "Only the States-General," Necker wrote in 1795, "could realize the hopes for a salutary reform in the interior administration of France."[55]

To bring that institution into being was the most important and all-absorbing challenge that he faced as he began his second ministry.

[1]Egret, La Pré-révolution française, 1787-1788 (Paris, Presses Universitaires de France, 1962).

[2]Ibid., 251-265.

[3]Ibid., 293.

[4]Ibid., 276-277.

[5]Ibid., 277-278.

[6]Ibid., 247.

[7]Ibid., 308.

[8]This information comes from the "secret memoirs" of Loménie de Brienne, a portion of which was published by Jean-Louis Soulavie in his Mémoires historiques et politiques du règne de Louis XVI, VI, 238-239.

[9]Also the Sinking Fund of Calonne must have been appropriated at some time during the summer of 1788.

[10]Egret, op. cit., 314-315.

[11]The resignation of the archbishop and the return of Necker were discussed in detail in a letter of Mercy-Argenteau to the emperor dated September 14, 1788. Correspondance secrète, II, 189-196.

[12]The quote of Sallier so often repeated about the king's view of Necker's appointment is not well documented. Sallier was a magistrate of the Parlement of Paris and certainly not an intimate at court. The statement he attributed to Louis XVI was: "They made me recall Necker. I did not want him. But it will not be long before they repent. I will do anything he tells me to do, and you will see what happens." Sal-

lier did not hear that statement himself, but from an-
other person who heard it from a third person! Guy-
Marie Sallier-Chaumont de la Roche, Annales françaises
(Paris, 1813), 199.

[13]Mercy-Argenteau, Correspondance secrète, II,
211.

[14]François-Adolphe Marthurin de Lescure, Correspondance secrète inédite sur Louis XVI, Marie-Antoinette, la cour et la ville (Paris, 1866), II, 285.

[15]"De la Révolution française," in Oeuvres
complètes, IX, 33.

[16]Considérations sur la Révolution française, 91.

[17]Charles-Alexandre de Calonne, Réponse à l'Ecrit
de M. Necker (Londres, 1788).

[18]"Nouveaux éclaircissements sur le Compte
rendu," in Oeuvres complètes, II, 243-602.

[19]Auguste de Staël, "Notice sur M. Necker," in
Oeuvres complètes de Necker, I, ccxi-ccxii.

[20]Lescure, op. cit., II, 321.

[21]Ibid., II, 286-287.

[22]Beatrice W. Jasinski, ed., Madame de Staël,
Correspondance générale (Paris, 1962), I, 253.

[23]Jacques Mallet du Pan, Mémoires et correspondance pour servir à l'histoire de la Révolution
française (Paris, 1851), I, 153.

[24]Lescure, op. cit., II, 284.

[25]Correspondance diplomatique, 89.

[26]Mémoires du baron de Besenval, II, 273.

[27] Lescure, Correspondance secrète, II, 296.

[28] Ibid., II, 291.

[29] M. F. Barrière, "Notice," Mémoires de Besenval, I, vi.

[30] "Mémoire instructif au comité des subsistences des états-généraux," in Oeuvres complètes, VI, 630-643. In his book written in 1791 Necker estimated the total cost of preventing famine came to 70 million livres. See Chapter 15 infra.

[31] "Sur l'administration de M. Necker, par lui-même," in Oeuvres complètes, VI, 23-24.

[32] Ibid., 28-29.

[33] Egret, La Pré-révolution française, 318.

[34] Mercy-Argenteau, Correspondance secrète, II, 113-114, n. 1.

[35] Ibid., 138.

[36] Ibid., 143.

[37] Ibid., 182.

[38] Lescure, Correspondance secrète, II, 266.

[39] Hardy, "Mes Loisirs," BN MSS Fonds français, 6687, fol.2.

[40] Ibid., fol. 9.

[41] Ibid., fol. 35.

[42] Antoine-François, comte de Ferrand, Mémoires du Comte Ferrand (Paris, 1897), 24.

[43]"Sur l'Administration de M. Necker," in <u>Oeuvres complètes</u>, VI, 21.

[44]<u>Ibid</u>., 23.

[45]Marmontel, <u>Mémoires</u>, III, 133.

[46]<u>Correspondance diplomatique</u>, 88.

[47]Marmontel, <u>Mémoires</u>, III, 134; <u>Mémoires du comte Ferrand</u>, 13; Mounier, <u>Récherches sur les causes</u>, 42; Bouillé, <u>Mémoires</u>, 118; Besenval, <u>Mémoires</u>, II, 323; Weber, <u>Mémoires</u>, 135; duc de Montmorency-Luxembourg, <u>Mémoires</u>, published in Paul Filleul, <u>Le duc de Montmorency-Luxembourg</u>, 274.

[48]Egret, <u>La Pré-révolution française</u>, 286.

[49]<u>Correspondance secrète</u>, II, 175-176.

[50]"Mémoires sur les Administrations provinciales," in <u>Oeuvres complètes</u>, III, 347.

[51]Mme. de Staël, <u>Considérations sur la Révolution française</u>, 127.

[52]"De la Révolution française," in <u>Oeuvres complètes</u>, IX, 37.

[53]<u>Ibid</u>., 39.

[54]<u>Considérations sur la Révolution française</u>, 91.

[55]"De la Révolution française," <u>op. cit</u>., 48.

CHAPTER 9

THE REPRESENTATIVES OF THE NATION

Once the decision had been made to embark on the dangerous course of convening the States-General Necker was concerned that it be truly representative of the "nation," and that it be invested with sufficient power to carry out its mission, namely, to draw up a new constitution for France. Although the concept of "constituent power" that was later to be elaborated by abbé Sieyes was foreign to his thought, Necker did believe that as soon as the States-General was assembled it would be recognized by the king and government as having full legislative powers. The transition from the absolute monarchy to a limited constitutional monarchy had already been accepted by the king. The most fundamental and lasting achievement of the French Revolution had already occurred before the meeting of the States-General on May 5, 1789. France was in fact a limited monarchy even if not yet in law. Necker expected therefore that the States-General would carry out its mission with a minimum of direction from the ministry. He thought it would be a mistake for the government to attempt to influence the selection of deputies to the States-General or to control their deliberations after they had assembled. Public opinion had rejected the Plenary Court of Loménie de Brienne because its members were all appointed by the king. He had also appointed the Assembly of Notables, but the Notables saved their honor by refusing to be bound by the guidelines laid down for them by Calonne. Necker believed if the government should attempt to control the activities of the new assembly it would soon be in the same position as the previous ministry, that is, considered by the nation to be its adversary. This was a culmination Necker sought to avoid.

Such a laissez-faire policy was difficult to understand for those brought up in the ancien régime. Friends and enemies alike severely criticized Necker for what they believed a failure of leadership. The Austrian ambassador wrote the emperor that the government was "without vigor (nerf)," allowing the most scandalous tracts to be printed and circulated. A prominent memoir writer whose opinions about Necker are often quoted, Pierre-Victor Malouet, even though a friend and confidant of Necker during the months preceding the convening of the States-General, was severely critical of his hands-off policy. Malouet thought Necker should have controlled the selection of deputies to the States-General to make certain the government would have a majority of supporters. He said Necker should have imposed the government's plan for a new constitutional order, and certainly should have decided the question of deliberation and voting by head rather than order well before the States-General convened. A deputy of the Third Estate from Bar-le-Duc, Adrien-Cyprien Duquesnoy, thought at the very least the ministry should have prevented the sending of such notorious scoundrels as Mirabeau to the States-General.[1]

The difference between Necker and his critics of course is that he reorganized the character of an open society. The French required not only precepts but experience on the road to freedom, and he was willing to give them the opportunity. Of course the States-General overshot the mark he had expected when it declared itself invested with total power, an idea that was the very opposite of Necker's liberalism. He did not, however, think he could be held responsible for that outcome, or that it was due to a failure of his leadership. Of course he admitted that firmness was necessary, particularly in a time of great popular excitement. But it is not a simple matter to know when firmness is called for and when the government must yield. The royal government was gravely weakened by nearly two years of political turmoil. It was easy for his critics to ignore that fact and propose bold, slashing initiatives. Necker could not ignore it. His own power was based upon his personal popularity and the confidence public opinion had in him. He was under no illusion as to how fragile was the foundation upon which he stood. His popularity could evaporate in a minute. He was eventually forced to take a stand against the power of public opinion when he saw it was threatening the personal security and property rights of citizens whose only crime was being an aristocrat. But he delayed that confrontation as long as he could, hoping that the States-General would be able to appease the popular wrath by promulgating the new constitution in a fairly short time.

Certainly one reason for the weakness of the government is that Necker was poorly seconded by his ministerial colleagues. He was unquestionably the most powerful minister in the royal councils because of his standing with the public and with the king. But he was not all-powerful; he had to persuade his ministerial colleagues, and some of them were most unfitted to lead the country into the kind of constitutional change that Necker envisaged.

The most important position after the ministry of finance for undertaking the great change that was to be effected in the constitution of the monarchy was the Keeper of the Seals. At the time of Necker's entry into the government on August 26 this post was still held by Lamoignon. Necker would have liked to have kept him at his post had it not been for the extreme hostility the magistrates of the parlements now had for their former colleague. The Plenary Court had already been suspended by Loménie de Brienne early in August (decree of August 8) since it had been found impossible to establish; nearly all those nominated to it by the king refused to serve. But the other reforms of the May edicts setting up the new inferior courts and abolishing inhumane procedures in criminal law, were acceptable, even desired by the public. The Parlement of Paris, feeling the flush of victory over the authors of the May edicts, demanded that everything be abolished. In the government's decree in council of September 23, 1788, the king explained in the preamble (which was written by Necker) that while the judicial reforms were still desired by the king, the May edicts proved to have "disadvantages." "The good is difficult to accomplish, we are acquiring that sad experience every day," the decree read somewhat plaintively; but since the States-General is soon to meet, these beneficial judicial reforms will be taken up by that assembly and will thereby have the sanction of "our people." Therefore all the courts set up by the May edicts were discontinued and the previous judicial system restored until changed by the States-General.[2]

The decisions promulgated by this decree had been made soon after the Parlement of Paris returned from its long "vacation" and resumed its duties in September. On September 16 Lamoignon resigned as Keeper of the Seals and was replaced by a magistrate whose selection was certainly aimed to conciliate the most conservative members of the Parlement. This was Charles-Louis François de Paule, comte de Barentin. He had served as First President of the Paris Court of Aides, since 1775, having replaced the illustrious Malesherbes who had entered the Turgot ministry that year. Barentin had none of his predecessor's brilliance nor any of the progressive ideas of the century. He proved to be one of the most stalwart defenders of the ancien régime. Jealous of Necker because of his popularity, that sentiment turned to bitter hatred as a result of the events of the summer of 1789. The uprising of July 12-14 in Paris forced him to resign and a few months later to emigrate. He joined the princes in the party of the émigrés at Turin. In 1797 when Necker's book on the French Revolution was published Barentin wrote a rebuttal, which for unknown reasons remained in manuscript at the time of his death in 1819. It was rescued from oblivion in 1844 and published, unfortunately for the reputation of the former Keeper of the Seals. The "Mémoire Autograph" is such a violent, unrestrained personal attack on Necker as to create doubt about the authenticity of the book at first reading. But it appears to be unquestionably the work of Barentin. None of the theses of the polemical brochures against Necker was denied by Barentin; he even believed there must be some truth to the legend that the threatened famine of 1789 from which Necker claimed to have saved the country, was "artificial," created by Necker himself in order to enhance his power over the popular and destitute masses! Barentin took issue with all the main ideas of Necker. He denied that the fiscal system of the ancien régime was unjust to the lower classes; the "public opinion" that Necker talked about so often was a figment of his imagination.[3] Secrecy was necessary in government, not publicity, and the principle of absolutism was defended by Barentin without qualification. Such was the colleague that Necker had to work with during his second ministry, and one that occupied such an important post. The only compensation for this misfortune was the Keeper of the Seal's ineffectiveness and nullity.

In the issues that were debated in the royal councils in late 1788 and during 1789 up to July, Barentin was invariably opposed to Necker's policies. Since it was not a cabinet system of government, and the vote by the council was not decisive, the king decided the issue. Barentin was usually seconded by the conservative Secretary of State for the King's Household, Laurent de Villedeuil, who had replaced the baron de Breteuil near the end of July. Also the minister of war, Pierre-Louis de Chastenet, comte de Puységur was an army general. The duke de Nivernais, a minister without portfolio, had been one of the most

301

vocal members of the Assembly of Notables in his opposition to Calonne. Inherently conservative by nature, he was yet not immune to persuasive arguments by Necker and therefore could not be counted on to hold ranks with the conservatives. The same was true of the naval secretary, César-Henri, comte de La Luzerne.

On Necker's side, his most loyal colleague was the minister of Foreign Affairs, Armand-Marc, comte de Montmorin-Saint-Hérem. Montmorin had succeeded to Vergenne's post on the latter's death in February 1787. He had tried without success to persuade the king to appoint Necker to the post vacated by Calonne in April 1787. Having devoted his career entirely to foreign affairs, Montmorin was not experienced in domestic matters, and could add nothing of his own to the debates. But his intellect and instincts told him that Necker was right on the issues in dispute. Montmorin was dismissed at the same time as Necker on July 11, 1789, and returned also after the popular revolution in Paris forced the king to recall Necker.

The third member of the trio of ministers dismissed by the king on July 11 and who returned with Necker after the July 14 uprising was François-Emmanual Guignard de Saint-Priest, a minister without portfolio. He was brought into the ministry at the behest of Montmorin in December 1788. Like his mentor, Saint-Priest's background was exclusively in the military and diplomatic service. In his memoirs written after the Revolution it appears that he was not an admirer of Necker, and did not share his ideas. Why he sided with Necker on the controversial issues in the council is a mystery, possibly explained by his following somewhat mechanically the lead of Montmorin. In 1788 he was asked to sit on the Council of Finance when états au vrai for the last two years of the American War were drawn up. His attentiveness during those deliberations can be judged by his recording in his memoirs that the American War, in its last two years, cost 1.2 billion livres in each of those years, about six times the actual cost.[4]

Foreign affairs was obviously his principal interest, and in this realm he was known to be the most favorable to Austria of any minister in the French government. He was thought to be the protégé of the queen, who along with Montmorin, was responsible for bringing him into the council of ministers. The court at Vienna had wished for Saint-Priest to succeed Vergennes when the latter died in 1787. Mercy-Argenteau did his utmost to persuade the queen to bring about this appointment and was disappointed that the post of foreign minister went to Montmorin, who was a known disciple of Vergennes, whom the court at Vienna had come to look upon as its particular bête noir. The queen intimated in a polite way to the ambassador that it was not for the court of Austria to choose the French foreign minister. Montmorin proved to be less objectionable than Vergennes had been from the standpoint of Austrian interests, but Vienna still entertained hopes that Montmorin would be replaced by Saint-Priest.[5]

The court at Vienna had also been favorable to Necker. We have seen the role of Mercy-Argenteau in bringing about the return of the Genevan banker to the administration of finances. But Necker's views on foreign policy were unknown. His support by Austria was due to the belief that he was the one person who could restore order to finances and thereby end the protracted internal crisis which weakened France's influence in international affairs, and her usefulness as an ally of Austria. "I have advised the queen," Emperor Joseph wrote to the Austrian ambassador in September, "not to place the least obstacle to any of Mr. Necker's projects, because that is perhaps the only means of improving the situation, or at least to disillusion the fanatical public in him by letting it be clear that he has had complete freedom of action."[6]

In the same letter the emperor revealed his primary concern, which was the war that had erupted between the Ottoman Empire and Russia in August 1787, and which Austria had joined in 1788 on the side of Russia. Military events were going badly for Austrian forces in the Balkans; the Turkish army had managed to cross the Danube and devastate the Sanjak; Russia's immobility on the Black Sea was inexplicable. What most worried the emperor was the danger that his old enemy, Prussia, could take advantage of Austrian defeats in the Balkans to make gains either in the German Empire or in Poland. The ties between Prussia and Great Britain were growing closer, and in 1788 Sweden attacked Russia in the Baltic. It was necessary, Joseph thought, that the Bourbon allies demonstrate their alignment with Austria. Spain offered her good offices to mediate a truce between Vienna and the Porte, and this was received favorably by the Emperor Joseph who now was eager to end the war. But he thought France should join Spain in that effort, and to make the mediation of the Bourbons effective, he thought both France and Spain should accept the proferred alliance held out to them by the Russian Empress, Catherine II.

The Austrian government tried strenuously in the early months of 1789 to get France to become an ally of Russia. The French Council of State seemed to be in favor of taking the step. Montmorin, and especially Saint-Priest urged the momentous step in foreign policy. According to Saint-Priest's memoirs, all the other ministers did also with the exception of Necker. But so powerful was the Director-General of Finances that he managed to veto the project and the king supported him. The queen also seems to have been influenced by Necker on the matter. In a letter to Mercy-Argenteau she explained her stand. An alliance with Russia would certainly mean greater expenditures, and it would be awkward to meet the States-General in May and have to justify that expenditure. It would give the States-General an excuse to intervene in foreign policy. Since France was in no condition to give any assistance to Russia in the war, the proposed alliance would be devoid of meaning; furthermore it might hinder rather than help France's diplomatic efforts to bring about a truce between Austria and the Porte. Mercy-Argenteau tried to argue the queen out of such eminent good sense, but to no avail, for she showed once again that she was not the pawn of Vienna at the court of Versailles.

Saint-Priest was greatly disappointed that France did not become Russia's ally, and for reasons which appear extremely bizarre. Since the States-General was soon to meet, and its convening was already accompanied by popular disturbances throughout the kingdom, Saint-Priest thought it would be useful for the authority of the monarchy to have foreign troops at its disposal rather than to have to rely on French troops to crush these popular disturbances. One can imagine what effect it would have had on the national movement in France to have attempted to crush it with Cossack squadrons borrowed from Catherine II! But Saint-Priest was by no means alone in thinking that the Revolution could be crushed by military force. He thought also, as several did at the time, that a foreign war would be the best remedy for the internal crisis. He was dismayed that France did not go to war with Prussia over the Holland affair in the summer of 1787: "Alas! War at that time would have spared us the horrible revolution which followed, by diverting the attention and the ambition of all those young Frenchmen who had just come back from America and were the principal authors of the troubles which came."[7] Such elementary sociological analysis of the forces coming into existence shows how isolated Necker was in his appraisal of the government's weakness and the strength of the national movement. Fortunately he was able, as Saint-Priest admitted, to deflect France from such a disastrous course as the Russian alliance.

The Austrian ambassador was more subtle than Saint-Priest in his analysis of the French situation. In January 1789 he had written to the emperor:

> . . . it is difficult to form a very clear and precise picture of the strange situation in which France finds herself reduced. She is threatened by a revolution too remarkable for one to be able to describe it in a historical diary filled with minute facts, but which shows the evolution of a national effervescence of which there are few examples . . . . It has been over a year that I first perceived and commented upon the symptoms. Since that time the government has heaped mistakes upon mistakes; perplexities and sources of opposition have multiplied from all parts; and by calling in too late the only man upon whose talents the fate of the country now depends, he has had thrust upon him a task so difficult to fulfill that he is himself appalled by it.[8]

Writing to Chancellor Kaunitz a month later, Mercy-Argenteau recognized that France was in no condition to go to war. But he thought a Franco-Russian alliance would be advantageous to Austria because it could prevent a threatening rapprochement between Great Britain and Russia.[9] In April he wrote the emperor that the French Council of State had made its decision: Montmorin and Saint-Priest were strongly in favor of the Russian alliance, "but the opinion of Mr. Necker prevailed. The last-named sees only the financial problems to which he subordinates all else. The preponderant influence he enjoys at the present moment is based upon an abyss and the terror which the convening of the States-General inspires." In his reply on April 25 the emperor seemed more sympathetic to the French situation. "I have found the reply of France touching on the alliance with Russia to be, in truth, very honest and sincere, in view of the increasing difficulties this country finds itself in at this time, and where everything depends upon the outcome of the States-General."[10]

The internal situation was certainly uppermost in Necker's thoughts, and absorbed his energy entirely. Although excited and eager about the coming of the States-General, he was also apprehensive and conscious of the risks. During the last three months of 1788 and during January of the following year a great number of decisions were made that were to be supremely important for the fate of the Revolution. Besides keeping the government from bankruptcy and the population from famine, Necker was faced with a barrage of decisions of great complexity. As he complained to the president of the Estates of Brittany when that province erupted in a violent struggle between the Third Estate and the nobility in January, "There is so much to write, and especially to discuss, and unfortunately I have only moments that are free in the midst of the torrent that engulfs us."[11] In early February he suffered from illness, according to the writer of the "Secret Correspondence."[12] By that time the machinery for electing the deputies to the States-General was in place, and except for innumerable quarrels between competing pretensions at the local and regional level, Necker could look forward with some confidence to the great day, the opening of the national assembly of estates.

The most important question was how the States-General would be organized, and how the deputies would be chosen. These matters had engaged the attention of the public since the decree of July 5, 1788 had invited different corporations and individuals to send information and advice to the royal government about them. The response had been overwhelming. That "public opinion" to which Necker attached so much importance was eager to take up the question of the organization and election of deputies to the States-General.

It was on September 24 that the Parlement of Paris held its first deliberating session after the long "vacation." Its first act was to register the royal decree of the previous day which revoked all the judicial reforms of Lamoignon and announced that the convening of the States-General would now take place in January of the following year. In its decree of registration the Parlement stated that the forthcoming assembly of estates would be convened according to the forms and rules that had governed the preceding States-General of 1614. This declaration was made without any particular deliberation or discussion. It was almost as an afterthought that it was incorporated into the decree of registration, as if the magistrates assumed as a matter of course that the rules of 1614 were still valid for 1789.[13]

Upon its return to Paris after the turbulent months since May 8 the Parlement was in a triumphant mood. Once again it had survived the attempt of the government to abolish its political role in the state. It was also in a vindictive mood. Much of the session of September 24 was taken up by a condemnation of the acts of the preceding ministry of Loménie de Brienne and Lamoignon. The exiled and imprisoned magistrates, including Duval d'Eprésmesnil, were now on their way back to Paris to take up their influential roles, and they were not in an humble frame of mind. They had no reason for believing that they would not continue to be the leaders of the nation and the guardians against ministerial despotism.

The magistrates soon became aware that the popular ferment had not died down since the dismissal of the unpopular ministers and the return of Necker. They learned that at the Place Dauphine from August 26 to August 29 a boistrous crowd had taken over the neighborhood, required passers-by on the bridge to dismount and salute the statue of Henri IV, and that residents illuminate their houses to celebrate the departure of Loménie de Brienne. On August 29 troops under the command of Marshal Biron suppressed the disturbances, not without a fusillade and casualties. A similar eruption came later in the middle of September. The Parlement undertook an inquiry into this incident and other instances of popular violence.

What most concerned the magistrates after September 24 was the vehement outcry of the leaders of the towns and cities against its decree on the organization of the States-General. Since July 5 much had been published and read about the history of previous meetings of States-General. Special attention was paid to that of 1614, since that was to be the model for the forthcoming assembly of estates. It was learned that the assembly held in Paris in 1614 was particularly humiliating for the Third Estate. The nobility and the prelates had behaved with arrogance; and the Provost of the Merchants had to present the grievances of the Third Estate in a kneeling position over several hours, and in the end nothing was gained from the government. An unprecedented amount of literature now poured from the printers denouncing the privileges of the First and Second Estates. It was the "awakening of the Third Estate," the beginning of a powerful movement whose enemy was no longer exclusively ministerial despotism but the "aristocrats" and the entire system of privilege. What was especially called for was that the organization prevailing in the provincial assemblies should also apply to the national assembly: the doubling of the Third Estate (a number of deputies for the Third equal to the combined number of the other two), and the deliberation and voting by head count in the common assembly.

The magistrates of the Parlement were stunned by the popular outcry against them, and they suspected the government, and particularly Necker was secretly behind the movement and purposely permitted the scandalous tracts. On December 5, under the influence of Duval d'Eprésmesnil, the Parlement of Paris published another decree that was an attempt to win back the support of the public. The decree called attention to the alarming popular unrest in the kingdom and reproached the government for not nipping the movement in the bud as it could have. Not only could the government prevent the scandalous literature from being published, but it could, if it wanted to, allay the fears of the populace that its basic desires from the coming States-General would not be met. Concerning the organization of the States-General the Parlement retreated from its position stated on September 24. The States-General should be based upon the bailiwicks and seneschalships as in 1614, but concerning the number of deputies for each order, "which has not been determined by any firm precedent for any order, it is neither in the power nor the intention of this court to provide one."[14]

The Parlement then stated that the popular unrest could be allayed if the king would grant clearly and unequivocally certain basic concessions that would be incorporated into the new constitution to be drawn up by the States-General: (a) that the States-General would be convened regularly and periodically; (b) that it would have the authority to guarantee to creditors of the state the reimbursement of their loans and the interest from specific tax revenues; (c) the States-General would have the right to give its consent to all tax measures of the government, which however must all be specific in duration and amount; (d) the States-General would have the right to approve the funds granted each year to all the departments of the government; (e) the king should state his resolution to suppress all taxes that are distinctive to the orders, and replace them with a common subsidy equitably partitioned; (f) the ministers of the government should be responsible to the States-General; (g) the States-General should have full legislative powers to approve all laws, and the sovereign courts will not be asked to register any acts of the royal government that are not so sanctioned; (h) the king's subjects should be guaranteed personal security against arbitrary arrest and imprisonment; (i) finally, the king should guarantee freedom of the press, so long as prompt and certain remedy is provided for those unjustly libeled.[15]

It was the Parlement of Paris that in July 1787 first launched the idea of the States-General as the only body that could approve tax proposals of the royal government. From that date the idea caught fire with the public. Now, on December 5, 1788, the Parlement formally decreed in quite specific articles what the new constitution should be. The monarchy was no longer to be absolute in theory or practice. The king would rule by sharing legislative power with a general assembly representing the nation. This was certainly not a return to the traditional monarchy of estates that preceded absolutism; it was rather an imitation of the English and the American system of government. It is true that the only concession to equality made by the privileged orders to the Third Estate was the definite pledge to give up all fiscal privileges and accept a tax system to which all would be subject based upon ability to pay. The "aristocratic revolution" that took place from the time of the Assembly of Notables in 1787 until the meeting of the States-General in 1789 can be called that only in the sense that its aims were the conquest of liberty rather than equality. Once it had given up its fiscal privileges the First and Second Estates did not intend to be shorn of other rights and privileges which were considered sacred property rights.

Necker was certainly conscious of the power of the Parlement of Paris, and the other sovereign courts as well, when they were supported by public opinion. He did not wish to repeat the mistakes of Calonne and Loménie de Brienne in underestimating them. It was necessary to avoid a needless confrontation with the Parlement of Paris especially, and this is what determined Necker's policy concerning the convocation of the States-General. The declaration of the Parlement that the coming States-General should be organized exactly like the preceding one of 1614 made no sense at all to Necker, and he suspected that the Parlement had made a serious blunder by that decree of September. "The dissatisfaction in the kingdom was universal at the time the Parlement recalled the forms of 1614," he wrote in his book on the French Revolution.[16] Here was an opportunity to capture public opinion from the sovereign courts that he did not allow to pass by.

The main reason Necker thought the forms of the last States-General meaningless for the one to be held in 1789, was because the two assemblies were entirely different. It was not only that one hundred seventy-five years separated the two assemblies and much had changed in the kingdom during that time. More to the point was that the coming States-General had come about in circumstances that were unprecedented for any previous assembly of estates, unless one went back to the year 1355, and no one seemed eager to refer to those unhappy days. But the fact was that the forthcoming States-General had been extracted, one could even say forced, from a reluctant ministry and monarchy. Although the terms "constituent power" and "constitutent assembly" were not yet in vogue, everyone knew the States-General to be convened in 1789 was intended to draw up a new constitution for France. In that respect it was unprecedented and all the rules and forms of previous States-General had no relevance for it.

As for the organization and the forms of procedure for a constituent assembly, Necker believed the most essential requirement was that it be representative of the nation, which meant what he conceived to be the dominant political forces in the kingdom. It must be an assembly that would have the confidence of the nation. But what was the "nation" and what kind of organization of the States-General could be certain to enjoy its confidence? Here Necker could see no end of fierce controversy and divisiveness. But he knew it would be a mistake either for himself or for the government as a whole to decide these questions. Despite his own personal popularity the government did not have the moral force to make those decisions. Was there any other moral support that could be called upon? Necker thought of the Assembly of Notables convened in February 1787. Certainly it was not a perfect solution to the problem, for it represented the highest aristocracy in the kingdom: princes of the blood, peers both secular and clerical, in fact the great majority of the Notables were of the First and Second Estates, and those who might be considered to represent the Third Estates were officials who had acquired nobility by purchase of office. Yet the important thing was not their social rank but their interest in serving the country, and in giving to the king their own insights on the questions to be presented to them. It was believed by the public that the Assembly of Notables of 1787 had performed creditably the task for which they had been called, namely to give their independent judgment on the reform proposals submitted to them. It was a group appointed by a previous ministry and could not be considered the handmaiden of the present one, and it had been summoned previously for a function entirely unrelated to that for which they were now called, namely to give their advise about the organization and the forms to be used for the forthcoming States-General. Finally, the Assembly of Notables was a solution to that problem about which the Parlement of Paris could make no reasonable objection.

The king was agreeable to that solution, and on October 5, 1788, the decree-in-council was published announcing the convocation of an Assembly of Notables for the following month.[17] The preamble explained to the public that while the king would desire to follow the procedures of the States-General of 1614, so many conditions had changed since that time it was necessary to make some revisions. The preamble pointed out for example that the Third Estate in 1614 was represented by only the larger cities; this left unrepresented the non-noble and non-clerical people of the other towns and in the countryside. Furthermore the deputies from the cities in 1614 were locally-chosen civic leaders of the Third Estate, whereas today the city officials were office-holders who had acquired their posts by purchase and were nobles. Many other matters were pointed out which made the previous States-General inapplicable for the present, such as the great change in the population of the bailiwicks that sent deputies in 1614, and also the fact that about one-seventh of the area of the kingdom had been annexed since 1614 and the local institutions in the newly acquired areas were not comparable to those of the provinces that had sent deputies in 1614. Lorraine, for example, had proportionally a far greater number of bailiwicks, while other newly annexed provinces had none at all. It was more than enough to reveal to the public the complete lack of seriousness of the Parlement's decree on the subject in September.

The second Assembly of Notables met on November 6 at Versailles. About 40 of the 144 members who had attended the first assembly the year before were unable for various reasons to take part, and were replaced by others of equivalent rank and stature. The princes of the blood again presided over the bureaux, now reduced to six because of the absence of the duc de Penthièvre. The duc d'Orleans was to preside over the Third Bureau, as before, but failed to show up for the first meeting, and a substitute was hastily ap-

314

pointed, the Archbishop of Bordeaux. Orleans did manage to preside in 10 of the 25 sessions.

The opening session took place with all the customary pomp and ceremony of such occasions under the ancien régime, which was described in great detail by the writer of the procès-verbal. "Mr. Necker," we are told, "sat at a small bench on the right, at the end of the table occupied by the four secretaries of state. He wore ordinary dress."[18] The proceedings were opened by a message delivered personally from the king, followed with a welcoming speech by the Keeper of the Seals. Necker then gave the lengthiest speech. It was a dress rehearsal for the opening of the States-General the following year. There was very little in Necker's speech that was ceremonial. In presenting the difficult matters for the Notables to decide upon he steered a delicate course between the desire to allow complete freedom of deliberation to the assembly but at the same time offer useful guidance that would be up to the deputies to accept or reject as they saw fit. No one who has read carefully this speech delivered before the Assembly of Notables and the later one of May 5, 1789 before the States-General could agree with the often-stated notion that Necker left the nation directionless on the great issues it faced in those years. He did not hesitate to present his own ideas, but did so in a deferential manner relying upon persuasion rather than issuing commands. He always addressed the representative assemblies, whether the Notables in 1788, or the States-General in 1789, and even the Constituent Assembly in the final, bitter months of his third ministry, with the greatest consideration and courtesy. His critics, who were of military, or magisterial, or aristocratic background were unable to appreciate this kind of delicatesse which is the necessary requisite today of all leaders of constitutional and democratic regimes. Necker's speech of November 6 before the Notables makes an interesting contrast to Calonne's at the first Assembly of Notables on February 22, 1787, in showing some awareness of the opinions of the audience he was addressing. Necker said that the king:

> knows the respect one must have for ancient practices of a monarchy; it is by their lineage that all established rights acquire renewed power, and assure public order by setting up necessary barriers to an inconsiderate love of novelty. But His Majesty is equally aware of those principles of justice which have no date or epoch and which impose upon him the duty of seeking through a just representation the desires of his subjects. You will observe, gentlemen, how much things have changed since the days of the last States-General. The great increase of money in circulation has created a new kind of wealth, and in the enormous public debt we see a large class of citizens who [as creditors] have a direct interest in the prosperity of the state in a way that was unknown in former days of the monarchy. Commerce, manufacturing, and all sorts of crafts, brought to a perfection which one could hardly have conceived of formerly, have vitalized the kingdom today by all the means that derive from a dynamic economy; and there are many precious citizens among us whose work enriches the state, and to whom the state, in return, owes esteem and confidence. Finally, the growth of enlightenment and the gradual emancipation from a multitude of prejudices has made us aware of the honor which we should hold for all those who devote themselves peacefully to fruitful work in agriculture . . . In the midst of these diverse citizens who have so many rights to recognition, the king still dis-

tinguishes what he owes particularly to the
first two orders of his kingdom.[19]

Then Necker spoke in equally eloquent terms
of the historical role of the Clergy and the Nobility.
The First Estate was responsible for the moral order
and for education, the Second Estate, "the generous
nobility from which the kings of France have received
so many glorious services," for the nation's military
security. He obviously tried not to offend the sus-
ceptibilities of any of the three orders. Yet it was
clear also that he was emphasizing the great change in
the position of the Third Estate in the nation, and
discreetly intimating the logic for the doubling of
the Third Estate. He hoped that was as far as he
would need to go.

After that introduction Necker told the assembly
that the administration was making available to them
all the data compiled by scholars and specialists regarding previous meetings of the States-General.
These experts would be on hand if any of the bureaux
had questions to refer to them. He outlined the specific topics the Notables were to deliberate upon in
four sections: First, what should be the composition
of the States-General in numbers, both the total number of deputies and the number for each order? The
second section had to do with the manner of convocation: to whom should the king's letters be addressed?
Should the circumscription for sending deputies directly to the States-General be the military governments, the financial generalities, the judicial circumscriptions called the "bailiwicks" (or
"seneschalships" in the southern and western
provinces), or the dioceses of the church? What rules
should determine who could take part in the selection
of the delegates? The third section of questions concerned the election of deputies that would go directly
to the States-General. What requirements if any
should there be for eligibility? Finally, the fourth

317

section of questions was about the instructions the deputies would take with them to the national assembly. Within the four-fold classification Necker submitted about 24 specific questions to the Notables to deliberate upon, but he said these were only suggestions, and that the Notables might wish to form other questions. In fact they did decide to draw up a list of 54 questions for deliberation. Each question was voted upon and the vote recorded in each bureau, although not the persons who voted.

From November 7 until December 12 the Notables seriously applied themselves to the task set before them. As in the first assembly the year before some bureaux kept more elaborate minutes of their deliberations than others. Again it was the First Bureau presided over by <u>Monsieur</u>, the Second Bureau under the comte d'Artois, and the Third Bureau under the duc d'Orleans and the Archbishop of Bordeaux that held the most interesting and detailed discussions. It is not sufficiently recognized in the general histories of the French Revolution the extent to which the Assembly of Notables of 1788 provided the framework for the States-General of 1789. The liberal and even democratic features that were to be later assailed by Burke and French conservatives were due to the Assembly of Notables rather than Necker or the government. Among these features were: the permission given to all Frenchmen aged 25 or over to participate in the primary assemblies of the Third Estate if they were inscribed on the tax rolls; the absence of a property franchise required of deputies to the States-General; the right of parish priests to attend directly the secondary assemblies of the First Estate; and the same right of nobles who did not possess fiefs to attend the secondary assemblies of the Second Estate.

Yet the final results of the deliberations of the Assembly were disappointing to Necker. He had hoped they would place greater importance than they did on

318

the economic and social changes in the kingdom since 1614. He had discreetly suggested that the Third Estate should be conceded the doublement, a number of deputies equal to the other two orders combined. This question was thoroughly debated in the assembly. An important minority did vote for the doubling of the Third Estate. The measure passed the First Bureau by a majority of one, due in part to the influence of Monsieur who at that time favored it, although he was to repent of his vote later. Only a minority in the Second, Third, and Sixth Bureaux favored it, and none at all in the Fourth and Fifth Bureaux. The total vote was 113 against the doubling and 36 in favor of it.

The question of the numbers of deputies for each order was related to another matter decided upon by the Notables that was a disappointment to Necker. In the States-General of 1614 each of the bailiwicks that sent deputies directly to Paris sent the same number of deputies regardless of their differences in geographical area, population, and tax contribution. Since 1614 such disparities between bailiwicks had grown ever wider. Necker presented the problem to the Notables in such a way as to leave no doubt about his own feelings: it was manifestly unjust for a bailiwick with 600,000 population to have only one deputy as did the bailiwick of 6,000 population. Again the First Bureau agreed with him, but not the others who argued that a single deputy could just as well represent the larger bailiwick as several deputies.

The Second and Third Bureaux explained in detail the reasons for their stand. It appears they decided to support the Parlement of Paris in its decree of September 24, calling for the States-General to abide by all the forms and procedures of 1614. The majority of the Second Bureau explained that "because of the many claims and pretensions that are springing up, the safest policy is to hold fast to what has been done .

319

. . If His Majesty is determined to make changes, what a crop of pretensions will blossom out!" Therefore the Second Bureau "stands by the plan of convocation of the estates that is most circumspect, wise, and most expedient, the plan which gives no legitimate grievance because it conforms to the plan of the last States-General." In addition the Second Bureau pointed out the difficulty of acquiring adequate information in time to apportion deputies on the basis of population and tax contribution. The Third Bureau presented similar arguments as did the Second. "If fear of a few inconveniences attached to old forms leads to a light-hearted adoption of important innovations, the Constitution of a great Empire could become so subject to versatility as to bring about the greatest of evils."[20]

To Necker such arguments were utterly frivolous. To stick by old customs which may have been suitable two hundred years before simply out of fear of change, and in the face of all reasonable and necessary change, was incomprehensible. He felt certain that such views were wholly out of step with the national opinion on the matters. In fact it probably was the fear by the first two estates of the increasing manifestations of resentment against them by the awakening of the Third Estate that explains why the majority of Notables voted as they did.

That "social fear," to use an expression of Georges Lefebvre, is what acted upon many of the Notables is evident in the attempt of the Prince de Conti, chairman of the Sixth Bureau, to get the Assembly to make representations to the king about the "seditious and scandalous writings" that were being published, and to propose that "all new systems be forever proscribed, and that the Constitution and the old forms be maintained in their integrity." The Bureaux agreed to make such representations. The king replied by a message written in his own hand that the representations were entirely foreign to the purpose for which the Notables had been summoned, and "I forbid them to occupy themselves with them." He added that he would be quite willing to receive the princes who were most concerned about the matter, and listen to their complaints, but not as a part of the business of the Assembly of Notables. It was that invitation which led several of the princes of the blood to present a memorial to the king at the time of the separation of the Assembly of Notables, calling attention to the great danger of the numerous attacks launched against the First and Second Estates by the writers and orators of the Third. "Let the Third Estate cease attacking the rights of the first two orders, rights which are no less ancient than those of the monarchy and should be as unalterable as its Constitution."[21] The Memorial of the princes stated what had been conceded by the Parlement's decree of December 5, that they agreed to the renunciation of all fiscal privileges and to the principle of the taxes being levied on everyone in accordance with his ability to pay. This principle also was formally sanctioned by all the bureaux of the Assembly of Notables. Whether it was a sufficient concession to halt the campaign initiated by the awakening of the different corporations, clubs, the journalists and the orators of the Third Estate whose influence radiated from the Palais Royal was becoming increasingly doubtful.

After its December 5 decree whereby the magistrates of the Parlement of Paris had hoped to recoup their popularity and stem the tide of opinion against them, they also began to move against the "licentious" writings. One of these, which contained ideas similar to the more famous essay of abbé Sieyes on privileges was condemned and publicly burned by the magistrates at the foot of the staircase of the Palace of Justice.[22] Then their attention fell upon a petition being circulated in Paris by the Six Corporations of Merchants of the city. Written by a physician named

321

Dr. Guillotin, soon to be famous for other reasons, the petition called upon the king to grant the doubling of the Third Estate for the States-General and the vote by head. The notaries of the city took part in gathering signatures for the petition to which they affixed their own. The Parlement of Paris began an "instruction" against the writing, calling upon the carpet the author as well as others responsible for the circulation of the petition. Those questioned by the court gave answers that were cool, precise, and ironic. They pointed out that the king had invited the citizens and particularly corporations to contribute their ideas on the forthcoming assembly of states in his edict of July 5. They also reminded the magistrates of the clause in their own decree of December 5 calling for freedom of the press. It soon appeared that the Parlement was getting nowhere with the questioning, and beginning to look ridiculous, so the matter was dropped.[23] On December 22 the Parlement issued a formal decree once again stating that it favors the suppression of all taxes based upon privilege: "the said court unanimously persists in the said decree (of Dec. 5) that there should be no doubt in the minds of citizens that it is the official desire of the court that all fiscal exemptions be abolished."[24]

Meanwhile, after the end of the Assembly of Notables Necker began to hold conferences with two or three ministers at a time in the presence of the king. He wanted to persuade them that the ministry must overrule three of the decisions of the Assembly: First, that which prescribed the same number of deputies for each bailiwick; Necker believed that the number of deputies should be proportionate to the population and tax contribution of each bailiwick. Second, the decision of the Notables to have the same number of deputies for each order at the States-General; Necker believed it necessary to give the Third Estate the doublement. Third, the Notables had decreed that at the bailiwick elections the three electoral assemblies--clergy, nobility, and Third Estate--must choose deputies that belong to its own order; Necker wished to make it possible for electoral assemblies of the Third Estate to choose persons that belonged to the other two orders.

Our knowledge about what transpired at these important ministerial conferences is limited to Necker's own discussion of them in his writings, particularly that on the French Revolution, and the memoirs of Barentin. Since the latter was written for the purpose of contradicting Necker it is not surprising that there is some variation in their accounts.[25] Necker, while admitting that not all ministers agreed with his proposals at first, said that in the final council meeting of December 27 all agreed with him except one member and that on one point only. He did not specify who the individual was, or the point in question, but it seems certain that it was Barentin, who was opposed to the last sentences in Necker's "Report" which indicated that he (Necker) would resign if the States-General failed in its purpose. According to Barentin four ministers were initially opposed to the proposals: Barentin, Laurent de Villedeuil, Nivernais, and Puységur.[26] The last two, however, were prevailed upon to change their minds, and only the first two remained adamantly opposed to Necker's proposals. The final decision was taken on December 27 in the presence of both the king and the queen. It was evident that the king and also the queen favored Necker's proposals. In that setting it is possible that Barentin and Laurent de Villedeuil, while still being opposed to the measures, did not make known their opposition forcefully enough to prevent Necker from believing that all ministers had agreed, finally, to the three important proposals.

The decisions taken on December 27 were published under the title Résultat du Conseil. It was an unusual format. Ordinarily royal acts were preceded by a preamble, more or less lengthy in which the king explains to his subjects the reasons for the measures given in the decree, which follow the preamble. The Résultat du Conseil listed first the commands of the king, which included the three proposals of Necker departing from the decisions of the Notables, the most important of which was the doublement. But instead of a preamble of the king, the formal clauses of the act were followed by a long essay entitled "Report to the king in his council, by the minister of finance." This essay explained in considerable detail the reasons for the decisions announced in the decree. Both the decree and the "Report" were discussed and approved by the king and his council, and so the latter had the force of law, even though written by the minister of finance. The reason for this unusual form, according to Necker's discussion in his book on the French Revolution, was that such a lengthy and detailed exposition of the decree would not be in keeping with the formal style ordinarily used for preambles of royal edicts and decrees.[27] Although Necker did not say so, it was more honest also. Even had it been written in the usual form everyone would know that the actual author was Necker rather than the king. By writing under his own name the minister of finance could speak more informally, personally, and most important, direct his discussion to the present state of public opinion and the high degree of excitement in the country about the organization of the forthcoming States-General.

The "Report" was certainly an unusual document in the history of the monarchy. It was characteristically Neckerian throughout: its length (which some no doubt thought excessive), its personal note in which Necker spoke directly to the king as he had done in the Compte rendu of 1781, the logic, the common sense, and above all the passion which suffused the whole essay. While alluding to it only indirectly, it is evident that Necker was greatly worried about the political situation and the serious division in French society. The "Report" was addressed to the king, but its ultimate audience was the public whose opinion he had so much cherished in the past, and of which now he began to be apprehensive. By using all his persuasive powers and eloquence Necker wanted to dampen down the violent quarrel that had erupted between the orders. To say, as many of his enemies did at that time, and some historians still believe, that he deliberately sought to deepen the schism, to turn the Third Estate against the privileged orders in order to rebuild the power of the king, or alternatively, to enhance his own power, is one of the most unjust and unperceptive allegations that could be made about Necker's political career. Exactly the contrary was true. Throughout his second ministry Necker's role was that of mediator, attempting to find the right compromise that would be not only acceptable but just to all sides, and reasonable in the light of the circumstances. Such was the intent of the "Report" of December 27, 1788.

Appropriately, the document began on a low key note, discussing the work of the Assembly of Notables, and pointing out that many of the problems concerning the convocation of the States-General had been satisfactorily resolved by them. But there were three important matters about which the notables were not unanimous, and because the public was so keenly interested in them, the king thought it advisable to reconsider them in his council. The three matters were then listed and discussed in turn. On the matter of the representation of the bailiwick, Necker said that by the end of December the government would be able to compile sufficient information about the population and wealth of the different bailiwicks to make it feasible to have representation based upon those two criteria. The rule of one deputy to each bailiwick may have satisfied the people of 1614, when there was not such keen interest, especially by the Third Estate, to send deputies to Paris. But it was not the feeling of the public in 1788, and it would be thought terribly unjust to have a bailiwick of half a million subjects send only one deputy, the same as the smallest baili- wick.

Because of the public excitement about the dou- bling of the Third Estate Necker addressed himself to that matter at great length. He described the argu- ments both for and against the doublement. Then he gave his own views, which have been amply described above. In arguing for the doublement, Necker sought to allay the suspicions of the privileged orders that the ultimate intent of the doublement was to bring about deliberation and vote by head at the States-Gen- eral. He asserted categorically that the traditional method of deliberation and vote by order could not be changed except by the agreement of each of the three orders and the approval of the king. One might won- der, then, why the doublement was so important for the Third Estate. Necker gave two reasons. First, the function of deputies at the States-General was like that of the Notables or members of the royal councils, to give advice and the benefit of their knowledge to the king. "One cannot deny," he wrote, "that a great variety of this type of knowledge is possessed by the Third Estate. There is a multitude of affairs about which it alone is really knowledgeable, such as both domestic and foreign commercial transactions, the state of manufactures, the means of encouraging them, public credit, interest and circulation of money, the abuse of tax collection and of privileges and so many other matters of which it alone has the experience."[28]

Another reason that the doublement was important was because Necker envisaged cases where the three chambers would want to join together for common delib- eration and voting. If there was a deadlock and the States-General should become paralyzed, Necker supposed that all three orders would vote to meet in common. If the Third Estate had only one-third the total deputation they might not be willing to do so. Thus the compromise plan that Necker was eventually to propose in his address to the States-General the following May was briefly alluded to in his "Report" of December 27. His reason for being low-key about it at this point was probably to avoid alienating the Notables any more than he had already by imposing the dou-blement.

The final argument that Necker gave for the dou-blement, which he expressed in the "Report" and which was certainly his innermost conviction, was that the doubling of the Third Estate was overwhelmingly endorsed by the public, indeed by the "nation." "Finally, the desire of the Third Estate, when it is unanimous, when it is in conformity with the general principles of equity, will always be the desire of the nation. Time will consecrate it; the judgment of Europe will encourage it; and the sovereign can only distribute his justice and advance his wisdom according to what the circumstances and opinions bring by themselves."[29]

The third question that Necker took up in his "Report" was the ruling of the Assembly of Notables that all deputies should belong to the order which sent them to the States-General. This was seemingly a matter of minor importance, but it gave Necker an opening to the most vital messages that he wanted to convey in this document. He argued that the Third Estate (for it was the only order in which this ruling was significant) should be permitted to choose deputies from among the nobility or clergy if they wished to do so. This would help to dampen the antagonism between the orders and build that spirit of national solidarity which was the aim of the king and the forthcoming States-General. Necker believed that the chief cause for dissension was the existence of

327

fiscal privileges and the inequity of the tax burden. If those injustices could be removed he thought there would be no more serious reason for conflict between the Third Estate and the privileged orders. "For the Third Estate, like the nobility, like the clergy, like all Frenchmen, is not their main concern to establish order in the financial administration, to moderate the tax burden, to bring justice to the civil and criminal law, tranquility and force to the kingdom, happiness and glory to the sovereign? It will never enter the minds of the Third Estate to seek to diminish the prerogatives, either seignorial or honorific, of the first two orders, or their property, or their persons. There is no Frenchman who does not recognize that these prerogatives are as respectable a property right as any other, that several are intimately linked to the essence of a monarchy, and never will Your Majesty permit the slightest infringement upon them."[30]

Looked at in retrospect, after all that happened in the Revolution, those thoughts seem naive indeed, and Necker was himself to lead the government in making greater concessions before resisting the onward march of the "commons" toward greater equality. But at the end of 1788 and in the first months of 1789 he had reason to believe that compromise was possible on the basis of the terms indicated in the passage quoted above.

The purpose of the "Report" was to foster the nationalist spirit at the expense of the spirit of particularism. In his exhortation to the three orders to moderate their passions and their claims, Necker became increasingly emotional. As he turned his remarks directly to the king, the "Report" became a veritable épanchement du coeur:

> Ah, how from all sides one wants to arrive
> at the port! Let no one make the efforts of
> Your Majesty vain by a spirit of discord,

and let each one make a small sacrifice out of love for the common good! Your Majesty can confidently expect it from the order of his clergy: it's for it to inspire everywhere the love of peace; it's for it to believe in the virtue of its king and to impart this belief to those who listen. It's for the order of the nobility not to give in to imaginary apprehensions, and to sustain the generous efforts of Your Majesty, at the moment that he is solely preoccupied in assuring the general happiness, at the time that he wants to call all hearts and minds to second his benevolent aims. Ah, Sire, only a little time, and all will turn out well. I hope that you will not always have to say what I heard you say once in speaking of public affairs: "For several years," you said, "I have had only moments of happiness." Moving words, when they are the expression of a sincere soul and the feelings of a king so deserving of being loved. You will find it again, Sire, this happiness; you will rule a nation which knows love, and which political novelty that it is not yet ready for, has distracted for a time from its natural character. But sustained by your actions and strengthened in its confidence by the purity of your intentions, it will think no more hereafter but to enjoy the stable and happy order which it will owe to you.[31]

Necker then went on to describe the "stable and happy order" that the king intended to bring about. Louis XVI had told his ministers that he would never levy another tax without the consent of the States-General of the kingdom; that he would consult with the coming States-General on the suitable intervals that it would be regularly convened; that he would consult

329

with them about the means of establishing regular institutions for the management of the finances of the
government, so that the nation would never again suffer from the mismanagement or the incompetence of a
minister. The States-General would be invited to take
up the questions that have arisen about the use of
lettres de cachet, and the matter of freedom of the
press, and publicity that will be given to all acts of
the government.

Here was, in short, the practical abdication of
Louis XVI as an absolute monarch. He intended to become a constitutional monarch, ruling in conjunction
with a national parliament. This was the harbor toward which Necker was steering the nation, and which
he thought was the national goal. Probably he was answering the challenge of the Parlement of Paris in its
decree of December 5, which reproached the ministry
for not making explicit just what the king was willing
to concede. Necker laid out in the final pages of his
"Report" a new order which would be permanent and not
simply for the duration of the reign of Louis XVI. He
pointed out to the king that absolutism is really for
the benefit of ministers; it is they who are impatient
of any sharing of power because it is in their interests. The king would be in a happier position by ruling with a national parliament. He would no longer be
subject to the conflicting and sometimes dubious advice of ministers. With the States-General he could
consult directly with his subjects. His actual power
would be more secure, the nation would be stronger
with this change in the constitution.

> The resolutions which Your Majesty has taken
> will leave him all the great functions of
> supreme power; for national assemblies with-
> out a guide, without a protector of justice,
> a defender of the weak, can themselves err.
> And if there is established in Your
> Majesty's finances an immutable order, if

confidence soars, as one may hope, if all
the forces of this great kingdom are become
vitalized, Your Majesty will enjoy in his
external relations an ascendancy which ad-
heres much more to real and well-ordered
power than to an authority that is irregular.[32]

Such was the superiority of a limited, constitutional monarchy over the absolute rule which had been
established in the seventeenth century. Necker assumed that it would be possible to find a just balance
between the national assembly representing the nation
and the necessary executive powers that must remain to
the king. It was to prove much greater a task than he
thought at the time when plans were made for the
States-General. But this was his vision of where the
nation was going at that time, and where it ought to
go. If he was wrong in the short run, perhaps he was
not in the long run. Constitutional regimes backed by
the spirit of the nation have proved to be stronger
than absolute regimes, and France never again returned
to the absolute monarchy of the ancien régime in which
there was no form of national representative assemblies.

The "Report" ended on a note that indicated that
Necker was not a naive optimist, but that he was fully
aware that the noble dream which he had just drawn for
the king might not come to fruition because of the
forces of division within the nation.

However, if a difference in the number of
deputies to the Third Estate becomes a subject or a pretext for discord; if one contests the right of Your Majesty to make a
preliminary decision demanded with such insistence by the greater part of his subjects, and which preserves in its entirety
the constituted forms of the States-General;

331

if each one, yielding to an unreasonable im-
patience, not willing to wait upon the
States-General the perfection of which they
have a different opinion; if one pays no attention to the difficulties in which the
government finds itself, and in the midst of
the present ferment, and in the midst of
this fight over custom versus equity, form
versus reason; finally if each one, discon-
tented that his own desires, not for the
long run but for the moment, are not met,
loses from view the permanent good that we
must work toward, . . .

If all that happens, Necker wrote in the final sentences of the "Report," then the only thing for the
king to do is to ask for the resignation of the minister who had counseled him to take those steps.[33] It
was this comment that Barentin, and perhaps some others, found difficult to accept, arguing that it was
out of place for a minister to make such a threat to
the public in a decree in council ratified by the
king. But Necker insisted upon keeping it in. He
knew that his position in the government was dependent
on his popularity, and he was putting that popularity
on the line.

The publication of the Résultat de Conseil had
the impact on public opinion that Necker had hoped.
Writing later in his book on the French Revolution he
asserted that it "spread a universal calm (over the
nation), and this tranquility, a hopeful sign, seemed
to announce, seemed to promise, the peaceful reunion
of the States-General and its propitious influence.[34]

The bitter opponents of the doublement reacted
violently against the Résultat de Conseil as was to be
expected. The Parlement of Paris turned against
Necker and sought to block his loan of 25 million
livres from the Discount Bank in January. The magis-

trates, led by Duval d'Eprésmesnil, claimed that the Genevan was purposely fomenting division between the Third Estate and the nobility.[35] But after the turn of the year it became apparent that the Parlement of Paris had lost its power with the public. The writer of the "Secret Correspondence" reported on February 2 that Duval d'Eprésmesnil, the hero of the national resistance against the May edicts only eight months previously, was now hissed by the crowds as he strode through the gardens of the Palais Royal. It was a dramatic revolution in his own personal career, but it might have been some comfort to him had he known that many others were to follow the same course, including his enemy, the Director General of Finances.

[1]*Journal d'Adrien Duquesnoy* (Paris, 1894), I, 36. "Un vil coquin" was this deputy's description of the Tribune of the People.

[2]*Oeuvres complètes de Necker*, VI, 395-399.

[3]Charles-Louis-François de Paule de Barentin, *Mémoire autographe de M. de Barentin, Chancelier et Garde des Sceaux sur les derniers conseils du Roi Louis XVI*, ed., Maurice Champion (Paris, 1844), 43-45.

[4]François-Emmanuel Guignard de Saint-Priest, *Mémoires* (Paris, 1929), I, 197.

[5]Mercy-Argenteau, *Correspondance secrète*, II, 80.

[6]*Ibid.*, 213.

[7]Saint-Priest, *Mémoires*, I, 204.

[8]*Correspondance secrète*, II, 217.

[9]*Ibid.*, 221.

[10]*Ibid.*, 234.

[11]Egret, *Necker*, 264.

[12]Lescure, II, 328. "Une espèce de érsipèle aux jambes."

[13]Flammermont, Remontrances, III.

[14]Ibid., III, 780-781.

[15]loc. cit.

[16]"De la Révolution française," in Oeuvres complètes, IX, 57.

[17]Oeuvres complètes de Necker, VI, 399-405.

[18]Procès-verbal de l'Assemblée des Notables tenue à Versailles en l'année 1788 (Paris, 1789), 46.

[19]"Discours de M. Necker," in Oeuvres complètes de Necker, VI, 412-413.

[20]Procès-verbal de l'Assemblée des Notables.

[21]"Mémoire des princes," in Archives parlementaires, I, 487-489.

[22]Flammermont, Remontrances, III, 785.

[23]Charles Chassin, ed., Les élections et les cahiers de Paris en 1789 (Paris, 1888-1889), I, 67-72.

[24]Flammermont, op. cit., III.

[25]Egret wrote that "the memory of Necker on the events of the debates in Council is summary and imprecise; Barentin's is more detailed and seems surer." La Pré-révolution française, 362, n. 6. I cannot see why that conclusion follows. Egret accepted Barentin's Mémoire autographe without question. A more accurate evaluation of that source was given by Jules Flammermont in his article "Le Second Ministère de Necker," Revue historique, 46 (May-June, 1891), 53, n. 3. While not sympathetic to Necker's policies, Flammermont wrote about Barentin's Mémoire autographe: "There are not words strong enough to condemn this audacious lier, who himself at every turn accused Necker of lying and calumny."

[26]Barentin, Mémoire autographe, 61-75.

[27]"De la Révolution française," in Oeuvres complètes. IX, 65.

[28]Oeuvres complètes de Necker, VI, 445.

[29]Ibid., 449.

[30]Ibid., 457.

[31]Ibid., 458-459.

[32]Oeuvres complètes de Necker, VI. 467.

[33]Ibid., 468-469.

[34]"De la Révolution française," in <u>Oeuvres complètes</u>, IX, 78.

[35]Lescure, <u>Correspondance secrète</u>, II, 321.

CHAPTER 10

THE CONVOCATION OF THE ELECTORAL ASSEMBLIES

The political reputation of Necker has suffered because of his supposed miscalculations. Both his contemporaries and subsequently the historians have placed on his shoulders the responsibility for the failure of the moderate revolution and the coming of the violent revolution. When Necker returned to Paris from Basel soon after the July days of 1789 Arthur Young saw his party pass through Belfort, and the English agronomist was moved to write in his journal: "Monseigneur Necker passed here today on his way to Paris, escorted by fifty bourgeois horsemen, and through the town by the music of all the troops." Young maintained that Necker had complete power during his second ministry to do whatever he wanted: "He had the greatest opportunity of political architecture that ever was in the powers of man; the great legislators of antiquity never possessed such a moment; in my opinion he missed it completely, and threw that to the chance of the winds and the waves, to which he might have given impulse, direction, and life."[1]

Some of his severest critics were those like Malouet and Jean-Joseph Mounier whose aims were the same as Necker's, to bring about the revolution in an orderly and peaceful way that would preserve the full executive power of the monarchy, the social order, and the sacred rights of property. Necker was criticized for not anticipating the deadlock that occurred immediately after the convening of the States-General in May. His critics believed he should have forced the two privileged orders to join with the Third Estate. Eventually Necker did advise the king to insist on the reunion of the orders but this came after the Third Estate had demonstrated its power in June by passing the resolution of abbé Sieyes declaring the assembly

of the Third Estate to be the representatives of the
nation. Thus the final union was achieved too late to
save the prestige of the monarchy and prevent the radical leaders of the Third Estate (the "factious ones")
from seizing control of the Assembly and ruining the
plans of the moderates.

Necker had waited until the eleventh hour to use
the force of the government against the privileged orders. His reason for doing so was to give a peaceful
solution a chance, to attempt to bring about a union
of the orders based upon compromise and not coercion.
He believed that what most concerned the Third Estate
was the matter of fiscal privileges of the clergy and
the nobility. If tax equality were assured, and both
the clergy and the nobility had left no doubt that
they were willing to give up all fiscal exemptions and
admit a tax system based upon ability to pay, then
Necker thought compromise on the question of the future organization of the States-General was within
possibility. His plan was to get an agreement of the
three orders to meet in a common assembly and vote by
head on matters that were of concern to all orders.
On matters of concern to the individual orders they
would be permitted to hold separate assemblies. Implied in Necker's compromise plan was the assumption
that the Third Estate did not intend to go beyond the
achievement of fiscal equality and attack other privileges that the nobles and the clergy did not intend to
give up. Necker's compromise plan was barely intimated in his "Report" of December 27, but he was to
spell it out clearly in his address to the States-General on May 5.

What were the chances of such a compromise? In
his later writings about his second ministry Necker
complained quite rightly that his critics who wrote
after the failure of his compromise plan had the advantage of hindsight. It was natural to think that
events must necessarily have had to turn out the way

340

they did. What should have been done to prevent the catastrophe is always clearer after the catastrophe than before, and therefore it is easy to put the blame on the minister in power who failed to foresee that particular denouement. But it is not true, Necker argued, that what did happen necessarily had to happen. The failure of compromise, and the violent revolution that followed, were not inevitable. The political situation was volatile; decisions that proved to be turning points were not taken without significant opposition.

As was true of Necker's first ministry, facile judgments are made about his second ministry without much knowledge of the circumstances. It has become a cliché that Necker financed the American War by loans rather than taxes, as if it were possible for him to do otherwise; or that he did not include the extraordinary costs of the war in his Compte rendu of 1781 because he wanted to deceive the public. A knowledge of the circumstances would show that he could not have published the extraordinary expenditures without revealing too much to the enemy. One of the issues that Necker's post-mortem critics continually reproached him about in his second ministry was the decision to have the States-General meet at Versailles rather than at some provincial city safely removed from the Parisian populace which was to overpower the monarchy in the October days of 1789. But could the king have taken such a step which would have advertised to the nation that he distrusted his people? In the exalted patriotic feeling of the early months of 1789 when there was such an outpouring of expressions of loyalty to the king and gratitude for his convening the States-General such a step was unthinkable.

In view of the information and evidence at his disposal there is reason to think that Necker's judgment of public opinion and what could be expected of it was not as mistaken as it might appear in retrospect. There is a tendency for history to see only the bitter animosities that divided the Third Estate from the privileged orders, and to overlook the great surge of ardent national feeling that subordinated particularist claims to the greater goal of national unity and harmony. The "spirit of 1788" alluded to in a previous chapter had not suddenly disappeared in the early months of 1789, as the famous passage so often quoted from the Journal of Mallet du Pan might lead one to think.[2] The best proof of this can be seen in the cahiers drawn up by the assemblies that sent deputies to the States-General, as will be shown in the following chapter.

To understand the great surge of patriotism stimulated by the elections of deputies to the States-General it is necessary to be reminded how thoroughly most classes of the population were drawn into the process. All males over the age of 25 who were inscribed on the tax rolls were allowed to participate and vote at the primary assemblies. The procedures for the selection of deputies had been for the most part worked out by the Assembly of Notables and codified in the Regulation of January 24, 1789. Necker's policy was to follow the recommendations of the Notables wherever possible. His only departures were in cases like the doublement, where he believed the Notables did not reflect the desire of the "nation." Where the national desires and the recommendations of the Notables were the same, then their decisions were adopted by the government. On most matters that needed to be decided upon, the work of the Notables was productive and their recommendations followed through by the government.

The electoral circumscriptions decided upon from which to send deputies to the States-General from the pays d'élections were the same as those used in 1614. These were the most ancient administrative institutions of the monarchy dating from the time of Philip

342

II in the High Middle Ages. In the provinces of customary law they were called "bailiwicks" (baillages),
in the provinces of Roman law or "written law" they
were called seneschalships (sénéschaussés). By the
eighteenth century they had become primarily judicial
in function, being directly below the thirteen parlements. There were a total of 92 of these jurisdictions that sent deputies directly to the States-General. Of this number 82 had deputed directly to the
States-General of 1614, and ten new jurisdictions were
created for the States-General of 1789. Each bailiwick or seneschalship was assigned a certain number of
"deputations" depending upon its population and wealth
or tax contribution. Each deputation consisted of two
deputies from the Third Estate and one each from the
other two orders. The pays d'élections sent 624
deputies, of which 312 were for the Third Estate and
156 for each of the other two.[3]

Shortly after January 24, 1789, letters were sent
out from the king to all the great bailiffs and
seneschals of the sword explaining the reasons for the
coming States-General and commanding the officers to
convene "in as short a time as possible" the assemblies of three orders to meet in a designated city,
usually the seat of the bailiwick, "for the purpose of
conferring with one another on what remonstrances,
grievances, or complaints they should propose to the
general assembly of our said estates; and for that
purpose to nominate, choose and elect (a designated
number) persons from each order worthy of this great
mark of confidence by their integrity and zeal."
Attached to the letter was the Regulation of January
24 giving precise details of how the deputies of the
assemblies were to be chosen.

The letters and the Regulation were permitted to
be copied on unstamped paper so as to make it possible
to distribute them widely among the population. The
bailiff's own instructions were added to the royal

343

documents and sent out to each parish, village, commune, and town, to be posted in market places, on
church doors, and read to the congregations from the
pulpits. The entire population was made aware of the
importance of the impending event. The fact that the
electoral process took place within a few weeks must
have added to the general excitement, extending to all
classes and to the farthest recesses of the kingdom,
and even overseas to the colonies.

The method by which the three assemblies of the
orders were chosen was a complicated, yet truly representative system, beyond reproach from the liberal or
even the democratic standpoint. Aside from the general instructions contained in the king's letters to
the grand bailiffs and seneschals about choosing
"worthy people" the government made no attempt to influence the choice of deputies. The king's officials,
such as intendants, procureurs du roi, sub-delegates,
were all strictly prohibited from trying to influence
either the choice of deputies or the drawing up of the
cahiers and instructions that the deputies carried
with them to Versailles. For such abstinence Necker
was severely criticized in later years. According to
Malouet's memoirs, the former intendant of the Navy
tried to persuade Necker to use all the powers of his
office to influence the choice of deputies among the
electoral assemblies. In the two or three months preceding the States-General Malouet was an intimate advisor of Necker and Montmorin, the two ministers who
together exercised the predominant power in the king's
councils. According to Malouet's memoirs, it was during those months that he wrote down his thoughts on
what the government should do in the circumstances of
that time. The elections to the States-General took
place in an atmosphere of increasing popular violence.
The coming States-General was a great question mark;
no one could be certain what would happen, and Malouet
had the darkest forbodings which were amply justified
by events. "Are you going to allow this great crisis

344

to approach without taking any preparations for defense, without any plan?" he supposedly queried the ministers. "You have the means to know who the men (favorable to the ministry) are and to choose them, or at least to direct their choice." It was by means of the police force, the intendants, and the king's attorneys in all the courts that Malouet believed such influences could be exerted.[4]

Others also criticized the ministry for its "lack of energy" and Necker answered this criticism in his books written after his departure from office. The criticism was totally unrealistic. Even if the king had wanted to, how would it have been possible to influence the choice of 1200 deputies? Who could know which of the individuals in the electoral assemblies would support the government's policies and which not? What could the government do to hold them to their promises supposing it would be possible to influence them by pressure or bribery? He made no mention of the fact, but it will be remembered that the king had appointed all the Notables in 1787 and that did not insure an assembly that was docile toward the minister who had convened them. The Plenary Court of Loménie de Brienne was also appointed by the government and almost unanimously boycotted by the appointees.

But the strongest argument against Malouet's advice was that it would have been contrary to the entire spirit of the king's decision to summon the States-General. "Even to succeed with great difficulty, and success would certainly have been problematic, was it for the king to offer an example of corruption and intrigue in the search for suffrages?" Only his enemies, the enemies of the government, would have wanted him to do so, for that would have given them a perfect weapon to undermine the government. It was necessary, Necker wrote, to remember the spirit in which the king had assembled the representatives of the nation:

I had thought that the call of the representatives of the nation around the throne being a great concept of both the heart and the mind, one should not, in carrying it out, tarnish its character. On the contrary, I thought that a feeling of elevation was the most appropriate in this noble enterprise, and one should take care to uphold it. I also believed that at a time when the convocation took place in the name of the fatherland, at a time when the assembly was inspired by a feeling for the public good, the ties of confidence and fraternity would acquire a renewed force. I thought especially that gratitude would exert a moderating influence on people and that the most generous act of the monarch would win him renewed affection. I would have blushed to think that servitude was more in accord with love than liberty. But the error which I committed along with all of France was not to have foreseen that in this century of philosophy, theories, and abstractions, those idols of the mind, obtain the greatest homage, to the exclusion of all other cults.[5]

To a later age which has become accustomed to a government's influencing the outcome of elections, particularly dictatorships which do not blush to report a majority of 99 percent in favor of the regime, Necker's views on this question must seem hopelessly naive. But France was taking its first steps in the life of representative government; and idealism, not cynicism, was the order of the day. It would have required a different sort of person than Necker to initiate the French in the ways of hypocrisy. It was sometime during this period that Necker told the king he would be useful only for certain kinds of policies. "If a Richelieu or a Mazarin is required, then Your

Majesty must let me resign," an offer that the king did finally accept on July 11, 1789, albeit momentarily.[6]

The Regulation of January 24 provided an extensive participation of all different classes in the selection of deputies and in the writing of cahiers. For the First Estate, all bishops, abbots, and other ecclesiastical people possessing benefices were invited to attend the principal bailiwick assemblies of their order. Parish priests, even those who were not beneficed but received their material support from salaries called the portion congrue, were also permitted to attend the bailiwick assemblies directly. All other ecclesiastical persons: monks and nuns, canons of cathedral chapters and others besides parish priests who did not possess a benefice, were convened at a specified place to send deputies. The cathedral canons could send one deputy for every ten of their number to the bailiwick assembly, other clergy attached to the cathedral one for every twenty. The regular clergy, monks and nuns, sent one deputy for every convent or monastery. The nuns of course sent representatives who were male clerics. Despite the liberal provisions of the Regulation no women attended the electoral assemblies of the principal bailiwicks.

It was one of the surprises of the electoral process that such a great number of parish priests, the congruists, were elected deputies to represent the First Estate at the States-General. This was to be of momentous consequence because the parish priests were strongly in favor of the demands of the Third Estate, and their defection from the assembly of the clergy to the "Commons" in the June deadlock was crucial in the victory of the Third Estate. Necker's critics thought it unfortunate there were not a greater number of prelates and condemned that provision of the Regulation. In his later writings Necker defended the parish priests as very suitable representatives not only of the church's interest but that of their parishioners. It is probable that in his heart of hearts he would like to have seen more prelates elected. His good friend, abbé André Morellet, with whom he had crossed ideological swords twenty years earlier over the affairs of the Company of the Indies, and who had just received a wealthy benefice, wanted very much to be elected to the States-General but his candidacy aroused no interest at his bailiwick assembly. In any case, Necker pointed out that it would have been inappropriate for the government to have dictated to the church its method of selecting its representatives. It was the Assembly of Notables, which included a great number of influential prelates, who had decided upon the method of election of the deputies of the First Estate.

As for the nobility, the Regulation provided that all nobles, those possessing fiefs and those who did not, even the most recently ennobled, could attend directly the bailiwick assemblies of the nobility. This measure was also criticized in later years since it was thought by some that only the fief-owning nobility should be permitted to attend. This "liberal provision" of the Assembly of Notables was contrary to traditional practices and shows that the Notables were not invariably governed by tradition. Women and even minors who owned fiefs were permitted to send a representative to the bailiwick assembly of the nobility.

All the deputies at the bailiwick assemblies of the Third Estate were sent there by primary assemblies. In the larger towns, which were specifically named in the Regulation, the craft guilds, the professional corporations, and other such organizations met and selected their representatives. Those who did not belong to a corps met at the mayor's hotel and elected deputies. In the smaller towns and villages the local judge or some officer designated for the purpose convened an assembly of all the inhabitants who were residents, aged 25 years or more, French citizens, males, and inscribed in the tax rolls. These assemblies drew up cahiers and selected representatives to go to the assembly of the Third Estate at the principal baili-wick city.

It was a very liberal franchise for that age, and of course Necker came in for criticism because of it, although the Assembly of Notables had originally made the recommendations.[7] Much of the criticism came from those influenced by the physiocratic doctrine, accord-ing to which only landowners were truly citizens. All transients, including wealthy capitalists were birds of passage and not really patriotic if the basis of their fortune was not in agriculture. In his reply to this criticism Necker pointed out that there was no precedent for requiring a property qualification for voting, and it would have been impossible to impose such a qualification in the limited time that remained before the scheduled convening of the States-General. Furthermore, he doubted that a property qualification could have been high enough to make any difference in the character of the persons who were eventually se-lected to go to the States-General.

The Regulation of January 24 applied only to the pays d'élections. Separate acts were drawn up by the royal council and sent out to the other regions not included in that act. These were the pays d 'états and the pays conquis . The former were provinces that had been brought under direct authority of the king of France by special treaties. The latter were the provinces brought into the kingdom since the last States-General of 1614. The Necker ministry hoped that the deputies from both types of provinces could be selected from bailiwicks as in the pays d'élections so as to make the electoral process as uniform as pos-sible throughout the kingdom. But here it encountered serious opposition, especially from the pays d'états, who did not consider themselves to be provinces just like any other. Some were apt to be proud of their separate character and insistent that special privileges and immunities originating from their treaties of admission into the kingdom be observed strictly. Such an attitude gave rise to pretensions and claims that were often contradictory. The nobility of Brittany were the most recalcitrant reactionaries. Surprisingly the province of Dauphiné which began by demanding the restoration of its old estates which would have placed it in the camp of the "aristocratic revolution," in fact became the outstanding exponent of just the opposite, the "national revolution." These two provinces illustrate the contradictory impulses that made the convening and organizing of the States-General such a redoubtable task.

The combination of hopefulness and apprehension that Necker must have felt after the promulgation of the Regulation of January 24 was probably well expressed by a dispatch of baron de Staël to Gustavus III of Sweden:

> The letters of convocation for the States-General have been sent today. The estates will assemble at Versailles on April 27, and the entire kingdom, beginning on the first of March, will assemble according to bailiwicks and draw up cahiers which will be taken to the States-General. This is a great day for France. Those who have followed the progress of this revolution, by a backward glance of only three years, can hardly conceive of the course of events nor the sudden change of opinions.[8]

But this positive note was offset by a dissonant one. Baron de Staël wrote also: "The interior affairs are not taking the path one would desire. The disunion between the privileged orders and the Third Estate is causing a great deal of embarrassment to the government. Brittany especially is difficult to control. I believe that the nobility and the clergy (of that province) will not send deputies to the States-General. It's a province entirely separate from France. It is a hotbed of insurrection (un foyer d'incendie").[9]

It was unfortunate for Necker's plans that the province which was one of the most backward in the kingdom from any aspect--social, economic, and political--was to play such an important role in the history of the Revolution. Arthur Young visited the province of Brittany in September 1788 before the conflict between the Third Estate and the nobility had erupted, when the chief conflict was between the Parlement of Rennes supported by the Estates of Brittany, against the royal intendant and military governor. Young wrote that "one-third of what I have seen of this province seems uncultivated, and nearly all of it in misery." While in Rennes in September Young witnessed the troops under the command of Stainville brought into the city to keep order. He was puzzled why the populace should identify with the Parlement of Rennes and the Estates. "The distinction between the noblesse and the roturiers is nowhere stronger, more offensive, or more abominable than in Bretagne" [Brittany].[10] From that province came the most radical deputies of the Third Estate, who refused to accept any compromise proposal to settle the dispute with the nobility on the matter of voting by head or by order. It was the Breton delegates who founded the society to become known as the Jacobins. And in Brittany also was to be found the most resolutely reactionary nobility, who refused to send deputies to the States-General but remained in the province to lead the counter-revolution which erupted during the period of Jacobin rule four years after the convening of the States-General.

During January 1789 the struggle in Brittany became a veritable class war between the nobility and the radical Third Estate. It began in late September 1788 when the pronouncement of the Parlement of Paris regarding the organization of the forthcoming States-General unwittingly triggered the "awakening of the Third Estate." In the 42 cities of Brittany there was an abrupt change in the governments, an oligarchical regime being replaced by one endorsing the demands of the Third Estate, notably the doublement and the vote by head at the forthcoming meeting of the estates of Brittany, due in late December. Unlike Languedoc, the vote in Brittany was taken by order. The Breton nobility had long dominated the estates of Brittany, where each nobleman had a right to a seat without representing anyone but himself. Practically alone among the nobility of France, the Breton nobles had refused to concede the principle of fiscal equality and to renounce tax exemptions and fiscal privileges.

It was this issue that brought about the troubles early in 1789. The city of Rennes had passed a resolution requiring their deputies at the forthcoming estates of Brittany to insist that the exemption of the nobility and clergy to a special Breton tax called the fouage be abolished. The origin of this tax was typical of the fiscal system of the ancien régime. In 1641 the estates of Brittany incurred a deficit of 300,000 livres which they met by issuing a loan for that amount. It was to be amortized with interest at the end of the year from a special tax levied on homes (foyers) of the non-privileged plebeian class. But at the end of the year the debt was not paid and the special tax became a permanent one levied each year, from which the nobility and the clergy continued to be exempt.[11]

The Breton nobles refused to agree to give up their exemption to the fouage. Whereupon the city of Rennes went a step further and required its deputies at the estates to insist not only that the exemption to the tax be abolished in future levies, but that the nobles and clergy be required to pay to the provincial government all the back taxes of the fouage which they had not paid since 1641 together with accrued interest! The deputies of that city were given an imperative mandate not to agree to anything at the estates until that demand had been met. It was obviously a provocative declaration of war rather than a serious attempt to bring about change by negotiation. When it appeared that the other cities of Brittany would follow the lead of Rennes in requiring their deputies to insist on that measure or withdraw from the assembly of estates, a stormy session was assured.

The intendant of Brittany at the beginning of December 1788 when the quarrel over the fouage became serious was Antoine-François de Bertrand-Moleville. Alarmed over the threat of civil disturbances that might erupt if the estates of Brittany became deadlocked, Bertrand-Moleville hurried to Versailles and sought to get the government to quash the decree of the city of Rennes in order to prevent the other cities from imitating it. The minister to whom intendants of the provinces reported and received their orders was the minister of finance. Hence, it was necessary for Bertrand-Moleville to persuade Necker to take the step. He succeeded in getting an interview with Necker, but found the director-general of finances not very eager to act on his proposals. "Mr. Necker replied with the utmost sang-froid that he could not assume himself the responsibility of such a grave measure without first getting the king's approval and that of the other ministers, and that he would take it up at a council meeting to be held that evening." The next day the intendant repaired to the ministry of finance to learn of the decision but he could not get another interview with Necker. He learned from officials in the Contrôle-Général that Necker did not think the situation was serious enough

353

to require such drastic action. Greatly disappointed,
Bertrand-Moleville resigned his commission as intendant on December 6. He had never been an admirer of
the Genevan banker, being one of the intendants hostile to Necker's reform ideas. In fact six months
previous to this incident, before Necker returned to
the finance ministry, Bertrand-Moleville had sought
without success to get the Parlement of Rennes to condemn his book on the administration of finances.[12]
Naturally this new incident did nothing to improve his
opinion of Necker. Bertrand-Moleville became one of
the most violent memoir writers against Necker in the
years after 1789, accusing him of being the cause of
all the misfortunes that fell upon France.

Necker's response to this situation (in Brittany)
was perhaps typical. He was not anxious to commit the
force of the royal government in disputes of this
kind, hoping that they could be settled without intervention. Again it was his laissez-faire policy for
which he was accused of "lack of energy" by those anxious to respond to the popular effervescence with
armed might. For Necker, force was the last resort
rather than to be invoked at once. In the case of
Brittany, when the estates met in December they did
become deadlocked, as feared, and on January 3 the
royal government suspended the meeting of the estates.
Ill-will between the Third Estate and Nobility did not
improve, and in fact, degenerated into open violence
in the streets of Rennes in late January, with the
servants and lackeys of the nobles fighting the youthful middle-class sons of the Third Estate. At Rennes
the hall where the estates met was surrounded by a
threatening crowd and the nobles virtually imprisoned
for three days. Finally the nobles emerged, swords
drawn, and were able to leave Rennes. The citizens of
the latter city received reinforcements from those of
Nantes, despite the attempts of the military governor
to prevent the arrival of the Nantois.

How Brittany would be represented at the States-General was indeed an intractable dilemma for Necker. He sought to resolve it by the Regulation of March 16 in which the nobles and prelates of Brittany met separately at the city of St. Brieuc to select their deputies to the States-General. The Third Estate and the parish priests met in seats of the seneschalships as in the pays d'élections. The prelates and nobles declined to send deputies to the States-General in protest against the doublement. The deputies of the Third Estate arrived at Versailles breathing fire and ready to continue the battle against the privileged orders.

If Brittany seemed to be the province where enmity between the orders was most intractable, the province of Dauphiné in the opposite corner of the kingdom appeared by the beginning of 1789 to offer the best model of a spirit of unity between the orders, and an example of willingness to mitigate particularistic claims in the interests of national goals. Grenoble had been the city where resistance to the May edicts was most determined, and where the parlement received popular support. When the magistrates of that body received lettres de cachet exiling them from the city, popular elements rose up in violent defiance on June 7, 1788 and prevented the magistrates from leaving. Troops were brought into the city by the military governor, the duc de Clermont-Tonnerre, but his lack of energy "almost amounted to complicity."[13] When his troops were met with a hail of tiles from rooftops he hastily withdrew them into quarters. The magistrates were finally able to leave the city and the calm that followed the "day of tiles" enabled the notables of the city one week later to convene an assembly at the Hôtel-de-Ville on their own initiative without the authorization of the government. The military governor "closed his eyes" to the illegal assembly. It met only briefly, long enough to call for a general assembly of the notables of Dauphiné to

355

meet on July 21 at a small town, a suburb of Grenoble named Vizille, for the purpose of drawing up a constitution for the provincial government of Dauphiné.

Nothing in the past had indicated that such an assembly of notables in Dauphiné could be anything but reactionary. During Necker's first ministry he had offered to establish a provincial administration of his type for the province. But the insistence of five nobles of ancient lineage that they had a right to sit in the assembly defeated Necker's project. When Loménie de Brienne attempted to establish a provincial assembly for Dauphiné in the summer of 1787 the Parlement of Grenoble rejected it and demanded the restoration of the old estates of the province which had last met in 1628. Nothing would seem less propitious for the "national revolution" than the predominance in Dauphiné of a proud nobility anxious to recover lost powers in the government of the province and a vast army of magistrates, officials, lawyers, notaries, all the people dependent upon the parlement of Grenoble for their careers and livelihood.

Yet the brief meeting at the Hôtel-de-Ville of Grenoble in June and the assembly at Vizille the month following proved to be momentous events in the bringing about of the "forgotten revolution." A number of enlightened nobles and magistrates were responsible for this result, but certainly a great amount of credit was due to a brilliant thirty-year-old lawyer of Grenoble who was royal judge in that city, Jean-Joseph Mounier. It was due to him that a coalition between the lawyers and the nobles was formed at the June 14 meeting at the Hôtel-de-Ville, and the larger assembly at Vizille. The purpose of the Vizille assembly was to lay the foundations for the new government for the province of Dauphiné, but it was clearly not to be a restoration of the old estates of 1628. Mounier persuaded the delegates that the Third Estate

356

should have double the number of each of the other orders, and that the meetings and voting should be done in a common assembly rather than in separate assemblies of the orders. The purpose of the revolutionary movement in Dauphiné was not to restore ancient privileges. It was to gain for all citizens rights that were not derived from tradition but from natural law. Furthermore, Mounier lifted the horizon of the delegates from the provincial to the national vista. The chief demand the assembly made to the royal government was to convoke the States-General. The estates of Dauphiné would not demand the right of abonnement of tax levies, nor the right to approve royal taxes and loans. This was to be the exclusive function of the States-General.

The Vizille assembly had been an unauthorized assembly, and represented only a part of the cities of the province, ten out of nineteen, and less than a fifth of the parishes.[14] The deputies were all notables of the three estates: 50 from the clergy, 165 nobles, and 276 from the Third Estate. Its petition to the government was in the form of a remonstrance similar to those of the parlements. By the beginning of August the ministry of Loménie de Brienne was no longer in a confident mood and the leaders of the Vizille assembly were permitted, by royal decree of August 2, to hold a regularly constituted and legal assembly at the city of Romans to draw up their constitution for the Estates of Dauphiné and to submit their project to the royal government for approval.

During September the Romans assembly worked out a compromise between the orders that was often difficult and placed in jeopardy. It was a rehearsal for the States-General that took place the following year, in that while all three orders had agreed to the doubling of the Third Estate in the estates of Dauphiné there had been no agreement on the question of deliberating by order or in a common assembly. Mounier led the

357

fight for deliberating and voting in common, but he did it in such a way as to avoid antagonizing the privileged orders. On September 18 the assembly nearly broke up over the question, but Mounier and the other moderates managed to prevent the denouement which occurred later at the States-General. A suitable, if precarious compromise was worked out to which each of the three orders, deliberating separately could adhere. There would be deliberation and voting in a common assembly in the estates of Dauphiné. But each order could determine the qualifications of its deputies. This enabled the nobility to require that deputies from that order must have had noble status for at least one hundred years and from all four grandparents, and must be landed proprietors paying at least 50 livres land tax. The recently ennobled were not permitted to serve as deputies for the nobility. The clergy excluded the congruists from representing that order of the estates of Dauphiné, allowing only priests who were proprietors of benefices. Both deputies of clergy and nobility had to pay a land tax of 50 livres per year. The clergy, like the nobility, would have 48 deputies each, the Third Estate 96 deputies. The leaders of the Third Estate at Romans required that their deputies be landed proprietors paying at least 50 livres in royal land taxes. Their deputies were to be elected by primary assemblies, the electors being required to pay a stipulated tax according to the city, 40 livres at Grenoble and lesser amounts in the smaller cities. The tenor of the Romans assembly it can be seen, was far from democratic. The ideas of the physiocrats were influential in that body, Mounier himself having absorbed some of the tenets of the sect. The Third Estate was not pleased about the exclusion of the ennobled and the evident prejudice in favor of the older noble families. In order to get the Third Estate's consent to that measure the nobles agreed not to permit their agents such as stewards or judges in the seigneurial courts to take part in the primary assemblies of the Third Estate. More remarkable was the Third Estate's insistence that not even farmers who leased land from noble or clerical proprietors would be permitted to vote in those assemblies, a clause which the nobles also reluctantly agreed to. The Third Estate was also insistent that all agents of the royal government: the employees at the office of the intendant, and royal officials of any kind, should not participate in the political life of the province.[15]

The new provincial government that the Romans assembly proposed for Dauphiné, despite its socially conservative character, was similar to Necker's provincial administrations and those of Loménie de Brienne, for their assemblies also had been composed of notables. The doublement, the vote in common assembly, the administrative functions such as assessing and collecting the taxes, administration of social welfare, construction and maintence of roads, all were similar to those of the reform ministers. But the Romans assembly, while giving up all special privileges of the province and subordinating the estates of Dauphiné to the forthcoming States-General, insisted upon more autonomy from the royal government. The powers of the intendant were even more restricted than in Necker's provincial assemblies of 1778 and 1779. The parlement also was shorn of its political powers and restricted to judicial functions alone. The king was not even mentioned in the constitution, the assembly of estates meeting periodically on the authority of the constitution rather than the king. The president of the assembly was elected by the assembly itself rather than appointed by the king as in Necker's assemblies. One final feature of the new constitution that was to be important later was the manner of electing deputies to represent the province at the States-General. The Romans assembly insisted that the estates of Dauphiné should be able to choose all the deputies of the province in the provincial assembly,

in contrast to the principle adopted by the Assembly
of Notables a month later, namely that the bailiwicks
and the seneschalships should send deputies directly
to the States-General.

It was near the end of September 1788 when the
Romans assembly had completed its project of a provincial constitution. It recessed until Novermber 1 in
order to take the project to the royal government and
get its approval. Necker was the minister who reviewed their work. The delegates who took the constitution to Versailles found the Director General of Finances a reserved, rather cold person, who had some
serious reservations about it. Primarily he was dis-
pleased that the king was not mentioned at all. He
told the delegates that with the coming of the States-
General he could see no reason for such suspicion of
royal authority. "It is important for the general
well-being to cease regarding the king and the nation
as enemies engaged in ceaseless combat." he told
them.[16] The convocation of the estates of the
province should be by order of the king, and the king
should appoint the president of the assembly. Also
Necker objected to the exclusion of certain classes
from the electoral process: the recently ennobled,
the renters of noble and church lands, the parish
priests who were congruists, the royal agents of the
intendants and the financial administration. Finally
the method of choosing deputies to the States-General
was to be decided upon by the forthcoming Assembly of
Notables and the assembly of Romans had pre-empted
their decisions by having the province of Dauphiné
represented at the States-General rather than the
seneschalships.

On the whole, however, the unity achieved by the
three orders and the nationalist spirit which animated
the assembly of Romans rather than provincial particularism were all positive features, and the delegates
were fearful that the royal government could upset the

360

delicate compromise between the orders that made these benefits possible. The delegates were surprised and relieved to find that the royal decree of October 22, 1788, modified their work much less than they had feared from the demeanor of the minister of finance. He did insist that the renters of noble and clerical land be given some representation, but on the whole the decree was written in a style laudatory to the Romans assembly, and Necker's initial criticism was greatly mitigated.[17] This may have been due to the personal influence of Mounier, who had not gone to Versailles with the delegation but wrote earnestly to Necker explaining why ratifying the work of the Romans assembly was crucial. "It is extremely important," he wrote, "to maintain in this province the confidence which your return to the ministry has inspired in it, and to do nothing to weaken its resolution to sustain the monarchy."[18] Necker's basic reluctance to interfere in local affairs once again prevailed.

Unfortunately the decree of October 22 did not end Necker's embarrassing relations with Dauphiné. On November 1 the Romans assembly reconvened and ratified the constitution for the province. Elections were held immediately for the new estates of Dauphiné which met on December 1 and sat until January 16, 1789. By the end of December the estates had chosen the twenty-four deputies to the States-General. Mounier was one of the deputies of the Third Estate, elected by acclamation as was Malouet at Riom. But in drawing up the cahier or instructions that the deputies were to take with them to Versailles the estates enjoined them to insist on the doublement of the Third Estate at Versailles and the vote by head rather than by order. They were not permitted under any circumstances to agree to vote by order. This was an "imperative mandate" of the kind often given to deputations in the States-General of the old type that preceded the absolute monarchy. It was ironic that the estates of Dauphiné should use an archaic weapon to insist on a

361

thoroughly modern principle that Necker wanted, the deliberation by head rather than order at the States-General. But Necker had wanted to bring this about by compromise and negotiation, not by force. If all deputations were bound by imperative mandates, the nobility for vote by order and the Third Estate the opposite, there would be no chance of a compromise settlement. The instructions that the king had sent out to all the bailiffs and senschals of the sword required the electoral assemblies to grant their deputies sufficient powers to agree to the general puposes of the States-General. In effect, the imperative mandates were illegal, or at least contrary to the spirit of the States-General of 1789. Necker wrote to the president of the estates of Dauphiné protesting that mandate and threatening to reconvene the assembly to revoke it. This was an eventuality dreaded by the leaders of the estates because it threatened once again to disrupt the tenuous unity of the three orders. Before the closure of the estates Mounier and other leaders of the Third Estate had made a great concession to the nobility by including in the imperative mandate the provision that "the sacred rights of property" would be interpreted to include the exemptions to the taille that was attached to land rather than persons. In some of the southern provinces the taille originally was not a personal tax levied on persons who were taillable, but on lands that were taillable. The exempt lands in the pays de taille réelle had become alienable for generations and the purchasers of the exempt land had to pay the value of the exemption. According to the mandate of the deputies for Dauphiné they were required to insist that if the taille were abolished, or all exemptions to the taille abolished, then the owners of non-taillable lands should be indemnified. It was typical of the thorny problems facing the National Assembly when "feudalism" was abolished later in the year in trying to distinguish between "oppressive and unjust feudal

privileges" and the "sacred rights of property."
Mounier and his friends believed the most essential
matter at this time was to get a constitution ratified
that guaranteed liberty, political liberty above all,
and that if concessions had to be made on economic and
social matters to the nobility or clergy in order to
prevent a schism in which everthing would be lost, including liberty, then those concessions were advisable
and even necessary. Again perhaps due to the influence of Mounier, Necker gave up the idea of reconven-
ing the estates of Dauphiné to revise their mandate.[19]
But the disgruntlement about the concessions made to
the nobles and clergy particularly in the rural peasant population, became serious in the weeks after the
estates had adjourned. The unity and harmony between
the three orders which Dauphiné had set as an example
for the rest of the provinces was in fact very fragile.

Yet it cannot be doubted that the example of
unity and patriotism of the province was an important
moral force in the kingdom during these months. Other
provinces and also the city of Paris wanted to imitate
the Dauphinois in that method of representation and
selection of delegates but were not permitted by the
government which felt bound to abide by the decisions
of the Assembly of Notables.

The personal prestige and influence of Jean-
Joseph Mounier continued to grow in these months. He
became a national figure, and probably the best representative of the spirit of the "forgotten revolution."
In February his brochure "New Observations on the
States-General of France" was published in Paris and
became one of the most widely read tracts during the
period preceding the convocation of the national assembly of estates. The main theme of the essay was to
demonstrate that France did not have a constitution in
the past which could be resurrected for the present
time and which could be authoritative on all matters.

Mounier rejected the authority of Montesquieu on the subject: the notion that the French were free under the absolute monarchy because of the independent judiciary institutions. The traditional States-General did not have legislative powers, so that there was no basis of comparision to the States-General that was now being convened. If the coming States-General should be divided into three separate deliberating assemblies representing the orders, one assembly alone could veto and block any act of the States-General. But that was not true of the traditional estates which could not do anything against the king's will. Furthermore, Mounier made a thorough historical investigation of the procedures of the traditional States-General and found that the custom of deliberating and voting in separate assemblies was a fairly recent innovation. It was a consequence of the Wars of Religion beginning in 1560, in which antagonism between the orders was dramatically accentuated. So even if one insisted that France did have a constitution already it was not such as could provide clear and definite rules on matters of greatest importance. The "fundamental laws of the monarchy" about which Montesquieu had made so much were really not very significant in the late eighteenth century. There were only two: the rule of succession to the throne according to the "Salic Law," and the rule that the people could not be taxed without their consent. If these were by no means negligible matters they did not make a constitution. What did Mounier mean by a "Constitution"?

> We do not have a constitution, and the happiness of the monarch and that of his subjects requires one. I understand by constitution, a body of fundamental rules upon which all the powers of the government are based, which allows to the social body the means of obtaining the laws necessary for maintaining public order; but they must be true laws, symbols of the general will,

which indicates to the people what they must obey, which restrains all agents of power within just limits, which sees to it that laws are not invoked in vain, that arbitrary decisions cannot be substituted for them, and that by conforming to what it commands, the most obscure citizen can enjoy all the independence of nature.[20]

Without such a constitution it was not possible for reforms to be carried out with permanent effect. All the reform ministers of the past could not prevail against the powers of particular interests, the holders of special privileges, because they had nothing firm to stand on in resisting the privileged classes. No matter how virtuous and capable the minister, whether a Turgot or a Necker, they were dependent on the will and resolve of the king, and when the king rules without a constitution his rule is arbitrary. Arbitrary power, whether it be that of a single person or that of many, was the greatest of evils. Mounier said that the despotism of many was far worse than that of a single person. He was referring to feudal, aristocratic tyranny, but those words were to be prophetic for the future when Mounier would feel the violence of popular tryanny. It could be said of Mounier, as Prince Mirsky wrote of Alexander Herzen, that "few people have ever felt as keenly the value of individual liberty and the horror of despotism."[21]

Along with his passion for individual liberty was Mounier's conviction that such liberty could not be gained except through the national constitution. This is why he rejected all pretensions of the individual provinces whether pays d'élection or pays d'état to preserve their existing privileges or recover former ones. Only the States-General should have the power to grant or withhold taxes, and exercise the legislative power under the constitution. Nationalism suffused Mounier's thought, but it was not the

365

nationalism of abbé Sieyes or of the later Jacobins. Full executive authority would be left to the king, the popularly elected lower legislative house would be balanced by an upper chamber of distinguished peers appointed by the king. The provincial governments were to retain a great deal of autonomy, but not as much as the cahiers indicated nor as the future Constituant Assembly was to grant them. As the most elequent spokesman of the "forgotten revolution" Mounier was a liberal but not a democrat.

A number of other influential essays were published in the last two months of 1788 and during the time electoral assemblies were being convoked by the bailiffs and seneschals of the sword. Abbé Sieyes by no means had the field to himself. In Languedoc there was some manifestation of an aristocratic reaction in that ancient liberties were being remembered and their restoration sought. It was in answer to one such brochure that the comte d'Antraigues was moved to write his "Memorial on the Constitution of the Estates of Languedoc."[22] He maintained that the existing estates of Languedoc were not really representative of the province. The assembly of estates consisted of 23 bishops who sat "by reason of their dignity" and were not representative of anyone else; there were 23 barons who "having purchased a landed estate were given the title of baron by the king and were appointed by him." The Third Estate consisted of double the number of each of the other orders, but they were mayors and consuls who held their office by purchase, and represented no one. Therefore d'Antraigues argued that it would be unjust for the assembly to nominate the deputies for Languedoc to go to the States-General as some reactionary aristocrats were calling for. D'Antraigues said it was the seneschalships which had traditionally sent deputies to the States-General and they should be the electoral districts for 1789. Like the leaders of Dauphiné, d'Antraigues denounced provincial particularism. The estates of Languedoc

366

should not insist on the right to approve royal taxes or loans for that province but should acknowledge the States-General as alone capable of that function. The same nationalism and desire for national unity among the three orders suffused the essay of d'Antraigues as it did those of Mounier.

In another essay that was more widely read than the above which was of interest only to Languedoc, "Memorial on the States-General, their rights and the manner of their convocation," Antraigues showed himself to be one of the true liberals of the nobility. The States-General would grant a constitution to France, and his view of the nature of the coming constitution was similar to that of Mounier's. He made a strong plea for the doublement of the Third Estate. The traditional States-General had no clear answer to the number of deputies each order should have, and "when there is no positive means of resolving such a great question, it is the immutable law of nature that should supply it." "The third Estate," he asserted, "is the people; it is the state itself. . . . It is in the people that national power resides; it is for it that the state exists, and for it alone that the state should exist."[23] One might think he was reading Sieyes essay, "What is the Third Estate?" but those were the words of an aristocrat of Languedoc writing in late 1788. But the conclusion d'Artraigues drew from those remarks were much less drastic than the abbé's. In this essay d'Artraigues called only for the doublement of the Third Estate at the States-General and did not mention the question of voting by order or by head. In fact he represented the nobility the following June in the conferences held at Versailles to resolve the question of verification of the powers of the deputies. He sat across the table from Jean-Joseph Mounier who was the spokesman of the Third Estate. What had caused Antraigues to change is not clear. But his most influential tracts in late 1788 and the first months of the following year were illustrations that the liberal nobility and the moderate Third Estate were not so far apart in their thinking, and that the desire for national unity was stronger than has usually been supposed.

When the royal letters patent were sent out to the provinces late in January, there was a conspicuous omission. No letters were sent to the capitol city of Paris. This was because of a dispute that had arisen between two rival authorities each of whom claimed the right to preside over the local assemblies of the city. One of these was the Provost of the Merchants and the Alderman, head of a very old municipal corporation which resided at the Hôtel-de-Ville. The other was the Provost of the Vicounty of Paris, who resided at the Châtelet, one block down the river from the Hôtel-de-Ville; the office of the Provost of the Vicounty was similar to that of the grand bailiff of the sword or seneschal of the sword in the provinces. Both authorities (Hôtel-de-Ville and Châtelet) were of ancient vintage. The officials of the Hôtel-de-Ville even claimed that their corporation was more ancient than the monarchy itself. It had begun as an association of merchants, a hanse, which had acquired trading privileges very early in the middle ages. The Capetians had granted not only privileges but certain functions of local government to the corporation. In the later middle ages the Provost of the Merchants and Aldermen became the acknowledged leader of the Third Estate not only in Paris but throughout the northern part of the kingdom, the Langue d'Oil. This was the office held by Etienne Marcel in 1356. In the last States-General held in the 16th century and in 1614 the Provost of Merchants received special permission from the king to preside over an assembly of the bourgeois of Paris; this assembly drew up its own cahier reflecting the desires of the inhabitants of the city, and elected deputies directly to the States-General, who sat in the assembly of the Third Estate.

In 1614 the Provost of Merchants himself led the delegation from Paris, and was elected President of the Assembly of the Third Estate.

Now, in January 1789, the Provost of the Merchants and the officials at the Hôtel-de-Ville were demanding the same privilege they had enjoyed formerly of convoking an assembly of the bourgeois of Paris and sending deputies directly to the States-General, by-passing the authority of the Provost of the Vicounty. But the Provost of the Vicounty at the Châtelet maintained that this had been an unusual favor granted by the king and was not in accord with the fundamental laws of the kingdom. According to regular traditional procedure the Provost of the Vicounty would convoke the assemblies of the three orders within the city just as the bailiffs and seneschals were doing in the provinces.[24]

At the time of the last States-General in 1614, and those held earlier in the 16th century, there were very few nobles resident in Paris. In the period preceding the establishment of absolutism by Richelieu and Louis XIV the nobility resided in their provincial château and when they had business at Paris, maintained only temporary residences. In the following period of absolutism the most influential members of the nobility built town houses and palaces in the capitol city and became legal residents of Paris in addition to maintaining their ancestral manors on their fiefs. It was estimated by the Minister of Police in 1789 that 4,000 nobles were residents of Paris. Many of them served in the king's government in various capacities; holding honorific posts in the King's Household, or serving as military and civilian officials; many were nobles of the robe, owning offices in the corps of magistrates. Now if the Provost of the Merchants were to receive the right of assembling the inhabitants of the city to send deputies directly to the States-General, what about

369

this considerable group of nobles? Would they take part in this assembly and vote for deputies who would sit at the assembly of the Third Estate at Versailles? Obviously not if the three orders were to be retained at the national level. Seemingly the new condition made illogical the claim of the Provost of the Merchants. The officials at the Châtelet did not fail to point it out. It was more logical for the Provost of the Vicounty to assemble three orders for the bailiwick of Paris-within-the-walls, and each of the three orders would send its own deputies to Versailles. According to the argument of the Châtelet, the rightful place of the Provost of the Merchants was at the head of the Third Estate in the general assembly of the three orders presided over by the Provost of the Vicounty. This was the reasoning which eventually prevailed at the royal council when, on March 28 it handed down a Regulation governing the elections of Paris to the States-General. According to the Regulation the city of Paris-within-the-walls was divided into 60 primary electoral districts for the members of the Third Estate; each district would send deputies to the general meeting of the Third Estate for the city. Similarly, Paris was divided into 20 departmental districts for the elections of the nobility. In each department the nobility would gather and elect deputies to the general city assembly of the nobility; the general assembly of the three orders would be presided over by the Provost of the Vicounty in the same manner as did the bailiffs and sénéschaux of the sword.

The Regulation of March 28 provoked an explosive outburst of indignation in the capitol city, first, among the officials of the Hôtel-de-Ville where the Provost of Merchants sent the king his resignation, then among the partial assemblies of the nobility. All maintained that the Regulation deprived the Commune of Paris of its traditional privilege of electing itself its own deputies to the States-General. In the partial assemblies of the Third

370

Estate, each district protested in its cahier the "destruction of the Commune." And no less emphatic were the partial assemblies of the nobility in the 20 departments. In each one of these assemblies of the nobility, resolutions were passed condemning the destruction of the Commune. The procès verbaux of the Third Department of the nobility, who assembled at the Palais-Royal was typical: The nobles resolved to "use all their efforts to bring about a general reunion of the commune in order to deliberate and vote by head, to draw up the cahier, and to have only a single assembly of the Third Estate and the nobility under the name of the Commune." The assembly of the nobility of the 5th Department protested the "abolition of the Commune of which the inhabitants of Paris have always taken part, without distinction of estate or of birth." The partial assembly of the 20th Department of the nobility meeting at Les Invalides included in the procès verbaux of their meeting the following resolution which was passed unanimously: "Considering that the permanent usage of the Commune of Paris has always been to proceed in common to the election of deputies, since there is in this city no other distinction in public assemblies than that of Bourgeois of Paris, the said inhabitants have a right to protest against the form prescribed by the Regulation [of March 28]."[25]

Similar resolutions were passed by all other assemblies of the nobility. There can be no question of the strong stand taken on this matter by the Parisian nobility. A substantial group of the nobles wished to resist the regulation of March 28 and to insist on the "restoration of the Commune." But it was decided in an informal meeting in which most of the partial assemblies were represented, that the situation was not propitious for such a tactic. The partial assemblies were being held late in April; the States-General was to open around the first of May. It was decided by the nobility that any resistance of

371

the people of Paris to the regulation would simply delay the opening of the States-General to which all eyes were now turned. But nevertheless, a formal protest was included in each cahier of the partial assemblies and in the cahier of the general assembly of the nobility against the "dissolution of the Commune," and the expectation was expressed that the States-General itself would restore the "rights of the Commune" in the general constitutional reorganization of the kingdom which everyone was anticipating.

The stand taken by the nobles domiciled in Paris on the Commune is pertinent evidence that the Second Estate was not closing itself off from the rest of the nation in the early months of 1789. The Parisian nobles were attempting to bring about the same kind of unity of the orders as had been achieved in Dauphiné. As the Breton nobility was the most intransigent opponent of the Third Estate, the Parisian nobles were its most determined allies. Jean-Sylvain Bailly, who was elected a deputy of the Third Estate from Paris, remarked in his Mémoires that "the attitude of the nobility of Paris was excellent; if it had been such in the rest of the kingdom the regeneration of the kingdom would have been the work of brothers."[26] Here in the capitol city was to be found the most liberal-minded and progressive of the members of the Second Estate.

There is reason to believe that the liberal nobility was not such a minority as is usually thought. Rather the greater part of the order came to Versailles with the intention of working with the Third Estate to realize the national goals of the States-General. This spirit can be seen by a study of the cahiers of the nobility drawn up in their bailiwick assemblies. From that source it is evident that what united the orders was far more important than what divided them. From that standpoint Necker's hopes and intentions of achieving a compromise in the

dispute over the method of deliberation and voting was
not so chimerical as is usually thought.

[1]Arthur Young, Travels in France during 1787, 1788, 1789, ed., M. Betham-Edwards (London, 1889), 211.

[2]"The public debate has changed course. It is only secondarily a matter of the king, despotism, the Constitution. [Now] it is a war between the Third Estate and the other two orders." Journal de Mallet du Pan (Paris, January 1789), I, 163-164.

[3]"Regulation of January 24, 1789," in Oeuvres complètes de Necker, 447-509. These 92 electoral circumscriptions were called "principal bailiwicks and seneschalships." There were 133 smaller bailiwicks and seneschalships called "secondary." They were included in the circumscription of the principal bailiwick and seneschalship, sending deputies to those assemblies.

[4]Mémoires, I, 252.

[5]"Sur l'administration de M. Necker," in Oeuvres complètes, VI 195.

[6]Ibid., 183.

[7]The bias against the Assembly of Notables is palapable in the Lavisse Histoire de France: "In order to oppose to the enlightened classes the masses of ignorant and dependent people they (the Notables) demanded the right to vote without any condition of tax payment for their servants, hired hands, and lackeys. Such intransigence by the Notables was a disappointment to Necker, and increased the resentment in the nation against the privileged classes." Tome IX, premiére partie, 315. On the contrary, the Assembly of Notables required that all who took part

in the primary assemblies be taxpayers, however modest their contributions.

[8]Correspondance diplomatique, 97.

[9]Loc. cit.

[10]Young, Travels in France, 124.

[11]Antoine-François de Bertrand-Moleville, Mémoires particuliers pour servir à l'histoire de la fin du règne de Louis XVI (Paris, 1816), I, 37.

[12]Ibid., 35-36.

[13]Jean Egret, La Révolution des Notables, Mounier et les Monarchiens (Paris, 1950), 8, 16.

[14]Ibid., 17.

[15]Egret, Les Derniers Etats de Dauphiné. Romans (Grenoble, 1942).

[16]Ibid., 56.

[17]Ibid.

[18]Egret, La Révolution des Notables, 24.

[19]Ibid., 34-41.

[20]Egret, Les Derniers Etats de Dauphiné, 186-187.

[21]D. S. Mirsky, A History of Russian Literature (New York, 1958) 221.

[22]Emmanuel-Louis de Launay, comte d'Antraigues, Mémoire sur la Constitution des Etats de Languedoc, (n.d., n.p.).

[23]D'Antraigues, Mémoire sur les Etats Généraux (1788).

[24] Charles L. Chassin, ed., _Les Elections et les Cahiers de Paris en 1789_ (Paris, 1888-1890), I. All the pertinent documents on the quarrel between the Châtelet and the Hôtel-de-Ville are in this volume.

[25] Chassin, _op. cit._, I, 163.

[26] _Mémoires d'un témoin de la Révolution_ (Paris, 1821-1822), I, 44.

CHAPTER 11

THE NATIONAL MANDATE

Among the severe critics of the government of Louis XVI for its lack of resolution in handling the revolutionary crisis in the final months preceding the meeting of the States-General was Alexis de Tocqueville. Recognizing the need to be just toward the ministers of the government and to be cognizant of the gigantic tasks that confronted them, he yet concluded that "what was done could not have been better calculated to make the conflict inevitable."[1] He was referring to the decision made by the government after the council meeting of December 27, 1788 to order the doubling of the number of deputies for the Third Estate at the forthcoming States-General. Tocqueville condemned the government for failing to order at the same time the deliberation of the three estates in a common assembly with the vote counted by head. He thought the government should either have taken sides with the privileged orders, the First and Second Estates, and ordered the same number of deputies for each of the three estates and the vote in separate assemblies; or it should have sided with the Third Estate and ordered at the same time as the doubling, the vote in common. Instead of doing one or the other the government imagined it could separate the two policies of numbers of deputies in each order and the question of voting.

> At that time M. Necker so advised the King; he was momentarily, the idol of the nation. His traits are effaced by distance now. Still, he was one of those men who never really know where they are going, for they do not follow their own inclinations but the ideas which they think are influencing others.[2]

Necker's own inclination, Tocqueville said, was to order both the doubling and the deliberation of the
three orders in a common assembly.

Of course it was not as clear to Necker in the
early months of 1789 "where he was going" as it was to
Tocqueville who viewed the events more than half a
century later. In the complex and unprecedented situation that Necker faced in the months before the convening of the States-General it may be surmised that
it was not clear to anyone where the country was going. There were of course some strong opinions expressed. Some were alarmed at the vehemence of popular feeling and the incidents of violence that were
already erupting around the country. It was that situation which had inspired the Memorial of the Princes
presented to the king in December 1788.[3] In January
1789 the marquis de Bouillé had a conversation with
Necker in the presence of Madame Necker in which he
tried to persuade the Director General of Finances of
the necessity of revoking the decision to double the
number of deputies of the Third Estate. According to
Bouillé's own Mémoires written years later he told
Necker that the consequences of the doubling would
"turn the people against the privileged orders, and
surrender the latter to popular vengeance." Necker,
according to Bouillé, "raised his eyes to heaven and
said we must have faith in human morality."[4]

> I replied that that was romantic fiction,
> and it would lead to a horrible and bloody
> tragedy. I earnestly urged him to prevent
> the catastrophe. Monsieur Necker smiled.
> Madame Necker told me that surely I was ex-
> aggerating and although she did not say so
> she obviously thought I was crazy.[5]

The marquis de Bouillé was one of those generals
who thought the only solution to complex political
problems was military force. He persistently believed

in later years that the revolution was unnecessary, that it could have been prevented if the government had acted immediately and decisively with armed force against the national movement. Of all his critics, this was the kind with which Necker had the least patience. He thought these critics simply did not know the reality of the situation. The government did not have the force that such a resolution of the crisis would require. Where the top military commanders and many officers and soldiers were caught up in the national movement, that movement could not be crushed by military force.[6]

It has already been shown in previous chapters that to accuse Necker of having no policy of his own, of allowing matters to drift, or of following the opinions of others rather than his own, is unjust. He did intend to bring about deliberation of the three orders in a common assembly, but he wanted to do this by a compromise agreement that would not require coercion of the two privileged orders. Each assembly would decide separately on what matters they would agree to deliberate in a common assembly and what matters would be left to the separate assemblies of the three orders. Force was the last resort, not the first, and to be used only when all attempts at compromise had failed. Necker's situation was not unlike that of other mediators in history who have attempted to prevent great catastrophes. They are distrusted by both sides during the negotiations, and if compromise fails they are condemned again for not realizing the futility of their efforts. Such was Necker's fate not only at the hands of his contemporary critics but by historians as well.

The justice of the compromiser's critics depends upon his judgment of the situation. If there is really no hope of averting the collision then the effort to mediate might well be mischievous.[7] But if there is some chance of success, even if a long shot, surely

379

the mediator deserves the sympathetic understanding of the historian. We should examine the state of public opinion in those months from the convocation of the electoral assemblies until the meeting of the States-General in May. Was there really no hope of maintaining the spirit of national unity among the three orders? Was it apparent in these months that the enmity between the Third Estate and the Nobility was so irreconcilable that it would have been evident to a far-sighted statesman that a peaceful solution was out of the question?

In such a major confrontation there is usually a wide spectrum of opinion in both warring camps. The decision of the government to order the doubling of the delegates of the Third Estate had already antagonized the princes and a certain element of the conservative nobility. If the government had ordered at the same time the coercive deliberation and vote of all three orders in a common assembly it would certainly have aroused more violent resistance. By delaying the decision and seeking some sort of compromise Necker hoped to appeal to that part of the nobility that was genuinely patriotic and supported the national movement. At the same time he wanted to appeal to the moderate element of the Third Estate that also was patriotic and nationalist and wanted to maintain that spirit of unity that had been moulded during the past two years since the meeting of the first Assembly of Notables. Neither the liberal, nationalist nobility nor the moderate section of the Third Estate intended that the forthcoming States-General should become deadlocked and thereby fail in its mission. That mission was to form a new constitutional regime based upon the principles that Necker had announced the king was willing to grant after the council meeting of December 27, 1788.[8]

Despite his severe condemnation of the "imbecility" of the government of Louis XVI, Tocqueville was aware of the power of the nationalistic movement. In fact he paid eloquent tribute to it.

I think that no epoch of history has ever witnessed so large a number so passionately devoted to the public good, so honestly forgetful of themselves, so absorbed in the contemplation of the common interest, so resolved to risk everything they cherished in their private lives, so willing to overcome the small sentiments of their hearts. This was the general source of that passion, courage, and patriotism from which all the great deeds of the French Revolution were to issue.[9]

One would think that of all historians Tocqueville should have appreciated Necker's efforts to maintain that spirit and protect it from the corruption of bitter divisive influences. "A common joy," wrote Tocqueville, "filled those divided hearts and bound them together for an instant before they were to separate forever."[10]

That the spirit of discord had made its appearance in the first days of 1789 was certainly true. On one hand, princes and conservative aristocrats railed against the doubling of the Third Estate. On the other, the essay of Emmanuel Sieyes made its appearance shortly after the beginning of January 1789. It is usually said in the histories of the French Revolution that this brochure entitled "What is the Third Estate?" was the most potent of all tracts that accompanied the "awakening of the Third Estate." Someone has written that after the appearance of this essay "all France thought like abbé Sieyes." And what was the thought of the abbé? He set forth what he said were the "true principles of the social order."[11] These were derived in some measure from Rousseau's _Social Contract_, but Sieyes elaborated upon them to show

how they applied to the political circumstances of the time. The final repository of political authority was in the "nation" consisting of all the inhabitants. No one citizen had more political power than another. Only citizens could be recognized as participating in the political process, all those who had a common interest. Privileges by definition and those who held them had no right to representation in the political order. The privileged orders were antithetical to the "nation"; they were like a cancer on the body politic, noxious to the health and well-being of the "nation."[12] They were as hostile to the "nation" as the English were in enclaves of France in time of war.[13] Sieyes' essay was a declaration of war against the "privileged", a term he used interchangeably with "aristocrats."

What was most fateful in this essay was the concept Sieyes introduced into the political life of France of "constituent power." All political authority reposed in the "nation." It could never divest itself of this authority. Like Aristotle's "unmoved mover" or Hegel's World-Spirit, the "nation's" political power was not derived from elsewhere; it was power in itself; there was no authority higher or outside it, such as divine law or natural law. All other political institutions were derivative of national power. The "constituent assembly" was an extraordinary assembly elected for a specific purpose and for a limited period of time. Its purpose was to frame the constitution for the nation. While performing this task the constituent assembly was supreme in the state; no person or institution could challenge its authority, not even the king, who was only "first citizen" with no power to intervene in the work of the constituent assembly. Once the constituent assembly had completed its work it dissolved itself and institutions it had created went into operation: the legislative assembly, the judicial tribunals, and the executive authority.

It would be hard to imagine a mentality more alien to Necker's. The abbé's political system was based upon "absolutely true principles" from which all else was derived. It was impermeable to compromise, concessions, or amendments to cope with experiential reality, as closed a system as a demonstration in geometry. He had utter contempt for the man of experience who distrusted theory, convinced that such a person had not come of age intellectually. "He was a very absent man," wrote Etienne Dumont, who knew Sieyes personally, "and was by no means of an open disposition. He gave his opinions, but without discussion; and if any one raised an objection, he made no reply."[14]

Yet the thought of Sieyes was to triumph in the coming States-General. His notion of "constituent power" was adopted by the Third Estate, who had named itself the "Commons" which was probably derived from Sieyes' essay. It was the motion of Sieyes of June 17 that declared the Commons to be "the National Assembly of the deputies of the French Nation, known and verified," and which exercised supreme power in the state, denying any role to either the first two estates or the king or his ministers in the formation of the constitution. But there is reason to doubt that all deputies who voted for that resolution quite realized its absolute, totalitarian character. And it is questionable that "all France thought like abbé Sieyes" in the five months that separated the appearance of his essay and the convening of the States-General.

To find out "what all France thought" in the months preceding the meeting of the States-General there are two sources of information. One is the great quantity of brochures that poured from the printing presses after July 5, 1788, when the government invited the nation to express itself on the method of convening the national assembly of estates. It has already been seen that abbé Sieyes by no means

had the field to himself. The published articles of
Jean-Joseph Mounier and the comte d'Antraigues analyzed in a previous chapter were sympathetic to the
Third Estate, but far removed from the incisive but
abstract deductions of abbé Sieyes.[15]

The second source of information is the great
quantity of cahiers drawn up by all the electoral assemblies in the early months of 1789. The many special studies that have been made of the cahiers since
that year seem to agree that the radical ideas of
Sieyes were not shared by the electoral assemblies.
Beatrice Hyslop found that only ten of the general
cahiers (out of a total of 190 for the Third Estate)
showed evidence of the influence of Sieyes. "The attack on the class structure itself," she wrote, "was
negligible."[16]

What was most noteworthy is the tendency of the
general cahiers of the Third Estate and the Nobility
to approach each other in their demands and aspirations as to what was to be achieved by the national
assembly of estates. Scholars who have read the general cahiers have found to their surprise that the
cahiers of the Nobility were more radical than supposed and those of the Third Estate were more moderate. Tocqueville was not only surprised but deeply
shocked when he read the cahiers of the Nobility. The
nobles demanded a general declaration of rights that
would guarantee individual liberty for all men. This
was not a vaguely expressed idea. The nobles spelled
out in specific detail just what rights should be included. On the form of government the cahiers of the
nobles stipulated a permanent national assembly would
come into existence that would meet periodically and
not await the initiative of the king, and that it
would have full legislative powers. "No law shall
take effect until it has been sanctioned by the
States-General and the King." The king would retain
full executive power but with constitutional safe-

guards, such as publicity for his acts and the requirement that he communicate with the States-General on matters of military and foreign policy. "In a word," concluded Tocqueville in this essay, "it is seen from these cahiers that the only thing the nobles lacked to effect the Revolution was the title of commoners."[17]

On the other hand, the cahiers of the Third Estate have been found to be remarkably moderate and unrevolutionary. They did not call for the destruction of the traditional orders nor for a democratic regime absorbing complete powers of "sovereignty." It is sometimes said that the secondary assemblies of the Third Estate did not really represent or express in the cahiers the actual feelings of the multitude. But studies made of the parish cahiers show that they were even more conservative than the general cahiers. In a sample study which included both general cahiers and a far greater number of parish cahiers, George V. Taylor found this to be the case. "The only possible conclusion," he wrote, "is that the revolutionary program and its ideology were produced and perfected after the voters had deliberated in the spring and that the great majority of them neither foresaw nor intended what was about to be done."[18] This author found that when these assemblies mentioned the constitution they did not have in mind what Sieyes and other radicals were writing about, who were imbued with the ideas of natural law, but rather the old traditional constitution. "The preponderant rationale of revolution in the spring [of 1789] therefore, was traditionalist, or Whiggish, rather than rationalist and philosophic."[19]

A French scholar who made a detailed study of the general cahiers of all three orders near the end of the nineteenth century had come to the same conclusion. Edme Champion wrote:

In all parts of France there was a resolve
to be satisfied with partial reforms. . . .
All the mandates without exception left to
the monarchial government its stability, to
the king sufficient power. For property and
religion what was essential in the old institutions was respected. Abuses were singled out, but only to reform them and not to
overthrow institutions.[20]

Champion disagreed with Tocqueville that the
cahiers of the Nobility were as revolutionary as he
claimed. Obviously there is a contradiction in the
views of the authorities just cited. The goals expressed in the cahiers of 1789 are described as shock-
ingly revolutionary, moderately reformist and unrevolutionary, or if revolutionary it was an archaic,
"traditional," or "Whiggish" type of revolution that
was contemplated.

If we confine our attention to the general
cahiers there can be no doubt that Tocqueville's analysis of the cahiers of the Nobility was correct, and
what he said about that order was true of the other
two, the Clergy and the Third Estate. If the three
orders had been permitted to deliberate and vote in
separate chambers when they arrived at Versailles in
May all three would have voted by a great majority for
a new constitution. This would have provided for a
permanent States-General or national parliament that
would meet periodically and not be dependent upon the
convocation by the king. This parliament would have
exercised full legislative authority. No act of the
government could have been passed without the concurrence of the assembly. In matters of financial administration the assembly would be given legislative initiative. In other matters, according to the majority
of cahiers in each order, the assembly would have
shared legislative authority with the king. That
meant the king would have an absolute veto on all mea-

sures sent to him by the assembly. Some of the cahiers of the Third Estate stipulated that the king should have only executive powers, and no part of legislative. In general, the principle of the separation of judicial, executive and legislative functions was endorsed with that one exception. Even those who wished to limit the king's powers to executive functions agreed that there should be no restrictions on that power, that the king's person was sacred, and that the monarchy would remain hereditary according to ancient laws of the kingdom. There was no suggestion that the king's role would be only that of chief magistrate.

The courts of the judiciary were to be stripped of all the administrative powers, all the pretensions of the parlements to veto legislation. The courts were to exercise judical functions only. The practice of venality of office would be abolished. Titles of nobility were no longer to be purchased, or acquired by holding office. The majority of cahiers of all three orders called for a charter of liberties guaranteeing the inviolability of persons and property. And this declaration of rights was to be based upon natural law principles fashionable in the eighteenth century.[21]

Even if the cahiers frequently referred to the "ancient constitution" the ultimate result of all their proposals was to found a modern constitution that has nothing "archaic" or traditional about it. None of the previous assemblies of estates had exercised such powers as now contemplated. The British example was sometimes referred to as a model. The United States had just launched its new government under the federal constitution at the time the electoral assemblies in France were drawing up their cahiers. While France was to remain a monarchy, and "distinctions were necessary in a monarchy," some ideas expressed in the cahiers such as the separation

387

of powers and the declaration of rights might have
been inspired by the new federal as well as the state
constitutions of the North American republic.[22] As we
shall see, what most electoral assemblies, even of the
Third Estate, assumed would come out of the deliberations of the States-General would leave the three orders with a separate assembly for each, but they would
agree on certain matters for deliberation in a common
assembly of the three orders with the vote being
counted by head. As we shall also see, this was not
an "archaic" idea, but a very reasonable and sensible
compromise on the question of deliberating and voting
by head or by order. This was the compromise that
Necker suggested and hoped for. Neither can it be
said that this proposal was "Whiggish" if by that it
is meant a parliament dominated by an aristocracy.
The method of selecting the deputies to the States-
General as finally enacted by the law of January 24
was remarkably liberal and even democratic for that
age. The future constitution could hardly have been
less so.

If the cahiers were "archaic" or traditional one
would expect to see them emphasize ancient rights and
privileges, and to insist on regional autonomy. On
the contrary, with the exception of some frontier
provinces such as Brittany, Burgundy, and Alsace, the
great majority of the cahiers of all three orders emphasized the national interest. Powers of sovereignty
would be at the national capitol and not shared with
the provinces. Provincial assemblies would have no
right to negotiate with the central government about
their quota of tax contributions.

These were the provisions in the majority of
cahiers of all three orders that were truly revolutionary in the sense that an entirely new political
order was to replace the ancien régime. They were
however in accord with the concessions that the king

granted in the recess of the council meeting of December 27, 1788.

There was in addition to these revolutionary measures a broad spectrum of agreement among the three orders as to the reforms that the States-General should carry out. Many of these reform proposals in the general cahiers had been the goals of reform ministers since the beginning of the reign of Louis XVI. The regime of the intendants would be ended everywhere and replaced by provincial assemblies and administrations on the model that Necker had introduced in Berri and Haute-Guienne during his first ministry. Their most important function would be assessing and collecting the taxes of the royal government. With very few exceptions the cahiers of the Clergy and the Nobility renounced all their fiscal privileges and exemptions. They accepted the principle that the tax burden should be borne by all citizens in accordance with their ability to pay. Existing taxes were to be abolished forthwith and a new system established which would be a land tax levied on all lands. Also a new system of indirect taxation would be levied uniformly throughout the kingdom, abolishing all regional privileges. The internal barriers to trade, the transit duties, péages, or tolls were to be eliminated and replaced by a single duty tax at the frontiers of the kingdom. There was little sympathy, however, for international free trade; many of the cahiers specifically repudiated some of the treaties that had lowered tariff barriers between France and neighboring countries.

Many of the reforms called for in all three orders were influenced by Necker's reform ideas set forth in his book published in 1785 on the administration of finances in France. The government was to give full publicity to all its acts. The budget would be submitted each year to the legislative assembly. The list of pensions and favors granted by the king to individuals would be published each year. The secret use of public money would be prohibited. There would be a general restatement and codification of the laws. The courts would be reformed in the manner desired by Keeper of the Seals Lamoignon. Fees and bribes to judicial officers would be outlawed. One could continue in this vein indefinitely and list all the beneficial reforms that were to become the enduring legacy of the French Revolution. All of them could have been accomplished without commotion if the States-General had been permitted to carry out the mission it was expected to when it convened at Versailles on May 5.

On the other hand there can be no denying the fact that substantial important differences existed among the orders, especially between the Nobility and Third Estate, according to the cahiers. The Third Estate wanted to "abolish feudalism" which meant ending personal servitude of peasants to landlords without compensation to the latter; and where the feudal obligation was considered based in property law, the peasants or communities should have the option of repurchasing them at a rate fixed by the States-General. The seigneurial courts of justice should be abolished, and the exclusive privilege of hunting. The non-nobles should have equal opportunity of advancement in the armed forces and in the royal government. Above all, the cahiers of the Third Estate asserted in the strongest terms that it would not submit to humiliating ceremonies at the forthcoming meeting of the States-General. But at the same time the nobles were assured that the Third Estate would respect all privileges and ranks and marks of distinction that the nobles had won by meritorious service to the king and nation.

With regard to the Clergy the cahiers of the Third Estate wanted to increase the rights of non-Catholics above what had been granted in the edict of November 1787. They did not think the government

390

should assume the debt of the French Catholic Church, which had been incurred as a form of taxation. The Third Estate expressed some apprehension of the restrictions the church placed on freedom of expression and of printing.

As for the two privileged orders, they did insist by a great majority that they should be allowed to keep their own separate chamber and deliberate on matters that pertained to their order. They were willing to meet with the Third Estate and deliberate and vote in common on matters that concerned the national interest such as fiscal laws. They insisted that maintaining their own organization within the States-General did not infringe upon the legitimate rights of the Third Estate. The Nobility left no doubt that it would relinquish all fiscal privileges and exemptions, and even stipulated that all taxes should be collected in the same manner, on the same rolls as was done for the non-nobles. But at the same time they insisted on the right to maintain all other distinctions and privileges. These included feudal dues which they said were property rights. They agreed to the abolition of all personal servitude where it still existed, and without compensation to the serf owners. But nobles insisted on retaining all honorific privileges that were not humiliating to non-nobles: the right to bear arms, to wear all insignia of their order, to keep titles and in general to inherit the names and prestige gained by illustrious ancestors.

The Clergy indicated its concern about the extreme license of the press and other threats it saw to the well-being of the Catholic religion. It was apprehensive of the desire to expand rights to non-Catholics, and insisted on its ban against mixed marriages between Catholics and Protestants. It agreed also to equality of the tax burden, but thought some consideration should be given to the huge debt it had incurred in order to make loans to the government.

391

The clergy also was apprehensive about the proposals being made for it to divest itself of its land holdings.

In short, both the Clergy and the Nobility had good reason to fear being coerced into deliberation with the Third Estate in a common assembly in which they could be crushed by a majority. They agreed with the Third Estate on a broad area of constitutional changes and reforms. But there were vital matters on which they did not agree. Therefore the majority of cahiers of both privileged orders insisted on the right to decide separately when they would meet in a common assembly and on what matters voting would be done by head.

The enemies of the privileged orders, like abbé Sieyes and the comte de Mirabeau, asserted that the concessions made by them, such as the promise to relinquish all tax privileges, were not made in good faith, and the proof of this was their insistence on deliberating and voting in separate chambers rather than in a common assembly of the three orders. This idea has persisted in the historiography of the French Revolution. It assumes that the deputies of the nobility came to Versailles carrying in their cahiers an imperative mandate against voting by head. If this were true the failure of the States-General would have been determined before it opened on May 5.

An examination of the cahiers of the nobility on this matter, the question of voting by order or by head, shows that they did not intend to be recalcitrant. Many that did have imperative mandates were usually restricted to specific constitutional measures that did not include the matter of voting by head or by order. Of the original general cahiers of the nobility 154 have been preserved today. On that number, twenty did not express an opinion on the question of voting. Of the 134 assemblies that did express an

392

opinion, only 46 gave their deputies what could be called an imperative mandate against voting by head under any circumstances whatever. And this is giving the benefit of a doubt to several cahiers in which it is not at all clear what the local assembly intended its deputies to do if voting by head were decided upon at the States-General. Some of them did expressly require their deputies to withdraw from the States-General if that measure were enacted. But others expressly stipulated that their deputy was not to withdraw from the assembly. His instructions only required him not to consent to that measure. "He will protest," they said, "but he will not withdraw."[23]

This would indicate that some of the 46 assemblies were aware of the danger of schism and had no premeditated idea of sabotaging the States-General. Even some of the assemblies who required their deputies to withdraw indicated that they were acutely aware of the danger of schism. The assembly of Cahors, for example, instructed its deputies as follows:

> The consequences of schism in the States-General can only be disastrous; our deputies will do all in their power to prevent it; and if it is necessary to withdraw due to the resistance of the other members of the assembly, our deputies will be the last to withdraw.[24]

It is well known that there was a minority of liberal nobles in the States-General who willingly joined the Third Estate in a common assembly in June. In the 134 cahiers studied, only 15 expressed a preference for voting by head. But eight others stipulated that the question should be decided at the States-General, and their deputies were authorized to agree to whatever was decided upon.

The largest number of cahiers of the nobility fell between these two extremes. This group, comprising 65 assemblies is the most significant for understanding the attitude of the Nobility. There can be no question as to the strong preference of this group in maintaining the traditional system of voting by order. But these assemblies also clearly realized the danger of schism. Therefore they gave their deputies sufficient powers to compromise with the Third Estate on the issue. We can roughly divide these 65 cahiers into four groups, depending on the degree of their liberality and readiness to compromise.

On the far right was a group of 14 assemblies who instructed their deputies to "do everything in their power" to maintain the traditional method of voting by order. So if the States-General insisted on voting by head their deputies were not required to withdraw from the assembly but only to have their negative vote recorded. A typical example of this class of assemblies was that of Angers. After charging their deputies to defend the vote by order, the assembly added:

> Our deputies will not retire from the general assembly; they will not adhere to any schism, but they will strive by all possible means to restore and maintain peace and concord, demanding only that their protest be duly recorded.[25]

A second group that we might call the "right center" consisted of 23 assemblies who instructed their deputies to use all their influence to maintain voting by order; but if a majority of the members of the Nobility should agree to join with all three orders in a common assembly, the deputies of this group were authorized to agree and follow the majority. On what we might call the "left center" was a group of 16 assemblies who were in favor of voting by head on matters concerning the raising of revenue or other matters affecting the general interests of the nation. But they wished to vote by order on all matters which concerned only the individual order. On the far left was a group of 12 assemblies who indicated their preference for voting by order but gave their deputies full powers to agree to whatever decision might be reached at the States-General. Typical of this group was the cahier of the Nobility of Guéret:

> The assembly recommends to its deputies that they employ all their efforts and zeal to maintain the old constitution and support deliberation by order; desiring, however, to contribute with all its power to the solidarity of the three orders, so necessary to the welfare of the State, the assembly authorizes its delegates to adopt the form of deliberation which is desired by the general assembly.[26]

The Nobility has had the reputation of being the most intransigent on this matter.[27] It is true that the other two orders showed even more flexibility in their cahiers on the issue than those of the Nobility. In a random sample of 35 cahiers of the Third Estate only four seemed to adopt a position of extreme inflexibility, anticipating what actually happened in June.[28] Another four assemblies did not mention the matter of voting in their cahiers.[29] Eleven simply stated the "wish" of the assembly was to vote by head, but made no other comment as to what should be done if that wish were thwarted.[30] Sixteen of the assemblies stipulated that their deputies would be flexible on the matter and obviously looked forward to a compromise in which the two privileged orders would maintain their separate assemblies.[31] There were certain matters on which the Third Estate clearly would not compromise, namely the question of eliminating all tax privileges and exemptions. But the greater number of the _cahiers_ of the Nobility would probably have agreed to a common deliberation and vote on fiscal matters.

As for the Clergy, it appeared to be the most flexible of the three orders, and the most sincerely desirous of a compromise after the States-General convened in May. The _cahiers_ indicate that a greater proportion than the other two orders did not mention the question of voting. In a random sample of 27 _cahiers_ of the Clergy nine clearly indicated a willingness to compromise.[32] Six appeared strongly opposed to voting by head.[33] Twelve did not mention the matter of voting.[34].

There can be little doubt that when the deputies went to Versailles what was uppermost in their minds was the great task of creating the new constitution and the bill of rights. It seems clear that the majority of them expected there would be a compromise on the issue of voting by head or order. The feeling expressed in the _cahier_ of the nobility of Bourges probably was representative of the general _cahiers_:

> The spirit of union and concord which has always reigned among the three orders has also manifested itself in our _cahiers_. The opinion of voting by head at the States-General has been the only issue to divide the Third Estate from the other two orders, upon which our constant desire has been to deliberate there by order. But the wise decision to defer this question to the States-General has, as it were, annulled this disparity of principle; and it is with the greatest satisfaction that the orders have seen their _cahiers_, although drawn up separately, dictated by the same spirit.[35]

If the general _cahiers_ were a reliable barometer of what "all France thought" on the eve of the Revolution, then Necker's strategy for compromise was by no means as hopeless as his critics claimed. But that raises another matter. If the three orders were as close as their cahiers indicated, then why did he fail to bring about the compromise he sought? Near the end of the last century an American historian who read the cahiers was astounded to find so much agreement among the three orders. The deputies who were sent to Versailles with these instructions in their pockets clearly did not intend what actually happened. "The more we examine these lines of division," wrote C. H. Lincoln in the American Historical Review,

> the more evident it becomes that the terrible character of the French Revolution was not caused by the gradual accumulation of burdens upon the shoulders of the peasants, causing the gradual growth of a spirit of hostility between the several orders, but that there must have been somewhere a great lack of organizing ability, a dearth of the spirit of what we term practical politics, to allow such forces of moderation to have been wasted and a small minority of the dissatisfied sections to carry with them an Assembly the majority of which was composed of well-meaning delegates anxious to avail themselves of some practical way out of the difficulties which surrounded them.[36]

Certainly as the day arrived at last, and the opening ceremonies of the States-General were over, Necker faced the severest challenge of his political career.

[1]Alexis de Tocqueville, The European Revolution and Correspondence with Gobineau , ed. and trans. by John Lukacs (Garden City, N.Y., 1959), 78.

[2]Ibid., 76.

[3]Supra, Chapter 9.

[4]François-Claude, marquis de Bouillé, Mémoires, ed., F. Barrière (Paris, 1859), 135.

[5]Loc. cit.

[6]Jacques Necker, "De la Révolution française," in Oeuvres complètes, IX, 174.

[7]Americans may well be grateful that the British and French efforts to mediate the conflict between the Union and the Confederacy in 1862 did not culminate in success.

[8]Supra, Chapter 9.

[9]Tocqueville, European Revolution, 86.

[10]Loc. cit.

[11]Emmanuel Sieyes, Qu'est-ce que le Tiers état?, ed., Roberto Zapperi, (Genève, 1970), 151.

[12]Ibid., 211.

[13]Ibid., 140.

[14]Etienne Dumont, Recollections of Mirabeau and of the Two First Legislative Assemblies of France (Philadelphia, 1833), 85.

[15]Supra, Chapter 10.

[16]Beatrice Hyslop, French Nationalism in 1789 according to the General Cahiers (New York, 1934), 88.

[17]Alexis de Tocqueville, The Old Regime and the French Revolution (Garden City, N.Y., 1955), 272.

[18]George V. Taylor, "Revolutionary and Nonrevolutionary Content in the Cahiers of 1789: An Interim Report," French Historical Studies (Fall, 1972), VII, 494.

[19]Ibid., 492.

[20]Edme Champion, Esprit de la Révolution française (Paris, 1887), 84, 79 n. 1.

[21]A total of 615 general cahiers were drawn up in 1789, of which 93 are missing, making a total of 522 extant. See Beatrice Hyslop, French Nationalism in 1789, 244. The above discussion of the cahiers is based upon my reading of 27 of 158 cahiers for the Clergy, 151 of the 154 for the Nobility, and 68 of the 190 for the Third Estate. Most of these were read in the Archives parlementaires, ed. by Mavidal and C. Laurent (Paris, 1867-1896), II-VI.

[22]Georgia Hooks Shurr, "Thomas Jefferson and the French Revolution," The American Society of the Legion of Honor Magazine (1979), I(3), 161-682.

[23]For example, Marches Communes, Archives parlementaires (hereafter cited as AP), III, 687-689; Toulouse, AP, VI, 31-35; Riom, AP, V, 563-568; Semur-en-Auxois, AP, II, 128-131.

[24]AP, V, 488-489.

[25]AP, II, 32-38.

[26]AP, V, 355-361.

[27]The entrenched opinion in the histories of the Revolution that the noble deputies were all bound by imperative mandates not to agree to deliberation by head is probably due to the evolution of the attitude of many nobles during the deadlock in May and June. As will be seen in Chapter 13 below the opinion of the nobles tended to stiffen in response to the intransigent attitude of the Third Estate. When the king ordered the reunion of the orders in a common assembly there was deep resentment on the part of those who at the opening of the States-General were more disposed to compromise on the question of voting by head. These deputies were inclined to exaggerate the importance of the imperative mandates. When one deputy named d'Ambly from Chartres accused his colleagues of violating their imperative mandates on that question the marquis de Sillery replied that "the Nobility from Champagne has been granted complete freedom to adopt whatever laws are proposed by the States-General. These mandates are imperative only for the constitution. I am as sensitive as Mr. d'Ambly, and if my mandate had been as imperative as his I would have fulfilled it with as great an exactness as he has." AP, VIII, 172. When the 47 noble deputies who voluntarily joined the National Assembly on June 25 were accused by some nobles in Paris of violating their mandates they wrote a letter addressed to "the noble citizens of Paris" explaining that they understood the imperative mandates to apply only to the requirement that the constitution must be passed and approved by the king before any credits are voted for the government. They pointed out that the cahier of the Nobility of Paris required specifically that "The States-General will be wise enough to prevent the veto of any order from realizing the passage of laws which concern the public welfare." Charles Chassin, ed., Les Elections et les Cahiers de Paris en 1789 , III, 436.

[28]Bourges, Dax, Montargis, and Nivernais.

[29]Vendôme, St. Pierre-le-Moutier, St. Flour, and Annonay.

[30]Provins, Senlis, Chartres, Dourdan, Gien, Moulins, Forez, Lyon, Clermont-Ferrand, Mende, and Puy-en-Velay.

[31]Nemours, Meaux, Castelnaudary, Armagnac, Soule, Nérac, Evreux, Beauvais, Etampes, Mantes, Montfort l'Amoury, St. Pierre-le-Moutier, Villefranche-de-Beaujolais, Riom, Gérat, and Montpellier.

[32]Mantes, Melun, Provins, Dourdan, Gien, St. Pierre-le-Moutier, Lyon, Villefranche-de-Berg.

[33]Etampes, Nivernais, Clermont-Ferrand, Riom, St. Flour, Puyen-Velay.

[34]Meaux, Nemours, Chartres, Montargis, Vendôme, Guéret, Moulins, Forez, Annonay, Béziers, Mende, and Montpellier.

[35]AP, II, 319.

[36]C. H. Lincoln, "The Cahiers of 1789 as an Evidence of a Compromise Spirit," American Historical Review (1897), II(2), 228.

CHAPTER 12

THE OPENING OF THE STATES-GENERAL

"At the moment," wrote Madame de Staël, to a correspondent early in 1789, "France is offering a great theatrical spectacle to all Europe."[1] Certainly as the delegates gathered at Versailles for the opening ceremonies on May 4 the eyes of Europe if not of the world were upon the scene unfolding. The atmosphere was highly charged with excitement. From what can be seen in the vast literature of memoirs and correspondence of that time, the excitement was that of festival rather than of a civil war or imminent violent revolution.

This optimistic outlook seems to have been reflected in most if not all the letters and dispatches of foreign ambassadors. The minister of the United States, Thomas Jefferson, had written in January to Richard Price that "upon the whole it has appeared to me that the basis of the present struggle is an illumination of the public mind as to the rights of the nation, aided by fortunate incidents; that they can never retrograde, but from the natural progress of things must press forward to the establishment of a constitution which shall assure them a good degree of liberty."[2] To the Secretary of State, John Jay, he wrote: "This country advances with a steady pace towards the establishment of a constitution whereby the people will resume the great mass of those powers so fatally lodged in the hands of the king." Jefferson interpreted the recess of the Council meeting of December 27 to have implicitly granted a constitution. But he was not unaware of the serious discord between the orders. On the matter of voting by order or by head he believed, mistakenly it turned out, that the Clergy would be most adamant against voting by head.

403

"With respect to the Nobles," he wrote to Jay, "the younger members are generally for the people, and the middle aged are daily coming over to the same side; so that by the time the states meet we may hope there will be a majority of that body also in favor of the people, and consequently for voting by persons and not by orders."[3]

Three days before the opening of the States-General Jefferson indicated awareness of some disturbing matters. "We have had in this city (Paris) a very considerable riot [the Réveillon riot] in which about 100 people have been probably killed." But he attached no political significance to the event. The serious grain shortage was a matter of concern. About the opening of the States-General on May 5 Jefferson wrote:

> The States-General were opened the day before yesterday. Viewing it as an Opera it was imposing; as a scene of business the king's speech was exactly what it should have been and very well delivered; not a word of the Chancellor's was heard by anybody, so that as yet I have never heard a single guess at what it was about. Mr. Necker's was as good as such a number of details would permit it to be. The picture of their resources was consoling and generally plausible. I could have wished him to have dwelt more on those great constitutional reformations which his "Rapport au roy" [of Dec. 27] had prepared us to expect. But they observe that these points were proper for the speech of the Chancellor.[4]

A similar report was given by the Swedish ambassador in his dispatch to King Gustavus on May 10.

Tuesday was the greatest day in the history
of France. Nothing could be more imposing
to the sight or the mind than the majestic
assembly of a powerful nation, gathered together by its king to work on the regeneration of the fatherland. The king's speech
gave assurances of love for his people and a
sincere desire for their happiness, and was
vigorously applauded. Cries of "Vivre le
Roi!" interrupted him. But the speech of
the Keeper of the Seals could not be heard
and perhaps that was just as well. The
speech of Mr. Necker captivated the attention of three thousand persons for three
hours.[5]

The British ambassador, the Duke of Dorset,
viewed the situation very much as did Jefferson, although more concerned about the popular unrest both in
Paris and in the provinces. He estimated that 200
persons lost their lives in the Réveillon riot and
there were popular distubances in Normandy. He
thought the grain shortage was serious. "Private letters mention the extreme distress that is felt there
and that in some particular districts the people are
actually starving."[6] About the opening day of the
States-General on May 5, Dorset was also impressed by
the marks of esteem given to both the king and the
queen by the people.

His Majesty delivered His Speech with great
dignity though He was interrupted in the
course of it by the repeated acclamation of
Vive le Roi accompanied by clapping of
hands. . . .As soon as His Majesty had finished His Speech the Garde des Sceaux delivered a set speech which he read in so low a
voice that it was impossible to collect a
single sentence of it. M. Necker afterwards
addressed His Majesty and the Assembly in a

405

set speech, the whole of which lasted three hours, but Mr. Necker, after reading a part of it, found himself obliged on account of hoarseness, the effect of a cold, to crave His Majesty's indulgence in permitting one of the Clerks to read the remainder.[7]

The Duke of Dorset thought Necker's speech was "laborious" but said it was "received with bursts of applause." After describing the contents of the speech, while ended at 4 o'clock, Dorset made some other remarks of interest, among them that "M. de Mirabeau was present and upon taking his seat was received with hissing and other marks of disapprobation."[8]

The resident minister of the Republic of Geneva to France was the famous physician, Jean-Armand Tronchin. His report to the government of Geneva was read with considerable attention.

After all the Orders had taken their places, all the princes, the queen and the king entered the hall to the liveliest acclamations and repeated cries of Vive le roi! Then after a silence the king gave his speech with the greatest dignity, which lasted three or four minutes. The acclamations resumed and then there was silence in order to listen to the Keeper of the Seals. His discourse was long, and very little heard. When our illustrious compatriot [Necker] began his speech the august assembly gave him great attention. His discourse lasted about two and one-half hours. He spoke perfectly clearly for about a quarter of an hour and then asked permission to have a reader finish it, his voice not permitting him to go further. The reading was often interrupted by enthusiastic applause. It dealt succes-

sively, in perfect order and with great
clarity, with all different aspects of administration.[9]

The eye-witness accounts of private memoir writers and correspondents were not so uniformly favorable
to Necker's May 5 address as were the ambassadors.
Aside from those who were inveterately hostile to his
policies there were some accounts by youthful and impressionable witnesses that have been preserved. The
marquis de Ferrières revealed himself sympathetic to
Necker in his letters to his wife, although his memoirs written later indicated that he had changed his
mind. Arriving in Paris in April Ferrières was appalled to see such violent attacks against Necker in
the pamphlet literature. "You cannot imagine the
frightful attacks upon him by the great lords, the financiers, and the parlements. He is denounced to the
king as the most dangerous man in France; others
ridicule his morality, his probity and his religion."[10] In his letters Ferrières believed that the
Réveillon riot was instigated by Necker's enemies to
embarrass him. Later, in his memoirs, he maintained
that Necker himself had instigated that affair. With
regard to Necker's May 5 speech Ferrières wrote his
wife that "Necker revealed the state of the finances.
His speech lasted three hours. I found it very
mediocre and much beneath what one would have expected
from a man who enjoyed such a great reputation."[11]
Madame de Chastenay, the daughter of a liberal nobleman who was a deputy, believed that it was poor judgment on Necker's part to pack so much detail into his
speech "which an assembly could hardly digest in a
full day's time."[12] The son of a deputy from Poitou,
23-year-old A. C. Thibaudeau also left a vivid account
of the opening of the States-General. He reported
that the king's speech made a good impression on the
assembly: "He pronounced his discourse without hesi-
tating, in a firm and sonorous voice and recieved enthusiastic applause." But Necker did not make a fa-

vorable impression on him. "He had a cold physiognomy, solemn and not very attractive, his head thrown back. In his bearing and speech there was more hauteur and declamation than dignity and eloquence. He was not at all attractive or impressive. I don't know if it was because he was Genevan that made him appear to be a foreigner rather than a Frenchman. His speech was of crushing length."[13] All three of these witnesses were intelligent, sensitive, and impressionable but not well informed about the important issues facing the country. This unflattering portrait of Necker was somewhat altered by young Thibaudeau a few days later when he had a chance to meet the Director-General personally. He accompanied his father who visited Necker at the latter's office. "It was the first time I found myself in the presence of so eminent a person by reason of his position and his fame. In entering [his office] I felt some trepidation in his presence." But he soon relaxed as his father and Necker discussed the deadlock that had ensued in the States-General. Necker said that he did not doubt that the king's intervention would resolve the matter. After the interview the younger Thibaudeau wrote: "Mr. Necker had a very impressive physical appearance, and I believe, like everyone else, that he is at bottom moral, capable, and patriotic. But he had such a glacial, austere air that I was not attracted to him. I would wish that he had more animation and warmth."[14]

Whatever the impression Necker might have made by his physical appearance, a reading of his speech belies the assertion that he was "cold" or that its style was excessively declamatory. It was vintage Necker, repeating once again the moral and ethical ideas for which he had become so famous. Above all, his deep feelings about the significance of the great event, though restrained, were clearly evident. He began on a note of humility: "Gentlemen, anyone called upon to stand before such an august assembly, and as imposing as this must feel at first a certain diffidence, reassured only by the hope of obtaining a little indulgence because his motives are above reproach." Then he alluded to the scene before him. "What a day is this, gentlemen, a time that will live eternally in the memory of France!"[15] The king had summoned the representatives of his people to carry out a great enterprise, one that would endure for ages. But not much time was spent in such effusive remarks before getting down to the main business at hand.

His speech takes 110 pages in the printed edition of Necker's complete works, about the length of the Compte rendu of 1781. It was indeed a long piece to expect his listeners to sit through. But Necker was not speaking to an audience at the Comédie. He was addressing the nearly 1,200 deputies who had come to Versailles for the serious business of creating a new order for France, however theatrical the pageantry of the opening ceremonies may have been. Most of the eye-witness accounts, even from those hostile to Necker, agree that the address of the Director General of Finances was enthusiastically applauded by the deputies, who showed no signs of weariness during the three hours. It was unfortunate for Necker to have succumbed to a head cold a few days before the assembly, for he was a good orator with a powerful bass voice. After the first fifteen minutes of his speech, as Dorset relates, Necker handed his manuscript to a clerk to read. But he took it back to deliver the eloquent closing passages.

In many ways the speech of May 5 resembled the Compte rendu of 1781. Most of Necker's "ideas," those that had appealed to the French nation since his first ministry, were again set forth clearly and cogently before this audience. Of course the situation of the royal finances was uppermost in everyone's mind, and it was to that subject that Necker addressed himself first.

I must, gentlemen, according to the king's orders, give you a faithful account of the state of his finances. A costly war and the conjunction of other unfortunate events has brought about a great disparity between revenue and expenditure. You will examine, gentlemen, the means which the king has ordered me to propose to you to restore the necessary equilibrium. You will search for and indicate the best means, and you will respond to the desire of the nation and the expectation of Europe in joining all your efforts to placing the finances of the greatest of empires in an order that will remain forever assured.[16]

The reason why the royal finances were the concern of both the government and the States-General was because financial panic was an important element of the political and social unrest. The creditors of the government were not all wealthy landowners and merchants, bankers, and tax farming companies. Many were of modest means who had invested life savings in government rentes. The great fear among the rentiers as among other creditors was a belief that the government was near bankruptcy and at the very least would carry out the kind of reduction of its obligations that abbé Terray did in 1770. The act of Loménie de Brienne of August 16, 1788, which precipitated his fall from power, was seen as a prelude to partial bankruptcy. That measure simply suspended amortization payments on the public debt that normally was amortized. But interest payments on that debt were not suspended, nor did the act of August 16 affect the rentiers since rentes were not amortized. The same act announced that up to three-fifths of government payments would be made not in cash but government bonds bearing 5% interest. This seemed to inaugurate a regime of paper money, another terror of creditors, for the "system" of John Law had not vanished from the national memory.

410

For those who were not government creditors, the great fear was that the enormous deficit inevitably meant a crushing new burden of taxes.

About two weeks after his appointment to the ministry, Necker had revoked that part of the act of August 16 concerning the payments of the government in 5% notes, and restored all payments by specie. But he continued the suspension of amortization payments on the government debt. This did no harm to the holders of those government bonds as long as that "paper" did not deteriorate on the securities exchange (the bourse). If they wished to liquidate those notes they could do so by selling them to other investors. This was only one of several reasons, from Necker's standpoint, why it was supremely important to adopt fiscal policies that would assure creditors of the soundness of the royal finances.

One can imagine the astonishment of the States-General on May 5 when they heard the Director General of Finances tell them that not only could he balance the royal accounts, he could do it without requesting additional taxes. And the means by which he would eliminate the famous deficit would cause no shock to the public, either creditors or tax-payers. He even ventured to say that he could put the king's finances in order even without the convening of the States-General, an affirmation that was greeted in stony silence by his audience instead of the usual applause. His enemies probably thought: "Here's that charlatan up to his magician's tricks again!" It is possible that Necker was well aware that his claim could be greeted with skepticism, and that is what led him to give such a complete account of the situation of the royal finances, and his proposals for ending the financial crisis.

Once again Necker explained the method of accounting, a subject familiar to readers of the Compte

411

<u>rendu</u> of 1781 and his treatise on French finances of
1785. The first account to look at was the government's fixed income and fixed expenditures. Necker
had decided to use the term "fixed" in place of
"ordinary" to designate these accounts, probably to
make them clearer to the lay public. "The revenues
and expenditures that are fixed do not belong to any
particular year; they are always the same, unless they
are changed by new enactments. . . The king receives
the same tax revenue as long as the edicts establishing those taxes are in force; and the king pays the
same sum of interest until capital of that debt is
amortized. These two examples, applicable to many
other items, will explain the true meaning of those
accounts designated as fixed revenue and expenditures."[17]

During his long exposition of the royal finances
Necker's concern was to make the accounts intelligible
to those unfamiliar with such documents. He sought to
minimize the details, and explained to the deputies
that the account of the royal finances would be published soon after the meeting. It was published under
the title of "<u>Compte général des Revenues et des
Dépenses fixes au 1 Mai</u>, 1789," and each deputy received a copy. It remains the most complete account
of the royal finances of the <u>ancien régime</u>, containing
every loan made by the government of France in which
obligations were still due.[18]

To meet a criticism that had been made of his
<u>Compte rendu</u> of 1781, notably by Calonne in the lat-
ter's "Reply to Necker" published in January 1788,
Necker told the assembly that the fixed revenues and
expenditures would be given in two forms. One would
be the same used in the <u>Comte rendu</u> of 1781 which
listed the income received from each sub-treasury
(<u>caisse</u>) such as the Receivers-general, the Farmers-
general, and others; the account would indicate the
sum turned over to the royal treasury, and the sum

412

which the caisse retained itself to defray royal expenditures. The expenditure account would show only the amounts spent by the royal treasury. The great advantage of this system, as Necker had explained back in 1781, was that the accuracy and authenticity of each item in the account could be verified independently of the ministry of finance. But this method had the disadvantage of not showing in a clear and immediately visible way the totality of expenditures for each category. For example the royal treasury paid only a small part of the annual sum to rentiers each year. Most of that expenditure was acquitted by the caisse of the Farmer's General, which turned the funds over to the Hôtel-de-Ville. To see the totality of expenditures for that category one would need to add up the sums paid to rentiers by the different caisses and the royal treasury. THe second account would list the total amount of income received and spent in each category regardless of which treasury or caisse made the disbursement or received the revenue.

What was the deficit of ordinary or fixed income in 1789? Necker first alluded to the previously published compte rendu, that of March 1788 by his predecessor, Loménie de Brienne. The total deficit given in that account was 160,827,492 livres. But that was not the "ordinary" deficit of fixed expenditures above fixed income. It included the extraordinary or non-fixed expenditures for 1788, those that were not recurring. The figure for this type of expenditure was 29,395,585 livres. In addition, Loménie de Brienne had included in the above deficit the reimbursements due on loans, which came to 76,502,367 livres. In 1789 Necker did not believe it was essential to include amortization payments as part of the fixed expenditures. This was a change in his thinking from 1781, for his account of that year had included 17 million livres for reimbursement of loans as "ordinary expenditures." But he did mention in the compte rendu of 1781 that some finance ministers would not think it necessary to include reimbursements, that is, amortization of capital, as part of the ordinary expenditure.[19] His predecessors during the Seven Years War had not done so. Now, in 1789, his "Compte Général" did not include amortization as an ordinary expenditure. His reasoning on this matter has already been explained above. A suspension of amortization payments did not harm the creditors of the government so long as there was no decline of the value of their notes on the bourse. If confidence in the government's credit could be restored, if creditors could be assured that there would be no default of any kind on the government's obligations, then amortization payments could be made when it was convenient for the government to do so.

By deducting the extraordinary expenditures and the amortization payments from the deficit given by Loménie de Brienne in the compte rendu of 1788 Necker arrived at a deficit of fixed income for that year of 54,929,540 livres. While Necker did not attack his predecessors in his exposition of the royal finances before the States-General (in this providing a notable contrast to Calonne's discourse of February 22, 1787 before the Assembly of Notables), it was not possible for him to avoid calling attention to omissions made by Loménie de Brienne in the compte rendu of 1788. The latter had not included in the fixed expenditure side of the account an item of 12 million livres for the life rente loan of November 1787, which clearly belonged there. He had also left out an expenditure of 800,000 to 900,000 livres on behalf of Dutch refugees from the political troubles of 1787 in the United Provinces. Nor had he included an item for unforeseen expenditures which normally was 5 million livres. That made a deficit of 76 million livres. But there were also omissions on the fixed income side of the compte rendu of 1788. Strangely, Loménie de Brienne had not credited the economies he had achieved in 1787. He had reduced pensions paid by royal gov-

414

ernment 5 million livres; the fixed expenditures for the war department were cut 8,000,000 to 9,000,000 livres; those for the Navy 4.5 million, and the department of foreign affairs 1.8 million livres. With these adjustments Necker found a deficit of 56 million livres for 1788.[20]

Since the publication of Loménie de Brienne's account in March 1788 nothing had happened to alter either the fixed income or the fixed expenditures. No new taxes or loans had been enacted, obviously because of the political situation in the last months of the ministry of the archbishop. So the deficit of fixed income was the same for 1789 as it was for 1788, 56 million livres. Necker laid before the States-General specific proposals for erasing that deficit. One of the most frequent criticisms made of Necker's May 5 speech was that he demonstrated that he was a good bank clerk, but nothing more, certainly not a great statesman. Since the estates had been convened in part to deal with the financial crisis, such a complaint must have seemed strange to Necker. In fact, what the country needed in the circumstances was a chief minister who was both an expert banker and a statesman.

Necker listed eighteen specific proposals whereby the fixed income could be increased and the fixed expenditures reduced in order to eliminate the deficit. During the next two years the revenue from the General Farm could be increased by 18 million livres because of the natural increase of imports and the resumption of certain indirect taxes that had been suspended. Revenue from other financial companies, for example the post office and the domain, could increase the revenue by another 5,000,000 or 6,000,000 livres. Certain provinces were exempt from some of the excise taxes. If the entire kingdom paid those taxes uniformly it would add another 7,000,000 or more livres of revenue. If the king took over the debt of the

415

clergy and amortized that debt by making use of the new Sinking Fund to be set up, that would add 4.5 million livres to the regular revenue of the king. The other proposals had more slender yields. Most consisted of the abolition of privileges in certain regions. The bourgeoisie of Paris, for example, were exempt from paying the entrance tax into the city on goods that they had brought from their privately owned lands in the provinces. Abolishing that privilege would yield half a million livres. The king's two brothers had agreed to a reduction in what had been allotted to their households. Such was the nature of the proposals to eliminate the deficit. Each of them taken separately would have seemed paltry, but when all were added up the goal of a balanced budget was reached. Furthermore the manner in which this was done was not such as to cause an unreasonable hardship on any of those affected.[21]

If it should be the judgment of the States-General that some of these measures would not be found suitable, Necker pointed to other possibilities. The privileged orders had almost unanimously agreed in their cahiers to renounce their fiscal privileges. Necker estimated that this would yield an initial increase of from 10 to 12 million livres in the ordinary revenue. He said that the deputies themselves might suggest other ameliorations in the vast array of taxes of so many different kinds. A reduction in the expenses of collecting taxes was an area of possible amelioration. He left no doubt that the finance minister would work closely with the States-General to place the king's finances on a sound basis, and he did not look upon himself as the only source of ideas as to how that might be done.

The fixed revenue and expenditures were only a part of the picture of the royal finances. Necker's skeptical critics would wonder about those "extraordinary expenditures." Was the Director General

416

cleverly concealing some of the government's expenditures under that category? By their nature extraordinary accounts could not be presented with the same certainty as the ordinary accounts. It was not possible to foresee what emergencies might occur in the months ahead. Extraordinary expenditures were those that did not recur each year. The money Necker had spent to import grain to meet the threatening famine was an example. These expenditures, according to Necker, were always to be met by income that was also non-recurring rather than by fixed income. It made no sense at all to meet extraordinary expenditures by raising the permanent level of income. If these extraordinary expenditures required new loans, then the regular annual costs of the loans would be added to the regular fixed expenditures, so that the lenders could be assured of the continued ability of the government to meet those payments.

Despite his reputation Necker was reluctant to issue loans. The government's debt was already so enormous that he did not relish adding to it. But he pointed out to the States-General that it would be to the advantage of the government's credit to float loans to achieve three purposes. The first was to reduce the sum of anticipations. This short-term debt, consisting of loans from the Farmers-General and the Receivers-General, was guaranteed by specified future tax revenue. It was a means of spending the king's tax income before it had been collected from the taxpayers. It was a very lucrative loan for the lenders because it yielded not only a good rate of interest, depending upon the government's financial posture, but also a broker's commission. The loans were due for reimbursement at the end of the year. But usually the minister of finance would renegotiate so that the capital remained unreimbursed and the creditors would receive their annual interest and commissions. It had cost the government in the ministry of Calonne and Brienne from seven to nine percent in interest and

commissions for anticipations. When Necker spoke to
the States-General the anticipations on future revenue
for the remaining months of 1789 was 172 million
livres. Necker proposed that a loan of 80 million be
raised to bring the capital of anticipations down to
90 million for 1790. The interest to pay for the loan
of 80 million had already been included in the fixed
expenditures for 1789. By reducing the amount of
anticipations that low Necker believed the interest
rate could be held down to 5½ or even 5%, thus
considerably reducing the fixed charges for the costs
of anticipations. In the Compte général of 1789 the
cost for anticipations appears as 15,800,000 livres.
The operation that Necker proposed would have reduced
that cost to 4,950,000 livres.

Necker's second proposal for a loan was for the
purpose of eliminating the retardation in the payment
of rentiers by the Hôtel-de-Ville. These payments had
been made current by Calonne. In the tumultuous ministry of Loménie de Brienne they had been allowed to
lapse again by six months. Necker believed the rentiers could not be asked to make further sacrifices.
A loan of 75 million livres would enable the Hôtel-de-
Ville to make those payments on the time originally
agreed upon. The third proposal for a loan was to
cancel direct taxes that were in arrears. It was
usual for two-fifths of the ordinary revenue from direct taxes to come into the coffers of the king six
months late, in the fiscal year following the year to
which they were assigned. By cancelling those taxes
in arrears Necker hoped to have all revenue from direct taxes come into the treasuries during the fiscal
year to which they were assigned. This would greatly
reduce the dependence of the government on anticipations. The amount of money involved in this operation
would be another 80 million livres.

Finally in his exposition of the situation of the
finances, Necker turned his attention to the royal

debt. He proposed the restoration of the Sinking Fund
which had been established by Calonne in 1784 and allowed to lapse by Loménie de Brienne. The Sinking
Fund could be financed from several sources, among
them the extinction each year of the life rente debt,
which Necker thought was about a million and a half
livres per year. Also the pension reform of Loménie
de Brienne provided that when a pensioner died only
one-half the pension would be continued in the pension
fund until the fixed expenditure for that item had
been brought down to the sum of 18 million livres.
That savings, Necker proposed, could go into the Sinking Fund. Each year a certain amount of the government debt would be amortized. How much depended upon
the financial situation and the decision of the
States-General.

Amortization was more important for some debts
than others. In the suspension of these payments by
Loménie de Brienne's act of August 16, 1788, not all
reimbursements were suspended. The sum of 13,053,848
livres continued to be spent for debts that had been
contracted with foreign countries such as Genoa, and
also the loans from the Pays d'Etats. The total
amount of reimbursements that were suspended on other
loans amounted to 114,084,090 livres. It should be
repeated that interest continued to be paid on all
loans, amounting to 44,855,968 livres. The payments
to rentiers were not touched by the act of August 16,
1788.

In view of the great importance the royal finances have acquired in present day thinking about the
French Revolution, some observations can be perti-
nently drawn from a study of Necker's Compte général
of 1789. He did not think so much in terms of the total capital debt as of the annual cost of the debt.
This was due in part to the fact that rentes were not
amortized, and they constituted by far the major portion of the debt. It was not difficult to establish

419

an accurate sum for the capital value of the perpetual
rentes upon which an invariable interest was paid.
But it was difficult for the life rentes, since the
government's obligations to the holder of life rentes
ended with the life on which those rentes were constituted. Necker thought it more useful to consider the
situation of the royal debt from the standpoint of the
fixed obligations that the government was required to
pay upon it each year.

The total amount of perpetual rentes to be paid
in 1789 was 56,796,924 livres. There was in addition
3,199,880 livres to be paid for "tontines" deriving
from the reign of Louis XV. The life rentes paid in
1789 amounted to 101,469,586 livres. That made the
total cost of rentes 161,466,390 livres. In addition
to the rentes, the public debt upon which interest
payments were due in 1789 amounted to 44,855,056
livres. That made a total of 206,321,446 livres that
were paid on the public debt. That sum amounted to
38.8% of the total fixed expenditures of 531,533,000
livres for 1789. There was in addition to the public
debt the "private debt" consisting of the interest
payments made to office holders for the capital they
had extended to the government and upon which the government paid them an interest of 5%. This amounted to
14,727,230 livres in the Compte général of 1789.
There were also the costs of the anticipations which
came to 15,800,000 livres. If the latter two sums are
added to the public debt, the total royal debt in 1789
cost 236,850,676 million livres, or 44.46% of all expenditures. It is an exaggeration, then, to say that
the costs of the royal debt were over one-half the expenditures of the government.[22]

With the resumption of specie payments by the
government in September 1788 Necker had greatly mitigated the damage of the "partial bankruptcy" of August
16. But apprehension was still widespread among the
rentiers and other creditors that some drastic reduc-

tion of the government's obligations was imminent. Necker sought to allay those fears. In doing so he inadvertently touched upon a sensitive nerve in the national assembly. He explained in detail the fiscal measures that would meet the government's financial crisis, and would not endanger the rights of any creditors. Although public opinion in France and throughout Europe had viewed the convocation of the States-General by the king as caused by the financial crisis, in fact, said Necker, the king could have resolved that crisis without the meeting of the estates. But he certainly had not intended to diminish the importance of the States-General. On the contrary, he went on to explain why the new constitutional order to be established by the States-General was vitally important for the long-term stability of the government's credit.[23] Even though it was possible for him to put the royal finances on a sound basis, creditors would need assurance that some minister in the future would not be able to dilapidate the finances. He did not refer to himself or his first ministry, or to Calonne in his May 5 speech, but the precedent must have been clear to his listeners. He had put the royal finances in order once before only to have his work undone by an imprudent minister.

This was only one of the small clouds on the horizon that day in May when such a festive and patriotic mood suffused the assembly at Versailles. Necker alluded to the provision in several cahiers that had required their deputies to insist on the new constitution being ratified by the king before taking up the financial situation. Without specifically opposing that demand Necker emphasized the importance of dealing with the fiscal crisis as soon as possible. The nation's interests were not different from the king's in maintaining the continuity of the government. "You will not forget," he said, "that the financial needs of the government are not separate from your own; they are one and the same because the expenditures for de-

421

fense, for policing the kingdom, treating the creditors of the government justly, rewarding truly meritorious service, and the needs of maintaining the dignity of the foremost throne in Europe, all these expenditures and others as well concern the nation as much as the monarch."[24]

It was definitely implied in Necker's message that he looked forward to a fruitful partnership of the king's government and the representatives of the nation. It was not a forced marriage in which the king was the reluctant groom. Necker made it clear in his speech that the States-General would meet periodically. This event was not a one-time expedient to rescue the king from an embarrassing financial predicament. The foundation for this union between king and nation was morality. This was not a vague rhetorical expression. It was given concrete meaning by Necker's ideas concerning the nature of government credit. He lashed out aginst the "Machiavellians" who counseled the king to deal with his creditors the way abbé Terray did in 1771, which was to reduce the government's obligations by defaulting on them. Necker seemed to fear that the States-General might be susceptible to these blandishments. His most eloquent passages in the May 5 speech were to counteract them and to dispel the idea of such an alternative. He admitted that by such a reduction the king could get by without loans for extraordinary expenditures. But once the king had made a commitment in a loan his word was sacred. He could not enforce the laws on his subjects and at the same time violate his own contractural obligations.

The principal of fidelity of the government to its contractual obligations was not simply a matter of justice. The well-being and safety of the state itself was involved. He reminded his listeners that modern wars cannot be paid for out of current revenue. If a war should come the nation could only be defended

422

by resort to loans. The stability of government credit was a matter of national security. In peacetime also there was much at stake in protecting the rights of creditors. The government's debt was so enormous that fluctuations in the market value of its loans on the Bourse invited speculators to gamble with them. If the value of government paper were stable through sound management, the capital that was devoted to speculation could be diverted to the private sector of industry. The rate of interest could be lowered to 4% which could have a powerful influence on economic growth.

"It is in that way, gentlemen," Necker told the assembly, "that momentous consequences flow from this first principle of fidelity that you will consecrate." "There is only one great national policy," he said, "a single principle of order, power, and well-being and that principle is unblemished morality. When one strays from it he is obliged to change directions at every moment and he is judged to be clever by his ability to extricate himself from a peril that is of his own making, and his talent for creating other perils that again require expedients, while with a policy of honesty and perfect fidelity everything correlates, holds together, reveals that beautiful moral system which is the cherished masterpiece of the Supreme Being."[25]

Necker never referred directly to his predecessors in his May 5 speech, but many of his listeners no doubt thought of Calonne's ministry and the expedients that the minister had resorted to in order to shore up a disintegrating government credit. Calonne's use of public funds to enter stock market speculation in order to preserve the value of government paper, his secret operations such as extending several loans of previous administrations; even his convening of the Assembly of Notables in 1787 was not a serious attempt to consult with a body of representatives of the nation. He expected the Notables to ratify the proposals submitted to them with a minimum of discussion and he was niggardly about turning over to their scrutiny documents concerning finances.

Having dealt with the finances at such length, one might have thought Necker had completed his mission. Several witnesses who have left memoirs give the impression that Necker's three-hour speech concerned only the finances. Jefferson expressed dissatisfaction that the minister had given so much attention to the details of finance and none to the new constitution that the States-General was to enact. Necker's critics at the time and even some historians not necessarily hostile to him have asserted that he seriously misjudged his audience.[26] Instead of rising to the occasion and acting the role of the statesman Necker gave a detailed report that a treasurer might have given a board of directors. But these critics must not have listened to or read the second half of Necker's May 5 speech. He certainly attempted to do what he has been reproached for not doing, to inspire the assembly with the great responsibility and the opportunity that lay before it.

It was in the second part of his May 5 address that Necker expressed most clearly and eloquently what the king and his ministers intended to be the primary work of the States-General. Far from being restricted to financial matters, as if the government had only assembled the estates to extricate itself from an embarrassing situation in the manner of Calonne, Necker left no doubt that the main task of the States-General was "the regeneration of the kingdom." Another expression he used was "the great enterprise." And this encompassed a broad range of reforms, both "that which pertains to the present time and that of the time to come." These were the reforms that had been in the air since the beginning of the reign, and the new political order that was to replace the absolute

424

monarchy, namely, a constitutional monarchy. And Necker indicated clearly that the national assembly was not convened to listen to the directives of the king's ministers. "The king," he told the deputies, "considers you, gentlemen, from this moment as associates in his councils, and he will listen attentively and with interest to all the overtures and propositions to be made to him on your part. But His Majesty will also communicate to you all the ideas which he thinks merit your attention. It is by a complete concert between the government and this august assembly that the affairs of the king and the nation will be better understood and dealt with."[27] It was a far cry from Calonne's intentions when he convened the Assembly of Notables in February 1787. But it was equally remote from the notion of "constituent power" reposing in the national assembly. According to abbé Sieyes the government had no role in the "regeneration of the kingdom" but to receive the dictates of the Constituent Assembly.

It was at the beginning of this second part of his address that Necker intended to reach the heights of eloquence, and it is probably unfortunate that he did not leave the details of the finances to be handed to the deputies in the published Compte général, for it may well be that the interest of the audience began to flag just at the moment he wanted to make his most urgent and emotional appeal. And this appeal was to the spirit of nationalism. The French people had every reason to be proud of their country. It was not only endowed by nature with rich material resources; its people were leaders in the progress of civilization. The "old barbarism"--no doubt a reference to the age of religious strife--had been overcome. "Ours is an epoch when the general enlightenment seems to have achieved perfection; an epoch when prejudices, when the residue of an ancient barbarism, lingers only in weakened bonds, ready to break asunder. It is a period when the entire universe looks to France to

425

place its rare and singular advantages to the honor and glory of humanity."[28] Not least among those favorable features was the character of the king. Louis XVI had willingly accepted the end of absolutism and the coming of the constitutional monarchy, as had his ministers. The ministers, he said, "were not led astray by any system, nor dominated by a single idea, and they esteem themselves happy to serve a king who does not separate his interests from those of the nation."[29]

But there were danger signals on the horizon not to be underestimated. He alluded to serious divisions within the estates; these must be overcome by "a wise and moderate spirit."[30] He exhorted the deputies to give up private and narrow interests in order to achieve the "grand and majestic universal interest." They should "make the title of Frenchman more glorious and profitable than that of an inhabitant of a province or of a bailiwick.[31] In his appeal to nationalism Necker indicated his own thinking about the social structure of the ancien régime. He did not anticipate that traditional aristocratic society was to be overturned all at once. But in the interests of the general welfare and happiness Necker urged that social distinctions be forgotten for a time in order to make the "great enterprise" succeed. "You can return to them whenever you wish," he said, apparently addressing the aristocrats, "those distinctions which pit citizens in opposition to one another because of status or birth; we do not ask you to forget them entirely; they even make up the social order, they form that chain so necessary for the regulation of society. But these rival considerations must be suspended for a time, and their sharpness mitigated, to be returned to only after a long period has been spent working in common for the general interest."[32] Here was a plea to allow patriotism to take precedence over class interests. It echoed a sentiment that appeared in the general cahiers of the nobility, as we have seen.[33]

After these preliminary remarks Necker summarized what the ministry considered the most urgent matters calling for deliberation and action by the national assembly. He said that the king did not intend to lay down the agenda for the assembly. The deputies could take up any matter they desired. The reforms he mentioned were those that had preoccupied the ministers. Detailed dossiers of information had been drawn up for each of those subjects which would be available to the different committees it was expected the assembly would appoint.

Necker proposed that the reforms be divided into two categories: those to be dealt with at the national level, and those to be carried out at the provincial level. Once again he emphasized the importance of decentralizing administration. As much as possible the government should be shifted from the capitol to the provinces. This had also been a frequent demand in the cahiers of all three orders. This was not a decentralization of authority, but of administration. There was no thought of creating semi-independent, autonomous provincial governments such as appeared later in the constitution of 1791. Nor was there any federal principle involved as in the United States' constitution which "enumerated" certain powers for the federal government but left all "residual powers" to the states. The purpose of Necker's provincial governments was to achieve a more efficient and equitable administration. The notables at the local level were intimately familiar with conditions unique to their region, while the ministers at the central government and their officials were not.

The most prominent subject for reform was of course the fiscal system. The unjust taxes were a common complaint in the cahiers, as they had been also of the reform ministers since the beginning of the reign. There were two categories of taxation, the direct taxes, which Necker believed would continue to be derived principally from landed income, and the indirect taxes. With regard to the former the national assembly would lay down the principles for assessing the direct taxes, such as abolishing the fiscal privileges and establishing fiscal equality among citizens. The national government would levy a repartitional land tax, not a proportional one, and would apportion the amount to be levied on each province based upon geographical extent, population, and wealth. But after that was accomplished it would be the provincial assemblies that would decide how best to divide the burden within the provinces. The diversity of economies, resources, and populations among the regions of France was Necker's rationale for this proposal. In addition to administration of the direct taxes, Necker proposed that provincial governments assume social welfare measures like work-relief for the unemployed, the maintenance of hospitals, care for the population in time of disasters, and public health. Also he proposed that the local government build roads and maintain arteries of communication.

The reform of indirect taxes would be the responsibility of the national government except for the excise taxes which he thought might be left to the provinces. On this matter of the indirect taxes, Necker told the deputies that abolition of tax exemptions was complicated because the exemptions were not held by individuals or social classes as in the case of direct taxation but by regions, the provinces that had been joined to the kingdom according to treaty often had those fiscal privileges inscribed in the treaties. How to make the gabelle, the tobacco monopoly, the transit duties uniform in the kingdom required careful negotiation, and Necker advised the deputies to proceed cautiously on those matters.

Reforms at the national level, in addition to the indirect taxes, concerned the economic well-being of the kingdom. Necker proposed that internal restraints on trade be abolished, that a national customs union be established which would include all provinces. He asked the States-General to review the monopoly of the company of the Indies and to study plans for making the Discount Bank more useful to commerce. The harmful effects of speculation in the stock exchange was referred to, and he thought the fiscal policies already discussed would end the influence of speculators. Once again, Necker emphasized the humanitarian aspect of reform: he called for the abolition of the corvée in Brittany where it still persisted, the end of forced conscription of peasants into military service; they would be replaced by paid professional troops. Finally, Necker made a plea for France to join England and other countries to enforce an international prohibition of the traffic in black slaves. The reform of the judicial system was under the authority of the Keeper of the Seals, but Necker mentioned that aspect of the reform measures to be considered by the States-General. He discussed at length the severe grain shortage and subsistence crisis, appealing for support of the government's policies to save the population from famine. The administration of the king's forests and royal domain were also matters to be investigated by the deputies.[34]

These were the reforms that were most prominent in the cahiers. In fact they had been in the reform programs of several ministers since the beginning of the reign. Necker's first ministry had grappled with them. He discussed them at length in his book on French finances published in 1785. They were part of Calonne's reform program, but shorn of physiocratic influences. They had been included in the reform program of the Notables, and of Loménie de Brienne. Why, then, can historians assert that "Necker misjudged his audience" in elaborating upon them? The historian Georges Lefebvre thought Necker's plans for the work of the States-General were so restricted as to be "laughable."[35] But there were no restrictions laid down by Necker in his May 5 address. He made clear that the States-General could occupy itself with everything, "that which pertains to the present time and that of the time to come. They must observe and follow the paths of national well-being in all their ramifications." A vast field as yet uncultivated lay before them, which gave promise of great fertility. "What country," he exclaimed, "has ever offered such great means for prosperity! What country ever gave birth to such encouragement and promise!" And he went on to describe all the great resources, natural and human, that lay ready to respond to the treatment of the States-General.

It is true that throughout his address Necker showed himself scrupulous about property rights. He did not consider fiscal privileges enjoyed by individuals a property right that required indemnity. But it was a different matter where the _taille_, for example, was not personal but attached to lands. In the southern parts of the kingdom, in the land of "written law" the exemption from the _taille_ was a privilege attached to lands and not persons. Those lands, which originally were owned by the nobility, had often been sold to non-noble proprietors, and the purchase price of the land had included the exemption from the _taille_. Therefore, in those southern regions the abolition of the _taille_ should be accompanied by an indemnity to the landowners. The same sensitive regard for property rights was characteristic throughout his reform proposals. It would be for the States-General to decide whether to abolish the Company of the Indies (restored by Calonne in 1785) but if they decided to do so they should be certain that the stockholders in the company were indemnified.

In the final minutes of his address Necker came to what everyone was waiting for, and he himself considered its climax, namely, the shape of the constitution. Here he could not be specific. While he had in mind the form he hoped would emerge from the work of the States-General, which would be a government similar to the English monarchy, he did not think it proper for him to propose it. Instead he remained in the realm of ideas, of abstractions, from which one could deduce his precise views. What most disturbed him was the danger of schism in the States-General resulting in total immobility. Therefore what he tried above all to achieve was to find a middle way between two extreme views. One view insisted that France had an ancient constitution which was still serviceable and needed no innovations. The opposite pole of the political spectrum maintained that France had no constitution at all, no binding precedents, and therefore the States-General was free to build upon a completely bare foundation, drawing all its materials from the fashionable ideas of the century. Each side hoped to see in the speech of the Director General of Finances substantiation for its view.

As he began to address this question, Necker let it be known that the government did not consider the rules and procedures adopted for convening this first States-General as immutable for the future. The deputies were bound by no historical precedents, not even those that had recently been used for their own convocation.

All the arrangements, gentlemen, which have served to assemble you together are remnants, as it were, of the old and respected trunk of the French constitution. But the changes which have taken place in our customs and in our opinions, the growth of the

431

kingdom, the increase of national wealth, especially the abolition of pecuniary privileges, if this abolition takes place, all of these circumstances and many others require perhaps a new order; and if the ministry limits itself at the moment in fixing your attention on this thought, it is not because it remains a stranger to such an important matter; but the regard due to the enlightenment of this august assembly must restrain us from proposing any guide other than its own reflections. We have gathered together for this time the debris of an old temple; it is up to you, gentlemen, to make the revision of it and to propose means for a better order.[36]

Having made this gesture of deference to the States-General, and indicating clearly that the deputies were free to alter the rules by which the present States-General had been convened, Necker then added a caveat. It was necessary to distinguish, he said, what was temporary and what would become permanent in the institutional arrangements. He gave no specific examples, but the tone in which he uttered this caveat showed clearly his irritation over the failure to make that distinction. During the elections to the States-General there had been numerous clashes of opinions and interests. It required the patience of Job and the wisdom of Solomon to resolve those quarrels by compromise, which even then could be very fragile. Yet the partisan spirit led each side to look upon the mediator as its adversary. From the historian's perspective what made the functioning of the States-General so difficult was that, unlike the American Constitutional convention called for the specific purpose of framing the new constitution, the States-General of 1789 was assumed to act as a legislative body all at once without training or experi-

ence for such a role. It represented the "Nation" and
nothing could be done after May 5 without its consent.
This tended to make the deputies apprehensive that the
measures taken for temporary, short-range purposes
would compromise the future and become inscribed in
the permanent constitution. This tended to make the
deputies inflexible on even the most trivial matters.
In fact it caused the deadlock in the days after May
5. Necker expressed the earnest hope that once the
Nation and the king were agreed upon principles of
justice, the government would cease to face constant,
carping opposition.

> The king, gentlemen, in thinking of this
> great edifice of well-being and power that
> you can help him raise, earnestly desires
> that it be built upon the most assured foun-
> dation. Search for it, indicate it to your
> sovereign, and you will find on his part the
> most generous assistance. The king, gentle-
> men, enlightened by a long period of in-
> tractible problems, and by the rush of
> events which in a sense double the years of
> experience, loves reason more than ever, and
> he is a good judge of it. Therefore, when
> the initial confusion that is inseparable to
> the convening of such a large body is over,
> when the dominant opinion of this assembly
> can be separated from the clouds that may
> obscure it for a time; finally, when the
> time is ripe His Majesty will justly appre-
> ciate the character of your deliberations.
> And if it is such as he hopes, if it is such
> as he has a right to expect, finally, if it
> is what the most enlightened part of the na-
> tion desires and asks, the king will second
> your wishes and your acts. He will think it
> to his own glory to see them fulfilled. And
> the mind of the best of princes being joined

so to speak to that which inspires the most
faithful of nations, will see arise from
this accord the greatest good and the most
solid power. It's up to you, gentlemen, to
bring into being such a great alliance, it's
up to you to form such a union. And in order to succeed you will avoid exaggerations;
you will not entertain imaginary evils, you
will suspect opinions that are too innova-
tive. You will not think that the future
can have no connection with the past, you
will not listen to speeches or choose projects that would transport you into an ideal
world; rather (you will choose) those
thoughts and counsels which, less spectacular but more practical, give rise to fewer
controversies, and to greater stability and
permanence. Finally, gentlemen, you will
not be envious of what time can achieve, and
you will leave something for it to do. For
if you attempt to reform everything that
seems imperfect, your work itself will be
so.[37]

The intention of the orator was evidently to
steer the assembly somewhere between two views. One
was the conviction that France already had a constitution, that which preceded the establishment of absolutism. The opposite view was that of abbé Sieyes:
France had never possessed a legitimate constitution,
and the one to be created now was bound in no way to
the past. By comparing the above passages of his May
5 speech with his other writings that came from his
pen during the years after his political career was
over it is possible to see that what Necker wanted to
come out of the "great enterprise" was a constitution
similar to the British. It would allow full executive
powers and functions to the king; it would provide for
a periodically assembled legislature of two chambers

exercising full legislative powers. The upper house
would not represent the privileged orders.[38] It would
be appointed by the king from a pool of public-spirited citizens regardless of social status who had
served the country with distinction. Necker's arguments in favor of bicameralism were the usual ones:
an upper chamber is necessary to balance a more popularly elected lower house (which Necker even referred
to in his May 5 speech as "the commons") which could
be swayed by demagoguery or otherwise make hasty and
ill-considered decisions. The upper chamber was to
represent the Nation just as much as the lower house,
but it represented the conservative opinion of the Nation, that which defended property rights, which resisted the tendency toward greater democracy and
equality. If such were Necker's goals regarding the
future constitution it might be wondered why he was
not a bolder helmsman in steering the States-General
in the direction he desired. It is necessary to insist that Necker was not a free agent. He did not
have the power or the authority to build the new constitution himself, Arthur Young to the contrary
notwithstanding. He could not, in his May 5 address,
boldly proclaim the British constitution as the model
for the States-General to follow. That would have irritated a strong nationalist strain of anglophobia in
the population. It would have alienated the king, who
at that time was opposed to having France adopt the
British model. There were also colleagues in the ministry whose opinions could not be flouted and who were
more conservative than Necker. The most important of
these was the Keeper of the Seals, Barentin.

These were the long-range projects Necker hoped
would come out of the States-General of 1789. Of more
immediate concern to the deputies and also to himself
was the manner in which the States-General would carry
out this "great enterprise." How would it organize
itself to begin its deliberations? Here the danger of

435

an immediate schism had to be faced. In the final part of his May 5 address Necker took up that matter: whether the estates should first organize themselves as separate deliberating bodies, or whether they should meet together first and then agree on what matters could be deliberated and voted upon in common, and what would be left to the separate assemblies. At the time of the publication of the Resultat de Conseil of December 27, Necker had expressed the hope that the three orders could come to an amicable agreement that some matters be dealt with in a common assembly and others could be left to the individual assemblies of the three orders. This was the way of conciliation, of negotiation. None of the three orders should be coerced. The Regulation of January 24 governing the elections to the States-General had provided in each bailiwick assembly for the election of deputies and the drawing up of cahiers in three separate assemblies. But the Regulation also permitted the bailiwick assemblies to meet in a common assembly, elect deputies and draw up a united cahier. About twelve general bailiwick assemblies did so. But this was done by free consent of all three orders meeting separately. Paris intro muros, we have seen, wanted very much to meet in a common assembly and elect deputies to represent the "Commune," but since Paris was treated separately rather than coming under the General Regulation, the government had declined to permit it.

In the speech of the Keeper of the Seals to the States-General, which preceded Necker's, the idea of a compromise was broached. In referring to the doubling of the Third Estate contained in the Résultat du Conseil of December 27, Barentin said:

> In acquiescing to this demand [the double-ment] His Majesty, gentlemen, has not

436

changed the old form of deliberation; and, although deliberation by head, in giving a single decision (résultat), appears to have the advantage of making better known the general desire, the king wills that this new form of deliberation should not come into operation except by the free consent of the States-General and with the approval of the king.[39]

What Barentin seemed to be hinting at was a solution to the problem contemplated in a large number of the cahiers of the nobility. That is, that on matters concerning the general interest of the nation, the order could vote by head in a common assembly; in matters of interest only to each order, deliberation and voting would be by order. This compromise solution was more clearly stated by Necker in his May 5 speech. He said the king was definitely worried about the possibility of a division in the States-General. One of the great questions which had risen in the kingdom, he said, was the manner of deliberation; and the "opinions for deliberation in common or by head seem to be shared with such an ardor as to become truly alarming." Necker made it clear that the question was one to be decided by the estates themselves but he very deliberately brought forth the "king's reflections" as to how the issue might be resolved.

Everything indicates, gentlemen, that if a part of this assembly demands that the very first of your decisions be a law to deliberate by head on all subjects which shall be submitted to your examination, the result of this step, if it is obstinately maintained, would be a schism in which the progress of the States-General would be stopped or suspended for a long time; one cannot foresee

what the consequences of such a division
would be.[40]

But, Necker urged, by proper timing and circum-
spection the issue could be resolved without creating
a division. He proposed that the Third Estate permit
the other two orders to separate right after the joint
meeting, and begin deliberations in their separate
chambers. He suggested that the Clergy and the Nobility take up immediately the question of abolishing
their fiscal privileges, which they had promised to do
in their cahiers. Necker said that the two orders
ought to be allowed the honor of making this sacrifice
gratuitously and not under duress, as it might appear
if the fiscal privileges were abolished in a common
assembly. He apparently thought that after this step
had been taken, the principal cause for dissension between the orders would be removed, and the form of deliberation and voting could then be taken up in a
calmer, less charged atmosphere. He proposed that a
joint committee be formed of representatives from each
order to discuss the matter.

> It is then that, in an atmosphere of calm-
> ness, the advantages and disadvantages of
> all forms of deliberation could be examined;
> it is then that perhaps those questions
> could be designated for which the best in-
> terest of the sovereign and state require to
> be discussed separately, and those subjects
> which it would be desirable to leave to a
> deliberation in a common assembly.[41]

Such was Necker's proposal. It will be recalled
that it was not contrary to the majority of the
cahiers of the Nobility on this question. Neither the
Nobility nor the ministry insisted on rigidly maintaining the traditional form of deliberation and of

voting without any change whatever. Of course the question as to what subjects would be allowed to be deliberated and voted upon in a common assembly was left vague. That was a matter to be resolved by negotiation and compromise by the estates themselves, the government taking no part.

It is only in retrospect that Necker's hopes appear illusory. On May 5 there was good reason for thinking that "the most enlightened part of the nation" would have agreed with the Director General of Finances. Certainly in the Nobility and the Clergy the most eminent and influential leaders were moderates who favored the reforms and the type of constitution that Necker appeared to suggest.[42] The attitude of the deputies of the Third Estate was more of a question mark. But the most prominent leaders such as Jean-Joseph Mounier and Samuel Dupont de Nemours were clearly moderates who shared Necker's ideas.

Yet he was not a naive optimist. He saw clearly the dangers threatening the country. The horrors of anarchy and civil war were agonizingly present in his mind. The proposals that he offered the States-General were honorable, and in fact about the only ones he could offer. His was a high-minded vision, and a patriotic one, of the great opportunities that lay at the feet of the government and the assembly if they could achieve that harmony of aims for which he so earnestly pleaded. His program deserved a better fate than awaited it.

[1]Madame De Staël, Correspondance générale, ed., Beatrice W. Jasinski (Paris, 1962), I, Lettres de Jeunesse, 274.

[2]The Papers of Thomas Jefferson, XIV, 423.

[3]Ibid., XIV, 432.

[4]Ibid., XV, 104-105.

[5]Correspondance diplomatique, 99.

[6]Despatches from Paris, 1784-1790, II, 191.

[7]Ibid., 192-193.

[8]Ibid., 194.

[9]Jean-Armand Tronchin to Marc-Alexandre Puerari, 7 mai 1789, in Edouard Chapuisat, Necker (Paris, 1938), 288-289.

[10]Charles Elie, marquis de Ferrières, Correspondance inédite (1789-1791) (Paris, 1932), 29.

[11]Ibid., 45. Charles-Elie, marquis de Ferrières, Mémoires pour servir à l'histoire de l'Assemblée constituante et de la révolution de 1789 (n.p., An VII), I, 15.

[12]Victorine, comtesse de Chastenay, Mémoires de Madame de Chastenay (Paris, 1896), I. 99.

[13]A. C. Thibaudeau, Biographe-Mémoires, 1765-1792 (Paris, 1875), 68.

[14]Ibid., 72-73.

[15]"Ouverture des Etat-Généraux," in Oeuvres complètes de Necker, VI, 507.

[16]Ibid., 510.

[17]Ibid., 512.

[18]Copies of the Compte général still exist at the Bibliothèque nationale under the call number Lf 76.124, in quarto folio.

[19]"In addition to several (explanatory) notes that are included in this account of Your Majesty's finances, there is one in particular to call to his attention: Included in the ordinary expenditures are 17,300,000 livres for reimbursements. However what one applies to reimbursements can reasonably be regarded as surplus, because it is an exedent of ordinary revenue above ordinary expenditure that is used. . . to extinguish part of the capital indebtedness. Thus, by adding those 17,300,000 livres for reimbursement, to the 10,200,000 livres of surplus which are indicated in this account of Your Majesty's finances, one could reasonably affirm that his ordinary revenue exceeds at this moment his ordinary expenditures by 27,500,000 livres." "Compte rendu au Roi," in Oeuvres complètes de Necker, II, 16-17.

[20]"Ouverture des Etats-généraux," in Oeuvres complètes de Necker VI, 515-517.

[21]Ibid., 518-527.

[22]For example, Albert Mathiez, La Révolution française (Paris, 1922-1924), 10. Mathiez gave the cost of the "service on the debt" as 300 million per year. In view of the importance given to the American War for causing the financial crisis that led to the French Revolution, it is worth noting that almost exactly 50% of the royal debt existing in 1789 was contracted prior to 1777. Of the total rentes paid in

1789 (161,466,390 livres) only 46,657,883 were derived
from loans made during the war years 1777 through
1783, including Calonne's life rente loan of December
of that year. The latter loan was specifically earmarked for the purpose of paying the "war debt" that
remained after the end of the war. That figure of
46,657,883 amounted to 28.89% of the total rente debt
facing the government in 1789. For the other charges
on the constituted debt in addition to the rentes existing in 1789, namely 44,855,056 livres, only
12,321,247 was derived from loans made during the
years of the American War, and in addition Calonne's
loan of December 1784, which was also earmarked to pay
off the last to the war debts. That amounted to 27%
of the obligations (other than the rentes) that was
derived from the American War. These calculations are
based on the Compte général of 1789 cited in footnote
18 above, with one exception: I have not included the
extensions of the life rente loan of March 1781 and
January 1782, which were made by Calonne in 1786,
since those loan extensions were not made to pay for
costs of the war. For those two loans I have used the
original amount given in the loan edicts: 3 million
livres for the loan of March 1781 and 12 million
livres for that of January 1782. The above calculations put into some perspective the responsibility of
the American War for the financial distress of the
government in the years 1781-1789. Around 28% of the
royal indebtedness in 1789 can be charged to the American War. That was not a negligible sum, and it could
be argued that it was the additional burden that broke
the camel's back. But few would deny that the war was
fought in the national interest (to say nothing of the
interest of the new nation in America) whereas it is
not clearly demonstrated that all of Calonne's additions to the debt were equally in the national interest.

[23]"Ouverture des Etats-généraux," in Oeuvres
complètes , VI, 559-561.

[24]Ibid., 557.

[25]Ibid., 534-535.

[26]Chapuisat, Necker, 172.

[27]"Ouverture des Etats-généraux," 568.

[28]Ibid., 565.

[29]Ibid., 565-566.

[30]Ibid., 566.

[31]Loc. cit.

[32]Ibid., 567.

[33]See Chapter 11, supra.

[34]"Ouverture des Etats-généraux," 568-599.

[35]Georges Lefebvre and Anne Terroine, eds., Recueil de documents relatifs aux séances des Etats Généraux, mai-juin 1789 (Paris, 1953), I, 220-221.

[36]"Ouverture des Etats-généraux," 601-602.

[37]Ibid., 604-606.

[38]In his analysis of Necker's May 5th speech Henri Grange wrote that for future assemblies Necker "called purely and simply for the disappearance of the orders, thereby bringing to an end the ancien régime." Les Idées de Necker (Paris, 1974), 412. This was also the opinion of Frédéric Braesch. 1789. L'Année cruciale (Paris, 1941), 98, cited by Grange.

[39]Archives parlementaires, VIII, 3.

[40]"Ouverture des Etats-généraux," 608.

^{41}_Ibid._, 610.

^{42}In his study of Necker's May 5th speech, Henri Grange makes this summary: "Sovereignty shared between king and assembly, a compromise on the question of voting by order or by head, indicating the latter for the future constitution, an electoral law putting an end to the distinction among the orders, bicameralism, periodic meetings of the assembly, the consent of the nation required for all taxes, full executive powers to the king, fiscal equality, decentralization, such was a very coherent program, designed for a precise political future. What evidently detracted from the force of these propositions was that they were inserted in a text the main objective of which was to reveal the financial situation of the kingdom rather than being the essential subject. Unfortunately, Necker could not do otherwise. At the time the king was a dead weight that blocked any overture." _Les Idées de Necker_, 415.

CHAPTER 13

THE FAILURE OF MEDIATION

The three months following the opening of the States-General were the most dramatic of Necker's political career. His popularity with the public continued to soar, contrary to what some authors have asserted.[1] It reached a peak in the last days of July when he returned to Versailles from his brief exile to begin his third ministry. Yet in the general histories of the French Revolution he has almost dropped from sight after Bastille Day. His third ministry is hardly mentioned at all. Was his popularity so ephemeral, and his importance in the history of the Revolution so slight?

After he left the king's service in September 1790, this time permanently, and returned to Switzerland to spend the rest of his days, Necker wrote voluminously about the events of the revolutionary decade. He compared his role in the Revolution to that of Michel de l'Hôpital, chancellor of Catherine de Medici at the beginning of the Wars of Religion in the sixteenth century. L'Hôpital had tried valiantly to mediate the quarrel between the two rival factions, the Protestants and the Catholics, but was overborne by the fanatics in both camps. As a result the kingdom was plunged into forty years of bitter religious strife, which was concluded finally by the Edict of Nantes, a treaty very similar to what Michel l'Hôpital had attempted to negotiate at the beginning of the civil war.[2] "History has vindicated L'Hôpital," Necker wrote in his memoirs on the French Revolution, and he asked somewhat wistfully, "will it me?"[3]

History seems to have neither vindicated nor condemned the Genevan banker, but simply to have ignored

445

him. The assumption seems to have been that Necker's attempt to mediate a compromise between the two conflicting orders, the aristocracy and the Third Estate was hopeless at the outset. By failing to realize the futility of mediation Necker missed his opportunity to make a decisive impact on events. The deadlock that immobilized the States-General in the weeks after May 5 seemed to diminish his stature, making him appear weak and vacillating where a policy of boldness was required. Jefferson wrote the American Secretary of State on June 17 expressing his disappointment and dismay at the direction events had taken. He placed the blame for it largely on Necker. "It is a tremendous cloud which hovers over this nation, and he at the helm has neither the courage nor the skill necessary to weather it...His judgment is not of the first order, scarcely even of the second, his resolution frail, and upon the whole it is rare to meet an instance of a person so much below the reputation he has obtained."[4] Jefferson enclosed with this letter an essay "On the Character of Mr. Neckar [sic]," the author of which he did not name but said it was an acquaintance of his who knew Necker well. "He is not indeed his friend, and allowance must therefore be made for the high coloring. But this being abated, the facts and ground work of the drawing are just." Unfortunately for the American minister the portrait was unjust and the facts supposedly found in it were untrue, the misspelling of the name being the least of them.   It contained the usual libels propagated by Necker's enemies: that he doubled his fortune during his first ministry by having a secret interest in a banking firm that marketed government loans, that the loans he made during the American War were the cause of the present financial distress, that the Compte rendu of 1781 was flagrantly in error and was corrected by M. de Calonne, and so forth. The essay contained several allegations Mirabeau had made in his 1787 essays denouncing Necker's first ministry and were being repeated at this time by Mirabeau's circle of Genevan friends who were violently hostile to Necker.[5]

It is usually thought that Necker's three-hour speech on the opening day of the States-General was a blunder on his part, that he misjudged the temper of his audience. "Let us say the word," wrote Chapuisat, "it was boring."[6] The contemporary reports by eye-witnesses do not all bear out that conclusion. The editor of the Correspondance littéraire, who was at that time Henri Meister, a close friend of Necker it is true, wrote about the speech: "I do not think there ever was a speech so long, and by the nature of the subjects treated, as boring, at least for a great part of the audience, that has ever been listened to with as much lively and sustained attention."[7] The Genevan ambassador wrote in his dispatch to his government: "When our illustrious compatriot appeared in the hall his modest temperament had to confront the most lively applause, which was repeated several times during the speech and also at its close. After the adjournment of the meeting cries of Vive Monsieur Necker accompanied him even to his residence. Never has a minister enjoyed such spectacular glory." But Tronchin also noted that "those who denigrate great virtues and talents were resuming their activities in numerous gatherings." He believed that the "illustrious compatriot" had the moral courage to bear the great burdens and anxieties that fell upon him and he prayed that his health would be equally firm. Fortunately, he wrote, Necker did not appear to be fatigued at the end of the long day.[8]

But the Austrian ambassador did not send such a glowing report to his master in Vienna. Mercy-Argenteau wrote that the king's address was well received, but that Necker's speech "which lasted three hours, excited only criticism and murmurs from the first, even among those of the Third Estate, who were disap-

447

pointed to find their hopes diminished for realizing
their aims." Mercy-Argenteau was also concerned about
the threat posed by Necker's enemies. "The ministry
is fearful, without vigor; only the Director General
of Finances faces the storm with courage; but he is
isolated, without important support and he finds himself threatened by a cabal which is all the more dangerous in that the two brothers of the king have rallied to it, and give greater momentum to the clergy
and nobility who are conspiring against the government.[9] As for the queen, a subject of constant preoccupation for the Austrian ambassador, Mercy-Argenteau
wrote that she was "often exhorted by the princes her
brothers-in-law, to support their proposals and to
transmit them to the king. She avoids doing so, and
attempts to persuade them that their duty is to favor
reasonable conciliation rather than force, which must
be avoided."[10]

Necker himself seemed to retain mixed feelings
about the success of his speech. Despite the vigorous
and repeated applause, what lingered in his memory,
and about which he wrote later, was the reception of
the audience to his statement about the royal finances. Eager to let the assembly know of his success
in bringing order to the finances without having to
ask for additional tax revenue he expected the same
praise as at the time of the Compte rendu of 1781. He
was dismayed that the assembly remained stonily silent
during that passage of his speech. It was a great
misunderstanding on the part of both the speaker and
his audience. Many of the deputies looked upon the
financial crisis as the guarantee of a new constitutional order. There was considerable distrust of the
ministry, not of Necker himself, but of those whose
conservative and reactionary instincts were known.
The mandates of many deputations had stipulated that
the government would not be left off the hook, so to
speak, until the new constitutional order had been
definitely established. Necker also looked forward to

448

the new constitutional order and despite his remarks
that the king could have resolved his financial problems without the convening of the States-General, he
expected the new regime would be the foundation of financial stability. Why, then, did he make such an
undiplomatic remark that could lend itself to misin-
terpretation?

Since the beginning of his second ministry Necker
was appalled by the weakness of the monarchy. It was
not that Louis XVI was unpopular. Quite the opposite,
for the cahiers without exception overflowed with
gratitude to the king for condescending to convene the
national assembly of estates. But Necker understood
the difference between the monarchy as an institution
and the personal popularity of the reigning monarch.
The monarchy was weak, and Necker saw the necessity of
restoring some of its traditional prestige if France
were to have a regime similar to Great Britain's where
the king exercised full executive power. After the
concessions made by Louis XVI in the recess of the
Council meeting of December 27, Necker was puzzled to
see that the government was still looked upon as an
adversary. This was especially apparent during the
elections of the deputies to the States-General.
Therefore Necker took every opportunity to extol the
king and to impress upon the nation why it should be
grateful for all the concessions he made. Hence the
many "pompous allusions"--as Georges Lefebvre called
them--to the king in his May 5 speech.[11]

It was of crucial importance on the day following
the opening of the States-General to see if the estates would follow the recommendations made by Necker
in his speech. That is, for them to meet first in
their separate chambers, for the privileged orders to
publicly renounce their fiscal exemptions, and then
for the three assemblies to appoint a commission to
negotiate about the mode of deliberation. This would
enable the estates to arrive at a compromise on the

449

issue of voting by head or by order. The plan that Necker proposed was that on national matters the procedure would be to meet in a common assembly, deliberate and vote by head. But it was supposed that on matters which concerned the individual order there would be deliberation and voting in separate assemblies. It was necessarily a vague suggestion. As to what matters would be decided in common and what separately, it was not for the government to determine. It was up to the leaders of the three orders to arrive at a solution by bargaining and compromise. Necker did not think the two privileged orders should make their fiscal exemptions a matter to be bargained about. If the Clergy and Nobility voluntarily gave up those privileges immediately, Necker hoped that such a gesture would establish a good atmosphere in which the three orders could work together in a spirit of harmony and willingness to compromise.

If looked at in the context of the time Necker's suggestion would not seem so hopeless as it does in retrospect. There is no question that the great majority of the cahiers of the Clergy and the Nobility had pledged to abolish the fiscal exemptions. The atmosphere of the opening days of the States-General was suffused with intense partiotism and a feeling of generosity. Men of good will in all three estates wanted to see the estates succeed in their mission of the "regeneration of the kingdom." There was a radical faction among the deputies of the Third Estate that wished for the dissolution of the privileged orders and for the Third Estate to declare itself the repository of complete sovereignty, following the ideas of abbé Sieyes. But this faction did not control the assembly of the Third Estate at the outset. There was also a faction in the assembly of the Nobility influenced by the princes who wrote the "mémoire" back in December who thought the estates should be dissolved, the deputies sent home, and the experiment in constitutional government brought to an end. But they also

450

were in a minority. If there could have been a common
assembly of all three orders in 1789 there is no doubt
that the moderates would have kept control of affairs
and prevented the extremists from dominating events as
they were to do. The Clergy was certainly in a conciliatory mood. The majority of the Third Estate were
strongly in favor of a common assembly but not one
that would exclude the other orders, and certainly not
one that would claim full powers of sovereignty
against both the privileged orders and the king. The
Nobility was strongly in favor of deliberating and
voting by order, but did not want to see the States-
General paralyzed by a deadlock. The majority of the
nobles were willing to compromise on the issue. The
deputies of the Nobility who were most strongly in
favor of maintaining harmony among the orders were the
most well-known and influential of that order. The
question to be asked then, is why did the moderates
fail to reach a compromise which could have left a
States-General free to act in harmony to bring about
the new order that the great majority of deputies
clearly desired?

In his parting remarks to the deputies on May 5
the Keeper of the Seals, Barentin, told them that the
first order of business the following day would be for
each order to meet in the hall prepared for them and
to verify the credentials of the deputies of their order. On May 6 the assembly of the Nobility did so,
organizing itself into a deliberating body, appointing
a commission to verify the credentials of its
deputies, and then adjourning until May 11. The Third
Estate was assigned the hall of the Menus Plaisirs
where the joint meeting had been held the day before.
The deputies immediately declared that they would not
organize into a deliberating assembly until those of
the other two orders came and joined them in a common
assembly. This was precisely what Necker had pleaded
with them not to do: to insist that the question of
voting by head or by order be decided at once, and

451

that nothing could be done until it was resolved in the way the Third Estate demanded. Unless the other two orders joined it in a common assembly the Third Estate announced that it would consider itself only "an aggregation of individuals."[12] The assembly of the Clergy began to organize so that it could verify the credentials of its members, but when it became aware of the attitude of the Third Estate it suspended those proceedings and sought to mediate a compromise for the purpose of "establishing harmony between the orders."[13]

It does appear that the two privileged orders wanted to be conciliatory. At first this was true of the Nobility. The deputy of the Third Estate from Montauban, Jean-Baptiste Poncet-Delpesch, wrote to his constituents that the Nobility was making "many conciliatory gestures toward the Third Estate, even though it does not appear that it is prepared to abandon the vote by order, which it regards as constitutional."[14] When a deputy of the Third Estate died unexpectedly, both privileged orders sent deputations to attend his funeral, the president of the order of the Clergy, Cardinal de La Rochfoucauld personally officiating. But Ligou's "witness" also reported in a bulletin to his constituents that "there were many hotheads in the order of the Third Estate which no doubt will eventually cool off." Until they did, he wrote, "it would be impossible to do any good."[15] He told his constituents that these deputies were proposing that if the two privileged orders obstinately refused to join the Third, the latter alone will constitute the nation and will act accordingly. This idea seemed outlandish to the deputy from Mantauban and he did not suppose that it could happen.

A deputy of the Third Estate from Bar-le-Duc, Adrien Duquesnoy, wrote in his Journal that "there reigned a puerile and ridiculous imitation of the English. They call each other 'the honorable member,' talk of 'motions,' 'amendments,' and 'the majesty of the Nation.'"[16] The assembly had adopted the name of "the Commons," probably not in imitation of the lower house of the British parliament but of medieval city-state democracies. The most resolute of the radical leaders of the "Commons" came from Brittany, Provence, Artois, and Paris intro-muros. The Breton deputies had arrived at Versailles fresh from their struggle with the nobility of the province. They rented quarters on the avenue Saint-Cloud which became "the Breton Club." Other deputies, as many as a hundred at a time, were invited to attend meetings of the Club. It was here that the strategy was prepared for maneuvering the assembly of the Third Estate in the direction the radicals desired. From Paris intro-muros came the great theoretician of the Third Estate, Emmanuel Sieyes, and Armand-Gaston Camus, the latter to become Necker's particular bête noire in the future Constituent Assembly. From Artois came Maximilien Robespierre who was to make the Breton Club his base of power when it moved to Paris in October and became the Jacobin Club. From Provence came the comte de Mirabeau who was to help the radicals up to a certain point, but who did not accept the idea of the supremacy of National Assembly over the king.

Probably only a minority were in favor of such a trenchant solution at the beginning of the deadlock between the Third Estate and the Nobility. The assembly of the "Commons" had several distinguished leaders who were moderates with no idea of overturning the power of the king or of the destruction of the orders. Jean-Joseph Mounier, Pierre-Victor Malouet, Jacques-Guillaume Thouret, Rabaut-Saint-Etienne, Pierre-Samuel du Pont de Nemours, were all moderates. But they threw their support to the cause of deliberation and voting in a common assembly. They feared that if the precedent of deliberating and voting in separate assemblies of the three orders were established, even for such routine matters as verification of the powers

453

of the deputies, it would determine the future
constitution, in which legislative powers would be divided equally between three separate chambers. This
was utterly unacceptable to the moderates, and on that
issue they joined with the radicals. It made a
formidable coalition, and it was strengthened by the
conviction, not unjustified, that Necker was sympathetic to their aims. Where the moderates differed
from the radicals at the beginning of the deadlock was
that they did not want to ignore the privileged orders. They wished to persuade them of the necessity
of joining a common assembly. The radicals wanted to
ignore the Clergy and the Nobility, who after all,
"represented only two to five percent of the Nation."

Certain circumstances surrounding the first days
of the States-General seemed to have helped create
that mood of obstinacy in the Third Estate. Their
cahiers had stipulated certain humiliating distinctions that the Third Estate had suffered in previous
States-Generals which their deputies were not to tolerate in the forthcoming meeting. Some matters that
would appear trivial to the observer seemed to acquire
great importance. One concerned the costumes to be
worn by the deputies on the opening days of the
States-General. The person who was in charge of such
matters was the Grand Master of Ceremonies, the marquis de Brézé. A devoted servant of the ancien
régime, steeped in routine, he mechanically prescribed
the traditional costumes worn by the three orders.
The Nobility was to be decked out in their tricornes
topped with a panache, and wearing a sword. The First
Estate was to appear in the traditional clerical robes
according to their rank and office. But all deputies
of the Third Estate were to wear the black costume of
the minor cleric, which "resembled that of a church
beadle," wrote one disgruntled deputy. The costume
bore a striking resemblance to that worn by the
Crispins and the Gerontes, those who played the role
of lackey, swindler or villain in the classical French

comedy. Naturally Brézé's decree was received with a furor of indignation. One deputy from Lyon wrote a formal letter to the ministry calling attention to the fact that his instructions did not permit him to accept "distinctions which humiliated the Third Estate."

Necker was quick to see the blunder and ordered a change in the decree.[17] The new costume prescribed for the deputies of the Third Estate was that of the maître de requêtes in the parlements. This seemed to satisfy most of the deputies, one of whom recorded that the new costume definitely enhanced the stature of the deputies among the citizens:

> The cloak has a thousand advantages; first,
> it lends an air of dignity which impresses
> everyone. If one dines at the ministry, it
> imposes respect on the lackeys and one is
> better served; if one steps out in society,
> women surround Monsieur the deputy, in order
> to get the latest news from him; when one
> walks in the streets the bourgeois yields
> you the path, and when one crosses the mar-
> ket place one hears oneself blessed by women
> and children; the cloak serves to develop a
> thousand graces, acquired and natural.[18]

Another matter about which the deputies of the Third Estate seemed particularly sensitive was the seating arrangements and the ceremonies on the opening days of the States-General. The attitude and policy of the ministry on this question paralleled that on the question of costume. Brézé amd the lesser officials studiously poured over the records of the preceding States-General, particularly that of 1614, and assumed that traditional usages must inexorably apply. The king and Necker showed an appreciation of the feelings of the Third Estate and intervened to prevent further blunders.

This can be seen in the changed seating arrangements in the opening assembly on May 5. In 1614 the privileged orders sat in the first rows and the Third Estate was relegated to the rear rows. In the new seating arrangements the Third Estate faced the king directly, and the privileged orders were ranged on either side of him. Apparently this solution was satisfactory to all concerned.[19]

One question that seemed to defy any attempt at compromise was that of "covering" (couverture). Traditionally when the king had finished his welcoming address to the assembly, the deputies, who meantime had been standing, took seats. At this time the privileged orders put on their hats, but the deputies of the Third Estate were required to remain uncovered.

Exactly what happened in the session of May 5 is not clear, since eye-witness accounts are contradictory. But the reports of Gouverneur Morris, Galart de Montjoye, and Malartic, all of whom were present, agree on the following: After the king had finished his address and was seated, the deputies of the nobility took seats and covered themselves. Some audacious deputies of the Third Estate also put on their hats as they sat down, but most remained uncovered. This caused considerable confusion within the ranks of the Third Estate, those who were covered urging the others to do likewise, the rest demanding that the radical deputies remove their hats. The king, perceiving the confusion and the cause for it, affected to be uncomfortable because of the heat and removed his hat. This automatically caused the nobility to remove theirs. So for the moment the Third Estate had achieved equality on that point![20] In the royal session of June 23 when the crisis between the orders had reached its climax, the king was no longer in a magnanimous mood. He put on his hat after finishing his address. But the Nobility knowing full well that the Third Estate, now firmly controlled by the radicals, intended to cover themselves, denied them the satisfaction of their triumph by remaining uncovered. Jean-Sylvain Bailly, deputy of the Third Estate from Paris intro-muros, relates in his memoirs that "by putting on my hat, I had resolved to manifest a right. As soon as I saw the majority uncovered, I removed it and everyone remained uncovered."[21]

Another issue which was never satisfactorily resolved and which was the most prominent grievance listed in the cahiers of the Third Estate was the question of kneeling. Traditionally, when the king entered the hall, the deputies of the privileged orders stood, and the deputies of the Third Estate kneeled. After the king was seated on the throne the deputies of the Third were permitted to be seated. But when the spokesman for the Third Estate advanced to address the throne he was required to kneel, whereas the spokesman for the privileged orders stood. The same distinction was observed in all audiences with the king.

Realizing the strength of this grievance, the ministry abolished the custom of kneeling in the opening ceremonies of the States-General. But the privileged orders insisted that the distinction be preserved in private audiences with the king. Apparently Louis himself inclined to this view, although it is not certain if it was the king or the Keeper of the Seals, Barentin, who insisted upon it. The issue finally exploded in a stormy interview between the Keeper of the Seals and Bailly, who had been elected "dean" of the assembly of the Third Estate. Some representatives of the Third Estate had been attempting to get an audience with the king to present their side of the dispute with the privileged orders which by now had resulted in a deadlocked States-General. Barentin hinted to Bailly that the delay in granting the audience was due to the insistence on the matter of ceremony. Bailly relates the incident in his memoirs:

He continued by revealing to me the true basis of the difficulty; he asserted that there was no thought of requiring the Third Estate to kneel while speaking; but there had been an enormous difference between the ceremony of the Third Estate and that of the other orders; one would indeed consent that the former should not speak on bended knee, but the other two orders demanded some difference; and this difference, infinitely difficult to find, caused the embarrassment. I immediately cut short this search by protesting to the minister that however slight the difference might be, the Commons would not suffer it. After this categorical answer, I withdrew; soon there was no more talk, either of ceremonial or of its nuances.[22]

During this conversation Barentin let it be known that he did not accept the idea that the king was relinquishing legislative powers to the States-General, but would continue to hold the monopoly in his own hands. This tended to stregthen the belief already held by Bailly and others in the Third Estate that the promises made in Necker's recess of the council meeting of December 27 were not agreed to by some in the Council. This must certainly have played into the hands of the radicals in the assembly of the Third Estate and weakened the moderates. Tending in the same direction was the activity of the comte d'Artois and his circle who were acting on the assembly of the Nobility to urge a recalcitrant stand. Artois had accepted the election of a bailiwick of Béarn in the south as deputy for the Nobility, but the king forced him to relinquish it. That did not prevent the prince from playing an active role as lobbyist.[23] Once again the king's younger brother was the focal point of Necker's enemies. The group included the comte de Vaudreuil, the duc de Coigny, the duc de Polignac, the duchesse de Polignac, all of whom met regularly at the home of the Polignacs to plan strategy to bring down the Director General of Finances. It was the counterpart of the Club Breton. Within the assembly of the Nobility the leader of the faction against any compromise with the Third Estate was that old leader of parliamentary opposition to the monarchy, Jean-Jacques Duval d'Eprésmesnil, who now openly proclaimed his goal was to bring down Necker.[24]

Meanwhile in the assembly of the Third Estate circumstances were reinforcing the aims of the radicals. Most of the deputies were unaccustomed to parliamentary procedures, and it was some time before they would agree to submit to disciplinary rules. Even Mirabeau had to use his influence to persuade the gentlemen of the Third Estate that it was impossible for all 600 to speak at once. It was not until the Parisians took their seats on May 18, and the head of that delegation, Bailly, was elected "dean" on June 4 that the assembly came under effective order.

What was most disruptive of calm deliberation was the willingness of the Third Estate to admit the public into the hall. The people, many of whom came from Paris, were not content to sit in the spectators' galleries but insisted on mingling with the deputies on the floor. The other two orders had not permitted any visitors or strangers to enter their assembly halls. Despite protests of Mounier, Malouet and the moderates, the radical deputies insisted that "the people" had a perfect right to enter the hall and listen to the deliberations. The trouble was that they were not content to listen. They made their own sentiments known with boistrous effect, and this was more than a little intimidating to the speakers. It was this situation, perhaps, more than any other that accounted for the rise of Mirabeau to power and influence. Many of the deputies of the Third Estate, probably a majority at first, were offended by the extreme violence of

459

Mirabeau's speeches.   But the spectators were much
more susceptible to the power of his oratory.

Gabriel-Honoré Riquetti de Mirabeau was forty
years of age when he came to Versailles to take his
seat in the assembly of the Third Estate, having been
sent there by the bailiwick of Aix-en-Provence.
Through the power of his personality he had established influence over a small society that met regularly at Versailles.   Several members were ex-patriate
Genevans who had been driven from the Republic after
the failure of the liberal revolt in 1782, a revolt
which had been crushed by the armed intervention of
France and Savoy-Piedmont.   Among the ex-patriates
were Etienne Clavière, future Girondin minister of finance, and Etienne Dumont, who left to posterity his
unflattering "Souvenirs of Mirabeau." Until his death
in 1789 an important member of the group was Necker's
old enemy in the international banking community,
Isaac Panchaud.   Another ex-patriate Genevan was
Jacques Antoine du Roverai who had the reputation of
being an expert parliamentarian.   His goal, as that of
the other Genevan members of the society, was to bring
about a government in France that would again intervene in Genevan affairs, this time to further the aims
of the revolutionaries of 1782 rather than thwart
them.

In the ancien régime when an assembly of estates
recovered authority from an absolute ruler it was often seen by foreign adventurers as an opportunity for
outsiders to influence the new government in a way
that would serve their interests rather than the national interests of the country unfortunate enough to
come under the power of the estates.   Such had been
the fate of the Holy Roman Empire, Sweden (before
1773), and Poland.   Du Roverai mingled among the
deputies of the Third Estate with all the assurance of
a modern lobbyist, taking a seat in the area which was
supposed to be reserved for deputies.   When he was no-

460

ticed passing notes to some of them, one of the moderate deputies called the assembly's attention to the presence of a foreigner on the floor behaving as if he were an elected deputy. In the hushed silence that ensued Mirabeau stood up and caught the attention of the deputies. He told them about De Roverai's background and catapulted him into the role of a hero for the cause of human liberty. His fiery oration concluded with the words:

> Behold then the stranger, the exile, the refugee, who has been denounced to you! Formerly the persecuted man sought refuge at the altar, where he found an inviolable asylum, and escaped from the ravage of the wicked. The hall in which we are now assembled is the temple which, in the name of Frenchmen, you are raising to liberty; and will you suffer it to be polluted by an outrage committed upon a martyr of liberty?[25]

His auditors demonstrated thunderously that they could not. The speech was not only heartily applauded by the spectators but by the deputies as well. It was, according to Dumont, Mirabeau's first success at the States-General, and the beginning of his ascendancy over the assembly of the Third Estate. Du Roverai saw in this volatile southerner an opportunity. Could not the king be persuaded to put into council a person who held such sway over the assembly? Since Necker was the most prominent man in the ministry at the moment, it would be necessary to persuade him to admit Mirabeau as a colleague, perhaps even as his superior in the Council. It was a bizarre scheme in view of Mirabeau's past savage essays denouncing Necker. Malouet had a passing acquaintance with the Genevan group, and since he had access to Necker, he was persuaded to approach the Director General of Finance and explain that Mirabeau had propositions to make to him. Necker agreed to see the deputy from

461

Aix-en-Provence, but without enthusiasm. When Mirabeau was introduced to him in his office Necker said bluntly" "Mr. Malouet has told me that you have some proposals to make to me. What are they?" Offended by this glacial greeting, Mirabeau replied: "My proposal is to wish you good day," and turned on his heel. It was the first personal encounter between the two antagonists, the tribune of the people and the popular minister. When he saw Malouet afterwards in the assembly hall, Mirabeau told him: "Your man is a fool. He will be hearing from me." To his Genevan friends Mirabeau said "Necker was a good kind of man, unjustly accused of possessing talent and depth of thought."[26]

This sneering judgment of Necker was rather mild compared to Mirabeau's previous onslaughts against the Director General of Finances. On May 6, the day after the opening of the session of the States-General, Mirabeau launched a new publication for which he invited subscribers. It was entitled "The Journal of the States-General" and was to provide its readers with a complete account of all the proceedings of that body. In the first issue Mirabeau gave free rein not only to his comtempt for Necker but to his resentment at the hostile manner in which he had been greeted when he entered the hall of the States-General on May 5. He had prepared an oration to be delivered at the States-General immediately after Necker's speech, in which he would challenge the financial figures given by the Director General. Mirabeau was deeply chagrined that the session was brought to an end immediately and his attempts to be recognized were ignored. Now in this first issue of the "Journal of the States-General" Mirabeau launched a broadside against the Director General of Finances. He denounced Necker as a person, an incompetent statesman, whose hesitations, whose nullity would defeat the great purpose of the States-General. Necker's May 5 speech was "nothing but wind" in which he concealed his secret intention

462

of destroying the States-General. This was demonstrated, said Mirabeau, by the very measures which Necker had proposed to eliminate the deficit. "What!" cried Mirabeau, "the deficit is our treasure!" It was the means by which the National Assembly would restore the French people to their liberty and defeat the wicked schemes of the ministers. Necker's lengthy discussion of the question of voting by head or by order simply boiled down to the fact that he was going to support the privileged orders against the Third Estate and insist on the deliberation and vote by order. Furthermore, affirmed Mirabeau, it was improper for the Director General to even mention the subject, for it was a matter over which the States-General had exclusive authority.[27]

This was, of course, an outrageous misrepresentation of what Necker had said in his May 5 speech, and it was treated as such by moderates in the three assemblies. The president of the Assembly of the Clergy, Cardinal de la Rochefoucauld, read passages to the assembly and it roused general indignation. The day after its publication Barentin ordered the suppression of "The Journal of the States-General." The order in council recognized that one of the promises made on December 27 was freedom of speech and of press. It would be up to the States-General to enact that principle into law that would provide safeguards against abuse of that freedom. Until that was done the government would continue to enforce existing laws on publications, which meant the continuation of censorship. Furthermore, the decree stated, the "Journal" was not an example of freedom of the press but of its abuse.[28]

This decree had an unfortunate impact on public opinion. In Paris where the electoral assemblies were still in session the assembly of the Third Estate and that of the Nobility protested the decree as a violation of freedom of the press. The Nobility of Paris acknowledged that the piece suppressed was "abominable" but thought the government should not have suppressed it. The assembly of the Third Estate at Paris said it did not approve or disapprove of the contents, but that the issue was freedom of the press. When Mirabeau's second issue came out in print, the name had been changed to "Letters to His Constituents." The government did not interfere with that publication, possibly because of Necker's influence and others in the ministry who wished to be as conciliatory as possible to public opinion. The new name did not imply that the publication was an official journal of the States-General, as might have been assumed by the other title, and which Mirabeau certainly did not discourage.

Naturally Mirabeau viewed these events as first, an attempt to shut him up and second, as a cowardly retreat of the government due to fear of him. In his first "Letter to His Constituents" he drew himself up in the garments of a martyr. He saw himself as the spokesman for twenty-five million Frenchmen demanding freedom of the press. Both the king and the nation unanimously wanted this concourse of wisdom. "And so! it is in that situation that we have been lured into an illusory and perfidious tolerance by a so-called popular ministry, which dares with effrontery to put a seal on our thoughts, to grant privilege to the traffic in lies, and to treat as contraband the necessary export of truth!"[29]

These assertions were as far removed from reality as was usually the case with Mirabeau's pronouncements, both oratorical and written, whose dominant characteristic was excess and exaggeration. Sensible observers of the French scene in 1789, both foreigners and Frenchmen, were appalled by the extreme license of the press. Arthur Young could not understand why the government would permit such free rein for publications of unrestrained violence. This was certainly

464

one of the circumstances that played into the hands of the radicals and defeated the aims of the moderates.

In his political goals Mirabeau differed however from the radical faction influenced by abbé Sieyes. He did not believe in the supreme power of the Constituent Assembly. He remained a monarchist and never became a republican. He wanted to preserve a strong monarchical government, but one in which the king would choose as his first minister the most influential member of the national assembly, which of course would be himself. He was not a devious person. His motives were open as a book. His ambition was to replace the popular minister who now seemed to have the undivided confidence of the king, and whose popularity inflamed that deep-seated envy which was the most dominant characteristic of the tribune. All methods were good to achieve that end: personal denunciation and abuse of the minister in power, demagogic sway of the multitude, personal influence over individuals by the force of his personality. Above all, his immediate goal was to defeat Necker's hopes to mediate between the Nobility and the Third Estate.

Throughout the negotiations between the orders to find some compromise on the question of verification of powers of the deputies from May 12 until June 10 Mirabeau exerted his influence to isolate the Nobility, but to appeal to the lower class of the Clergy, who were parish priests and generally sympathetic with the aims of the Third Estate. Mirabeau wanted to ignore the Nobility and the prelates who were insisting on deliberation by order, but in a way that would not alienate the king. To do this he took up the cause of the radicals in the Commons even though his goal was different from theirs, for the radicals wanted to declare the Commons the supreme sovereign power in the state.

As mentioned above, on May 12 the assembly of the Clergy took the initiative in attempting to bring harmony to the three orders. It passed a motion creating a commission for the purpose of "concerting and conferring with the commissions of the other two orders on the question of the verification of powers." The chamber of the Nobility immediately accepted the invitation and appointed a commission to enter into negotiations. In the assembly of the Third Estate there was a stormy debate between the moderates and the radicals. The latter led by Isaac-René Le Chapelier from Brittany wanted the Commons to ignore the invitation. He argued that if it were accepted it would require the organization of the Commons into a deliberative assembly which would establish once and for all deliberation and voting by order. Furthermore the Commons could afford to ignore the other two orders because they had the weight of numbers if their sympathizers in the other two orders would take their places in the assembly. Le Chapelier wanted the Third Estate to hold fast, to say and do nothing, and inevitably the force of gravity would give a clear majority to the Commons.[30] This was also Mirabeau's strategy.

The moderates were as insistent on deliberation in a common assembly as the radicals. But they wanted all the deputies of the Clergy and the Nobility to join the common assembly, not just those who already were so disposed. The moderates wanted to persuade the privileged orders rather than ignore them, for they did not want a schism in the States-General. Even before the invitation from the Clergy on May 6, Jean-Joseph Mounier had sought to establish contact with the other assemblies to explain the policy of the Third Estate. He proposed a resolution in the assembly to send a deputation to the Nobility and the Clergy asking them to join the Third Estate in a common assembly in order to verify the credentials of all deputies. He related in his memoirs that the overwhelming majority supported this resolution. He per-

466

sonally took the act of the assembly to the other chambers, found that the Nobility had adjourned until the following Monday, but the Clergy was strongly disposed toward conciliation. "When I returned to report to the assembly of the Third Estate, I believed that everyone was satisfied with what I had done. But the factious ones, desperate at the first sign of peace, spread the word among those easily influenced that it was demeaning for the Commons to make such an overture." They disputed whether the resolution of Mounier had received a majority of votes. Because of the confusion about rules of order it was possible for that argument to be of some cogency.[31] When Malouet offered a motion to set up a commission to confer with the other two orders it was voted down by a majority. Next Rabaut-Saint-Etienne introduced a motion to set up a commission but with greatly reduced powers. The mandate of the commissioners permitted them only to demand (réclamer) that the deputies of the Clergy and Nobility join them in a common assembly or to listen to any proposals that might be made to them and to report back to the assembly of the Commons. But they had no power to negotiate, or to make any proposals of their own. Finally, Rabaut's motion declared that the deputies "would never relinquish the principle of voting by head, or the indivisibility of the States-General."[32] This would seem to rule out any chance of compromise according to Necker's suggestion in his May 5 speech. The Third Estate would not agree under any circumstances to voting by order. Yet the fact that Rabaut's motion indicated a willingness to talk to the other orders would hold out some hope for compromise, if the Third Estate could be satisfied that their basic aims would be decided in a common assembly in which the vote would be taken by head.

Mild as Rabaut's motion was it was violently denounced by the Breton delegates who asserted that France could get along very well without the 200,000 or so members of the privileged orders. They drew upon the not very happy precedent of the Protestants driven out of France by Louis XIV, whose numbers exceeded those of the privileged orders and which had no harmful consequences.[33] Such an argument revealed the basic illiberalism of the radicals and gave an indication of what would come if they should prevail. It was particularly offensive in the circumstances since Rabaut-Saint-Etienne was a Protestant pastor from Nîmes. But the assembly passed his measure by a majority and a commission was appointed to meet with those of the other two orders.

The first meeting of the three commissions was held on May 23. It opened with a statement by the spokesman for the Clergy, the Archbishop of Arles, that his order intended to bear all the taxes of the government in the same proportion and in the same manner as all other citizens. Substantially the same statement was made by the spokesman of the Nobility, the duc de Luxembourg, who said that this renonciation of fiscal privileges appeared in nearly all the cahiers and was "as certain as it was irrevocable."[34] This was of course what Necker had requested in his May speech. But unfortunately these statements did not have the impact Necker had hoped because they did not amount to a formal, binding commitment. The Clergy was not yet organized as a deliberating assembly. The minutes of the Nobility show that many insisted that such a concession should be used for bargaining with the Third Estate, and that fiscal privileges should not be formally renounced until and unless the deliberation and vote in separate orders were guaranteed. Therefore the commission was authorized only to state that the principle of renunciation of fiscal privileges was stated in most all cahiers of the Nobility. The Clergy gave their commission authorization to say that the Clergy intended to give up all fiscal privileges but not to put it into writing.[35]

The spokesman for the Third Estate was the eminent Parisian lawyer, Guy-Jean Target. He made no comment about the statements concerning fiscal privileges but said that the purpose of the meeting was to discuss the matter of joining the three assemblies together for the common verification of the credentials of the deputies. He asked why the first two orders had not joined the Third Estate for that purpose. The reply of the Nobility was that in constituting themselves as a separate assembly and verifying the credentials of their members they had acted according to the king's instructions and the traditional practices of preceding States-General. A prominent spokesman for the Nobility was the comte d'Antraigues who said that the present States-General was bound to follow the rules of the preceding ones until it verified the powers of its deputies and became constituted as a deliberative body that could act. Then it could alter the old rules as it saw fit. Later in the assembly of the Nobility, d'Antraigues stated the argument:

> From the first day of your reunion, you took for guides the usages of preceding States-General. Did it lie in your power to change them? Certainly not. These usages transmitted by preceding national assemblies of estates were your law. You could, once constituted, deliberate whether it would be advisable to abolish them or modify them, with the consent of the three orders. But before being constituted you do not have the power to reject the usages and laws of the preceding States-General.[36]

The answer to this argument was given by Mounier: there was no ancient constitution which could be binding on the present. The States-General now sitting had no precedent. Its purpose is to draw up a new constitution for France, to carry out a vast array of reforms called for by the cahiers, to revamp entirely the fiscal system, and to have all fiscal measures of the government sanctioned by periodic meetings of the estates. What previous States-General had ever had such power and responsibility? In view of such great differences between this and previous States-General it made no sense to say that the present assembly was bound by the rules of its predecessors, even temporarily. Since the Third Estate represented at least 95% of the population how could the Clergy and the Nobility justify exercising two-thirds of the legislative power, with each having a veto on all legislation?[37]

Imperceptibly, Mounier had slipped into the question of what the new constitution would be that was to come out of this States-General. It was a different question than that of verifying the credentials of the deputies. Paris intro-muros had verified the credentials of the electors who came to the archepiscopal palace in a common assembly, even though the cahier of the Nobility of that bailiwick called for voting by order at the States-General, and the cahier of the Third Estate for voting by head. The commissioners of the Nobility said that an agreement resolving the matter of verification of credentials did not decide the issue of deliberation and voting in common or separate assemblies of the three orders. That question would be taken up later. D'Antraigues, we have seen, was one of the enlightened nobles from Languedoc who enthusiastically supported the convening of the States-General in 1788. His vision of the forthcoming assembly was not reactionary but forward-looking. He did not dream of returning to the monarchy of estates of two centuries earlier, nor was he ignorant of all the changes that had taken place since 1614. He was not defending an old order but wanted to have the new order come in with due deliberation and consultation among the three estates. Necker's proposal suggested that the Clergy and Nobility would retain their organization for certain matters that concerned their respective orders. Deliberation and voting in common

470

would be done for matters that concerned the nation as a whole. Fiscal matters were certainly included in that category, but there is no reason to think, as some historians do, that Necker intended to limit deliberation in the common assembly to those matters. What concerned d'Antraigues and the moderate and public-spirited nobility was the seeming impulse of the Third Estate to resolve all questions by the weight of numbers. As has been seen in Chapter 11 above, the Clergy and the Nobility were forward-looking in their vision of the new constitution. But that included respect for the rights of minorities. There were some matters concerning honorific privileges and religion that the two privileged orders did not want to give up, at least not without a negotiation, without being consulted. Unfortunately moderates like Mounier could not grasp what was a legitimate concern of the two orders, or did not grasp it in time to prevent the division among the moderates, and the triumph of the extremists in both assemblies of the Second and Third Estates.

The essential matter from the viewpoint of the well-wishers of the nation was to get the States-General organized and brought to the urgent tasks that were becoming more critical by the day: the food shortage, widespread popular unrest, the government finances. Before any of those vital matters could be taken up the States-General had to write the new constitution, and it could not even get started for what many considered a _pointillérie_, a small matter of form. Almost everyone was anxious to get the States-General moving, and yet it remained blocked.

It is usually thought that the assembly of the Nobility was the main reason for the deadlock. But a study of the negotiations would indicate that the majority of the Second Estate initially wanted to cooperate with the Third Estate in forging a new constitution that would be progressive and not reactionary,

471

but would offer sufficient guarantees against the possible tyranny of the majority. The assembly of the Third Estate right at the beginning acted convulsively rather than coolly and deliberately. Nothing except their own strength authorized them to maintain that the other two assemblies should, as a matter of course, join them in a common assembly for the verification of the credentials of all deputies. The moderates who might have been expected to contain the "hotheads" failed to do so, and even supported them in the initial error of insisting, contrary to Necker's entreaty, that the question of voting in common or separately be decided at once rather than to be a subject of negotiation after the States-General had been formally constituted.

Nothing was concluded at the first session of the commissioners on May 23. It was agreed to meet two days later to resume conversations. At the second session the delegates from the Nobility requested the delegates from the Third Estate to make a compromise proposal as a basis for negotiations. The Third Estate replied that they were not authorized by their assembly to do so. Both the Clergy and the Nobility then offered suggestions for a compromise. The proposition of the nobles was that a joint committee of the three orders be appointed to verify the powers of those deputies which were contested. This joint committee would not have the final decision on the contested cases. Its decisions would have to be ratified by the three assemblies separately. The proposal of the Clergy went further. It suggested that those cases in which the committee failed to agree would be decided by a general assembly of the three orders. The deputies from the Third Estate only said they would refer the proposals back to their assembly. Thereupon the session adjourned without fixing any date for another meeting. It was agreed that if there were occasion to renew conversation the assemblies would notify each other.

On May 26 the assembly of the Nobility, after hearing the report of their commissioners who had attended the joint meeting, resolved that verification of the credentials of their deputies in the present States-General would be done by order, but that the Nobility would inform the other two assemblies about their contested deputations; that the examination of the advantages and disadvantages of that procedure would continue to be discussed with the other two orders for future meetings of the States-General. This left the door open for negotiations on the subject of the constitution and the vote in common or by head.

Moderate and sensible as the resolution of the Nobility was, it played into the hands of the radicals of the Third Estate who had been saying all along that negotiations with the Nobility were futile. Now Mirabeau launched a furious assault against the Nobility. He denounced the proposals to have a committee consisting of commissioners from the three orders review the cases of disputed delegations. "We cannot delegate our power of verification to a commission," he thundered, "the consequences of doing so would be to limit the States-General, circumvent it, denature it, finally surrender to a dictatorship. Such a pretension would be criminal as well as absurd. It would be a usurpation of sovereignty, which would be tyranny. . ."[38] He denounced the Nobility for constituting itself a deliberative assembly on May 6, "which amounted to usurpation of complete sovereignty." After this remarkable "export of truth" the tribune then gave his support to a resolution that the Commons send a formal invitation to the Clergy to come take their seats in the assembly of Commons. It was known that nearly half the deputies of the Clergy who were parish priests wanted to join the Third Estate in a common assembly. Mirabeau's resolution was to tug at them. The resolution was passed by the assembly almost unanimously.

Excitement in the assembly of the Commons was very high in the afternoon of May 26. They had made a bold move to split the Clergy, in order to acquire sufficient numbers to enable them to act as the representatives of the nation, ignoring the Nobility and the prelates who would remain in the assembly of the Clergy. Expectations were high that the parish priests would come and take their seats in the hall of the Menus Plaisirs. But no one came. The Commons sent a deputation to the assembly of the Clergy to inquire about their decision. The deputation was told that the Clergy was deliberating on the matter and had not arrived at a decision. The Commons remained in session until after midnight vainly waiting for the mass exodus of deputies from the Clergy that failed to appear. Even the parish priests were reluctant to make such a move that would inevitably antagonize the Nobility and destroy whatever possibility remained for restoring harmony between the orders.

Indeed when the assembly of the Nobility heard of the overture of the Commons to the Clergy they were furious. Now it was possible for the circle influenced by the princes to get the assembly to act according to their desires. For some days they had listened to the orations of Duval d'Eprésmesnil which were becoming more and more violent against the Third Estate. He was a worthy counterpart of the tribune of the people. Many in the chamber of the Nobility were offended by his extremism; the duc de Luynes, for example, reminded the orator that his own father had been a member of a class which he was now castigating in such unmeasured terms. It was one of the ironies of the assembly of the Nobility that those who were most insistent on preserving what they called the traditional practices were in fact of recent nobility. The most illustrious names were more often in the ranks of the moderate or the liberal nobility, as de Luynes was himself. But now d'Eprésmesnmil managed to get the assembly to pass by a majority a resolution

474

which effectively blocked any chance of the type of compromise Necker had been hoping for. The resolution, passed in the morning of May 28, stated:

The chamber of the nobility, considering that at the present moment, its duty is to rally to the constitution and to set an example of firmness as it has already given proof of its disinterestedness, declares that deliberation by order and the veto of each order are constituent elements of the monarchy, and that the nobles will constantly maintain these principles as necessary for the preservation of the throne and of liberty.[39]

The implications of this resolution were that the Nobility was closing the door to any hope of mediation. It had taken a stand as intransigent as that of the Third Estate. The resolution passed the assembly by a majority but not without vigorous dissent, even among those whose mandates called for voting by order. The latter argued that the timing was inappropriate when efforts were being made to reach an agreement among the orders. The resolution passed by a majority of 197 votes against 44. But the deputies from Paris intro-muros and Dauphiné had not yet had their credentials verified and were not included in the voting. Had they been included the minority would have been strengthened, for both deputations were strongly in favor of harmony between the orders.

The sentiment in favor of the resolution was strengthened by the reception that same morning of a letter from the king expressing his disappointment and concern that the States-General was not able to take up the tasks for which he had summoned it. He therefore was inviting the commissions of the three orders who had been negotiating among themselves, apparently without success, to come to the residence of the

475

Keeper of the Seals the following evening at 6 p.m. There, under the chairmanship of Barentin, and in the presence of the other ministers, attempts at conciliation on the question in dispute would be resumed. The intervention of the government to bring an end to the impasse was not viewed with enthusiasm by the Nobility. It feared a forced mediation in which the king would command the three orders to meet in a common assembly to verify the credentials. Now the resolution of d'Eprésmesnil assured them that they could not be pressured into such an outcome. They agreed to accept the invitation of the king on those terms.

The Clergy was still deliberating on the invitation from the Commons when the king's letter arrived. The summons was accepted at once and with great relief since the Clergy was embarrassed by the invitation from the Commons. The great majority of the Clergy, prelates as well as parish priests were anxious to reach a peaceful compromise. Some memoir writers maintained that it was the Clergy who took the initiative in asking the government to intervene and attempt mediation.[40] But in Barentin's message to the king about the matter, he refers to such a rumor and said it was not true. The ministry took the initiative in reopening negotiations.[41] Necker wrote in his memoirs on his second ministry that the initiative for convening the meeting was his.[42]

When the king's letter arrived at the assembly of the Third Estate it aroused a vigorous debate as to whether the royal invitation to renew negotiations should be accepted. The radicals such as Le Chapelier from Brittany and Camus from Paris condemned the government's intervention, asserting that the king had no right to interfere in a matter that was exclusively the business of the States-General. The moderates just as strongly urged acceptance of the invitation. Mounier, according to Creuzé-Latouche, "spoke forcefully for participation and for the confidence which one should have in the good intentions of the king, and also of the ministers."[43] But the moderates were facing a hostile audience in the galleries. According to the minutes of the session a deputy from Riom, no doubt Malouet, asked that in view of the great importance of the matter to be discussed the visitors in the hall should be required to leave. The radical deputies protested that no matter how important the business before the assembly the people had a right to observe and listen to the debates. Malouet's motion failed to pass, but the "dean" of the Commons did attempt to discipline the spectators, admonishing them to refrain from manifesting their views in favor of or in opposition to issues and speakers.[44]

Mirabeau, like the radicals, denounced the intervention of the government. But he separated the wicked intentions of the ministers, whom he said were deliberately fomenting the deadlock in the States-General in order to bring about its dissolution, from the intentions of the king. He urged that the Commons approach the king directly and present their case against the Nobility. But they could not boycott the meeting at the residence of the Keeper of the Seals without offending the king. Therefore Mirabeau got the assembly to agree to send the commissioners to the meeting but under two conditions. First, that a deputation be sent to the king with a petition, and second, that the minutes of the conferences at the Keeper of the Seals be signed by all commissioners who attended. The purpose of the second condition was purely obstructionist, since it provided endless opportunities for chicanery. The Nobility had earlier objected to the new term the Third Estate had adopted for itself, the "Commons," and passed a resolution that their commissioners were not to sign the minutes of the meetings if the name "Commons" appeared in them. The commissioners of the Third Estate wrote the minutes of the first session and the name "Commons" appeared forty times![45] The prospects for successful mediation did not look promising.

The petition which the assembly of the Commons drew up to be presented to the king expressed the undying devotion of the Commons to the king's "sacred person." They maintained that the schism in the States-General was due entirely to the refusal of the privileged orders to join them in a common assembly. They invoked the historic alliance between king and people against the feudal aristocracy.

> Sire, your faithful Commons will never for-
> get what they owe to their king; they will
> never forget that natural alliance of the
> throne and people against the diverse aris-
> tocracies whose power can be established
> only on the ruin of royal authority and pub-
> lic felicity.[46]

Meanwhile the first meeting of the commissioners of the three assemblies took place on the evening of May 30. It was opened by a statement from Necker: "You can see, gentlemen, all the dangers which surround us. Are not there some means for conciliation?" One of the deputies from the Nobility replied to the Director General: "You should have foreseen the danger and prevented it." He said that the credentials of the deputies should have been verified by the government before the meeting of the estates, as had been done in the past. Brette's "secret agent" reported that it was a lively exchange, but that Necker finally remained silent.[47] He had not come to quarrel with either side but to mediate. Brette's "secret agent" remarked about the scene:

> It is an extraordinary thing that the con-
> duct of Mr. Necker is stongly condemned by
> all parties. The Nobility reproaches him
> for his populist principles; the Third Es-

tate criticizes him for his lack of resolution and for favoring the aristocrats. It must be admitted that the task of a minister is a difficult one; with the best intentions when one wishes to please everyone, one ends up pleasing nobody.[48]

The first session was taken up with an endless dispute about how the minutes should be recorded and who should sign them. There was another fruitless excursion into historical precedents and why they should or should not apply in the current dispute. At the second meeting the Clergy and the Nobility proposed that since the question of voting by head or by order was what lay behind the dispute about verification of credentials of deputies, why not grasp the nettle and see if that fundamental issue could be compromised in the present discussion? The commissioners of the Commons said they were not authorized by their assembly to discuss that matter. In the assembly of the Commons Malouet introduced a motion to grant them that power but his motion was decisively defeated. It would appear that the Third Estate was confident of victory in the dispute and could see no reason to compromise. The stalemate seemed more firmly entrenched than ever.

On June 4, at the third and last session, Necker presented the government's proposal on a settlement of the question of verification of powers. He set forth lucidly the fundamental issue in the dispute: each order was legitimately concerned about the verification of credentials because where there were disputed elections of deputies, each assembly would want to seat the deputy that held its views. It would not be fair to the Third Estate to allow the privileged orders to resolve contested elections in their orders all by themselves without allowing a voice to the Third Estate. Similarly it would be unfair to the privileged orders to have all contests resolved in a common assembly of the three orders, because the Third Estate, with their allies in the other two estates, would clearly have a majority. Their preponderant voting power could increase the number of their own partisans at the expense of the Nobility. Therefore Necker proposed that the contested delegates and delegations be resolved first by a commission representing the three orders. Their decisions would be referred back to the three assemblies who would vote upon them. If there could be no agreement among the three assemblies on a case it would be resolved by the king. Finally the compromise proposal would not prejudice whatever decisions might be made for the verifications of powers of future States-General. And of course, it would not prejudge the important issue of voting by head or by order.

Necker thought this as fair a proposal as could possibly be made. He could not understand why there would be any objection to it. Therefore he admonished the commissioners:

> What true citizen would fail to sustain the intentions of the best of kings? And who would wish to burden his conscience of all the misfortunes that could be the consequence of the schism which threatens your first steps, gentlemen, that you are taking, in a task where the welfare of the state calls you, where the Nation is impatient for you to get on with the task, and the greatest dangers lurk around you. Ah! gentlemen, even if you could attain such a desirable goal by the schism of hearts and minds, it would be too dearly bought. The king therefore invites you to take his proposal, and he urges you with all his love to accept and grant him that satisfaction.[49]

480

On the following day, June 5, Necker's proposal was read to all three assemblies. The Clergy by a great majority accepted the plan and sent deputations to the other two assemblies informing them of their actions and urging them to do likewise. On June 6 the Nobility informed the other assemblies that it had accepted the king's plan of conciliation but with some amendments. The Nobility stood by its previous decision that it would be the final judge of individual deputies in their order, but that in cases where entire deputations were in dispute the Nobility would accept Necker's plan for having the king be the final arbitor. Since the Nobility had already admitted in previous negotiations that the Third Estate had a legitimate interest in verifying the credentials of entire delegations which included deputies from all three orders, its action of June 6 did not amount to a great concession. It was looked upon by most observers as a refusal, despite the language of the resolution. Necker had no doubt that it was such and he was appalled and outraged by it.

In the assembly of the Commons the decision was to delay deliberation on the "Memoir of Conciliation" until the conferences were concluded and the minutes of each session signed. It was a tortuous process that was not completed until June 9. The commissioners of the Nobility still objected to the use of the word "Commons" in the minutes but finally agreed to the proposal of the Keeper of the Seals that the secretary of the government's delegation could sign the minutes for them.[50] On June 10 the head of the delegation at the conferences for the Commons, Dupont de Nemours, began to read the minutes of the final session, as he had done in the past. He was interrupted by Mirabeau who told the presiding officer (Bailly) that a deputy had a motion to present. This was abbé Sieyes who got up to read a long speech. He said the Nobility had rejected the king's proposal for compromise so it was unnecessary for the Commons to debate

481

on it. Further conciliatory conferences were useless.
It was essential that the States-General be organized
and begin the task of drawing up the new constitution.
Sieyes moved that the assembly send a final message to
the privileged orders that it would begin immediately
to call the roll of all deputies, Clergy and Nobility
as well as Commons, and that those who were absent
would be declared in default.

This maneuver, which had been carefully planned
at the Club Breton, did not succeed in stifling debate
on Necker's conciliatory proposal. The moderates, including Dupont de Nemours, insisted on a full discussion before voting on the motion. More than half the
deputies were concerned about the impact this would
have on the king. It was one thing to coerce the two
privileged orders, but a different matter to coerce
the king. When the vote was taken 247 deputies would
support it only if an address was presented to the
king explaining that the Commons did not intend to attack royal authority. Eventually in a later session
that same day the motion with that amendment was
passed. About 44 deputies voted to have the matter
carefully deliberated in the bureaux of the Commons,
Dupont being among them.[51]

The radicals were anxious to get the motion carried and not so scrupulous about how the royal government would react. Their position was argued by Camus
who said that Necker's proposal "contained principles
that were a violation of public rights, destructive of
liberty, . . . it gives the Royal Council the right to
intervene, and the Council has no authority over the
States-General." Camus acknowledged that the king
shared legislative powers with the States-General, but
not the Council, whose ministers were responsible and
subservient to the States-General. Just how the king
would exercise his legislative authority without a
council of ministers Camus did not say. But here was
the germ of the future Constituent Assembly. The king

482

would be "sacred" and the throne hereditary, but the ministers of the government would be lackeys of the Assembly. As for Necker's plan of conciliation Camus said "we must protest against the person who strikes at our rights." He said further that the plan of conciliation was contradictory to the promise made at the time of the doubling of the Third Estate granted in the recess of the Council meeting of December 27. The Commons, he said, would not gain anything by that concession if it were forced to deliberate and vote in a separate chamber from the other two orders.[52] This argument was patently in bad faith because Necker's proposal stipulated that it would not prejudge the question of voting by head or by order.

Others besides Camus, even moderates, argued that the quarrel that had immobilized the States-General was not one in which the government should intervene. They asserted it would be dangerous for it to do so, for such intervention could lead to the destruction of the States-General and of all hope for a constitutional regime. "Divide and rule," wrote Bailly in his memoirs, "is ever the maxim of all governments."[53] He argued against Necker's plan of conciliation because "it would be dangerous to allow the king to decide contested cases."[54] This was a notion that had been consistently propagated by Mirabeau: the government was malevolently provoking and deepening the schism in the States-General so that it could restore the absolute power of the monarchy. It was unfortunate for Necker that such an able and intelligent person as Bailly should have allowed himself to be influenced by Mirabeau and should have so badly misjudged the situation. Far from being a threat to the States-General, the government was dangerously weak. It is true that there was a clique of courtiers which included princes of the blood who did intrigue to bring about the dissolution of the States-General by armed force. But events proved they were impotent against the power of the national movement. The government was weak not because of the personal qualities of the ministers but because of the "force of circumstances," as Necker constantly pointed out in his books written in later years. The government could only act in concert with an overwhelmingly dominant public opinion, or "national will," and attempt to direct it in the channel that the moderates desired. The moderates in the Third Estate should have given their support to the ministers such as Necker and Montmorin who were attempting to realize their aims. Instead, some of the most influential of the moderates did just the opposite: they gave their support to the radicals. They, and the nation, were to pay dearly for their mistake. Bailly himself was to be one of their most celebrated victims, perishing on the guillotine some four years later.

To accuse Necker of being "despotic" because he attempted to mediate the deadlock in the States-General was singularly unjust in view of his abstention from any attempt to influence the election of deputies to the States-General. He had been circumspect in his relations with the deputies since their arrival at Versailles. He was hospitable and open to them, but did not try to influence them on specific policies or to build a personal following. He believed that such a sensitive regard for the independence of the States-General was the right and honorable policy. Yet it was the one that drew vehement criticism at the time and later by both friends and enemies. Malouet, we have seen, thought it was the greatest imprudence not to control the selection of deputies, and to refrain from laying before the States-General a specific constitution. Mounier wrote in his memoirs that Necker could have prevented the disastrous outcome by forcing the reunion of the orders. The commissioners of the Nobility and some of Necker's ministerial colleagues, notably Barentin, believed that the deadlock could have been prevented had the government insisted on its right to verify the credentials of the deputies before the opening of the States-General. Everywhere Necker was accused of "weakness," "indecisiveness," and "lack of energy." As he saw it, the one thing no one would tolerate in that period was a display of energy by the government, particularly if it went counter to the dominant opinion.

After the passage of the fateful motion of Sieyes on June 10 the Commons notified the other two assemblies of its act, and "invited" rather than "summoned" (as had been in Sieyes' original motion) them to take their places in the general assembly. The roll call of all deputies was begun the next day and completed on June 16. In the meantime there were desperate efforts to revive mediation. On June 16 the king sent two reproachful letters, one to the Nobility and one to the Third Estate, saying that if either had accepted his plan of mediation the other would not have dared to take the responsibility for failure of the government's peace proposal. "More deference on the part of the Nobility," he wrote, "could have led to the conciliation that I desired."[55] To the Third Estate he wrote: "The reservation that the Nobility made in its acceptance of my plan should not have prevented the order of the Third Estate from deferring to my wishes. The example of the Clergy, followed by that of the Third Estate no doubt would have led the Nobility to desist in its reservation."[56] In fact there was pressure from within the chamber of the Nobility to reconsider the "reservation" which had meant a rejection. That act had passed by a vote of 158 votes in favor and 76 votes against.[57] The latter figure included of course the minority of nobles who had wanted to join the Commons at the outset, numbering 47 or 48 deputies. The remainder were not "liberal" nobles but "moderate," that is, those who genuinely sought a compromise that would end the deadlock but not be a capitulation to the majority. Lally-Tollendal led the argument in favor of Necker's proposal in the chamber of the Nobility. In his memoirs he indicated that the opinion could have shifted decisively had there been more time. In considering the final answer to the Commons on June 13 there was considerable debate in the assembly of the Nobility. The final resolution, after several amendments, passed by a narrow majority of 116 votes for and 110 votes against.[58] The resolution restated the positions the order had taken on May 27, May 28, and June 5, which meant a rejection of the invitation from the Commons to take their seats in a general assembly.

But time was running out for the mediators. On June 16 the Commons had completed the roll call. On June 17 Sieyes offered his second motion that "since 96% of the nation was present, the assembly could not remain inactive because of the absence of a few bailiages or a few classes of citizens." Furthermore, he said, "since it pertains only to the representatives who have been verified to form the national will, and all the verified representatives are in this assembly, we must conclude that it is in the power of this assembly, and this assembly alone, to represent the general will."[59]

The motion passed by a great majority, 491 to 90. But the minority was vocal and indignant. Even Mirabeau abstained from voting since he did not want to offend the king. "We cannot tell the king," said Mirabeau, "that the nobles and the clergy are not representatives of the nation, for he has convoked them as such, and they have been presented to him as such."[60] Malouet, who had been fighting a rear-guard action against the radicals from the beginning, was exasperated:

> It would seem, gentlemen, that you are thought to be strangers to all (prudent) considerations, independent of all obstacles, dominating all wills, and arriving in the midst of the centuries without regard to

the past, without concern for the future. This, gentlemen, is not our position. . . do not forget that the Clergy and the Nobility, called, as we were, to the regeneration of the state, have a right, as do we, to this high destiny. Woe to those who would wish to dissolve such a holy community![61]

A deputy from the Third Estate of Castelnaudary wrote later that "I had never seen in my mandate anything which could allow me even to presume that we had the right to claim to represent the nation. . . I dreaded the consequences of what I considered an adventure. I believed I could see in it the dissolution of the States-General . . . and I voted against constituting (the Commons) as the national assembly."[62]

Malouet wrote in his memoirs that both Necker and Montmorin were astonished and infuriated at the passage of Sieyes' resolution. Necker evidently believed his influence among the deputies of the Third Estate was sufficient to forestall such an outcome. It would seem that the success of the radicals was due in part to what in American politics is called "cloakroom buttonholing." A deputy from the Third Estate from Bordeaux, Pierre-Paul Nairac, wrote in his journal:

This motion of abbé Sieyes was carefully prepared in special committees, and arrangements were made to have it adopted in advance by provinces and members of the assembly who had shown themselves to be ardent partisans (of the radicals). I am not so much concerned right now as to what the ultimate consequences to the nation might be as I am disturbed by the precipitation with which the action was taken, and the gathering of votes that preceded it. If the voice of wise men is stifled by violent means, if a partisan spirit continues to replace prudence, there is reason to fear that the resolutions of the chamber will be a series of projects harmful to (the purpose of the States-General), contrary to the public welfare, and directed in general against the minister of finances which a powerful party wishes to thwart. . .[63]

Jean-Joseph Mounier was aware of the resolution that Sieyes would present to the Club Breton the evening before it would be introduced to the Commons and he sought to deflect it by a counter-motion. This was to assert that "the majority of deputies, deliberating in the absence of the minority of deputies, duly invited, have resolved that deliberation will be (in common, and votes counted) by head and not by order, and we will never agree to the members of the Clergy and Nobility deliberating separately." Mounier succeeded in getting this motion passed by a majority of the deputies who attended the Club Breton. While insisting on deliberation and voting in a common assembly it continued to recognize the existence of the privileged orders whose deputies had failed to appear at the roll call. The next day Mounier was astounded that "most of those who the evening before had supported my opinion suddenly abandoned it and voted for the motion of Sieyes."[64] A deputy from the Third Estate from Laon, Jacques François Laurent de Visme, also expressed surprise at the sudden shift in opinion: "What was astonishing is that this idea which yesterday one thought absolutely necessary to avoid became acceptable."[65]

Certainly one explanation was the increasing pressure and threats on the deputies coming from the popular classes that inundated the hall of the Menus Plaisirs, or who watched outside if they could not gain entrance. Etienne Dumont was a direct observer of events in those days and wrote that "the people of Versailles have got to insulting those whom they call

488

'aristocrats' on the streets and at the door of the assembly hall. The power of this word is acquiring all the magic of such partisan slogans . . ."[66] Mounier wrote bitterly that "that day (June 17) was the beginning of the most violent measures against freedom of deliberation. A list of names was compiled of all those who had rejected the motion of M. Sieyes; it was circulated in Paris; all those who appeared on it were called traitors."[67] Even those sympathetic to the radicals noted this behavior of the people. Crueuzé-Latouche saw the placards on which the names of "bad citizens" were inscribed. He saw the names of almost all the deputies from Paris, except Bailly, Sieyes, Poitnet, and Des Meismes: the names of Malouet, Thouret, Lebrun, Dupont de Nemours, appeared on the placards. Mirabeau escaped condemnation because he had abstained rather than voted against the motion of Sieyes.[68]

The first acts of the National Assembly showed clearly that the ideology of abbé Sieyes had triumphed for the moment. Turning its attention first to the finances the newly-formed Assembly declared that all existing taxes were illegal since they had not been approved by the Assembly. But as a temporary measure the Assembly granted the government permission to collect them for the duration of the Assembly. The Assembly would turn to the constitution next and when that was completed it would dissolve itself and the new constitutional regime would begin. Meanwhile the Assembly would deal with emergency matters that could not wait. The national debt was to be examined and consolidated, then placed under the protection of the honor and loyalty of the French nation.[69] Also a committee on subsistence would be set up immediately to examine the question of the food shortage and the threat of famine.

The failure of Necker to mediate a way out of the deadlocked States-General was the greatest political

489

set-back in his career. His plan for the work of the States-General that he had suggested in his May 5 speech now lay in tatters. It would be necessary to use the prestige and power of the government to impose an arbitration. The king and his minister must now decide on a solution that would be a compromise, no doubt, but an enforced one, resisted by one side or the other. But this was fraught with great risk because of the weakness of the government, or rather, the fact that the ministry was divided. Some of the ministers, which included Necker, would tend to favor the Third Estate; but there were conservatives in the ministry, especially the Keeper of the Seals, who would favor the privileged orders. It was with apprehension and foreboding that Necker prepared for the next great challenge: to win the king over to his thinking about what needed to be done.

[1]For example, Ambrose Saricks, _Dupont de Nemours_ (Lawrence, Kansas, 1965), 147.

[2]J. H. Mariéjol, _La Réforme et la Ligue. L'édit de Nantes_ (Paris, 1900-1911, 53.

[3]"De la Révolution française," in _Oeuvres complètes de Necker_, IX, 323.

[4]_The Papers of Thomas Jefferson_, XV, 190.

[5]_Ibid._, 191-192. The editor of the Jefferson papers, Julian Boyd, wrote that "the most likely candidate" for the authorship of this essay sent to John Jay was Dupont de Nemours. This seems highly unlikely because Dupont did not write that kind of libels, and although he differed strongly with Necker on economic and political doctrines, the two were always on cordial personal terms. Necker invested money in Dupont's American venture as did his brother, Louis Necker de Germany. Both maintained an active correspondence with Dupont de Nemours and his two sons, as can be seen in the index of John Beverly Rigg's _Guide to the Manuscripts in the Elutherian Mills Historical Library_ (Greenvillle, Delaware, 1980), 1177. I am indebted to Alfred Necker, present-day descendant of Louis Necker de Germany, now living in Geneva, for calling my attention to the business relationships between the Duponts and the Neckers.

[6]Edouard Chapuisat, _Jacques Necker_(Paris, 1938), 174.

[7]_Correspondance littéraire, philosophique et critique_, XV, 453.

[8]Chapuisat, _Necker_, 300.

[9]Mercy-Argenteau, Correspondance secrète, II, 238-239.

[10]Loc. cit.

[11]Georges Lefebvre and Anne Terroine, Recueil de documents relatifs aux séances des Etats-Généraux (mai-juin) (Paris, 1953), I, 218-243. In his discussion of Necker's May 5 speech Lefebvre wrote that he revealed his intention to reduce the States-General to an advisory body without legislative powers. I cannot see that such an interpretation is justified. In his book devoted to Necker's thought, Henri Grange has shown that Lefebvre misread a passage of the speech where Necker said: "Et nous autres, Messieurs, nous seconderons, non pas de notre pouvoir, puisque ce pouvoir ne consiste que dans notre obéissance aux ordres du Roi," to mean that Necker was referring by "we" to the States-General, but it is clear that he meant only himself and the other ministers whose powers were derived entirely from the king. See Henri Grange, Les Idées de Necker (Paris, 1974), 409.

[12]Archives parlementaires, VIII, 28.

[13]Ouverture des Etats généraux, procès-verbaux et récit des séances des ordres du Clergé et de la Noblesse, jusqu'à leur réunion à l'Assemblée nationale (Paris, 1891), BN Le 27.6. Contrary to the title this does not include the procès-verbaux of the Nobility.

[14]Daniel Ligou, ed., La première anné de la Révolution vu par un Témoin (Paris, 1961), 21.

[15]Ibid., 21-22.

[16]Journal d'Adrien Duquesnoy, député du Tiers-Etat de Bar-le-Duc sur l'assemblée constituante. 3 mai 1789-3 avril 1790 (Paris, 1894).

[17]Lefebvre and Terroine, Recueil de documents, 74.

[18]Ibid., 80.

[19]Lefebvre, Recueil, 48.

[20]Ibid., 51-52.

[21]Ibid., 52.

[22]Jean-Sylvain Bailly, Mémoires d'un Témoin de la Révolution (Paris, 1821), I, 104-105.

[23]Ferrières, Correspondance inédite, 50 passim.

[24]Marquis de Clermont-Gallerande, Mémoires particuliers pour servir à l'histoire de la Révolution (Paris, 1826), I, 62-63.

[25]Etienne Dumont, Recollections of Mirabeau, 82.

[26]Pierre-Victor Malouet, Mémoires, I, 316-318; Dumont, op. cit., 78.

[27]Lettres du comte de Mirabeau à ses comettans pendant la tenue de la première Législature (Paris, 1791), no. 11.

[28]Réimpression de l'Ancien Moniteur (Paris, 1847), I, 25.

[29]P. J. B. Buchez, Histoire de l'Assemblée constituante (Paris, 1846), II, 278.

[30]François-Alphonse Aulard, ed., Récit des séances des députés des Communes depuis le 5 mai 1789 jusqu'à 12 juin suivant (Paris, 1895), 19.

[31]Jean-Joseph Mounier, Recherches sur les causes qui ont empêchés les Français de devenir libre (Geneva, 1792), 276.

[32]Récit des séances des Députés des Communes
depuis le 5 mai 1789 jusqu'à 12 juin suivant, 19.

[33]Duquesnoy, Journal, I, 20.

[34]Archives parlementaires, VIII, 46.

[35]Récit des principaux faits qui sont passés dans
la Salle de l'ordre du Clergé, depuis le commencement
des Etats-Généraux, 14 mai 1789, jusqu'à la réunion
des trois ordres dans la Salle commune de l'Assemblée
nationale, par M. Vallet, curé de St. Louis (Paris,
Imprimérie nationale, 1790), 33. For the assembly of
the Nobility: Procès-verbal des séances de la Chambre
de la Noblesse aux Etats-Généraux tenus à Versailles
en 1789 (Paris, Imprimérie nationale, 1792), BN Le
27.5a.

[36]Archives parlementaires, VIII, 52.

[37]Jean-Joseph Mounier, Recherches sur les causes
qui ont empêché les Français à devenir libre, I, 231-
232.

[38]Réimpression de l'ancien Moniteur, I, 43-44.

[39]Procès-verbal des séances de la Chambre de
l'Ordre de la Noblesse, 110.

[40]Daniel Ligou, La première année de la
Révolution vu par un Témoin, 28. Also Jacques-Antoine
Creuzé-Latouche, Journal des Etats-généraux et de
début de l'assemblée nationale (18 mai-19 juillet
1789) (Paris, 1946), 30.

[41]A. Aulard, Lettres et Bulletins de Barentin à
Louis XVI (avril-juillet 1789) (Paris, 1915), no. 19.

[42]"Sur l'Administration de M. Necker," in Oeuvres
complètes de Necker, VI, 80-81.

[43]Creuzé-Latouche, Journal des Etats-Généraux, 29.

[44]Récit des séances de la Chambre des Communes depuis le 5 mai 1789 jusqu'à 12 juin suivant (Thursday, May 28).

[45]Procès-verbal des séances de la Chambre de l'Ordre de la Noblesse.

[46]Archives parlementaires, VIII, 60.

[47]Brette, "Documents inédits," La Révolution française, XXIII, 461.

[48]Ibid., 541.

[49]"Sur d'Administration de M. Necker," in Oeuvres complètes de Necker, VI, 85.

[50]Brette, "Relation des événements depuis de 6 mai jusqu'à 15 juillet. Bulletins d'un agent secret," La Révolution française, XXIII, 523.

[51]Creuzé-Latouche, Journal, 95.

[52]Ibid., 85.

[53]Mémoires, I, 80.

[54]Ibid., 145.

[55]Procès-verbal des séances de la Chambre de l'Ordre de la Noblesse, 248.

[56]Bailly, Mémoires, I, 174.

[57]Procès-verbal de la Noblesse, Friday, June 5.

[58]Lally-Tollendal, Mémoire, 29; Procès-verbal de la Noblesse, 226.

[59]Archives parlementaires, VIII, 109.

[60]Ibid., 125.

[61]Ibid., 119.

[62]Lefebvre, Recueil de documents, I, part 2, 52, n. 61.

[63]Ibid., 54, n. 62.

[64]Mounier, Exposé de la conduite de M. Mounier (Paris, 1789), 6.

[65]Lefebvre, op. cit., 57, n. 75.

[66]Souvenirs sur Mirabeau (Paris, 1951), 69.

[67]Mounier, Exposé de la conduite, 708.

[68]Lefebvre, Recueil de documents, I, 55, n. 66.

[69]Bailly, Mémoires, I, 168.

CHAPTER 14

THE SWAY OF CIRCUMSTANCES

To many observers at the time and to historians of later day what seems inexplicable about Necker's conduct in the first weeks of the States-General was his "strange silence" and his seeming inactivity when the monarchy was passing through a fateful political crisis. Silent he may have been but inactive he certainly was not. His home was open to deputies of the States-General; he and Madame Necker were lavish hosts and many were seated at the evening dinner table. The comte d'Angiviller, director of the king's Buildings, who lived across the street from the Contrôle-général, watched with dark suspicion the many comings and goings at the Necker household. For Angiviller was a staunch conservative of the ancien régime who had conceived a violent hatred of Necker during the first ministry.[1]

Much of Necker's working day was taken up receiving visitors whose interviews in his office were not usually as abrupt as that with Mirabeau. Then, the two great emergencies faced by the government, the finances and the grain shortage occupied much of Necker's time and energy. He had kept the government afloat financially by a series of expedients which he was anxious to bring to an end once the new constitutional regime was founded and the government's credit thereby guaranteed. The grain shortage and threat of famine became increasingly serious in the early weeks of the summer. It continued to be until well into the fall months of 1789.

As to what the conversation might have been during those evening suppers and in Necker's office, the evidence is fragmentary. The Secret Agent reported

that the assembly of the Commons seemed to be convinced that Necker was in favor of the stand they were
taking in the deadlock, and that it was incumbent on
the minister to let the assembly know if this were not
true.[2] When the king's letter calling for the conference of commissioners to meet at Barentin's hotel arrived it was announced that Necker would be one of the
ministers present at the meeting. A cheer went up
from the Commons, who seemed to believe the Director
General of Finances was their man in the government.[3]
It is possible that Necker revealed to some of the
deputies his own thinking, that he was willing to go
much further in acceding to the demands of the Commons
than was indicated in his May 5 speech. But this is
rather improbable given Necker's strong repugnance at
what he called "intrigue." According to a conversation Joseph-François Coster, Necker's First Secretary
at the Contrôle-général had with Bertrand Moleville,
the former said that "Mr. Necker remains firmly resolved to have no secret relations with any member of
the assembly, whoever it might be . . . It is contrary
to his morals and against his principles to exert any
influence whatever . . . The duty of the minister is
limited to bringing the representatives of the nation
to the door of the States-General. From the moment
that they enter it is their own conscience and wisdom
that must guide them."[4]

Such abstinence may seem excessive to later democratic societies, where it is not deemed inappropriate, even in presidential regimes, for the president
to court members of the legislature to gain their support for his policies. Necker was aware of this criticism of his second ministry and discussed it fully in
his later books. He insisted it would have been inappropriate for a minister of the government to lay down
policy and lobby to get it accepted by the deputies of
the States-General.[5] It certainly would have been inappropriate for a single minister to have attempted
such a policy. Mounier suspected that Necker's

498

"strange silence" was due to division of opinion within the king's council as to what policy the government should pursue, and this seems to have been the right explanation.

According to Madame de Staël it was around May 20 that Necker presented two important documents to the king and sought his approval for them. One was a "tableau of the situation of the monarchy," in which Necker pointed out the weakness of the government. The disaffection was infiltrating the regular army regiments so that it was illusory to think, as some were attempting to persuade the king, that the popular movement could be overcome by military force alone. It was necessary for the government to make a great new concession to what Necker thought was the overwhelming opinion of the people. "What must be done now, Sire, is to accede to the reasonable desires of France. Deign to accept the English constitution; you will not suffer any constraint by the reign of laws; they would never impose stricter bonds on you than your own scruples; and, by going beyond the desires of your nation you can make a gift today of what tomorrow it may force from you."[6]

The second document was evidently a prototype of that which Necker eventually submitted to the king for the Royal Session held a month later. This was a joint session of the three estates like that of May 5 in which the king invoked his authority to enforce a compromise. But on May 20 Necker was planning for the king to make a Declaration to achieve the same end rather than to hold a Royal Session which would recall unpleasant memories of the lits de justice in past confrontations between the royal government and the sovereign courts. It would have forestalled the act of the Third Estate declaring itself the national assembly. In this Declaration the king would command the three orders to meet in a joint assembly to deliberate and vote on all matters that concerned the general interest, referring specifically to financial matters. The privileged orders would be allowed their separate assemblies to deliberate and vote on matters of concern to themselves. These included honorific privileges and feudal rights, and affairs concerning the Catholic religion and the church. The Declaration would indicate the king's intention to ratify a constitution providing for a bicameral legislature. The king would reserve the right of veto on all legislation and would exercise executive powers.

Our knowledge about this Declaration comes exclusively from the book of Madame de Staël on the French Revolution. It was not mentioned by Necker in his writings dealing with his second and third ministries, probably because it was superceded by his memorial written for the Royal Session of June 23. But it indicates that as early as May 20, well before the conferences began to mediate the dispute between the Nobility and the Commons Necker was having grave doubts about the success of mediation, and was not as passive in face of the deadlocked States-General as is usually thought. Madame de Staël writes that the king agreed to the Declaration. For some reason he did not act upon it. Possibly he wanted to see if mediation would resolve the schism. Necker indicates in his books that Louis XVI had a deep prejudice against the British system of government, and hesitated for some time to accept it. Then Necker also hoped for the peaceful settlement of the dispute that would not require the government to enforce a compromise.

Whatever the reason for the failure to publish the Declaration, it gravely weakened the king's authority to force a compromise. The act of the Third Estate on June 17 declaring itself to be the only representative of the French people was one in which it could not easily retreat. This was a serious blow to Necker's prestige also, not only with those who believed he could have prevented the deadlock by more imaginative and vigorous leadership, but with the king himself. Louis might well have had the same misgivings about Necker as he had two years earlier about Calonne when it appeared that his principal minister was unable to get the consent of the Assembly of Notables for his reforms. Now that the deadlock had reached this point it was not possible for the king and the government to remain inactive. But the alternatives open to it were narrow. It had to decide whether to favor the Third Estate or the privileged orders. The first alternative did not mean that the government would have to accept the claim of the Third Estate to hold the monopoly of legislative power, much less the notion of supreme sovereign power, an idea that still seemed preposterous to most people. But if one chose to favor the Third Estate it would be necessary to go much further than Necker had in the recess of the council meeting of December 27 and in his speech of May 5. Both had required the assemblies of the three orders to agree separately before they would meet and vote in a common assembly. Now Necker saw it was necessary for the king to enforce a union of the three assemblies for deliberating and voting on all matters that concerned the national interest. This would certainly be resisted by an important faction in the assemblies of the Clergy and the Nobility. More seriously, it would meet violent opposition among the princes and the courtiers who had protested the doubling of the Third Estate back in December.

The proposal that Necker had made to the States-General in his May 5 speech was necessarily vague, as has been seen. To say that the three orders would deliberate and vote in common on all matters that concerned the national interest, and would allow the privileged orders to deliberate and vote separately on matters that concerned only themselves was not a specific program. To the radical Third Estate there were no matters that were not of concern to the nation, certainly not those regarding honorific privileges and feudal dues. To the intransigent factions in the other two assemblies there could be no voting in a common assembly on any subject, whether of national interest or not. Somewhere between those two extremes a compromise would have to be found if the States-General were to break out of the deadlock. Now that the government had to force a compromise it could no longer be vague. Just what it meant by affairs conerning the national interest as opposed to those to be left to the particular orders would have to be spelled out. This is what Necker did in the memorial that he wrote to the king for the Royal Session.

It is too often said that because of Necker's high ideals and his dedication to the cult of morality in government that he lacked the suppleness of the statesman. On the contrary, throughout his ministerial career there were always two considerations that shaped his policy. First, what was the most ideal, the best policy, and secondly, what was possible in the circumstances? He did not think the States-General was the best vehicle to carry out the great reforms that the nation wanted, but it had been promised by the king and public opinion insisted on the convocation of the estates. He hesitated about the doubling of the Third Estate near the end of the year 1788. But he felt that public opinion was so insistent for the doubling that it could not be refused. Now he believed that public opinion was again forcing an issue that could not be denied, the unification of the three orders in a common assembly. He did finally, in July, at the beginning of his third ministry, take an intransigent stand against violence and unjust executions of those said to be enemies of the nation or of the people. And this, according to some, is what broke his career in mid-course. If he had acted like Mirabeau--made the most of the opportunity to advance one's political standing--he might have preserved his popularity longer, but he would no longer have been Necker, as he often said to those who urged him to follow the precepts of the Florentine Secretary.

As for his political ideas and his view of the new constitutional regime that would be best for the nation, Necker's thinking was similar to the moderates of the Third Estate. No more than Mounier did he think that the traditional States-General had any relevance for the France of 1789. The States-General of 1614 and its predecessors had little in common with the assembly convened by Louis XVI. They had no real legislative power but were called only for consultation. They granted extraordinary subsidies to the royal government, but the total amount was small compared to its regular income. Necker pointed out that all the subsidies granted by all previous States-General would not have kept the French government in 1789 operating for more than ten days.[7] The estates had no regular, constitutional standing. They were summoned only occasionally by the kings. The States-General of 1789, despite its name, was more like the English Parliament or the American Congress. It was a modern, not a medieval legislative body that would exercise full legislative power, meet periodically according to constitutional provision, and have unquestioned control over the finances. No tax levy could be imposed on the people without the sanction of the national assembly. Ministers would be responsible to the assembly for criminal conduct. But otherwise the king would appoint the ministers of the executive government. The king would be left with full executive powers including command of the armed forces.

For such a regime it made no sense at all to have the legislative assembly divided into three separate assemblies, two of which would be representative not of the nation and national interests but of the exclusive concerns of the privileged orders. That the Nobility and the Clergy should have such a position in earlier assemblies of estates was understandable for the society that existed in the late medieval and early modern period, and the limited character of those assemblies. Necker's social analysis of the French Revolution was as sophisticated as any of his contemporaries. He understood the great changes that had taken place in French society in the past two centuries: the increase in wealth on one hand had made the Third Estate economically much more important than it had ever been. The progress of learning and science had also strengthened the non-noble and non-clerical part of the nation. On the other hand, the evolution of society had brought about a deterioration of the moral influence of both the Nobility and the Clergy. The former no longer fulfilled that social and political role it once did. Since the time of Richelieu the Nobility in France had become a Court Nobility that lived off the bounty of the king rather than having an independent base of political and economic power. The moral position of the old nobility was further weakened by the practice of ennoblement of commoners. The moral prestige of the Church had also altered from what it enjoyed in earlier centuries. The prelates had become wealthy and worldly, living the life of the great secular nobles and being little distinguished from them. For these reasons Necker could not understand the nobles' and the prelates' determined insistence that the old traditional organization of the States-General should remain unchanged.[8]

On the other hand Necker was far removed from the political thought of abbé Sieyes and the radical Third Estate. The idea of sovereign power existing in any one political entity was alien to liberal thinking. Necker understood that every power needs to be checked, and that a constitutional regime means that even the majority cannot have everything its own way. When he presented his plan for conciliation to the commissioners of the three orders at the home of Barentin on June 4 he explained that it would not be fair to the privileged orders to have the powers of disputed deputations decided by a common assembly in the three orders. The Third Estate would be in a position to outvote the privileged orders and if so disposed would be able to increase their number of deputies whose policies were agreeable to their own. The radical deputy, Creuzé-Latouche, protested this reasoning, saying it was insulting to suggest the Commons could abuse their power.[9] This is ever the delusion of single-party regimes. It is right for them to exercise the monopoly of power at the exclusion of all others because they have a monopoly of all the virtues and all the talents. As to how Necker would protect the minority from abuse of power by the majority he could not be specific at this time. Ideally he would have achieved that aim by a bicameral legislature in which the upper house would represent not a particular social class but a conservative principle in the national interest. Presumably it would be a chamber of peers similar to the British House of Lords, but he never described it in detail. He only indicated in a general way his thoughts on that institution. But whether he could get the British type of Parliament accepted in France was none too certain. Failing that there were other alternatives to achieve the same goal. One he had mentioned several times: allow the privileged orders their own assembly to deal with matters that were particularly theirs. Another possibility which was finally adopted in the Constituent Assembly was to give the king a suspensive veto power on measures passed by the single-house legislature.

Today it might be asked if it was a wise policy to attempt to mediate between the privileged orders and the Third Estate. Was not abbé Sieyes correct in asserting that without the privileged orders France would be not something less but something greater? Were they worth bothering about, could not one watch their destruction with equanimity, particularly in view of Necker's own social analysis of the decline of

505

those two classes over the past two centuries? Granted that the two social orders were not what they had been, they were still not ready to be swept into the trash can of history, as the twenty-five years following the establishment of the Constituent Assembly amply demonstrated. Nobility and the Catholic Church could not be brushed aside so lightly; neither could royalty, which was also flouted by the resolution of the Commons of June 17. In discussing Necker's Declaration of May 20 which he had attempted to get the king to put into effect, Madame de Staël was struck by the resemblance of that document to the Charter proclaimed by Louis XVIII at Saint-Ouen in June 1814. "Is it not permitted to wonder," asked Madame de Staël, "if that bloody circle of twenty-five years could not have been traversed in a single day if (the king) had accepted at that time [in May 1789] what the nation wanted, and what it has not ceased to want?"[10]

The memorial that Necker presented to the King and to three of his ministerial colleagues in the days just before the Royal Session of June 23 contained all the provisions mentioned by Madame de Staël in his Declaration and much more besides. The king would command the reunion of the orders and the vote in common on matters of general interest. These would include the financial measures, taxes and loans, and accountability. The king would no longer ask the privileged orders to give up their fiscal privileges but would abolish them himself. Also, and the most significant clause, the deliberations on the new constitution would be done in the common assembly and the vote taken by head. The king would acknowledge some of the most frequent demands in the cahiers of the Third Estate: he would open up all civil and military appointments to sons of the Third Estate, he would abolish franc fief, the tax on plebeian owners of fiefs, and he would permit arrangements to be made for the purchase of economic feudal dues by peasants sub-

506

ject to them. There followed a list of individual
rights that the king would recognize: rights to security of persons and property, freedom of the press and
of assembly, in fact all the rights later appearing in
the Charter of 1814. But these concessions were balanced by conservative measures. The king would insist
on two chambers for the legislature. The honorific
privileges of the nobility would be respected, the
king reserved the plenitude of executive power, and
all acts of the legislature must have the king's approval. Also Necker proposed that the public be
barred from the two deliberative assemblies.[11]

As Necker analyzed the situation these were the
demands that public opinion insisted upon and it would
be impossible to refuse them. By making these concessions in time the conservative features of his proposal could be saved from further erosion. It was
necessary to invoke the king's authority in the circumstances. "But before deploying it one must appreciate the extent of his means and the force of resistance. . . . One cannot avoid studying the disposition
of opinions, to take account of circumstances, and to
fit the language of command to the rules of prudence
and a policy that has been carefully considered."[12]
It was just this willingness to consider all the aspects of the political situation that Necker found so
lamentably lacking among those who had influence on
the king.

The king agreed to call a meeting of the Council
of State at the château at Marly on June 19. According to Necker, his memorial had been approved by the
king beforehand, and also by three ministers, Montmorin, Saint-Priest, and La Luzerne. As Necker described the meeting in his book on the French Revolution written years later, all the members of the council agreed to the proposals that the king would include in his address to the Royal Session, to be held
on Monday, June 22. As the meeting was about to ad-

journ, an official entered the council room to give the king a message. Louis asked the ministers to wait until he returned. In about a half an hour he reentered and said that the decision on Necker's memorial would have to be postponed for further discussion in an enlarged council. Necker and others protested that delay was dangerous in view of the circumstances, but they could not shake the king's decision.

While the king was out of the room and the ministers were awaiting his return Montmorin said to Necker: "There is only one explanation for this: only the queen would dare to interrupt a council meeting. Apparently the princes have persuaded her to use her influence to delay the king's decision."[13] The Secret Agent who sent dispatches to the War Department wrote on June 13 that "the clergy, the nobility, and the parlements are joining together to bring about the fall of Mr. Necker. We have discovered the plot and we can give this information as positive. The blow is to be delivered at Marly."[14] The blow was to be dealt at Marly where the king would be more isolated from political pressures than at Versailles. About this same time there appeared a new rash of printed libels, similar in nature to those that had preceded the disgrace of Necker in 1781. He was accused of deliberately causing the grain shortage to strengthen his own power, to create a clientele of unemployed and starving workmen that would be dependent on subsidies from the government. The popular disturbances were said to be engineered by Necker's agents.[15] He was accused of extorting forced loans from the Discount Bank causing it to go bankrupt (a new charge that was not made back in 1781)![16]

The next council meeting was held on Saturday, June 20. Necker was unable to attend because of the illness and death of his sister-in-law, Madame Necker de Germany, which required him to go to Paris. It was at Paris, late in the afternoon that Necker heard of the events at Versailles concerning the national assembly. The Council had originally decided to hold the Royal Session on Monday, June 22 at the hall of the Menus Plaisirs where the States-General had been opened on May 5 and which continued to be the hall used by the Third Estate. Somehow, because of the confusion caused by the king's desire to continue discussion about the Royal Session in further council meetings, no one bothered to let the dean of the national assembly, Jean-Sylvain Bailly, know that the Menus Plaisirs would have to be prepared for the Royal Session and could not be occupied by the national assembly on Saturday, June 20. Or at least it was not until early in the morning, at 7:00 a.m., only two hours before the assembly had arranged to open a session, that Bailly was informed by the Master of Ceremonies, the marquis de Deux-Brézé, that the hall would not be available. When Bailly and all the deputies appeared at the entrance of the Menus Plaisirs what they saw was an impressive police force, and even troops guarding the approaches to the assembly hall. The deputies had been in a high state of excitement since the resolution of June 17. If not all had recognized the revolutionary implications, certainly they did realize the provocative nature of that resolution. It was hardly more than a year before that the government of Loménie de Brienne had decided to use force against the Parlement of Paris and to issue the May Edicts. At that time the leaders of the opposition persuaded all members of the Parlement to take an oath that they would not recognize nor accept membership in any new system of courts that the government might set up. Perhaps it was this precedent that was on the minds of the deputies that led them to find another assembly hall, the Tennis Court, where it is said the comte d'Artois had planned to play tennis that day! All deputies except one, including the 90 who had voted against the resolution of June 17, now took the famous oath that they would not disband until they had framed a constitution for France. The resolution was introduced by Jean-Joseph Mounier who had himself led the opposition to the resolution of June 17.

While Necker was at his brother's house he learned of these events. He recognized in them another serious blow to his own hopes for conciliation. He immediately sent a message to the Paris Lieutenant of Police, Louis-Thiroux de Crosne, stating emphatically that the government was not intending to dissolve the States-General, and that the assembly hall had been closed for "an absolute need." He asked de Crosne to publish this to the excited public in both Paris and Versailles.[17] Later when he wrote his memoirs on the events of 1789, Jean-Joseph Mounier deeply regretted the part he had taken in the famous Tennis Court Oath. It was all due to a misunderstanding, and the consequences were formidable. The populace was again convinced that the government was going to crush the States-General by force, and this played into the hands of those Mounier called "the factious ones," that is, the leaders of the radical Third Estate.[18] He confessed that he had wanted to recover the favor of the popular classes that he had lost by opposing the resolution of Sieyes. But he hoped that the union of the three assemblies would strengthen rather than weaken the authority of the king. The unilateral action of the Third Estate did just the opposite. The oath made the National Assembly independent of the king. "How I reproach myself today for having proposed it!," he lamented, and he could not conceal his admiration for the lone deputy, named Martin, who had the courage to oppose the fateful motion.[19]

The Tennis Court Oath was not the only significant news Necker received from Versailles on June 20. He learned that the day before the Assembly of the Clergy had split almost evenly on a resolution that the Clergy join the commons for the purpose of verification of powers. The prelates and their supporters, led by Cardinal de La Rochefoucauld, refused to go along with the resolution. It meant a schism in the Clergy, with about 148 deputies joining the Commons the following Monday when the latter, now the National Assembly, convened in the Church of Saint Louis. This bolstered Necker's conviction that the circumstances called for the king to order the union of the three assemblies. But he was worried about how his memorial was going to fare in the coming council meetings. He sent a letter while in Paris on June 20 to the king suggesting that a Royal Session might not be the best forum in which to present his program. He evidently feared that because of these events it would alienate the Third Estate and the increasing number of their supporters in the other two orders. He thought that "a simple letter of invitation would be preferable," but added that "there is not a moment to lose."[20] Everything should be done, in other words, to avoid giving the session the appearance of a _lit de justice_.

Necker returned to Versailles on Sunday, June 21, where the next council meeting was to take place. Evidently there had been one on Saturday at Marly, but little is known about it, and Necker did not mention it in his memoirs. On Sunday afternoon when the Council reconvened in its normal council room at the château of Versailles Necker found present the two brothers of the king, the comte de Provence and the comte d'Artois. In addition were four counselors of state whose views were known to coincide with those of the princes. Artois was not very effective in council meetings and usually remained silent. But this time he intervened with brash arrogance. According to Jefferson's dispatch to John Jay, Artois "attacked Mr. Necker personally, arraigned his plan, and proposed one which some of his engines had put into his hands; for his own talents go no further than a little poor wit. Mr. Necker, whose characteristic is the want of firmness was brow-beaten and intimidated and the king shaken."[21] According to Necker's own account he was

far from brow-beaten but vigorously defended his memorial against the onslaught:

> It was primarily the union of the orders
> that they wished to prevent . . . The
> ministers present who were most
> distinguished for their intelligence and
> their wisdom supported me firmly, and only a
> momentary advantage was gained over us. The
> king decided only, that in order to find
> some compromise between the two views
> debated in his presence there would be a
> meeting at the house of the Keeper of the
> Seals, and one of the magistrates called
> into the council was charged to work out a
> compromise with me.[22]

At the house of Barentin that evening Necker
found his opposite number in the negotiations was
Jean-Jacques Vidaud de la Tour, a counselor of state
and former first president of the Parlement of Grenoble. He was a "hard-liner," in opposition to even the
mildest of reforms. But it was an unequal contest.
Necker was able to get the opposing program modified
to such an extent that he could support it, although
he had to give up provisions that "really hurt" because he thought his original proposal had gone as far
in making concessions to the conservative side as was
safe and prudent. The arguments that the opposite
side invoked were jejeune in the extreme: "always the
respectful obedience to the French constitution, and
this constitution, always obeyed and no place written,
must by the authority of tradition irrevocably forbid
the reunion of the orders."[23]

But in the final council meeting held on Monday
Necker was dismayed to find that his strenuous fight
the preceding day had gone for nothing. According to
the dispatch of Baron de Staël, "the comte d'Artois,
fortified the evening before by the adherence of the

queen to his views, was more violent than ever."[24] The king was finally persuaded to rule against Necker's memorial entirely and to accept for the Royal Session a speech prepared for him by Vidaud de la Tour. Among the other ministers Barentin came out strongly for the side of Artois, as did the minister of the King's Household, Pierre-Charles Laurent de Villedeuil, and the minister of war, Pierre-Louis de Chastenet, comte de Puységur. Both Montmorin and Saint-Priest continued to give their strongest support to Necker's views. After the council meeting on Sunday afternoon the king requested both Montmorin and Saint-Priest to give him in writing their views on the dispute. Both did so Monday morning before the final meeting of the council on the subject. Montmorin called attention to the financial crisis. If the States-General should be dismissed it would not be possible to raise tax revenue. "However, the revenues of Your Majesty have already been spent in advance; the royal treasury cannot continue the most essential payments, and provide the expenditures which the drought has made necessary and which have been met up to now by means of credit that are almost miraculous."[25] He said that those who are insisting the king must stand by the old constitution "do not know the situation, or do not see it as it really is." Admittedly the Third Estate had usurped power by declaring itself the National Assembly, but "however extravagant and blameworthy it is, the public judges the matter differently," Necker's plan was essential to conciliate the Nation, even if it should fail to conciliate the Third Estate. He saw the matter exactly as Necker did, it was necessary to bend with the wind, to recognize the "sway of circumstances."

The result of the Council meeting of June 22 was the most bitter of all Necker's political defeats. He believed that his proposal had made the concessions that were absolutely necessary, but had gone no further. Now the king's decision meant the thwarting of

513

the national will, and could not fail to play into the hands of the radicals of the Third Estate. The speech that the king would deliver at the Royal Session would command the three orders to retire to their separate chamber to deliberate and vote by order. The possibility of deliberation in common was permitted but only if each order agreed to it and also the king. The king would not command the abolition of fiscal privileges but leave it up to the privileged orders. The constitution would be formed by each order deliberating and voting separately. The right of each order to veto all acts was guaranteed as "part of the traditional constitution." The speech written by Vidaud de la Tour did retain the promise of personal liberties that Necker had drawn up. But without specific guarantees, Necker asked what those liberties, expressed only formally in the constitution, would be worth? Finally the king's address set aside as invalid the resolution passed by the assembly of the Third Estate on June 17.[26]

To convene the three orders and read such a stern lecture to them would certainly be a dash of cold water in the faces of the Third Estate and their new allies. Necker reflected on his course after the council meeting of Monday afternoon. He decided that he could not possibly attend the Royal Session on Tuesday and thereby allow the impression that he had give his approval of the king's speech to the assembly. He saw clearly that he could not remain in the ministry; but he did not want to resign at the council meeting itself. He feared that the king might give him a direct order to attend the Royal Session. Jefferson wrote to Jay that both Montmorin and Necker submitted their resignations at the council meeting but they were not accepted. According to Jefferson, Artois said to Necker: "No sir, you must be kept as hostage; we hold you responsible for all the ill that shall happen."[27] Jefferson did not name his source but certainly his information was not correct, for Montmorin never did resign and attended the Royal Session the following morning. Etienne Dumont was at Versailles on the day of the Royal Session. In his book "Souvenirs sur Mirabeau" he told of meeting a person that afternoon, an official in the Austrian embassy, who related to him that he had seen Necker that morning who was en-route to the Royal Session. The Austrian said that he talked him out of going and was strongly supported by Madame Necker and Madame de Staël. Dumont suspected the authenticity of this story since the official was not of a stature to have exercised so much influence on Necker.[28] His skepticism was well taken, for Necker gave perfectly cogent reasons in his books written later why he could not attend the Royal Session on June 23.

The spirit displayed by the government in the morning of the Royal Session was the opposite of what Necker had thought necessary. Instead of doing every-thing to avoid offending the Third Estate it seemed that the officials in charge of the Royal Session did everything possible to irritate the alrady suspicious and apprehensive deputies. They were required to en-ter the hall of the Menus Plaisirs through a side street, the rue des Chantiers, while the deputies of the first two orders were seated ceremoniously through the front doors on the main avenue de Paris. The deputies of the Clergy who joined the National Assem-bly the day before were not permitted to sit with the Third Estate but had to take their seats with the First Estate. The streets were filled with police and soldiers. About 4,000 troops were massed in the imme-diate vicinity of the Menus Plaisirs, and no visitors were allowed into the assembly hall. Within there were guards everywhere as if the authorities even feared an insurrection inside. Outside the crowd was kept at a safe distance.[29]

As the royal procession came from the château to the assembly hall Etienne Dumont was able to observe the faces of the king and those around him. The expression of the comte d'Artois showed that he was basking in the pride of triumph, that of the king was just the opposite, sad and mournful. Dumont was struck by the contrast of this day with the opening day of the States-General back on May 5. "The ceremony was exactly the same, but what a contrast in the feeling! The former day was a national festival, the rebirth of liberty; but in the latter the same pomp which had enchanted all spectators was suffused with terror. The brilliant costumes of the nobility, the magnificence of the throne and royal pomp seemed to be the accompaniment of a funeral procession."[30]

When the king spoke to the assembly observers noted that his voice faltered, in contrast to the magnificent impression he had made on May 5. The Declaration on the Present Form for the States-General began by resolving the question of deliberating and voting by order or by head:

> The king wills that the traditional distinction of the three orders of the State be preserved in its entirety since it is an essential part of the constitution of his kingdom; that the Deputies, freely chosen in each of the three orders, form three chambers, deliberating by order, and which can, with the approval of the sovereign join to deliberate in common; (but otherwise) the orders alone form the corps of the representatives of the Nation. Consequently the king declares as null and void the deliberation of the Order of the Third Estate on the 17th of this month, as well as any deliberations which might flow from it.[31]

But the king did repeat the "exhortation" given on May 5 that the three orders agree to unite "for this session of the States-General only" in order to deliberate in common of matters of common utility. But he carefully circumscribed the subjects that could be deliberated and voted upon in common assembly. Exempt from common deliberation were the feudal and seigneurial rights of the fief-owners, the economic and honorific privileges of the first two orders, all matters concerning religion and ecclesiastical organization, and the corporate organization including both regular and secular corporations. The most important exclusion from common deliberation was the future organization of the States-General, in other words, the constitution. Even for those matters that were permitted to be discussed and voted upon in a common assembly the king said he would look favorably upon a rule requiring a two-thirds vote to pass, which in effect would permit the veto of the orders even in the common assembly. More than that, the king said if as many as 100 deputies in the common assembly should object to any law passed by the assembly it would need to be deliberated and voted upon the next day. The rights of the minority were amply protected! As for the imperative mandates, the king said they were illegal, since the royal acts convening the States-General had stipulated that the deputies must be given full powers by their constituents to decide on the matters that were to be resolved by the States-General. However, the king said, if deputies who had taken an oath to abide by their mandates felt they could not in conscience go against them, he would permit them to ask their constituents for new instructions. But he required that they attend the sessions of the States-General; they could refrain from voting until their mandates were revised.

The above were the harsh provisions of the royal declarations as far as the Third Estate was concerned. But the declaration then went on to repeat the concessions made by the king in the recess of the Council meeting of December 27 and in Necker's speech of May 5. The States-General would be convened periodically;

517

it would exercise control and supervision over the royal finances; it would have full legislative power. All the basic human rights and liberties called for by the cahiers were to be granted. This part of the declaration was what had been preserved from Necker's original project for the Royal Session, and is what gave some observers, Bailly for example, the belief that there was really not very much difference between the two. Foreign observers seemed to have been impressed by the extent of the king's concessions. Arthur Young supposed that the States-General would accept the royal declaration. In his autobiography written in later years Jefferson seemed to think that France would have been spared all the upheaval that followed the Royal Session if the king's proposals had been accepted.[32] They did not realize what was clear to Necker, that public opinion was insisting on the union of the three orders and it was too powerful to be ignored.

The final message of the king in the Royal Session was that each order was to repair to its own chamber the following day and begin the task of drawing up the constitution. He asserted that if the schism should continue despite his orders, then the only recourse for him was to send the deputies home and take upon himself the task of "the regeneration of the kingdom." The king and his retinue left the hall and returned to the château through a crowd that watched in silence. Only some children shouted Vive le Roi in contrast to the thunderous Vivats that accompanied the royal procession on May 5.

On the previous day at the church of Saint Louis the National Assembly passed a resolution that it would resume deliberation in the Menus Plaisirs immediately after the Royal Session. The government, whether it was aware of this or not, had forbidden any meetings of the orders on the day of the Royal Session. As soon as the king and his party had left the

518

hall, accompanied by the first two orders, workmen entered the hall to dismantle the preparations they had made the previous Saturday. Amid the din of saws and hammers the deputies began their session. The Master of Ceremonies, the marquis de Deux Brézé, approached them to repeat the orders of the king, that they were to leave the hall and refrain from further deliberation. There are conflicting reports by eye-witnesses as to what was said and by whom. It appears that no one else heard Mirabeau's celebrated riposte to Deux Brézé that he reported to his constituents in Provence, or at least not in the same ringing phrases.[33] But evidently he did say something to the effect that "we are here by the will of the people and will not leave except by force." Bailly was annoyed by Mirabeau's intervention. He wrote in his memoirs that nobody was threatening force, and anyway it was out of place for Mirabeau to speak in the situation.[34] De Brézé replied to Mirabeau that he could only recognize him as the deputy of the Third Estate from Aix-en-Provence and not the spokesman for the entire assembly. Bailly then spoke on behalf of the assembly, telling De Brézé that they had previously resolved to deliberate at that time and place and they intended to proceed accordingly, and that "we have declared that the members of this assembly are under the safeguard of the nation."[35] De Brézé could only report this to the king and ask for new instructions. When he did so the king said with a shrug of weariness, "oh well, let them stay."[36] It was the first step in what was to become a precipitate retreat from the elaborate demonstration of force and determination that he had mobilized for the Royal Session. It was before De Brézé came to the assembly that Mirabeau got his famous motion passed declaring the inviolability of the deputies and that anyone who laid hands on them would be "subject to prosecution under the crime of lèse-nation." This was a newly-coined term, indicating that

the National Assembly now considered itself endowed
with a majesty hitherto reserved for the king.

Whether Necker's own proposal for the Royal Session would have succeeded any better is impossible to
say. Contemporaries as well as historians have
doubted that it would. In his Mémoire autographe Barentin maintained that there was actually little difference between Necker's document and the Declarations
of the king.[37] But this was an attempt, according to
Necker, to implicate him in a policy which he had
strenuously opposed and knew could only be disastrous.
It was a disaster to royal authority and to the efforts of so many to restore that unity of the nation
which had been so pronounced on the opening day of the
States-General.

Necker's absence from the Royal Session was conspicuous and gave rise to rumors that he had resigned
from the ministry. This caused a shock wave among the
deputies and throughout the population at Versailles
and Paris similar to that which came later on July 12.
About four or five o'clock, according to eye-witnesses, the National Assembly had adjourned and a
great number of deputies variously estimated from 400
to 500 were seen going to the Hotel of the Contrôle-
général, which was the residence of the Neckers. They
were accompanied by a great crowd of townspeople from
both Versailles and Paris. Observers placed the number between four and six thousand who thronged into
the courtyard of the château as well as the grounds of
the Contrôle-général only a short distance away. Abbé
Coster wrote in his journal that "cries of Vive
Necker! resounded as far as the château. The people
wanted to see him and beg him to remain at the helm of
affairs."[38] According to Mounier who accompanied the
deputies to Necker's residence to beg him not to resign, the Director-General, in effect, read them the
riot act. "He reproached them for their excessive
claims and their seditious speeches at the clubs,

their neglect of the respect and gratitude they owed to the monarch for the concessions he had made. The deputies redoubled their entreaties and acknowledged that their conduct should have been more measured, and they ought to have followed his advice. There could have existed then a rapport between the minister and a great number of deputies."[39]

Meanwhile at the château both the king and queen were alarmed at the size of the crowd and the vehemence with which it demanded "give us back Mr. Necker!" It was the queen who took the initiative and sent a message to Necker to see her at the château. He was escorted by a crowd of deputies and townspeople whom the French Guards did not prevent entering the corridors of the château, although bodyguards stood firmly at the doors of the apartments of the king and queen. Necker had a private audience of about a quarter of an hour with the queen who asked him to withdraw his resignation. He was then taken to the king's apartment for a much longer conference, variously reported from one to two hours. Little is known of what transpired between them except that the king asked Necker to remain at his post and the latter agreed to do so. According to Necker's account in his later books he attempted to persuade the king that the power of public opinion was such that it was necessary to make further concessions than those given at the Royal Session. But Necker did not make any demands on the king in return for his agreement to remain in the government. He always venerated the king and queen though recognizing their weaknesses, and he could not bring himself to demand the dismissal of the ministers who had opposed him and were responsible for the disastrous Royal Session. In his book on the Revolution written in later years he seemed to admit that this was a mistake. "It was a moment when I could have exacted everything from the king, and I found myself powerless to demand anything. A surge of generous feeling dictated my conduct, which certainly could be criticized but at the same time comprehended. I was not long in repenting it, and I understood once again that a sentiment of virtue in a private person can become a fault, and a very grave one, in a statesman."[40]

Ironically Necker was accused by his enemies of just the opposite fault. He was said to have deliberately sought to stir up the crowd for his own political advantage. The comte d'Angiviller wrote in his memoirs that he was present in the château and personally conducted Necker to the exit. The duc de Châtelet, commandant of the French Guards, begged Necker not to return to his residence through the excited crowd in the courtyard but to take a secret passage through the gallery of mirrors. Angiviller said he had a key to that door and could lead Necker to it. But, wrote Angiviller, Necker insisted on walking through the crowd back to his residence.[41] The marquis de Clermont-Gallerande was also convinced that Necker had some part in stirring up the masses, but he had the honesty to report in his memoirs: "I saw him pass in the midst of his triumph, and if he had instigated (the popular movement) I must say in his favor that it did not appear in his demeanor. There was an expression of gloom and melancholy in his face."[42] According to abbé Coster the king had requested Necker to return to the Contrôle-général through the crown and announce to them that he would remain at his post.[43]

About a quarter of an hour after Necker had left the château Louis XVI came down to the courtyard and mounted his coach to go to Marly. According to Clermont-Gallerande there was still a crowd in the courtyard who watched the king get into the coach and leave. "There was not a single expression of affection for him. The contrast (with the way they had greeted Necker when he came into the courtyard) was too striking not to be felt by everyone."[44] The author speculated that this scene may have made a deep

impression on the king, and led him to the decision to
dismiss the popular minister as soon as he was in a
position to do so without danger. This is plausible
but not necessarily true, for the king was not vain,
or inclined to jealousy, at least not toward commoners. His apprehensions about the ambitions of the
Duke of Orleans were on a different level. It appears
that the attitude of the king was more of bewilderment
as to the course he should follow in the face of such
contradictory advice. Always dependent on others for
arriving at difficult decisions, but not without intelligence, Louis XVI could understand the basic arguments on both sides of the question that faced him.
In the days to come he was probably increasingly irritated by the arrogance of the radicals in the National
Assembly regarding his own powers in the new constitutional order. They did not seem to heed Necker's ad-
monition to restraint and moderation when they had be-
seeched him not to resign. They were obviously fearful of an impending act of force on the king's part.
Perhaps, Louis XVI might have thought, a show of determined force was just what is needed to keep those
"factious ones" in a reasonable state of mind. But
Necker argued with him that force would have just the
opposite result, it would weaken the moderates and
strengthen the radicals. Therefore it was necessary
to make concessions in time before being forced to
them. One policy the king absolutely opposed, which
was favorable to Necker's influence, was any violent
action against his subjects that would result in
bloodshed and ignite civil war.

When Necker left the château to return to the
Contrôle-général he was still accompanied by deputies
and the crowd of citizens. Evidently he was fatigued
after the conference with the king and asked Target to
tell the people that he would not resign, that the
king had asked him to remain in the government. It
was a highly-charged emotional scene that Adrien Duquesnoy recounted in his journal that afternoon.

523

Necker and Madame Necker mingled with the crowds in the salons of the <u>Contrôle-général</u>. Madame Necker, we are told, "preserved a calm and serene air, despite the tears that were shed around her."[45] Necker continued to urge the deputies to be moderate. "You are very strong now," he said, "but do not abuse your power." During the evening there was a joyous celebration with firework displays in the street in front of the <u>Contrôle-général</u>. Far into the night the crowds coursed through the streets, stopping in front of houses of the deputies and shouting "Vive M. Necker." It was the beginning of that strange apotheosis of a person who had certainly not sought it and who was apprehensive about it. The basis of his support had always been that class called "the notables," who were a mixture of great lords, prelates, wealthy landowners of all classes, educated and enlightened magistrates, and the intelligentsia. This was not a popular class. But now there was formed a coalition of the notables and the popular classes led by radicals of the Third Estate. For the latter it was a marriage of convenience. They needed Necker's great prestige and supported him as long as they feared the "bayonets" of the government. Once that threat was removed the radicals parted company with the Genevan whom they then sought to "depopularize."

Adrien Duquesnoy was one of the moderate deputies who shared Necker's goal of reconciliation of the three orders rather than confrontation and class struggle. He was forcibly impressed by the events of June 23. "Public opinion," he wrote in his journal, "thus has placed men in their rank: the greatest king of Europe, surrounded by all the majesty of the throne, could not prevent marks of disapprobation; and a man born in obscurity commands the love and respect of the entire nation."[46] There now opened up a great opportunity if the Council would follow Necker's leadership and if the Genevan had the requisite qualities of leadership.

524

If the council has the good sense to profit
from this moment of enthusiasm, Mr. Necker
can accomplish an infinite amount for reconciliation, but I believe that he himself
lacks, as I have often said, sufficient
force; (he needs to have) less confidence in
the virtues of men, perhaps a deeper knowledge of the character of those he is called
upon to govern, less timidity; finally, it
is not sufficient to have principles and to
be firmly committed to them, it is also necessary to know how to get them accepted, and
the most suitable means to bring men to the
goals he proposes. A too-honest soul sometimes is very dangerous in a minister. If
Mr. Necker judges other men after himself he
surely does them too much honor.47

Perhaps this was an accurate assessment of
Necker's strengths and weaknesses in the situation.
He himself seemed to have admitted some of the above
in his account years later of the events of that memorable afternoon. Just as he also wrote later that
Louis XVI would have been an ideal sovereign in a
British-type monarchy, so Necker would have been an
ideal prime minister. But those institutions were not
yet in place in France. Twenty-five years of tumultuous trial and error would pass before they were.
But at this moment Necker had achieved an unprecedented peak of popularity. He was no longer just the
minister of Louis XVI. He was, for a brief time, the
minister of the nation. The next month was to be the
most dramatic of his own career, and the most fateful
in the history of the Revolution.

[1]Charles-Claude Flahaut de la Billardie, comte de Angiviller, _Mémoires_ (Paris, 1933), 155.

[2]Armand Brette, "Relations des événements depuis le 6 mai jusqu'au 15 juillet 1789. Bulletins d'un agent secret," _La Révolution française_ (July-December, 1892), XXIII, 448.

[3]_Ibid._, 459.

[4]Cited in Lefebvre, _Recueil de documents_, I, 45, n. 27, who in turn cites G. Rudé, "Notes sur les manuscrits de Bertrand de Moleville au British Museum," _Annales historique de la Révolution française_ (1956), XXVIII, 55.

[5]"Sur l'Administration de M. Necker," in _Oeuvres complètes de Necker_, IX, 143.

[6]Madame de Staël, _Considérations sur la Révolution française_, 151.

[7]"De la Révolution française," in _Oeuvres complètes de Necker_, IX, 143.

[8]_Ibid._, 115-126.

[9]Creuzé-Latouche, _Journal des Etats-généraux_, 89.

[10]*Considérations sur la Révolution française*, 152.

[11]"Sur l'Administration de M. Necker," in *Oeuvres complètes de Necker*, VI, 90-93.

[12]"De la Révolution française," in *Oeuvres complètes de Necker*, VI, 90-93.

[13]*Ibid.*, 198-199.

[14]Brette, "Bulletins d'un agent secret," *La Révolution française*, XXIII, 530.

[15]Clermont-Gallerande, *Mémoires particuliers*, I, 98.

[16]"Bulletins d'un agent secret," *op. cit.*, 530.

[17]Georges Lefebvre and Anne Terroine, *Recueil de documents relatifs aux séances des Etats-généraux*, I, part 2, 184-185.

[18]Jean-Joseph Mounier, *Recherches sur les causes*, I, 296, n. 1.

[19]*Loc. cit.*

[20]Lefebvre, *Recueil de documents*, I, part 2, 180.

[21]*Papers of Thomas Jefferson*, XV, 207.

[22]"De la Révolution française," in Oeuvres complètes de Necker, IX, 200-201. Baron de Staël wrote to Gustavus III that "The Royal Session was postponed until June 23 because of the resistance of Mr. Necker to the new proposals." Correspondance diplomatique, 103.

[23]"De la Révolution française,", op. cit., 202.

[24]Correspondance diplomatique, 103.

[25]Flammermont, "Le Second Ministère de Necker," Revue historique (May-August, 1891), XLVI, 63.

[26]P. J. B. Buchez, Histoire de l'Assemblée constituante, I, 331-339.

[27]Papers of Thomas Jefferson, XV, 207.

[28]Souvenirs sur Mirabeau, 78.

[29]Brette, "La Séance royale de 23 juin 1789. Ses préliminairies et ses suites d'après deux documents inédites: La correspondance de Barentin et le journal de l'abbé Coster," La Révolution française, XXII, 131-132.

[30]Souvenirs sur Mirabeau, 77.

[31]Collection des édits, déclarations et arrêts du Conseil d'état, BN F. 23632 (327), 23 juin 1789.

[32]Flammermont, "Le Second Ministère de Necker, Revue historique (May-August, 1891), XLVI, 46. Flammermont of course strongly disagreed with Jefferson, insisting that the most important achievements of the Revolution such as the abolition of feudalism were not in the Royal Declaration of June 23.

[33]Brette, "La Séance royale," La Révolution française, XXII, 434.

[34]Bailly, Mémoires, I, 214.

[35]Francisque Mège, Gaultier de Biauzet, Député de Tiers-Etat aux Etats-Généraux de 1789 (Paris, 1890), I, 138, n. 1.

[36]Octave Aubry, La Révolution française (Paris, 1942), I, 66. According to some sources the king at first tried to use the royal bodyguards to disperse the National Assembly, but the appearance of the liberal contingent of nobles at the Menus Plaisirs who demonstrated solidarity with the Third Estate led the king to acquiesce, and say "Let them stay." Cf. Louis Gottschalk, Lafayette in the French Revolution. Through the October Days (Chicago, 1969), 65.

[37]Mémoire autographe de Barentin, 214-216.

[38]Brette, La Révolution française, XXII, 66-68.

[39]Mounier, Recherches sur les causes, I, 304.

[40]"De la Révolution française," in Oeuvres complètes de Necker, IX, 125.

[41]Mémoires de Charles Claude Flahaut, comte de la Billardie d'Angiviller, 155-160.

[42]Clermont-Gallerande, Mémoires particuliers I, 93.

[43]Brette, "La Séance royale de 23 juin 1789," La Révolution française, XXIII, 67.

[44]Clermont-Gallerande, op. cit., 93-94.

[45]Duquesnoy, Journal, I, 122.

[46]Ibid., 123.

[47]Ibid., 123-124.

CHAPTER 15

THE MINISTER OF THE NATION

"From the 23rd to the 27th of June," wrote Mercy-
Argenteau to the Emperor, "we have been in the most
imminent danger of famine, bankruptcy and civil war."[1]
All three were serious but it was evidently the danger
of civil war that most concerned the Austrian ambassador. He referred to the "infernal cabal" which was
being directed against Necker. Describing the events
just prior to the Royal Session he said that "if the
insane idea supported by members of the royal family
to arrest Necker had been followed, or if that minister had resigned voluntarily as he had planned, the
people would have revolted, the massacre of the privileged orders would have ensued and rebellion would
have been openly declared." Necker, he wrote, was accused by the "intriguers" of being a subversive who
sacrificed everything to the people, while in reality
he yielded only to necessity because without troops
all resistance would have been impossible.[2]

On June 23 after the Royal Session the king had
retreated from his demand that the Third Estate leave
the hall of the Menus Plaisirs, and he had persuaded
Necker to remain at his post. But it was not clear
what those concessions implied. Did the king intend
to stand by the declarations he had made at the Royal
Session? Or would he acquiesce to the resolution of
the Third Estate in declaring itself on June 17 to be
the National Assembly of the French nation? Obviously
the two positions were incompatible. Yet Louis XVI
still attempted to stand by his declarations and the
policy he had asserted at the Royal Session, even
though he made piecemeal concessions to the popular
demands. His policy was in some respects a retreat to
Necker's project for the Royal Session, for it does

531

not appear that Necker mentioned the resolution of the Third Estate of June 17, thinking it best to pass it over in silence. He probably believed that the claim was so extreme that the king would be able to enforce his plan of union relying upon the moderates in the national assembly once the union of the three orders was effected.[3]

The most important difference between Necker's plan for the Royal Session and that finally adopted by the king was that Necker would have exerted the king's authority to bring about the union of the three orders, while the declarations of the king at the Royal Session still left the matter up to each order to decide. This was the kind of invitation Necker had extended in his May 5 speech, and it had not succeeded. But the king did urge the two privileged orders to agree to a union in order to get the States-General moving. The events after the Royal Session on June 23 and the two days following clearly had shaken the most adamant of the deputies of the Clergy and Nobility. The bailli de Virieu, minister of Parma, wrote to his government that "the fermentation of minds has been so great from Tuesday the 23rd to Friday the 26th that one would think, in looking and hearing the Parisians, that a violent fever had gripped them . . . All talk that one hears indicates they are capable of anything if the Nobility and the Clergy persist in their declarations."[4] The fact that slightly more than half of the deputies of the Clergy and an important minority of the deputies of the Nobliity did withdraw from their respective assemblies and joined the Third Estate during the two days following the Royal Session increased the pressure on those who remained.

On the day after the Royal Session the National Assembly came to the _Menus_ _Plaisirs_ palace to resume its deliberations. The leaders expected that the deputies of the Clergy who had joined them at the

Church of Saint Louis the day before the Royal Session would also join them on Wednesday, the 24th. They discovered that the same military and police forces were keeping the palace under surveillance as they had the day before. The commanders had received instructions not to permit any strangers into the hall and certainly no deputies from the other two orders. Bailly sought out the commandant and vigorously protested both the show of military force and the exclusion of all who were not members of the Third Estate. He discovered to his surprise that the officers and men of the units had become politicized--they were aware of the tension between the National Assembly and the government and were sympathetic to the former. "We are citizens also," some of the soldiers told the deputies.[5] An officer of the guards told Bailly of a secret passageway into the palace of the Menus Plaisirs that could be used by the deputies of the Clergy, and that he had the key to the door. In this way 151 deputies of the Clergy entered the National Assembly on June 24. A day later, Bailly learned that the officer who had disobeyed orders was arrested, and he made the strongest protest to the minister of the King's Household who had authority over the local police. Laurent de Villedeuil said he would refer the matter to the king, which he did, and the king ordered the officer released. Two days later Laurent de Villedeuil ordered reinforcements of French Guard units to come from Paris to Versailles to bolster the troops who could not be relied upon. They were ordered to carry guns that were loaded and ready to be used against the crowds. Two companies of Guards at Paris abandoned their arms on June 25, and went to mingle with the people at the Palais-Royal, where they were enthusiastically greeted and feted in the bars and restaurants.

The temper of the people became evident in other incidents. After the Royal Session Barentin sought to have the king's declaration broadcast to the public

533

through town criers. He learned the following day that they had not done so, and upon inquiring into the reason, was told that the criers had all come down with colds![6] The crowds at Versailles were aware of the proceedings of the assembly of the Clergy which had refused to join the National Assembly. The assembly hall of that order was invaded and some of the outspoken opponents of the Third Estate such as abbé Maury were verbally abused. On June 24 as the assembly of the Clergy adjourned their meeting the Archbishop of Paris, mistakenly thought by the crowd to be one of the "hard-liners," was stoned as he left in his carriage. When he reached his residence it was surrounded by the crowd and he was in imminent danger. The Guards français saved his life but at the same time did not have to charge into the demonstrators. The officer who commanded succeeded in calming the crowd by bringing nine deputies of the National Assembly to the scene.[7]

When the National Assembly was finally able to get down to business on June 24 its first concern was its relationship with the government. A message was sent to Necker expressing the assembly's gratitude for his remaining in the government. Whether Necker anticipated this and wrote to the assembly on his own initiative, or whether he responded to the message from the assembly is not clear. In any case, as Adrien Duquesnoy wrote in his Journal: "A letter has just been brought to Mr. Bailly from Mr. Necker expressing his appreciation of the demonstrations of esteem, confidence, and love that he had received the day before from the order over which he presides. This letter, written with great wisdom and feeling has made a profound impression, and its reading was followed by applause and cries of Vive M. Necker. The president has asked permission to let Mr. Necker know of the great impression which his letter has made on the assembly."[8] It was the beginning of a honeymoon between Necker and the National Assembly that, alas, was to alter dramatically by the end of the year. Bailly visited Necker personally that evening, along with the Archbishop of Vienne, Le Franc de Pompignan, to convey the official message of the assembly. It was the first meeting between the famous astronomer and the Director General of Finances. Prior to that time Bailly did not seem to have much regard for Necker. Now there began a fruitful if brief period of collaboration between the two, which provided an example of what Necker expected would be the normal relationship between the president of the National Assembly and the chief minister of the government. That was one of mutual respect in which there was no great concern about which was superior, the legislative or the executive power. Bailly acquired considerable esteem for the capabilities and the judgment of the Director General of Finances.

On June 25 the minority of the deputies of the Nobility who had been constantly in favor of union with the Commons, numbering 47, left the majority and came to take their seats in the National Assembly. They were warmly cheered as they entered the hall, for they included, as Adrien Duquesnoy wrote, "some of the most illustrious names in the kingdom: La Rochefoucauld, a Rochouart, the duc d'Orleans, Mathieu de Montmorency, Crillon, Alexandre de Lameth, La Tour-Maubourg, Luynes, d'Aiguillon, Lally-Tollendal."[9] At the head of the delegation was Stanislaus de Clermont-Tonnerre, deputy of the Nobility from Paris, who spoke to the assembly, expressing regret that the "brothers" who had not come over with them had really wanted to but felt bound by mandates "more or less imperative" that prevented them from voting by head. This was certainly true of some of the noble deputies who had not come over, Lafayette being one of them. It probably included most of those 77 deputies of the Nobility who had strongly supported the motion back on June 5 to accept "purely and simply" the compromise proposal of Necker on the question of the verification of credentials.[10]   It will be remembered that that number had not included the noble deputies from Paris and Dauphiné whose powers had not yet been verified.

Meanwhile it was becoming increasingly apparent to the "brothers" in the assembly of the Nobility who had remained behind that their continued separation from the National Assembly was untenable, given the violent manifestations of public opinion. On the same day that the 47 deputies left the assembly of the Nobility the majority that remained passed a resolution to send a letter to the king informing him that they would heed his request to join the other two orders to deliberate and vote in common on matters of general interest, particularly those concerning finances. The Nobility affirmed their determination to relinquish all fiscal privileges. But the letter stipulated that this act did not foreclose future decisions, and that the Nobility would continue to insist on the right, granted by the king himself at the Royal Session, to continue to exist as a separate order and to have its own assembly for deliberation and voting on matters that concerned the Nobility. The letter further pointed out that the mandates of several deputies prevented them from joining in a common assembly, and asked the king to reconvene the bailiwick assemblies so that their mandates could be revised.

On the following day, June 26, the assembly of the Nobility sent a deputation led by the duc de Liancourt to the National Assembly to inform them of the letter the Nobles had addressed to the king. Now there was a clear-cut issue between the "ancient constitution" and the resolution of the Commons of June 17. Could the Assembly representing the nation receive a deputation from another assembly that theoretically was not supposed to exist? The liberal Nobility that had joined the National Assembly the day before sought to persuade the assembly that it should receive the deputation as a gesture of conciliation.[11]

536

Fréteau de Saint-Just, one of the liberal nobles urged this course. He was opposed by Mirabeau who not only insisted on the "rigor of principles" but cast some personal aspersions on Fréteau's motives and character. The assembly strongly disapproved of such lack of courtesy and shouted Mirabeau down, crying "Order!"[12] Bailly himself wrote in his memoirs that "I feared rigorous and extreme resolutions which deepened divisions."[13] The National Assembly voted to receive the deputation of Liancourt. After hearing what he had to say another debate ensued: could the National Assembly recognize the legitimate existence of the assembly of the Nobility? The rigor of the resolution of June 17 could not be denied and Bailly was compelled to say to the deputation that "he could recognize them only as deputy-nobles, our fellow-citizens and brothers whom we again invite to take their seats in the National Assembly."[14] Adrien Duquesnoy wrote in his journal that he believed this coldness was a mistake because "a considerable party (of Nobles) seemed on the verge of leaving their assembly if the president (Bailly) had been the least bit accommodating."[15] Not satisfied with that triumph, Mirabeau and Camus sought to prevent any mention of the deputation of Liancourt in the minutes, but again Mirabeau was rebuffed by the assembly who refused to sanction such an unbrotherly act. The "rigor of principles" did not yet exercise absolute sway over the assembly.

When the duc de Liancourt reported these events to the assembly of the Nobility it caused a burst of indignation, even among those who had been the most favorable to joining the National Assembly if they could get their mandates changed. Therefore the nobles were not in a favorable mood when, on the following day, June 27, they received a letter from the king thanking them for yielding to his entreaty to join with the other orders and "engaging" them to do so immediately. The king said he would reconvene the bailiwick assemblies to revise the imperative mandates. In the meantime he ordered those who felt restricted by such mandates to attend the National Assembly anyway, but they could abstain from voting until their mandates were revised. A similar letter was sent by the king to the president of the Clergy, Cardinal de La Rochefoucauld: "I enjoin (engage) my faithful Clergy to unite with the other two orders to achieve my paternal goals."[16] It was Necker who had persuaded the king to take this step. But the comte d'Artois also wrote a letter to the president of the assembly of the Nobility, the duc de Luxembourg, expressing fear of the populace for his own and the king's safety and saying "there is no other way to save (us) than to hasten the reunion."[17] Another source has it that Artois wrote: "All is lost, even the troops are turning to the side of the people."[18]

On Saturday, June 27, one week after the Tennis Court Oath, the union of all three orders took place. At 2:00 p.m. that day the rest of the Clergy, 143 deputies, took seats in the National Assembly. Two hours later the majority of the Nobility arrived. It was evident from the expressions on their faces that this was not a joyous event for them. They would have come freely, of their own will, if they believed they were acceding to the king's request made at the Royal Session, and that all the principles stated by the king at that session would remain in effect. That is, if they could be certain that their orders would continue to be recognized as legitimate, that deliberation and voting in separate assemblies on matters that concerned their own orders would be permitted. But on this day they obviously felt that the reunion had been forced upon them by the king, and they feared that it could mean the acceptance by the king of the Commons' resolution of June 17. This was Bailly's interpretation of the king's letters to the privileged orders. He wrote in his memoirs that "the king tacitly recognized the constitution of the National Assembly establishing the vote by head, effecting the destruction of the orders and repudiating the Royal Session."[19]

Whether this was the king's assumption is doubtful, and it certainly was not the view of the deputies of the Clergy and the Nobility who entered the National Assembly that Saturday afternoon. Cardinal de La Rochefoucauld told the assembly that the Clergy had sent a letter to the king agreeing to his request to join with the other two orders to deliberate in common on matters of urgent national interest, "but without prejudice of the clergy's right, according to constitutional laws of the monarchy, to assemble and to vote separately." He asked the National Assembly to have this letter inscribed in the minutes of the session of June 27. This statement caused an uproar in the National Assembly, and a vigorous expression of disapproval, Mirabeau's voice rising above all the others to declare: "It's unheard of to admit those into the National Assembly who do not recognize its sovereignty."[20] According to Barentin's letter to the king the Tribune told the assembly "the king does not have the right to tell the National Assembly anything."[21] Early in the following week the Nobility held a separate meeting and passed a resolution similar to that of the Clergy: they insisted on the continued distinction of the orders, their independence and right to deliberate and vote separately, and even when acceding to the king's request to join the other two orders it would be necessary for many deputies to have their mandates revised by the bailiwick assemblies to permit voting by head. The Nobility did not, however, probably in view of the storm provoked by a similar resolution of the Clergy, attempt to get the resolution inscribed in the minutes of the National Assembly. Even so, the radicals of the National Assembly succeeded in getting a resolution passed immediately afterwards that , in effect, declared imperative mandates to be illegal, of no binding power on any of the deputies. It was another instance of invoking that resolution of June 17. On that rock the National Assembly was to insist on its total sovereignty. It was the absolute monarchy turned upside down. The callousness with which the imperative mandates were set aside, disregarding the consciences of those who quite honestly believed they could not go against their mandates, was illustrative of the way the assembly was to treat similar sensitive matters in the future. "The assembly," wrote baron de Staël to Gustavus III at the end of the year, "has not treated anyone with consideration . . . No prejudice, no title, is respected. They want to do everything at once, as if they had forgotten that you have to persuade men, even when you want their own good."[22]

The irony of the situation was that with even a little prudence and spirit of conciliation the nobles could have been brought willingly to the reunion of the orders. At the separate session held by the Nobility on July 3 there were 138 deputies who voted; 89 voted in favor of the resolution, 49 against. If the latter figure could have been added to the 47 deputies who joined the National Assembly on June 25 the conciliatory nobility would have outnumbered the recalcitrant. Those who believed they could not join until their imperative mandates were changed were only too eager to bring that about, and it is probable that the bailiwick assemblies would have responded rapidly, as that of Paris did. As it turned out, the Clergy and Nobility who were forced to join the common assembly were extremely disgruntled at the arrogance of the radical Third Estate. In that frame of mind they might well have been susceptible to support violent measures to bring the Third Estate to heel. It appears probable that events during these days led the Keeper of the Seals, Barentin, to advise the king that it was necessary to exert the king's authority against the Third Estate. On June 25 Barentin had written to the king:

The Third Estate has flouted the will of
Your Majesty . . . it is necessary for the
king to preserve the principles of the
monarchy. It is not enough, Sire, to have
consecrated them, they must be maintained.
And the more they are placed in contempt the
greater is the duty of the king to bring to
heel those who stray from the truth . . . I
would not propose any action to your Majesty
that would be contrary to the kindness of
his heart, and yet he owes it to himself, to
his subjects who are truly attached to him,
finally to the legitimacy of his power that
he not suffer any revolution in his reign.[23]

The radicals of the Third Estate were no more
pleased by the forced reunion than the conservatives
of the Nobility and the Clergy, for it greatly
strengthened the moderates. Creuzé-Latouche wrote in
his journal that "one must fear that aristocratic max-
ims and those not in harmony with good citizenship of
so many members of the Clergy and the Nobility must
divide the assembly and on occasion become dominant."[24] Even before the enforced union the presence
of the Clergy who had come voluntarily gave a pronounced moderate tone to the National Assembly. When
a radical deputy from Provence asked the National Assembly to denounce the Archbishop of Aix, Boisgelin,
for not joining the National Assembly as he was required to do by his mandate, the Archbiship of Bordeaux, Champion de Cicé, opposed the motion saying
that "one should not give up hope for a complete reunion of all deputies," and he succeeded in carrying
the assembly with him.[25] Duquesnoy wrote in his journal that it was "remarkable after the 151 deputies of
the Clergy and the 47 deputies of the Nobility had entered the assembly how they had already given the assembly the appearance of sobriety, and there reigns a
calmness hitherto unknown."[26] The deputy from Bar-le-
Duc thought it most unfortunate that the deputation of

541

the Nobility was received with such ill grace when Liancourt appeared at the National Assembly on June 25 to announce the willingness of the remainder of the Nobility to join the common assembly. "The reply of the president to this deputation seems to me very much out-of-place, harsh, rude and liable to permanently prevent a reunion which we should so much desire to bring about."[27] On June 30 after the reunion had come about Duquesnoy was disturbed by the evident lack of cordiality that still remained between the orders:

> There are persons in the commons who would despair if the reunion should be successful because their reputations are founded on discord; their projects would be realized through a failure of communication between the orders. There is no doubt that there exists in the (privileged) orders enemies of public well-being, whose only wish is to see the failure of the States-General . . . They should be opposed by methods that are gentle and frank, by a policy that is conciliatory and far-sighted; and that is just what has not been done; far from it, we have given plausible grounds for their animosity; and they now have a right to complain about us.[28]

But the public did not seem to be aware of these clouds over the reunion of the orders. The only desire of the populace at both Versailles and Paris was to see the orders united in a common assembly so that the States-General could get down to the urgent tasks that awaited it: the financial crisis, the subsistence crisis, the new constitution and the guarantee of basic human rights and liberties. When news spread about the king's letters to the Clergy and the Nobility ordering their union with the National Assembly there was another outburst of popular feeling similar to that of the afternoon of June 23 when it was

542

learned that Necker would remain at his post. The
minister from Parma wrote that the people of the capitol were "intoxicated with joy. Please God that it
will be of long duration!"[29] At Versailles there was
again a crowd in the courtyard of the château where
people wanted to see the king and thank him. He appeared on the balcony of the marble courtyard, along
with the queen, who, it seems, had not had time to
prepare herself as customary when she appeared in public. She came out on the balcony with her hair down
and in tresses, without rouge, "without any make-up,"
wrote the minister from Parma. But this endeared her
all the more to the crowd as she brought the young
dauphin out also. It was not only the royal couple
that received the enthusiastic benedictions of the
people. Everyone knew that Necker had been responsible for this result, and they descended again on the
Contrôle-général. "This day," wrote Duquesnoy in his
journal, "is for Mr. Necker the day of the greatest
glory that can ever occur to a person."[30] Mounier
wrote his impression on the tenor of the crowds. The
popular joy was spontaneous and genuine, "unspoiled by
any violence or hatred. All ranks, all corps, all individuals were moved by the same hope. The congratu-
latory addresses of this great event breathed the love
of peace, loyalty to the king, and the most decent respect for the Clergy and the Nobility."[31] Even
Duquesnoy was more optimistic by July 2 when he
recorded in his journal: "Everything is now proceeding in a favorable direction, and . . . it is still
possible that we shall be fortunate. It is not that
we have not committed some stupid mistakes, but they
are not irreparable."[32] On July 13, after he had
learned of Necker's dismissal by the king two days before, Lally-Tollendal spoke to the National Assembly
in which he described those few days of hope after the
reunion of the orders:

Amidst all the diversities of opinion patriotism still dominated all hearts. The ef-

543

forts of the minister to achieve pacification and the repeated invitations of the
king had at last produced their effect. A
reunion had taken place. Each day saw another ground for disunion disappear. A project for a constitution, drawn by an experienced hand, conceived by a wise mind and a
pure soul, had rallied all hearts. We were
marching ahead; we had finally got down to
our work and France was beginning to breathe
again.[33]

The constitution was a matter of first priority
since many of the cahiers had stipulated that their
deputies were not empowered to vote for new taxes or
approve loans until the new constitution had been
drawn up and ratified by the king. Therefore the
first committee established after the reunion of the
three orders in a common assembly was the committee of
the constitution. Mounier and Lafayette were on the
committee. The latter called upon his friend Jefferson to be a consultant.[34]

But another matter of great urgency was the
"subsistence crisis," the severe grain shortage and
the danger of famine. Next to the ministry, the
Clergy had been most concerned about this matter. Being in close contact with the poorer classes it was
aware of the anxiety and suffering, which was an important cause of the general unrest and popular rebel-
liousness. The Clergy was anxious for the States-General to reach a compromise on the issue of verification of powers so that it could turn its attention to
the subsistence crises. On June 6 the Clergy, at the
time it urged acceptance of Necker's plan of compromise on the issue of verification of powers, sent a
special deputation to the other orders to plead the
necessity of ending the deadlock.[35] It called upon
the Nobility and the Third Estate to concert in forming a committee to act on the subsistence crisis. The

radical leaders of the Third Estate could only see this as a devious maneuver to get the Third Estate constituted as a separate deliberative order. It gave the opportunity for a hitherto obscure deputy from Arras to give vent to an anti-clerical tirade, and to accuse the Clergy of hypocrisy in its professed concern for the poor when it was such a wealthy landowner, exacting tithes from the peasant population. This was the first important speech of the deputy to attract the attention of the assembly, and whose name was given at the time as Robert Pierre, which was to be changed to Robespierre.[36] The deputation was told by speakers in the Commons that they were as much concerned about the suffering of the people as the Clergy, and that is why it was necessary that the deputies of that order come and take their seats in the national assembly, so that the subsistence question as well as other urgent matters could be dealt with.[37]

No one was more interested in getting the States-General settled down to the tasks for which it had been convened than Necker. Since the beginning of his second ministry the previous summer he had been grappling constantly with two crises, the financial and the subsistence crisis. Both were closely related since the enormous amount of grain purchased abroad had to be paid for in hard cash or in credit that was impeccable. This required an increase of extraordinary expenditure in addition to the daily outlay for ordinary expenditures which also had to be paid in cash; such items as soldiers' pay, salaries for civilian employees, the maintenance of all public facilities, interest payments on certain types of debts that could not be delayed without causing serious damage to credit. As has been seen, it seemed "almost miraculous" to his colleague, Montmorin, that Necker was able to maintain these expenditures. But it was a miracle that could not be sustained indefinitely. Necker had called upon the Discount Bank for loans in

the form of bank notes which were used to pay some of
the government's obligations that did not require
specie payments. The tax-collecting officials, the
receivers at the level of the election and the generality, were required to accept these bank notes as
payment for taxes. The use of bank notes was not
harmful to the monetary system as long as the amount
in circulation was moderate. But this resource could
not be counted upon indefinitely if the government
were to avoid forced circulation which would lead to a
drastic depreciation on the stock market or bourse.
The notes were allowed to circulate as money only in
Paris by decrees in council and were for a specified
time period. A decree in council of June 14 extended
the period from June 30 until December 31. The preamble of the decree, no doubt written by Necker, stated
that "the public confidence in the notes is legitimate
and well-founded."[38]

Much of Necker's success in maintaining the solvency of the royal government was due to his personal
character. Foreign bankers and merchants trusted him
and felt they could rely on his word. There is probably no better illustration of Benjamin Franklin's
aphorism made famous by Max Weber: credit depends on
character. But this could not be a permanent solution
to the financial crisis. Necker had stepped into an
emergency situation, holding up the wavering edifice
by personal courage and skill, but impatiently waited
for relief. It was the great disillusionment of his
public life to find that the National Assembly, once
constituted, was more interested in abstract theory
than such practical, down-to-earth requirements as
money and grain. And finally the assembly berated him
when his messages began to take on a complaining tone!

It has been seen in a previous chapter that the
subsistence crisis and the threat of famine were due
to the crop failure of the summer of 1788 when hailstorms in July and drought reduced the normal crop

yield by one-half. The crisis lasted for about fifteen months, from September 1788 until nearly the end
of the year 1789. When Necker took over the responsibilities of Director General of Finance, a post similar to the "Home Secretary" of the British government,
he ordered an investigation and a report on the grain
supply, both what was in stock and what the future
crop might yield. The danger of famine became immediately apparent to him and his first act was to restrict export of grain, first from some provinces, and
then on September 7 a decree in council totally prohibited export of grain out of the kingdom. His survey included the grain situation in other countries as
well in order to see what the chances were of relying
upon foreign imports. His survey showed that the
grain harvest that summer had been short in most other
European countries, and that the price was nearly as
high as in France. This meant that merchants guided
by the profit motive could not be expected to ship
grain to France unless the government paid substantial
bonuses or subsidies for imported grain. But even
this would not bring in sufficient grain supplies in
the emergency. It was necessary for the king's government to enter the grain trade and purchase supplies
on the king's account. Furthermore it was necessary
to keep the price level of bread within the means of
the poor so that subsidies had to be paid to bakers to
prevent them from operating at a loss.

In his book written in 1791 Necker estimated the
total amount of grains of all kinds purchased during
the crisis came to 3,600,000 quintaux, which measure
is equivalent to the English hundred-weight. The total cost he estimated at 70 million livres.[39] It was
not easy to find such a quantity when other countries
of Europe were also suffering a shortage. Great
Britain, for example, prohibited all export of grain
and flour, despite the urgent appeals of Necker and
the French ambassador at London. As Necker said, he

547

ransacked the granaries of Europe and America to keep the French population from famine.

The supply of bread for Paris was a matter of constant anxiety for Necker. The capitol city had become a haven for the unemployed and the starving who flocked in from the immediately surrounding provinces. During the severe winter of 1788-1789 about 120,000 poor came from these regions searching for work and relief. Charitable workshops were set up for them, projects such as leveling the butte of Montmarte which gave employment to 12,000 workers.[40] The population of Paris, estimated usually as 600,000 people, was particularly vulnerable to the threat of famine because of the enormous quantity of grain needed for daily subsistence. Necker lived in constant dread that some accident might prevent the delivery of the crucial supply for each day: a shipwreck at sea or on the river, or spoilage of grain in transit. As order broke down in the July days there was added to these natural hazards the intervention of local citizen-militias in the provinces who tried to impede the shipments of grain from the harbors of Normandy to Paris. Necker did not leave the administration of subsistence to subordinates but carefully supervised the operations himself. He wrote in his book of 1791:

> It was especially the thought that a great city such as Paris, could be without bread for twenty-four hours, which made my soul quake, and troubled my imagination. I controlled this terror during the day, but it reasserted itself with force during my dreams, and in the morning, for several months, I was awakened by palpatations of the heart, one of the causes of the illness which so many anxieties and painful experiences gave me and from which I will never recover.[41]

The subsistence crisis had an impact on the financial crisis in other ways besides the mere cost of grain and its shipment from other countries. It created a serious balance of payment deficit in the country so that hard money or specie became even more scarce, and the foreign exchange rate became adverse for the French livre. The need to organize guard units to protect supplies transported through hostile country also contributed to the cost not included in the above figure of 70 million livres.

It was to be expected that Necker's enemies would make the most of the catastrophic harvest of 1788 to discredit his ministry. He never deigned to acknowledge much less reply to the grosser libels. But one criticism that he did not ignore was the charge by the "Economists" (the Physiocrats) that he was responsible for the subsistence crisis by abandoning the free trade policy of his predecessor. It was alleged that the prohibition of export of grain, the intervention of the government in subsidizing imports, and the direct purchase of grain on the king's account, all had frightened away the grain merchants, interferred with the free-market mechanism, and was in fact the true cause of the grain shortage. It was maintained that the decree in council of June 1787 which had granted unlimited freedom of export outside the kingdom had provided a safety net: this was the clause which permitted provincial governments of the intendants or the provincial assemblies to restrict export from their provinces if there was danger of a shortage. Necker explained in his 1791 book that such a regional focus was not sufficient for the national needs. It could happen that some coastal provinces would have a surplus and merchants would benefit by export to foreign countries, at the same time that interior provinces such as the Isle-de-France were suffering serious shortages. Necker was not ignorant of the virtues of free enterprise. He had made his own fortune in part by speculation in the grain trade. He knew as well as anyone the inhibiting effect that governments can have on private commerce. The difference between himself and the Economists was that he could not accept free trade as a panacea for all situations. The principles of free trade and the virtues of laissez-faire frequently are true, but not when they are absolute dogmas. If there is a catastrophic failure in the harvest one year, no doubt the rise in prices will stimulate landowners to increase their acreage. But in the meantime populations cannot be allowed to starve, no matter how wonderfully the free market mechanism often operates. If the grain havest has been unusually poor in neighboring countries, the market will not bring imports to make up for the crop failure in France.[42] All this seems fairly obvious. Yet there were attacks on Necker from the free trade dogmatists. Arthur Young wrote in his diary that the food shortage in France was due to state intervention, revealing that he was a free trade dogmatist, although he was not a physiocrat.[43] When the National Assembly wished to send Necker a vote of thanks for what he had done to preserve the country from famine, it was opposed by Jérôme Pétion who advanced the Physiocratic theses that if the government would have maintained freedom of export and kept out of the market there would never have been a shortage of grain.[44] He advanced the somewhat piquant objection to government subsidies to bakers in order to hold down the price of bread as giving an unnecessary aid to the wealthy, who can also purchase bread at the same price. Evidently Pétion would have preferred to see the masses starve rather than to give the rich an undeserved benefit of low prices for bread.

It appears that Pétion's Physiocratic objections were not taken seriously by the chairman of the Subsistence Committee who was none other than Pierre-Samuel Dupont de Nemours, one of the founders and most prominent publicist of the sect in its period of greatest influence. The chairman of the Subsistence

Committee approved the way Necker had handled the grain crisis, and could only suggest ways that the Assembly could assist him in carrying on as he had in the past. Mirabeau, whose father was a founder of the Physiocratic school, of course would not allow an oportunity to pass by to discredit the Director General of Finances. But he did so, not by accusing Necker of being an interventionist, but of not being enough of an interventionist.

As soon as it was appointed by the assembly the Subsistence Committee began its investigation of the crisis. It asked Necker to provide it with whatever information the Director General of Finance might have available. Necker sent a lengthy memorial to the committee on the subject, giving the amounts of grains imported, the subsidizing of imports, and the assistance given to bakers so that the price could be kept within the means of the poor classes. It was on July 6 that Dupont gave the first report of the committee to the National Assembly. He had scarcely begun his report when Mirabeau intervened to ask the chairman if he knew of "certain propositions" Mr. Jefferson made to Necker for the importation of American grain, and also that an individual residing in England had offered to sell flour made of peas "at a very modest price." Mirabeau demanded if the committee did have knowledge of these facts, why did it withhold them from the Assembly? Dupont replied that "absolutely the committee had no knowledge of what Mr. de Mirabeau had just related."[45] Mirabeau then asked for a delay of twenty-four hours in which he would report on those vital matters to the assembly, which was granted but without enthusiasm, for, as one witness wrote, it was felt that valuable time should not be wasted in allowing Mirabeau to pursue his personal vendetta against the Director General of Finances.[46]

During that twenty-four hour period Adrien Duquesnoy, who was a personal friend of Necker's, went to warn him about Mirabeau's planned attack on him, the allegation being that Necker had refused to follow up on an invitation from the American minister to purchase flour in the United States. "I found him not in the least agitated," wrote Duquesnoy in his journal, "but possessed of the tranquility of the man of integrity, and he preferred to wait until Mirabeau had presented the details of his charges before replying to them."[47] As it turned out, Necker did not have to defend himself. The American minister, when he heard of the charge, himself took the initiative in writing to Lafayette that the charges were untrue, and he personally paid a call on both Necker and Montmorin to show them a copy of the letter. As Jefferson described the incident in his report to the Secretary of State, John Jay:

> Monsieur de Mirabeau, who is very hostile to Mr. Necker, wished to find a ground for censuring him in a proposition to have a great quantity of flour furnished from the United States, which he had supposed me to have made to Mr. Necker, and to have been refused by him; and he asked time of the states general to furnish proofs. The Marquis de la Fayette, immediately gave me notice of this matter, and I wrote him a letter to disavow having ever made any such proposition to Mr. Necker, which I desired him to communicate to the states. I waited upon Mr. Necker and Monsieur de Montmorin, satisfied them that what had been suggested was absolutely without foundation from me, and indeed they have not needed this testimony. I gave them copies of my letter to the Marquis de la Fayette, which was afterwards printed. The Marquis, on the receipt of my letter, showed it to Mirabeau, who turned then to a paper from which he had drawn his information and found he had totally mistaken it. He

promised immediately that he would himself declare his error to the States-General, and read to them my letter, which he did.[48]

When Mirabeau spoke to the Assembly on July 8 he did admit an error on his part, but he was far from contrite about it, insisting that despite that error his condemnation of Necker's handling of the subsistence crisis was still true:

I must retract the word propositions, which I ventured the other day, relative to the offer of the Americans for grain supplies. I have a letter from Mr. Jefferson in which he declares he did not make propositions on this matter, and even that upon the inquiry of the Director General of Finances a few months ago, he informed the Americans that France would provide an excellent market for grain and flour. It is none-the-less true that the intentions of the government have been badly followed up, due to lack of orders, and that a profound ignorance and the failure of coordination in the payment of subsidies have deprived France of American grain.[49]

Furthermore, the Tribune let it be known that this was only the tip of the iceburg. "A multitude of facts of the same kind have come to my attention," he informed the Assembly, "and throw broad daylight on both the commerce of grain and the theory of this commerce (as practiced by the ministry)." He announced that he was preparing a memorial "on these facts and their consequences" which he asked permission to present at some presumably short time in the future. But immediately Mirabeau found another issue that was more productive of glory than the grain shortage. It was on July 8 that he delivered his famous oration on the danger of the foreign troops in the service of the king of France that were being withdrawn from the frontier and stationed in posts around Paris and Versailles. It was evidently a powerful oration, perhaps his most effective so far in the National Assembly. Several who had been distrustful of Mirabeau's demagogic powers, for example, Bailly, now began to look upon him with considerable admiration.[50]

But Bailly did not believe any of Mirabeau's allegations about Necker's sins of commission or ommission in his handling of the subsistence crisis. On the contrary he thought the Director General of Finances deserved the gratitude of the nation for saving it from a catastrophic famine. He wrote in his memoirs that "the measures of the government on the subsistence crisis have been as wise as farsighted. For that, one must credit both Mr. Necker and the king, and I can testify that without those measures, in the month of July and August Paris would have been afflicted with famine, and the constitution would have been annihilated even before it was established."[51] Bailly strongly condemned Mirabeau's "talent for arousing the popular classes."[52]

The subsistence crisis was intimately related to another major component of the general crisis that afflicted the country in the late spring and early summer months. There was mounting popular unrest in the cities, villages, and the countryside. The Réveillon riot that occurred in Paris in late April was the first important manifestation of popular violence. It was in some ways typical of incidents that were to spread like a contagious disease in the summer. The grievances of the workers in the Réveillon paper factory had to do with low wages. But perversely their anger was directed at the factory owner who paid the highest wages in the industry and was noted for his benevolent treatment of workers. His factory was broken into on April 28 by a mob who believed, according to a rumor which was false, that Réveillon had made derogatory remarks about the workers' grievances. The volatility of the crowds and their susceptibility to false rumors gave an opportunity for the demagogues, for those with particular gifts for inflaming the crowds, either through the printed or the spoken word. The Réveillon riot was subdued and order restored by the use of French Guard units, and a long inquest was begun to identify the persons who had spread the false rumors.[53]

The government of the ancien régime did not have a large police force especially trained to cope with civil disorder. The Maréchaussée, so called because these troops were under the direct military command of the eleven marshals of France, numbered about 4,300 men in 1789, about one-fourth the number of the gendarmeries that existed a century later who had the same function.[54] The courts that passed judgment on cases involving acts of violence were the thirty-three prevotal courts under the jurisdiction of the marshals. A Declaration of the king of May 21, 1789, made them the courts of last resort for such offenses. It amounted to a declaration of martial law throughout the country, the purpose of which was to bring promptly to justice those accused. The latter included those who "incited popular riots and excessive violence which has occurred in different provinces."

> The same riots, disorders, and excesses have multiplied in several provinces of our kingdom, not only in the cities where there are market places but also in the countryside, along the roads and rivers under the pretext of the scarcity of grain; these excesses lead to pillage, to preventing grain shipments from reaching their destinations, to alarming farmers, peasants and proprietors, and give way to brigandage of all sorts, which can have serious consequences if such

derelictions are not punished promptly and severely.[55]

The panic that seized the French popular classes in periods of scarcity tended to frighten off capitalists from entering the grain market. There was danger not only in the transport of grain by having it seized enroute, but even in the storage of it for the most necessary needs. Rumors spread rapidly that there was not actually a grain shortage but a "famine plot," a collusion of grain merchants to hold grain off the market in order to raise its price to exorbitant levels and to enrich the monopolizers by deliberately causing the people to suffer. The story that Necker himself, an experienced grain speculator was secretly behind this famine plot was spread by the libellists. The Secret Agent attended a meeting at the house of "a seigneur of the highest distinction," where the plans for overthrowing Necker were discussed. Among the allegations to be presented to the Parlement of Paris was that he had deliberately caused the grain shortage in order to raise revenue for the royal government. "I have always said," the seigneur told the Secret Agent, "that this man would be smothered in a sack of wheat."[56] The same allegation was made by the radicals on the opposite side of the political spectrum. On June 29, four days after this meeting alluded to by the Secret Agent there was a discussion of the subsistence crisis in the National Assembly. A deputy from Bordeaux stated that "the reasons for the grain shortage are well known; it's useless to blame it on the monopolizers. The hail storm, an unfortunate crop year, those are the only causes which have deprived us of abundance." To refute that statement a deputy of the Third Estate named Bertrand Barère got up to say:

> The grain shortage afflicts the capitol and
> the provinces; the cries of distress are
> heard from one end of the kingdom to the
> other; and yet we are assured that there is

556

being concealed enough wheat to last for
more than six months. Must we perish in the
midst of abundance? Are we to humour those
men who traffic in human misery? . . . Let
us resolve, gentlemen, to uncover, to foil,
the baleful projects of the enemies of the
people, the enemies of humanity.[57]

It is significant that Barère was not appointed
to the Committee on Subsistence which gave little credence to such allegations. When a representative of
the Parisian bakers appeared before the committee to
claim that the government was maintaining vast re-
serves of grain at Corbeil, held by the Lelu Company,
he was quickly dismissed, and told to take his allegations to the government itself.[58] Dupont, as chairman
of the committee, did not find any reason to reproach
the government's handling of the crisis. Yet all he
could suggest was that the National Assembly find some
means for helping the government finance the enormous
grain purchases. But this was not possible because of
the imperative mandates which required the constitution to be ratified first before any financial measures could be approved, or at least such was the argument of the radicals. In the final analysis, the
Committee on Subsistence soon ceased to exist and the
task of provisioning the country remained entirely up
to Necker.

It seems impossible to deny that Necker saved the
country from a grave catastrophe by his close supervision of the provisioning of Paris and the other
provinces surrounding the Isle-de-France. He did so
not only by his use of the administrative tools of the
government, but also with his own personal resources.
A few days before his dismissal by the king on July
11, he had sent an offer to the Hope banking firm in
Amsterdam to ship grain to Paris, putting up his own
fortune as collateral for the necessary funding. At
the time of his dismissal from the ministry on July 11

557

he had not yet received confirmation of his offer from Amsterdam. Therefore when he was told by the king to leave the country on July 11 and stopped first at Brussels he sent a message to the Hope firm assuring them that his changed circumstances did not alter his offer to pledge his own fortune to guarantee the grain shipments to Paris. Ironically, the first letter Necker's successor, baron de Breteuil, found on his desk that morning of July 13, was the answer to Necker from the Hope firm acknowledging and accepting his offer.[59]

Yet Necker's heroic efforts and success in preventing a famine are not mentioned in present-day histories of the French Revolution. And despite the special studies in the twentieth century showing how baseless was the legend of the "pacte de famine," Necker's reputation still seems tarnished by the calumnies of his own day. In the first volume of his financial history of France, Marcel Marion wrote that "the grain shortage was more artificial than real . . . By reason of excessive regulation and cries of alarm (Necker) managed to produce a famine by opinion much more terrible than a real famine; and the effects, in spite of the abundance, were felt in several parts of the kingdom . . . If Necker had not been minister, there would not have been a grain shortage in 1788; the harvest had been satisfactory, and the ravages of hail less extensive than thought."[60] The only evidence Marion offered for those astounding assertions was the statement by Arthur Young quoted above, and the speech of a certain Boislandry made in the Constituent Assembly on November 30, 1790. The evidence that contradicts those statements is certainly more ample. Practically without exception the writers of memoirs and diaries mention the devastating crop failure of 1788, and the subsistence crisis that followed. For example, baron de Besenval, who had little regard for Necker, gives the following picture of the circumstances existing in the military zones placed under his command for eight years prior to 1789:

> For eight years the king had given me command of the interior provinces including the Isle de France, with the exception of the city of Paris, the Soissonais, the Berri, the Bourbonnais, the Orleanais, the Tourraine and the Maine. The task of supervising such an extensive territory was greatly increased during the month of April 1789 by the scarcity of grain which began to be felt and which threatened a famine. The diminution of this commodity of prime necessity, the fear of the future, caused anxiety and general ferment. The market places became scenes of violence, and the convoys which the government sent to the places of greatest need, were intercepted; this obliged me to distribute troops under my command in order to protect a great number of markets over which I was compelled to maintain order, to protect the transport of grain, to pacify the country where brigands, emboldened by the general ferment, committed acts of violence.[61]

Despite the great extent of territory and the limited number of troops under his command Besenval claimed that he did succeed in maintaining order up until the 12th of July. The situation was like that of a seething kettle of water ready to boil over at the slightest provocation. Such it was at Paris and Versailles. But in those two cities the problem of maintaining order was complicated by the attitude of the troops that were assigned to the task. These were companies of French and Swiss Guards. It has already been seen that two companies mutinied in Paris on June 25, refusing to bear arms against the demonstrators supporting the National Assembly. At Versailles they did not have to mutiny since the officers were also sympathetic to the Assembly and followed the desires of the leaders such as Bailly. Even in Paris sympathy was pronounced among all the other guard units. The bookseller Hardy wrote on June 25 in his Journal that "there is not a single soldier in the barracks of the French guards, even though the officers have exhausted all means to retain them."[62]

The commandant of the guard units was the duc de Châtelet, who at the beginning of the following week undertook to restore discipline. On Tuesday, June 30, two soldiers of the Paris guards that had mutinied showed up in civilian clothing at the National Assembly to present a memorial denouncing the duc de Châtelet. They were arrested by a detachment of hussars sent by the duke and taken to Paris, where along with eleven other prominent leaders of the mutiny of the previous week, they were placed in the military prison of the Abbaye de Saint-Germain-des-Prés. Their comrades at the Palais-Royal immediately brought their case to the attention of the crowds and orators at that center of the popular movement. According to a note by the Secret Agent, that same evening at about 7:00 p.m., a fiery orator led three to four hundred persons to the Abbaye and forcefully released the prisoners who were taken back to the Palais-Royal and placed under the protection of the crowds.[63]

The next morning, July 1, as Bailly went to the assembly hall to open the session he was met by representatives of the Palais-Royal crowd, who told him of the events of the preceding day and asked that the freed prisoners be granted a pardon by the king. Bailly sensed the possibility of grave crisis in the incident, and leaving the assembly he went immediately to confer with Necker. Both viewed the situation in the same light. It would be disastrous for the authority of the government simply to acquiesce in the accomplished fact. Yet it was equally perilous to at-

tempt to return the soldiers to prison. At the conference Bailly clearly indicated his concern over the
situation in Paris. The popular movement was getting
out of control. Necker proposed that the city government establish its own police force consisting of
bourgeois militia units. In the present critical situation both Necker and Bailly agreed that the assembly
should recommend to the king that he grant clemency to
the soldiers, after they had been returned to
prison.[64]

At the National Assembly this was the first serious matter to be deliberated upon after the reunion of
the orders. The deputy Gaultier de Biauzet was favorably impressed with the maturity of the discussion,
"The matter passed as if there had never been a
schism, or differences in the matter of voting. Thus
the common good is achieved by simple force of circumstances which must prevail over (partisan) opinion."[65]
The assembly agreed that in theory it was a matter for
the executive power, but in practice the consequences
were so grave that it was appropriate for the Assembly
to take up this matter. The final decision was to ask
the king for clemency for the ex-prisoners, but at the
same time, ask the people of Paris to "immediately return to order."[66] The king agreed to this decision.
According to Gaultier de Biauzet the soldiers returned
to prison on July 4 with the promise from the Parisian
Assembly of Electors that they would be pardoned by
the king. This was done, the king sending his letters
of pardon to the Archbishop of Paris, and the matter
was seemingly closed.[67]

But it was not closed. The popular forces in
Paris had flexed their muscles and found they could
compel the government to treat with them. The week
before, when the majority of the deputies of the
Clergy and the minority of Nobles had joined the National Assembly, on June 25, the crowd at Versailles
demanded the right to enter the Menus Plaisirs and

561

witness the proceedings. They were obviously ready and willing to force their way in if permission were not granted. It required all the persuasive powers of Bailly, Clermont-Tonnerre, and the Archbishop of Vienne to keep them out, and they did so only with the promise that freedom of entry would be granted by the following day and continue thereafter. It must have been this event that alerted Bailly to the gravity of the situation. "The people are aroused," he wrote in his memoirs, "and they are a formidable instrument. Have we been wise in so arousing them? It's a great question."[68]

The idea of establishing a citizen militia to guard against intolerable disorder had been suggested by others besides Necker. At Paris this was increasingly urged by the Assembly of Electors. These were the deputies of the Third Estate of Paris intro muros who had been sent to the archepiscopal palace by the sixty districts into which the city had been divided for the Third Estate. After performing the task of electing the deputies for their order to go to the States-General the electors at the archepiscopal palace decided to remain in session to supervise their deputies at the States-General and see that they followed their instructions. The electors met at first in a museum at the Place Dauphine in Paris. On May 10 their leaders asked the Provost of the Merchants at the Hôtel-de-Ville, Jacques de Flesselles, for a hall in that building. The reply, approved by Barentin and Laurent de Villedeuil, was that the electors had completed the task for which they had been called into existence, and therefore the petition was denied. But when the king ordered the Clergy and the Nobility to join the National Assembly on June 27 he had also told the privileged orders that he would call back into session those electoral assemblies that had bound their deputies by imperative mandate not to vote in a common assembly. Now the electoral assembly of the Third estate in Paris demanded again the right to sit

562

in a hall in the Hôtel-de-Ville. Flesselles reversed himself, explaining in a letter to Barentin that the king's letters to the two privileged orders authorized it, and "furthermore, in the present agitation, so long as it remains so powerful, it would be prudent and wise for the Bureau of the Hôtel-de-Ville to accede to this request."[69] The electoral assembly had also taken the initiative to inform the National Assembly that the electors stood by and supported the resolution of June 17. Now they were permitted to occupy the Great Hall in the Hôtel-de-Ville. Soon seventeen nobles who had been electors of the Nobility in Paris and twenty-five electors of the Clergy came to join the 407 bourgeois members. It made an imposing assembly for the city government of Paris, and it assumed the de facto function of a representative assembly for the city. The electors saw to it that their respective district assemblies in the sixty districts also continued to remain in session. On July 11 it was this assembly that decreed the formation of a citizen guard to maintain order in the city of Paris.[70] Each district was to recruit 800 men to be trained and armed, to form a total citizen guard of 48,000 men.

It was to be expected that the defection of the French Guard units in Paris would direct the attention of the minister of war to other military units that would be less susceptible to the slogans of the Palais Royal. These were regiments stationed on the different frontiers composed mainly of recruits of non-French origin, "from the dregs of society of all European countries," the minister of Saxony described them.[71] Beginning on June 22 the king ordered the Swiss regiment of Reinach to come from Alsace to Paris; on June 26 three more regiments of infantry and three of calvary were ordered from the frontiers to take up posts around Paris between the dates of July 7 to July 16. On July 1st more orders were sent out by the minister of war. A total of from 25,000 to 30,000 men were to be in position by July 16. All units were placed under the command of a 70-year-old marshal who had distinguished himself in the Seven Years' War, Marshal de Broglie. His second in command was baron de Besenval.[72] The former was described by Jefferson in a letter to Thomas Paine as "a high flying aristocrat, cool and capable of every mischief."[73] The latter was an intimate of the circle of Madame de Polignac, the center of intrigues, along with the comte d'Artois, to bring about the disgrace of Necker.

What the intentions of the government were might seem fairly obvious in the circumstances: to restore the authority of the king's government, authority which had been so scandalously flouted by the resolution of June 17, and by the events following the Royal Session of June 23. But the evidence is fragmentary as to what specifically was to be done. The overthrow of Necker was certainly the objective of the circle of the courtiers around the comte d'Artois. Mounier wrote in his memoirs that the purpose of this armed force was to enable the government to dismiss Necker and prevent the kind of scene that occurred in the afternoon of June 23 when fear of the crowds prevented the king from dismissing Necker.[74] No doubt it was hoped that the mere appearance of an imposing armed force would be sufficient to cow the popular movement, but if necessary the artillery brought from the frontiers would be used. According to the comte d'Artois' good friend, the marquis de Clermont-Gallerande, the king's younger brother told him "we must cut the knot and it will cost many heads; more than one will have to be blown off the shoulders."[75] But what about the States-General? Would it simply be dissolved and the deputies sent home, and the political situation restored to what it had been before 1787? There were persistent rumors that the States-General would be dissolved but elections would then be called for a new assembly which would convene at some city away from Paris and the popular pressures of the Palais-Royal.

According to this plan the king would move the court to Compiègne.[76]

An obscure matter was what had transpired at the meetings of the king's Council just before the dismissal of Necker and his ministerial colleagues. Evidently Necker attended them up to the day before his dismissal. He knew of the decision to bring troops up to the capitol, and had argued against it, but still had granted the necessary money to the war ministry, according to the envoy from Saxony.[77] In these final meetings of the Council, according to some memoir writers, Necker was subjected to increasingly violent abuse by the comte d'Artois who attended them. Baron de Gleichen wrote that at a secret Council meeting on Thursday, July 9, "Mr. Necker suffered several insults from the princes, the comte d'Artois saying that he deserved to be hung."[78] According to another source it was at this meeting that the decision was made to bring the baron de Breteuil into the ministry, "but no precise plan was proposed since Necker was present."[79] It must have been at this meeting on July 9 that the personal confrontation between Necker and Artois took place described by the marquis de Ferrières. As Necker came to the doorway of the council chamber Artois barred his way, shook his fist in Necker's face and said to him: "Where are you going, you foreign traitor? Is your place at the Council, you sorry bourgeois? Go back to your little city, or you will die at my hand!" Ferrières wrote that "at that vulgar abuse, Necker took a step backward, remained perfectly erect, said not a word in reply, then went on into the council chamber."[80]

After Mirabeau's oration on July 8 denouncing the assembling of the troops in the vicinity of the capitol the National Assembly sent a formal protest to the king on the subject. He replied that the troop disposition was necessary because of the disorder at Paris, but denied having any intention to strike at the freedom of the National Assembly.[81] Some historians have concluded that this was calculated hypocrisy, that the king had already agreed to the project of the "hard-liners" to dissolve the States-General well before July 11.[82] But this was not the belief of several who were in a position to observe the king's actions. Bailly thought the king was being influenced by secret counselors but was himself unaware of where they were leading him. "The king is of very good faith, and would only take measures (that he believed) necessary for order and public tranquility."[83] This was Necker's belief also when writing his book on the Revolution published in 1796: "I was never certain just what their purpose was," he wrote, alluding to the secret counselors, "and I believe the king himself was not aware of all their secret plans."[84] Other observers thought the intentions of the counselors was to allow the king to believe sincerely that the only purpose of the troop movement was to assure peace and public tranquility, but at the propitious moment, to take advantage of an opportunity that would no doubt come, to engage the government in an operation that would lead to the result desired: the crushing of the popular movement in Paris and the dissolution of the States-General. Jefferson wrote to John Jay on July 19 that after the reunion of the orders on June 27, "Within the Assembly matters went on well."

> But it was soon observed that troops, and particularly foreign troops, were on their march towards Paris from various quarters and that this was against the opinion of Mr. Necker. The king was probably advised to this under pretext of preserving peace in Paris and Versailles, and saw nothing else in the measure. But his advisors are supposed to have had in view, when he should be secured and inspirited by the presence of the troops, to take advantage of some favorable moment and surprise him into an act of

authority for establishing the Declaration of the 23rd of June, and perhaps dispersing the States-General.[85]

In a dispatch sent on July 9 to King Gustavus by baron de Staël, the Swedish ambassador described Louis XVI as a person who was being pulled in opposite directions and could not make up his mind which to follow. His natural tendency was to find some middle way between two opposite sources of advice, but that course was becoming impossible. "The inconsistency in the conduct of the king of France presents an extremely bizarre spectacle in the present circumstances. In turn guided by Mr. Necker and the intrigue of which the queen and Monseigneur the comte d'Artois are the leaders, he makes a concession to one and then to the other, without definite plan, exposing himself to all the dangers of conflicting policies."[86] De Staël said that Necker was continually trying to persuade the king that he would have to decide on one policy or the other. Either to give full support to those who were opposing the revolution which was imminent, supported by the nobility, the clergy and the parlements, those who were openly proclaiming that they do not want the States-General, and appoint a ministry that would pursue that policy consistently. "But if, on the contrary, he is with reason appalled at the frightful misfortunes that policy would bring, then he must frankly favor the public cause and since he cannot avoid the revolution he must place himself at the head of it in order to lead it."[87]

In his books written in later years Necker indicated that he was well aware of the "intrigue" but was too engrossed in the pressing affairs of the moment to give it much heed. As always, his conduct was forthright and above reproach. He was not a "bureaucratic in-fighter" to use a modern term. He simply let the king know that if his service was no longer pleasing to the king he would submit his resignation. He promised also that if such was the king's decision Necker would retire discreetly to his estate in Switzerland and avoid a repetition of the scene of that afternoon of June 23. The king replied "I take you at your word," which was rather equivocal, Necker later admitted, but it was said in such a friendly and kindly manner that he gave it little thought.[88]

Although well aware of the "intrigue" and also warned by friends that he was in imminent danger of being arrested and taken to the Bastille, Necker still could not believe that the king would dismiss him. "It seemed to me morally impossible that the king should make such a decision, at a time when public opinion had given such a clear demonstration of its support for me, at a time when I was better able than anyone to restrain the impetuosity of the deputies of the Third Estate, and to compete with them for the support of public opinion; at a time when finally, by unheard of effort I had saved the country from bankruptcy and famine."[89]

Yet with a little imagination one can sympathize with the inclination of Louis XVI to yield to the alternate course. Certainly the statements coming from the radicals in the National Assembly, "the factious ones," were enough to exasperate even the mild disposition of this Bourbon king. The strength of the national movement was yet untested. No one could be cetain if it were limited to Paris and the National Assembly, or if it were equally strong throughout the kingdom. The extreme license of the press was a scandal that appalled foreign observers. As for the regular army units, perhaps if the king should take a strong stand against the movement in Paris he could overcome the tendency of soldiers to be influenced by it. If he did go to Compiègne and raise his standard against the National Assembly as Charles I did at Nottingham against the Long Parliament, perhaps the soldiers would have followed decisive leadership. If the nationalist movement proved stronger than anticipated, the king and his court could move to Metz, where the royal standard would be in close proximity to the lands of the Hapsburgs and the Empire and perhaps get important assistance from them. Probably these were ideas entertained by some of the ministers such as Breteuil who was appointed Necker's successor on July 11.

In retrospect it can be seen that such calculations were totally erroneous. The revolutionary movement in France attracted widespread sympathy and support throughout Europe at that time, especially among the intellectual classes. The other sovereigns in Europe showed little inclination to intervene in French affairs and bring to power those who enjoyed very little respect outside France. The Emperor Joseph advised the comte d'Artois after the October days of 1789 to return to France and accept the revolution, and to give up all thought of overthrowing it with the help of foreign troops.[90] Within France the forces of counter-revolution proved to be as weak as the national movement was unexpectedly strong. The envoy of Saxony agreed with most diplomatic observers that the dismissal of Necker was an act of unparalleled folly:

> The frivolity of the comte d'Artois has alone been the cause of all the misfortunes that have afflicted this country. . . . The personal hatred of the individuals who surround this unfortunate prince against Mr. Necker has been the reason for his dismissal, and it's to a cabal of 200 courtiers that one must attribute the subversion of the entire kingdom and the torrents of blood that at present are flowing from all parts (of the kingdom). It's this cabal which has fomented the obstinancy of the Nobility which, if it had followed from the beginning

the mediation proposed by the minister, would have reconciled all.[91]

On Saturday afternoon, July 11, Necker was preparing to sit down at dinner with Madame Necker, Madame de Staël, his brother, Louis Necker de Germany, along with the usual number of guests. At 3:00 p.m. the Secretary of State for the Navy, the comte de La Luzerne, entered and delivered to Necker a message at the table. It was from the king, telling him that he was relieved of his post in the ministry of finances, and requiring him to leave France as quickly and quietly as possible. He was to keep this message in absolute secrecy. Necker did not betray to the others the emotional impact this message had on him. He was not concerned about himself. Personally it was a great relief to let down the burden which had given him little joy since assuming it in August of the previous year. But he recognized at once the consequences for the king and for the nation. It meant either a violent popular revolution or a civil war. Either would be destructive of the kind of social and political order that he believed the nation wanted and which was best suited for it.[92]

After dinner Necker informed his wife of the king's message but no one else. They went for their usual drive after dinner, ostensibly to visit their friend the maréchale de Beauvau. Instead they went directly to their residence at Saint-Ouen to ask some faithful servants to accompany them, then drove to Saint-Denis where post-horses were hired. At midnight the Neckers left Saint-Denis for Brussels, under an assumed name and without passports, wearing the same clothing in which they had dined at Versailles. They were several hours from Paris before anyone, not even Madame de Staël, was aware of their departure. At the frontier Necker showed his letter from the king and was allowed to enter the Austrian Netherlands. At Brussels where the Neckers remained for two days, they

570

were joined by Ambassador and Madame de Staël. Necker continued on through Frankfort to Basel, on his way to Coppet, when, at Basel, he heard of the events at Paris. Some of the first refugees from the July revolution, among them his arch foe, Madame de Polignac, were staying at the same inn at Basel on July 20 when Necker arrived. From them he learned of the revolution of July 12-14 at Paris. And it was here that the courier caught up with Necker who had been sent with letters from both the king and the National Assembly begging him to return and resume his post as Director General of Finances.

It was shortly after noon on Sunday July 12 that the news of the dismissal and exile of Necker became known in Paris. Gradually news of the entire ministerial shake-up leaked out. Baron de Breteuil was named Necker's successor as de facto prime minister, holding the title of head of the Council of Finances, the position held formerly by Vergennes. Necker's close allies in the ministry, Montmorin and Saint-Priest, were also dismissed. Montmorin was replaced by La Vauguyon as foreign minister. La Luzerne and Puységur were not allies of Necker but were dismissed to make way for De la Porte at the Naval Department and Marshal de Broglie at the War Department. Barentin kept his position as Keeper of the Seals as did Laurent de Villedeuil as Secretary of State for the King's Household. Both had been strong adherents of the comte d'Artois. In fact all the new ministers as well as the two who remained in the government were known "hard-liners" who wanted to restore the king's authority. There is some evidence that Breteuil did not intend to strike at the States-General, but if so he made no pronouncement to that effect. No proclamation was published to the French people explaining the reasons for the ministerial shake-up or what policies the new ministry intended to pursue. The people were left to draw their own conclusions and that was that the

571

30,000-man army had not been assembled outside Paris for a peaceful exercise.

The person who commanded this army in the Paris area was no longer Broglie, who was now war minister, but his second in command, baron de Besenval. Late in the afternoon of July 12 he ordered a contingent of German cavalry numbering 100 men to occupy the Place Louis XV. Whether this was like the first move in a chess game, just to see what the other side will do, is not known. But the contingent of 100 horsemen attracted a crowd around the square, first just to stare at the troops then to throw rocks at them, or stones that had been piled up nearby for the construction of a bridge. The cavalry charged but the people were able to take refuge behind the rocks. Three of the cavalrymen were killed in the clash, and the commandant decided to withdraw to the main body of troops at the Champ de Mars. It was the first taste of victory for the crowds, and gave them the urge to find arms wherever possible. Gun shops, tool sheds, and private homes were ransacked. The French Guard units now joined the crowds, and soon there was added the units of citizen militia organized by the Assembly of Electors at the Hôtel-de-Ville. The battle was on, and during the next two days the crowds were to win a complete victory.

Meanwhile at Versailles when Bailly's successor as president of the National Assembly, the Archbishop of Vienne, Le Franc de Pompignan, learned of Necker's departure from the ministry he attempted to convene an extraordinary session of the assembly Sunday evening but could not get a quorum. The next morning all deputies were present at 6:00 a.m. Consternation and fear of what the ministerial shake-up meant was evident in all faces. "It was like a family that had lost its father," wrote Bailly in his memoirs. "Such was the opinion at that time about Mr. Necker. The destiny of the fatherland seemed to be bound up with his own."[93] It was a time of emotional and eloquent oratory. Mirabeau remained silent that day which belonged to those who admired Necker. The most memorable of these orations was delivered by Lally-Tollendal. He recalled the days of hope that followed the reunion of the orders on June 27, which has been cited above. "Then, after so many obstacles had been overcome, in the midst of hope as well as of great need, perfidious counsellors took from the most just of kings his most faithful servant, and from the nation the minister-citizen in whom it had placed its confidence." Then the orator referred to the violent libel campaign that had been launched against Necker about a month earlier. He asked who the calumniators were? It was a campaign whose authors were unknown. But what, he asked, were the accusations made against the nation's minister?

> In the absence of accusers I look for the
> crimes which they have denounced. This min-
> ister whom the king gave to his people, how
> could he have so suddenly become an object
> of aversion? What has he done in a year's
> time? We have just seen it, I have said it,
> I repeat it: when there was no money he
> paid us; when there was no bread he nour-
> ished us; when there was no more authority
> he quieted the rebels. I have heard him ac-
> cused in turn of undermining the throne and
> making the king a despot, of sacrificing the
> people to the nobility and the nobility to
> the people. I have seen in this accusation
> the usual fate of just and impartial men,
> and this double reproach seems to me a dou-
> ble hommage.[94]

After the oratory was over the deputies began to deliberate as to what the National Assembly should do in the circumstances. The reunion of the orders on June 27 had brought about a National Assembly that was preeminently moderate rather than radical. The assumption of moderate leaders was that the constitution they wanted to come out of the States-General already existed de facto. Therefore the National Assembly should conduct itself accordingly and not infringe on the executive powers of the king. This was of course in direct conflict with the radical view under the influence of abbé Sieyes in which there were no restrictions on the power of the assembly and certainly not by the king. It is doubtful if the majority of the deputies, even those belonging to the radical side, quite understood the implications of Sieyes' political principle.

The moderates were able to prevail in their view that the only recourse of the National Assembly was to send a petition and a deputation to the king. The archbishop of Vienne headed that deputation that took a message to the king later in the day of July 13. It pointed out the alarming situation in the kingdom, the danger of the movement in Paris spreading to other cities, the need to pacify Paris by sending away the foreign troops and allowing the formation of a bourgeois militia to maintain order. The National Assembly recognized that it was the king's prerogative to choose his ministers, "but the assembly cannot conceal that the change of ministers is the actual cause of the present misfortunes."[95]   Finally the assembly asked the king to agree to the above principles and allow a deputation from the assembly to go to Paris, announce the king's concessions and thereby attempt to appease the troubles.

The king's reply showed that he was still under the influence of his new advisors: "I have already made known my intentions and the measures which the disorders in Paris have forced me to take. It's for me to judge of their necessity, and in that respect I cannot make any change." He said Paris was too large a city to be entrusted to a bourgeois guard, and while he did not question "the purity of their motives," the presence of a deputation from the assembly to Paris would do no good; finally, he told them to get back to the business for which they had been summoned, to form the new constitution.[96]

In this stand-off between king and assembly it was events at Paris that shifted the balance to the assembly. Early in the morning of July 13 the tocsin pealed out from the parish churches in Paris which became the focal points for the district assemblies and the organization of the national guard. At the Hôtel-de-Ville the Assembly of Electors appointed a committee known as the "permanent committee" to govern the city in place of the former corporation of merchants. There was no resistance to this municipal revolution. French Guard units joined untrained citizens in the militia formations and gave them military instruction. Arming 48,000 citizen soldiers was not a simple matter. On July 13 the prison of Saint-Lazare was broken into by a crowd, the prisoners released, and the supply of grain stored there brought to the market place and sold. The "barrier" which was the customs boundary of the city manned by the General Farm to collect all duties on produce entering the city, was a special object of attack by the crowd, who pillaged the customs houses in search of grain and other produce subject to the duty known as "octrois" and which was an important source of revenue for the king. The next day, July 14, the popular forces attacked first the Invalides fortress which was taken without resistance, despite the presence of 5,000 troops under the command of Besenval a short distance away at the Champ de Mars. He believed that his troops were not reliable to attempt to quell the insurrection, and near the end of the day withdrew his troops to the pont de Sèvres, outside of the city, leaving it in the hands of the insurgents.[97] Late in the afternoon came the assault on the Bastille. Despite attempts of the military governor to negotiate with the new authorities at the

Hôtel-de-Ville, somehow when the drawbridge was lowered to receive the emmisaries of the Hôtel-de-Ville,
some shots were fired from the fortress killing four
in the crowd. The Parisians, now aroused to fury,
stormed the Bastille, took the military governor and
his deputy to the Place de Grève in front of the
Hôtel-de-Ville and decapitated them, mounting the
heads on pikes and parading them around the city as
trophies. Soon after the person who had been Provost
of the Merchants until the day before, Jacques de
Flesselles, was also beheaded by the crowd, who believed they had discovered in his seized correspondence some compromising letters.

When the National Assembly at Versailles learned
that the municipal revolution in Paris was increasing
in violence it sent another urgent petition to the
king, this one much longer and more insistent. The
National Assembly now declared that the ministers of
the government were criminally liable for any acts
contrary to the rights of the Nation and the decrees
of the National Assembly. The assembly affirmed once
again that it stood by its decrees of June 17, June
20, and June 23, and repeated that the government's
debt was under the guarantee of the nation. Finally
the declaration said that "Mr. Necker as well as the
other ministers who have been dismissed carry with
them the esteem and the regrets of the Assembly."[98]

Late in the evening of July 14 the vicomte de
Noailles returned from Paris and informed the assembly
that 200,000 men were under arms and that the Bastille
was under siege. A short time later a deputation from
the Assembly of Electors at the Hôtel-de-Ville came to
Versailles with the news of the fall of the Bastille.
The National Assembly was thoroughly alarmed by this
news. It believed that the king was probably not being informed of these events by his new advisors. At
11:00 p.m. the duc de Liancourt determined to see the
king and give him this information personally. A mem-

ber of the La Rochefoucauld family, a prominent phi-
lanthropist of the ancien régime, he had sufficient
moral authority to persuade the bodyguards to allow
him into the king's bedroom. This was the occasion
for his famous reply to the king's question after
hearing the news: "It's a revolt then?" "No, Sire,
it's a revolution."

What went on in the king's mind during the night,
and what conversation passed between himself and his
advisors and among the advisors themselves is almost a
blank page in the history of the Revolution. But according to the duc de Cars, baron de Breteuil urged
the king and the government to flee to Metz; the foreign minister, La Vauguyon also advised such a course.
But when Marshal de Broglie found that the king was
adamantly opposed to this step he declined to try to
change his mind. This according to de Cars, Broglie
later regretted, and both Breteuil and La Vauguyon
remained convinced in later years that such a move
would have saved the monarchy and crushed the Revolution.[99]

Of course it is impossible to say what might have
happened if the king had decided in favor of such a
move. But it is certain that this decision of Louis
XVI was a crucial event in the Revolution. Even if
resistance at Metz to the revolutionary movement had
collapsed rather soon the king and his queen would
have emigrated to friendly territory as did the comte
d'Artois. The latter must have tried to persuade the
king to go with him. Had he done so and openly taken
up arms against the National Assembly it is probable
that the latter would have named the duc d'Orleans
lieutenant-general of the kingdom and possibly the
successor to the throne. At worst, yielding to Breteuil's advice would have meant eventual abdication in
favor of Philippe d'Orleans and emigration; at best,
it would have meant civil war, the consequences of
which would be incalculable. The king's decision to

submit to the National Assembly, to walk from the château to the assembly hall on July 15 without escort, accompanied only by his two brothers, and then to place himself a day later under the power of the revolutionary régime at Paris was an act of great personal courage for which he has received little credit in the histories of the Revolution. His brother, the comte d'Artois, along with other princes of the blood and their advisors left Paris that night and escaped from the Revolution.

Meanwhile the National Assembly sent a deputation to Paris on July 15 to acquire exact information as to what happened. Lally-Tollendal was a member of the deputation. Upon returning to the assembly he reported that "there was a single cry at the Hôtel-de-Ville, in fact throughout the entire city for the dismissal of the ministry and for the return of the virtuous man who is now removed from the court after having served the country so well, namely, Mr. Necker."[100] Mirabeau offered a motion that the assembly address a memorial to the king calling for the dismissal of the unpopular ministers, but said nothing about Necker. His motion was immediately amended by others to call for the return of Necker, and this passed by an overwhelming vote, practically unanimously. When the king arrived at the assembly hall he agreed to the request and suggested that the National Assembly address a letter to accompany his own to Necker, requesting him to return to his post.

The unpopular ministers left the following day. Along with Necker, Montmorin, Saint-Priest, and La Luzerne were also recalled to the ministry. Only Montmorin was in Paris at the time, and for several days he and baron de Besenval were the only ones in the government to keep the king company. On July 16 the king, escorted by the deputies of the National Assembly and the National Guard of Paris, went to the capitol where he accepted the tricolor emblem of the

Revolution, given to him by Jean-Sylvain Bailly, the newly appointed mayor of Paris by the Assembly of Electors. On his progression to the Hôtel-de-Ville crowds lined the streets shouting "long live the Nation!" On his way back to Versailles the crowds shouted "long live the King and the Nation!" Jefferson wrote to John Jay on July 19 that "tranquility is now restored to the Capitol: the shops are again opened; the people resuming their labours, and if the want of bread does not disturb the peace, we may hope a continuance of it."[101]

Meanwhile the emissary entrusted with the two letters from the king and the National Assembly caught up with Necker at Basel on July 20, as already mentioned. The king's messages read:

> I had written you, Sir, that at a quieter time I would let you know of my good feelings toward you. However, the wishes of the States-General and of the city of Paris having been manifested, I undertake to hasten the moment of your return. I therefore invite you to come as soon as possible to resume your place by me. When you left you spoke of your devotion to me. There could be no greater proof of this in the present circumstances than heeding the request which I now make of you.[102]

Necker did not hesitate to reply and accede to the king's wishes. There was no struggle, no inner turmoil or indecisiveness about it. He could do no other than return to the king's side. But it was a violent change in the perspective that now opened before him. As stated previously, his dismissal was a personal relief, the lifting from him of a great burden. He and Madame Necker looked forward to the life of quiet retirement on the banks of Lake Geneva, at the barony and Château de Coppet. His true

579

feelings after receiving the letter from the king were probably most frankly expressed in a letter to his brother, Louis Necker de Germany, the same day:

> I was approaching the refuge and rejoiced. But this refuge would have been neither calm nor serene if I were to accuse myself of lacking in courage, and if it could be said or thought that I might have prevented this or that misfortune.
>
> I return, then, to France, but as a victim of the esteem with which I am honored. Madame Necker shares this feeling even more strongly, and our change in plans has been made with regret by both of us. Ah! Coppet, Coppet! Soon I may have good reason to regret thee! But one must submit to the laws of necessity, and the will of an inscrutable destiny. Everything is in movement in France. There has just been another outbreak of violent rebellion at Strassbourg. It seems to me that I am returning into a gulf. Adieu, my dear friend.[103]

[1]Correspondance secrète du comte de Mercy-Argenteau, II, 252.

[2]Ibid., 253.

[3]This is a conjecture on my part because unfortunately historians do not have a copy of the project Necker presented to the Council at Marly. He explained in his book on the French Revolution that he had left his copy in the hands of a friend, a woman whom he did not name, when he left Paris in September 1790 to return to Switzerland. When this friend had to leave precipitately to escape the Terror she burned the document, thinking it would be compromising. Necker wrote that he was certain that a copy would turn up which was in the king's possession at the time, and also copies were in the hands of the princes, the brothers of the king. Such a copy has not yet turned up. In 1955 at the time of the exposition at the Bibliothèque nationale of "Necker et Versailles" the historian Georges Lefebvre was permitted to search for this manuscript in the archives of the Château de Coppet and also in the documents kept at the Château de Broglie in Normandy. The lost document was not found, in fact one brief letter to the king by Necker was the only document found relating to this period of the States-General. Necker, "De la Révolution française," in Oeuvres complètes, IX, 180-182; Lefebvre, Recueil de documents, I, part 2, La Séance de juin 23 , 61, n. 98.

[4]Vicomte de Grouchy et Antoine Guillois, eds., La Révolution française racontée par un Diplomate étranger (Paris, 1903), 99-100.

[5]Creuzé-Latouche, Journal, 146.

[6]Aulard, ed., _Lettres et bulletins de Barentin_, 24.

[7]Creuzé-Latouche, _Journal_, 152; Francisque Mège, _Gaultier de Biauzet_, 139.

[8]Duquesnoy, _Journal_, 127.

[9]_Ibid._, 128-129.

[10]Lally-Tollendal, _Mémoires, ou Second Lettre_, 41.

[11]Bailly, _Mémoires_, I, 240.

[12]Mège, _Gaultier de Biauzet_, 142.

[13]Bailly, _Mémoires_, I, 239.

[14]Creuzé-Latouche, _Journal_, 159.

[15]_Ibid._, 134-135.

[16]Bailly, _Mémoires_, I, 249.

[17]Duquesnoy, _Journal_, I, 139.

[18]Creuzé-Latouche, _Journal_, 165.

[19]Bailly, _Mémoires_, I, 255.

[20]_Ibid._, 274.

[21]Aulard, ed., _Lettres et bulletins de Barentin à Louis XVI_, 57.

[22]_Correspondance diplomatique_, 152.

[23]Aulard, _Lettres et bulletins de Barentin à Louis XVI_.

[24]Creuzé-Latouche, _Journal_, 166.

[25]Duquesnoy, Journal, I, 130.

[26]Ibid., 131.

[27]Ibid., 134.

[28]Ibid., 143.

[29]Jean-Louis Virieu, La Révolution française racontée par un diplomate étranger, 105.

[30]Duquesnoy, Journal, I, 139.

[31]Mounier, Recherches sur les causes, II, 8.

[32]Duquesnoy, Journal, I, 149.

[33]Lally-Tollendal, Mémoires, ou Second Lettre, 76.

[34]Georgia Hooks Shurr, "Thomas Jefferson and the French Revolution," The American Society of the Legion of Honor Magazine (1979), I(3), 161-182.

[35]Daniel Ligou, La première année de la Révolution, 37.

[36]Dumont, Souvenirs sur Mirabeau.

[37]Ligou, La première année de la Révolution, 37.

[38]Chassin, Les Elections et les cahiers de Paris, III, 425-426.

[39]"Sur l'Administration de M. Necker," in Oeuvres complètes, VI, 306.

[40]Chassin, Les Elections, II, 547-549.

[41]"De l'Administration de M. Necker," in Oeuvres complètes, VI, 314.

[42] Ibid., 299-301.

[43] Arthur Young, Travels in France, 154.

[44] Creuzé-Latouche, Journal, 191.

[45] Archives parlementaires, VIII, 197.

[46] Creuzé-Latouche, Journal, 188-189.

[47] Duquesnoy, Journal, I, 163.

[48] Papers of Thomas Jefferson, XV, 284-285.

[49] Archives parlementaires, VIII, 208.

[50] Bailly, Mémoires, I, 303.

[51] Ibid., 288-289.

[52] Ibid., 295.

[53] The bookseller Hardy seemed to be susceptible to all sorts of rumors. He wrote in his Journal on May 12: "One hears of nothing but uprisings and insurrections in different cities of the kingdom, toward which the government is obliged to send detachments of troops. Everywhere the pretext is the high price of grain, which is continuing to be monopolized by tactics as inconceivable as they are criminal and reprehensible." Quoted in Chassin, Les Elections et les cahiers de Paris, III, 413.

[54] Paul Boiteau, Etat de France en 1789 (Paris, 1860), 238-240.

[55] Collection des édits, déclarations et arrêts du Conseil d'état, BN F. 23631 (321).

[56] Brette, La Révolution française, XXIII, 532.

[57] Archives parlementaires , VIII, 136.

[58] Duquesnoy, Journal, I, July 6, 1789.

[59] "De l'Administration de M. Necker," in Oeuvres complètes, VI, 310.

[60] Histoire financière de la France, I, 429-431.

[61] Mémoires du baron de Besenval, II, 342-343.

[62] Quoted in Chassin, Les Elections et les cahiers de Paris en 1789, III, 449-450.

[63] Ibid., III, 458.

[64] Bailly, Mémoires, I, 264-267.

[65] Mège, Gaultier de Biauzet, 153.

[66] Bailly, Mémoires, I, 270.

[67] Mège, 162.

[68] Bailly, Mémoires, I, 313.

[69] Chassin, Les Elections et les cahier de Paris, III, 445.

[70] Bailly, Mémoires, I, 320-321.

[71] Correspondence of Salmour, envoy of Saxony, in Jules Flammermont, Les Correspondances des agents diplomatique étrangers en France avant la Révolution (Paris, 1896), 232.

[72] Jacques Godechot, La Prise de la Bastille (Paris, 1965), 267-268.

[73] Papers of Thomas Jefferson, XV, 267-268.

[74] Jean-Joseph Mounier, _Exposé de la conduite de M. Mounier dans l'Assemblée nationale et des motifs de son retour en Dauphiné_ (Paris, 1789).

[75] Clermont-Gallerande, _Mémoires particuliers_, I, 98.

[76] J. F. Pérusse, duc de Cars, _Mémoires_ (Paris, 1890), I, 67.

[77] Flammermont, _Les Correspondances des agents diplomatique_, 232.

[78] Charles-Henri, baron de Gleichen, _Souvenirs_ (Paris, 1868), 63.

[79] Godechot, _La Prise de la Bastille_, 232.

[80] _Mémoires de Marquis de Ferrières_ (2nd ed., Paris, 1822), I, 89.

[81] Brette, _La Révolution française_, XXIV, 169.

[82] Godechot, _La Prise de la Bastille_, 225.

[83] Bailly, _Mémoires_, I, 302.

[84] "De la Révolution française," in _Oeuvres complètes_, IX, 225.

[85] _Papers of Thomas Jefferson_, XV, 285.

[86] _Correspondance diplomatique_, 105.

[87] _Loc. cit._

[88] "De la Révolution française," in _Oeuvres complètes_, IX, 227.

[89] _Ibid._, 225.

[90] Mercy-Argenteau, _Correspondence secrète_, I, 279.

[91]Flammermont, _Les Correspondances des agents diplomatiques_, 237.

[92]"Sur l'Administration de M. Necker," in _Oeuvres complètes_, VI, 98-99.

[93]Bailly, _Mémoires_, I, 332.

[94]Lally-Tollendal, _Mémoires ou Second Lettre à ses commettants_, 77.

[95]Bailly, _Mémoires_, I, 338-339.

[96]Letters of Tronchin to the Genevan government in Edouard Chapuisat, _Jacques Necker_, annex VII, 306-309.

[97]_Mémoires de Besenval_, II, 363.

[98]Chapuisat, _op. cit._, 309.

[99]Duc de Cars, _Mémoires_, II, 82.

[100]_Archives parlementaires_, VIII, 240.

[101]_Papers of Thomas Jefferson_, XV, 290.

[102]"De la Révolution française," in _Oeuvres complètes_, IX, 236.

[103]Vicomte d'Haussonville, "Le Salon de Madame Necker," _Revue des Deux Mondes_ (1881), 43(1), 76.

CHAPTER 16

THE STRUGGLE FOR LIBERTY AND ORDER

On July 30 the resident-minister of Geneva at
Paris wrote that "the day before yesterday, at 10:30
a.m., our illustrious compatriot arrived at Versailles, and in good health. His voyage from Basel
was a continous triumph, and the most moving homage
was given to virtue and great merit; at each step of
the journey there was a renewal of the most touching
scenes, all the way to Versailles."[1] As he traveled
through towns in eastern France citizens not only
lined the streets to cheer as his carriage passed
through, they unhitched the horses and personally drew
the vehicle carrying Necker, his wife and Madame de
Staël. The latter was once again ecstatic about the
homage paid her father, and literally swooned with joy
at the Hôtel-de-Ville at Paris on July 30 when Necker
succeeded in getting the Assembly of Electors to grant
an anmesty to all suspected of acts of lèse-nation,
and which was accompanied by thunderous approval of
Parisians who filled the Place de Grève where Necker
addressed them. The tremendous enthusiasm of the
crowds who cheered Necker along the way from Basel to
Versailles was unprecedented for a ministry of the
king.

While he certainly must have been strongly moved
by these demonstrations of affection from the populace
Necker was not so ecstatic about them as his daughter.
Once again, as in August 1788 he was more conscious of
the tremendous responsibility he had undertaken. As
he traveled through eastern France he received more
and more information about the mentality of the population and the real meaning of July 14. Reports
reached him of acts of violence against individuals
who were obviously innocent of any conduct that could

589

reasonably provoke such acts. The population was extraordinarily aroused and was susceptible to a variety of false rumors. Those suspected of monopolizing grain were among the victims, since the threat of famine was ever present, particularly at Paris and the surrounding regions. Individuals who had been appointed to the ministry after the dismissal of Necker were most in jeopardy. There was a fear of another such attempt to crush the revolution. All nobles and prelates came under suspicion. The cry "war on the aristocrats" began to ring out and set crowds in motion. In its lack of discrimination and in its unreality it resembled the cry "death to Jews" that rang out a century later. And in this summer of 1789 there were anti-semitic riots in Alsace. Particularly suspect were the British, whom it was thought were about to take advantage of the weakness of their traditional rival and invade France, despite the efforts of the British ambassador to point out the absurdity of such suspicions.[2]

While the need to maintain order was obvious the government was deprived of the means to enforce it. The events of July 11-14 had revealed the impotence of the royal government when it attempted to act against the national movement. At Paris a revolutionary city-government had replaced the corps of merchants and aldermen that traditionally ruled the city. A "permanent committee" appointed by the Electoral Assembly was now in control, which had appointed the mayor and the commander of the bourgeois militia without any regard for the royal government. In fact the mayor, Jean-Sylvain Bailly, had to promise the "permanent committee" that he would not attempt to get the king's sanction for his appointment. The command of the citizen militia, a force of 48,000 bourgeois, was given to the marquis de Lafayette, and was also independent of royal sanction. The same pattern of Paris was repeated in other major French cities throughout the country. The troops of the line, the regular professional army, had shown that they could not be relied upon to enforce the king's will against the national movement. Before July 14 the king had some means for inspiring respect and fear because his actual physical power was an unknown quantity. Because of the attempt to use military force against the revolutionary movement, Louis XVI had revealed to all the world that he had no force.[3]

In these circumstances Necker saw that his most important task was to restore that moral authority of the king in the public mind. His explanation of why that authority had been lost is an important part of Necker's political thinking. He was aware that some would draw the conclusion that the loss of royal authority was due to a failure of nerve, a reluctance to use armed force to overcome a movement that was clearly subversive. Necker drew just the opposite conclusion from the events of the past two years. It was "inconsiderate acts of authority" that had eroded and finally depleted the royal power. The dismissal of the Assembly of Notables in 1787, the exile of the Parlement of Paris later, the royal session of November 1787, the May edicts of 1788, the Royal Session of June 23, 1789, and finally the movement of troops around Paris and the dismissal of ministers who obviously had the confidence of the nation in July, these were the "causes" of the revolution of 1789, not the refusal to administer "whiffs of grapeshot."

How did he think he could recover that authority of the monarchy that had been so badly shattered by an aroused and alienated public? The first thing, obviously, was to avoid the mistakes of the past: no more "inconsiderate acts of authority." "A policy of prudence," he wrote later, "one without fault could alone achieve that goal and restore to the government the influence and prestige it had lost."[4] Necker shared the basic idea of later nineteenth-century liberalism: People can only be ruled by persuasion, by moral ideas

591

and by reason, not by bayonets. He believed that the majority of those who made up the "public opinion" of that day were reasonable and would give their support to policies that were just and moral. Like his contemporary, Jefferson, whom he resembled in little else, Necker's view of the future was basically optimistic and his faith in humankind was strong. He believed that virtue and reason would prevail over ignorance and fanaticism.

These principles explain his conduct throughout his political career, but at no time so much as at the beginning of his third ministry in July 1789. Popular fury had been unleashed by the government's "inconsiderate acts of authority." While Necker's policy was based upon reason and persuasion it was not lacking in firmness and stamina in opposing unreason. On his way back to Versailles from Basel whenever he spoke to crowds he strongly remonstrated against acts of violence being committed throughout the country against the innocent and the defenseless.

Most of those who had been appointed to posts in the short-lived ministry of Breteuil had sought to escape from Paris and Versailles or to go into hiding. There seemed to be a strong thirst in the populace to punish those who had taken part in what came to be called "the great conspiracy." Baron de Besenval who had been given command of the troops in the Paris region by the Secretary of War, Marshal de Broglie, resigned his command on July 16, as did all the new appointees. But he remained for a time with the king in the château at Versailles. When it became evident that his life was in danger he was given a letter of safe-conduct, a passport, by the king to return to his native Switzerland. A short distance from Paris he was recognized, despite his disguise, by local authorities and arrested. It was characteristic of the time that every small town came under the rule of local committees staffed by ardent patriots, who ruled in conjunction with the local bourgeois militia. As happens with those who suddenly find themselves pushed from lowly stations of life into positions of power, these citizens did not take an humble view of their authority and responsibility, as Arthur Young discovered on his "travels" during that revolutionary year. They did not think the king's passport prevented them from investigating a person on their own authority and they sent word to the Paris city government that they had arrested Besenval and asked for further instructions. It was fairly certain that had he been sent to Paris under armed guard the city authorities would not have been able to save Besenval from the same fate that befell the commandant of the Bastille. As his party was passing through the town of Nogent a short distance from where Besenval was being detained, Necker learned about the arrest from a local landed nobleman who was not acquainted with Besenval but knew that his life was at stake. Necker wrote a message to the municipal officers and entrusted the local nobleman to deliver it. "I know positively, gentlemen," Necker told them, "that the baron de Besenval, arrested by the militia at Villenaux, had the permission of the king to go to Switzerland; I earnestly ask you, gentlemen, to respect this safe-conduct, for which I will be your surety."[5] The municipal officers did not release their prisoner as Necker requested, but again asked the Paris city government for instructions.

It was soon after this incident on his journey from Basel that Necker arrived in Versailles, as related by Tronchin in his dispatch to the government of Geneva. When the National Assembly learned of his arrival the deputies asked for him to appear in the hall, according to Tronchin it was an emotional scene. "His entrance into the Assembly was greeted by the most lively applause and continued for some time."[6] Necker was so overwhelmed by this reception that he found it difficult to speak in his ordinarily powerful voice, and not everyone could hear the words as

recorded by the Moniteur: "Mr. President, I have has-
tened to come to this august Assembly in order to show
my respectful acknowledgment of the kindness and the
interest which it has shown me. It places upon me
great duties, and it is by sharing in its sentiments
and profiting by its wisdom that, in the midst of such
difficult circumstances, I will preserve some
courage."[7] He was then conducted to the chair opposite the president of the assembly, the duc de Liancourt, who made a prolonged eulogy of the returned
minister of the nation. "This eulogy," wrote
Tronchin, "was interrupted three times by unanimous
applause, and what is most remarkable is that upon his
leaving, by a spontaneous movement the entire assembly
stood at once, an honor that no person has ever received in this august assembly."

The following day, July 30, the Hôtel-de-Ville at
Paris also asked Necker to appear before them, both
the Assembly of Electors and the newly appointed Representatives of the Commune. Necker did so and on
this day he recovered his voice. His procession
through the streets of Paris to the Hôtel-de-Ville was
the crowning point of his homecoming. "The entire
population of Paris," wrote Madame de Staël, perhaps
with some exaggeration, "crowded into the streets, men
and women were seen at windows and on roof tops crying
'Vive M. Necker!'"[8] A crowd that she estimated at
about 200,000 poured into the Place de Grève in front
of the Hôtel-de-Ville to hear Necker speak.[9] Lally-
Tollendal wrote that about 40,000 people crowded into
the Place de Grève, which seems a more realistic figure.[10] He spoke first to the Assembly of Representatives of the Commune who had been sent to the Hôtel-
de-Ville by the sixty district assemblies of the Third
Estate of Paris, and next he entered the more numerous
Assembly of Electors who still sat in the Grande Salle
assigned to it and which this day was overflowing with
visitors. Then Necker appeared on the balcony of the

Hôtel-de-Ville to speak to the enormous throng below.
To all three audiences he gave the same message:

> Gentlemen, the king has received me with the
> greatest kindness and has assured me of his
> complete confidence. But today, gentlemen,
> the salvation of the state lies in the hands
> of the National Assembly and in yours, be-
> cause at this moment hardly any power re-
> mains in the government. It is to you, gen-
> tlemen, who can do so much both because of
> the importance of this city of which you are
> the leaders and because of the influence of
> your example throughout the rest of the
> kingdom that I call upon to devote your
> greatest care to the establishment of order
> that will be most perfect and durable.
> Nothing can flourish, nothing can prosper
> without this order; and what you have al-
> ready done, gentlemen, in so short a time,
> is the sign of what you can do; but until
> that objective is reached confidence will
> remain uncertain, a pervasive insecurity
> will trouble civic peace, and keep from
> Paris a great number of wealthy consumers,
> and prevent foreigners coming to spend their
> wealth.[11]

Only with the return of peace, said Necker, would
Paris recover its prosperity and its splendor as the
preeminent city of Europe. But there must be an end
to the proscriptions and violent scenes which have
tarnished the city in recent days. He called upon
Parisians to cast a veil of forgetfulness over the
past, to grant a general amnesty to all who might be
suspected of acts contrary to good citizenship. "Ah!
allow your good fortune to become even greater by remaining pure and unstained; above all, preserve and
honor, even in moments of crisis and calamity, that
character of kindness, justice and gentleness that has

always distinguished the French nation." Then he related the incident of the detention of baron de Besenval, and read the letter he had written to the militia leaders asking for his release and permitting him to go to Switzerland. The officials had not complied with this request, Necker said, and he now asked the municipal government of Paris to do so, as well as to pass a general act of amnesty that would bring an end to all arbitrary arrests for suspicion of the crime of lèse nation.[12]

Stanislas de Clermont-Tonnerre accompanied Necker on this visit to the Hôtel-de-Ville and wrote later in his memoirs: "I was struck by his reasoning, moved by his passion, transported by his eloquence, as was the entire assembly."[13] Clermont-Tonnerre followed Necker by delivering a powerful seconding speech, and formally made the motion in the Assembly of Electors to agree to Necker's pleas. The Declaration of the General Assembly of Electors, passed on July 30, stated that the city of Paris "granted a pardon to all its enemies, proscribed all acts of violence contrary to the present decree, and henceforth considers as enemies of the nation only those who disturb the public peace."[14] The decree was greeted with the same enthusiasm as Necker's speeches calling for it. It was published and posted in all streets and sent to other municipalities. Most gratifying to Necker was the thunderous approval given to his speech and the decree of amnesty by the crowd in the Place de Grève. In later years Necker thought this was the greatest moment of his career. "Ah! how happy I was that day! Every instant is engraved in my memory, and even today I cannot recall them without emotion. I had obtained the return of peace, and with no other means than the language of virtue and reason."[15]

Alas, his triumph was only for a day. That evening certain district assemblies of the city, influenced by Mirabeau, protested both the releasing of

Besenval and the declaration of amnesty. A timid Assembly of Electors revised its Declaration accordingly. It stated that it did not intend to let all enemies of the nation go scot free, but only that they should be judged according to law and not by popular passion. Baron de Besenval was to be kept in prison pending his trial, and protected from mob violence. The greatest disappointment for Necker was that the National Assembly adopted this revision of the Hôtel-de-Ville. Stanislas de Clermont-Tonnerre was as devastated as Necker by this turn of events, and wrote in his memoirs that Necker should have resigned rather than to acquiesce in it. It appeared to Clermont-Tonnerre that fear alone caused this retreat from the principles that Necker had expounded so eloquently the day before, fear of the popular forces, and of being implicated in the charge of lèse nation.[16]

But others criticized Necker from the opposite standpoint, for making a political blunder of the gravest consequences. Bailly, the mayor of Paris, when he heard of Necker's plan to ask for the release of Besenval and for a general amnesty, tried in vain to change his mind. It seemed to Bailly that Necker had been out of the country since the gigantic upheaval and was simply not well informed about the situation. A prudent policy would have been to adopt those principles in the revision of the Hôtel-de-Ville's declaration. By calling for a total amnesty Necker was naively playing into the hands of his great antagonist, the politically astute Tribune of the People. And it is sad to relate that this was the beginning of Necker's decline in popular favor. "From that day forward," wrote Madame de Staël, "began the reverse of his destiny."[17] Most painful of all was the steady deterioration of his relations with the National Assembly. Hardly more than a year passed from that day in July 1789, when the assembly gave him a standing ovation to the day in September 1790 when he told the assembly that for reasons of health he was

compelled to lay down his burden. There was not a
stir in the assembly, no mark of regret or sympathy,
only silence. Nothing could have been more wounding
to a person who believed that he had served the nation
with the greatest devotion, and without any thought of
his own advantage. His enemies had claimed that
vainglory was his dominant passion. But there was
none of it in his second and third ministries, no
exhilarating feeling of success which he had
experienced in his first ministry, nothing but
frustration, intense hard work, the shouldering of
enormous responsibilities, and not even a thank-you at
the end!

On several crucial issues Necker had demonstrated
that he was flexible, and could change his course if
he felt that "the circumstances" and the state of public opinion required it. But those were issues that
did not involve morality, or at least not so clearly.
Whether or not to grant the doublement, or to make
more concessions to the peasants on the matter of feudal rights, or to the workers' demand for government
regulation of the grain trade, all were clearly distinct from the issue of the violation of individual
rights to life and property. To compromise on those
issues would be like yielding to blackmail. As for
the revision of the Declaration of the Hôtel-de-Ville
on July 31, Necker's thinking was no doubt similar to
that of Jean-Joseph Mounier on the same subject. It
was not enough to see that a person was given a fair
trial, he must also be assured of not being arrested
in the first place without cause. In a speech he made
in the National Assembly Mounier asked "if it could be
permitted to arrest and imprison a person unless he is
taken actually committing a crime, or sufficient evi-
dences exists to make advisable his arrest. . . . Public clamor can only authorize arrest if he is seen to
commit the crime. But if by public clamor you mean
vague suspicions, popular rumors, what citizen could

depend upon that public and personal liberty we are summoned to defend."[18]

It was ironical that the individual whose case Necker took up with such passion at the Hôtel-de-Ville on July 30 was Besenval. No one was less sympathetic and less capable of understanding Necker's reform policies than this professional army officer who was an habitué of the circle of the Polignacs, the Vaudreuils, and the princes of the blood who were aggrieved at Necker because his reforms were adverse to their particular interests. Narrow in his outlook on public affairs (he believed sincerely that the English were fomenting the troubles in France in 1789), having no appreciation of the need to establish public control over the royal finances (he believed that the Committee of Finance set up by Vergennes and Joly de Fleury in March 1783 was nothing but a base intrigue to cause the ouster of both Castries and Ségur from the ministry), Besenval saw everything through the eyes of the courtier.[19] But his conduct on July 13 and 14 showed more political sense than might have been expected. He realized that the troops under his command were not sufficiently reliable to attempt to crush the revolution, and withdrew them to the Pont de Sèvres, leaving the city in the hands of insurgents. After July 31, he was kept in a safe prison outside Paris until his trial in late 1790, in which he was acquitted of all charges brought against him. As for Necker, Besenval wrote in his memoirs: "I know only one thing: Mr. Necker saved my life. Without changing my opinions on his political operations and his errors, I owe him gratitude and loyalty to my dying day."[20]

That Necker should have resigned from the government after the repudiation of his plea for amnesty and the freedom of Besenval, as Clermont-Tonnerre thought, was morally impossible so soon after his triumphal return to Versailles. Furthermore, his efforts were not totally lost, as the eventual survival of Besenval demonstrates. In the struggle against the forces of disintegration, against the radicals and the "factious ones" a battle had been lost but not necessarily the war. Necker always regretted his resignation from the first ministry in May 1781. The situation that had seemed intolerable at the time changed in a few months with the death of the comte de Maurepas, and had he been more patient, less prideful he would have been the successor of the Mentor. Now, at the end of July 1789, Necker still believed it was possible to steer the revolution on to the course which he thought was the national will since the beginning of the troubles in 1787.

The most crucial matter in Necker's third ministry (as it is called since his return to Versailles on July 28) was his relations with the National Assembly. The upheaval in Paris on July 13-14 seemed at first to have strengthened the moderate forces in the assembly. The resentment of the nobles and prelates who felt they had been forced to join the assembly on June 27 had almost disappeared in the crucible of the July days. The leader of the majority of the nobles who joined the assembly on that day, the duc de Liancourt, was elected president of the National Assembly on July 18. Several measures passed by the assembly indicated such a temper: the seating of Malouet, whose credentials were questioned by the radicals of the assembly because he had been sent by his constituents at Riom by "acclamation" rather than by a regular vote; and the concern of the assembly to preserve the separation of powers and the independence of the executive authority. As Mounier wrote, "after the 23rd of June the noble deputies in most of the kingdom had received permission from their constituents to vote in a common assembly, and those which had not yet obtained that permission declared on July 16 that they believed themselves authorized to vote, persuaded that they were only anticipating the wishes of their constituents."[21] The second letter that the National Assembly sent to the king on July 14 reaffirmed the resolutions of June 17, 20, and 23, and this letter was voted upon by the Clergy and the Nobility who had joined the assembly on June 27. Only the duc de Praslin said he still felt bound by his oath and could not approve the act of June 17. But after the letter was approved by the assembly by acclamation even he got up to say that he was "speaking only from his mandate, but that he personally felt like the rest of the assembly."[22] Thus by the revolution at Paris in the July days the States-General ceased to exist and became definitively the National Assembly.

It remained to be seen whether the National Assembly would become the Constituent Assembly as defined by abbé Sieyes or whether it would be succeeded by a liberal regime based upon British and American political institutions and experience. Necker clearly favored the latter. He rarely referred to specific individuals but it certainly must have been the system of abbé Sieyes that he had in mind when he told the States-General on May 5: "You will dismiss all exaggerated schemes, you will repel all reveries, you will distrust ideas too audacious, you will not believe that the future can have no connection with the past." On July 21 Sieyes got the National Assembly to include his proposed constitution as an annex of the minutes. It stated that "all public powers without exception are an emanation of the general will, all come from the people, that is to say, the Nation. The two terms are synonymous."[23] Although Mirabeau had abstained from voting on June 17 he took up the ideas of abbé Sieyes after the Royal Session of June 23 with his usual ebullience. In a debate with Mounier on July 16, Mirabeau objected to the idea of the separation of powers, of the independence of the executive, legislative, and judicial functions from each other. That scheme, said Mirabeau, in reality was hatched by the aristocrats in order to continue their domination of

601

the legislature. But their plot had been foiled by the events of July 14. "The head of the Nation overcame the aristocratic legislature by a simple appeal to the people, to the people who can never have but a single interest, because public well-being is essentially their own. Their representatives, armed with an invisible power and almost a veritable dictatorship when it is the organ of the general will, would only be impotent pigmies if there could be substituted for their sacred mission the passions of particular interests."[24] This tended to raise the somewhat secular ideas of the abbé to the mystical realm of divine right. But Mirabeau was no more consistent in his political philosophy than in other matters. He opposed Necker's loan of 30 million livres early in August because the mandates of the deputies had stated that no loans or taxes could be approved by the assembly until the constitution had been formed, this despite his own earlier disavowal of the binding nature of the mandates and that the National Assembly had set aside all imperative mandates on July 16. Essentially Mirabeau's political philosophy could be summed up by adding to Sieyes' assertation that "the terms Nation and People are synonymous" one additional term, namely, Mirabeau.

During the second half of July and throughout August and September the great issue was thrashed out between those called somewhat contemptuously "Anglophiles" by their opponents, who in turn were called with equal partisanship "the factious ones." At the beginning of this period few outside observers would have thought the latter would triumph at the end of the "October days," (October 5-6, 1789). Jefferson was keenly interested in the shape of the constitution that would emerge from this struggle. He had been invited by the chairman of the Constitution Committee, Champion de Cicé, to attend a meeting on July 22 to give his ideas on the subject. Later, on August 3, he wrote to Diodati that "the National Assembly have now

602

as clean a canvas to work on here as we had in America
. . . As far as I can collect from conversation with
their members, the constitution they will propose will
resemble that of England in its outlines, but not in
its defects."[25] The constitution that Jefferson went
on to describe in this letter matched rather closely
Necker's hopes. The king would be "possessed completely of executive powers, and particularly the public force." Representation in the national parliament
would be equal and not based on traditional orders.
Whether it would be a single house or a two-house legislature "could not as yet be foreseen." The parliament would assemble periodically without requiring the
consent of the king. "There is a difference of opinion whether the king shall have an absolute or only a
qualified Negative . . ." Jefferson ended this letter
on an optimistic note. "I will agree to be stoned as
a false prophet if all does not end well in this country. Nor will it end with this country. Here is but
the first chapter of the history of European liberty."

He was not a false prophet in the long run. But
for the short run he must have regretted that statement. For the "factious ones" triumphed over those
who wanted the kind of constitution Jefferson had described to Diodati. This was the greatest defeat of
Necker's political career. He attributed it to a single cause, the breakdown of public order, which was in
turn due to the eclipse of the executive power of the
royal government. With the population in turmoil,
with the old institutions no longer respected but new
ones not yet established; with the prevotal courts no
longer able to punish crimes, with tax revenue falling
off sharply because the people understood that the old
fiscal system was unjust but did not realize that they
must continue to pay the old taxes until new sources
of revenue could be implemented by new departmental
administrations; finally, with local committees of
citizens and militia assuming powers to arrest anyone
they chose, to disrupt the free flow of commerce, and

603

particularly grain shipments passing through their ill-defined jurisdiction, the old regime simply broke down before a new one could be established.

The National Assembly was in an anomalous position. Called by the king to enact a constitution and legislative laws, it had also to attempt to administer the country because of the collapse of royal authority. But the breakdown of order made it impossible for the National Assembly to deliberate calmly on the constitution because it was constantly preoccupied with manifold crises from without. As Necker and the moderates or "anglophiles" saw it, the main task was to get the populace quieted down so that order could be restored, the subsistence crisis met, the economy operating again so that regular sources of revenue could once more flow to the government to finance the armed forces, the administration, and also to guarantee the government's obligations toward its creditors, for this was one source of the unrest.

Instead of trying to calm the excited populace, the "factious ones" exerted themselves to the utmost to keep it stirred up. Popular orators competed with each other to fan the flames. A press of shameless violence and mendacity attacked ministers of integrity who were valiantly striving to cope with the crisis. And at the National Assembly the efforts of those who attempted in good faith to use the influence of the assembly to help the ministers were thwarted by those who wanted to keep the populace riled up until they had achieved their aims, which they eventually did with that "dictatorship of the people" that Mirabeau proclaimed as the great goal of the revolution.

What was of immediate concern to the most responsible leader in the National Assembly after July 14 was the continued fury of the certain strata in the population. This impulse to kill immediately those that incurred hostility was a concern to the new sources of authority that appeared in the towns and cities. It was not just the "aristocrats" who were alarmed by this popular temper but many bourgeois as well who had risen to places of authority in the citizen committees and the militia. Savage as the spectacles were in which individuals were hanged, decapitated, and heads placed on poles like trophies, there was surprisingly little disorder of any other sort. Jefferson was able to walk in the streets of Paris alone after July 14 and felt no apprehension about his personal safety. He thought that Paris had got through her revolution rather well, and he hoped that the rest of the country could do likewise. There was no looting of property, and the personal possessions of the victims were scrupulously given to the authorites or the relatives. It was a reign of terror that seemed to be well organized and disciplined.

But there was no slackening of this impulse to kill. Two hussar soldiers were taken by the crowd in Versailles right at the door of the National Assembly, and it required the most insistent pleas of the deputies to get them released. In the area of Poissy and Saint-Germain-en-Laye a miller named Sauvage was suspected of monopolizing flour and was summarily decapitated. A similar fate was about to fall on a certain farmer named Thomassin, but the municipal officials and some prominent inhabitants of Poissy managed to save him temporarily, until a deputation from the National Assembly led by the Bishop of Chartres arrived. Even so it required all the persuasion they could muster to prevent the violent death of Thomassin, who was taken back to Versailles in the carriage of the bishop.

These events prompted Lally-Tollendal on July 20 to propose that the National Assembly publish a proclamation to the nation calling for an end to disorder, explaining that the king had dismissed the unpopular ministers, and that there was no reason for

605

the continuation of the sort of activity that had led to the fall of the Bastille. In addition, his proclamation would grant the authority of the National Assembly to establish citizen-guard units in other cities similar to what had been done in Paris. Lally's proposal was applauded by the assembly and he supposed it would be enthusiastically endorsed. "But what was my surprise," he wrote later in his memoirs, "when I saw a group rise up to resist it, and to maintain their opposition for three days with the greatest determination."[26]

What was most surprising, and exasperating, were the arguments that these opponents brought against his proposal. Some said that Lally was exaggerating the seriousness of the violence. "Its all eloquence," said one deputy, "how can you speak of troubles in the provinces when the most perfect tranquility reigns."[27] Others maintained that this violence was salutary, just as that which had led to the fall of the Bastille, and that the forces of despotism were far from being defeated. These acts that Lally called barbarous were carried out for the cause of liberty. Robespierre said "we must love peace, but we must also love liberty. Let us examine the motion of Mr. Lally. There is in it a bias against those who are defending liberty. But is there anything more legitimate than rising up against a horrible conspiracy to destroy the nation? Let us not do anything hastily. How do we know that the enemies of the state are not still plotting against it?"[28] To Lally-Tollendal this was not only sophistry but blasphemy: "When it comes to liberty," he cried, "It's myself who is defending it. It is you who are undermining it. Remember that it is always fanatical zeal that turns people from the faith, and in the kind of sacerdotal robes we are clothed in, let us not blaspheme this holy liberty when we have been sent here to found its cult and proclaim its gospel."[29] As for the argument that he was exaggerating the scope of the violence, he replied:

606

They want us to keep calm when a conflagra-
tion is reaching all the provinces, where in
Brittany citizens are everywhere in arms;
where in Normandy streams of blood are flow-
ing; where in Burgundy the people have committed the gravest excesses, pursuing the
commandant, a respectable man, as a traitor
and a criminal; where the innocent are ex-
piring due to public hatred. And on the
other hand, we are to remain alarmed when
the troops have been sent away, when the
perfidious ministers have been banished from
the king's presence, and the faithful minister who enjoys the complete confidence of
the nation is recalled. I fail to see how
so much security can justify so much terror.[30]

It was a bitter disappointment for Lally that his
proposal was sent to a committee for further study,
which in effect meant shelving it. But the matter did
not rest there. Two days after the above discussion
events occurred in Paris that could not be ignored
even by the most optimistic. On July 22 when Lally
entered the assembly hall a young man threw himself at
his feet and implored his intervention to save the
life of his father who had been arrested by a committee of citizens at Compiègne and was being taken to
Paris where he faced certain death at the hands of an
angry mob. This was Louis-Jean Bertier de Sauvigny,
for many years intendant of the generality of Paris,
where he had acquired a reputation as one of the most
humane and enlightened of administrators, a reputation
not unlike that of Turgot a generation earlier. Arrested at the same time near Paris was Joseph-François
Foulon, who had been appointed undersecretary of the
War Department under Marshal de Broglie in the brief
ministry of Breteuil. He was turned over to local
militia by the peasants residing on his lands, and
brought to the Place de Grève in front of the Hôtel-

607

de-Ville of Paris. The city authorities, both the Permanent Committee, the Assembly of Electors, the mayor, Bailly, and Lafayette, commander of the National Guard, tried to reason with the crowd and allow the two suspects to be put in prison pending a trial. The crowd wanted the Electors to appoint a temporary court among themselves to carry out the trial immediately. It was a difficult assignment to ask of anyone, as Bailly explained in his memoirs: "The position of judges appointed to the court was extremely critical. They were expected to hand down death sentences, failing which they would themselves become suspect and could have their throats cut. If they gave the death sentences they would betray their own consciences. Thus, they had to choose between their consciences and their lives."[31]

Lafayette tried to reason with the crowd: "I only want the law to be observed," he told them, "without which there can be no liberty, the law without which I would not have contributed to the revolution in the New World, and without which I will not contribute to the revolution here."[32] Bailly observed in the Place de Grève "certain persons with a decent appearance mingled with the crowd to incite it toward severity. One well-dressed individual . . . cried in anger 'Why is it necessary to have a trial for a man who has already been judged for thirty years.'"[33] All the persuasion of the Hôtel-de-Ville failed to save the two culprits from the angry mob, and their fate was described at the National Assembly in lurid detail the following day by Gouy d'Arcy:

Can one believe in a century of enlightenment that a people could be led to tear out the entrails of a man and carry his heart at the end of a lance, carry the head of another through the streets in triumph and drag his body throughout the capitol! Can one believe that cries of joy, of happiness,

608

of enthusiasm were uttered at the sight of the remains of a man, that around him they danced to the sound of music!

Do not think, gentlemen, that it was only the class called common people who participated in these excesses; a great number of citizens accompanied the populace, encouraged it, animated it, and several did not hesitate to wash their hands in human blood.

I shudder to think of the possible consequences of these atrocities. People become accustomed to bloody scenes and the shedding of blood can become a game. Barbarism can become habitual, proscriptions indefinite, individual hatreds can serve as a pretext, etc.

I do not intend to frighten you, but gentlemen, I must tell you what I know; there exists a list of proscribed; sixty persons are on it and several honorable members of this assembly are among the number.

I conclude that we must take immediately effective steps and promptly end this disorder.[34]

It appears that these events, in the city that was supposed to be calm after the taking of the Bastille, did make a profound impression on the National Assembly. Lally once again introduced his proposal for a proclamation urging the populace to calmness. By the end of the session on July 23 he succeeded in getting his resolution passed but not without some amendments. The most important was a statement that enemies of the nation and those guilty of crimes against it should be punished, but that this was the function of the representatives of the nation in the National Assembly. Lally was reluctant to make such a concession to what he thought a popular ferment that was without any reason or justification. But he had to be content with getting the assembly to agree that killing people by angry crowds without a trial could not be tolerated in civil society.

Even so the resolution was vehemently opposed by the leaders of the "faction." Barnave, Camus, Volny, and Mirabeau still asserted that the proponents of the proclamation did not see the matter in proper perspective. So there have been a few executions of aristocrats by popular violence? But think of the violence perpetrated by the aristocracy for two or more centuries! "Is this blood that has been shed so pure?" asked Barnave in what is probably the most famous statement of this argument. Mirabeau gave full vent to it in the eighteenth letter to his constituents:

> Ah! if the anger of the people is terrible, it's the sang-froid of despotism that is atrocious; its systematic cruelties create far more victims in a day than popular insurrections in years . . . and to put it in a word, two hundred years of public and individual oppression, political and fiscal, feudal and judicial, crowned by the most horrible conspiracy of which there is hardly a parallel in the annals of history, that is what has provoked the people.

> There remain too many guilty for there not to be much terror. Let no one think that all obstacles have been surmounted, that the aristocracy is without hope, and arbitrary power without resources. Carthage is not destroyed; there remain a great number of means for thwarting our goals, of sowing discord in an assembly where already

the trap of a constitution is being prof-
fered under false pretenses, which has no
solidity, which will give birth to violent
troubles in the state, which will raise the
country against the city, province against
province, sow distrust between the people
and their representatives in order to destroy the fruit of their labors.[35]

Several themes can be seen in the above passage
that were to become familiar in succeeding periods of
the Revolution, among them the justification of terror
because of the danger of counter-revolution and the
intimation that the real enemy now is within the revolutionary movement, namely, those who disagree with
you on the form of the constitution or some other issue. It was evident that the target in Mirabeau's
sights was not the despotism of the old regime, but
the Anglophiles. Mounier understood this clearly when
he got up after one of Mirabeau's speeches to say "one
can have a great deal of talent and grand ideas, and
also be a tyrant." The recorder for the _Moniteur_
added that Mounier "appeared to have his eyes fixed on
Mr. de Mirabeau," and that the remark provoked
"murmurs" in the assembly.[36]

Lally-Tollendal readily admitted that the people
had suffered a long period of mistreatment under the
old regime and said he would be their advocate in that
matter. But the issue now was whether suspects should
be tried and convicted by orderly judicial procedures
or be summarily arrested or put to death by a furious
crowd. He was highly indignant at Mirabeau's assertion that there were only a few incidents of popular
violence and that Lally was exaggerating the situation. In a footnote to the minutes of the session of
July 31 when Lally attempted to persuade the National
Assembly to endorse Necker's pleas for a general
amnesty, he again answered Mirabeau, giving a long
list of examples that left no doubt of the widespread

existence of popular violence, atrocities, and injustice. What made these acts especially odious was the defenselessness of the victims. He wrote in his memoirs:

> Ah! I was inflamed by the Americans of today and the Dutch of yesterday when I saw torrents of blood shed for liberty. But robbery justified by sophistry! conflagrations spread by lies! murder inspired by rhetoricians! when there is no resistance! when the nobles consented to everything, when they were unable to oppose anything, when all had renounced their economic (utiles) privileges, it must break the heart of anyone who is not devoid of all feeling of morality and humanity.[37]

The atrocities committed in Paris on July 22 turned the attention of the deputies of the National Assembly once again to the capitol city. The statement of Gouy d'Arcy about that list of sixty proscribed persons in the hands of leaders of the Parisian crowds was not a new development. This type of pressure had already been used on the assembly in June. But now the crowd and their leaders had demonstrated their ability to carry out the liquidation of whomever they chose. Clermont-Tonnerre wrote in his memoirs that this list of proscribed persons "contained the names of the most respectable deputies,"[38] and that it was drawn up by "the sieur Saint-Huruge." Clermont-Tonnerre proposed that the National Assembly move to some other city in order to be free of this type of pressure, but his proposal was not acted upon. Clermont-Tonnerre, Mounier, and Lally-Tollendal were certain that the crowds in Paris were firmly organized and controlled, and that terror was steadily eroding the influence of the moderates, or "Anglophiles" in the National Assembly.

After the passing of Lally's resolution on July 23, two new developments were to have important consequences on the course of the Revolution. First was Mirabeau's attempt to establish a base of personal power in the sixty district assemblies in Paris. Second was the act of the National Assembly in setting up an "Investigating Committee" to gather information about the violent attacks on individuals throughout the country.

It was on July 25 that Mirabeau introduced a motion in the National Assembly to establish a permanent government for the city of Paris, ending the provisional regime established by the Assembly of Electors during the July revolution. He maintained that the Assembly of Electors were usurping power, they no longer had any legal right to govern, and the electors were not in accord with the sentiments of the sixty electoral assemblies. He proposed that the rule of the Assembly of Electors be ended, that the National Assembly send one of its deputies to each of the sixty district assemblies "in order to establish a center of correspondence among all the assemblies for the purpose of getting them to march together." Mirabeau proposed that a new assembly be elected by the districts, that it draw up a permanent statute for the city government, and replace the Assembly of Electors. "The most marked dissension exists between the districts and the electors," said Mirabeau, the latter "has finally established in its bosom a permanent committee which has no rapport at all with the districts."[39]

Bailly wrote in his memoirs that Mirabeau's attack on the Assembly of Electors was unjust and the electors were "profoundly afflicted by it."[40] According to Duquesnoy the Assembly of Electors had acted as a restraint on the Parisian crowds, and had managed to prevent much violence that would otherwise have occurred.[41] It was not true, wrote Bailly, that the electors were usurping power, or clinging to it despite their disaccord with the districts. On the contrary the electors, although they had assumed a great deal of the functions of government, were only too anxious to lay it down. Positions of responsibility in the Parisian government at the time were not a much-sought privilege. Those in authority were apt to fall under suspicion and be denounced by the popular orators and the press. Bailly watched Mirabeau's activities in Paris with a wary eye. "I am assured," he wrote in his journal on July 26, "that Mirabeau makes sometimes two trips a day to Paris. They tell me he goes among the districts at night. I can understand now the object of his proposition. He would like to seize the districts with the chain of the sixty deputies. He wishes to propose a plan of municipal government according to his own notion, and no doubt entertains the idea of holding a new election for mayor." And of course Mirabeau would be the candidate.[42]

Bailly acted quickly to foil Mirabeau's scheme. He had the sixty district assemblies each send two representatives to the Hôtel-de-Ville to form a new assembly known as the "Assembly of the Representatives of the Commune." The purpose of this assembly was to draw a permanent statute for the municipal government of Paris. When the 120 representatives assembled however they assumed it was their mission to replace the Assembly of Electors and become the governing body as well as the constituent assembly for the city. This was contrary to Bailly's intentions, but it was not unwelcome to the electors who were only too happy to be relieved of their responsibilities.[43] When Necker appeared at the Hôtel-de-Ville on July 30 and spoke to the Assembly of Electors the latter was near the end of its career. The last assembly took place the following day, when, alarmed at its temerity of the day before in granting a general amnesty, it was easily persuaded to revise that decree and assure the people that it was not their intention to "allow the enemies of the nation to go unpunished." This was the last act of the electors. The Assembly of the Representatives of the Commune replaced them. The representatives had agreed the day before to release Besenval, but it was only the electors who had granted the general amnesty. Bailly had refused to sign that decree. It had been passed during his absence. He wrote in his memoirs that it was not only impolitic but illegal. Clermont-Tonnerre had no right to introduce the motion in the assembly, not being an elector himself, and the city government had no right to pass laws for the nation. His attitude was deplorably legalistic, ignoring entirely the enormous moral question at stake, namely whether the populace should be restrained or incited; and it was a legitimate concern for any jurisdiction, even a village commune, to express its opinion on such a matter. But Bailly did achieve his main purpose in creating the Assembly of Representatives of the Commune: he prevented Mirabeau from establishing a formidable political machine by having those sixty deputies of the National Assembly, who would certainly have been under his influence, sent out to the district assemblies.

But Mirabeau had enough influence among some district to cause the failure of Necker's plea for a general amnesty and for the release of Besenval. Although direct evidence of Mirabeau's role is not ample, what exists makes his primary responsibility a reasonable inference. The opinion of Bailly is the most credible. He wrote in his memoirs that "I must say for the benefit of history that I remember very well the frequent nocturnal visits he [Mirabeau] made to the districts, and that he was strongly suspected of being the author of the demand against the Hôtel-de-Ville, and of the ferment of the districts, and especially that of the Oratoire. I do not know for certain that this is true, having no proof, which however would be difficult to acquire."[44] The marquis de Ferrières states quite categorically in his memoirs that Mirabeau delivered in the district of the Oratoire that evening of July 30 "a violent discourse the purpose of which was to revoke the pardon granted to Mr. de Besenval."[45]

It was certainly not a majority of the districts assemblies who were activated that night. Emissaries were sent out from the Oratoire to some others, notably the Blanc-Manteau district. Here was another example of what seemed to be a recurring phenomenon of 1789: an organized and stongly aroused minority could act upon the majority and influence the most crucial decisions. It was fear and timidity that caused the electors to back away from their decree of amnesty. At the National Assembly the same forces were at work. When the events of the Hôtel-de-Ville were related to the assembly there were "murmurs" and disapproval of Necker's initiative. Lally-Tollendal warmly defended Necker's pleas for amnesty, reading the entire speech that Necker had delivered at the Hôtel-de-Ville the day before. Despite Lally's undoubted oratorical ability, it did not produce the same magical effect as Necker's. The president of the National Assembly announced the reversal of the decree of amnesty by the Hôtel-de-Ville and soon thereafter admitted to the bar of the assembly hall a delegate from the district of the Blanc-Manteau. "The electors in the name of the city have pronounced a general amnesty," he told the National Assembly, "this decree had produced the most terrible impression. Crimes have been committed; the law requires that they be punished. And suddenly a general pardon is pronounced, in the name of all citizens by those without legitimate authority." The speaker called attention to the decree of the National Assembly of July 23, which was the revised motion of Lally and which had admitted that those who had committed crimes against the nation should be punished. The speaker also pointed out that on July 28, only three days before, the National Assembly had created a special investigating committee to look into all such alleged crimes and gather information about them. Both the above acts were contrary to the decree of amnesty of the Hôtel-de-Ville.[46]

It was at this juncture that Mounier got up to say that he had supported the act of July 28, but this Committee of Investigation was not created to be a vehicle for spreading popular accusations. Citizens should not only be guaranteed a fair trial but should not even be arrested without firm evidence. At that point Mirabeau arose to refute Mounier:

> The word pardon and the order to release Mr. de Besenval are as reprehensible as they are impolitic. Even we do not have the right to pronounce an amnesty . . . We accuse the great criminals, and therefore we do not judge them. We cannot declare those to be innocent which public notoriety has designated as guilty, nor deprive any individual, any corporation of the right to indict. The power of granting pardon, in-so-far as it exists, resides eminently in the hands of the monarch; I say in-so-far as it exists, because it is a great question whether the power of pardon can exist, in what hands it resides if it does exist, and if crimes against the nation can ever be pardoned.[47]

The contrast between Mounier and Mirabeau was clear. The municipal judge from Grenoble insisted that a person was presumed innocent until proved guilty. The orator from Aix-en-Provence, the Tribune of the People, declared that once popular suspicion falls on a person it is an indelible stain that no one can wash away. This was a startling application of vox populi, vox Dei. But the same position was taken by others in the National Assembly that day.

617

Robespierre, Volney, and Camus all maintained that the way to quiet the popular wrath of the people was to punish the guilty. And who were the guilty? Those who were enemies of the people, aristocrats, officials, conspirators, counter-revolutionaries. The reign of terror was already implicit in that debate in the National Assembly on July 31.

Whether there was any validity to those charges depended upon how realistic were the fears of the "aristocrats" and the "counter-revolutionaries." Adrien Duquesnoy did not think there was any basis for those fears. He wrote in his Journal on July 31:

> They talk ceaselessly about plots, conspiracies, etc. In truth, I cannot believe that they exist. They appear to be a vain and ridiculous smoke-screen put up by men who are concealing sinister projects . . . . . If there were conspiracies, they are no longer to be feared; our enemies are disarmed and in flight; our only, our unique enemy, is us, it's our restless anxiety which is carried beyond all bounds. Surely the nation and posterity expects something more substantial from us than the punishment of conspirators; they expect liberty which is equally removed from despotism and anarchy. They expect of us well-being (bonheur) and that is not to be found in blood and violence.[48]

The Committee of Investigation was set up on July 28 on the motion of Adrien Duport and Volney. It was a committee of twelve deputies charged to hear and to receive all information coming to them regarding crimes against the state. It seems to have been a concession to the Parisian populace, who demanded with insistence that a tribunal also be set up by the National Assembly to try all those suspected by the

618

Committee of Investigation. Both the Committee of Investigation and the tribunal were resisted by the "Anglophiles." The deputy of the nobility from Dauphiné, François-Henri comte de Virieu, one of the liberal nobles from that province, strongly opposed the Committee of Investigation. "Do you say that it will not be dangerous because it will be set up by the nation? I say it will be more dangerous. The despotism of the multitude is the most fearful of all. I ask you, what are the limits of our power? Who will judge us? Who will remind us of our principles? No, it is dangerous to unite in our hands all power, all authority."[49]

For those sensible remarks and others like them, the comte de Virieu's name was to be found at the head of that list of proscribed in the hands of Saint-Huruge!

At the end of the debate on July 31 the legal and no doubt politically smart decision was made by the National Assembly to endorse the amended decree of the Hôtel-de-Ville: the enemies of the nation were not to be pardoned, and the baron de Besenval was to remain in custody and not allowed to go to Switzerland.

The struggle for order had been lost. It remained to be seen whether liberty could survive in a climate of anarchy and violence. To contain the spreading disorder it would be necessary to restore effective power to the government, and end the paralysis brought on by the events of July 12-14.

[1]Chapuisat, Jacques Necker, 131.

[2]Despatches from Paris, 1784-1790, II, 250-251.

[3]Necker, "De la Révolution française," in Oeuvres complètes, IX, 241.

[4]Ibid., 242.

[5]"Discours à l'Hôtel-de-Ville," in Oeuvres complètes, VII, 7.

[6]Chapuisat, Jacques Necker., 313.

[7]Réimpression de l'Ancien Moniteur (Paris, 1847), I, 216-217.

[8]Considérations sur la Révolution, 158.

[9]Madame de Staël, Mémoires sur la vie privée de mon père (Paris, 1818), 63.

[10]Mémoires, ou Second Lettre, 100.

[11]"Discours à l'Hôtel-de-Ville," in Oeuvres complètes, VII, 5-6.

[12]Ibid., 8-11.

[13]Stanislas de Clermont-Tonnerre, Oeuvres complètes, I, xxiii - xxiv.

[14]"Extrait des délibération de l'assemblée des électeurs, du 30 juillet 1789," in Necker, Oeuvres complètes, VII, 12.

[15]"Sur l'Administration de M. Necker," in Oeuvres complètes, VI, 106.

[16]Clermont-Tonnerre, op. cit., I, xxvi-xxix.

[17] Mémoires sur la vie privée de mon père, 63.

[18] Réimpression d'Ancien Moniteur, I, 254.

[19] Mémoires de baron de Besenval, II, 114-150, 344-351.

[20] Ibid., II, 372.

[21] Mounier, Recherches sur les causes, II, Chap. 32.

[22] Bailly, Mémoires, I, 344.

[23] Archives parlementaires, VIII, 260.

[24] Ibid., VIII, 243.

[25] Papers of Thomas Jefferson, XV, 326.

[26] Mémoires de M. le comte de Lally-Tollendal ou second lettre à ses commettants, 79.

[27] Archives parlementaires, VIII, 253.

[28] Loc. cit.

[29] Mémoires de Lally-Tollendal, 83.

[30] Archives parlementaires, VIII, 254.

[31] Bailly, Mémoires, II, 110.

[32] Ibid., 112.

[33] Ibid., 114.

[34] Archives parlementaires, VIII, 265.

[35] Réimpressions de l'Ancien Moniteur, I, 181-192.

[36]Loc. cit.

[37]Mémoires, ou second lettre à ses commettants, 106.

[38]Clermont-Tonnerre, Oeuvres complètes, I, xxxiv.

[39]Réimpressions de l'Ancien Moniteur, I, 191.

[40]Mémoires, II, 169.

[41]Duquesnoy, Journal, I, 249.

[42]Bailly, Mémoires, II, 154.

[43]Ibid., 170.

[44]Ibid., II, 185.

[45]Quoted by the editor of Bailly, Mémoires, II, 155, n. 1.

[46]Réimpression de l'Ancien Moniteur, I, 250.

[47]Ibid., I, 254.

[48]Journal d'Adrien Duquesnoy, I, 243.

[49]Archives parlementaires, VIII, 295.

CHAPTER 17

THE STUGGLE FOR EXECUTIVE POWER

"It's been a long time," wrote the Swedish ambassador to King Gustavus on August 13, 1789, "that we have heard anything of executive power."[1] This was a crucial matter, he continued, because without the restoration of effective authority in the executive government all the various ills that afflicted the country could not be remedied. The National Assembly had been the focus of attention since the July upheaval, and was looked upon as the repository of moral authority in the nation. But it could not supplant the executive government in coping with the diverse problems that so urgently required attention.

It has been seen that when the king recalled Necker to his post on July 15, he also recalled to the ministry Montmorin, Saint-Priest, and La Luzerne. Montmorin resumed the portfolio of foreign affairs, and Saint-Priest, who had been minister without portfolio before July 11, now took over the department of the King's Household formerly held by Laurent de Villedeuil. La Luzerne resumed his post as Secretary of State for the Naval Department. When Necker returned to Versailles on July 27, he proposed four new appointments to the ministry which were immediately accepted by the king. Three had been prominent leaders in the National Assembly, and the fourth, Marshal de Beauvau, had been influential in the two Assemblies of Notables in 1787 and 1788. He was known as a liberal noble who had consistently supported Necker's policies including the doubling of the Third Estate in the Second Assembly of Notables. The person who replaced Barentin as Keeper of the Seals was the Archbishop of Bordeaux, Champion de Cicé, also a well-known Neckerist, who had led the majority of the deputies of the Clergy into the National Assembly on June 22. Since that time Champion de Cicé had been chairman of the constitutional committee in the National Assembly and continued to participate in the deliberations of the committee after joining the ministry. This was the kind of close collaboration that the Anglophiles expected would become habitual between the executive government and the National Assembly. Even if the ministers were not elected members of the National Assembly, as they were in the British House of Commons, it was expected that they would be invited to appear before committees and to address the entire Assembly when the occasion warranted.

The new minister of war who replaced Marshal de Broglie was also a general, Jean-Frédéric de La Tour du Pin, comte de Paulin. He was one of the liberal nobles who had joined the National Assembly on June 24. The third member of the National Assembly to be appointed to the ministry was the Archbishop of Vienne, Le Franc de Pompignan, another of the liberal prelates who joined the National Assembly on June 22. Marshal de Beauvau served as minister without portfolio.

For the first time since the beginning of the political troubles in 1787 the government was now a fairly united ministry. All ministers were in favor of a constitutional regime for France which was to be a new regime. None maintained that France should remain loyal to some traditional constitution. Equally, there were no radicals among them. All were moderates in their conception of what the new regime should be. They were, in a word, Anglophiles like Necker. No doubt there were some personality clashes, as Egret has mentioned.[2] But these no ministry could be entirely without. The important matter was that Necker now had ministerial colleagues entirely different from Barentin and Laurent de Villedeuil who had opposed him on the most crucial issues, and at the most critical time.

When the king sent word to the National Assembly of his appointment of the new ministers the assembly demonstrated enthusiastically its approval. "We now have a popular ministry," Adrien Duquesnoy wrote in his _Journal_ , "a ministry named by the voice of the people. Never has this been seen before."[3] On August 7 all ministers appeared before the National Assembly and were greeted with applause. Champion de Cicé was the first to address the assembly: "Gentlemen, we have been sent to you by the king to place before you the concerns which are disturbing the paternal heart of His Majesty." While the deputies of the National Assembly had been quite properly engrossed in laying the foundations of the future constitution, there had arisen "a covert but painful anxiety which pervades the nation." Popular uprisings were occurring in almost all cities of the kingdom. "Terror is spreading, property is being destroyed or appropriated without restraint, the law is without power, the courts are supine." The Keeper of the Seals urged the assembly to accelerate its work in building the new institutions to replace those that had been destroyed. "The circumstances require that you take measures immediately to repress the alarming impulse to pillage with impunity, and that you restore to public institutions the power that has been lost."[4]

The message of the Keeper of the Seals was certainly not news to the gentlemen of the National Assembly. Since the beginning of August reports had reached them of the uprising of the peasants in the countryside against the seigneurs, the noble landlords. For some time there had been a "tax-payers' strike." The common people had been told that the royal taxes were unjust and were going to be abolished. Therefore it was not easy for them to understand that the unjust taxes must still be paid until

625

new and presumably more equitable sources of revenue could replace them. Now it was the peasants who took into their own hands the abolition of their dues to the seigneurs. These were of great variety and nomenclature: personal servitudes called mainmorte, economic dues in both produce from the land and money payments, hunting privileges of the nobility on the lands cultivated by the peasants, game refuges maintained by the nobility, banalities of various kinds, inheritance taxes and sales taxes for transfer of peasant lands, the tithes exacted by the Church, in sum, all the residue of obligations on the peasants and privileges for the seigneurs that had originated in a quite different age, the feudal age.

The violence in the countryside erupted just as the National Assembly was getting down to the task for which it had been summoned, the formation of the new constitutional order. The urban revolution had been accomplished, although violence was still endemic in some cities. But the deputies had hoped to be free of further shocks so they could accomplish just what the Keeper of the Seals was now begging them to do, to get the new order into place as soon as possible. Now it appeared that the peasants were not at all interested in whether the national parliament would consist of one or two chambers, or whether the king should have an absolute or only a qualified veto on legislative acts. The peasants were concerned about the question of "feudalism." The deputies were appalled and frightened by this new outburst of what seemed to be a jacquerie, a savage peasant uprising that was purely destructive. Yet it soon appeared that this peasant rebellion of 1789 was not simply a violent, unreasoning explosion of popular wrath. The peasants were intent on destroying the terriers, or the documents that recorded the various dues owed by them to the seigneurs. There were some cases of châteaux being burned, and even less evidence of their inhabitants being murdered. But on the whole the rebellion seemed

626

to be well organized and directed to a specific goal, the burning of the _terriers_.

In that light it appeared to the deputies of the National Assembly that if the purpose of the peasants was a rational one, it should be possible to reason with them. As one deputy put it, "There are only two ways to calm an excited populace, either by armed force or by persuasion. We have no force; we must try persuasion." Hence that _folle nuit_, the "crazy night" of August 4, 1789, as it has gone down in French history. The most famous names of the aristocracy, the Noailles, the Aiguillons, the Montmorency, all got up to publicly renounce their "unjust privileges." All personal servitudes were abolished without compensation to the landlords. Their economic dues which were considered to have the character of private property were to be abolished with compensation to the landlords, at a rate to be determined by the National Assembly. Seigneurial courts were abolished without compensation and a new system of royal courts would provide justice free of the exorbitant fees of the courts of the _ancien régime_; the hunting rights of the nobility on peasant lands were abolished without compensation. The game refuges were renounced and the peasants could now kill game on their own lands.

Much more than "feudalism" was abolished on that night of August in 1789. It witnessed, in the words of Ernest Labrousse, "the theatrical demolition of the _ancien régime_."[5] The tax exemptions of the Nobility and the Clergy were now unequivocally renounced, and the royal taxes were to be levied on all classes and in the same manner. The entire system of venality of office was abolished as was the separate status of the provinces who enjoyed special privileges by treaty, the _pays_ d'états. The prelates abandoned church tithes. Both Nobility and Clergy accepted the principle of the career open to talent, that there would be no discrimination on the basis of class to appointments and advancement in the royal government. In short, the entire system of privilege upon which the ancien régime was based, was officially "abolished" by the National Assembly on that dramatic night. "What a great and memorable night!" Adrien Duquesnoy wrote in his Journal, "they wept, they embraced one another. What a nation! What glory, what honor to be French!"[6] Of course it was discovered on the morning after that "abolishing feudalism" was not such a simple matter as passing a resolution. Other "peculiar institutions" have been abolished by official proclamation, but leave a legacy of difficult social and moral questions to be resolved.

Three days after that memorable night the ministers of the government appeared before the assembly and the deputies heard themselves exhorted by the Keeper of the Seals to "hurry up with the constitution" in order to quell the mounting tide of violence. They must have wondered what more they could do after the night of August 4. Necker spoke to the assembly after the address of Champion de Cicé, and he had an answer for them. He said that while the architects were absorbed in drawing up plans for the new structure, the building materials were being eroded away. That is, society itself was threatened by the breakdown of order and the continued impotence of the government. The most imminent and dangerous threat of all was bankruptcy. If the government were unable to meet its financial commitments the social and political order would break down completely. If the troops could not be paid, the frontiers would be unguarded; within the country there would be no police force to cope with the anarchical tendencies already so formidable and difficult to contain; if the government could no longer meet its obligations to creditors, to the rentiers, the ensuing financial panic would ensure the ruin of confidence in the political order.

It was absolutely necessary, Necker warned, to keep the government supplied with money to meet these essential expenditures. And the needs of the next two months, for August and September, would require thirty million more livres than the finance minister could find in the treasury. Therefore Necker asked the assembly to approve a loan of 30 million livres which, if successful, would sustain the government until the end of September. By that time he assumed that the assembly would have completed its work on the constitution and the new regime would enjoy enough confidence from the nation to restore tranquility once again, to protect commerce and property, and above all, the safety of individuals. The mounting exodus of wealthy landowners and others of property was gravely undermining the economy, causing more unemployment, which in turn increased the expenditures of the government in order to care for the destitute.

The situation faced by the government was set forth by Necker in stark clarity. Those critics who find his prose inflated, bombastic, emphatic, should read his speech of August 7 to the National Assembly. The last time Necker had addressed the assembly on national policy was May 5. Now, three months later, he described to them a desperate situation. The regular income from both direct and indirect taxation had fallen off sharply because of the "taxpayer's strike." The income from the gabelles was cut in half due to the inability of the General Farm to supervise the sale of salt and to prevent contraband. The same severe reduction had occurred in the income from the tobacco monopoly and the excise taxes. The customs barrier surrounding Paris was only imperfectly restored since July 13. The same distress was experienced by the receivers of the direct taxes: the twentieths, the taille and the capitation tax. They were unable to meet their contractual obligations to the government because of the taxpayers' strike. Necker did not give an estimate of the proportion of revenue from direct taxation that had fallen off, but later documents indicate it was similar to that for indirect taxation, about 50% was being collected.

At the same time that regular income of the government was being impeded by the resistance of taxpayers the extraordinary emergency expenditures were being greatly increased. The danger of famine was not yet alleviated and enormous purchases of grain by the government were continuing. The great distress of the population, especially the high rate of unemployment, forced the government to sell the grain and flour it purchased much below the cost; and disorder in the country was impeding the transport of grain, forcing the government to provide armed convoys. The harvest in the summer and fall months of 1789 was bountiful, and the subsistence crisis was now due to the prevalent disorder rather than a scarcity within the kingdom. The unemployed had to be supported by government workshops in which the workers were paid twenty sous each per day. There was additional expenditure for tools and equipment to provide for this work relief. It should be noticed in passing, that the government did not share the doctrinaire liberal notions of a later age which opposed state assistance to care for the indigent whose situation was caused by economic and political factors beyond their control. In the debates in the National Assembly at that time, in the first days of August, one can see the beginnings of this ideology. Malouet argued eloquently for greater public assistance, for the establishment of workshops throughout the country, and he was supported by other liberals of the nobility. But the doctrinaire liberals of the Third Estate, Dupont de Nemours and Guy-Jean Target among them, called for stern enforcement of the laws against the destitute who were involved in the disorders. They were less concerned about their economic plight.[7]

Necker made it clear to the deputies that it was
by no means certain that the government could successfully issue a loan of 30 million livres. The last
loan of such a proportion had been issued in November
1787. Since that time no finance minister had ventured to issue a regular treasury loan, fearing that
the tumult in the country and the determined opposition of the Parlement of Paris to all new loans and
taxes would make its success extremely improbable.
But Necker believed that a loan sanctioned by the National Assembly, which he supposed enjoyed a moral
prestige in the country that unfortunately the royal
government did not, would create a favorable climate
for its issue. He told the assembly that instead of
appealing to the capitalists by a high rate of interest, it would be better strategy to appeal to their
patriotism. After all, the capitalists had as much as
stake as anyone in keeping the government from col-
lapsing. By offering the loan at 5% Necker thought
this spirit of patriotism could make it successful,
even though it was possible for capitalists to earn
between six and seven percent by purchasing government
notes on the stock exchange. That is, by purchasing
notes of previous issues of the government which had
fallen on the stock exchange, the investor could earn
that rate of interest (6% to 7%) because the government was committed eventually to redeem those notes at
par value. But it would be necessary to offer investors in the new loan certain advantages that the
holders of the old notes did not enjoy. The former
should be offered specific terms of amortization, either at the time of purchase of the notes, or at any
later time they might choose. Further, Necker proposed that if the investor in the loan of 30 million
livres placed their capital in negotiable bonds, those
bonds would be guaranteed from forceful conversion to
contracts of 5%. Finally, Necker suggested that the
names of all subscribers be placed on a scroll in the

National Assembly as a kind of honor roll in appreciation of their patriotism.

In his final remarks to the National Assembly on
August 7 Necker drew upon all his eloquence to insist
on the seriousness of the crisis facing the government. But he also held out hope that the crisis could
be overcome if the government and the assembly could
act in concert:

> The king, gentlemen, is ready to follow your
> views, and the ministers in whom he has
> placed his confidence, will act according to
> his intentions in order to contribute, along
> with you, to the well-being of the nation.
> Let us unite then to save the state, and let
> all men of good will enter this coalition;
> nothing less than the power of such an al-
> liance will overcome the difficulties with
> which we are surrounded. The distress is so
> great that everyone is able to perceive it;
> but at the center, where the ministers of
> the king are placed, the picture is truly
> frightening. Everything is fluid, a prey to
> individual passions, and from one end of the
> country to the other one sighs ardently for
> a reasonable plan for a constitution and of
> public order which will restore calm and of-
> fer a hope of peace and happiness.[8]

After Necker had finished speaking, one deputy
got up to move that his loan proposal be approved by
acclamation of the assembly. But this did not suit
the deputies' sense of the dignity of the National Assembly and its prerogative of deliberation on all fiscal measures.[9] After the ministers left the hall a
debate took place between the "factious ones" and
their opponents, the moderates. The former did not
want the loan to be approved by the assembly, nor did
they want it to succeed. They rejected the proferred

alliance between the government and the assembly held out to them by Necker. Instead their aim was to take advantage of the financial distress of the government to force it to accept the kind of constitutional regime desired by the radicals. A variety of pretexts were invoked. Camus said that the exclusion of the loan from the dixième d'amortissement was a privilege granted to subscribers to the loan and this violated the prohibition of privileges passed on the night of August 4. Mirabeau and others maintained that the mandates of the cahiers expressly forbid the approval of any loans or taxes by the deputies until the new constitutional order had been established. Necker was aware of this obstacle, and mentioned it in his speech of August 7. He said those who attended the primary and the secondary assemblies could not have foreseen the troubles of the past three months and the great danger now threatening the state. He argued that if the electoral assemblies knew of the seriousness of the threat facing the nation they would have recommended in advance the authorization of the loan now presented to the deputies. But this made no impression on the "factious ones." Mirabeau now insisted upon the sanctity of the imperative mandates of the cahiers even though he had voted to set aside all such mandates in June when the Nobility had invoked them to justify their refusal to join the National Assembly. On July 16 the National Assembly had formally set aside all imperative mandates and Mirabeau had voted for that measure. Now the tribune said he could not go against his conscience and violate the oath he had taken to abide by his mandate. He proposed to the assembly that Necker's plan for a loan be sent around to all the provincial assemblies (most of which had not yet been organized) for their ratification. As Duquesnoy wrote, the proposal, if adopted, would have killed the loan.[10] Near the end of August Mirabeau again reversed himself on the imperative mandates at the time the great issues on the constitution were being debated. Now he said the mandates of the deputies could not prevail against constituent power exercised by the National Assembly.[11]

The assembly voted to have the finance committee study the loan and report back the following day. The chairman of the finance committee, the comte d'Aiguillon, did so on August 9. The committee, he said, had found the preamble of the loan not well written: "it was too long, too verbose." But the most serious imperfection was the rate of interest Necker had proposed, namely 5%. Jerôme Pétion proclaimed that such a rate of interest was "illegal." Dupont de Nemours declared that 4 1/2% was the proper interest to grant to investors. Finally the loan edict was passed by the assembly at the rate of interest proposed by Dupont.[12] What most distressed Necker was to find the edict shorn of all the attractions he had deliberately put into it for investors. The clauses concerning the terms of amortization, the guarantee against forcible conversion into contracts of 5%, even the honor roll to be set up in the hall of the assembly were all denied by those who believed they could improve upon the proposal of the minister of finance.

Lally-Tollendal vigorously sought to protect Necker's loans from these "improvements." He reminded the deputies that they had made a solemn promise not to default on the government's obligations to creditors. He pointed out the dangers of defaulting on obligations, the need to support the armed forces whose pay would be suspended if the government went bankrupt. "Finally," he warned, "let us reflect that if this loan fails, in eight days our cities will be without security, our frontiers without defense, and we could destroy in an hour what has taken fourteen centuries to build."[13]

What bewildered Lally was the callous indifference of the deputies toward the prospective investors in the loan. "Ordinarily," he wrote later in his memoirs, "one encourages, even flatters investors. Here they are intimidated and threatened."[14] Nor could he understand the lack of concern about the imminent bankruptcy of the government and the catastrophe that would follow from it. The reason for the nonchalance of many deputies became apparent in the two days following the passage of the loan edict. During the debate on the loan a marquis de la Coste asserted that the church lands belonged to the state.[15] On August 8 François-Nicolas Buzot, the future Girondin, and Alexander Lameth proposed that the lands of the church be taken over by the state.[16] On August 10 Mirabeau spoke up to say that "we must as of today take back the lands of the Clergy, pay its debts, and the salaries."[17] Already it seemed that the deputies had seized upon the solution to the problem of the government's finances. And they were not just the "factious ones." Moderates also relied upon the church lands as collatoral for the government's future credit operations. On September 24 Dupont de Nemours presented an elaborate plan to cope with the royal finances by nationalizing the lands of the church. The income would not be great, as his figures, based upon physiocratic principles showed, but the mere nationalizing of the lands would serve as collatoral for government loans.[18]

It is doubtful if those who seized upon this quick remedy for the immediate financial crisis of the government had thought very carefully about the seriousness of the step. Certainly there were plans, often indicated in the cahiers, to reform the church's economic position in the kingdom. There were lands held by beneficiaries, which created wealth for individual prelates, abbots and archbishops, without making an equivalent contribution to the well-being of the church. The monastic lands were subject to reform, and other abuses long discussed, such as the tithes, the plural holding of church offices, the an-

635

nates paid to Rome. But it was quite a different matter to nationalize the entire church and for the state to take over its administration. This brought the church under the control of a very secular state, and few realized at the time how this would involve the state in the spiritual realm, and the difficulties the spiritual would have in accepting such an intrusion of the secular. Here was to become the most serious schism in the national revolutionary movement, even more serious than the alienation of the "aristocrats." In the end, it was an unnecessary and gratuitous affront to those prelates and parish priests who had been the strongest supporters of the Revolution. Necker claimed in later years that he could have resolved the government's financial crisis with one-tenth of the resources which the National Assembly eventually had at its disposal, and without alienating such an important class of citizens.[19]

When Necker heard of the terms of the loan passed by the assembly on August 9 he realized that it could not succeed, a supposition that was borne out in less than two weeks. On August 22 Necker sent a letter to the president on the National Assembly asking to appear the following Wednesday to discuss the loan. But he succumbed to illness that week and had to have his message read to the assembly on Thursday, August 27. It was understandably a reproachful letter. Since the opening of the loan on August 9, Necker told the deputies, only 2.6 million livres of the loan had been subscribed, and since the amount of subscription had declined precipitately in recent days the loan must be considered a failure. He explained why it was important that the deputies understand the reasons for the failure. The Genevan banker undertook to instruct them on the finer points of government loans and their marketing. The capitalists could earn above 6 1/2% by purchasing old government "paper" that had deteriorated on the bourse. Although amortization payments had been suspended the previous summer, the government was still bound to honor them at par value. therefore the capitalists could invest in that depreciated paper and earn an interest of above 6 1/2%. Why, then, did Necker think they would be willing to invest in this new loan at only 5%? Simply because the new loan that he had proposed had guaranteed amortization of the loan, and the patriotism of the investors, influenced by the credit of the National Assembly and the coming constitutional regime, made the loan a safe investment. Attracting investors to government loans was an art that required psychological as well as financial finesse. Successful loans occurred when a band-wagon effect seized investors and the loan was subscribed to in a matter of days. One-half percent may seem like a small difference, but when that was added to all the other enticements he had offered, and with the psychological uplift caused by the widespread hopes for a constitutional regime, it could be significant. All these calculations has been rudely upset by the way the National Assembly handled the loan.[20]

Leaving the dismal subject of the failure of the loan, Necker moved on to see what could be done in the present circumstances. It would not do simply to raise the interest rate again to 5%. The psychological moment had passed and the loan would no longer have the same effect had it been offered first on the terms he had proposed. Now it was necessary to appeal to the profit motive alone. Necker suggested that a loan of 80 million livres be offered in which the subscribers would pay one-half in hard money and one-half in government notes of previous loans that had fallen in value on the stock exchange. The government would honor those notes at par rather than market value. The loan would be amortized in ten years, one-tenth each year. Thus investors could exchange the notes of the government loans of which the amortization payments had been suspended the previous year for notes whose amortization the government was pledged to meet. This would mean only 40 million livres would be received in cash, if the loan succeeded, but that would be enough to tide the government over the present emergency. The rate of interest of the loan would be 5%; those who had already subscribed to the one of 30 million would be permitted to exchange their subscriptions to the new loan of 80 million livres. This type of loan had been tried before with success, notably by Joly de Fleury in December 1782. It meant that the government would in reality be paying more than the 5% indicated in the loan edict, in fact the same rate that capitalists could make by purchasing depreciated government paper at market value on the stock exchange. As has already been noted, this was between 6 1/2% and 7%. But it was the kind of loan that improved the credit posture of the government because it "bought up" so to speak the old paper that was declining on the stock exchange and which had cast an unfavorable reflection on the government's credit.[21]

Necker made it clear in his message to the National Assembly that it was by no means certain this loan would succeed in supplying the 40 million livres essential to see the government through the present financial crisis. "I must inform the National Assembly that in the present state of affairs and of public opinion, neither the loan which I have sketched nor any other can fully succeed unless you can raise morale and confidence from its present abasement by a determined and persistent series of policies."[22] In this message of August 27 he described what he thought those policies should be. As in his May 5 speech they were suggestions, but in view of the circumstances they were now offered somewhat more urgently. First, it was necessary to assure the creditors and the prospective investors of the determination of the assembly and the government to achieve a balance between ordinary expenditure and income; in other words, to eliminate the ordinary deficit which he had found to be 56 million livres back in May. This was already substantial, and while he had made several proposals as to how it might be eliminated, he had welcomed suggestions from the States-General. Now the ordinary deficit had widened because of the precipitate decline in the payment of taxes and by the enormous expenditures for grain imports. It would be necessary to slash ordinary expenditures from the budget and for the National Assembly to invoke all its authority to see that the taxes were paid until the new fiscal system could be put into effect.

With regard to the decline in tax revenue, the most dangerous situation was the salt tax, the gabelle. It normally yielded about 60 million livres to the government. It was generally agreed that this was one of the most oppressive and objectionable kinds of taxation, and everyone looked forward to its replacement by some more equitable form. But until that was done, the 60 million livres still had to be collected to prevent further erosion of the finances and the government's credit posture. With the breakdown of government executive power in the summer of 1789 the General Farm was unable to prevent smuggling on the frontier between the free-salt zone and the zone of the grandes gabelles. Furthermore in other parts of the kingdom the people were taking matters into their own hands by forcing the administrators of salt depots (greniers) to lower the price of salt to the level of the market. The gabelle was still being paid in a great part of the kingdom, and these examples of insubordination could spread rapidly.

But what could be done? Here Necker acknowledged that it would be unwise to attempt to enforce the collection of the salt tax according to the long-standing system which practically everyone expected to be changed in the new order. Instead of such an unfeasible policy Necker proposed that the price of salt be reduced throughout the kingdom to a uniform rate of six sous per pound of sixteen ounces. This would yield about 30 million livres, one-half the ordinary income. The loss could be recovered in part by the increased sales of salt at the lower price, and also because of the elimination of the large police establishment needed to prevent smuggling between the free salt zone and that of the grandes gabelles.[23]

Two other suggestions were laid before the assembly by Necker in this message. One concerned the Discount Bank. Since the beginning of the political crisis early in 1787 the directors and stockholders of the Discount Bank had given essential help to the government in the financial emergency. This required the bank to issue bank notes which circulated only in Paris. The conversion of these notes to hard specie had been suspended. This was not due to excessive issue of the notes but rather to the penury of hard money in the country, which was caused by several factors such as the unfavorable balance of trade and the flight of the wealthy from the country. Necker had called upon the bank for financial loans during his second ministry. But he now told the deputies of the assembly that this recourse had been exhausted. The issue of bank notes to circulate as money was safe only up to a certain point. If one passed beyond that limit the confidence of the public in this money would deteriorate. But the bank could be useful for another reason than granting short-term loans. Necker suggested that some representatives of the Discount Bank be invited to join the finance committee to give advice on credit and to examine the different projects which had been publicized to transform the Discount Bank into a national bank. Another project that might be considered by this committee was the levy on all fortunes of a patriotic contribution which had been tried successfully in Holland in the early 1750s. This was not a tax levy but a loan, which would be redeemed by the government when the new order was established and the financial crisis had been weathered.[24]

It appears that Necker's message of August 27 was a success as far as exerting influence on the National Assembly. The deputies were clearly chastened by the failure of the loan and the gentle but insistent reproof they had received from the Director-General. After the message was read to the assembly Talleyrand moved the acceptance of the loan of 80 million livres, leaving the terms up to the government. He also proposed that a special committee be set up to work with the finance minister on matters such as the budget and the loans. The assembly seemed to have recongized its dependence on the experts. Adrien Duquesnoy was struck by the paradoxical situation of an assembly wielding such great responsibility and yet being unprepared for it. "How many of these deputies are really qualified to sit here?" he asked. ..."we are excessively ignorant of finances, very feeble in commerce and in foreign affairs."[25] Even Mirabeau seconded Talleyrand's motion, although a few days earlier he had denounced the finance minister as being at fault for the failure of the loan, for "had counted too much on patriotism." But he admitted it was a mistake for the assembly to fix the rate of the loan at 4 1/2%.[26]

Nearly a month later, on September 23 the assembly passed a decree on the gabelles implementing Necker's proposal that a uniform price of six sous per pound be charged throughout the kingdom by the government monopoly. But nothing was done about inviting the directors of the Discount Bank to advise the committee on finance. On September 16 Mirabeau launched a vehement attack on the Discount Bank. He denounced the suspension of conversion of its notes to gold on demand, asserting it was unnecessary. It appears that his "expert" source of authority on the subject was his friend Etienne Clavière. Mirabeau accused the directors of the bank of planning to introduce paper money without any solid backing. His speech mounted in violence against the bank. All the ills that af-

641

flicted the country were due to the dishonest directors and the profit-greedy stockholders. Such a demagogic attack on the directors of the bank, who had
been compelled to suspend conversion only because of
their patriotic zeal to help the government in its
crisis, was not new. Since 1785 the Discount Bank had
been one of Mirabeau's favorite targets. He always
accused it of fraud and exaggerated the danger of
flooding the country with its paper notes.[27]

During the latter part of August the moderate Anglophiles seemed to be gaining strength in the assembly. There was an increasing awareness on the part of
the deputies of the necessity of preserving executive
power for the king. On August 13 a solemn _Te Deum_ was
celebrated in the chapel of the château in which the
deputies participated along with the king and _Mon-
sieur_, his brother. The assembly was moved to bestow
upon Louis XVI the title of "Restorer of French liberty." The following day the king responded by a message of confidence and hope in the future cooperation
between the king and the assembly: "I gratefully accept the title," he wrote, "which you have bestowed
upon me. It is in keeping with the aims that I had
proposed when I summoned you. I approve of the conduct of the National Assembly and I will always cooperate with you for the establishment of French liberty."[28] On August 17 Duquesnoy wrote in his journal:
"The spirit of wisdom has made some progress, no
doubt, since now one can speak in the National Assembly of the need to fortify executive power, and to
give it the means of action to command respect, which
one would not have dared to say fifteen days ago."[29]

The increasing confidence of the moderates was
shown by the beginning of party organization during
August. A central committee of fifteen deputies was
formed which maintained a correspondence with sub-com-
mittees, according to Malouet, of more than 300
deputies. "The moderate party," he wrote in his mem-

oirs, "was on the verge of obtaining a majority in the assembly, when the popular party began to take alarm. All those whom we had imprudently irritated, seeing us as the enemy, and our policies as counter-revolutionary, concluded that it was necessary for their security to move the assembly from Versailles to Paris."[30]

During the evening of August 29 the minister from Parma reported that "an orator held forth at the Palais-Royal inviting his fellow citizens to hang all the aristocrats in the National Assembly."[31] Mounier wrote in his memoirs: "They claimed that the defense of the royal veto was a final effort of the aristocracy" to achieve their idea of a constitution. This was the constitution promoted by the Anglophiles, who were now termed "aristocrats." Somehow this one issue of the constitution seemed to have caught the attention of the popular classes in the cities. Not only Paris but Rennes in Brittany was set ablaze by this single issue of royal veto. The city government of Rennes declared that all who favored that measure (the veto) were enemies of the fatherland.[32] According to Mounier, "the orators at the Palais-Royal claimed that the life of Mirabeau was in danger, that the aristocrats had sworn to destroy him, and that it was necessary to give him bodyguards. At once a list was made up of proscribed in which I had the honor of being the first on the list. They resolved to go to Versailles, with a crowd of about 15,000 for the purpose of punishing those called 'aristocrats', and to take into custody the king, the queen and the dauphin."[33]

This movement in Paris of August 30 did attempt to carry out the project of going to Versailles to force the king and his family as well as the National Assembly to take up residence in Paris. The Parisians feared that at Versailles there was danger of the royal court and the National Assembly moving to a provincial city in order to escape from their control.

There is some evidence that the leaders of the moderate party wanted to do just that. Malouet wrote that
both Necker and Montmorin had agreed to a proposal of
the moderate party around the first of September to
move the king and Assembly to Soissons or Compiègne,
but the king adamantly refused.[34] The alarm at the
threat of Paris was shared by all the moderates.
Clermont-Tonnerre asked the Assembly if, after having
refused to obey armed despotism, referring to the July
days, were they going to submit to the despotism of
popular ferment?[35] The clubs and their leaders of the
popular class at the Palais-Royal had drawn up a list
of deputies that were in effect, condemned for their
support of the royal veto. A list was published
throughout the city of Paris and even at Versailles of
those called "bad citizens." Thousands of letters
were sent out to the provinces to warn the patriots of
the danger of these "bad citizens" and "fly to the
rescue of the state," which they said was in danger.[36]

The immediate threat of the Parisians going to
Versailles en masse was conjured for the moment by
Lafayette who managed to prevent them from crossing
the Sèvres bridge with his National Guard troops. But
the situation remained smoldering. Baron de Staël
wrote to King Gustavus on September 17 that "we are in
the same situation as the inhabitants of the area
around Mount Etna or Vesuvius when the rumblings from
the interior of the volcano indicate another eruption
is imminent."[37] Once again the managers of the
Parisian crowds at the Palais-Royal succeeded in intimidating the National Assembly and to some extent
perhaps the royal government. The moderates lost the
momentum they had been gaining in the assembly and the
"factious ones" seized the initiative. On September
10 the assembly voted by 490 to 21 in favor of a single-house legislature, which defeated the hopes of the
Anglophiles for bicameralism. The moderates on the
constitutional committee, Mounier, Bergasse, Champion
de Cicé, Lally-Tollendal, and Clermont-Tonnerre were

644

replaced by those in favor of the unicameral legislature: Thouret, Target, and Rabaut-Saint-Etienne.[38] None of the latter were among the "factious ones" certainly, but they believed it was unrealistic in the circumstances to get a bicameral legislature accepted.

For some days Necker had realized that there was no chance of getting a two-house legislature, so vehement was the popular suspicion of the "aristocrats." Now the immediate question was the relations between the future single-house and the royal government. It had been assumed in the general cahiers and by the moderates that the king would retain a share of legislative power. He would be able to make proposals for new laws to submit to the legislature, and those passed by that body would require the king's consent in order to become law. This was called the "absolute" or the "definitive" veto of the king. Shortly after the beginning of September Necker came to the decision that a major new concession would have to be made to public opinion. The king must give up the power of an absolute veto and be satisfied with a "suspensive veto" in which he could delay for two subsequent legislatures any proposal which he or his ministers thought unwise or not well considered by the legislature. But if a third elected legislative body insisted on the proposal the king must give it his sanction.[39]

In a memorial written to Louis XVI and presented at a meeting of the Council Necker argued that this kind of veto would be not only expedient in the circumstances, but actually preferable in the new French constitution. Looking into the future to see how the constitution probably would work, Necker saw the danger of a confrontation between the executive and the legislature. If the legislators were strongly supported by public opinion and the king and his advisors believed the measure in question unwise or ill-considered, an absolute veto might cause political convul-

645

sions. "What is most to be feared," Necker wrote, "is the power of an initial movement (of public opinion), the influence of a period of excitement. But all proposals that are subject to calm deliberation, to reflection, will be decided according to reason and justice."[40] The British government achieved this not by the power of absolute veto, which the British king theoretically had, but by the existence of a two-house legislature. The British sovereign used the veto so seldom as to make it an unimportant feature of the constitution. The reason he did not use it was out of prudence. It would be dangerous to veto an act supported by public opinion. But there must also be some restraint on public opinion, and this was provided by the upper house of Parliament. Since France was not going to have an upper house, the suspensive veto would provide that necessary period of calm deliberation and avoid a dangerous showdown between the legislature and the executive. If the king and the ministers were prudent, the absolute veto would never be used, and there would be no restraint on an impulsive legislature supported by an aroused opinion. The suspensive veto until a third legislature sanctioned the measure would allow time for reflection and perhaps compromise.

As with his other attempts at mediation, Necker's compromise proposal alienated both those who insisted on an absolute veto and those who maintained that the king had no right to any kind of a veto however attenuated. In his memoirs written a year later Mounier bitterly condemened what he considered Necker's desertion of those who were trying to preserve the power of the monarch. He wrote that the assembly would have passed the absolute veto if Necker had continued to support it. And he saw this desertion as due to fear of the Parisian democracy. Mounier believed that there was no hope of preserving a strong executive power for the king after giving up the veto. The king became only an official, subject to the whims of the assembly, and no longer a king.[41] On the other hand the "factious ones" maintained that the king should not be permitted even a suspensive veto. Mirabeau said a royal veto "can never prevail against a law solicited by the General Will."[42] However Mirabeau indicated at the same time he might support some kind of concession on the matter if it appeared that the king was being given a veto power which in reality would be ineffective. Abbé Sieyes was willing to support a suspensive veto but for only one legislature rather than two. Necker argued that such a brief suspension would be just as bad as the absolute veto, in that a ministry would fear repudiation by the second legislature, and therefore would never use the veto.[43]

On September 11 Necker sent a letter to the president of the National Assembly with an enclosure of his memorial to the king on the subject of the veto. He requested that the letter and the memorial be read to the assembly. This seemed to affront the deputies' sense of the dignity of the National Assembly, and they refused to permit his communication to be read. However, only four days later, on September 15 the National Assembly voted for Necker's plan, namely the suspensive veto until the third legislature.[44] It appeared that his influence in the assembly was still considerable, even if he had alienated some of the important moderates like Mounier.

It was certainly not Necker's intention to weaken the full executive power of the monarchy by giving up the absolute veto. In his concluding remarks in his letter to the president of the assembly he once again called attention to the necessity of a strong executive government: "...do not lose sight, gentlemen, that if you neglect the precautions necessary for preserving to the executive power its dignity, its ascendancy, its power, this kingdom is threatened by the disintegration of order; and this disorder can destroy in unforeseen upheavals the edifice you have sought to

erect with so much care."[45] He told the deputies that
all of Europe as well as France was watching with intense interest their actions in these crucial days.
"Do not gamble with those precious hopes by a spirit
of disunity, the natural effect of exaggeration in
opinions. The good that you can do seems to me boundless; but it is by moderation that will give it stability; that alone is the power where can be found the
concord and the unity of all the means by which you
can bring about the prosperity of the state."[46]

What made the defense of the king's executive
power so difficult for Necker and the moderates was
the paradoxical situation of having to govern at the
same time as the great decisions were being made about
the constitution. The enemies of the moderates made
the most of this awkward situation to force the acceptance of their constitution which eventually left the
king simply an official of the government subject to
the dictates of an omnipotent assembly. This appeared
over the question of the king's consent to the August
decrees of the National Assembly, those passed on the
"crazy night" of August 4 and the days following. On
September 15 the king received a formal request from
the National Assembly to promulgate those decrees.
His reply was evidently written by Necker. The message pointed out that those decrees were often statements of general policies which required more specific
legislation, and the king would have to await those
measures before granting or withholding his consent.
But in the intermediate period, he announced that "I
approve the general spirit of your decrees, but there
are a small number of articles to which I could only
give a conditional adherence at this moment." He made
it clear that these were only his reflections and
those of his council, and they were by no means
definitive or categorical. "I will modify my opinions, even renounce them without difficulty if the observations of the National Assembly request it, for it
is always with regret that I would differ with its

manner of perceiving and thinking."[47]   The polite,
even deferential tone was typically Necker's style in
the government's handling of its relations with the
National Assembly.

The style of Necker was also clearly visible in
the strong desire expressed by the king to admit those
reforms so long called for by the nation: the abolition of "feudalism," the end of unjust privileges, the
equality of all citizens before the law and particularly with respect to the government's taxation. He
indicated reservations about the August decrees only
in those matters where the assembly was inclined to
ignore legitimate rights. On the matter of feudalism
the king reminded the deputies that he had abolished
personal servitude of peasants on his own patrimonial
lands back in 1779 and had hoped thereby to set an example to other fief owners. Such debasing and unjustifiable servitude should certainly be abolished without any compensation to the fief-owners. But there
were certain types of obligations that did not have
that stigma of humiliation and which justice required
compensation to the fief-owners. The king proposed
that for that category of feudal dues the government
itself should assume the financial burden of compensation. Other feudal dues that originated in servitude
but had been commuted to money payments had entered
the value of the lands, just as the case of the taille
reéle, and therefore the owners of those lands who had
purchased them in good faith should receive compensation from those subject to the dues. Even dues which
the National Assembly had decreed should be abolished
without any indemnity required some qualification.
The foreign nobles who held fiefs in Alsac had been
promised by treaties that their feudal rights would
not be interferred with by the government. Those nobles should certainly not be deprived of their property except by a new treaty to which they would agree
and receive compensation, presumbaly also from the
government of France.

The same principle applied to some other articles of the decrees which the king said he could not accept without some qualifications. The abolition of all venal offices, particularly judgeships, should be done but the owners of those offices must be compensated fairly by the government. As for the abolition of the church tithes on the land, the king wondered if the deputies realized that the bulk of this sum levied by the church came mostly from the large landed estates. The ordinary peasant was not much affected. It would not be just to give such a windfall to the wealthy. It would be more reasonable to have that revenue come into the government treasury so that the nation would benefit, not just the few. At the conclusion of this message the king again stated that the assembly was invited to consider and deliberate on these reflections, that he was not insisting upon them. With most of the articles he indicated his complete agreement, such as the abolition of hunting privileges, the accessibility of all subjects to public office, the abolition of the plurality of benefices, and the abolition of provincial privileges.[48]

When the king's message was read to the National Assembly the radical deputies exploded with indignation. Le Chapelier from Brittany asserted that the National Assembly has constituent power and therefore does not ask the king to consent to the August decrees but merely to promulgate them, a statement that drew applause from the assembly. Mirabeau asserted that since the assembly exercises constituent power no one can prevail against it, and the August decrees came under that power. Mirabeau's brother, the vicomte de Mirabeau, was also a deputy in the National Assembly, sent by the Nobility of Limoges. Endowed with some of the eloquence of the family and all of its common sense, he supported the king's message, pointing out its reasonable tenor. His brother the tribune retorted that "when the National Assembly pronounced a great truth the king has no right to question or amend

650

it." This seemed to announce a doctrine of assembly infallibility. The duc de La Rochefoucauld came forward with a motion that since the king had accepted the August decrees in principle and only had reservations regarding details, the assembly might ask him to publish the decrees at once, indicated his approval with the understanding that the details could be worked out through negotiations with the executive government when the time came to implement the decrees with specific laws. He suggested the king should begin negotiations with the foreign princes in Alsace over their rights in that province. The motion of La Rochefoucauld aroused extraordinary hostility among the "factious ones." Volney arose to propose that the deputies should move on with the constitution, get it established, then hold elections for a new legislature in which the likes of La Rochefoucauld would no longer be around. The vicomte de Mirabeau then got up to say that "it might be a good thing if none of us appeared in the next legislature." This bizarre proposal, probably not offered seriously by the vicomte, was eventually adopted by the National Assembly with the result that no deputy to the States-General of 1789 was allowed to stand for election to the Legislative Assembly of 1791. La Rochefoucauld's motion passed in the assembly and was sent to the king, who replied immediately that he would publish the August decrees without delay.[49]

Such was the nature of the deliberations going on at the National Assembly as Necker sat in the office of the Contrôle-général and watched the steady erosion of the finances. Nearly a month had passed since his message of August 27 proposing the loan of 80 million livres and making urgent requests for the assembly to act in specific ways that would help him withstand the steady drift toward bankruptcy. But the assembly had acted upon only two of his requests: the deputies had passed his loan of 80 million and allowed him to fix the terms, and on September 23 they had passed his suggested measure on the gabelle. But the assembly had done nothing about the precipitate decline of other sources of tax revenue; they had not taken steps to assure creditors of their determination to efface the deficit of fixed revenue; nor had they invited directors of the Discount Bank to appear before the finance committee to discuss means of transforming the bank into a national bank. While the deputies debated about the constitution the deficit was growing wider, the resistance of taxpayers was spreading, and the general disorder was continuing. All these matters affected the credit posture of the government, and the result was that the loan of 80 million livres was not being subscribed to very eagerly; and Necker had counted upon that 40 million livres of hard money to meet the expenditures for the remainder of September.

On September 24 Necker again appeared at the National Assembly at his own request. The time had passed for him to be considerate of the feelings of the deputies, or to treat them with that deferential attitude he had always observed in the past. "Gentlemen," he began, "the finances about which I have spoken to you a number of times, have reached the final stage of crisis." All the expedients which he had used since returning to the Contrôle-général more than a year before, were now exhausted. There was nothing more that he could do to avert disaster. It was up to the National Assembly. "The public has been waiting impatiently for the National Assembly to attend to the finances; but the time necessarily consumed by a numerous legislative body has prolonged its deliberations so that after five months in session it has not yet got around to the royal finances."[50]

The fact that foreign and domestic capitalists were withholding their money from government loans was only a reflection of their lack of confidence in the present situation of the government. The tourists were staying away, which deprived the country of a

652

source of hard money to pay for imports which were now terribly in excess of exports, and the trade deficit caused the extraordinary dearth of hard money in the country. Contributing to the same end was the flight of the wealthy out of the country because of the lack of security for persons and property. The foreign bankers who ordinarily had their correspondents in Paris subscribe to loans had given them no commissions. It was the task of the National Assembly to raise up from that abyss the prestige of the government and to demonstrate that it could cope with the crisis.

Coming to the immediate financial crisis, Necker said that 40 million livres were necessary for the remainder of September and the first days of October; 60 million additional would be needed for the rest of the year. "As of yesterday morning," he told the assembly, "the treasury had exactly 12,800,000 livres in the form of notes of the Discount Bank, specie, and promissory notes." It was true, of course, that when he assumed the directorship of the finances thirteen months ago there was much less than that sum in the treasury, only about 400,000 livres. But since that time all the resources available had been used up and no more expedients were possible. From this day until the end of the month, that is scarcely one week away, he faced expenditures that were absolutely necessary, that could not be delayed: payment of the troops, interest on the royal debt, pensions that are necessary, essential help that must be given to several semi-private treasurers who habitually serve the king with their credit: all these would cost from eight to nine million livres. So there would be only three to four million to begin the next month, one week away. And 30 million livres would be necessary for October, and 70 million for the last three months of the year.

"It tears my soul to have to present to you such a picture of our distress," Necker told them. And he

653

compared the present situation to the years of the American War when he had raised 150 million livres a year for extraordinary expenses without anxiety; and also the months preceding the meeting of the States-General when he had held such high hopes for the regeneration of the kingdom that would be a consequence of that great event. "Those times are too near to my memory not to present the most devastating contrast to the present circumstances."[51]

Having presented the situation in its stark reality, Necker then proceeded to suggest what could be done. The most important matter was to restore people's confidence. They would endure sacrifices if they believed they were going to build a stable future. In restoring that order and confidence the financial situation was of the first importance, and the National Assembly must make a concerted effort to implement policies toward that goal. First of all it was necessary to show prospective creditors that the government could eliminate that deficit between ordinary or fixed expenditures and income. Secondly, means must be found to raise the extraordinary income to meet the needs of the remainder of the current year and the beginning of the next.

As for eliminating the deficit, Necker said it would be inappropriate for the finance minister to present an assortment of ameliorations which would not be very convincing to the public, and which would engross the assembly in time-consuming deliberations. Means must be found that are clearly visible and can be understood by the public, and can be either accepted or rejected by the assembly with a minimum of discussion. Regarding the 56 million deficit between fixed expenditure and income that he had reported on May 5, circumstances had altered that figure by late September. The loan of 80 million livres required a yearly reimbursement of 10 million livres, whereas only 5 million had been listed for the ordinary expenditure for anticipations in the account of May. This meant that the deficit now stood at 5 million more livres, or 61 million. It was true that the last loan had not been subscribed to but it must be assumed that it will be, and the interest and amortization costs of that loan must be included in the fixed charges of the royal treasury. The essential part of Necker's proposal for dealing with the deficit was a drastic slash in expenditures: 15 to 20 million from the department of war, 5 million from the King's household, 1 million from the ministry of foreign affairs, 5 to 6 million from pensions; the cost of anticipations had already been reduced by force of the government's discredit, and this would pare off about 8 million from the account submitted in May; the reform of the system of direct taxation on land would yield an additional 15 million livres by reason of the abolition of privileges.

After these and other resources that Necker showed were available and possible he concluded this part of his address by insisting on the basic soundness of the financial and economic positions of the monarchy. There was no need to despair. He pointed out that the remedies herein proposed were not such as to create convulsions in the state. "I do not propose to you, gentlemen, any great subversion to restore order to the finances, no great revolutionary idea, none of which imagination makes out to be genius; everything must be simple in matters of this kind, everything must have continuity, especially at a time where confidence, so necessary a link between the present and the future, is lacking."[52]

Next he turned to the extraordinary income that the government must find to meet the needs of this year and the beginning of the next. It would be unwise to attempt another loan in the present state of the government's discredit. What Necker proposed was "an extraordinary levy on all incomes." This would be a one-time only levy to meet the present crisis. It would be a levy of one-quarter of all incomes. A very important matter in the execution of this levy was how the determination of the revenue of the contributors should be arrived at. The only possiblility for Necker was to take the contributor's own declaration of his revenue. Should he be required to swear under oath the exact measure of his annual income? Necker repudiated this idea. The state should not come between an individual and his religious conscience. Let the contributor simply say "I say truly that . . ." and list his means. Necker's delicacy on this matter was a striking contrast to the roughshod way the National Assembly treated religious conciences at the time it exacted an oath from all priests and bishops to support the Civil Constitution of the Clergy. Necker believed that patriotism would be sufficient to render most declarations honest. In the minutes of the National Assembly it can be seen that practically every day people appeared at the bar of the assembly to make some monetary offering to the state out of sheer patriotism.

This contribution would not be a tax revenue that the citizen was giving up permanently to the state. It would be in the nature of a forced loan. Each contribution would be registered in the parish, in a kind of honor roll. The loan would be reimbursed successively as the recovery of the royal finances permitted. As with his first loan proposal of 30 million, Necker counted heavily upon the spirit of patriotism, that strange exaltation which seemed to have seized the population. He supposed this new nationalism would stengthen the devotion of the French people to the king and the royal government. It scarcely occurred to him that the "factious ones" could ever succeed in capturing this exalted feeling and turning it against the king, who was destined to be called "the last despot."

In the final part of his address to the National Assembly on September 24 Necker urged the deputies to act immediately on three proposals. First, the private citizens be permitted to bring their gold and silver utensils or jewelry to be melted down at the mint to help meet the desperate shortage of hard money. They would receive in return bonds yielding interest. The king and queen had set an example by so disposing of their plate. Second, Necker urged the Assembly to authorize the transformation of the Discount Bank into a National Bank to increase its utility to the government and the public. Third, Necker again pleaded with the assembly to pass a proclamation to the people telling them that the taxes must continue to be paid, both direct and indirect, until the new constitutional order makes other arrangements. Unless this "taxpayers' strike" is halted extraordinary measures like the patriotic levy would only fill the void momentarily. "Nothing will work, gentlemen, nothing can bring about amelioration if the payment of taxes is interrupted, if these collections are not protected by the publicity of your intentions and the firm expression of your will, if the collections do not have the support of law, and if these laws are not sustained by executive power, and if this power should confront resistance superior to its force."[53]

In his last remarks Necker gave vent to some of his innermost feelings. He said he could not understand why so many well-known friends of liberty were spending their time in deliberating upon the constitution and were oblivious to the imminent danger that surrounded them. Could they not suspend those deliberations for awhile to take care of urgent matters? The constitution was already well on the way to completion and it would be no violation of their instructions from their constituents to attend to the present emergency. The assembly must assume responsibility for the present as well as for the future. It is evading the hard decisions. It is easy to declare the abolition of unpopular taxes, but such policies must be accompanied by concrete rather than vague proposals as to how that revenue will be made up.

Despite the bluntness of his message Necker was given a warm reception by the National Assembly on September 24. After his departure from the hall the deputies listened to a long speech by Dupont de Nemours who argued that a better way out of the financial crisis would be for the government to take over the property of the church. Necker's scheme of a patriotic levy would not work, he said, because only landed proprietors who received a "net profit" each year could pay the levy, and it was doubtful if even they could contribute one-fourth of their income. The church received income of about 100 million livres from the tithes, which the state would take over. In addition the church received annual income from its lands which Dupont estimated at 60 million livres. Of course the churches would have to be maintained at government expense, the clergy paid their salaries, and the church's debt serviced.[54] Dupont had all the figures calculated with great precision. What he did not have was the incalculable moral cost of the state's taking over such a large establishment when it's own administration was so weak and when the great majority of clerics were strongly opposed to it.

But fortunately the assembly was more influenced by Necker at the moment and acted promptly on his proposals. The committee on finance was ordered to study them and to report back the next day. It did so and recommended approval. Mirabeau made a motion for acceptance which the editor of the Moniteur wrote was "greeted with almost convulsive applause."[55] Encouraged by this demonstration of support Necker asked to appear again before the assembly on October 1 to lay before the deputies a "project of a decree" in which he spelled out in specific articles all his proposals. Had the assembly been accustomed to writing legisla-

658

tion Necker might have left the task up to it; but evidently he was afraid of further lengthy speeches and delays, and time was of the essence for his proposals. After reading his "project for a decree" Necker concluded: "There, gentlemen, is the project or sketch of the decree which could be the final step in implementing your deliberation regarding the finances. I submit these ideas to your judgment and allow myself once again to say that nothing is more urgent." He concluded by telling the assembly that he was making his own contribution of 100,000 livres which , he said, was considerably more than the proportion of one-fourth his annual income which was called for by the decree. The <u>Moniteur</u> records that "he left the hall in the midst of almost unanimous applause."[56]

It appeared that the moderates were in a fairly strong position in the National Assembly. On September 28 Mounier was elected presiding officer. The vote was light, only 560 being counted. Of that number, 365 went to Mounier and 143 to his closest rival, Jérôme Pétion, who was favored by the radicals. Target received the remaining 52 votes. But the "factious ones" were fertile in tactics that could turn the tables. In the National Assembly, at the Club Breton on the avenue de Saint-Cloud, at the Palais-Royal in Paris plans were afoot to change the balance in favor of the radicals, even though the manipulators behind the scenes remain obscure. On the floor of the National Assembly Mirabeau spoke after Necker's departure to criticize some of the statements made by the Director-General. Necker had used the expression "as much as it is in the power of the National Assembly." This, said Mirabeau, was insulting to the National Assembly which had the power to do whatever it chose![57] Adrien Duport intervened to say that the financial measures just proposed by the government should not be approved by the National Assembly until the king has given his assent to the Declaration of Rights and the constitutional measures that had been decided by the National Assembly, namely the single-house legislature and the suspensive veto.

The assembly did not specifically at this time accept Duport's suggestion to link its support of Necker's financial project with the king's ratification of the constitution. But it did pass by a great majority a resolution that the sub-committee of finance that had been appointed to work with Necker on financial laws would meet with him to work out the final decree on his project. At the same time the assembly enjoined its presiding officer, Mounier, to take to the king the constitution and the Declaration of Rights and ask for his ratification of them.

The special twelve-member sub-committee of the main finance committee did its work promptly and reported to the National Assembly on October 2, presenting its own "project for a decree" which followed exactly that of Necker. But the assembly did not act upon the project until it received word of the king's response to the constitution and the Declaration of Rights. The king's reply finally came on the morning of October 5. As for the constitutional provisions, the king accepted them, but with one "positive condition," namely that the king be granted "the plenitude of executive power." He accepted the Declaration of Rights on principle but recognized that some articles might lead to diverse interpretations. The primary impression left by the king's reply was that while he may have reservations about the precise manner in which some articles may be implemented, they were not serious enough to delay the promulgation of the constitution and Declaration which he was obviously anxious to do in order to restore tranquillity to the country. It was evident that Necker was the author of the communication for it reflected his own ideas and anxieties about the situation.

But even the mild reservations of the king's message drew an angry riposte from the radicals of the National Assembly. "The king has no right to go against the will of the people," declared Muquet de Nanthou, and Robespierre said that "he who can place conditions on a constitution has the right to veto it." Bertrand Barère asked how the "executive power could modify the national power which has created it," meaning by the latter "constituent power." Mirabeau proposed that the assembly insist that the king "clarify" his reply so that the deputies would have no doubt about his acceptance.[58] The assembly adopted that resolution but also asked "the full force of executive power be used to assure the capitol of grain and flour supplies which it needs." The distress of the Parisians in the matter of grain supplies had reached the ears of the National Assembly.

Soon much more was to reach them. During the afternoon of October 5, Mirabeau had a premonition of that "earthquake" baron de Staèl had talked about in September. Mirabeau hurried up to Mounier who was presiding over the session and spoke in a confidential but excited voice: "Mounier, Paris is marching upon us!" "I know nothing about it," replied Mounier. "Whether you believe it or not doesn't matter to me," rejoined Mirabeau, "I'm telling you Paris is marching upon us. Say that you are ill, go the the château and alert them. You can say you have the information from me . . . time is pressing, there is not a minute to lose." Mounier was amused. "So Paris is marching upon us," he said jokingly, "well, so much the better, we will have a republic even sooner."[59]

But Mounier was soon to realize it was not a matter to banter. The Parisians were indeed coming, and their arrival was to seal the fate of executive power and much else, including his own political career. It was to spell the demise of the moderates, and the end of Necker's influence on the course of events.

661

[1] *Correspondance diplomatique*, 110.

[2] Jean Egret, *Necker*, *Ministre de Louis XVI* (Paris, 1975), 329.

[3] Duquesnoy, *Journal*, I, 265.

[4] *Réimpression de l'Ancien Moniteur*, I, 302-303.

[5] Roland Mousnier and Ernest Labrousse, *La XVIII Siècle*. *Révolution intellectuelle, technique et politique* (*1715-1815*) (Paris, 1955), 371.

[6] Duquesnoy, *Journal*, I, 267.

[7] *Archives parlementaires*, VIII, 337-339.

[8] "Discours de M. Necker, premier ministre des finances, à l'assemblée nationale, le 7 août 1789," in *Oeuvres complètes*, VII, 20.

[9] Tronchin to Puari, August 8, 1789, Chapuisat, *Necker*, 315.

[10] Duquesnoy, *Journal*, I, 274.

[11] *Mémoire de M. le comte de Lally-Tollendal, ou Second Lettre à ses commettants*, 126-127; *Archives parlementaires*, VIII, 364 *passim*.

[12] *Archives parlementaires*, VIII, 376.

[13] *Ibid.*, VIII, 367.

[14] *Mémoires de Lally-Tollendal*, 126.

[15] Duquesnoy, *Journal*, I, 278.

[16] Daniel Ligou, *La première année de la Révolution vu par un Témoin*, 52-53.

[17]Ibid., 55.

[18]Archives parlementaires, IX, 147-168.

[19]"Sur l'Administration de M. Necker," in Oeuvres complètes, VI, 123.

[20]"Rapport de M. Necker, premier ministre des finances, lu à l'assemblée nationale le 27 août 1789," in Oeuvres complètes, VII, 23.

[21]Ibid., VII, 29-30.

[22]Loc. cit.

[23]Ibid., 37-38.

[24]Ibid., 32-33.

[25]Duquesnoy, Journal, I, 325.

[26]Archives parlementaires, VIII, 460.

[27]Ibid., IX, 17-23.

[28]Ligou, La première année de la Révolution.

[29]Duquesnoy, Journal, I, 294.

[30]Malouet, Mémoires, I, 339.

[31]Vicomte de Grouchy and Antoine Guillois, eds., La Révolution française racontée par un diplomate étranger, 131.

[32]F. Bussière, "Le Constituant Foucauld de Lardimalie," La Révolution française (Jan.-June 1892), XXII, 204-241.

[33]Mounier, Exposé de la conduite, 39.

[34]Malouet, Mémoires, I, 342.

[35]Archives parlementaries, VIII, 513.

[36]Ligou, La première année de la Révolution, 69.

[37]Correspondance diplomatique, 125.

[38]Jacques Godechot, Les institutions de la France sous la Révolution et l'Empire (Paris, 1959), 77.

[39]"Lettre de M. Necker, premier ministre des finances, à M. le president de l'assemblée nationale, Versailles, le 11 septembre 1789," in Oeuvres complètes, VII, 48.

[40]Ibid., 52.

[41]Mounier, Recherches sur les causes, II, 79.

[42]Ligou, La première année de la Révolution, 71.

[43]"Lettre de M. Necker," in Oeuvres complètes, VII, 62.

[44]Godechot, Les institutions de la France.

[45]"Lettre de M. Necker, " in Oeuvres complètes, VII, 62.

[46]Ibid., 66.

[47]"Lettre du Roi à l'assemblée nationale sur les décrets du 4 août et les jours suivans," in Oeuvres complètes, VII, 67.

[48]Ibid., 79-80.

[49]Archives parlementaires, IX, 33-35.

[50]"Discours prononcé par M. Necker, premier ministre des finances à l'assemblée nationale, le 24 septembre 1789," in Oeuvres complètes, VII, 83-84.

[51]Ibid., 90.

[52]Ibid., 102.

[53]Ibid., 114.

[54]Archives parlementaires, IX, 147-168.

[55]Ibid.

[56]Ibid., IX, 321.

[57]Ibid.

[58]Ibid., IX, 345.

[59]Buchez, Histoire de l'Assemblée constituante, II, 120.

CHAPTER 18

THE OCTOBER CATASTROPHE

In the historical writing on the Revolution of 1789 there seems to be fixed belief that the October days were a reenactment of the July days. In both cases the populace of Paris arose in arms to defeat a counter-revolution. Had it not been for their intervention the result would have been a restoration of the ancien régime. The National Assembly would have been dissolved, the king's absolute authority restored, and the events of the previous two years would have remained a mere episode in the history of France like the Frondes of the previous century. With regard to the July days there is good reason for such a point view. The party whose leaders were the comte d'Artois, the duc de Breteuil, Barentin, and Laurent de Villedeuil were certainly committed to the goal of the counter-revolution.

But there is reason to question whether the October days were a repetition of the earlier event. First of all, there was no overt and visible act on the part of the king or his inner circle that could be compared to the dismissal of Necker on July 11. There were rumors of plots during September according to which the plotters were not planning to crush the Revolution by armed force at the outset, but rather to have the king and his government escape from the influence of the Parisian democracy. Usually the city of Metz was the designated strategic position from which the king would rally to his standard the loyal part of the nation and begin a civil war against Paris. It was rumored that the great hope of the "aristocrats" was help outside France. The queen's brother, Emperor Joseph, would lend his army to accompany the king back to Paris and crush the national movement. The known dissatisfaction of the emperor with the war in the Balkans and his desire to withdraw from it tended to reinforce the conviction of such a plot, at least on the part of those who were already convinced of it.

That the king was seriously intending once again to crush the revolution is not well supported by evidence. At the end of the nineteenth century the French historian, Albert Mathiez, published a series of articles in the Revue Historique which tried to substantiate the thesis of a counter-revolutionary plot.[1] He maintained that the crucial event was the king's "refusal" to sanction the August decrees, the Declaration of Rights, the single-house legislature, and the suspensive veto. But it has been shown in the previous chapter that those assertions were not true. The king did accept the "spirit" of the August decrees and specified those he could accept without qualification, which was most of them. But there were others that he could not accept without qualification and he explained why. It was Necker, of course, who wrote the king's message sent to the National Assembly, and each reservation of the king was substantiated by cogent reasons. The rights of the foreign nobles in Alsace, the fact that abolition of tithes would give an unjustified windfall to land proprietors, the need to compensate those who would otherwise suffer a legitimate property loss--those were all spelled out in the message the king sent to the National Assembly on September 18.[2] The National Assembly responded by asking the king to "promulgate" the August decrees. He replied that "promulgation" was done for laws which "had all the formalities necessary to give them immediate execution."[3] The August decrees were not specific enough to become laws in their existing form. But since the king had already indicated his agreement with the general spirit of the decrees he would immediately "publish" them and thereby demonstrate his approval. The same attitude was expressed about the

Declaration of Rights. This was a statement of general principles which were subject to different interpretations, but he was willing to accept them with that understanding. He had accepted the suspensive veto and the single-house legislature. His message on these constitutional matters did stipulate that the king must be left with full executive powers. The difference between the king's position on all those matters and the radical party in the National Assembly was clear-cut. The notion of "constituent power" could not be accepted by the king because it excluded himself and his ministers from any participation in the framing of the constitution. In the messages he wrote for the king that were sent to the National Assembly, Necker did not specifically refer to this issue. He did talk of "exaggerated opinions" which the doctrine of constituent power certainly was. But he hoped during September that "moderate opinion" would prevail, and his hopes were not unfounded. It was the "October days" that upset his expectation.

Mathiez maintained that the "refusal" of the king to accept the August decrees and the other constitutional decisions of the National Assembly left that body no alternative but to carry out another popular revolution in alliance with the Parisian democracy. He wrote that the moderates who were defeated in the National Assembly on the matter of the bicameral legislature and the absolute royal veto saw no alternative but to join forces with the "aristocrats" of the counter-revolution. Such an alliance was formed, he said, and this threw down the gauntlet to the popular party, the "patriots" who up to the time were attempting to reach an accommodation with the moderates. The popular party he wrote, believed it was necessary to destroy the abuses of the ancien régime before the new order could be built. "The resistance which they encountered (by the king) could not but irritate them . . . They feared especially the Clergy whom they accused of encouraging the king to resist. To prevent

the counter-revolution which was being prepared the
(patriots) sought the support of the clubs and the
Parisian districts."[4]

The only evidence Mathiez produced to substantiate this alleged coalition of the moderates with the
aristocrats was some memoir writers, notably Malouet
and Montlosier. The latter was a political naïf who
had little knowledge and preparation for the role he
was to play as deputy of the Nobility to the States-
General.[5] Malouet was a sincere and honest moderate,
but of unsteady character. He spoke too often in the
assembly when the cause for which he fought would have
been better served by his silence. Etienne Dumont
wrote about Malouet: "He was continually making blunders in the assembly, to whose forms he could not ac-
custom himself. Everything he did was in the wrong
place. . . . but he had intellect, firmness of mind,
good intentions and experience."[6]

While the evidence to support the belief in the
counter-revolutionary plot is feeble, the reasons for
doubting it are compelling. Who were the individuals
who could have been its promoters? Between July and
October the government had issued 200,000 passports to
émigrés.[7] The cream of the crop of the counter-revolution left the country. The comte d'Artois and the
princes who had signed the memorial against the doubling of the Third Estate back in December were all
émigrés. The Polignacs, the Vaudreuil, the ministers
of the July days were either out of the country or in
hiding. There were some fiery orators in the National
Assembly who were hostile to the Revolution: the abbé
Maurys, the Cazalès, the d'Eprésmesnils. But they
were, as Jefferson put it, "a head without a body."[8]

Much is made of the decision of the king and his
advisors to recall the Flanders regiment from the
frontier post of Douai and to station it at Versailles
after the middle of September. This was comparable to

670

the secret orders to bring back from the frontier those regiments which were placed around Paris early in July. But there was a vast difference between the two operations. As a result of the August 30 manifestation at the Palais-Royal the minister of war, La Tour du Pin, and the Secretary of State for the King's Household, Saint-Priest, whose area of administration included the Isle-de-France, became concerned about the security of Versailles, the château, and the royal family. They asked the commandant of the Versailles National Guard, the comte d'Estaing, if he had sufficient military capability to secure the city of Versailles. After a conference with his staff, d'Estaing requested that the Flanders regiment be brought from the frontier and placed under his command. All the troops in the Versailles National Guard were untrained and unpaid militia. D'Estaing believed it necessary to supplement them with more professional troops. It was the municipal government of Versailles that made the formal request to La Tour du Pin for the reinforcements. D'Estaing, a good friend of Lafayette and a veteran also of the American war, had no sympathy with the counter-revolution. Unlike the troop movements of July the stationing of the Flanders regiment was not done secretly. The National Assembly was informed of the decision and the reasons for it. Lafayette himself was not informed of it and was irritated because it seemed to indicate a lack of confidence in his own assurance that he could control the Parisians. The soldiers and officers of the Flanders regiment were required to take the oath of allegience to the nation, which would mean no support for the counter-revolution. The regiment was a force of 1,000 officers and men, in contrast to the 20,000 elite troops brought from the frontier in July. In Paris the National Guard under Lafayette's command numbered 30,000 men. Included were 5,000 well-trained and paid former French Guards, those who had joined the national movement in June. They were fiercely national-

671

istic and intensely suspicious of the counter-revolution. Defending the château at Versailles were some units of Body Guards who were unquestionably loyal to the king. Altogether the troops in the entire Paris area under direct command of the king numbered 3,676 men.[9] What incredible folly it would have been to attempt a showdown with the patriotic National Guard units, even if only to enable the king and his court to flee from Paris to Metz! The Flanders regiment did not consist of foreign mercenaries, as did the regiments stationed around Paris in July, but native French troops who proved to be susceptible to the nationalist exhortations of the Parisians. In the showdown on October 5 they refused to fire on them.

It is true no doubt that some generals and lesser-grade officers were anti-patriotic and willing to place their swords in the cause of counter-revolution. But like the right-wing orators in the National Assembly they were a head without a body. As for the expectations placed in Emperor Joseph, it has already been seen that he had no sympathy for the counter-revolution, and had written a letter to the comte d'Artois earnestly advising him to return to France and make his peace with the Revolution. There has been some suggestion that the queen, enormously unpopular with the Parisians, was involved in the plot, and also the Austrian ambassador, Mercy-Argenteau. But the evidence is not very credible, and anyway even if they were involved their acts could not have gotten very far in the face of opposition from the imperial brother and master.

Finally, if there had been such a plot it would have required a preparation much more elaborate than the one made in June 1791 when the royal couple did attempt to escape from Paris. There is no evidence of any such preparation prior to October 5. The descent of the Parisians on the city and château of Versailles was a bolt out of the blue. The king was hunting when news arrived at the château of the coming of the Parisians. The deliberations that took place in the hurriedly convened council meeting show that flight would have been an extremely improvised operation.

The conclusion of these observations must be that the notion that the king was seriously planning another coup against the revolution by force, or alternately was planning to escape from the control of the Parisians in order to raise the banner of civil war against them is nothing but a myth. It was certainly not the king and Necker who were the aggressors in the October days. They made every effort to be conciliatory with the National Assembly, even going further than moderates like Mounier thought wise. The initiative that set in motion the events of the October days did not come from Versailles but from Paris.

The events in Paris during August and September paralleled in some ways those at Versailles. To cope with the serious threat of famine, to patrol the city and maintain order, to try to exercise restraint over the demagogic orators at the clubs of the Palais-Royal, and the incredible press, a strong executive authority was needed. Bailly was faced with a situation similar to Necker's. He tried to reason with the Assembly of Representatives of the Commune and explain why they could not assume all the responsibilities of government. There were indeed important functions for the assembly in representative government. But assemblies also had to realize what they were not competent to do, what must be left to the executive government of the city, consisting of the mayor, and the commandant of the National Guard and their staffs. The assemblymen did not see themselves consigned to such a modest role. They wanted to take charge of everything, such as sending messages to the government and National Assembly at Versailles behind the back of the mayor. The original number of 120 representatives that took over from the Assembly of Electors on July

31 was increased to 180 deputies during August. In mid-September Bailly wanted to enlarge the number to 300 representatives thinking it would be made clearer that the assembly was not in charge of administration. He also wanted to get the assembly to appoint a select council of 20 members who would assist the mayor in the executive government. He got the 300 representatives but not the select council. For the representatives thought they were councilors as well as representatives, and now it was 300 who intervened in everything. It was in vain that Bailly tried to get them to understand that "the executive power must be strong and constantly active and can never be thwarted in its march."[10] Eventually, he got the Council but he had to submit to one of sixty members, one councilman chosen from each district. Even more frustrating was Bailly's relations with the sixty district assemblies and their executive committees. They acted like sixty independent republics, each thinking it represented the General Will. Each looked upon the Assembly of Representatives as their servant and did not hesitate to revoke its decrees and substitute their own. Bailly tried to persuade them that sixty districts could not each wield sovereign powers. He granted that authority reposed in the sixty assemblies, but they had sent representatives to sit in the assembly of the Commune, and those deputies must be allowed to make the decision for all sixty assemblies. It was the district assemblies who had organized batallions of National Guard troops during the July days. They sought to govern their batallions, even to the minute details concerning their uniforms rather than leaving such matters to the commanding general of the Parisian guard, the marquis de Lafayette.

The dispute between Bailly and the assemblies was illustrated by the problem of subsistence that continued to threaten the city with famine. The harvests had been completed during the last two weeks of August, and it was a bountiful crop. Necker was anxious

for the new grain to appear on the market so the royal
government could be relieved of the great financial
burden it had shouldered since the beginning of his
second ministry. Near the end of August he began to
discontinue import subsidies and government purchases
of grain. But somehow there was a long delay before
the new crop appeared in the market places. Some observers, including Jefferson, attributed this not to
the shortage of grain but of flour. There had been a
lack of wind and low water in the streams which impeded the milling of flour. There were problems also
in returning to the system of free enterprise after
such a long period of dependence on the government.
Bakers seemed to fear going out to purchase grain because popular prejudice against "monopolizers" made it
dangerous for them to maintain large stocks. The real
cause of the problem of subsistence continued to be
the turmoil in the country, the breakdown of habitual
authority for regulating the commerce in grain. Local
authorities tended to impede the transit of grain
through their jurisdictions. In Paris the district of
Saint-Nicholas-des-Champs sent a deputation to investigate the central marketplace, the Halles, and complained to the assembly of the Commune that they were
not given the informtion requested. The Commune itself was besieged by countless deputations from the
district assemblies demanding information about the
subsistence problem. "This evening," wrote Bailly on
August 22, "we had to listen to ten to twelve deputations, and it occupied our time from six o'clock until
midnight."[11]

Bailly and the subsistence committee of the Commune took charge of the provisioning of the capitol,
relieving Necker of some of the burden although the
royal government continued to provide the finances.
Now it was Bailly's sleep that was troubled by the
threat of famine. "The supplies of grain were always
so short at this time that the life of the inhabitants
of Paris depended each day upon the exactness of the

675

shipments to the mills, on that of the millers, and on the diligence of shipments to Paris." The failure of a day's supply due to some accident could be catastrophic. On one occasion a full day's supply had to be brought to Paris from Poissy by wagons since it would not have arrived at the city in time by the usual transport by water. Bailly had dispatched wagons to bring the supplies; an officer at Poissy did not know of the critical situation at Paris and ordered the wagons to return empty to Paris. Quite by accident Bailly heard of this and just in time ordered the convoy to return and bring the sacks of flour from the boats at Poissy. By such a slender thread hung the preservation of the Parisian population from famine!

The mayor was assisted by devoted public servants and the subsistence committee of the Commune. Some had been electors of the Electoral Assembly and therefore fell under suspicion of the popular elements. The Parisians were extremely irritable about the bread supply. "The most absurd rumors circulated," wrote Bailly, "directed against officials who were doing their utmost to avert a famine." On one occasion some "evil-intentioned individuals" broke into a storage place where spoiled flour had been kept away from other supplies and distributed it to the populace, alleging that this was the way the people were being abused. What was most disturbing for Bailly was the reports he received of popular gatherings that could turn into a general insurrection. "Concern over subsistence was a means always at hand to mobilize the crowds to serve other ends then (remedying) the problem of subsistence."[12]

While the mayor felt grievously hampered by the assemblies he did not think they were among the malevolently-disposed. The members of the assemblies, both at the Commune and the districts were on the whole honorable, patriotic, and upright citizens. He could not say the same for the ringleaders of the crowds that frequented the Palais-Royal. The crowds were intensely politicized. The orators and journalists at the Palais-Royal presented political problems such as the royal veto which required calm and educated discussion as apocalptic; the issue at stake was the blackest despotism versus true liberty. And their proposal for dealing with the despots was forthright. In the fifteenth issue of his journal, L'Ami du Peuple, Jean-Paul Marat challenged his readers: "Ignorant people, will you always be victims of your blindness? Open your eyes at last, come, come out of your lethargy, purge the committees, keep the healthy members, sweep away the corrupt, those royalist pensioners, those sly aristocrats, those infamous men, those false patriots. You can expect nothing from them but slavery, misery, desolation.."[13]

The orators at the Palais-Royal on the evening of August 30 denounced the "horrid plot" of the aristocracy to give the king a veto on legislation. A motion was made in one of the clubs (de Foy) that, if the aristocrats in the National Assembly did not desist in their efforts to give the king a veto, an army of 15,000 would to go Versailles and see that the Nation recalled its unfaithful representatives and replaced them with others. The marquis de Saint-Huruge, until recently an inmate of the insane asylum at Charenton, was the foremost orator. He was commissioned to take the message to the National Assembly. The message said that 15,000 men were ready to march to Versailles and inflict on the traitors who supported the veto the fate of Foulon and Bertier de Sauvigny.[14] Saint-Huruge resolutely set out on his mission, accompanied by a group of followers that Bailly estimated at 100 to 200. As mentioned in the previous chapter he was intercepted by Lafayette and troops of the National Guard at the Sèvres bridge and forced to turn back.

Failing in the attempt to go to Versailles on the 30th, the same group, the Café de Foy at the Palais-Royal, sent a deputation the next day to the representatives of the Commune proposing that the district assemblies review the deputies at Versailles, replace them if needed, and give them an imperative mandate against the veto. In addition the National Assembly would be called upon to suspend the vote on the veto until the other provinces could be consulted. "Nothing," wrote Bailly, "was more seditious and dangerous than such propositions. They would destroy the representative system." He said that the editor of "The Revolutions of Paris," Elysée Loustalot, was the author of these preposterous demands. But Bailly suspected Mirabeau also.[15] He noted the paradoxical fact that Mirabeau was the favorite of the Palais-Royal crowd, who believed his life was in danger from the "aristocrats." In fact Mirabeau secretly supported the absolute veto of the king, which for anyone else except the Tribune would have earned a place on the proscribed list of Saint-Huruge.[16] The assembly of the Commune simply dismissed the deputation from the Palais-Royal out of hand. Furthermore the assembly passed a formal decree condemning the activities of the Palais-Royal, leaving no doubt that it had had enough of them. The decree called upon the commander of the National Guard to keep the Palais-Royal under surveillance and prevent "attrouppments" which in that day did not mean peaceful assemblies, but referred to crowds provoked into existence for violent and unlawful purposes. The decree was sent to all sixty districts for the citizens to read and sign, showing that they "disavowed such excesses and disorders of which the city of Paris will eternally blush if true citizens could be suspected of having any part of it."[17]

After the beginning of September the National Guard troops continually patrolled in the area of the Palais-Royal. As in the National Assembly at Versailles it seemed that the city of Paris was firmly in the hands of the moderates. The assembly of the Commune was indignant when the deputies of the Palais-Royal signalled at the time they were led out of the hall, by a crude gesture, that the members of the assembly would end up on the "lanterne" which was their favorite mode of executing their enemies.[18]

What tended to destabliize this situation during September was events concerning the trained and paid components of the National Guard, the 5,000-man contingent which had formerly been the French Guards. These were the soldiers who had defected from the command of the duc de Châtelet back in June. They had been the shock troops for Revolution during the July days. Perhaps because they felt some guilt about their original disobedience to the king, and their violation of the oath taken to support the king, the former French Guards were acutely sensitive to any rumor of a threatened counter-revolution. They were apprehensive about the units of bodyguards that had replaced them at Versailles as principal defenders of the king, the royal family, and the court. The French Guards would not really feel secure unless they could resume their old posts as protectors of the king. They wanted, in other words, to supplant the king's Bodyguards. On August 25 at the time Louis XVI celebrated "the day of Saint-Louis," he invited Bailly, Lafayette, and a detachment of National Guard troops to come to Versailles and participate in the ceremony. It soon appeared that the entire National Guard wanted to be included in the invitation! Lafayette and Bailly feared that they might all go uninvited and they got a decree from the assembly of the Commune forbidding any armed Parisian going out of the city.[19]

About the middle of September the former French Guards, now usually referred to as the "grenadiers," were becoming more insistent that the king was being influenced by "aristocrats" and that they should replace the Bodyguards at the château. On September 17 a meeting of grenadiers decided to carry out the project. Lafayette heard of it and managed to persuade them to abandon it. But it was this incident that alarmed the ministry at Versailles. What if the grenadiers did come, could the court and the National Assembly be protected? Lafayette was aware of this anxiety and wrote a letter to Saint-Priest assuring him that he had thwarted the grenadiers' project and he could be depended upon to keep the troops of his command obedient. It was then that Saint-Priest put the matter to the commandant of the Versailles National Guard with the consequences described above. The coming of the Flanders regiment caused a violent stir in the districts and among the National Guard troops in Paris. Deputations from the districts interpellated the assembly of the Commune and Bailly about the matter, demanding complete information. Bailly obliged by sending letters to both Saint-Priest and La Tour du Pin asking about the troop movements. La Tour du Pin replied that the Flanders regiment was stationed at Versailles due to the request of the municipal government there, and that the National Assembly had been informed of the decision. Saint-Priest replied that "well-founded rumors that armed men were coming to Versailles to prevent the arrival of the Flanders regiment had caused the king to decide on some military measures."[20] The assembly of the Commune sent commissioners to inquire into the matter and sought to allay the fears of the districts. But then the rumors began to circulate in the press about the plans for the king and the government to escape from the influence of Paris and to go to Metz to raise the standard of the counter-revolution. The situation of public opinion among the districts remained tense, as it did among the troops of the grenadiers and the National Guard.

Near the end of September the National Guard of Paris had been organized by Lafayette into a force of 30,000 men. Only 5,000 grenadiers were paid, the re-

maining batallions being unpaid militia, and were
still the creation of the sixty districts. But their
morale was very high. They were intensely patriotic
and intolerant of those who did not share their exaltation. On Sunday September 27 a brilliant and moving
ceremony took place in the cathedral of Notre Dame in
Paris during which the standards of the different
batallions received their "benediction." It was offi-
ciated by the Archbishop of Paris in the presence of
Bailly and Lafayette. The archbishop must have shud-
dered when the exuberance of the occasion led the
batallions to fire off volleys from their rifles inside the cathedral! But the day demonstrated to
Parisians who witnessed the ceremonies that Lafayette
now commanded a force of well-drilled and disciplined
men. He was potentially the most powerful individual
in the kingdom. But he never aspired to become the
military dictator of the Revolution. He was sincerely
devoted to both the Revolution and the king, with an
unselfishness that resembled Necker's. He was a citizen first and a soldier second, like his mentor and
model, Washington. As in the case of Necker, his upright character earned him the contempt of those who
think only egotism and corruption are befitting a
statesman.

The last entry of Bailly in his memoirs was dated
October 1.[21] The subsistence crisis was still his
foremost concern. Although the harvest had been completed six weeks earlier there was still a shortage of
flour in Paris. He continued to subsidize Parisian
bakers by paying them nine livres per sack of flour,
which Necker had authorized him to do. But there
seemed to be tension between the bakers and the
Parisian government. Bailly suspected collusion among
the bakers to withhold bread from the market by refusing to bake. Long lines formed at the bakeries, which
greatly disturbed the mayor. It was the women of the
families who stood in those long lines, and who were
becoming increasingly exasperated. They could not un-

681

derstand why there should be shortage given the bountiful harvest. They were susceptible to false rumors
of the most absurd kind, such as that the Archbishop
of Paris was secretly giving money to bakers to prevent them from baking their usual quota. Again there
was that violent impulse to punish those who were responsible for their misery, and the demand for prompt
justice was joined with the elemental demand for
bread. It was an explosive situation, one that called
for extreme prudence on the part of the government at
Versailles.

    The Flanders regiment arrived at Versailles on
September 23. A week later its officers were invited
to attend a military banquet hosted by the royal Bodyguards. Officers and a few soldiers of other units,
notably the Versailles National Guard, were also invited. This was not an unusual occurrence in the ways
of military life at the time, but it was unusual for
the royal Bodyguards. It was also a rare privilege
for them to hold the festive event in the theatre of
the opera at the château. The opera adjoined the marble courtyard; above the courtyard was the balcony of
the royal apartments. The decision of the king and
queen to make an appearance at the banquet was another
unusual occurrence. It seems to have been made on the
spur of the moment, at the suggestion of a lady-in-
waiting of the queen's court. She thought her mistress was "in a sad mood" and needed something to
cheer her up.[22] The queen seemed to hesitate, but finally yielded to the suggestion and persuaded the king
to come also, who had just returned from a hunting
trip. The dauphin and princess were taken along also.
The entrance of the royal family into the banquet hall
created quite a stir. The queen's gesture of going
around the tables, holding the dauphin in her arms,
and greeting officers and soldiers individually made a
profound emotional impact. The royal family stayed
only a short time in the banquet hall and then withdrew to their apartments. But their presence was as

intoxicating as the ample quantities of wine served at the tables. Repeated toasts were drunk in honor of the royal family. The party became rather boistrous as the evening wore on. The revellers spilled out of the opera hall into the marble courtyard. The demonstrations of loyalty to the king and the queen were by no means unusual or shocking. But rumors spread that the officers shouted slogans disrespectful of the National Assembly, and that the Bodyguards, who still wore the white insignia of the royal house rather than the tricolor, persuaded the officers of the National Guard of Versailles and the Flanders regiment to do likewise, casting off and trampling underfoot the tricolor cockade.

In the days following the banquet Parisian radical journals made the most of the incident. Loustalot asserted that "there must be a second revolution! Everything is preparing for it. The soul of the aristocratic party has not left the Court." Marat and Camille Desmoulins were even more shrill in their denunciation of the "insult" to the national emblem. Deputations from the more militant district assemblies again appeared at the Commune demanding that the representatives carry out a thorough investigation of the outrage to the nation. Whether the revellers of October 1 did or did not express counter-revolutionary slogans, or purposely fail to toast the Nation along with the king and queen, or whether they did flaunt the white standard of the Bourbons and or the black one of the Habsburgs and desecrated the tricolor has been a disputed subject between royalist and republican historians. Mathiez insisted that such acts did occur and that they were a clear manifestation of a serious counter-revolutionary plot: "It has been sometimes denied that the national emblem [the tricolor] was trampled upon and replaced by the black or the white cockade. But the most authentic witnesses attest that those facts were true."[23] But four out of the five witnesses that he cited were not present and got their information at second-hand. Baron de Staël did indeed tell Gustavus III that the revellers "had imprudently outraged the national cockade and distributed others" but he was in Paris rather than Versailles at the time of the banquet and was relying upon what he had heard.[24] De Staël was alienated from the queen at this time and might have been particularly receptive to criticism of her conduct. The British attaché at Paris wrote to the Duke of Leeds about the incident: "Happy would it have been had their festivity ended in noise and singing, but unfortunately they forgot themselves, and in the height of imprudence and mistaken zeal they all tore the National Cockade from their hats and trampled them underfoot, with many oaths against all those who wore them and whom they considered as traitors to the king. The Gard du Corps [Bodyguards] supplied themselves with black Cockades in the room of those they had thrown away. . . ."[25] But the Bodyguards had never worn the national cockade and still were sporting the white emblem of the Bourbons at the time of the banquet.[26] So it is evident that this witness was reporting from hearsay and his source was not reliable. Mathiez also cited the journal of Duquesnoy and the memoirs of Gaultier de Biauzet, both of whom were members of the National Assembly and most likely were not invited to the banquet. The fifth witness of the event was an aide-de-camp of the comte d'Estaing, who was present at the banquet and wrote in a note to his chief that along with vivats for the king and the queen were denunciations of the National Assembly and the Duke of Orleans. But nothing was said in this note about the national cockade or the white and black.[27]

A study of the October days published later than Mathiez's, in 1924, attempted to separate rumors from reality and concluded that the revellers did express strong support of the king and queen, but that there was not sufficient evidence to prove they had insulted

684

the national cockade.[28] The American biographers of Lafayette have concluded that the truth of this matter is still uncertain, but they write that "for our purposes what was thought in Paris to have happened in Versailles is more important than what actually happened."[29] This might be suitable in a biography of Lafayette but will hardly do in a biography of Necker. Since the October days were so crucial in his own career, and indeed for the entire course of the Revolution it is necessary to separate myth and rumor from reality. It makes a great deal of difference if the October days were a defensive reaction of the Revolution from a serious threat to crush it and restore absolutism; or, whether the event was inspired by rumors that were untrue. The probabilities seem to be that those who were managing the crowds in Paris took advantage of the imprudence of the royal couple in going to the banquet hall and they either invented or exaggerated the incidents by which they aroused the Parisian populace. The fact that the officers and soldiers of the Flanders regiment placed themselves immediately under Lafayette's command when they learned of the mass exodus from Paris to Versailles casts serious doubt on the truth of the reports printed in Paris journals that they desecrated the national emblem. Unfounded, baseless rumors circulating in Paris was typical of the time, and Loustalot, Camille Desmoulins, and Jean-Paul Marat were not distinguished for objective and impartial journalism.

At Paris the assembly of representatives at the Hôtel-de-Ville and the commandant of the National Guard were clearly more alarmed about the situation in that city than any supposed counter-revolutionary plot at Versailles. When Marat falsely alleged that a representative had stolen some documents the assembly passed a decree condemning l'Ami du peuple and inviting the accused to bring Marat to court.[30] This decree was published and posted in all the sixty districts. On October 4, which was a Sunday, the assem-

685

bly decided it was necessary to remain in session all day because of the alarming unrest in the population. Lafayette appeared before the assembly that morning to assure the representatives that he was taking every precaution to maintain order in the city. At the same time the assembly took care to denounce the wearing of the white cockade of the Bourbons or the black of the Habsburgs. The wearing of the tricolor cockade was made obligatory on all citizens and Lafayette was ordered to enforce those decrees, which also were posted in all districts. The assembly was obviously doing its utmost to prevent acts or conduct that would incite the Parisians to violent activity beyond its ability to cope with it.

On Monday morning, October 5, women shopped early for the daily supply of bread. Bakeries were probably closed, or at least many of them, on Sundays, and the women arrived early to get in line. It can readily be imagined how they felt when the bakeries failed to open, or if they arrived at the counter inside and found the stock sold out. They gathered around in crowds in the streets, giving vent to their feelings. One natural-born leader seized a military drum at an arsenal and with it summoned the others to follow her to the Hôtel-de-Ville to make known their feelings to the assembly of representatives, the mayor and the commander of the National Guard. The assembly had stayed in session late that night so there were few in the Hôtel-de-Ville. Bailly and Lafayette were not yet on the scene. Thousands of women crowded into the Place de Grève opposite the Hôtel-de-Ville calling for bread. They were joined by crowds of rough-appearing men from the poor districts of Saint-Antoine and Saint-Marceau who were armed with picks, shovels, axes, hatchets, anything they could seize as a possible weapon. With these they broke into the Hôtel-de-Ville and the women roamed throughout the building. They discovered an arsenal containing 700 to 800 rifles and two cannon. A hero of Bastille Day, one

686

Stanislas Maillard arrived and was recognized by the crowd. He managed to assume leadership of the movement. Now the crowds were shouting "on to Versailles." They would take their grievance about the bread shortage to the king himself and the National Assembly. Maillard succeeded in getting much of the crowd to leave the Hôtel-de-Ville and move to the Champs-Elysée as a staging area preparatory to going to Versailles.

Gradually representatives and officials of the Commune showed up. The city came alive. All sixty of the district assemblies were activated by the ringing of the tocsin. The districts responded to the request of Jean-Baptiste Gouvion, Lafayette's second in command of the National Guard, to send militia units to the Place de Grève. When Lafayette arrived he found the National Guard units and especially the companies of grenadiers firmly resolved not to take any action against the civilian crowds. Even more, they demanded that the commandant accompany the National Guard and the civilian crowds to Versailles and support their petition. It was a mutinous situation that Lafayette faced. He asked in disbelief if they were taking up arms against the king to whom they had taken an oath of obedience. The reply of the leaders of the grenadiers was:

> My general, we are deputies of the six com-
> panies of the grenadiers. We do not think
> you are a traitor, but we believe the gov-
> ernment is betraying you. It is time to put
> a stop to it. We will not turn our bayonets
> against women who are asking for bread. Ei-
> ther the Committee on Subsistence is corrupt
> or it is incompetent to administer its af-
> fairs. In either case it must be changed.
> The people are suffering; the source of the
> trouble is at Versailles. We must go find
> the king and bring him to Paris; we must ex-

terminate the Flanders regiment and the
King's Bodyguards who have trampled under
foot the national cockade. If the king is
too weak to wear his crown, then he should
give it up. We will crown his son, name a
council of Regency, and everything will be
better.[31]

Again, as he had two weeks earlier, Lafayette
used all his persuasive powers to try to talk them out
of this project. For several hours, from about 11:00
a.m. to nearly 4:00 p.m. there was a standoff.
Lafayette was determined not to be dictated to by men
under his command. But eventually his iron will weakened when he saw that the grenadiers could not be
shaken from their resolve. Grosser men than the
grenadiers began to indicate clearly that they were
quite ready to make Lafayette the next victim to hang
from a lamp post in the _Place_ _de_ _Grève_. He had only
two alternatives: to sacrifice his own life then and
there, or lead the National Guard to Versailles, more
their prisoner than their commander, hoping he could
yet mitigate the catastrophe that threatened. The assembly of representatives agreed with him on the second alternative and named four representatives to accompany him on the trek to Versailles.[32]

Meanwhile from seven to eight thousand women set
out before noon from the Champs Elysées for Versailles. Maillard managed to control them so that
there was little looting or destruction of property en
route. But the women were accompanied by those ruffi-
ans from the Saint-Antoine and the Saint-Marceau districts. There were also some National Guard units in
the first crowds that reached Versailles about 3:00
p.m. It was dismal weather. A driving rain added to
the misery of hunger. But Maillard impressed upon the
women the necessity of peaceful rather than a threatening demonstration. Maillard was admitted along with
some women to present their petition to the National

688

Assembly. They demanded that the king and the National Assembly both take steps to alleviate the bread shortage. They asked that the president of the National Assembly conduct them to the king. Mounier had just been enjoined by the assembly to go to the king and ask again for his sanction of the constitutional measures and the Declaration of Rights, this time "purely and simply" without those reservations in his first message. Mounier therefore consented to have some representatives of the Parisian women accompany him to the king's apartment and present their petition. On his way to the château he could see the size of the crowds from Paris. The gates to the main square of the château (the Place d'Armes) were guarded by the King's Bodyguards. They admitted Mounier and twelve women to go to the château. The women delegates were received sympathetically by the king. A seventeen-year-old girl who read the petition fainted in his presence and he helped revive her. The female deputation left the council room assured by the king that he would take immediate steps to remedy the bread shortage. A decree was drawn up by the Keeper of the Seals which gave specific instructions to officials on the matter, a copy of which was given to the women. They were excited by the encounter with the king and left shouting "Vive le Roi." But when they returned to their comrades they found themselves under a cloud of suspicion. They were accused of having accepted bribes from the king and his counsellors![33]

In fact relations between the Parisian crowds standing outside the iron grill that enclosed the Place d'Armes and the King's Bodyguards were anything but cordial. The Guards were already the target of the grenadiers, whose aim was to replace them as the king's protectors. Some violent incident occurred and for a moment it appeared that the Parisians would fire their cannon into the midst of the King's Bodyguards. This was prevented by pacification efforts on both sides, in addition to the rainy weather which prevented the powder from igniting. The crucial element in the armed forces was the disposition of the Versailles National Guard. As soon as the Paris crowds appeared the Commandant of the Versailles National Guard, the comte d'Estaing and his second-in-command the comte de Gouvernet (who was the son of the war minister, La Tour du Pin) left their posts and went to the château. They had received orders from the municipal government of Versailles to assist the king in escaping from Versailles to safety.[34] Apparently the municipal government thought the king would be well-advised to get away. Some troops were already stationed at the château of Rambouillet, half-way between Versailles and Chartres, a safe distance from the Parisian crowds but not a long journey for the king. Because of the absence of the two generals the command of the Versailles National Guard devolved upon a lieutenant-colonel, one Laurent Lecointre, who proved to have the coolest head in Versailles on that day.

As soon as the authorities at the château learned of the imminent arrival of the Parisians they stationed the King's Bodyguards in front of the iron grill of the Place d'Armes. A contingent of dragoons was stationed on their right, and to the right of the dragoons, reaching down to the stables, was the Flanders regiment. While waiting for the deputation of women to return from their interview with the king, the Parisian women mingled with the dragoons, winning them over to the side of the Parisians. Scarcely less effective was Colonel Lecointre. He found that the troops under his command were steadfastly sympathetic to the Parisians and would not turn their arms against them. So Lecointre contacted the commander of the King's Bodyguards, the comte de Luxembourg, and asked what he intended to do. The latter said he was under orders not to fire on the Parisians, and to do nothing to provoke them. Lecointre assured him that this was the intention of the Versailles National Guard. Next he accosted the officers of the Flanders regiment and found that their disposition was entirely pacific. The officers said they had never intended to do harm to the "bourgeois." The soldiers of the Flanders regiment demonstrated this friendly feeling by distributing a large quantity of cartridges to the National Guard troops.[35] But it was still very difficult to establish peace with the King's Bodyguards. A deputation of about fifty Guards led by the comte de Luxembourg left the château unarmed to attempt negotiations with the Parisians. Luxembourg told them that the Bodyguards intended the following day to take the oath of loyalty to the nation and to adopt the tricolor standard. But these efforts proved abortive. Shots rang out from both sides, and the deputation of Luxembourg had to beat a hasty retreat. It was now a stand-off between the King's Bodyguards defending the château and the Parisians, who had the Versailles National Guard firmly on their side. The dragoons and the Flanders regiment were at least neutral.

Now the drama took place inside the château. What should the king do? Flight from the terrible control of the Parisians was certainly a strong impulse. Only one minister in the government, Saint-Priest, advocated this course. Necker strongly opposed it. The other ministers, according to Necker's later work on the French Revolution were too timid to take a stong stand on the question. So the debate was between Necker and Saint-Priest.[36] During the discussion an attempt was made to take some royal carriages out of the stockade. The Versailles National Guard firmly spiked it. It was evident that the château was practically under siege. That the Bodyguards could get the royal family out of Versailles and to Rambouillet Necker thought was feasible. But there would be bloodshed, and this directed his thought to the political implications. The National Assembly would be left behind, and terrible vengeance could be wreaked on all those moderate deputies who were on the proscribed lists of the Palais-Royal. Those in the government who could not escape would similarly be held hostage. The very act of flight would play into the hands of the king's enemies. His attempt to escape from the Parisians would have been misinterpreted. He wrote later that "they [the Parisians] would have attributed his flight to a long-prepared plot. They would have propagated the idea that the people and the National Guard of Paris had come to Versailles expressly to foil such a plot; and one knows by experience to what extent one can become master of [public] opinion by that multitude of dismal brochures which, directed by an identical spirit and with any energy without parallel, covers today the entire landscape of France."[37]

There were other considerations just as compelling. The government coffers were empty. How could the king set up a new government outside Paris and Versailles? The latter cities would have maintained control of the administrative apparatus together with what funds were still to be found. Finally, the subsistence of Paris still hung by a delicate thread. Supplies of grain would have been interrupted by the outbreak of civil war. Famine in the city would have been a certainty. It was this consideration which made a particularly strong impression on the king during the debate between Necker and Saint-Priest. "I must say in tribute to the king that this consideration had a powerful influence on him," wrote Necker; "it was Paris which had just used violence against him, and it was in part for the interests of the Parisians that he decided to remain with their city and resist the personal motives which could have induced him to flight."[38] There were other political considerations: the king would necessarily have sought refuge in a city not too far from Paris, and the ardent nationalist feeling and fear of civil war would be just as strong in the provincial city as in Paris. There was one further consideration that Necker did not discuss in his 1791 book, but later in

692

his memoirs on the French Revolution. The Palais-
Royal who had probably stirred up the Parisians to
swarm to Versailles were expecting that the king would
flee from them. Their scheme was to have the Duke of
Orleans proclaimed lieutenant-general of the kingdom.
The flight of Louis XVI could be interpreted as a de
facto abdication, as the flight of King James from
England in 1688 was interpreted by Parliament. "Do
not do what your enemies want you to do," was Necker's
advice to the king.[39]

But if the king were not to flee from the control
of the Parisians it would be necessary to treat with
them. There was some bewilderment as to what exactly
the Parisian crowds wanted. The cry for bread was
clear enough, but there were evidently further demands
of a political nature. From the château the impreca-
tions against the King's Bodyguards and the queen
could be heard. It was they who were suspected of being the promoters of the plot to take Louis XVI to
Metz and get help from abroad for the counter-revolution. It was concern for the safety of the queen that
made Louis XVI consider escaping to Rambouillet. Even
after the initial decision was made not to flee he
seems to have had second thoughts. At least there was
another attempt to see if carriages and horses could
get through the barrier. It was found they could not.
The only possibility was to remain and face the demands of the Parisians. With respect to securing the
bread supply at Paris, the king sent the following
message to the National Assembly: "I am deeply moved
by the deficiency of provisions at Paris. I shall
continue to support the zealous efforts of the municipal government with all the means and resources in my
power, and I will give the most categorical orders
that the transport of grain on all routes be free, and
there be no restraints on those shipments destined for
Paris."[40] Later in the evening Mounier returned from
the château to the National Assembly with the king's
express promise that "I accept purely and simply the

articles of the constitution and the Declaration of
the Rights of Man that the Assembly has presented to
me." Both these pronouncements of the king were read
to the assembly, printed and distributed. Some of the
leaders of the women's procession and Maillard received printed copies of these royal promises, and believed that their mission had been accomplished. With
the assistance of the king's government who provided
horses and carriages for them, they returned to Paris
about the time that Lafayette and his troops arrived
at Versailles.[41]

It was of course impossible to transport all the
women back to Paris by royal carriage. Many had taken
shelter in the Menus Plaisirs assembly hall, making it
difficult for the presiding officer to maintain an atmosphere of parliamentary decorum. Others remained
outside in front of the Place d'Armes, giving their
moral support to the National Guard troops that faced
the King's Bodyguards across the iron grill. About
9:00 o'clock in the evening word reached the court in
the château that Lafayette was approaching Versailles
with an army of National Guard troops numbering about
20,000 men. What their purpose was in coming to Versailles and what they would do were both mysterious.
Some were relieved at the news. The king and Necker
were confident that Lafayette was not a person who
would lead an army against the king. But there was
some question as to the extent of his control over the
troops.

On the way from the Place de Grève in Paris to
the outskirts of Versailles Lafayette succeeded in
gaining the moral authority over the National Guard
that he seemed to have lost momentarily earlier in the
day. As soon as he gave the order to march at 5:00
o'clock in the afternoon the mutinous situation he had
faced for several hours ceased. Before entering Versailles the march was halted and Lafayette got the
troops to take an oath of loyalty to the king and to

the nation. He impressed upon them the necessity of avoiding any violent or aggressive move against the troops under the king's command. By that time Lafayette had received emissaries from the Versailles National Guard and the Flanders regiment placing those two units under his command. Upon entering Versailles Lafayette went first to the National Assembly to assure Mounier, the presiding officer, of the peaceful intentions of his army. "Then what do they really want," Mounier asked, "why have they come here?" Lafayette reiterated that they did not intend to "impose any laws." But he said it would be prudent in view of the present state of public opinion in Paris for the king to send away the Flanders regiment and "to say something favorable about the tri-color emblem."[42] It was still that infamous banquet on the night of October 1 that rankled the former French Guards!

Lafayette then left the National Assembly, presented himself at the iron grill guarded by the King's Bodyguards, and asked to be admitted into the king's presence. He was to enter with only two representatives of the assembly of the Paris Commune accompanying him. Some grenadiers were appalled at this and broke ranks in an attempt to hold him back. They feared he would be arrested once inside the château, or possibly that he would desert the cause of the Parisians and take up that of the king. He argued for some time with them, and finally had to break away from their grasp.[43] Once inside the château he encountered hostility from the court. "There goes Cromwell," jeered one courtier. As he was introduced to the king Lafayette said: "I come, Sire, to offer my own life to save that of Your Majesty." Then he related the circumstances of his being forced to lead the Paris National Guard from the Place de Grève to Versailles. He assured the king of the loyalty of the troops, informing him of the oath they had taken before entering the city. As for the desires of the

Parisians which were supported by the National Guard, Lafayette left those matters to the two representatives of the Paris Commune, who presented to the king four distinct requests. First, they wanted the king to place his safety in the hands of the Paris and the Versailles National Guards. Second, that the king communicate to the Paris Commune his plans for the provisioning of Paris during the coming winter months "in order to assure the multitude whose fears increase at the approach of winter." Third, the people of Paris urgently requested a constitution and new courts that can deal with the great numbers of prisoners, who are a burden to the city government; they urged that the king "deign to expedite the work of the representatives of the nation (the National Assembly) and that he give his sanction to it. Finally, the two representatives requested that the king give proofs of his love for the French nation by coming to dwell "in the most beautiful palace of Europe, in the midst of the greatest city of his realm, and among the most numerous part of his subjects."[44]

Concerning the first request the king replied in the affirmative, that he was willing to place the security of his own person and the château in the hands of the National Guard. D'Estaing was also present and the king said both National Guard commanders could work out between them the implementing of that task. This left undecided the role of the King's Bodyguards. Lafayette apparently thought the grenadiers, those former French Guards who had deserted the king's obedience back in June, would be satisfied with recovering their former posts in the outer bulwarks of the château. He assumed they would not insist on replacing the Bodyguards who had traditionally secured the innermost sanctums of the château. In the event, Lafayette arranged the defenses of the court on that assumption. He made those arrangements in cooperation of the comte de Luxembourg, commander of the Bodyguards.[45]

With regard to the second and third requests the king said in effect that he had already taken the action desired. On the question of subsistence he had already given orders to his ministers to meet that problem. He had agreed to accept the constitutional measures and the Declaration of Rights sent to him by the National Assembly, and he had accepted them without any qualifications. On the fourth proposal, that he move to Paris, the king was not so immediately forthcoming. He was an outdoor man, accustomed to the nearness of the château to the hunting preserves and the forests. The Louvre had been the palace of the effete Valois, and he could never be at home there. He discussed the matter with his courtiers but gave no final answer that evening. Sometime before the October days Lafayette had entertained the idea that if the king were to take up residence at the Louvre it would calm the agitation so stridently fanned by the radical journals that the king was determined to escape from the influence of Paris, go to the frontier and initiate a civil war against his subjects. But Lafayette would never have tried to force the decision on the king.

As he left the château Lafayette must have felt a great crisis had been safely weathered. The armed clash which had threatened for several hours across the barrier of the iron grill had been avoided. The court was certainly relieved of anxiety and grateful for what Lafayette had accomplished. It is true that the grenadiers did not get everything they wanted, that the King's Bodyguards still held the innermost sanctum of the château, and that the National Guard only the outer grounds, that the queen was still unpopular with the Parisian crowds who were at Versailles and that the king had not promised to move from Versailles to Paris. For those who had initiated the movement in the first place, who had insisted that Lafayette accompany them to Versailles, all such matters would have to be reconciled before they would be satisfied.

The comte de Luxembourg had dispersed the King's Bodyguards, leaving only a small number in the courtyard of the château. The bulk of the Bodyguards were moved to the Trianon area a considerable distance away. Lafayette had observed this, but trusting that his own troops including the granadiers would abide by the oath they had taken not to do violence to the king or his Bodyguards, he thought nothing of it.

At dawn on the morning of October 6 the Place d'Armes was swarming with people. They were in the same mood as the day before, hostile to the King's Bodyguards and to the queen. The gate from the Place d'Armes to the Court of the Ministers was opened at 5:30 a.m. by grenadiers of the Parisian National Guard. It is difficult to believe that this was done out of simple negligence, or because it had been the custom in former times when the French Guards had been in charge of that gate. Suddenly at 6:00 a.m. the crowd from the Place d'Armes rushed into the Court of the Ministers and then on into the marble courtyard. What happened next is not very clear, due to conflicting testimony. The marble staircase leading to the royal apartments was occupied by a bodyguard, who was soon joined by his brigadier. There was a standoff for a moment when the crowd hurled insults and threats. According to some accounts both guards fired into the crowd killing as many as five or six.[46] From the inquest conducted by the Court of the Chatelet a year later on the October days it appeared that only one demonstrator was killed, and it was uncertain if he was shot by the bodyguard or fell and struck his head by accident. The King's Bodyguards were still under strict orders not to fire on the crowds or do anything to incite them. One non-commissioned officer of the King's Guards "vigorously denied that any bodyguard fired any shot throughout October 5-6."[47] In

698

any case the crowd rushed up the marble staircase, killing two of the Bodyguards and broke into the château in pursuit of others. It was the queen's bodyguards, evidently, that drew them to her chamber. She was rudely awakened by one of her guards and told that they could not prevent the crowd from entering her chamber. She escaped without a second to lose by way of a secret passageway into the king's apartment. The king was not there, having gone out by the regular passageway to see about her safety. The King's Bodyguards, both inside and outside the château were hunted down and killed. The heads of two were affixed to the end of pikes and triumphantly carried off to Paris.[48]

Several of the National Guard units immediately entered the château to protect the royal family and their bodyguards. Even the grenadiers joined in this operation. If they were responsible for the riot in the first place they were anxious to get the genie back in the bottle once they had accomplished their goal. The king appeared on the balcony above the marble courtyard and made his first announcement that he would heed their request to go to Paris. Lafayette hurried from his father-in-law's house where he was resting and with remarkable energy restored order. He persuaded the king to receive the oath of loyalty from the grenadiers. The king agreed to do so, but told them that his Bodyguards were not guilty of the accusations made against them. His acceptance of the loyalty from the grenadiers amounted in fact to a pardon of their disobedience back in June. Now the grenadiers were willing to make peace with the King's Bodyguards.

Once order had been restored inside the château it was necessary to deal with the milling, shouting crowds out in the marble courtyard. Lafayette appeared on the balcony with the king and queen on either side of him; also the dauphin and princess, and two ministers, Necker and Champion de Cicé came out. The king repeated that he would go to Paris, which seemed to win the crowd to him. A non-commissioned officer of the King's Bodyguard appeared on the balcony to receive from Lafayette the national tricolor standard and to take the oath to the nation. The final balcony scene was the queen alone with Lafayette, who told the crowds that she was also going to Paris with the king. He kissed her hand which seemed to melt the hearts of crowd, for it symbolized the union of the monarchy and the nation. But Lafayette also lectured the crowd about the violence that had been committed and the innocent guards that were put to death. He scolded them for having been mislead by "factious men" and his speech was received with enthusiastic approval.[49] It was a scene very much like that at the Hôtel-de-Ville on July 30 when Necker had won over the crowd to his plea of general amnesty.

At 1:00 o'clock that afternoon the procession, numbering from 50 to 60 thousand persons began the slow journey to the Hôtel-de-Ville at Paris, and ultimately, for the royal family, the palace of the Tuileries. The weather was a striking contrast to the day before; brilliant sunshine lit the landscape. The climate of opinion was also a contrast to the previous day. The king and queen received an enthusiastic reception by the mayor and the assembly of representatives as they entered the city, and by the Parisian populace as they made their way to the Hôtel-de-Ville for a moving ceremony of welcome. It was late at night before the weary royal family could retire, so many of the common people wanted to visit them in their new home, the Tuileries palace. They were completely dependent on the National Guard and Lafayette for protection. But the people were kindly-disposed, and responded to the genial manners of both Louis XVI and Marie Antoinette. And the original cause of the troubles seemed to have disappeared. The next day the American chargé, William Short, was astounded to see

all the bakeries abundantly supplied with bread. He
wrote to Jefferson that "nobody can divine the cause
of this rapid change from scarcity to plenty."[50]

Necker, his wife and Madame de Staël returned to
Paris also that afternoon but by a different route
than the royal procession. The Neckers took up residence again in the hotel of the Contôle-général at No.
9, Rue des Petits-Champs. As they approached Paris
they passed through the Bois-de-Boulogne. "The
weather was of rare beauty," wrote Madame de Staël,
"hardly a leaf stirred, and the sunshine was of such
splendour as to leave nothing somber in the landscape.
No exterior object matched the sadness in our hearts.
How many times in the course of life do we experience
this contrast in the beauty of nature and the suffering imposed by men!"[51]

Necker must have felt that the atmosphere of public opinion on the morrow of the October days was similarly deceptive. The relations between king and people seemed euphoric. The forces of moderation were
still imposing in the National Assembly, the assembly
of the Commune, and in the government. There was a
kind of reaction against the October days in public
opinion, and sympathy for the royal family. But there
could be no denying the fact that it was the minority,
the "factious ones," who had actually determined
events during those two days of October 5 and 6. Once
again a resolute minority had engineered affairs the
way it wanted them to go. Yet there was nothing else
to do but make the best of it. Necker had no faith in
Mounier's attempt to return to Dauphiné and try to
raise the provinces against the Parisian democracy.
He realized there was no such support. All he could
do was to try to work again within the limits of the
reality of circumstances. If people were reasonable
and fair-minded they would eventually support policies
based upon virtue and reason.

[1]Albert Mathiez, "Etudes critiques sur les journées des 5 et 6 octobre 1789," Revue historique 67, (1898), 241-281; 68 (1899), 258-294; 69 (1899), 41-66.

[2]"Lettre du Roi à l'Assemblée nationale," in Oeuvres complètes, VII, 71-80.

[3]Ibid., 80-81.

[4]Revue historique, 67 (1898), 265-268.

[5]Reynaud de Montlosier, Mémoires de M. de comte de Montlosier sur la Révolution française, le Consulat, l'Empire et les principaux événements qui l'ont suivi, 1755-1830 (Paris, 1830), 2 vols. Montlosier was a scientist by profession. During the first weeks of the States-General he was a dinner guest at the Neckers. His strongest impression which he recorded in his memoirs was not the conversation at the table but Madame Necker's dental work.

[6]Dumont, Recollections of Mirabeau, 217-218. Malouet's memoirs are not always reliable. Sometimes he recorded events that seem extremely improbable. During the deadlock of the States-General in June he reported a conversation he had with Necker in which the Genevan regretted having allowed the Third Estate to assemble in the hall of the Menus Plaisirs because that permission strengthened their claim that the three estates must meet in a common assembly. Therefore, according to Malouet, Necker seriously thought of having the Menus Plaisirs blown up in such a way as to make it appear the result of an earthquake. This anecdote is unbelievable. If such a conversation did take place the only explanation conceivable is that Necker had a well-known sense of humor and Malouet did

not. Also dubious is Malouet's assertion that Necker and Montmorin tried to persuade the king to move the government to Soissons or Compiègne after the threat from the Palais-Royal on August 30. Both opposed such a move on October 5, as we shall see, and the arguments Necker made against such a move on that day were just as cogent a month earlier.

[7]Mathiez, _Revue historique_ 68 (1898), 258.

[8]_Papers of Thomas Jefferson_, XV, 458.

[9]Bailly, _Mémoires_, II, 387.

[10]_Ibid._, II, 318-319.

[11]_Ibid._, II, 295.

[12]_Ibid._, II, 293.

[13]Quoted in Mathiez, "Les Journées des 5 et 6 octobre, 1789," _Revue historique_, 68 (1898), 266.

[14]Bailly, _Mémoires_, II, 329, n. 2.

[15]_Ibid._, II, 327.

[16]_Ibid._, II, 327.

[17]_Ibid._, II, 343-344.

[18]_Ibid._, II, 341.

[19]_Ibid._, II, 297-300.

[20]_Ibid._, II, 384.

[21]_Ibid._, II, 405.

[22]P. J. B. Buchez, _Histoire de l'assemblée constituante_, 2nd ed., II, 94.

[23]Albert Mathiez, "Etudes critiques sur les journées des 5 et 6 octobre 1789," _Revue historique_, 68, (1898) 289.

[24]_Correspondance diplomatique_, 130.

[25]Browning, _Dispatches from Paris_, II, 262.

[26]Buchez, _op. cit._, II, 93.

[27]_Ibid._, III, 348.

[28]Henri Leclerq, _Les Journées d'Octobre et la fin de l'année 1789_ (Paris, 1924).

[29]Louis Gottschalk and Margaret Maddox, _Lafayette in the French Revolution through the October Days_ (Chicago, 1969), 328.

[30]Buchez, _op. cit._, II, 103.

[31]Buchez, _op. cit._, II, 117.

[32]_Ibid._, II, 119.

[33]_Ibid._, II, 123.

[34]_Ibid._, II, 121.

[35]_Ibid._, II, 125.

[36]"De la Révolution française," in _Oeuvres complètes_, IX, 273-274.

[37]"Sur l'administration de M. Necker," in _Oeuvres complètes_, VI, 163.

[38]_Ibid._, VI, 64.

[39]"De la Révolution française," in _Oeuvres complètes_, IX, 276.

[40]Buchez, _op. cit._, II, 128.

[41]Ibid.,II, 128.

[42]Ibid, II, 131-132.

[43]Gottschalk, op. cit., 355.

[44]Buchez, op. cit., II, 137.

[45]Gottschalk, op. cit., II, 137.

[46]This was the report sent by the British diplomat, Fitgerald, in his dispatch to the Duke of Leeds. Dispatches from Paris, II, 263.

[47]Gottschalk, op. cit., 368-369.

[48]Evidently it is not true, as so often reported, that these gruesome trophies were part of the procession that conducted the royal family to Paris later in the day.

[49]Gottschalk, op., cit., 375.

[50]Papers of Thomas Jefferson, XV, 511-512.

[51]Madame de Staël, Considérations sur la Révolution française, 212.

CHAPTER 19

NECKER AND THE CONSTITUENT ASSEMBLY

The October days (October 5-6, 1789), like many
of the journées of the Revolution, appear as boundary
marks only in retrospect. At the time it was not so
clear what they meant in the history of the Revolution
or how they would influence the course of events.
From one perspective there was reason to hope that the
change in residence of the royal family from Versailles to Paris might calm the agitation of the popular elements in Paris and their fears that the king
would try to flee from the Revolution in order to return and crush it with the help of his brother mon-
archs. The king and queen were given a hospitable,
even enthusiastic reception by the Parisians in the
days following the trek of October 6. If this should
continue, and if the National Assembly also moved to
Paris as the deputies had promised, was there not hope
that eventually order would be restored under the new
constitution? The deputies from the Paris Commune who
addressed the National Assembly on October 10 asking
them to move from Versailles to Paris said that "the
storm was over which threatened to crush the capital
and the entire country."[1]

It was not long before such hopes were seen to be
illusory. The British chargé d'affaires wrote his
foreign minister on October 22 that "I could have
wished to inform your Grace that as the Parisians had
obtained their warmest wishes in receiving the King
and the States General within their walls, that peace
and quiet were restored to this Capitol, but that is
by no means the case, and the prospect we have before
us is not in any aspect flattering."[2] If the king and
queen were popular, many of the deputies of the National Assembly were not. Particularly threatened

were those of the Clergy who were known to oppose the confiscation of church lands. Deputies who had favored the bicameral legislature and the royal veto were still on the list of the proscribed kept by the leaders of the popular movement in Paris. On October 10 while the National Assembly was still at Versailles a noble-deputy related that he and Gouy d'Arcy were stopped by a crowd at the Sèvres bridge and threatened with immediate execution because one of them was believed to be the comte de Virieu, the moderate deputy from the Nobility of Dauphiné. Only when the crowd was satisfied that neither of the deputies was Virieu were they permitted to continue on their way. In such circumstances Malouet asked: "Can the Assembly be indifferent to the danger which threatens its members? Can they deliberate when they are denounced? . . . The people are misled, stirred up by having its victims pointed out to them, but who are unquestionably innocent. It is unthinkable for the assembly to remain quiet when its members are proscribed."[3] It was not only the deputies who were fearful of popular violence. Several private hotels and residences of foreign ambassadors in Paris were marked with white chalk, a sign their residents had fallen into disfavor.[4]

As for Necker and the other ministers, their primary concern on the day after taking up residence in Paris was the safety of the royal family. The king and queen were completely in the power of the citizen-militia, themselves under the uncertain command of Lafayette. The mood of the crowds, if friendly at the moment, was extremely volatile and capable of being swayed by obscure leaders whose aims were suspect. The fundamental reasons for the popular unrest were still present. If the bread supply seemed to William Short to have been surprisingly plentiful on October 7, this was of brief duration, probably due to the supplies brought from Versailles the day before. Necker and Bailly were soon again preoccupied with the threat of famine in the city.[5] The scarcity of bread and flour was now caused more by the breakdown of the government than an overall shortage in the supply of grain. Local authorities interferred with the transit of grain supplies. The excited populace was inclined to take matters into its own hands whenever it suspected grain dealers or bakers were trying to profit by their suffering. Added to this was the persistent fear of "aristocrats," the fear of counter-revolution, and the accompanying determination to punish the suspects. This in turn accelerated the exodus of foreigners and notables from the country, which affected the general economic situation. Production and distribution in both agriculture and industry continued to decline. It was a vicious circle. Fear of aristocrats impeded the attempts of the government to cope with the subsistence crisis and unemployment. The ability of the government to continue this effort was seriously endangered by the decline of revenue. About one-half of the ordinary income from taxation was being received by the tax collectors. If the government should have to default on payments for ordinary expenditures it would mean bankruptcy and final chaos.

In view of these circumstances it seemed to Necker that men of good will could not fail to support the government in coping with the crisis. The most obvious need was to restore executive power. Only a strong, determined government could carry out the exemplary punishments that would end the popular violence against persons and property. But Necker also realized that executive power could not be restored unless the people were assured that the aims of the Revolution were to be carried out: the constitutional monarchy in which a national assembly exercised full legislative powers; the guarantee of liberty and equality inscribed in the Declaration of Rights; the promises made in the August decrees to end "feudalism." Both policies had to be pursued jointly, the establishment of the new order, and the restora-

709

tion of the executive power of the government, if the
descent into anarchy were to be halted.

Everything depended upon "confidence." This was
a key word in Necker's vocabulary, whether it concerned private business, public finance, or social and
political order. Only by a restoration of the confidence of the people in its government could France
again become the leader of European civilization, the
nation with the most flourishing economy, the center
of the arts and sciences, where "enlightenment" would
spread beyond the confines of Europe to other peoples
around the world. The essential question was how to
rebuild confidence. It was a subtle, intangible relationship. Here Necker's thought had some affinity
with that of Edmund Burke. The confidence of a people
in its government required time and continuity. This
was an idea he had tried to impart to the States-General on May 5: "You will not be envious," he said,
"of what must be left to time, you will not believe
that the present can have no relationship with the
past."[6] As in his first ministry when he competed
with the Physiocrats' doctrines, his bane during his
second and third ministries were the miracle-workers,
those with dramatic and simple solutions, and governed, as he put it, by an "excess of theory." On one
hand were the counter-revolutionaries, those who believed that the Revolution could be crushed with armed
force if only the king and his ministers had the necessary resolution. Or those who believed the way to
handle the finances was that of abbé Terray, to carry
out a reduction of the government's obligations if not
outright repudiation. On the other side were those
who believed in the supreme sovereignty of the Constituent Assembly, the repository of the General Will.
Or those who believed that the solution to the financial problems was to confiscate the land of the
church, not just some of it, as Necker finally agreed
to reluctantly, but all at once, and to liquidate with
it the entire royal debt.[7] Both those on the right

710

and on the left were supremely contemptuous of the "virtuous Genevan" for his presumed mediocrity and his pusillanimity. Mirabeau constantly maintained that the real cause for the crisis was Necker, who refused to recognize his own nullity and would not step aside for an abler person, which of course would be Mirabeau. Necker was well aware of this criticism and wrote in later years that "it also takes courage to remain faithful to moderate opinions, and never abandon the beleagured post, whose guard is so difficult."[8]

If Necker were to realize his goals it was necessary to have the support of the National Assembly. Neither the government nor the assembly could overcome the crisis acting separately, and certainly not by acting against each other. There were still substantial forces of moderation in the country, not only in the National Assembly but in the Paris Commune of 300 representatives, and throughout the lesser courts below the parlements. The latter were on vacation before November and the National Assembly abolished them before they could resume their functions. The parlements were by this time totally unsympathetic with the Revolution. But the lesser courts, including the Châtelet at Paris were moderate in opinion and were trusted by the moderates in the National Assembly. It was the Châtelet that adjudicated the cases of those suspected of lèse-nation. All these forces of moderation were pitted against the "factious elements" represented in most of the 60 sections in Paris, the Palais-royal, and the Jacobin Club.

The October days dealt a serious blow to the moderates in the National Assembly because many deputies refused to go to Paris where they believed it impossible to carry out the mission of the assembly under threats from the popular organizations. Jean-Joseph Mounier and Lally-Tollendal were among those, numbering about 55 or 56, who left Versailles to return to

their constituents.[9]   Many become émigrés, both
Mounier and Lally going to Geneva. The National Assembly was alarmed at the number "who had suddenly become ill" and passed a decree requiring proof from a
physician that they were genuinely ill before receiving a leave of absence.[10] Several prominent leaders
of the moderates did go to Paris with the assembly,
including Malouet, La Rochefoucauld, Clermont-Tonnerre, and even the comte de Virieu! But they
protested the activities of the radical clubs and demanded that the assembly pass a resolution declaring
the inviolability of the deputies from any arrest or
harm at the hands of the populace. Mirabeau succeeded
in defeating the resolution arguing that it was unnecessary, since it duplicated the decree of the National
Assembly passed back on June 23. The two situations
were entirely different. In June after the Royal Session the deputies were in danger of being arrested by
the royal government. Now in October it was popular
forces in the city that threatened them, and who made
up a roster of deputies who were to be taken to the
"lanterne" (lamp-post) for hanging.

Mirabeau himself was not on the proscribed list,
even though he had begun to veer away from the policies of the "factious ones" and to support moderate
policies. But he was always careful to conceal this
from the populace in Paris, including the
"poissardes," those fish-women for whom he was still
"our little mother Mirabeau." During the debate on
the royal veto in September Mirabeau had been secretly
in favor of the absolute veto for the king rather than
the suspensive veto. Yet he managed to remain off the
list compiled by the radical leaders of those deputies
who supported the royal veto, and who were accordingly
to be taken to the lanterne. After his return to
Dauphiné from Versailles Mounier wrote an essay to the
National Assembly justifying his refusal to go to
Paris. He related an incident which was a piquant illustration of Mirabeau's duplicity. Meeting the tri-

712

bune of the people one evening at the home of a royal
painter, Mirabeau told Mounier that he entirely agreed
with his position on the subject of the royal veto.
Later in the evening Mounier struck up a conversation
with another guest who turned out to be the author of
the radical pamphlet called "The _Lanterne_ of
Parisians," which called upon Parisians to hang (at
the lamp-post) all those deputies of the National Assembly who favored a veto for the king. Among those
named in the brochure who were consigned to that fate
was Mounier himself, Lally-Tollendal, Clermont-Tonnerre, Bergasse, and Thouret. But Mirabeau not only
was not included in the list of proscribed but was
given very high praise by the author. Later Mounier
observed the two talking together with great cordiality, and eventually left the house together. Mounier
learned that the Parisian "writer of pamphlets" was a
house guest of Mirabeau's during his stay at Versailles.[11]

As seen in the previous chapter, Necker's plan
for the "patriotic contribution" was presented to the
National Assembly on September 24. Two days later it
was accepted by the assembly without amendments,
"almost convulsively," as the editor of the _Moniteur_
described it. This was due to Mirabeau's eloquent defense of Necker's plan, in one of his most famous orations. Earlier in May he had called the royal deficit
"the nation's treasure" because it was the means of
forcing the government to grant a constitution. Now
in September he described "hideous bankruptcy" in im-
agery that rivaled Dante's depiction of the inferno.
It came as a surprise to many observers that Mirabeau
would ever support a proposal of Necker's. Now he got
the assembly to pass the "patriotic contribution"
without any discussion or changes.[12]

It may have been this unexpected support for his
loan plus the indication that Mirabeau was leaving the
radicals to support moderate policies that led Necker

713

to agree once again to an interview with Mirabeau. After the October days the tribune and his backers once again thought that chances of getting Mirabeau appointed to the ministry were propitious. What better way to bring about that cooperation between the government and the assembly than to bring the most powerful orator of the National Assembly into the government? Unlike the first meeting between the two this was a friendly conference, lasting about five hours. According to Madame de Staël, Mirabeau actually had considerable esteem for her father despite his public denunciations of Necker in both writings and oratory. But there was hardly any chance that Necker would agree to accept Mirabeau as a colleague in the ministry. The cynical opportunism of the tribune was repugnant to Necker's innermost ethical being. "You have too much intelligence," Necker told him, "not to realize sooner or later that morality is the nature of things."[13]

Intelligence Mirabeau certainly possessed to a high degree. He had a clear view of the general crisis threatening the country. He had abstained from voting for Sieyes' resolution of June 17 which declared the National Assemby to be the representative of the French people, and implicitly, the repository of the General Will of the nation. Mirabeau admitted to Etienne Dumont that this was the great mistake of the assembly, from which all later troubles were derived. This confession was made in 1790 when Mirabeau had fallen out with the National Assembly and secretly sought its dissolution. According to Dumont he said: "How right we were when, in the beginning, we tried to prevent the commons from being declared a national assembly. This is the origin of the evil."[14] Indeed it was, and while Mirabeau refrained from voting for the resolution of June 17 he had played no small part in bringing it about by sabatoging Necker's attempt to mediate the quarrel between the Nobility and the Third Estate. Now, in October, he recognized clearly enough that the problem was anarchy, and that was due to the collaspe of executive power. But again no one had played a greater role than Mirabeau himself in bringing about that result. For his activity in the Parisian districts had defeated Necker's attempt to halt the popular violence against persons suspected of being "enemies of the people." Mirabeau could have said about himself what he told abbé Sieyes on the day after the "crazy night" of August 4 when, to the distress of Sieyes, the National Assembly abolished church tithes along with feudalism: "My dear abbé, you have let loose the bull and you now complain that he gores you!"[15]

Up until September 25 Mirabeau had opposed Necker consistently, and had done his utmost to undermine his popularity earned during the July days. Now Mirabeau was ready to turn the tables, to desert the popular classes in Paris, his poissardes, and throw his support to the moderates. The trouble with such duplicity was that he was distrusted and hated by too many people. If he could hoodwink the poissardes it was not so easy with regard to the leaders that now came to the fore in the National Assembly following the October days. These were notables who had decided to embrace the cause of the common people and form an alliance with the Parisian radicals. The future "triumvirate" of 1791 was now beginning to control the assembly. Alexander Lameth, a nobleman who had served as an officer in the American war, Adrien Duport, the former magistrate of the Parlement of Paris, and Antoine Barnave, a countryman of Mounier from Dauphiné, now managed to get the National Assembly on November 7 to pass a decree forbidding any member of the assembly to serve in the executive government. This cut the ground completely from under Mirabeau's schemes to become a minister, for he had no other solid base of power than as a deputy of the National Assembly.

The decree of November 7 was a blow to Necker as well as Mirabeau, for one feature of the British parliament that Necker most admired was the intimate association between ministers of the government and Parliament in forming legislation. If he did not expect the ministers to be deputies, he looked forward to a procedure whereby ministers would appear before the committees of the National Assembly or before the entire assembly to answer questions, propose legislative measures, or simply to present information. Despite the sneering judgment of Necker by the leaders of the assembly that the Genevan was a "mediocrity," he would have outclassed them all on the front bench. Etienne Dumont wrote that the members of the National Assembly were inept at extemporaneous speaking. There were some exceptions, such as Clermont-Tonnerre, but they were few. Most read their speeches from prepared texts and they were of unconscionable length. They needed the help of experts and secretaries to write these interminable monologues. Not least of those dependent upon such help was Mirabeau. His famous "workshop" included expert bankers and financiers who always provided him with the information for his articles and speeches.[16] For a person of his fame he was astonishingly ignorant; however endowed with literary and oratorical ability the tribune was a temperament primarily, not an intellect. But Necker was not only an effective orator, he was his own "fact-man," he did his own research, and his knowledge of French internal affairs was hardly equalled by anyone in the National Assembly. Yet, as the procedures of the assembly developed after July, Necker was limited to sending messages to the assembly, or, if he did appear in person to read them, there was no chance for the give and take so famous in the British Parliament.

After the interview between Necker and Mirabeau on October 15 the tribune resumed his tactic of trying to undermine and bring down the ministry. In fact he had hardly ceased that policy. The oration he delivered on September 26 in support of Necker's financial plan submitted two days earlier, which seemed to surprise so many observers, was actually part of a general strategy that he was developing. He did not expect the "patriotic contribution" to succeed, and this time he did not want the Prime Minister of Finance to lay the blame for its failure on the assembly because of alterations, as in the case of the loan of 30 million livres the previous August. The idea was now germinating in Mirabeau's mind that the ministry should be separated from the king. The latter would be "sacred" and "inviolable" but not the ministers, who would be responsible to the National Assembly, and subject to impeachment for criminal conduct. This principle could be expanded to encompass negligent conduct, or even unsuccessful projects which were initiated by the ministers. On October 3 when the assembly was drawing up its message to be sent to the king who had agreed "conditionally" to the Declaration of Rights and the constitutional measures, Mirabeau made four distinct proposals: that the king be asked to discipline the officers of the Flanders regiment, forbid other military units to "insult the misery of the people," that any act of the king must be countersigned by a minister who would thereby be held responsible for it by the National Assembly, and finally that "His Majesty clarify his reply about his conditional acceptance of the constitutional provisions so there would be no doubt about his acceptance."[17] Only the last of those stipulations was included in the final document sent to the king on October 4. But they show the thinking and the strategy of the tribune in the weeks ahead.

Necker was not the only target of Mirabeau. Shortly after the October days he launched an attack against Saint-Priest, Secretary of State for the King's Household, for allegedly "insulting" the women who came to the château on October 5 to present their grievances to the king. Mirabeau claimed that the

717

minister had told the women that "they never lacked bread when they had a single king. Now that they had 1200 (alluding to the National Assembly) they should present their petition to their new masters." Saint-Priest indignantly denied ever making such a statement. The British chargé wrote on October 15 that "the good sense and prudence of that minister would never have permitted him to hold" such an idea, and that Saint-Priest's letter was "much admired and depended upon by all for integrity, altho' Mons. de Mirabeau persists in the accusation and insists on the Comité de Recherches taking cognizance of the affair."[18]

The Keeper of the Seals, Champion de Cicé, was also called on the carpet, not only by Mirabeau but by other deputies of the National Assembly when it was discovered that decrees passed by the assembly were not being promulgated in some provincial cities. It was suspected that the ministry was in fact blocking surreptitiously the acts of the assembly. Champion de Cicé appeared at the bar of the assembly and repeated what had already been pointed out in the king's messages on the August decrees and the Declaration of Rights: it was one thing to announce a general principle or policy; but laws that were to be enforced required more specific language and formality. "I take the liberty to point out to you," he told the deputies, "that the conditions necessary to construct a law and to make it enforceable have not yet been decided upon (by the National Assembly), except the articles of the constitution which you have decreed and the king has accepted purely and simply at Versailles on October 5."[19] It was a good example of how suspicion rather than confidence inhibited the establishment of the new order desired by both assembly and ministry.

Overshadowing the entire scene like a pall were the endemic acts of violence in which innocent people suspected of participating in the "famine plot" were put to death. A particularly atrocious case occurred on October 21 at Paris when a young baker was put to death and his wife subjected to appalling cruelty. There was a pronounced reaction to this incident both in the assembly of the Paris Commune and in the National Assembly. The outcome was the passage of a decree of martial law, which set forth in detail how popular riots were to be controlled and suppressed. But several of the districts protested this act and established a "committee of correspondence" which threatened to become a counter-government to the 300 representatives. The sympathizers of the Parisian redicals in the National Assembly also objected to the decree of martial law, maintaining that the incidents of violence were only excuses for the government and the moderates to crush the Revolution. Robespierre said that "when the people are dying of hunger, they come together; therefore it is necessary to go to the cause of the riots in order to pacify them. It is necessary to take measures to discover the authors, and to crush the growing conspiracy."[20] He called upon the assembly to set up a permanent tribunal to try cases of lèse-nation rather than leaving those cases to the Châtelet court.

Mirabeau gave his support to the decree on martial law, but he did not fail to make use of the situation to attack the ministry. He agreed with Robespierre that the chief cause of the popular unrest was hunger, and once again, as early in July, he laid the blame for the subsistence crisis on the ministry and chiefly Necker. In the decree of October 21 authorizing the drawing up of the law against riots, Mirabeau got the following clause included: "That the ministers of the king will declare positively what means and resources the national assembly can furnish in order to assure the bread supply of the nation and particularly that of the capitol, in order that the National Assembly, having done all that it can on that matter, can depend that the laws will be enforced, or hold the ministers and other agents of (the executive government) responsible for their lack of enforcement."[21]

This was a summons to the ministers to undertake a legal obligation to keep the country supplied with bread. Underlying it was the assumption that the National Assembly could provide the government with the necessary means, and therefore there was no more need for a subsistence crisis. To Necker who had been grappling with the crisis since his return to the ministry the previous year, such a statement was sublimely ridiculous. In a memorial which he wrote on October 24 but was signed by all the ministers, he explained once again courteously but firmly why the National Assembly was not facing reality. The grain supply is not a fiat of the government, it is determined by "the favor of Providence," namely the character of the harvest. Foreign imports could not make up for a bad year. He reviewed again what the government had done to grapple with the grain shortage: export had been prohibited, imports from other countries were carried out whenever possible, but in Europe there was everywhere a shortage so that neighboring countries had also prohibited export. The breakdown of order had compounded the crisis. Even though the National Assembly had confirmed by two decrees the complete liberty of internal freedom of the grain trade, resistance had been endemic. "The maritime cities of Brittany cannot receive from the interior of that province essential provisions, much less can the rest of the country benefit from that surplus in Brittany. Roussillon refuses to Languedoc the help it needs; upper Languedoc takes umbrage at the demands made upon it by the rest of the province. Lyon receives with infinite difficulty the smallest assistance from Burgundy; consequently Dauphiné controls its exports. Other provinces follow the example. And at Le Havre, Caudebec, and Rouen supplies purchased by the king for the

720

city of Paris have been and continue to be retained."
To require the ministers to undertake a legal obligation to see that the nation was adequately supplied
would be like requiring a general to guarantee that he
would win a battle. The ministers were already doing
everything possible to meet the food crisis. Necker
reminded the deputies that he had asked for the National Assembly to set up a subsistence committee with
which he could communicate the acts of the government
and receive the moral support of the assembly. But
this committee had ceased to exist as early as July.
The government was left with all the responsibility
and received no help from the assembly. And to dis-
charge that responsibility, what a multitude of obstacles it faced!

> All France is under arms. The militia
> chiefs are not appointed by the king, and
> they receive no direct orders from him. The
> former subordination of the troops is under-
> mined by all kinds of insinuations. The
> courts, mindful of what is going on in your
> assembly, are concerned about your coming
> dispositions, and their discouragement is
> everywhere evident. Respect for magistrates
> in the highest positions of the administra-
> tion is daily weakened; and that moral au-
> thority which supplements real power is al-
> most extinct. At the same time a proper
> freedom of the press is transformed into un-
> limited license, surrendering the reputa-
> tions of all those devoted to public service
> to the most infamous lies. And to make the
> situation most dangerous, these are spread
> among the lowest classes of people, in order
> to destroy all ties of sentiment and esteem.

The memorial asserted that the ministers would not undertake such a legal commitment as was being asked of
them. If this were unacceptable to the deputies, the

ministers would yield their posts to anyone rash enough to make such a commitment. Necker said to the National Assembly approximately what he said to the king prior to July 11: if it were thought that some-one else should be in his position, he would gladly yield it. "Today it requires much less effort to sac-rifice high positions than to keep them; and you would readily believe this if you knew, as we do, all the pains and anguish which accompany these positions, and how much steadfastness is required in the devotion to the good not to be discouraged."[22]

It was about two weeks after sending that memo-rial to the National Assembly that it decreed no mem-ber of the assembly could hold a portfolio in the min-istry. The government and the assembly were now more separated than ever. The National Assembly found it much more congenial to issue decrees that promised greater concessions to the popular classes. But it left it to the government to exact what was necessary in the way of sacrifices, and in incurring the consequent unpopularity.

The same attitude of the National Assembly with regard to the subsistence crisis was paralleled in its handling of the financial crisis. It was much easier to talk about confiscating the church lands to meet the deficit of the ordinary income as well as the ex-traordinary needs that Necker had constantly laid be-fore them. It was more pleasant to abolish old taxes rather than to find ways of making up the necessary revenue by passing new tax measures. Necker's attempt to get the assembly to set up a Treasury Board to as-sist him in financial administration met the same fate as the subsistence committee. His continual efforts to establish a close working relationship with the fi-nance committee of the National Assembly met one re-buff after the other.

The notion that the church lands were the solution to the financial crisis of the government had been propounded in the National Assembly by people as diverse as Dupont de Nemours, Mirabeau, and Tallyrand. On November 2 the National Assembly formally appropriated the lands of the church for the state. The next question was how to use those lands for the immediate financial relief of the royal government. The idea had already been broached that the lands could be administered by a special authority set up for the purpose, in fact this could be a national bank. The assets of the bank, consisting of land, would be the security for bank notes. The circulation of bank notes as a medium of exchange had become common in Europe in the eighteenth century. There was no question about the soundness of bank notes if they could be converted on demand into gold or silver specie. It seemed a simple step from notes based upon metallic specie to those based on land. Theoretically the security should be just as good, and in fact landbanks existed in North America during the eighteenth century. There was an obvious difficulty: it was not so easy to convert bank notes into land as into gold and silver specie. Land was an awkward medium of exchange. In fact it was no medium of exchange at all, and was far from being the equivalent of gold and silver money. For that reason the idea of nationalizing the church lands did not necessarily lead to the issue of paper money based upon those lands. Dupont de Nemours, for example, remained steadfastly opposed to the issue of paper money. But the idea was supported by the left side of the National Asssembly and by the radicals in the Parisian districts, and in the Jacobin Club. Mirabeau also supported the issue of paper money based on church lands although prior to that time he had denounced the issue of notes by the Discount Bank in the most violent terms, ironically, totally without foundation.[23] The notes of the Discount Bank circulated only in the city of Paris, and were required to be redeemed within a year. The government tax officials could receive payments of taxes in the form of these bank notes. It is true that the Discount Bank had to suspend convertability of its notes into gold and silver due to the general crisis of 1789, and particularly because of the extreme dearth of metallic currency. But it was due to Mirabeau that in September 1790 the <u>assignats</u> became no longer interest-bearing bonds but outright fiat money, with no backing except the faith of the holders of that paper in the government.[24] Such a reversal on this matter was only one example of the ability of the tribune to meet himself going in the opposite direction with perfect aplomb. "He was not consistent in anything," baron de Staël wrote, "not even in corruption."[25]

Necker had been opposed to the wholesale confiscation of the lands of the church. Not that he was unwilling to consider some reforms, and the taking over of lands in the hands of wealthy beneficiaries who provided nothing in return by the way of service to the nation. But he doubted that the nationalization of the lands was a panacea for the financial crisis. First of all, the church was not so wealthy as commonly believed. Talleyrand had estimated the wealth of the church lands and left completely out of his account the debts of the church, which considerably diminished his optimistic picture.[26] But what Necker feared most was the unlimited issue of paper money. Here was a simple and easy solution to the government's finances that he was certain would be disastrous. A limited amount of paper money in circulation would be acceptable. But the quantity should be kept as low as possible in comparison to the circulation of metallic currency. As usual, his was the voice of moderation and experience as opposed to the theorists and the advocates of simple, sweeping solutions.

724

To forestall these potentially catastrophic ideas
that were so much talked about Necker proceeded in his
usual fashion: try to control them by advancing part
way to meet them.   On November 14 he made his first
appearance before the assembly since the beginning of
October.   He read a long memorial entitled "Project
for a National Bank."   His basic proposal was to
transform the Discount Bank into a National Bank.
This would not greatly change what it had been doing
in the past.   But the national name would give it
somewhat more respectability than if it remained a
private institution.   The capital of the bank would be
increased by 50%.   It had been 30 million livres before 1787, the stockholders being all private investors.   When Calonne borrowed 70 million livres from
the bank in January 1787 he did so by having the capital increased by 70 million livres, and the new stockholders placed that capital in the hands of the government as a loan.   That made a total of 100 million
livres capital, which Necker now proposed to increase
to 150 million.   The bank would be reorganized, its
directorship augmented and the National Assembly would
be invited to appoint commissioners to supervise the
operations of the National Bank.   The 150 million
livres of shares in the hands of stockholders would be
one kind of security for the bank notes that would now
be authorized, up to but no more than 240 million
livres.   These notes would be spent by the government
for extraordinary expenditures needed both for the remainder of 1789 and for 1790.   Necker explained that
the Discount Bank had advanced bank notes to the government amounting to 90 million livres to meet the
needs of the last months of 1789.   But these notes had
to be redeemed by the government at the end of the
year.   Looking ahead, he said it was not possible to
predict precisely what the extraordinary needs would
be for 1790, but it appeared that 80 million livres
should be a minimum estimate.[27]

725

In order to repay the 90 million due the National Bank for 1789 and the 80 million the coming year, Necker proposed setting up a special treasury called the Extraordinary Treasury (<u>Caisse</u> <u>de</u> <u>l'Extraordinaire</u>) which would receive the extraordinary income from which the National Bank notes would be redeemed. What sources of extraordinary income did Necker expect would come into the Extraordinary Treasury? First were the proceeds from the patriotic contribution issued by the government and approved by the National Assembly in the first days of October. This loan was not being filled as rapidly as hoped, but it was still not considered a failure. Necker estimated later, in February 1790, that Paris had pledged about 30 million livres for the "patriotic contribution." But the fulfillment was not to be completed until 1792. Thus there was hope that eventually this loan would be successful. Despite the troubles and the seriousness of the government's financial posture in these months it is easy to forget that patriotism was still important. If one-half of the tax revenue were not being paid, it is easy to overlook the fact that many local governments were meeting their quotas, at a time when the impulse to renege was very strong because of the great number who were not. Additional extraordinary income would be derived from both royal domain lands and church lands that would be sold to private purchasers. But Necker's project did not include any plan for issue of notes based on those lands. There would be an increase in the circulation of the notes of the National Bank, but these notes would continue to circulate only in Paris, and not in the provinces. Necker did suggest that the National Assembly might wish to extend the circulation to other cities, such as Lyon.

The project that Necker presented to the National Assembly on November 14 was typical in its moderation and also its hopefulness. In the long run, the country's situation was by no means desperate. If the new order could be established Frenchmen had every reason to be optimistic. The main danger Necker saw on the immediate horizon was that impulse for wholesale solutions that would cause even greater convulsions.

The National Assembly considered Necker's project for over a month and passed a decree on December 19 which incorporated some but not all the proposals in the project. The deputies declined to transform the Discount Bank into a national bank. And they ordered an extension on the debt of 90 million livres which had been due for repayment by the end of the year. They allowed the Discount Bank to make another loan of 80 million livres to meet extraordinary expenditures of the government in the first months of 1790. The decree allowed the capital of the Discount Bank to be increased up to 200 million livres. These loans would be in the form of bank notes, which would have forced circulation only in the city of Paris. The Extraordinary Treasury was set up that would grant prescriptions, according to Necker's project, and would derive extraordinary income for the government from the three sources that Necker had indicated: the proceeds from the patriotic levy and from the sale of domain and church lands. The amount of land to be sold would be 400 million livres worth. Bonds bearing 5% interest were to be issued to subscribers. The holders of those bonds would be given preference in the sale of domain and church lands. These bonds were to be redeemed in five years. They are usually called the first "assignats;" they were not called that at the time but billets d'achats. They were not to be paper money, not given forced circulation, not even in Paris.[28]

Such a transformation of his project must have been a great disappointment to Necker. He wanted to head off the issue of bonds backed by domain and church lands, because he feared it would be the camel's nose in the door. He had tried to persuade the National Assembly in his address of November 14 that such a measure was unnecessary. The notes of the newly formed National Bank would have been sufficient for the extraordinary needs of the remainder of 1789 and the first part of 1790. They would circulate only in Paris. While the _billets_ _d'achats_ based on the nationalized lands were not legal tender they would be negotiable throughout the kingdom. The solution to the long-range achievement of financial stability lay elsewhere than issuing more paper. The National Bank would have strengthened the weaknesses of the Discount Bank, which were due to the financial distress of the royal government, and also the extreme dearth of metallic currency which caused the Bank, not to suspend conversion entirely, but to carry it out in limited amounts regularly. As already mentioned, the notes of the Discount Bank were not of indefinite duration. They were committed to be convertible into specie at some stipulated time, usually in a year.

Necker told the assembly on November 14 that if they could achieve three things by the beginning of 1790 the financial crisis would be resolved. First, see that the ordinary accounts were balanced; second, get the provincial (departmental) assemblies established so that the regular income of the government could be collected; and third, "restore executive power which can assure obedience to the law." Once those three fundamental bases were established and the new constitution promulgated Necker saw the end of the nation's troubles. The credit situation of the government was not all bleak. There were some means of bringing metallic money into the country through loans. Negotiations were proceeding to assign the debt owed France by the Americans to the Dutch, who would provide a cash loan; the patriotic contribution, as mentioned above, was not hopeless. The loan of 80 million livres decreed by the National Assembly back in August was being slowly subscribed, but it was succeeding. Thirty-two million of the 80 million had been subscribed to, although only one-half was in specie. But it seemed probable that the loan would be eventually fulfilled. Furthermore, the regular extinction of the life rente obligations was a favorable factor in the government's credit. Once again, as on May 5, 1789, Necker's message was one of hope rather than bleak discouragement. All that was necessary were policies that were prudent, moderate and would cause the least trauma.[29]

Although the National Assembly had decreed on December 19 that the Extraordinary Treasury could issue billets d'achats up to 400 million livres, it would take time for the operation to be implemented. It could provide no immediate assistance to the government in meeting the needs for the remainder of 1789 and during 1790. Necker's methods were still the only ones possible in the short-run. After the beginning of 1790 he tried again to persuade the National Assembly of the need for caution in relying upon bonds backed by the nationalized lands of the church. He planned to address the National Assembly about the middle of February, when illness overtook him, no doubt the result of overwork and strain. But he had drawn up his memorial and sent it to the president of the National Assembly on March 6, explaining that he was not yet recovered sufficiently to read it in person. He began the memorial by pointing out that the hopes he had expressed in his address to the assembly the previous November had not been borne out. The gap between ordinary revenue and expenditure had not been closed. The loss of revenue from the abolition of the gabelles had not been made up; the payment of ordinary tax revenue was still behind schedule, the credit of the government was so unfavorable that anticipations could not be renewed in their entirety. Looking to the ten months left in 1790 Necker placed the minimum need at 294 million livres. How could this void be filled? Again he proposed a variety of expedients in preference to some single, drastic solution. The future was full of promise once the temporary crisis could be weathered. Examples of the "shot-gun approach" to the problem were: the Discount Bank could make another loan of moderate size; the National Assembly could reduce ordinary expenditures by 30 million livres; anticipations could be renewed later in the year if the National Assembly took certain actions; the new departmental assemblies could speed up the collection of tax revenue; the patriotic contribution would begin to come into the treasury in May; near the end of the year a loan of modest proportions would be feasible; the intention he had expressed in November to make the payments to _rentiers_ more current could be delayed, however regretfully.[30]

In this gamut of proposals there was no mention of the Extraordinary Treasury or the assets it was to receive from the sale of church lands, no mention of the 400 million livres in _assignats_ authorized by the National Assembly's act of December 19. Knowing that this subject would be foremost in the minds of many of the deputies Necker entered into a detailed discussion of the use of paper currency. He explained why he preferred to use notes of the Discount Bank rather than _assignats_ based upon the future sale of land. The bank notes were redeemed in a specific time period and circulated only in Paris. He acknowledged that some would want to raise that sum of 294 million livres by the issue of _assignats_. This, he said, would put too much paper into the monetary system:

> A sum of two to three hundred million, added to that of 160 million, the amount of bank notes currently in circulation, would be a terrifying sum. The National Assembly has decreed that 400 million can be realized from the sale of domain or church lands; but we must await to see specifically which lands will be sold, the time when they will be sold, the number of purchasers. Finally,

the confidence which cannot be impaired by a limited amount, can be by a greater amount; as in everything, a proper measure is the most indispensable of conditions.[31]

It is apparent that Necker expected the government to benefit from the sale of church lands only when the lands were sold and the cash in the treasury. He realized very well that such was not the view of many of the deputies. Their scheme was to issue the assignats to the public and to make them legal tender throughout the kingdom. The amount to be issued would be determined by the needs of the government. Necker argued that paper money should be resorted to when absolutely necessary and in the most restricted amount. "In general, absolute remedies are often desired in the greatest emergencies; but this is rather the result of impulse rather than of reflection. Because it is when the emergencies are at their greatest that injustice and the rigor of extreme means become most painful and often dangerous."[32] It would be unjust to several classes to give forced currency to paper money with such uncertain guarantees. Creditors would be wronged. The government itself would receive all its revenue in paper, and there were some expenditures that had to be made in specie, such as pay for troops, police forces, or purchases in open markets and overseas. The violence and destruction that would ensue with such a flooding of the monetary system was incalculable.

The chief intent of Necker's memorial of March 6 to the National Assembly was to get the deputies to face realities. But he was increasingly aware that his influence was ebbing, even while his responsibilities were enormous. It was an impossible situation and could not last. For one reason, his health was such that he would have to have some relief soon, even if a few weeks vacation to go to Plombières. Many in his position would no doubt have laid down the burden at once and washed their hands of it. But Necker was too public-spirited, too conscience-ridden, to entertain such a thought. The sentiments he had expressed at the time he embarked upon the third ministry were still overriding: his retirement to Coppet would not be peaceful as long as there was some possibility that he could avert greater disasters than had already occurred.

These sentiments were imparted to the deputies in his memorial of March 6. Following these remarks he presented the assembly with an astonishing proposition. For a long time, he said, he had entertained the idea and had discussed it with the king, of setting up a Treasury Board to take over the administration of finances. This project now was particularly appropriate in view of the constitutional order the National Assembly was completing. "This Board would do what I am doing today; that is, it would pay for all daily expenditures, determine the mode of payment, supervise the collection of revenue, in fact direct all operations of the public treasury without exception or reservation."[33] It would be composed of members of the National Assembly, who would have the title of commissioners of the treasury. In short, this Treasury Board would assume the entire direction of the finances and would render unnecessary the continuation of the offices of controller-general and director-general of the public treasury.

Necker went on to explain the advantages of the proposed new administration. First it would mitigate the distrust of the deputies toward the executive government. It would also strengthen the credit posture of the government. One could be certain that no abuse would occur in the handling of public funds; no expenditure would be presented for the king's approval until it had been deliberated upon by the commissioners. It would be a more effective, more diligent, more exact administration than was now possible under a single administrator. Necker ackowledged that this would require some revision of that decree of November 7 which had forbid any deputy to assume a post in the executive government. But he argued again the necessity of the legislature and the executive working in partnership. And the finances were the branch of administration where this was particularly necessary:

> At this time how important it is that you be constantly reminded of the crucial nature of the finances. I dare say that in one way or another they are tied to all the questions which agitate the National Assembly. Therefore, at this moment of peril, do not refuse this union which I now propose for the establishment of an active committee of the treasury whose membership will be primarily chosen from your assembly. You still have great opportunities to save the finances. . . . What can I do alone, far from you, except to send a few memorials of which the subjects can be so easily forgotten about if there are not people among you who are continually occupied with them. . . .[34]

This project had been the heart of Necker's reform since the time of his first ministry. The financial problems of the monarchy could only be resolved by establishing this kind of administration which took the management of the royal finances out of the secret chambers of power and placed in full view of the public. The finances could not be left to the discretion of a single person, no matter how honest or competent. The establishment of this type of independent board to supervise the finances was the most insistent demand of the Assembly of Notables of 1787. Now the National Assembly was given a specific invitation to carry out what the nation had so long desired, and which was clearly in the national interest.

733

However important the finances were, it was still the political and social instability that concerned the ministry and the king. The lower classes were still apprehensive of counter-revolution. Some alleged plots had been uncovered which attracted much publicity. And yet there was little real danger from conter-revolution. What was tearing the country apart was the rise of factions. The political revolution had succeeded. It would never be overthrown, even with the return of the Bourbons in 1814. But partisan strife was now the deadly enemy. Within the National Assembly were a few refractory conservatives who thought the only way out of the turmoil was the restoration of the old order. On the opposite side of the hall were those who believed the Revolution had only begun and was far from completed. And they were convinced that their enemies in the assembly, the moderates, were allies of the counter-revolution. There was a persistent belief that the king was not sincerely attached to the revolution, that he felt himself a prisoner after the October days, and his heart was really with the counter-revolution. Necker did not think this was true, and he persuaded the king to try to lay that misconception to rest once and for all. He wrote an address for the king to deliver in person to the National Assembly.

"On the 4th [of February, 1790]," wrote William Short to Jefferson, "the King went to the national assembly and delivered a speech . . . He went on foot, announced his coming by a short letter to the President and desired to be received without ceremony."[35] It was the final attempt of both Necker and Louis XVI to persuade the nation of the sincerity of the king's acceptance of the Revolution and thereby attempt to bring an end to the factionalism in the assembly and the popular violence in the countryside. "Gentlemen," he began, "the gravity of the circumstances in which France finds itself has brought me before you. The progressive weakening of all ties of order and subor-

734

dination, the suspension or the inaction of the courts of justice, the discontent arising from privation, the antagonisms and hatreds which are the unfortunate consequence of a long period of dissension, the critical situation of the finances, the uncertainty about the state's solvency, all conspire to keep in constant anxiety the true friends of prosperity and well-being of the realm."[36]

The king reviewed what had been accomplished and what he had sanctioned. The new regional reorganization of the old provinces into departments was what he had envisaged back in 1778 when he established the first provincial assembly. But this was only the beginning. Time would continue to reform what is imperfect in the laws and customs. But any enterprise that attempts to overturn the principles of the constitution would bring about the most fearful calamities. "Let us then in good faith yield ourselves to the hopes with a unanimous spirit. Let everyone know that the representatives of the nation and the monarch are united in the task of realizing these hopes, so that peace and concord can come to the kingdom." The king referred to the abolition of the orders in the future national asssemblies, and left no doubt of his acceptance of that change. At the same time, he observed that nothing could destroy the respect earned by distinguished families in the past, implying that the nobility would continue to exist as a social class but without fiscal or political privileges. He also called for the continued respect to be given to the ministers of religion. There was no reason however to fear that the king was not sincerely in favor of the work so far of the National Assembly. Finally, he called for the assembly to try to end the endemic violence in the country by restoring executive power in the government.[37]

According to William Short the king's speech of February 4 made a strong impression on the National

735

Assembly. With the exception of the two extremes on the right and the left, "the measure taken by the King produced a degree of enthusiasm on all present of which there are few examples."[38] The king was escorted back to the Tuilleries palace by the deputies, the queen appeared with the dauphin, which greatly moved them, for the king had stressed his intention to raise the dauphin to become a constitutional monarch. The enthusiasm led all deputies of the National Assembly to take a formal oath "To swear fidelity to the Nation, the Law and the King, and to support the New Constitution, such as it is decreed by the Assembly and sanctioned by the King, to the extent of his power."[39] The spirit of the deputies of the National Assembly spread to the 300 representatives of the Paris Commune who took the same oath.

Both Louis XVI and Necker had reason to feel that the day was a triumph. The king's appeal for unity, patriotism, and the moderate revolution seemed to have provoked a powerful response in the country. But it proved to be only temporary. The spirit of faction, of partisanship and rival ideologies was destined to triumph in a matter of months. And it was to bring to a conclusion what Necker had called "an inscrutable destiny," namely, his own public career.

[1]Archives parlementaires, IX, 403.

[2]Fitz-Gerald to the Duke of Leeds, 22 Oct. 1789, Despatches from Paris, II, 270.

[3]Archives parlementaires, IX, 397.

[4]Baron de Staël, Correspondance diplomatique, 136.

[5]That Necker was still concerned about the bread supply is apparent according to Gouverneur Morris, A Diary of the French Revolution (Boston, 1939), I, 260 passim. Government subsides for imported grain and flour were restored at the beginning of September.

[6]"Ouverture des Etats-généraux, in Oeuvres complètes, VI, 606.

[7]Such was Talleyrand's scheme which he presented to the National Assembly on October 10. He was among those "intriguers" who aspired to the ministry, and his proposal for the government to take over all lands of the church was in a sense his "platform." At that time he was the bishop of Autun. Archives parlementaires, IX, 393-404.

[8]"La Révolution française," in Oeuvres complètes, IX, 323.

[9]Dumont, Recollections of Mirabeau, 171.

[10]Archives parlementaires, IX, 396.

[11]Jean-Joseph Mounier, Exposé de la conduite de M. Mounier dans l'Assemblée nationale et des motifs de son retour en Dauphiné, 38. This incident was wit-

nessed by Etienne Dumont who wrote that "Mounier's account of this conversation was quite correct." Recollections of Mirabeau, 172.

[12]Archives parlementaires, IX, 193.

[13]Madame de Staël, Considérations sur la Révolution française, 237.

[14]Recollections of Mirabeau, 230-231.

[15]Ibid., 146. During and after the October days there was a widespread belief that Mirabeau was implicated in the alleged conspiracy of the duc d'Orleans and his circle to instigate the popular exodus from Paris to Versailles assuming that the king would take flight and leave the way open for the duke to become regent for the dauphin, or lieutenant-general of the kingdom. The Châtelet court at Paris conducted an investigation to determine if the duke and the tribune had engaged in such a criminal conspiracy. The results of their investigation were turned over to the National Assembly. A report to the assembly concluded that the evidence was mostly hearsay and not solid enough to support a criminal indictment or a move to expel the two from the National Assembly. Buchez, Histoire de l'Assemblée constituante, III, 315-380. Dumont wrote that Mirabeau said nothing to him about the matter, but certain incidents made him think that Mirabeau was "in the secret of the occurrences of the 5th and 6th of October." Recollections of Mirabeau, 164. He thought "if the king fled, Mirabeau would have proclaimed the duke of Orleans lieutenant-general of the kingdom, and would have become his prime minister." Ibid., 165.

[16]J. Bénétruy, L'Atelier de Mirabeau. Quatre proscrits Genevois dans le Tourmente révolutionnaire (Geneva, 1962).

[17]Archives parlementaires, IX, 473.

[18]Fitz-Gerald to the Duke of Leeds, 15th Oct. 1789, Despatches from Paris, II, 269.

[19]Archives parlementaires, IX, 473.

[20]Buchez, Histoire de la Constituante, II, 173.

[21]Ibid., 175.

[22]"Mémoire des ministres du roi . . . sur les subsistences," in Oeuvres complètes, VII, 136-149.

[23]S. E. Harris, The Assignats (Cambridge, 1930), 7.

[24]Ibid., 15-16.

[25]Correspondance diplomatique, 143.

[26]Archives parlementaires, IX, 488.

[27]"Projet d'une Banque nationale," in Oeuvres complètes, VII, 149-197.

[28]William Short to Thomas Jefferson, December 25, 1789, The Jefferson Papers, XVI, 43-44.

[29]"Projet d'une Banque nationale," in Oeuvres complètes, VII, 186-189.

[30]"Moyens de Combler le Déficit," in Oeuvres complètes, VII, 237-242.

[31]Ibid., 248-249.

[32]Ibid., 251.

[33]Ibid., 254.

[34]Ibid., 261.

[35]Papers of Jefferson, XVI, 160.

[36]"Discours prononcé par le roi, à l'assemblée nationale, le 4 février 1790," in <u>Oeuvres complètes</u>, VII, 214.

[37]<u>Ibid</u>., 222-223.

[38]William Short to John Jay, <u>Papers of Thomas Jefferson</u>, XVI, 163.

[39]Fitz-Gerald to the Duke of Leeds, 22 Oct. 1789, <u>Despatches from Paris</u>, II, 270.

CHAPTER 20

THE END OF A CAREER

Encouraged by the reception of the king's speech
of February 4, Necker began to prepare another report
on the financial situation which he would present in
person to the National Assembly. Unfortunately, illness overtook him in January, as it did about the same
time the year before, and lingered through February.
On March 6 he sent his report to the president of the
National Assembly with a note that he was not yet well
enough to present it to the assembly in person.[1] The
memorial was read to the assembly after which a member
requested that it be printed and distributed to the
deputies, as was done.

On March 12 the finance committee gave its report
to the assembly containing its recommendations on the
matters submitted by Necker's memorial.[2] As William
Short wrote to Jefferson, the finance committee
"rejected almost every article of the memorial, as
well the amount of the exigencies as the means of
procuring it."[3] Short predicted that the "assembly
will adopt much more the report of the committee than
the plan of the minister." He also wrote that
"Necker's friends and those who are in his confidence
say he will certainly resign in a very short time."

The report of the finance committee to the National Assembly was given by the marquis de Montesquieu. It disputed several of Necker's figures on
the amount of money needed for the remainder of 1790.
Necker had said the shortfall in the collection of indirect taxes would be at least 60 million livres, and
he "feared that it would be even more." The finance
committee found that the shortfall would be only 30
million livres. Necker had said the loan of 80 million livres authorized by the assembly the previous
August was not yet subscribed to by 33 million livres.

The finance committee said only 10 million of that loan remained to be subscribed to by investors. The committee said the interest the government paid on that loan was 6.5%, and not 5% as stated by Necker. Other such faults were found in Necker's memorial of March 6.

The finance minister immediately replied to those alleged inaccuracies. There was no doubt that the shortfall in the collection of indirect taxes was greater than he had indicated in his memorial. It was now 71 million livres, and this was authenticated by the documents of tax-farming companies. The committee provided no documentation about the loan of 80 million livres, and Necker's was conclusive: the loan still was not yet subscribed to by 33 million livres. As for the interest rate on the loan the committee was obviously confused. The obligations of the borrower was stipulated at 5%. But the lender could earn 6.5% interest because he was able to subscribe to the loan by paying one-half his investment in cash and one-half in depreciated government paper that he held which the government honored at face value. The committee's report asserted that anticipations were the most costly form of loan the government could make. Necker said they were now only 5% for the 60 million livres owed. These were only examples of the many mistakes he pointed out in the committee's report. To such an impartial observer as William Short it appeared that Necker's refutation of the committee on finance was convincing.[4] It was a group of amateurs disputing with the expert professional. The committee did not understand many of the technical aspects of the subject over which they exercised such great power. This demonstrated forcefully the cogency of Necker's recommendations for a Treasury Board staffed by deputies who could acquire the expert knowledge so conspicuously lacking in the average deputy.[5]

In its recommendations to the National Assembly the finance committee rejected Necker's continued reliance on the Discount Bank. All the notes outstanding of the bank, amounting to 170 million livres were to be reimbursed by _assignats_ drawn upon the _Caisse de l'Extraordinaire_. The latter institution would also advance to the Royal Treasury an additional 132 million livres in _assignats_, which the finance committee thought was the sum of the needs for the remainder of 1790. The "project for a decree" submitted by Montesquieu provided that 400 million livres in _assignats_ be printed and that their security be based on the sale of national property of that amount. The decree already passed by the assembly on December 19 was now to be carried out. The caution of Necker regarding the issue of paper notes was disregarded. The spokesman of the finance committee did admit "caution" was necessary, but added that by the use of _assignats_ the assembly can "in an instant thwart the attacks of the enemies of the fatherland and of the Revolution." This was the beginning of that elevation of the _assignats_ to become a symbol, even an emblem of the nation and the Revolution, as was the tricolor standard.[6]

What was most disappointing to Necker was the rejection by the finance committee of his proposal to establish a Treasury Board consisting of members of the National Assembly. Sensing that his arguments in the memorial of March 6 might not be entirely persuasive, he wrote another on March 12, which was published in the minutes of the session on that day, following the report of the finance committee. He had anticipated what the objections might be. The committee resisted the appeal to revise the decree of November 7 excluding deputies from accepting posts in the executive government while remaining deputies. In his memorial of March 12 Necker protested, once again, the attitude of the National Assembly that its role was adversarial rather than cooperative with the executive government. "Ministerial despotism" may have been the

743

main issue before the Revolution. But now the Revolution had been accomplished and there was no longer any reason to persist in confrontation. He emphasized once again the importance of constant communication between the government and the assembly. The finances were too complex to be dealt with by those with only a casual knowledge. There must be some deputies who have or can acquire a day-to-day familiarity with the administration of finances. Responsibility for administration must be shared by the assembly. It was too great a burden for any individual no matter how capable. The finances should be placed under the direction of a board, and the members must have the status of deputies of the nation.[7] The committee insisted that such a collegial administration would weaken the responsibility to which an individual minister could be held by the assembly for malfeasance. From Necker's standpoint, that was just the trouble. The deputies wanted to enjoy all the power and prestige of representatives of the nation, but none of the responsiblity for government.

What was becoming increasingly evident during March was the absence of any strong support for Necker in the National Assembly. No one spoke up in his defense, as Lally-Tollendal had done so often and eloquently before the October days. When abbé Maury, that combative defender of the ancien régime, accused Necker in the latter days of March of not keeping the assembly informed about the government's finances, he was according to Fitz-Gerald, "excessively applauded from every side of the house." The British chargé added that "Necker will resign upon his going to the waters at Vichy, and his return seems not to be reckoned upon by any."[8] What puzzled Necker was why the assembly should have applauded the abbé for making such a patently untrue and unjust allegation. In a riposte to this charge, Necker reviewed all the information he had given to the assembly beginning with the publication of the compte général of May 5, 1789. It

744

seemed to Necker that abbé Maury must have been illiterate not to have seen all that information.[9]   The abbé accused the finance minister of failing to provide the assembly with a definite financial plan, as if Necker had not been constantly preoccupied with keeping the goverment solvent until the new institutions of the Revolution could be in place. Again, it was a case of theory taking precedence over the concrete and practical problems of administration.   The abbé's illiteracy about the royal finances should have served as a prime example of the desirability of a Treasury Board consisting of members of the assembly.

The incompetence of the finance committee in dealing with the problems of financial administration, the ignorance of the abbé Maury, these were only irritations to Necker compared to the bombshell dropped by another committee of the National Assembly, the committee set up to investigate pensions granted by the government. Early in April selections from the "Red Book" were published by the committee and distributed to the press for publication. The Red Book was a list of a certain type of disbursements made by the royal government called "ordonnances de comptant."   These were differentiated from ordinary disbursements in that they were not subject to the elaborate "purifying" procedures of the chambers of account. They were controlled only by the Council of Finance in the presence of the king and then sent to the archives of the Louvre. The receipts of ordinary disbursements were burned after the chambers of account had finished with them.

The publication of excerpts from the Red Book was accompanied by a "Forward" which maintained that all disbursements by ordonnances de comptant were secret, kept not only from the chambers of account but from everyone except the king and his ministers.   The "Forward" was written by the chairman of the committee on pensions, that stern Jansensist, Armand-Gaston Camus. It clearly gave the public the impression that all expenditures in this form were kept secret because those who had authorized them would have "blushed" to have revealed them to the public. The published list of ordonnances de comptant went back to the year 1779, amounting to over 116 million livres in that year. If the records of such accounts revealed a scandal, then Necker could not escape ignominy.

For a minister who had always proclaimed his goal was to bring the administration of finances out of the secret chambers of the court into public view, who for that reason had constantly reduced the sum of disbursements by ordonnances de comptant each year, so that in 1789 it was less than 12 million livres, and who was trying to get the assembly to take a major part in financial administration, such an article as the "Forward to the Red Book" seemed a terrible injustice. He could ignore libels from obscure or patently irresponsible writers, but here was a dart hurled from the very body of deputies of the nation with which he had sought so ardently to form a working relationship. In a riposte written to the "Forward" Necker did not base his case on the argument that he was less guilty than other ministers who had indulged in this questionable type of disbursement. His main argument was that the writer of the "Forward" did not have an accurate knowledge of ordonnances de comptant. They were originally used for making payments that were kept secret. But in the course of time the decision was made by a lesser official in the treasury to have certain expenditures acquitted by comptant in order to avoid the lengthy and cumbersome process of being audited by the chambers of account. These accounts were verified in the Council of Finance and then the records were sent to the Louvre archives where they were still available for the inspection of the committee on pensions. Necker had his secretary find the exact account of the acquits de comptant for 1779 and this was added to this essay; it could be seen that no item

would have cause the administrator to "blush." Most
were for ordinary, fixed expenditures. The one item
of expenditure by comptant that attracted attention
was the money granted to the king's two brothers.
Necker admitted this was considerable and said the
king had thought so too. But it was well known that
he had constantly opposed excessive grants to the
princes which was the main reason he had incurred
their enmity during this first ministry.[10] The greatest proportion of the disbursements by ordonances de
comptant were neither secret nor scandalous. The purpose of the author of the "Forward to the Red Book"
was polemical. "The Red Book," wrote René Stourm,
"printed in thousands of copies, reproduced in ex-
tracts in all newspapers, perfidiously commented upon
in the clubs, exaggerated and falsified from person to
person, served to point out to the populace the names
of its future victims."[11]

While Necker was absorbed in refuting the allegations of the committee on pensions the financial situation became precarious. The National Assembly was
still deliberating on his proposals of March 6 and the
report of the finance committee of March 12. On April
10 Necker appeared before the assembly and announced
that unless some action was taken there was grave danger that the troops on the eastern frontiers would not
receive their pay. He said the treasury must find 40
million livres for the next two months and he proposed
another advance from the Discount Bank. Now the National Assembly was forced to come to a decision, either to follow the advice of the prime minister of finances or that of its finance committee. Beginning on
April 15 the duc d'Aiguillon opened the debate on the
use of assignats. It will be remembered that 400 million had been created by the assembly the previous December and turned over to the Caisse de
l'Extraordinaire. That institution was to redeem the
assignats with hard money from the proceeds of the
sale of nationalized church lands. But the sale took

place slowly; the _assignats_ were only bonds of 5% interest and were subject to the dictates of the market like other promissory notes. The city of Paris had offered to assume responsibility for selling one-half the authorized amount of church land. The other municipal and local governments also offered to assist in the sale of the nationalized lands. The duc d'Aiguillon proposed that they be permitted to do so, that the interest rate be reduced from 5% to 3%, that the _assignats_ be printed in denominations as low as 100 livres, and that they be given forced circulation throughout the kingdom. That is, it was a proposal that the _assignats_ become paper money that would be legal tender for all transactions. This was quite a different matter than to issue the _assignats_ as bonds backed by church lands. Several who had favored the nationalization of the church lands, like Dupont de Nemours, vigorously opposed giving forced circulation to the _assignats_. "The fact that the National Assembly declares the _assignats_ to be as good as gold does not make them so," he said during the debate. "The _assignats_ are only a promise to pay; they are anticipations based upon land."[12] But he could not shake the conviction of others who argued that since the _assignat_ was backed by land it was perfectly sound. Dupont admitted that theoretically it would be, and even thought that if placed on the free market it would not decline. But he said it was opinion that decided the question, and the best chance of the _assignats_ being successful was to avoid forcing them on the public. Others made strong arguments against the proposal of d'Aiguillon, particularly the Archbishop of Aix, Boisgelin. It was not an issue that necessarily divided the moderates from the radicals, the right side of the aisle from the left. Moderates like the duc de La Rochefoucauld strongly supported forced circulation, arguing that unlike the system of John Law, whose paper money was based upon some mythical Eldorado, the _assignats_ were backed by tangible land wealth. Finally, on April 16 and 17 the final decrees were passed by the National Assembly ordering that the 400 million assignats, bearing an interest of 3%, would become legal tender throughout the kingdom. To meet the immediate needs of the government the Discount Bank would advance 20 million of its notes to the Caisse de l'Extraordinaire, which would endorse them by writing on the backs: "promise to furnish assignats," which would be done as soon as they could be printed.[13]

The act of the National Assembly on April 18 transforming the assignats into paper money had an unexpected consequence. Since the decree of the National Assembly the previous November which nationalized the lands of the Church, the Clergy were concerned about what would happen to the Church and to the Catholic religion. The animosity toward the deputies of the Clergy among the Parisians after the October days had revealed a strong, latent anti-clericalism in the Parisian popular classes. Many deputies of the Clergy still supported the Revolution, and even joined the Jacobin club. Such a one was Dom Gerle, a monk of the Carthusian order, who, during the debate on the assignats made a motion that the Catholic religion be declared the religion of state. His intention was to allay the fears of his Catholic colleagues by demonstrating that it was the wealth of the church, not the Catholic religion, which was the reason for the vehement anti-clericalism of the Parisian populace. To the surprise of the Carthusian monk, his motion set off a violent explosion of anti-clericalism. Crowds demonstrated outside the assembly hall, and in the spectators' galleries demanding the defeat of the motion. The deputies of the Clergy supported by many of the Nobility protested such threatening conduct by repairing to a convent of the Capuchins and signing a Declaration that if Dom Gerle's motion were not enacted they would secede from the National Assembly and present their grievances personally to the king. Ac-

749

cording to William Short about 300 deputies signed the petition, making it the most serious schism so far in the career of the National Assembly.[14]

It was an explosive situation, potentially as dangerous as the confrontation across the Place d'Armes at Versailles on October 5. Fortunately, cooler heads managed to control the situation in April, as they did the previous October. Lafayette again distinguished himself as a pacifier. He succeeded in calming the excited populace in the area around the National Assembly. Leaders of the Jacobins did not want the crisis to erupt in violence. An informal agreement was made to prevent the spectators in the galleries from demonstrating. The motion of Dom Gerle was withdrawn and a tenuous compromise was achieved on the basis of not mentioning religion at all in the National Assembly. But it was a tense situation. The highly charged feelings of the Parisians spread to the provinces, especially in the south, where there were clashes between Catholics and Protestants. "The symptoms of a religious war grow fast," Fitz-Gerald wrote to the Duke of Leeds.[15]

During May the struggle between the two parties that foreign diplomats were beginning to call the "aristocratic party" and the "popular party" became increasingly violent. Every matter taken up by the National Assembly threatened to provoke another convulsion like the debate on assignats. Whether judges should be elected by the people or chosen by the king, what should be the salaries allotted to bishops, almost any subject was apt to stir up anew the fires of partisanship. In this situation a major foreign policy crisis erupted for the first time since the summer of 1787. Spain and Great Britain had never resolved their rival claims along the west coast of North America. Early in May the Spaniards seized two British trading ships off the coast of Nootka Sound, in waters they claimed were under Spanish sovereignty. The

British public and Parliament were roused to a wartime fever by the incident. Suspicion and misapprehension existed on all sides, most of it, as usual, unfounded. In France there had long been apprehension that the British might take advantage of French internal weakness to settle their accounts with the Spanish Empire in the western hemisphere, at a time when Spain's traditional ally in the "Family Compact" was seemingly helpless to sustain its traditional support in the international balance of power. It was feared that Spain would be sacrificed as were the Dutch patriots in 1787.

Within France the popular party at Paris were suspicious that their rivals were maneuvering to get France involved in war, thinking this would strengthen royal power and enable it to crush the revolution. Therefore when Montmorin appeared before the National Assembly with a proposal that France should be prepared to give diplomatic and eventually military support to its traditional ally, the storm broke. The deputies had not yet taken up the constitutional question as to the respective powers of the king and the National Assembly on foreign policy and the right to declare war. Therefore a major debate now ensued in which there were three distinct viewpoints. The "popular party" insisted all powers of decision on war and peace be invested in the legislature. The counter-revolutionaries wanted it left in the hands of the king. The "aristocratic party" which their opponents congenitally and wrongly associated with the counter-revolution, wanted some kind of balance between the executive and legislative bodies in making decisions on foreign policy.

A majority of the deputies of the National Assembly favored the latter opinion. Mirabeau for the first time came out openly in support of the moderates, and offered a motion that allowed the king to share in the conduct of foreign policy, which passed

the assembly. The tribune suddenly was no longer the
favorite of the poissardes. The populace that swarmed
threateningly around the assembly hall and entered the
spectator galleries now wanted to take the tribune to
the lanterne along with the other moderate deputies.
"The distance between the capitol and the Tarpian Rock
is rather short," Mirabeau commented ruefully. Again
Lafayette found it necessary to deploy troops to protect the National Assembly from violence at the hands
of the crowds.

As for the Nootka Sound controversy a majority of
the deputies favored extending support to Spain and
ordering the ministry to take steps to build up the
fleet at Toulon. The ministers, except for Necker,
were in favor of strong support for Spain, and authorized extraordinary expenditures for the navy. Necker
predictably advised a more prudent policy, one of restraining the Spaniards and attempting to find a negotiated settlement. He believed that war would mean
the ultimate disaster for France in view of the social
and political division within the country. Fortunately, good sense prevailed, as the British and
Spaniards decided the matter was not worth a general
war and compromised on the dispute. As for France,
the incident revealed how serious the internal divisions were that threatened the country. All issues
were seen through the prism of partisan passion so
that the true national interests were distorted.

In late May Necker appeared before the National
Assembly to lay before the deputies the situation of
the finances for the remaining eight months of 1790.
He was ordered to present such a statement to the finance committee after his proposals of March 6 had
been so drastically altered. The committee had substituted assignats for the renewal of anticipations
and the new advances from the Discount Bank that
Necker had suggested. The committee had also reversed
Necker's plan to delay the reimbursement to rentiers,

752

and decided they would be paid currently. These changes were made possible by the decision of the National Assembly on April 17 to carry out the immediate issue of 400 million livres of assignats.

Necker was not content with sending his report to the finance committee. He wrote to the president of the National Assembly asking permission to appear before the assembly and read his report personally. This was granted on May 29. Over a year had passed since the opening date of the States-General when he had addressed the delegates. In that speech Necker's ostensible purpose was to present to the States-General the state of the royal finances, which he did in exhaustive detail. But that was not the foremost subject on his mind. He told the delegates that the finances were not in such serious shape as so many thought. The greatest danger, it appeared to Necker, was the deep divisions of opinion between the orders. His speech on May 29, 1790, was very similar. The financial situation was not so bad. What was critical was the lack of restraint on partisan passions. This was what preoccupied him and what he wanted to talk about with the deputies although he did devote the first half of his address discussing the finances in characteristic detail.

What was significant in his review of the financial situation was his implicit acceptance on behalf of the king of everything the National Assembly had decreed up to that time. Even if he had not agreed with those decisions there was no thought of resisting them now. His main concern was to look to the future and do whatever possible to prevent further erosion of financial integrity of the government, of public order and the effectiveness of constitutional government. The departmental administrations were given the kind of authority in government and the assessing of taxes that Necker had always wanted. The nationalization of the lands of the church and the government's assumption of responsiblity in administering the Catholic cult was by this time decided. Necker had not wished to see this, but he accepted the decrees of the assembly. The "sovereign courts" of the ancien régime disappeared. The venal offices of the magistrates were abolished although the government was committed to paying interest in the unredeemed capital of those offices. A new judicial system was established which was as democratic as the new church administration. The assembly had not made as much progress as Necker had hoped in revamping the tax system. But the gabelle had been reformed so that a uniform, moderate price for salt was established throughout the kingdom, yielding about one-third the sum of the old gabelles. In March other indirect taxes collected by the administration of the royal domain were mostly eliminated. The revenue lost from those reforms had to be made up. They had not yet been, but Necker expressed confidence that they soon would be, either by new kinds of indirect taxation that would not to be so objectionable as the old, such as a general stamp tax, or by an addition to direct taxes. Necker thought the tobacco monopoly should be retained. The internal transit duties (traites) had not yet been abolished but Necker expected they soon would be. As for reform of the direct taxes, the taxation committee of the National Assembly had not yet gotten to them, but Necker assumed that they soon would, and that the departmental administrations would have no difficulty in assessing and collecting them.

The financial statement that Necker presented to the assembly on May 29 was not a compte rendu of ordinary, fixed revenue and expenditure such as he had presented to the States-General on May 5. Rather it was a "budget" of both ordinary and extraordinary income and expenditure for the remaining eight months of 1790. In that sense it was admittedly "speculative" and dependent upon assumptions that might or might not materialize. The bottom line of this financial report

was that by the end of the year there would remain in
the treasury 11,400,000 livres to begin the next year.
Thus the anxiety about meeting the needs of the immediate future were laid to rest.   There remained an
anxiety: the continued dearth of metallic currency,
particularly after the issue of 400 million livres in
paper assignats. But Necker announced to the assembly
that the assignats so far issued, mounting to 45 million livres, were holding up well on the bourse and
there was no reason to fear their imminent depreciation.   The patriotic contribution was not the total
failure so many (including Mirabeau) had expected it
to be.   It was true that only Paris had so far submitted its pledges, but the amount thus far was 46 million livres, about one-third the total amount anticipated, and the levy was not scheduled to be complete
until 1792.   The National Assembly was expected to reduce ordinary expenditures by about 25 million livres
in the near future.   This would eliminate finally the
deficit of ordinary revenue.   There would be a new
charge to pay the interest on the capital of the offices of magistrates that had been abolished, and also
for a debt-in-arrears for which interest had to be
paid.   Necker proposed also that another 60 million
livres in "contracts" be used to reimburse those who
had suffered losses due to popular violence.   To offset these new charges, however, new sources of income
would be realized by the reforms.   The end of exemptions for the direct taxes would yield an estimated 32
million in the last eight months of 1790.[16]   The two
vingtièmes and the four sous per livre surcharge on
the first vingtième was equal to 9% of the income from
land, and the yield of the vingtièmes had been much
below what should have been realized from that proportion.   Necker assumed that the new departmental administrations would be able to levy that full amount,
which would be another increase in revenue from direct
taxes that could reasonably be expected.   Other possibilities for increased revenue were in the postal ad-

ministration by the abolition of franking privileges, improvement in the administration of the domain land, and the extinction of obligations each year owed the holders of life _rentes_. In his estimate of the resources for the future, or at least for the next eight months, Necker clearly did not envisage any further resort to _assignats_. The reason for his going into such detail, and giving a rather optimistic portrayal of the financial situation was to head off any further issue of paper money. He thought 400 million in _assignats_ already authorized and partly issued could be absorbed without causing major dislocation, but no more. However he did say that the acquisition of all the lands of the church by the government could lead to legitimate expectation of revenue for the government over and above the costs of administering the cult.[17]

Such was the optimistic tableau of Necker's budget for the remainder of 1790. From the fiscal viewpoint the future was not at all foreboding. "What ideas does this brief sketch of our immense resources not awaken in us," he exclaimed. "It is a pleasure to present such a tableau, both to the friends and to the enemies of France." But that outburst of hope as he contemplated the future was immediately followed by _caveats_, "ifs," and "howevers." If the endemic violence still continuing in the town and countryside could not be brought under control and a strong executive established, then France would not be able to enjoy her bountiful resources. "We are rightfully alarmed by the general insubordination which reigns in the kingdom, and the spectacle of disorder which erupts everywhere, causing the most painful uncertainty." The new constitutional regime itself was threatened by this disorder. "All parts of your vast edifice are not yet cemented but by novel conceptions which are untested by experience." The steady decline in the power and influence of the government must be ended, and this was a moral power, not a physical one.

"It cannot escape your attention that in a kingdom of 25 thousand square leagues which contains a population of 25 million souls the maintenance of order can never be achieved solely by the use of military force. Such a means could not be sufficient in the time of the most perfect subordination of the army; it can be much less so today." In order to realize this moral order divisions and partisan passions must be moderated. The distrust of the government had no basis in reality. The king deserved the loyalty of the assembly. As for the ministers, they would be ready to give up their posts to others that the assembly might prefer, if they could get the confidence of the king. But the greatest menace, Necker said, was the ability of demagogues to mislead the people, to stir them up for personal advantage. And this was harmful to the welfare of the common people themselves, who needed social peace more than anyone to return to full employment and the care that a benevolent government can bestow upon those in need.[18]

Partisan passions within the National Assembly, class struggle in the countryside, these were the twin evils. "Ah, if our passions could but be subdued, how everything would be clear sailing. How easily one could find the truth if the sentiment of peace, of unity should animate our hopes! Liberty can be of two kinds: that which is won by force and violence and that won by fraternity. All that is needed in this most memorable of epochs is a spirit of gentle fraternity, the lack of which obscures our future in the eyes of Europe."[19] Necker was particularly concerned about the victims of violence and brutality in the countryside. He proposed to the assembly that the government indemnify as much as possible the victims of injustice. The money spent to heal the social wounds would be well spent and future generations would not regret it. He anticipated the famous indemnity act of 1825 under the Restoration.

The minister of peace and concord, this had been Necker's role since he entered the goverment and was faced with the revolutionary crisis. He could not desist from this opportunity to lay before the assembly what was in his heart. He apologized for being carried away by his feelings and straying so far from the subject for which he was invited to speak. He referred to his coming retirement from public affairs. As he left the hall the recorder noted "Mr. Necker was generally applauded." It was a respectful if not enthusiastic send-off, for this was to be Necker's last appearance before the National Assembly.

What remained to be seen after May 29 was how well the assembly carried out what was required if the financial needs of the year were to be met and leave that surplus of 11 million livres to begin the year 1791. Necker's account was admittedly speculative, and dependent on several contingencies. Two months later he sent a memorial to the National Assembly which called the deputies' attention to the fact that a number of those contingencies were not being realized.[20] The delay in the collection of direct taxes by the departmental assemblies was not being overcome, but in fact getting further behind, despite the exhortations sent by both the minister of finance and the National Assembly to those newly-installed administrations. The National Assembly had not yet partitioned out to the departments the 49 million livres that were to replace the decline of revenue from indirect taxes, due to the reforms of March. The National Assembly had also failed to cut ordinary expenditures by 60 million livres for the fiscal year, of which 25 million Necker had included in his "speculative tableau." In fact the National Assembly had increased some expenditures where it was expected to make reductions. Soldiers' pay, for example, had been increased by over 7 million livres per year. Pensions had also been increased by about the same amount. Two and a half million livres had been added to the item for mendicity.

The ordinary allottment for the navy had been increased. It was necessary, wrote Necker, for the assembly to attend to all those matters if the necessary
expenditures for the year were to be met, and a surplus left in the treasury to begin the next year. He
seemed to suspect that the deputies were relying upon
the nationalized church lands to meet the situation,
but Necker warned that extraordinary income cannot be
used to meet a deficit of ordinary income. "Ordinary
expenditures," he wrote, "must always be met by ordinary income."

How seriously the deputies took this memorial became apparent a month later when Necker heard that the
finance committee had sent a recommendation to the National Assembly that the government print one billion,
nine-hundred million more assignats and use them to
retire the entire exigible royal debt. Necker was
horrified by this act of the finance committee, who
had not bothered to let him know of their recommendation to the assembly. In a memorial dated August 27,
1790, he vigorously opposed the measure. The first
objection was that such a great quantity of paper
would flood out the already scarce hard money. The
assignats were at that time limited to denominations
of 200 livres and over. Specie was absolutely necessary for some kinds of payments. The basic needs of
the common people could only be paid for in silver
coin. Necker had exerted great efforts, almost the
same effort, he said, with which he had met the subsistence crisis, to bring more hard money into the
country. But the conditions were not propitious, particularly because of the unfavorable exchange rate
with foreign currency and the unfavorable balance of
trade. The greatest danger of such a flood of paper
was a disastrous inflation, and this would cause incalculable convulsions.

Incomparably, the greatest danger is to introduce an immense amount of paper money

into circulation. This would bring about discontent, complaints, and recriminations, not only from one class of society, but the universality of citizens. It would affect their interests not just once but each day, each hour, each instant. It would keep the manufacturers in constant anxiety as to their means of paying their employees, and everyone as to the means of meeting their daily expenditures. It is to place at risk the subsistence of cities where the influx of unlimited paper money would prevent them from purchasing grain in the free market . . . it would make uncertain the payment of troops, of public works, of charitable workshops, and all other expenditures the delay of which would cause commotion and ferment. Finally it would give to those of sinister intentions the means of setting the entire kingdom in flames.[21]

The proponents of this scheme had argued that one billion, nine-hundred million in _assignats_ was equal to the value of nationalized church lands. That may be true in theory, Necker argued, but the experience shows that an excessive amount of paper currency drives out hard money and leads to inflation. Even the 33 million of _assignats_ already subscribed and now in circulation were not holding up on the bourse against hard money.

Finally, Necker pointed out the likelihood of run-away speculation as a consequence of the disposal of the church lands.

Let there be no doubt, in the hands of speculators the greatest number of citizens will be affected in some way by the enormous operation, which, by upsetting all relations, by changing the price of everything, by introducing frenzied gambling, will strike at all fortunes, and become the cause for the most dangerous (popular) commotion.[22]

What seemed most appalling to Necker about this proposal which threatened such dire consequences was its utter needlessness. The committee on finance was under the impression that the royal government was faced with an exigible debt, that is, a debt the payment of which was falling due, amounting to the sum of one billion, nine-hundred million livres. In a separate memorial sent to the National Assembly Necker showed where the gentlemen of the finance committee were under a grave misapprehension. Most of that "exigible debt" did not require immediate payment, only the interest charges had to be met. If the National Assembly would take those steps he had constantly urged to achieve a balance between the fixed revenue and expenditure the royal finances would not be in a dangerous situation.

Necker's two memorials did achieve his goal. The plan of the finance committee was shelved when it reached the National Assembly. "It was my last service to the nation," he wrote later in his memoirs. A week later he submitted his letter of resignation to the National Assembly, on September 3, explaining that the situation of his health did not permit him to delay going to the spa at Plombières.[23] If his health had permitted probably he would have remained at his embattled post to continue resisting the advocates of unlimited paper money. Later in September the National Assembly authorized the issue of another 800 million in _assignats_. Necker had thought the original issue of 400 million was twice too much. Furthermore the decree of the National Assembly, following a motion of Mirabeau, changed the _assignats_ from bonds yielding interest to paper money alone. It was the greatest irony that this person, who had written a celebrated essay in 1787 denouncing "agiotage"

761

(speculation) and the Discount Bank's issue of paper notes that it could not immediately redeem in gold, now inaugurated a regime of paper money that was to make the "system" of John Law seem puny in comparison.

But this was only one of the anomalies of Necker's career, as he sought to untangle himself from his responsibilities. During the summer he had been charged with making questionable payments to the comte d'Artois, certainly the most dangerous and fateful enemy of his career. Camus was the author of this slander, and demanded that Necker be required to pay from his own purse the amount in question, nearly 2 million livres. In his defense Necker showed first, that the government's obligation was not to Artois but to the prince's creditors, and was perfectly legal and proper; second, that he had not paid the prince anything since he entered the government in August 1788 because he thought that was a debt that could be delayed.[24] In July Necker had sent to the National Assembly a compte rendu of the revenue and expenditure from May 1, 1789 to May 1, 1790. It had been prepared with his usual thoroughness and care. Yet some members found certain items questionable, and insisted that the prime minister of finances should not be permitted to leave Paris until they were cleared up.

In his letter of resignation on September 3, Necker told the assembly that all items had been cleared up, only those of a routine nature being left to employees of the Contrôle-général. However, he said, because of questions being raised about his compte rendu he was leaving as surety his house in Paris, his country estate at Saint-Ouen, and his funds in the royal treasury amounting to 2 million livres.

> The emnity, the injustice which I have experienced have given me the idea of this surety. . . . But when I think of my conduct in the administration of the finances, it

will be permitted me to reflect on the (strange) singularities which have accompanied my life.[25]

The cup of bitterness was not yet emptied. When his letter of resignation was read to the National Assembly there was complete silence, no expression of regret, no mark of gratitude for the two years of heroic effort he had devoted to directing the Revolution, coping with the subsistence crisis and the finances. A week later he and Madame Necker, whose health was steadily deteriorating, left Paris to return to Switzerland. A short distance from Paris, at Arcis-sur-Aube, they were arrested by the local national guard, at the behest of a crowd influenced by the radicals. Necker was permitted to write to the National Assembly asking for their passport, for he had only the king's letter. The National Assembly wrote to the local government at Arcis to permit the Neckers to continue their journey. There was some attempt on the part of the president to say something about Necker's service to the country as a reason why he should not be molested in passage through the country. But the radical deputies prevented even that recognition, and the letter of the assembly sent to Arcis was as terse as possible. Necker continued on to the eastern frontier but his party was again arrested at Vesoul and detained for several hours while national guard troops went through the baggage searching for compromising documents. None were found and the Neckers finally reached Coppet, having given up the plans to stay at Plombières.[26]

Singular indeed was this career! It was not so surprising that he should be mistreated by the radical elements that were inexorably advancing to control the destinies of the country. Others suffered a worse fate. But what remains perplexing is why this person who served without any financial remuneration, who spent his health in grappling with the intractable

763

crisis of 1789, should be so ill-remembered today in the nation he served with such devotion and capability.

Necker lived another 14 years after his public career was over. He remained passionately absorbed in the events that followed his departure. Several volumes came from his pen in those years, devoted to the situation in France, continuing to offer advice and counsel. Unlike others who had participated in the revolution at first with enthusiasm and then turned violently against it, Necker did not abandon the moderate Revolution. He continued to advise the émigrés to make peace with the new order and give up their hopes for a counter-revolution. He continued to deplore the absence of executive power for the king, the violence against property and persons, the descent into anarchy. "How he must have suffered during his retirement," wrote that cosmopolitan European, the baron de Gleichen, "this man so jealous of his reputation, so passionately devoted to the public welfare, whose sense of virtue was so delicate, in seeing his glory eclipsed, his highest hopes deceived, and the horrors that desolated France."[27]

[1]"Mémoire du premier ministre des finances, lu à l'assemblée nationale, le 6 mars 1790," in Oeuvres complètes, VIII, 226-227.

[2]Archives parlementaires, XII, 141-150.

[3]Papers of Thomas Jefferson, XVI, 234.

[4]Papers of Thomas Jefferson, XVI, 269.

[5]"Observations de M. Necker sur le rapport fait au nom du comité des finances, à la séance de l'assemblée nationale du 12 mars," in Oeuvres complètes, VII, 299-314.

[6]Archives parlementaries, XII, 146.

[7]"Projet d'établissement d'un Bureau de Trésorerie," in Oeuvres complètes, VII, 289-299.

[8]Fitz-Gerald to the Duke of Leeds, 19 March, 1790, Despatches from Paris, II, 298.

[9]"Observations sur un Discours de l'abbé Maury," in Oeuvres complètes, VII, 314-324.

[10]"Observations de M. Necker sur l'avant-propos du Livre Rouge," in Oeuvres complètes, VII, 333-334.

[11]Les Finances de l'ancien régime et de la Révolution (Paris, 1885), II, 159.

[12]Archives parlementaires, XIII, 55.

[13]Ibid., XIII, 91.

[14]Papers of Thomas Jefferson, XVI, 401.

[15]30 April 1790, Despatches from Paris, II, 307.

[16]It may be recalled that Necker had not included this item as a regular fixed income in the Compte général of 1789, but had mentioned it only as a new source of income that could be expected, and which he estimated then at 12 million livres. This rather modest estimate of the value of exemptions from the taille was greatly increased a year later: 32 million livres for eight months, at which rate it would be 48 million livres per year or four times what Necker had earlier estimated.

[17]"Mémoire lu à l'assemblée nationale, par M. Necker, le 29 mai 1790. Budget des huit derniers mois de 1790," in Oeuvres complètes, VII, 363-392.

[18]Ibid., 384.

[19]Ibid., 388-389.

[20]"Mémoire adressé à l'assemblée nationale, le 25 juillet 1790, par le premier ministre des finances," in Oeuvres complètes, VII, 392-401.

[21]"Mémoire adressé à l'assemblée national, le 27 août, par le premier ministre des finances contre l'emission de dix-neuf cent millions d'assignats," in Oeuvres complètes, VII, 430-447.

[22]Ibid., 443.

[23]"Retraite de M. Necker," in Oeuvres complètes, VII, 448-450.

[24]"Réponse à deux accusation," in Oeuvres complètes, VII, 402-407.

[25]"Retraite de M. Necker," in Oeuvres complètes, VII, 450.

[26]"Sur l'administration de M. Necker," in Oeuvres complètes, VI, 348-354.

[27]Charles-Henri, baron de Gleichen, Souvenirs (Paris, 1868), 66-67.

CONCLUSION

It is premature at this juncture to offer a final estimate of Necker's political career, or his place in the history of the great revolution. A third and final volume is planned for this purpose. During the decade of revolution that followed his departure from France he wrote copiously about the situation. These works deserve the attention of the historian and the biographer. Furthermore a review of the treatment Necker's career has received at the hands of historians since his death is in order. It might also be possible to address some of the controversial problems of interpretation that still rage around the historiography of the French Revolution.

These matters have not been within the scope of this volume. The purpose is rather to give Necker a sympathetic hearing. Whatever might be the final judgment on his career, history owes him an accurate description of his thinking about the manifold crisis, his intentions and policies in coping with it, and to see them in the context of the circumstances he faced. In my opinion this has not been done hitherto. The biographers who have been most sympathetic toward him have not delved into the financial aspects of his administration, and this is essential for a just and impartial evaluation. Those historians who have made contributions to the financial history of the revolution have generally been hostile to Necker.

Despite the above disclaimers, there are matters raised in this volume that are controversial. The traditional view of the role of finances in bringing on the revolution is considerably modified. Necker did not think the revolutionary crisis was caused by the financial predicament of the royal government. Its debt was enormous, and the carrying charges on it approached one half the annual fixed expenditures. Yet Necker thought the financial situation could have been resolved without convulsions. The amount of increased taxation proposed by both Calonne and Loménie de Brienne to meet the deficit was not an alarming sum. The proposals of both ministers to overcome the deficit were moderate. When Necker came to the helm in August 1788 he believed he could put the finances in order without summoning the States-General.

In Necker's view the crisis was not financial but political. The Assembly of Notables of 1787 insisted that the public interest required some institutional restraints on government spending. The nation could no longer admit that the king or the minister who had received his confidence could spend money at will, and then when the deficit reached an alarming figure, summon an assembly of notables to get their assent to a permanent increase in tax revenue. The notables were influenced by Necker's first ministry. What they wanted was to institutionalize Necker's policies so that the nation would no longer be subjected to irresponsible management of the royal finances. This was their chief concern; not, as so often said, simply because they refused to give up their fiscal privileges.

Necker shared this belief. He had seen his own reforms largely abandoned by his successors. There must be some institutional changes that would ensure the permanence of the policies he advocated. But did this require the summoning of the States-General? At first he would have preferred to work with the Assembly of Notables. He believed the greatest mistake of the archbishop was to dismiss the notables. Necker had no confidence in the magistrates of the sovereign courts as representatives of the nation's interests. He condemned the decree of the Parlement of Paris calling for the States-General as irresponsible. Yet Necker's own experience with the second Assembly of Notables in 1788 was disillusioning. In the final analysis, as he wrote in his memoirs at a later time, only the States-General could assure the nation of the

changes it demanded. He therefore welcomned the first
revolution. His vision of what was needed and what
the most educated part of the nation desired was a
limited monarchy based upon the British model. This
was the direction in which he sought to steer the revolution.

He failed to achieve that goal because of enemies
on both the right and the left. Before July 11, 1789,
the threat was from the right, from the circle of the
comte d'Artois and Necker's own ministerial colleagues
who wanted to restore the absolute power of the king
by military force. After the July days and his return
to the ministry he found his enemies were on the left,
those who proclaimed the supreme power of the Constituent Assembly to the exclusion of all other authorities including the king and his ministers. From
Necker's viewpoint this was the absolute monarchy
turned upside down. The National Assembly was qualified to represent the nation but not to administer the
government. Necker's repeated attempts to form a
working partnership between the government and the assembly met one rebuff after the other. It is amazing
that he stayed the course as long as he did.

A work that undertakes to examine Necker's role
in the revolution of 1789 with the historian's sympathetic understanding will of course seem unsympathetic
to those individuals and social forces that brought
about his failure. If one is basically out of sympathy for Necker's aims in the revolution, then Calonne,
Mirabeau, and the leaders of the Parisian democracy
could be described in a different light. If Necker's
goals were unrealistic or inherently undesirable for
the time, then Mirabeau's attempts to bring down the
popular minister could be applauded.

It is probably not possible to eliminate values
entirely from historical writing. If the historian is
disposed to value compromise and the spirit of na-

tional unity above that of faction and class hatreds, then Necker's career would appear more significant than for one who believed in the inevitability of class struggle and violent revolution. But that concession to "historical relativism" needs to be modified. First, one's values are not a license for misrepresentation and distortion of the evidence. In his efforts to be just to Necker the writer of this work has sought to avoid being unjust to Necker's enemies. Second, whatever one's values on revolutions or politics, Necker's career in 1789 is a dramatic story well worth knowing for anyone interested in the history of the great revolution.

BIBLIOGRAPHY

A. Primary Sources

1. Manuscripts

Archives nationales (AN), Paris.

C^1-C^5. Assemblée des Notables, 1787.

144 AP 130. Mémoires d'Henry-François de Paule d'Ormesson, contrôleur-général des finances.

Bibliothèque nationale (BN), Paris.

MSS Fonds français: 6684-6687, Journal du Libraire Hardy

MSS Fonds français, nouv. acquis. 22590, Recueil de pièces imprimées et manuscrits sur l'assemblée des Notables tenue à Versailles en 1787; 23615-23617, Recueils de papiers d'état provenant des archives de la famille de Loménie de Brienne.

MSS Fonds Joly de Fleury. 1038-1040, Assemblée des Notables, 1787; 1432, 1434-1444, 1448-1449, documents from his financial ministry.

2. Printed Documents

Archives parlementaires de 1787 à 1860. First ser. 47 vols. Paris: 1867-1896. Edited by Jérôme Mavidal and E. Laurent.

Aulard, François-Alphonse, ed. <u>Lettres</u> <u>et</u> <u>bulletins</u>
<u>de</u> <u>Barentin</u> <u>à</u> <u>Louis</u> <u>XVI</u>, <u>avril-juillet</u>, <u>1789</u>.
Paris: 1915.

Bloch, Camille. <u>Procès-verbeau</u> <u>du</u> <u>comité</u> <u>des</u> <u>Finances</u>
<u>de</u> <u>l'Assemblée</u> <u>constituante</u>. 2 vols. Rennes:
1922-1923.

Brette, Armand, ed. <u>Recueil</u> <u>de</u> <u>documents</u> <u>relatifs</u> <u>à</u>
<u>la</u> <u>convocation</u> <u>des</u> <u>Etats-généraux</u>. 3 vols.
Paris: 1894-1904.

Chassin, Charles L., ed. <u>Les</u> <u>élections</u> <u>et</u> <u>les</u> <u>cahiers</u>
<u>de</u> <u>Paris</u> <u>en</u> <u>1789</u>. 4 vols. Paris: 1888-1889.

<u>Collections</u> <u>des</u> <u>édits</u>, <u>déclarations</u> <u>et</u> <u>arrêts</u> <u>du</u> <u>con</u>-
<u>seil</u> <u>d'état</u>. (BN F. 23628-23632.)

<u>Collection</u> <u>Rondonneau</u>, <u>archives</u> <u>nationales</u>. (AN 97,
379, 389, and 407.)

Flammermont, Jules, ed. <u>Remontrances</u> <u>du</u> <u>Parlement</u> <u>de</u>
<u>Paris</u> <u>au</u> <u>XVIII</u>^e <u>siècle</u>. 3 vols. Paris: 1888-
1898.

Isambert, François-André; Jourdan; Decrusy, eds. <u>Re</u>-
<u>cueil</u> <u>général</u> <u>des</u> <u>anciennes</u> <u>lois</u> <u>français</u>. 29
vols. Paris: 1822-1827.

Mathon de la Cour, Charles-Joseph. <u>Collection</u> <u>de</u>
<u>comptes</u> <u>rendus</u>: <u>Pièces</u> <u>authentiques</u>, <u>états</u> <u>et</u>
<u>tableaux</u> <u>concernant</u> <u>les</u> <u>finances</u> <u>de</u> <u>France</u> <u>depuis</u>
<u>1758</u> <u>jusqu'en</u> <u>1787</u>. 2d ed. Lausanne: 1788.

<u>Observations</u> <u>présentées</u> <u>au</u> <u>Roi</u> <u>par</u> <u>les</u> <u>Bureaux</u> <u>de</u>
<u>l'Assemblée</u> <u>des</u> <u>Notables</u> <u>sur</u> <u>les</u> <u>Mémoires</u> <u>rémis</u> <u>à</u>
<u>l'Assemblée</u> <u>ouverte</u> <u>par</u> <u>le</u> <u>Roi</u> <u>à</u> <u>Versailles</u> <u>le</u> <u>23</u>
<u>février</u> <u>1787</u> (1st et 2nd divisions). (BN 8° Le
21.10.)

Ouverture des Etats-généraux, procès-verbeau, et récit
des séances des ordres du Clergé, et de la Noblesse, jusqu'à leur réunion à l'assemblée
nationale. Paris: Imprimérie nationale, 1791.
(BN 8° Le 27.6)

Ouverture de conciliation: Ouverture fait par les
commissaries du Roi aux commissaires des trois
ordres, à la conférence tenue chez M. le garde
des sceau. Versailles: Imprimérie nationale,
1789. (BN 4° Le 29.15.)

Procès-verbal de l'Assemblée des Notables tenue à
Versailles, en l'année 1787. Paris: Imprimérie
royale, 1788.

Procès-verbal des séances de la Chambre de l'ordre de
la Noblesse aux Etats-généraux en 1789. Paris:
Imprimérie nationale, 1792. (BN 8° Le 27.5A.)

Récit des principaux faits qui se sont passés dans la
salle de l'Ordre de Clergé, depuis le commencement des Etats-généraux, la 4 mai 1789, jusqu'à
la réunion des trois ordres dans la salle commune, par M. Vallet, curé de Saint-Louis, député.
Paris: Imprimérie nationale, 1790. (BN 8° Le
27.3.)

Récit des séances des députés des Communes depuis le 5
mai, 1789, jusqu'à 12 juin suivant. Edited by
François-Alphonse Aulard. Paris: Soc. hist. de
la Rév. française, 1895.

Recueil de documents relatifs aux séances des Etats-
généraux, mai-juin 1789, préparé par l'Institute
d'histoire de la Révolution française de la
Faculté des lettres de Paris sous la direction de
Georges Lefebvre. Vol. I, pt. 1: Les préliminaires. La séance de 5 mai 1789. Edited by
George Lefebvre and Anne Terroine. Paris: 1953;
pt. 2: La séance du 23 juin. Paris: 1962.

3. Printed Books, Journals, and Pamphlets

Allonville, Armand-François. Mémoires secrets de 1770
  à 1830. 6 vols. Paris: 1838-1845.

Angiviller, Charles-Claude Flahaut de la Billardie de.
  Mémoires. Edited by Louis Bobe. Paris and
  Copenhagen: C. Klincksieck, 1933.

Antraigues, Emmanuel Louis-Henri de Launay de. Mémoire sur la constitution des Etats de la province
  de Languedoc. Vivarais: n.d.

_____ Mémoire sur les Etats-généraux. n.p. 1788.

_____ Second Mémoire sur les Etats-généraux. n.p.,
  n.d.

Augeard, Jacques-Mathieu. Mémoires secrets. Paris:
  H. Plon, 1866.

Bachaumont, Louis Petit de. Mémoires pour servir à
  l'histoire de la république des lettres en France
  depuis 1762 jusqu'à nos jours. 36 vols. London:
  J. Adamson, 1777-1789.

Bailly, Jean-Sylvain. Mémoires d'un Témoin de la
  Révolution. 3 vols. Paris: Baudin fils, 1821-
  1822.

Barentin, Charles-Louis-François de Paule de. Mémoire
  autographe de M. de Barentin, Chancelier et Garde
  des Sceau, sur les derniers conseils du roi Louis
  XVI. Edited by Maurice Champion. Paris: 1844.

Beauvau, Marie-Charlotte de Rohan-Chabot de. Souvenirs de la maréchale princesse de Beauvau; suivis

des mémoires de maréchal de Beauvau. Paris:
1872.

Bertrand-Moleville, Antoine-François de. Mémoires
particuliers pour servir à l'histoire de la fin
du règne de Louis XVI. 2 vols. Paris: L. G.
Michaud, 1816.

Besenval, Pierre-Victor de. Mémoires. Edited by M.
F. Barrière. 3 vols. Paris: 1851.

Blondel, Jean. Introduction à l'ouvrage intitulé de
l'administration des finances par M. Necker.
n.p., 1785. Also attributed to Antoine Bourboulon. (BN 8° Lb 39.331.)

Bouillé, François-Claude de. Mémoires. Edited by F.
Barrière. Paris: 1859.

Bourboulon, Antoine. Réponse de sieur Bourboulon au
Compte rendu au Roi par M. Necker. London:
1781. (BN 8° Lb 39.278.)

Brette, Armand. "Relations des événements depuis le 6
mai jusqu'au 15 juillet 1789. Bulletins d'un
agent secret." La Révolution française. 23
(1892), 348-368; 443-471; 520-547. 24 (1892),
69-84; 162-178.

_____ "La séance royale de 23 juin 1789. Ses préliminaires et ses suites d'après deux documents
inédites: La correspondance de Barentin et le
journal de l'abbé Coster." La Révolution française. 22 (1891), 5-44; 120-154; 416-452. 23
(1892), 55-76.

Browning, Oscar, ed. Despatches from Paris, 1784-
1790. Selected and edited from Foreign Office
correspondance. 2 vols. London: 1909-1910.

Buchez, P. B., and P. C. Roux, eds. Histoire parle-
mentaire de la Révolution française. 40 vols.
Paris: 1834-1838.

Bussière, F. "La constituant Foucauld de Lardimalie."
La Révolution française. 22 (1891), 204-241.

Calonne, Charles-Alexandre de. Discours prononcé par
M. de Calonne dans l'asssemblée des Notables
tenue à Versailles le 22 février 1787. Versailles: P. D. Pierres, 1787.

_____ Lettre adressé au Roi le 9 février 1789.
London: 1789.

_____ Réponse à l'écrit de M. Necker. London: T.
Spilsbury, Jan. 1788.

_____ Requête au Roi, adressé à Sa Majesté par M. de
Calonne, ministre d'Etat. London: T. Spilsbury,
1787.

Chastenay, Victorine de. Mémoires. 2 vols. Paris:
A. Rosebot, 1896.

Clermont-Gallerande, Charles-Georges de. Mémoires particuliers pour servir à l'histoire de la Révolution qui s'est opérée en France en 1789. 3
vols. Paris: J. G. Dentu, 1826.

Clermont-Tonnerre, Stanislas de. Oeuvres complètes de
Stanislas de Clermont-Tonnerre. 2nd ed. 4 vols.
n.p. An III.

Cormeré, Guillaume-François Mahy de. Recherches et
considérations nouvelles sur les finances ou mémoires sur leur situation actuelle, cause du déficit . . . 2 vols. London: 1789.

Creuzé-Latouche, Jacques-Antoine. Journal des Etats-
généraux et du début de l'assemblée nationale (18

mai-29 juillet 1789). Paris: Henri Didier, 1946.

Des Cars, Jean-François de Pérusse. Mémoires. 2 vols. Paris: 1890.

Dumont, Etienne. Souvenirs sur Mirabeau et sur les deux premières assemblées législatives. New edition edited by J. Bénétruy. Paris: 1951.

_____ Recollections of Mirabeau and of the First Two Legislative Assemblies of France. Philadelphia: Carey & Lea, 1833.

Duquesnoy, Adrien-Cyprien. Journal d'Adrien Duquesnoy. Député du Tiers de Bar-le-Duc, sur l'Assemblée constituante (3 mai, 1789-3 avril, 1790). 2 vols. Paris: 1894.

Ferrand, Antoine-François-Claude de. Mémoires. Paris: 1897.

Ferrières, Charles-Eli de. Mémoires pour servir à l'histoire de l'Assemblée constituante et de la Révolution de 1789. 3 vols. Paris: An VII. 2nd ed. n.p., 1822.

_____ Correspondance inédite (1789-1791). Edited by H. Carré. Paris: 1932.

Flammermont, Jules, ed. Les Correspondances des Agents diplomatiques étranger en France avant la Révolution. Paris: 1896.

Gleichen, Charles-Henri de. Souvenirs. Paris: 1868.

Grimm, Friedrich Melchior. Correspondance littéraire, philosophique, et critique par Grimm, Diderot, Raynal, Meister. 16 vols. Paris: 1877-1882.

Hennet, Albert-Joseph-Ulpien. Théorie du crédit public. Paris: Testu et Delunay, 1816.

Jefferson, Thomas. The Papers of Thomas Jefferson.
Edited by Julian Boyd. Vols. 11-16. Princeton,
New Jersey: 1959-1961.

Lafayette, Gilbert de Motier de. Mémoires, correspondance et manuscrits du général Lafayette,
publié par sa famille. 6 vols. Paris: 1837-
1838.

Lally-Tollendal, Trophine-Gérard de. Mémoires de M.
le comte de Lally-Tollendal ou second lettre à
ses commettants. Paris: janvier, 1790.

_____ "Necker." La Biographie universalle. 30
(1811-1849), 9-25.

Lescure, François-Adolphe Mathurin de. Correspondance
secrète inédite sur Louis XVI, Marie-Antoinette,
la cour et la ville, de 1777 à 1792. 2 vols.
Paris: 1866.

Ligou, Daniel, ed. La première année de la Révolution
vue par un témoin, 1789-1790. Les Bulletins de
Poncet-Delpesch, député de Quercy au Etats-
généraux de 1789. Paris: 1961.

Loménie de Brienne, cts. Athanase-Louis de, and
Etienne-Charles Loménie de Brienne. Journal de
l'assemblée des notables de 1787. Edited by
Pierre Chevallier. Paris: C. Klincksieck, 1960.

Mallet du Pan, Jacques. Mémoires et correspondance
pour servir à l'histoire de la Révolution française. 2 vols. Paris: 1851.

Malouet, Pierre-Victor. Mémoires . 2 vols. Paris:
1868.

Marmontel, Jean-François. Mémoires. Edited by M.
Tourneux. 3 vols Paris: 1891.

Mège, Francisque. Gaultier de Biauzat, député du
Tiers-état aux Etats-généraux de 1789. 2 vols.
Paris: E. Lechvalier, 1890.

Mercy-Argenteau, Florimond-Claude de. Correspondance
secrète du comte de Mercy-Argenteau avec l'empereur Joseph II et le prince de Kaunitz. 2 vols.
Edited by A. d'Arneth and J. Flammermont. Paris:
1889-1891.

Metra, François. Correspondance secrète, politique et
littéraire, ou mémoires pour servir à l'histoire
des cours, des sociétés et de la littérature en
France depuis la mort de Louis XV. 18 vols.
London: J. Adamson, 1787-1790.

Mirabeau, Honore-Gabriel de Riqueti de. Correspondance entre le Cte. de Mirabeau et le Cte. de
la Marck pendant les années 1789, 1790, 1791. 3
vols. Paris: 1851.

_____ Lettres de comte de Mirabeau à ses commettants. n.p., 1791.

_____ Lettres sur l'administration de M.Necker.
n.p., 1791.

_____ Mémoires de Mirabeau. Edited by Lucas-
Montigny. 8 vols. Paris: 1834-1835.

Montlosier, François-Dominique Reynaud de. Mémoires
sur la Révolution française, le Consulat,
l'Empire et les principaux événements qui l'ont
suivi, 1755-1830. 2 vols. Paris: 1830.

Morellet, André, Lettres de l'abbé Morellet à Lord
Shelburne, 1772-1803. Paris: Plon, Nourit et
Co., 1898.

_____ Mémoires. 2 vols. 2nd ed. Paris: Ladvocat,
1882.

Morris, Gouverneur. A Diary of the French Revolution.
Edited by Beatrix Cary Davenport. 2 vols.
Boston: Houghton-Mifflin, 1939.

Mounier, Jean-Joseph. Exposé de la conduite de M.
Mounier dans l'Assemblée nationale, et des motifs
de son retour en Dauphiné. Paris: 1789.

_____ Recherches sur les causes qui ont empêché les
Français de devenir libre. 2 vols. Geneva:
1792.

[Necker, Jacques]. Compte général des Revenues et des
Dépenses fixes au 1 de mai 1789. Versailles:
Imprimérie royale, 1789.

Necker, Jacques. Oeuvres complètes de M. Necker
publié par le baron de Staël, son petit-fils. 15
vols. Paris: Treuttel et Würtz, 1820-1821.

Norvins, Jacques Marquet de Montbreton de. Mémorial.
3 vols. Paris: 1896.

Panchaud, Benjamin (Isaac). Réflections sur l'état
actuel du crédit public de l'Angleterre et de la
France. n.p., Nov. 1781.

[Papon, Jean-Pierre]. Histoire du Gouvernement français depuis l'assemblée des Notables tenue le 22
février 1787, jusqu'à la fin de décembre de la
même année. London: 1788.

Pasquier, Etienne-Denis. The Memoirs of Chancellor
Pasquier. Trans. by Douglas Garman. London:
Elak Books, 1967.

Rilliet de Saussure. Lettre sur l'Emprunt et l'Impôt.
Geneva: 1779. (BN 8° Lb 39.6262.)

Saint-Priest, François-Emmanuel Guignard de. Mémoires. 2 vols. Paris: 1929.

Sallier-Chaumont de la Roche, Guy-Maire. Annales
français (mai 1789-mai 1790). 2 vols. Paris:
1832.

Sieyes, Emmanuel. Qu'est-ce que le Tiers-état?
Edited by Roberto Zapperi. Geneva: Droz, 1970.

Soulavie, Jean-Louis. Mémoires historiques et politiques du règne de Louis XVI. 6 vols. Paris:
1801.

Staël-Holstein, Anne Louise Germaine de. Considérations sur la Révolution française. Edited by
Jacques Godechot. Paris: Tallandier, 1983.

_____ Correspondance générale de Madame de Staël.
Edited by Beatrice W. Jasinski. 3 vols. Paris:
1962.

_____ Mémoires sur la vie privée de mon père.
Paris: 1818.

Staël-Holstein, August Louis de. "Notice sur M.
Necker." Oeuvres complètes de M. Necker. Vol. I
(1820), 1-cccli.

Staël-Holstein, Eric Magnus de. Correspondance diplomatique de baron de Staël-Holstein, Ambassadeur
de Suède en France. Paris: Hachette, 1881.

Thibaudeau, A. C. Biographe-Mémoires, 1765-1792.
Paris: H. Champion, 1875.

Virieu, Jean-Louis. La Révolution française rancontée
par un diplomate étranger. Correspondance du
bailli de Virieu, ministre plénipotentiaire de
Parme (1788-1793). Edited by the vicomte de
Grouchy and Antoine Guillois. Paris: 1903.

Weber, Joseph. Mémoires de Weber, frère de lait de
Marie-Antoinette, Reine de France. 2 vols.

Paris: 1822. The first three chapters are identical to Lally-Tollendal's article on Necker in the Biographie universelle, cited above.

Young, Arthur. Travels in France during 1787, 1788, 1789. Edited by Bethan-Edwards. London: 1889.

B. Secondary Works

Andlau, B. d'. La Jeunesse de Madame de Staël (de 1766 à 1786) avec des Documents inédits. Genève: Librairie Droz, 1970.

Beach, Vincent W. "The Count of Artois and the Coming of the French Revolution." The Journal of Modern History, 30 (December, 1958), 313-324.

Beik, Paul H. "The Comte d'Antraigues and the Failure of French Conservatism in 1789." American Historical Review, 56, n. 4 (July, 1951), 767-787.

Bénétruy, J. L'Atelier de Mirabeau. Quatre proscrits Génévois dans le Tourment révolutionnaire. Genève: 1962.

Boiteau, Paul. Etat de la France en 1789. Paris: 1860.

Bosher, J. F. French Finances, 1770-1795. From Business to Bureaucracy. Cambridge: University Press, 1970.

_____ "The Premier Commis des Finances in the reign of Louis XVI." French Historical Studies, 3, no. 4 (1964), 475-495.

Bouchary, Jean. Les Manieurs d'Argent à Paris à la fin du XVIIIe siècle. 3 vols. Paris: M. Rivière, 1939-1943.

_____ Les Compagnies financières à la fin du XVIIIe siècle. 3 vols. Paris: 1940-1942.

Braesch, Frédéric. 1789. L'Année cruciale. Paris: Gallimard, 1941.

_____ Finance et Monnaies révolutionnaires. Etudes et Documents. 3 vols. Nancy: Roumegoux, 1934.

Castries, René de la Croix de. Le Maréchal de Castries, 1727-1800. Paris: Fayard, 1955.

Champion, Edme. Esprit de la Révolution française. Paris: 1887.

_____ La France d'après les Cahiers de 1789. Paris: A. Colin, 1897.

Chapuisat, Edouard. Necker (1732-1804). Paris: Librairies du Recueil Sirey, 1938.

Chaussinand-Nogaret, Guy. Mirabeau. Editions du Seuil, 1982.

Dawson, Philip. "The Bourgeoisie de robe in 1789." French Historical Studies, 4, no. 1 (1865), 1-21.

Diesbach, Ghislain de. Necker, ou la faillite de la Vertu. Paris: Perrin, 1978.

Doyle, William. Origins of the French Revolution. Oxford: University Press, 1980.

_____ "The Parliaments of France and the Breakdown of the Old Régime." French Historical Studies, 6 (Fall, 1970), 415-459.

_____ "Was there an Aristocratic Reaction in Pre-revolutionary France?" Past and Present, 57 (Nov. 1972), 97-122.

Egret, Jean. Les Derniers Etats de Dauphiné. Romans. Grenoble: 1942.

_____ "Lafayette dans la première assemblée des Notables." Annales historiques de la Révolution française (Jan.-March, 1952).

_____ Necker, Ministre de Louis XVI. Paris: Champion, 1975.

_____ La Pré-révolution française. Paris: Presses universitaires de France, 1962.

_____ "Un conseiller d'Etat à la fin de l'ancien régime: Jean-Jacques Vidaud de la Tour." Revue historique, 198 (1947), 189-202.

Filleul, Paul. Le duc de Montmorency-Luxembourg, Premier baron Chrétien de France, Fondateur du Grand Orient. Sa Vie et ses Archives. Paris: Labérgerie, 1939.

Flammermont, Jules. "Le second ministère de Necker." Revue historique, 46 (mai-août, 1891), 1-67.

Forster, Robert. "The Survival of the Nobility during the French Revolution." Past and Present, 37 (July, 1967), 71-86.

_____ "The Provincial Nobles: A Reappraisal." American Historical Review, 68 (April, 1963), 681-691.

Garrett, Mitchell B. The Estates General of 1789. The Problem of Composition and Organization. New York: Appleton-Century, 1935.

Glagau, Hans. Reformversüche und Sturz des Absolutisimus in Frankreich, 1774-1788. Munchen: R. Oldenbourg, 1908.

Godechot, Jacques. La Prise de la Bastille. Paris: 1965.

_____ Les institutions de la France sous la Révolution et l'Empire. Paris: 1951.

Gomel, Charles. Les Causes financières de la Révolution française. 2 vols. Paris: Guillaumin, 1892-1893.

Goodwin, A. "Calonne, the Assembly of Notables of 1787 and the Origins of the Revolt Nobiliare." English Historical Review, 61 (1946), 202-234; 329-377.

Grange, Henri. Les Idées de Necker. Paris: C. Klincksieck, 1974.

Gruder, Vivian R. "No Taxation without Representation: The Assembly of Notables of 1787 and Political Ideology in France." Legislative Studies Quarterly, 7, no. 2 (May, 1982), 263-279.

_____ "Paths to Political Consciousness: The Assembly of Notables of 1787 and the 'Pre-revolution' in France." French Historical Studies, 13, no. 3 (Spring, 1984), 323-355.

Guimbaud, Louis. Un grand Bourgeois au XVIIIe siècle. Auget de Montyon. (1733-1820). Paris: 1909.

Harris, Robert D. "Equality as Interpreted by the French Revolutionaries." Unpublished Ph.D dissertation, University of California, Berkeley, 1960. Listed in Xerox University Microfilm, Vol. 10, p. 106.

_____ "French Finances and the American War." Journal of Modern History , 42, no. 2 (June, 1976),
233-258.

_____ "Necker's Compte rendu of 1781: A Reconsideration." Journal of Modern History, 42, no. 2
(June, 1970), 161-183.

_____ Necker. Reform Statesman of the Ancien Régime. Berkeley, University of California Press,
1979.

Harris, Seymour. The Assignats. Cambridge: University Press, 1930.

Haussonville, Othenin d'. "Le Salon de Madame
Necker." Revue des deux mondes, 37 (1880), 47-
98; 38 (1880), 63-106; 42 (1880), 790-828.

Hyslop, Beatrice Fay. French Nationalism in 1789
according to the Cahiers. New York: Columbia
University Press, 1934.

_____ A Guide to the General Cahiers of 1789 with
the Texts of Unedited Cahiers. New York:
Columbia University Press, 1934

Kelly, George Armstrong, "The Machine of the Duc
d'Orleans and the New Politics." Journal of
Modern History, 51, no. 4 (Dec., 1979), 667-684.

Lacour-Gayet, Robert. Calonne. Financier, Réfor-
mateur, Contre-Révolutionnaire, 1734-1802.
Paris: Hachette, 1963.

Lincoln, C. H. "The Cahiers of 1789 as an Evidence of
a Compromise Spirit." American Historical Review, 2, No. 2 (1897), 225-228.

Lucas, Colin. "Nobles, Bourgeois and the Origins of the French Revolution." Past and Present, 60 (August, 1973), 84-126.

Marion, Marcel. Histoire financière de la France depuis 1715. 8 vols. Paris: A. Rousseau, 1914-1928.

Mathias, Peter, and Patrick O'Brien. "Taxation in Britain and France, 1715-1810. A Comparison of the Social and Economic Incidence of Taxes Collected for the Central Governments." Journal of European Economic History. 5 (Winter, 1976), 601-650; 7 (Spring, 1979), 209-213.

Mathiez, Albert. "Etudes critiques sur les journées des 5 et 6 octobre 1789." Revue historique, 67 (1898), 241-281; 68 (1898), 258-293; 69 (Jan.-April, 1898), 41-66.

_____ La Révolution française. Paris: 1922-1924.

Mosser, Françoise. Les Intendants des Finances au XVIII siècle. Les Lefevre d'Ormesson et le "Département des Impositions" 1715-1777. Genève: Librairie Droz, 1978.

Murphy, Orville T. Charles Gravier, Comte de Vergennes. French Diplomat in the Age of Revolution, 1719-1787. Albany: State University of New York Press, 1982.

Necheles, Ruth F. "The Curés in the Estates General of 1789." Journal of Modern History, 46, no. 3 (Sept. 1974), 425-444.

Pugh, Wilma H. "Calonne's 'New Deal'." Journal of Modern History, 11 (Sept. 1939), 289-312.

Rampelberg, René-Marie. Le Ministre de la Maison du Roi, 1783-1788. Baron de Breteuil. Paris: Economica, 1975.

Ravitch, Norman. "The Taxing of the Clergy in Eighteenth-Century France." Church History, 33 (June, 1964), 157-174.

Renouvin, Pierre. L'Assemblée des Notables de 1787. La Conférence de 2 mars. Paris: 1920.

_____ Les Assemblées provinciales de 1787. Paris: A. Picard, 1921.

Rose, R. B. "The French Revolution and the Grain Supply." Bulletin of the John Rylands Library, 39, no. 1 (Sept. 1956), 171-187.

Saricks, Ambrose. Pierre Samuel du Pont de Nemours. Lawrence, Kansas: 1965.

Schelle, Gustave. Dupont de Nemours. Paris: 1888.

Scott, Samuel F. "Problems of Law and Order during 1790, the 'Peaceful Year' of the French Revolution." American Historical Review, 80 (Oct. 1975), 859-889.

Sepet, Marius. Les Préliminaires de la Révolution. Paris: Retaux-Bray, 1890.

_____ "Le serment du Jeu de Paume et la déclaration du 23 juin, 1789." Revue des questions historiques. Nouvelle ser., 5 (Avril, 1891), 491-546.

Shafer, Boyd C. "Bourgeois Nationalism in the Pamphlets on the Eve of the French Revolution." Journal of Modern History, 10 (March, 1938), 31-50.

Shurr, Georgia Hooks. "Thomas Jefferson and the French Revolution." American Society of the Legion of Honor Magazine, 1, no. 3 (1979), 161-182.

Susane, G. La Tactique financiére de Calonne. Paris: A. Rousseau, 1901.

Stourm, René. Les Finances de l'Ancien Régime et de la Révolution. 2 vols. Paris: Guillaumin, 1885.

Taylor, George V. "The Paris Bourse on the Eve of the Revolution, 1781-1789." American Historical Review, 67, no. 4 (July, 1962), 951-977.

_____ "Revolutionary and Nonrevolutionary Content in the Cahiers of 1789; An Interim Report." French Historical Studies, 7, no. 4 (Fall, 1972), 479-503.

Tocqueville, Alexis de. The European Revolution and Correspondance with Gobineau. Edit. and trans. by John Lukacs. Garden City, NY: Doubleday Anchor, 1959.

_____ The Old Regime and the French Revolution. Trans. by Stuart Gilbert. Garden city, NY: Doubleday Anchor, 1955.

Acquits de comptant,
10, 56, 216. See
also Ordonnances de
comptant
Aligre, Etienne-Fran-
çois d', 55, 63,
117
Amécourt, Lefebvre d',
63
American War, 33, 36,
55, 95; cost of,
31; debt from, 22,
60-61, 107, 111
Amortization payments:
in comptes rendus,
158; suspended by
Loménie de Brienne,
265; in Necker's
Compte Général of
May 1789, 414, 419
Angiviller, Charles-
Claude Flahaut de
la Billardie d',
45, 52, 497, 522
Anticipations, 81,
138, 165, 171, 173,
179, 245, 264-265,
272, 417-418, 730,
752
Antraigues, Emmanuel-
Louis-Henri de Lau-
nay d', 366-368,
384, 469, 470
Artois, Charles-
Philippe d', 21,
35, 45, 105, 126,
168, 182, 210, 228,
244, 266, 318, 458,
509, 511, 512, 538,
564, 569, 578, 667,
670, 762, 771
Assembly of Electors
(of Paris), 562,
572, 590, 594, 597,
613-614
Assembly of Notables:
of 1787, 23, 49,
92-93, 95, 195,

196, 232, 262, 380;
convening of, 105,
106; deliberation
on Calonne's re-
forms, 117-132; fi-
nal recommenda-
tions, 210-213; of
1788, 271, 273,
313-321, 342, 348
Assembly of Repre-
sentatives (of the
Paris Commune),
594, 614-615, 673-
674, 678, 685, 686,
688, 736
Assignats, 724, 727,
730-731, 743, 747-
750, 752, 755, 756,
759-761
Augeard, Jacques-Math-
ieu, 43-44, 46, 74
August decrees: night
of August 4, 1789,
626-628; other,
648-651, 668, 718
Avertissement, 135-
136.

Bachaumont, Louis Pe-
tit de, 3-4, 42-43,
45, 49, 50, 63, 86,
87, 103, 105, 143,
168-169, 197, 210
Bailly, Jean-Sylvain,
371, 457-458, 459,
483, 509, 518, 519,
537, 538, 554, 562,
566, 572, 579, 590,
597, 608, 613, 615,
674-676, 678, 679,
680, 681
Barentin, Charles-
Louis-François de
Paul de, 300-301,
323, 332, 435, 436,
451, 457-458, 476,
484, 498, 504, 512,
513, 520, 533, 540-

541, 562-563, 571,
623, 667
Barère, Bertrand, 556-
557, 661
Barnave, Antoine-
Pierre, 263, 610,
715
Bastille, 575-576,
593, 606, 609
Beauvau, Charles-Juste
de, 2, 105, 130,
131, 281, 623
Bergasse, Nicolas,
263, 644
Bertier de Sauvigny,
Louis-Jean, 607
Bertrand-Moleville,
Antoine-François
de, 353-354, 498
Besançon, Parlement
of, 225
Besenval, Pierre-Vic-
tor de, 28, 43, 45-
46, 142-143, 239-
240, 258, 272, 288,
558-559, 564, 572,
575, 578, 592-593,
596-597, 599, 619
Bonvallet Desbrosses,
159-160
Bordeaux, Parlement
of, 7, 225
Bosher, J. F., 28,
189-190
Bouillé, François-
Claude de, 106,
378-379
Bourboulon, Antoine,
6, 168
Bourgade, Marquet de,
168, 170
Bourse, 56, 57, 94,
179, 245, 411;
speculation on, 58-
59, 423
Bouvard de Fourqueux,
Michel, 195, 197
Boyd, Julian, 491
Braesch, Frédéric, 233

Breteuil, Louis-Au-
guste Le Tonnelier
de, 44, 82, 138,
153, 196, 221, 227,
282, 301, 558, 565,
571, 577, 592, 607,
667
Breton Club, 453, 482,
488, 659
Brienne, Etienne-
François Loménie
de. See Loménie de
Brienne
Brienne, Louis-Marie
de, 137, 229
Brissot, Jacques-
Pierre, 59, 111
Brittany: estates of,
7, 261, 307, 351;
province of, 276,
280, 351-355
Broglie, Victor-
François de, 106,
281, 564, 571, 577,
607
Bureau of Commerce, 53
Burgundy: province
of, 276, 280, 281
Buzot, François-Nico-
las, 635

Cahiers (of grie-
vances), 93, 342,
344, 347, 349, 366,
371-372, 384-397,
454, 457, 468, 470,
506, 633
Caisse d'amortisse-
ment, See Sinking
Fund
Calonne, Charles-
Alexandre de, 6,
23, 24, 73, 75,
103-104, 194, 195,
219, 225, 226, 228,
239, 245, 271, 285,
423-424, 425, 771;
appointment to
Contrôle-Général,

43; career prior to 1783, 44-46; prodigalities of, 45-52; quarrels with Parlement of Paris, 55-63; reform projects of 1786, 77-78, 83-90; financial expedients, 80-81; ideas on credit, 83; explanation for deficit, 94-97, 145-146, speech before Assembly of Notables of Feb. 22, 1787, 106-117; resignation of, 137-140; correspondence with Necker, 147-150; emigration of, 154; apologia, 154-155, reply to Necker's April essay, 269-270; as counter-revolutionary, 193-194

Camus, Armand-Gaston, 453, 476, 482-483, 537, 617, 745-746, 762

Capitation tax, 15, 123-124, 159

Castries, Charles, marshal de, 2, 37-38, 43, 45, 104, 139, 147-148, 195, 228

Catherine de Medici, 445

Catherine II, empress of Russia, 304

Catholic Church. See French Catholic Church

Centième denier des offices, 171, 172

Chambers of Account, 36, 164-165, 166, 244

Champion, Edme, 385-386

Champion de Cicé, archbishop of Bordeaux, 315, 541, 602, 623-624, 625, 644, 718

Chapuisat, Edouard, 447

Charles I, king of England, 136, 568

Chastenay, Victorine de, 407

Châtelet: court of, 73, 368-373

Châtelet, Florent-Louis-Marie de, 267, 522, 560

Cherbourg: construction of naval port, 38, 108, 198

Choiseul, Etienne-François de, 5

Clavière, Etienne, 59, 111, 460, 641

Clermont-Gallerande, Charles-Georges de, 83, 522, 564

Clermont-Tonnerre, Stanislaus de, 535, 562, 596, 597, 612, 644, 712

Clugny, Jean-Etienne-Bernard Ogier de: compte rendu of (1776), 161, 169, 182, 187

Coigny, Henri de Franquetot de, 228, 239, 458

Committee on Finances: established in Feb. 1783, 36-39, 43, 49, 62, 203, 226; called for by Assembly of Notables,

204, 205, 207, 208, 210, 213, 215
Company of the Indies, 53, 84
Compte rendu au Roi: of 1781, 523, 46, 95, 111, 128, 130-131, 139, 166, 183, 188-191, 446; of 1787, 48-49, 129, 145-146, 198, 201, 269-270, 341; of 1788, 155, 233-236, 270, 341; of 1789, 411-420, 762; general, 137, 155-157, 165-166, 242, 246
Comptes effectives, 113, 131, 150-151, 156, 158, 161-162, 165-166, 183, 201
Condé, Louis-Joseph, prince de, 50, 103
Constituent Assembly, 116, 312, 382, 425, 707-736 passim, 771
Constituent power, 297, 312, 382, 634, 650, 669
Constitution: in 1789, 659-661, 689, 693, 717
Conti, prince de, 42, 118, 320
Cormeré, Guillaume-François Mahy de, 53
Corvée, 14, 90, 117, 124, 132, 160, 211, 223, 429
Coster, Joseph-François, 498
Council meeting of Dec. 27, 1788, 322, 377; Resultat of, 323-333, 389, 403, 404, 436, 449, 458, 483, 501

Council of finances, 36, 164, 205-206, 221. See also, Royal Council of Finance and Commerce
Council of War: creation, 229-230
Court of aides, 36, 244, 300
Court of Peers, 238, 242. See also Parlement of Paris
Creuzé-Latouche, Jacques-Antoine, 476, 489, 505, 541
Crosne, Louis-Thiroux de, 510

Dauphiné: province of, 261, 280, 355-363, 372
Declaration of Rights, 659-660, 668, 689, 693, 717, 718
Desmoulins, Camille, 683, 685
Discount Bank, 40-42, 53, 81, 86-87, 108, 115, 117, 273, 429, 545-546, 640-642, 657, 723-724, 725, 727-728, 730, 743, 749, 752
Dixième d'amortissement, 54, 60, 633
Domain of the Occident, 171, 172
Don gratuit, 15, 171, 172, 262
Dorset, Duke of, 51, 103, 405-406
Doublement, 20, 319-320, 326-327, 332, 342, 352, 361, 367
Droits de contrôle. See Stamp tax
Dufresne, Bertrand, 236

Dumont, ██████ ██3,
460, ██████ ██6,
737-██
Dupont ██████
Pier██ ██████ 3-
54, ██████ ██, 118,
119, 439, 453, 481,
482, 491, 550-551,
630, 634, 635, 658,
723, 748
Duport, Adrien, 238,
618, 659, 715
Duquesnoy, Adrien-Cy-
prien, 298, 452-
453, 523, 524-525,
534, 535, 537, 541-
542, 543, 551-552,
613, 618, 625, 628,
633, 641
Du Roverai, Jacques-
Antoine, 460-461

Economists. See
Physiocratic doc-
trine
Eden Treaty, 54, 83
Egret, Jean, 185-186,
236, 261, 264, 278,
283, 336, 624
England. See Great
Britain
Eprémesnil, Jean-
Jacques Duval d',
238, 246, 251-253,
308, 310, 333, 459,
747, 476
Espagnac, abbé d', 50
Estaing, Henri d',
106, 671, 684, 696
Etat au vrai, 164-165,
302

Farmers-General, 42,
49, 115, 138, 413,
415, 417, 629, 639
Ferrand, Antoine-Fran-
çois-Claude de, 283

Ferrières, Charles-
Elie de, 407, 565,
615-616
Five Great Farms, 18
Flammermont, Jules,
336
Flanders Regiment,
670-672, 682-685,
687, 690-691
Flesselles, Jacques
de, 562-563, 576
Forgotten revolution:
the, v, 356, 363,
366
Foulon, Joseph-
François, 607
Franche-Comté: pro-
vince of, 280
Free gift. See Don
gratuit
French Guards, 533,
534, 555, 559-561,
572, 575, 671, 679,
695. See also
Grenadiers
French Catholic
Church, 15, 90;
convocation of
1788, 262; debt of,
125, 132, 133, 390-
391; tithes, 128,
627; nationaliza-
tion of lands. 635,
658, 723-728, 730,
753-754

Gabelles, 7, 14, 18,
89-90, 116, 125,
197, 211, 428, 629,
639-649, 729, 754
General Farm. See
Farmers-General
Gleichen, Charles-
Henri de, 565, 764
Gojard, Achilles-
Joseph, 163, 202,
235, 236, 258, 264
Gomel, Charles, 46-47
Gouy d'Arcis, 609, 612

Grain trade: regulation of, 222-223, 273-274, 547. See also Subsistence crisis
Grandes gabelles, See Gabelles
Grange, Henri, iv, 444, 492
Great Britain, 304, 306, 449; tax system, 11-17; Bank of England, 40-41; Parliament, 41
Genadiers, 679, 680, 687-688, 689, 697-700
Grenoble: Parlement of, 225, 356; city of, 261, 276, 346, 355, 512
Guémenée, prince de, 42, 50
Guibert, comte de, 229-231, 240
Guienne: province of, 276, 280

Hardy, Sebastien. See Journal de Hardy
Haussonville, Othenin, vicomte d', 256
Hennet, Albert-Joseph, 66, 98
Hôtel des monnaies, 52
Hôtel-de-Ville: of Paris, 54, 686-687, 700; rentes paid by, 52-53, 199, 413, 418, 562-563, 576, 594-595; claim to represent Paris at States-General, 368-373. See Assembly of Representatives of the Commune
Hyslop, Beatrice, 384

Imperative mandates, 361, 363; in cahiers of Nobility, 393-396, 517, 539, 633
Intendants of finance: abolition of offices, 34, 64-66

Jacobins, 351, 366, 453, 711, 750
Jefferson, Thomas, 403-404, 405, 424, 446, 511, 514, 518, 544, 551-553, 566, 579, 602-603, 670
Joly de Fleury, Jean-François de, 15, 23, 49, 97, 139-140, 168, 228, 285, 638; financial ministry of, 31-39; war loans of, 32-33; opposition to Necker's reforms, 33-35; financial statement of March, 1783, 35, 157, 181-182, 197; special committee on finance, 36-37; departure from office, 36-37; "Observations on Compte rendu of Necker," 170-177; refutation of Calonne, 179-183
Joseph II, emperor, 1, 35, 78, 136, 196, 266, 280, 303, 304, 306, 569, 667, 672
Journal de Hardy, 5-6, 74-75, 281-282, 283, 560, 584

Kindleberger, Charles P., 199-191

798

King's Bodyguards, 679, 682-683, 684, 687, 689, 690, 691, 693, 696, 697-699
King's Household, 52

Lafayette, Gilbert de Motier de, 106, 207-208, 229, 251, 263, 544, 552, 590, 608, 644, 671, 674, 677, 679, 680-681, 686-688, 694-700, 750, 752
Lally-Tollendal, Trophime-Gérard de, 485-486, 543-544, 573, 594, 605-607, 609-610, 611-612, 613, 634-635, 644, 711, 744
La Luzerne, César-Henri de, 302, 507, 570, 571, 623
Lambert, Claude-Guillaume, 236, 266
Lameth, Alexander, 635, 715
Lamoignon, Chrétien-François de, 194, 195, 196, 221, 237, 239, 244, 246-247, 265, 286, 299, 308, 390; judicial reforms of, 255; resignation of, 278
Land subsidy. See Subvention territoriale
Languedoc: province of, 280, 352; estates of, 366-368
La Rochefoucauld, cardinal de, 452, 538
La Tour du Pin, Jean-Frédéric de, 624, 671, 680

Law, John: system of, 41, 46, 410, 762
Le Chapelier, Isaac-René, 466, 476, 650
Lefebvre, Georges, 430, 449, 492, 581
Lemaître affair, 73-75
Le Trosne, Guillaume, 83, 87
Lettres de cachet, 138, 244, 249, 281, 330, 355
L'Hôpital, Michel de, 445
Liancourt, François-Alexandre de, 536-537, 542, 576, 594, 600
Lit de justice, 95, 276; of Dec. 23, 1785, 62-63; of July 1787, 243-245, 247, 499, 511
Loans: of French government, 32, 39-40, 54, 56-57, 59-63, 111, 171-172, 181, 204, 246-247, 249
Loménie de Brienne, Etienne-François de, archbishop, 15, 105, 152, 153, 196, 202, 262, 308, 357, 410, 413, 414, 418, 419, 509; appointed to head of council of Finance, 203-204; relations with Assembly of Notables, 205-207, 211-214, 219-221; relations with sovereign courts, 220-221, 238-254; economies and ameliorations, 227-233; compte rendu of 1788, 233-237; and convocation of

799

States-General,
263, 265; resig-
nation of , 265-
268; character of ,
285-287
Louis XIV, king of
France, 2, 21, 128,
369, 468
Louis XVI, king of
France, 1, 11-12,
27, 62, 91, 104,
138-140, 152-153,
195, 197, 206, 244,
268-269, 281, 282,
289, 304, 404-406,
426, 449, 456, 478,
485, 500-501, 507-
525, 537-538, 543,
566-569, 574-580,
642, 648-650, 668-
669, 679, 682, 689,
691-700, 734-736
Loustalot, Elysée,
678, 683, 685

Machiavelli, Nicolò,
288, 422
Malesherbes, Chrétien-
Guillaume de Lam-
oignon de, 287, 300
Mallet du Pan, Jac-
ques, 271, 342
Malouet, Pierre-Victor
de, 194, 298, 339,
344-345, 453, 459,
461-462, 467, 477,
479, 484, 486-487,
600, 630, 642-643,
644, 702-703, 708,
712
Marat, Jean-Paul, 677,
683, 685
Maréchaussée, 281, 555
Marion, Marcel, 29,
47-48, 77, 558
Marie Antoinette,
queen of France,
21, 43, 45, 74, 78,
95, 97, 152, 195,

228, 266-269, 304-
305, 448, 521, 543,
672, 682-683, 698-
700, 736
Marmontel, Jean-
François, 153, 195,
196, 219
Mathiez, Albert, 668-
670, 683
Maupeou, René-Nicolas
de, chancellor of
France, 44, 104,
237, 239, 251
Maurepas, Jean-
Frédéric Phélypeaux
de, 1, 74, 161, 169
Maury, abbé, 534, 744-
745
May Edicts (May 8,
1788), 253-255,
262, 263, 278, 286,
355
Mazarin, Jules, cardi-
nal, 9, 285, 288,
346
Meister, Henri, 447
Memorial of the
Princes (Dec.
1788), 321, 378,
450
Mercy-Argenteau,
Florimond-Claude
de, 1, 35, 43-44,
51, 77-78, 86, 195,
236, 237, 266-268,
279-280, 286, 303,
305, 306, 447-448,
531, 672
Metra, François, 7-8,
27
Mirabeau, Honoré-
Gabriel, de, 58,
87, 111, 262, 270,
298, 392, 406, 446-
447, 453, 459, 460-
465, 466, 473, 477,
481, 486, 519, 537,
539, 551-554, 596,
601-602, 610-611,

800

613-617, 633, 635,
641-642, 647, 650-
651, 658, 659, 661,
678, 711, 712, 713-
718, 719, 723, 738,
751-752, 761-762,
771
Mirabeau-Tonneau, A.
B. L. R., 650-651
Miromesnil, Hue de, 6,
36, 73, 82, 92,
104, 138, 140, 194,
196
Monsieur. See Pro-
vence, comte de
Montmorin-Saint-Hérem,
Armand-Marc de,
104-105, 153, 195,
197, 219, 302, 303,
304, 344, 487, 507,
508, 513, 514, 571,
578, 623, 751
Morellet, André, abbé,
126, 134, 152, 195,
209, 279, 348
Morris, Gouveneur,
456, 737
Mosser, Françoise, 64-
65
Mouchy, Philippe de
Noailles de, 106
Mounier, Jean-Joseph,
1, 339, 356-366,
384, 439, 453, 459,
466-467, 469-470,
471, 476, 484, 488,
489, 498, 510, 520,
543, 544, 564, 598,
599, 600, 611, 617,
643, 644, 646-647,
659, 660, 661, 689,
693, 695, 701, 711,
712-713
Murphy, Orville T., 67

Nantes, Edict of, 445
National Guard: of
Paris, 561-563,
578, 674, 679, 680-

681, 687; of Ver-
sailles, 671, 682,
683, 689-690
Necker, Germaine. See
Staël-Holstein,
Anne-Louise-Ger-
maine de
Necker, Jacques:
preoccupations dur-
ing years of re-
tirement from first
ministry, 1-29; re-
action to Calonne's
disclosure before
Assembly of Nota-
bles, 146-152;
April 1787 essay,
152-154; view of
Loménie de Brienne,
219-220; policy on
grain trade, 223,
return to ministry,
265-269; financial
measures, 271-272;
the subsistence
crisis, 273-274;
view of States-Gen-
eral, 275-278; and
the Revolution,
284; opposes Rus-
sian alliance 304-
305; convenes the
second Assembly of
Notables, 312-320;
address to States-
General on May 5,
1789, 408-439; at-
tempts to mediate
deadlock of States-
General, 479-481;
plans for Royal
Session of June 23,
515-520; relations
with National As-
sembly after June
23, 534-535; dis-
missed by the king
on July 11, 568-
571; and return,

579-580; view of situation at beginning of third ministry 589-592; at the Hôtel-de-Ville on July 30, 594-596; loan proposals to National Assembly, 631-639; views on the constitution, 645-658; and the October days, 691-701; policy after the October days, 709-711; financial proposals, 722-733; resignation, 761-764

Necker, Suzanne, 4, 378, 515, 524, 763

Necker de Germany, Louis, 570, 580

Nootka Sound incident, 750-752

October days, 341, 669; Mathiez's view, 667-670; refuted, 670-673

Ordinary accounts (of income and expenditure), 158-161, 199

Ordonnances de comptant. See Acquits de comptant

Ordonnateurs, 36, 62, 202, 226, 237

Orient, porte d', 50

Orleans, Louis-Philippe-Joseph, duc d', 50, 248-249, 314, 318, 577, 738

Ormesson, Henry Lefèvre d', 39-43, 65, 86, 97

Ottoman Empire, 279, 304

Palais Royal, 321, 333, 371, 533, 560, 564, 644, 659, 677, 678, 692, 711

Panchaud, Isaac, 53, 59, 111, 168, 233, 270, 460

Parlement of Paris, 4, 33, 74-75, 81, 93, 204, 221, 226, 272, 276, 279, 285, 300, 332-333, 631; remonstrances of, 1, 55-56, 57, 59-63, 75-77; indictment of Calonne, 154, 203; organization of, 238; jurisdiction curtailed by May edicts, 253-254; ruling on organization of States-General, 308-310; ideas on constitution, 310-311; attempts to censor seditious writings, 321-322

Pays conquis, 18, 349

Pays d'élection, 18, 116, 223, 342, 343, 365

Pays d'état, 18, 116, 137, 223, 349, 365, 627

Peace of Versailles, 31, 42

Pensions, 3, 35, 49, 57, 203, 205, 206-207, 231, 419

Penthièvre, Louis de Bourbon, duc de 42, 49, 314

Pétion, Jerôme, 550, 634, 659

Physiocratic doctrine,
19, 53, 83-84, 88,
89, 90-91, 118,
120, 128-129, 169,
222, 349, 358, 549-
550, 635, 710
Pièces justificatives,
151, 161-163, 201,
270
Plenary Court: of May
edicts, 253-254,
263, 276, 286, 297,
299, 345
Polignac, Jules, duc
de, 51, 103, 458
Polignac, Yolande,
duchesse de, 43,
459, 564, 571
Poncet-Delpesch, Jean-
Baptiste, 452
Provence, Louis-
Stanislas-Xavier
de, 117, 129, 150,
194, 207, 210, 228,
244, 318, 319, 511
Provincial assemblies,
19-20, 87-89, 118-
121, 132, 133, 137,
263, 428; of Berri
and Haute Guienne,
19-20, 120-121,
212, 223-224, 389;
powers of inten-
dants over, 224-
225; established in
Brienne ministry,
224-225
Prussia, 229, 304, 305
Public opinion (in
France), 2, 136,
145, 209, 239, 276,
279, 287, 289, 299,
307-308, 324, 341,
484, 518, 536, 592,
680
Puységur, Pierre-Louis
de Chastenet de,
301, 323, 513, 571

Rabaut-Saint-Etienne,
Jean-Paul, 453,
467-468, 645
Radix de Sainte-Foy,
Claude-Pierre, 45;
affair of, 35
Rambouillet, château
de: purchased by
king, 49; contem-
plated as refuge
for king on Oct. 6,
690
Recoinage of gold
louis, 75, 77, 200
Red Book, 47, 745-747
Regulation of January
24, 1789, 343-344
Rennes: city of, 354;
Parlement of, 7,
351, 354
Renouvin, Pierre, 186
Resultat du conseil,
Dec. 27, 1788. See
Council meeting of
Dec. 27
Réveillon riot, 404,
405, 407, 554-555
Richelieu, Armand-
Jean, cardinal de,
9, 45, 285, 346,
369, 504
Rilliet de Saussure,
41
Robespierre, Maximi-
lien, 453, 545,
606, 617, 661, 719
Romans assembly, 357-
360
Rousseau, Jean-
Jacques, 8
Royal Council of Fi-
nance and Commerce,
225-226
Royal Session of June
23, 499-502, 507,
515-520, 532, 564
Russia, 279, 304, 306

Saint-Charles, Bank of
58-59
Saint-Cloud, château
de: purchased by
queen, 50
Saint-Germain, Claude-
Louis de, 4, 230
Saint-Huruge, marquis
de, 612, 619, 677,
678
Saint-Priest,
François-Emmanuel
Guignard de, 302-
303, 304-305, 306,
507, 513, 571, 578,
623, 671, 680, 691-
692, 717-718
Sallier-Chaumont de la
Roche, Guy-Marie,
292
Sancerre: county of,
50
Sartine, Gabriel de,
37
Saxe-Teschen, arch-
duchesse de, 5
Séguier, Jean-Louis
de, 247
Ségur, Louis-Philippe
de, 37-38, 43, 195,
227, 228
Short, William, 700-
701, 734, 735, 741,
742, 750
Sieyes, Emmanuel-
Joseph, abbé, 297,
339, 366, 381-383,
392, 425, 450, 453,
465, 481, 485, 486,
489, 504, 574, 601-
602, 647
Single duty tariff,
89, 116, 124, 222,
389, 429
Sinking Fund, 53, 55,
56, 108, 292, 416,
419
Staël-Holstein, Anne-
Louise-Germaine de,
4, 46, 146, 256,
268, 269, 287-288,
289, 403, 500, 506,
515, 589, 594
Staël-Holstein, Au-
guste de, 270
Staël-Holstein, Eric
Magnus de, 4, 54,
78, 271-272, 286,
350, 404-405, 512,
540, 567, 623, 644,
683-684, 724
Stamp tax, 57, 86,
125, 197, 212, 284
States-General: of
1614, 309, 343,
503; of 1789, 93,
137, 207, 242-243,
262, 265, 268, 270,
273, 280, 285, 287,
288, 291, 297, 306,
341, 344, 446, 503;
organization of,
307-310; for pays
d'élection, 343-
349; for Brittany,
351-355; for
Dauphiné, 355-363;
for Languedoc, 366-
368; for Paris,
368-373; opening
of, 403-439 passim
Stock exchange. See
Bourse
Strafford, Lord, 136
Subvention territori-
ale, 122, 125, 133,
207
Subsistence crisis,
222-223, 273-274,
405, 429, 544-554,
674-676, 681, 693,
708-709, 720-722

Taille, 14, 90, 116,
117, 123-124, 132,
159, 211, 223, 362,
430

Talleyrand-Périgord,
Charles-Maurice,
99, 641, 724, 737
Target, Guy-Jean-Bap-
tiste, 74, 263,
469, 523, 630, 645,
659
Taylor, George V.,
188-189, 385
Tennis Court Oath,
509-510
Terray, Joseph-Marie,
abbé, 22, 34, 95,
97, 113, 136, 237,
239, 251, 410, 422,
710
Thibaudeau, A. C.,
407-408
Third Estate: awaken-
ing of, 309-310,
320, 321, 381
Tithes. See French
Catholic Church
Tocqueville, Alexis
de, 377-378, 380-
381, 384-385
Treasury Board, 722,
732-733, 742, 743,
745
Tronchin, Armand-Jean,
406-407, 447, 589,
593
Turgot, Anne-Robert-
Jacques, 1, 34, 97,
187, 285, 300, 607

United Netherlands,
108, 228-229, 305

Vauban, Sébastien Le
Prestre de, 87, 128
Venality of office,
20-22, 33-34, 203-
205, 227-228, 232-
233, 387
Vergennes, Charles
Gravier de, 12, 40,
43, 82, 104; crea-
tion of committee

on finance, 36-37,
92
Vidaud de la Tour,
Jean-Jacques, 512-
513, 514
Villedeuil, Laurent
de, 206, 236, 282,
301, 323, 513, 533,
571, 623, 667
Vingtième tax, 7, 15-
16, 23, 159; third
vingtième, 32-33,
35, 60, 175; reform
of, 84-85, 116,
121-123, 125, 126-
127, 135, 207-208,
212, 245-246, 249-
251, 755
Virieu, bailli de,
533, 543
Virieu, François-Henri
de, 619, 708, 712
Vizille assembly, 356

Weber, Joseph, 45

Young, Arthur, 339,
351, 435, 464, 518,
550, 558, 593